RUSSIA

A HISTORY

RUSSIA
A HISTORY

EDITED BY
GREGORY L. FREEZE

Oxford   New York
OXFORD UNIVERSITY PRESS
1997

Oxford University Press, Great Clarendon Street, Oxford OX2 6DP

Oxford New York
Athens Auckland Bangkok Bogota Bombay
Buenos Aires Calcutta Cape Town Dar es Salaam
Delhi Florence Hong Kong Istanbul Karachi
Kuala Lumpur Madras Madrid Melbourne
Mexico City Nairobi Paris Singapore
Taipei Tokyo Toronto Warsaw
and associated companies in
Berlin Ibadan

Oxford is a trade mark of Oxford University Press

British Library Cataloguing in Publication Data
Data available

Library of Congress Cataloging in Publication Data
Data available
ISBN 0–19–215899–6

1 3 5 7 9 10 8 6 4 2

Typeset by Selwood Systems
Printed in Great Britain
on acid-free paper by
Butler & Tanner Ltd
Frome, Somerset

Contents

LIST OF COLOUR PLATES

LIST OF MAPS

Editor's Preface

This volume seeks to provide a systematic, state-of-the-art account of Russian history from its recorded origins to the present day. It is distinguished, first and foremost, by the fact that it draws upon the most recent scholarship, which in many areas has considerably changed the way we think about the Russian historical experience. It also gives a relatively stronger emphasis upon the modern period, with roughly one-third on the medieval period, one-third on the imperial, and one-third on the Soviet era. Most, but especially later, chapters are deeply informed by the newest research and revolution in archival access, which has permitted the use of a broad array of previously classified sources. Indeed, archival access for material on twentieth-century topics was until recently all but denied; in the last few years researchers have used materials, the very existence of which we did not even suspect. With this greater access, with a gradual depoliticization of what was once an intellectual Cold War battleground, historians can now tell their story far more dispassionately, far more intelligently than was the case only a few years hence.

Several important themes run throughout this book and deserve to be underscored here. One is the protracted, difficult process of development, not only in the economic domain, but also in state and society. In contrast to mesmerizing images of an all-powerful autocrat, whether it be Ivan the Terrible or Stalin the Terrorizer, in fact the rulers and regimes of Russia have had but a tenuous hold on society, especially outside the capitals and major cities. The authority did indeed gradually increase, but it remained highly vulnerable, circumscribed by geography, compromised by bureaucratic incompetence, pervasive corruption, and evasion and resistance from below. Although tyrants like Ivan and Stalin could brutally extinguish large numbers of people, they did so more prophylactically than purposefully; in many cases the sheer violence was meant to coerce compliance because the regular instruments of rule and repression were so episodic, sporadic, or downright unreliable. That curious combination—a veneer of omnipotence, a huge void of operational power—periodically dissolved into 'times of trouble', as in 1598, 1917, and 1991, when the impotence of the regime became transparent to all. In recent years the floundering, corrupt regime has been aptly described by some as 'Anarchistan', by others (frustrated in making sense of the new disorder) as 'Absurdistan'.

It was certainly not for lack of will that an Ivan, a Peter, a Lenin failed to establish tight operational control over society. But to do so they had to overcome enormous (if not insuperable) hurdles—the sheer dispersion of the populace, the dearth of means and men to govern, a primitive infrastructure with poor means of communication and transportation. As many historians have emphasized, mother nature gave Russia great resources and great problems; alongside the rich soil and vast natural resources, the country had to overcome serious obstacles—such as a great northern location, vast distances between critical resources, barriers to easy and cheap access to international markets. Plagued by natural disasters, hamstrung by structural problems, the Russian economy (whether pre-revolutionary capitalist, Soviet socialist, or post-Soviet semi-capitalist) has had enormous difficulties adapting to the highly competitive world of international markets. Its people poor, regardless of regime or economy, Russia has had little 'surplus product' to allocate for state-building. Ultimately, a poor state was a weak state, one that could barely afford to educate, organize, and pay an army of qualified bureaucrats. Indeed, what few resources it did have paled in comparison with the demand, especially from the military, let alone for basic social services.

The development of society has been variously described as 'backward' and more often as 'peculiar', for it does not fit easily into any West European mould. Whereas the latter traversed an evolution from a system based on 'estates' (hereditary, juridical orders) to 'classes' (based on wealth and occupation), with 1789 representing a great divide in the transition, Russian society took an entirely different line of development. Most striking of all, it only began to construct a system of estates in the eighteenth and nineteenth centuries, as it amalgamated a plethora of tiny service orders into larger estates. Serfdom took a similar line of development, consolidating and intensifying in the seventeenth and eighteenth centuries—just as the last vestiges dissolved in Western Europe. Memory of serfdom was fresh in historical consciousness; some in Stalinist Russia wryly decoded the initials of the All-Russian Communist Party (VKP) as *Vtoroe krepostnoe pravo*—'the second serfdom'. Perhaps most symptomatic of the peculiar social history was the commune, which not only continued to exist into the modern era, but even became more powerful and resilient until its violent repression in the collectivization drive of the early 1930s.

Another elemental fact is Russia's multinational composition: Russia, even in the Muscovite period, was already becoming *Rossiia*, a latinized variant of *Rus*—the original name for Russia. Even in the medieval era Russia came to include various non-Russian, non-Slavic peoples, and the accumulation of other ethnic and national groups gained momentum in the eighteenth and nineteenth centuries. By the mid-nineteenth century a 'Russian heartland' included myriad ethnic groups, not only in central European Russia, but all across the vast borderlands that stretched from Finland and Poland to the Caucasus and Central Asia. The realm of tsars and general secretaries included scores of minorities, every imaginable confession, and powerful national and religious movements. The latter posed an increasingly serious threat to the stability of the empire itself, attracting an ever greater share of the regime's attention and scant resources. But with little effect: from the late nineteenth to late twentieth century, these areas were a constant source of seething discontent and disorder, often providing the driveshaft of revolution that would topple one regime in 1917 and another in 1991. In that important sense, if one is to understand Russian historical development, it is essential to appreciate the role of non-Russians in shaping the development—and disintegration—of the Russian state. It is thus important to 'de-Russify' Russian history and to recognize the powerful, transcendent role of its non-Russian minorities.

For all too long Russian history has been dominated by myths and counter-myths, concocted by those seeking to legitimize the existing order and those seeking to destroy it. This book represents an important attempt to rethink Russian history, not so much to provide new facts, but a new understanding of that country's complex, often contorted, but ever-fascinating course of historical development.

GREGORY L. FREEZE

Brandeis University, 1997

LIST OF CONTRIBUTORS

John T. Alexander is professor of history at the University of Kansas. His major publications include *Autocratic Politics in a National Crisis* (1969), *Emperor of the Cossacks* (1973), *Bubonic Plauge in Early Modern Russia* (1980), and *Catherine the Great* (1989). He is currently preparing a comparative biography of Peter the Great and Catherine the Great, and a study of the four Russian empresses of the eighteenth century.

Gregory L. Freeze is professor of history at Brandeis University. His major publications include *The Russian Levites: Parish Clergy in Eighteenth-Century Russia* (1977), *The Parish Clergy in Nineteenth-Century Russia: Crisis, Reform, Counter-Reform* (1983), and *From Supplication to Revolution: A Documentary Social History of Russia* (1988). He is currently completing a two-volume study, 'Religion and Society in Modern Russia, 1730–1930'.

William C. Fuller, Jr. teaches in the Department of Strategy at the United States Naval War College. He is the author of *Civil–Military Conflict in Imperial Russia, 1881–1914* and *Strategy and Power in Russia, 1600–1914*. He is currently completing a book about treason and espionage cases in Russia during the First World War.

William B. Husband is associate professor of history at Oregon State University. He is author of *Revolution in the Factory: The Birth of the Soviet Textile Industry, 1917–1920* (1990). He has published a series of articles on the rewriting of history in Russia since 1987; he is currently completing a social and cultural history of Soviet atheism, 1917–32.

Nancy Shields Kollmann is professor of history at Stanford University. A specialist in Russian social and political history, she has written *Kinship and Politics: The Making of the Muscovite Political System* (1987) and *Honor and Society in Early Modern Russia* (in press).

Martin McCauley is a senior lecturer in politics, School of Slavonic and East European Studies, University of London. He has specialized on the Soviet Union/Russia for over twenty-five years and has published widely, including a recent book entitled *The Khrushchev Era 1953–1964*. He was involved in editing the English edition of Gorbachev's *Memoirs* and is also writing a book on Gorbachev as a politician.

Gary Marker is professor of history at the State University of New York at Stony Brook. He is the author of *Publishing, Printing, and the Origins of*

Intellectual Life in Russia, 1700–1800 (1985) and co-author of *Reinterpreting Russian History* (1994). He also has edited *Ideas, Ideologies, and Intellectuals in Russian History* (1993) and *Catherine the Great and the Search for a Usable Past* (1994).

Janet Martin is professor of history at the University of Miami, Coral Gables, Florida. She is the author of *Treasure of the Land of Darkness: The Fur Trade and its Significance for Medieval Russia* (1986) and *Medieval Russia, 980–1584* (1995).

Daniel Orlovsky is professor of history at Southern Methodist University, Dallas, Texas. He is the author of *The Limits of Reform: The Ministry of Internal Affairs in Imperial Russia, 1802–1881* and a forthcoming history of the Provisional Government of 1917, *Russia's Democratic Revolution*, as well as several studies of white collar workers and professionals in the revolutionary and early Soviet period.

David L. Ransel is professor of history and director of the Russian and East European Institute at Indiana University. He is the author of *The Politics of Catherinian Russia: The Panin Party* (1975) and *Mothers of Misery: Child Abandonment in Russia* (1988). His current work includes a study of the life of an eighteenth-century Russian merchant family, and the transformation of maternity and early child care in rural Russia during the twentieth century.

Lewis Siegelbaum is professor of history at Michigan State University. He has written extensively on Russian and Soviet labour history. Among his books are *Stakhanovism and the Politics of Productivity in the USSR, 1935–1941* (1988); *Soviet State and Society between Revolutions, 1918–1929* (1992), and *Workers of the Donbass Speak: Survival and Identity in the New Ukraine, 1989–1992* (co-authored, 1995).

Hans-Joachim Torke is professor of Russian and East European history at the Free University of Berlin. His publications include *Das russische Beamtentum in der ersten Hälfte des 19. Jahrhunderts* (1967) and *Das staatsbedingte Gesellschaft im Moskaner Reich* (1974).

Reginald E. Zelnik is professor of history at the University of California at Berkeley. He is author of *Labor and Society in Tsarist Russia* (1971), editor and translator of the memoirs of Semen Kanatchikov (*A Radical Worker in Tsarist Russia* (1986)), and, most recently, author of *Law and Disorder on the Narova River: The Kreenholm Strike of 1872* (1995).

GLOSSARY OF TERMS, ABBREVIATIONS AND ACRONYMS

Barshchina	Corvée labour (rendering of serf obligations through personal labour)
Batrak	Landless peasant (in Soviet jargon, a peasant who had no land and earned his support as a hired agricultural labourer)
Bedniak	Poor peasant (in Soviet jargon, a peasant whose farm income was insufficient and who had to hire himself out to kulaks)
Bezprizorniki	Homeless, orphaned children in the 1920s
Boyar duma	Boyar council in medieval Russia
CC	Central Committee
Centner	Hundredweight, or 100 kg. (from the German *Zentner*)
Cheka	Extraordinary Commission (created in December 1917 to 'combat counter-revolution and sabotage')
Chernozem	Black-earth region of southern Russia
Chetvert'	Unit of dry measure for grain, equivalent to 288 pounds of rye in the seventeenth century
CIS	Commonwealth of Independent States (established in December 1991 as an association of most of the former Soviet republics)
Cominform	Communist Information Bureau (established in 1947 to coordinate Communist Parties in the Western and Eastern blocs)
CPD	Congress of People's Deputies (last Soviet parliament elected in 1989)
CPRF	Communist Party of the Russian Federation (the reconstituted CPSU in the post-Soviet era)
CPSU	Communist Party of the Soviet Union
Dikoe pole	The untamed southern steppes (literally meaning 'wild field')
Duma	State parliament of tsarist Russia, 1906–17, and post-Soviet Russia; elected city councils after the urban reform of 1870
GDP	Gross domestic production
GKO	State Defence Committee (chief military organ during the Second World War)
Glasnost	Openness or publicity (a reference to the relaxation of censorship controls in the 1850s and again in the last 1980s)
Gosudarstvenniki	Civil servants who were devoted primarily to serving the interests of the state (*gosudarstvo*), not their own social estate
GULAG	Main Administration of Camps (responsible for management of the labour camps)
Iasak	Tribute exacted from non-Russian subject populations in Eastern Russia and Siberia

Kadets	Pre-revolutionary liberal party (name being an acronym of 'Constitutional-Democrats')
KGB	Committee for State Security (secret police)
Kolkhoz (pl. *kolkhozy*)	Collective farm (literally, 'collective enterprise', where the peasants nominally own the land, fulfil state grain procurements, and receive compensation as 'workdays' that they have contributed)
Komsomol	Communist Youth League
Kulak	Rich peasant (derived from the word for 'fist'; after 1917 formally used to designate any peasant who 'exploited' the labour of others)
Lishentsy	Disenfranched (those members of the former 'exploiting classes', such as nobles, bourgeoisie and clergy, who were deprived of civil rights and subjected to various other forms of discrimination from 1918 to 1936)
Manufaktura	Primitive handicrafts and industrial enterprises in early modern Russia
MTS	Machine Tractor Stations (state units established in 1935 to provide tractor and technical services to the kolkhoz)
Narkomindel	People's Commissariat of Foreign Affairs
Narkompros	People's Commissariat of Education
NEP	New Economic Policy
Nepman	Traders and entrepreneurs who engaged in 'free enterprise' during NEP
NKVD	People's Commissariat of Internal Affairs
Nomenklatura	System of appointment lists, emerging in the first years of Soviet power and eventually coming to define the country's political élite
Oblast (pl. *oblasti*)	Soviet territorial unit, roughly equivalent to a prerevolutionary province
Obrok	Quitrent (payment of serf obligations in kind or money)
Oprichnina	The separate state 'within a state' established by Ivan the Terrible in 1565; more generally used to designate this reign of terror, which lasted until 1572
Orgburo	Organizational Bureau
Perestroika	Reconstruction (the term adopted to designate a fundamental reform in the Soviet system from the mid-1980s)
Pomest'e	Conditional service estate in Muscovy, but by the eighteenth century equivalent to hereditary family property
Posad	Urban settlement in Muscovy
Prikaz	Term for 'chancellery' in the sixteenth and seventeenth centuries
Proletkult	Proletarian culture movement
PSR	Party of Socialist Revolutionaries
Rabfak	Workers' faculty (special schools for workers with little or no formal eduction)

Rabkrin	Workers' and Peasants' Inspectorate (organ to control state and economy, 1920–34)
RSDWP	Russian Social-Democratic Workers' Party
RSFSR	Russian Soviet Federal Socialist Republic
SD	Social Democrat
Seredniak	Middle peasant (in Soviet jargon, a peasant who was self-sufficient, neither exploiting the labour of others nor working in the employee of others)
Smychka	Soviet slogan designating an 'alliance' or 'union' of the workers and peasants in the 1920s
Soslovie	Social estate (in the sense of the French *état* or German *Stand*)
Sovkhoz	State farm (literally, 'soviet enterprise,' where the state owns all assets and the peasants provide hired labour)
Sovnarkhoz	Council of National Economy: provincial and district organ to manage industry and construction (1917–34); system for decentralized economic management (1957–65)
Sovnarkom	Council of People's Commissars
SRs	Members of the neo-populist Party of Social Revolutionaries
Streltsy	Musketeers (military units of riflemen organized in the seventeenth century)
Sudebnik	Law code in medieval Russia
Third Section	Tsarist organ of secret police, established as a 'section' of the emperor's personal chancellery in 1826
Ulozhenie	Title of first inclusive law code adopted in 1649 (formally called the *Sobornoe ulozhenie*)
Vesenkha	Supreme Council of the National Economy (central industrial organ, 1917–32)
Voevoda	District governor in the seventeenth and eighteenth centuries
Volost	Township
Votchina	Hereditary family landed estate
Vyt	Unit of land area and taxation (of varying size)
Zemskii sobor	Council of the realm (informal assemblies convoked for purposes of consultation from the mid-sixteenth to the mid-seventeenth centuries)
Zemstvo	The provincial and district organs of elected self-government from 1864 to 1917; in the sixteenth century it refers to a system of community self-rule
Zhenotdel	Women's section in the party

NOTE ON TRANSLITERATION AND DATES

Transliteration follows a modified version of the Library of Congress system. For the sake of readability, the 'soft sign' has been omitted for the better known terms (e.g. Streltsy, not Strel´tsy). In the case of those names which have already achieved recognition in the West, that form will be followed here (e.g. Peter, not Petr; Trotsky, not Trotskii; Beria, not Beriia). The same applies to certain terms (e.g. soviet, not sovet; boyar, not boiar).

Dating until February 1918 follows the Julian ('Old Style') calendar, which lagged behind the modern Gregorian ('New Style') calendar: eleven days in the eighteenth century, twelve days in the nineteenth century, and thirteen days in the twentieth century. Hence the 'October Revolution' on 25 October, for example, actually occurred on 7 November in the modern calendar. Dates from 14 February 1918 (when the Soviet government adopted the Gregorian calendar) conform to those in the West, whether for international or domestic matters.

FROM KIEV TO MUSCOVY
THE BEGINNINGS TO 1450

JANET MARTIN

In these early centuries East Slavic tribes and their neighbours coalesced into the Christian state of Kievan Rus. Its ruling Riurikid dynasty oversaw increasing political complexity, territorial expansion, economic growth, and frequent warfare, but was defeated by Mongol invaders. During the ensuing Mongol era a junior dynastic branch extended its authority and laid the foundations for a new state—Muscovy.

THE formative centuries of the Russian state are perhaps best divided into three main periods: the era of Kievan Rus from its roots in the ninth century to the Mongol invasion of 1237–40; a century of 'Mongol dominance' from 1240 to c.1340, during which Kievan traditions and structures lost their potency and the Rus principalities adapted to Mongol or Tatar suzerainty; and the period from c.1340 to the mid-fifteenth century, when the foundations of the new state of Muscovy were laid.

Kievan Rus

The lands that made up Kievan Rus were located in the forest zone of Eastern Europe along a group of rivers, the Dnieper, the western Dvina, the Lovat-Volkhov, and the Volga, the headwaters of which all emanate from the Valdai hills. They were populated mainly by Slavic and Finnic tribes. The members of those tribes supported themselves, to some degree, by fishing, hunting, and gathering fruits, berries, nuts, mushrooms, honey, and other natural products in the forests around their villages. But the Slavs were primarily agriculturalists. In natural forest clearings or in those they created by the slash-and-burn method, they typically cultivated one or more cereal grains and also raised livestock as well as supplementary crops, such as peas, lentils, flax, or hemp.

Although each tribe followed its own leaders and worshipped its own set of gods, they interacted with one another, at times exchanging goods, at others fighting one another. The more adventurous among their members transported the most valuable goods their societies produced (for example, fur pelts and captive slaves) to the markets of distant neighbours—Bulgar on the mid-Volga, the Khazar capital of Itil at the base of the Volga, and the Byzantine outpost of Kherson on the coast of the Crimean peninsula. There they exchanged their goods for oriental finery and, most conspicuously, silver coin.

The transformation of these tribes into the state of Kievan Rus is shrouded in uncertainty. Legends and literature recorded much later, archaeological evidence, and the notations of foreign observers, however, suggest that by the early ninth century Scandinavian adventurers (known variously as 'Varangians' and 'Rus') had entered the Slav lands. Primarily attracted by the silver at the Volga market centres, they plundered Slav villages and carried their booty to the same markets that the Slavs themselves had visited. In the course of the ninth century the Varangians established more permanent ties to the native populace: each band of Varangians protected its own group of Slavs from competing Scandinavian pirates in exchange for regular tribute payments. Those stable relationships were mutually beneficial. The Slavs were relieved of the sporadic, violent raids, while the armed Rus bands received regular supplies of goods used in their exchanges for silver and oriental luxury products. Gradually, the

Rus leaders acquired the character of princes, and the Slav populace became their subjects.

According to a legend in the Primary Chronicle (compiled during the eleventh and early twelfth centuries) one of the first Rus princes was called Riurik. The legend states that Riurik and his brothers were 'invited' by Slav tribes to rule their lands. Tribes that dwelled in the general vicinity of the Lovat and Volkhov rivers and the lands to their east had ejected previous Scandinavian protectors, but then became embroiled in warfare among themselves. Unable to reconcile their differences, the chronicler explained, they called upon Riurik in 862 to restore peace and rule over them.

Riurik, the legend continued, survived his two brothers to become sole ruler until his own death in 879 or 882. A regent, Oleg, then ruled on behalf of Riurik's young son Igor. After Oleg's death (912) Igor reigned until 945; a tribe called the Drevliane killed him after he attempted to collect more than its standard tribute payment. Igor's wife, Olga, assumed the regency and took cunning revenge upon her husband's murderers. Their son, Sviatoslav, claimed his father's place in 962.

By that time the realm of the Riurikid clan had expanded substantially. According to the chronicle, the tribes subject to the Riurikids had increased to include the Krivichi (in the region of the Valdai hills), the Poliane (around Kiev on the Dnieper river), and the Drevliane (south of the Pripiat river, a tributary of the Dnieper). The Riurikids, furthermore, had taken command of the Dnieper, a major commercial artery. From the vantage-point of Kiev they could control all traffic moving down towards the Black Sea, the Byzantine colony of Kherson, and towards the sea route to the Don river and the Khazar Empire. Oleg in 907 and Igor, less successfully in 944, conducted military campaigns against Constantinople, which resulted in treaties permitting the Rus to trade not only at Kherson, but at the rich markets of Constantinople itself, where they mingled with merchants and had access to goods from virtually every corner of the known world.

Sviatoslav (962–72) continued to expand his forefathers' domain. He first subdued the Viatichi, who inhabited lands along the Oka and Volga rivers and had previously paid tribute to the Khazars, and in 965 he launched a campaign against the Khazars themselves. His venture led to the collapse of their empire and, subsequently, the destabilization of the lower Volga and the steppe, a region of grasslands south of the Slav territories. Although he did rescue Kiev from the Pechenegs (a nomadic Turkic population that occupied the steppe) in 968, Sviatoslav devoted most of his attention to establishing control over lands on the Danube river. Forced to abandon that project by the Byzantines, he was returning to Kiev when he was killed by the Pechenegs in 972.

Shortly after Sviatoslav's death his son Iaropolk became prince of Kiev, but conflict erupted between him and his brothers. After one died in battle against him, another brother, Vladimir, fled from Novgorod, the city that he governed, to raise an army in Scandinavia. Upon his return in 980, he first engaged the prince of Polotsk, one of the last non-Riurikid rulers of the East Slav tribes. Victorious, Vladimir married the prince's daughter and added the prince's military retinue to his own army, with which he then defeated Iaropolk and seized the throne of Kiev. Vladimir also subjugated the Radimichi (east of the upper Dnieper river), and in 985 attacked the Volga Bulgars; the agreement he subsequently reached with the latter was the basis for peaceful relations that lasted for a century. Vladimir's triumphs over competing rulers and neighbouring powers established him as the sole ruler of the East Slav tribes and gave his heirs a monopoly over the right to succeed him. His family, which traced its lineage to Riurik, the progenitor of the dynasty, ruled the lands of Rus until 1598.

Over the next generations Vladimir and his successors continued to extend their domain and to create an apparatus to govern it. The political structure they devised for Kievan Rus was based on the concept that its lands were the possession of the dynasty. Thus, as his father had done, Vladimir assigned a portion of his realm to each of his principal sons. Thereafter, the Riurikid princes continued to share the lands of Kievan Rus and the responsibilities for administering and defending them.

Princely administration gradually replaced tribal allegiance and authority. As early as the reign of Olga, officials representing the Kievan ruler began to replace tribal leaders. Vladimir extended this practice by assigning particular lands to his sons, to whom he also delegated responsibility for tax-collection, for protection of communication and trade routes, and for local defence and territorial expansion. Each prince also had his own military force, which was supported by tax revenues, commercial fees, and booty seized in battle. After Vladimir's son Grand Prince Iaroslav (d. 1054) issued a law code known as the *Russkaia pravda*, the Rus princes also became enforcers of Riurikid law. The administration of justice, which upheld both Riurikid authority and social order, yielded revenues in the form of court fees and fines. The *Russkaia pravda*, as amended by Iaroslav's sons and later provisions that continued to be added to it until the thirteenth century, remained in force long after the Kievan era; it was not formally replaced until the law code (*Sudebnik*) of 1497 was adopted.

Over the two centuries following Vladimir's death (1015), Kievan Rus became an amalgam of principalities, whose number increased as the dynasty itself grew. The main principalities in the centre of the realm were Kiev, Chernigov, and Pereiaslavl. Galicia and Volhynia (south-west of Kiev) gained the status of separate principalities in the late eleventh and twelfth centuries, respectively. During the twelfth century Smolensk (north of Kiev on the upper Dnieper) and Rostov-Suzdal (in the north-east) similarly emerged as powerful principalities. The north-western portion of the realm was dominated by Novgorod, whose strength rested on its lucrative commercial relations with Scandinavian and German merchants of the Baltic as well as on its own extensive empire that stretched to the Ural mountains by the end of the eleventh century. After 1097 each of these principalities (with the exceptions of Novgorod and Kiev) was identified with its own branch of the dynasty.

The Riurikid dynasty also converted Kievan Rus to Christianity and thereby provided it with a uniform religious and cultural framework. Christianity, Judaism, and Islam had long been known in these lands, and Olga had personally converted to Christianity. When Vladimir assumed the throne, however, he set idols of Norse, Slav, Finn, and Iranian gods, worshipped by the disparate elements of his society, on a hilltop in Kiev in an attempt to create a single pantheon for his people. But for reasons that remain unclear he soon abandoned this attempt in favour of Christianity. He thereupon gave up his numerous wives and consorts and married Anna, the sister of the Byzantine Emperor Basil. The patriarch of Constantinople appointed a metropolitan to organize the see of Kiev and all Rus, and in 988 Byzantine clergy baptized the population of Kiev in the Dnieper river.

Christianity was not confined to Kiev. When Prince Vladimir dispatched his sons to their portions of his realm, each was accompanied by clergymen and charged with establishing and defending Christianity as well as the dynasty's own authority. In some regions the introduction of the new religion and its clergy met overt resistance. When representatives of the new Church threw the idol of the god Perun into the Volkhov river in Novgorod, for example, their action provoked a popular uprising. Elsewhere resistance was passive; the populace simply continued to honour their traditional gods and practise their rituals in relatively private settings. Thus, although the lands of Rus formally entered the Christian world in 988, it was centuries before the population transferred their faith and loyalties to the Christian Church.

In the mean time, however, the Church, supported by the Riurikid princes, transformed the cultural face of Kievan Rus, especially in its urban centres. The change occurred first in Kiev, which was not only the seat of the senior Riurikid prince, but also the ecclesiastical centre of Kievan Rus. Vladimir removed the pagan idols he had previously erected and in their stead ordered the construction of Christian churches. The most notable was the Church of the Holy Virgin (also known as the Church of the Tithe), which was built in stone and flanked by two other palatial structures. The ensemble formed the centre-piece of 'Vladimir's city', which was surrounded by new fortifications. A generation later Prince Iaroslav expanded this sector of the city by replacing the walls built by his father with new fortifications that encompassed the battlefield on which he defeated the Pechenegs in 1036. Inset into its southern wall was the Golden Gate of Kiev. Within the protected area he constructed a new complex of churches and palaces, the most imposing of which was the stone-built Cathedral of St Sophia—the church of the metropolitan and the symbolic centre of Christianity in Kievan Rus.

These projects brought Byzantine artists and artisans to Kiev. Following Byzantine architectural models, they designed and decorated the early Rus

The Cathedral of St Sophia in Kiev, sketched to re-create its appearance in the late eleventh century.

churches and taught their techniques and skills to local apprentices. The visiting artisans were most heavily concentrated in Kiev, which became the centre of craft production in Kievan Rus during the eleventh and twelfth centuries. Native and visiting artisans—blacksmiths and stone-cutters, carpenters and potters, leather workers, goldsmiths and silversmiths, glassmakers and bone-carvers—produced an array of products, including stone blocks and brick for the new cathedrals, armour and weapons for the princes' retinues, fine jewellery for members of the élite, and pottery and buttons for commoners. The adoption of Christianity also stimulated an expansion of Kievan commerce: marble and glazed tiles, icons and silver frames, and numerous other items used in the construction, decoration, and rites of the churches were added to the silks and satins, wines and oils, and other staple imports from Byzantium.

The expansion of Kiev's commercial and craft activity was accompanied by an increase in its population. By the end of the twelfth century between 36,000 and 50,000 persons—princes, soldiers, clergy, merchants, artisans, unskilled workers, and slaves—resided in the city. Kiev, the political capital of Kievan Rus, had become the ecclesiastical, commercial, and artisanal centre of the realm as well.

Other towns underwent similar, but less dramatic development. Novgorod was also influenced by Christianity and Byzantine culture. Although it had initially been a centre of violent opposition to Christianity, its landscape too was quickly altered by the construction of new, wooden churches and, in the middle of the eleventh century, by its own stone Cathedral of St Sophia. Although Novgorod's economy continued to be centred on its foreign trade, by the twelfth century some artisans were emulating Byzantine patterns in new crafts, such as enamelling and fresco-painting. Novgorod's flourishing economy supported a population of 20,000 to 30,000 by the early thirteenth century. Similar developments occurred in Chernigov, where the Church of the Transfiguration of Our Saviour (1035) had heralded the arrival of Christianity. The construction of the stone Church of the Mother of God in Smolensk (1136–7) and of the Cathedral of the Dormition in Vladimir (1158) proclaimed that wealth and Christianity were spreading across the Riurikid realm.

While architectural design and the decorative arts of mosaics, frescos, and icon-painting, all associated with church construction, were the most visible aspects of the Christian cultural transformation, new literary genres, including chronicles, saints' lives, and sermons, also appeared in Kievan Rus. Although much of the ecclesiastical literature was translated from Greek originals, the clergy of Kievan Rus also began to make their own contributions. The outstanding products of indigenous literature from this era were the Primary Chronicle or 'Tale of Bygone Years' (compiled by monks of the Monastery of the Cave which was founded in the mid-eleventh century outside Kiev) and the 'Sermon on Law and Grace', composed (c.1050) by Metropolitan Hilarion (the first native Rus to be head of the Kievan Church).

By agreement with the Riurikids the Church also assumed legal jurisdiction over a range of social practices and family affairs, including birth, marriage, and death. Ecclesiastical courts had jurisdiction over church personnel and responsibility for the enforcement of Christian standards and rituals in the larger community. Although the Church received added revenue from its courts, the clergy were only partially successful in their efforts to convince the populace to abandon their pagan customs. But to the degree that they were accepted, the spiritual guidance, the promise of salvation, and the social norms and

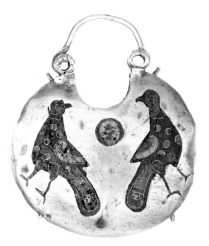

Gold and enamel pendant typical of the jewellery crafted in Kiev in the twelfth century. Pendants of this sort were suspended from head-dresses worn by married women.

Miniature from the fifteenth-century Radzivillov Chronicle illustrating carpenters engaged in construction at Novgorod.

Notes and memoranda associated with daily activities were often engraved on the soft inner surface of birchbark. Among the surviving samples is this document written and drawn by Onfim, a young boy in thirteenth-century Novgorod.

cultural forms of the Church provided a common identity for the diverse tribes comprising Kievan Rus society.

As the Riurikid dynasty and Christian clergy displaced tribal political and spiritual leaders, their political and religious-cultural structures transformed the conglomeration of East Slav tribes into a dynamic and flourishing state. The political system balanced a diffusion of administrative and military power against principles of dynastic sovereignty and seniority; it elevated Kiev to a position of centrality within the realm; and it provided an effective means of defending and expanding the realm.

Within this system each prince supported his own military retinue, and had the authority and the means to hire supplementary forces; he was also responsible for conducting relations with his immediate neighbours. Thus the princes who ruled Novgorod in the eleventh century pushed the Rus border west to Lake Peipus, provided security for the trade routes to the Gulf of Finland, and also participated in the creation of Novgorod's northern empire. Similarly, the princes of Suzdal in the twelfth century extended their domain to the north and east—at the expense of the Volga Bulgars. And, through the first half of the eleventh century, the grand princes of Kiev conducted relations with western neighbours (Poland and Hungary), Byzantium, and the Pechenegs on the steppe.

The dynastic system, however, also encouraged co-operation among the princes when they faced crises. Concerted action was prompted particularly by the Polovtsy, another population of Turkic nomads that moved into the steppe and displaced the Pechenegs in the second half of the eleventh century. Prince Vsevolod Iaroslavich of Pereiaslavl, who commanded the first line of defence for the southern frontier, was defeated by a Polovtsy attack in 1061. When they launched a new campaign in 1068, Prince Vsevolod and his brothers, Iziaslav of Kiev and Sviatoslav of Chernigov, combined their forces. Although the Polovtsy were victorious, they retreated after another encounter with Sviatoslav's forces. With the exception of one frontier skirmish in 1071, they then refrained from attacking the Rus for the next twenty years.

When the Polovtsy did renew hostilities in the 1090s, the Riurikids were engaged in their own intradynastic conflicts. Their ineffective defence allowed the Polovtsy to reach the environs of Kiev and burn the Monastery of the Caves.

Grand Prince Iaroslav's foreign policies included arranging marriages for his children with foreign princes and princesses. This detail, taken from a painted frieze in Kiev's St Sophia Cathedral, depicts one of his daughters.

But after the princes had resolved their differences at a conference in 1097, they once again mounted impressive coalitions that not only repulsed Polovtsy attacks, but pushed deep into the steppe and broke up the federation of Polovtsy tribes responsible for the aggression. These campaigns yielded comparatively peaceful relations that facilitated trade between Kievan Rus and the Polovtsy and kept the trade route linking Kiev and Constantinople secure for the next fifty years.

But the political organization of the Riurikids also contributed to repeated dynastic conflicts over succession to the throne of Kiev. Although the princes were dispersed, it was understood that the senior member of the eldest generation of the dynasty was heir to the Kievan throne. Succession thus followed a lateral pattern, with the throne of Kiev passing to a grand prince's brothers and cousins, then to their sons.

The proliferation and complexity of the Riurikid family, however, generated recurrent confusion over the definition of seniority, the standards for eligibility, and the lands subject to lateral succession. Disagreements over succession provoked intradynastic warfare; the outcome of the conflicts refined the 'rules'. For example, a challenge to the seniority of Iaroslav's sons was mounted by a grandson of Iaroslav's elder brother (concurrently with the Polovtsy attack on the Rus lands in 1068–9); following its failure, eligibility for succession was restricted to those princes whose fathers had been grand prince of Kiev. In 1097, when wars over lands to be transferred along with the Kievan throne became so severe that they impaired a successful defence against the Polovtsy, a princely conference resolved that each principality in Kievan Rus would henceforth be the possession of a single branch of the dynasty. The only exceptions were Kiev itself, which in 1113 reverted to the status of a dynastic possession, and Novgorod, which had asserted the right to select its own prince by 1136.

But even as confrontations and conferences resolved disputes, the evolving rules of succession to the grand princely throne failed to anticipate new disputes stemming from the growth of the dynasty and state. As a result, throughout the twelfth century the dynasty was embroiled in numerous controversies, often triggered by attempts of members of younger generations to bypass their elders and to reduce the number of princely lines eligible for the succession. These conflicts escalated as dynastic branches formed rival coalitions, drew upon the enlarged populations and economic resources of their own principalities to enhance their military capabilities, and also fought for control over secondary regions, especially Novgorod, whose wealth and power could give a decisive advantage in the battles for the primary objective, Kiev.

The greatest confrontations involved the heirs of Grand Prince Vladimir Monomakh (1113–25). By the time of his death, his sons had become the exclusive heirs to the grand princely throne; first Mstislav (1125–32), then Iaropolk (1132–9) ruled as grand prince. An attempt by Iaropolk to arrange for his nephew (Mstislav's son) to be his successor provoked objections from his younger brother, Iurii Dolgorukii, the prince of Rostov-Suzdal. The struggle persisted until 1154, when Iurii finally ascended to the Kievan throne and restored the traditional order of succession.

The stylistic features of the Church of the Intercession are reflected also in the Church of St Dmitrii, constructed in Vladimir in the 1190s.

An even more destructive conflict commenced after the death in 1167 of Grand Prince Rostislav Mstislavich (who had appropriately succeeded his uncle Iurii). When a member of the next generation (Mstislav Iziaslavich, the prince of Volhynia) attempted to seize the throne, a coalition of princes formed to oppose him. Led by Iurii's son Andrei Bogoliubskii, it represented the senior generation of eligible princes, but also included the sons of the late Grand Prince Rostislav and the princes of Chernigov. The conflict culminated in 1169, when Andrei's sons led a campaign that resulted in the flight of Mstislav Iziaslavich and the sack of Kiev. Andrei's brother Gleb, as prince of Pereiaslavl (traditionally the main seat of the house of Monomakh), became grand prince of Kiev.

Prince Andrei personified the growing tensions between the increasingly powerful principalities of Kievan Rus and their centre Kiev. As prince of Vladimir-Suzdal, he concentrated on the development of Vladimir and challenged the primacy of Kiev by building the Church of the Dormition in 1158 and his own Golden Gate. He also constructed his own palace complex of Bogoliubovo outside Vladimir, conducted campaigns against the Volga Bulgars, celebrated a victory over them in 1165 by building the Church of the Intercession nearby on the Nerl river, and extended his influence over Novgorod. Andrei used his power and resources, however, to defend the principle of generational seniority in the succession to Kiev. But his victory was short-lived: when Gleb died in 1171, Andrei's coalition failed in its attempt to secure the throne for another of his brothers. The renewed struggle ended instead with a prince from the Chernigov line on the Kievan throne; his reign and the accompanying dynastic peace lasted until 1194.

By the turn of the century, eligibility for the Kievan throne was confined to three main lines: princes of Volhynia, Smolensk, and Chernigov. When the prince of Volhynia (representing the junior generation) claimed the throne, the rules of eligibility and succession were temporarily waived due to the sheer power that he was able to muster. Although the primacy of the senior generation was restored upon his death in 1205, new rivalries emerged. By the mid-1230s, princes of Chernigov and Smolensk were locked in a prolonged conflict over Kiev. But in this case the combatants were of the same generation and each was the son of a grand prince; dynastic traditions were offering little guidance for determining which prince had seniority.

The dynastic contests of the early thirteenth century had serious consequences. During the hostilities Kiev was sacked twice more, in 1203 and 1235. The strife revealed the divergence between the southern and western principalities (which were deeply enmeshed in the conflicts) and those of the north and east (which were indifferent). Intradynastic conflict, compounded by the lack of cohesion among the components of Kievan Rus, undermined the system of shared power that had previously ensured the integrity of the realm. Kievan Rus was thus left without effective defences when it had to face a new, overwhelming threat from the steppe—the Mongols.

The Rus Principalities under Mongol Domination

In 1237–40, the Mongols extended their empire, founded by Genghis Khan, over the lands of Rus. Their first victim was the north-eastern principality of Riazan. After besieging and sacking its capital, the Mongols next destroyed the fortified outpost of Moscow and then advanced northward towards the capital of the main principality in the north-east, Vladimir. By the time they arrived there in early February 1238, its prince, Iurii Vsevolodich, had left the city to gather an army; meeting little resistance, the invaders laid siege, stormed, and sacked Vladimir as well as the neighbouring town of Suzdal. When Prince Iurii belatedly brought up his army to face the Mongols, it suffered a crushing defeat in a battle on the Sit river (4 March 1238). The Mongols then proceeded westward towards Novgorod, but broke off their campaign to summer in the steppe. The following winter they subdued the Polovtsy and the peoples of the North Caucasus.

The Mongols resumed their assault on the lands of Rus in 1239, when they conquered Perciaslavl (March) and Chernigov (October). A year later, after conducting additional campaigns in the steppe and the Caucasus, they laid siege to Kiev. The date of its fall—December 1240—marks the collapse of Kievan

A Mongol horseman armed with bow and arrows.

13

Rus. The Mongols continued their advance westward, subduing Galicia and Volhynia and pressing into Poland and Hungary. They halted their advance only in September 1242, when their leader Batu was recalled to Mongolia for the selection of a new great khan.

The Mongol campaigns devastated the lands of Kievan Rus. Among its major towns, Riazan, Vladimir, and Suzdal in the north-east, and Pereiaslavl, Chernigov, and Kiev in the south-west had been severely damaged. The ruling élite was also decimated. At the Battle of Sit alone, Prince Iurii Vsevolodich, three sons, and two nephews had all been killed. The invaders also ravaged the villages and fields in their path; peasants who were not slain or enslaved fled to safer locales. Where the Mongols passed, farming, trade, and handicrafts ceased. The Mongol invasion shattered the economic vitality and cultural vibrancy characteristic of Kievan Rus.

The Mongol invasion, however, did not disturb all the norms and traditions of the Kievan Rus. The devastation was neither ubiquitous nor total. In the north-east some towns, such as Rostov, Tver, and Iaroslavl, had not been touched. Although initially strained by the influx of refugees, these communities ultimately benefited economically from the labour and skills brought by their new residents. Novgorod, which similarly escaped the Mongol onslaught, continued to engage in commercial exchanges with its Baltic trading partners and import vital goods, including silver, to the Rus lands.

Lines of authority also remained unbroken: the metropolitan of Kiev and all Rus was still the leader of the Orthodox community, and the Riurikid dynasty remained the ruling house of Rus. While the Mongols pursued their westward campaign, the Riurikid princes were left to restore order, organize recovery efforts, and attempt to avert further invasion and destruction. They followed dynastic custom: the senior surviving prince of the eldest generation assumed the highest position in the north-east. When Prince Iurii Vsevolodich of Vladimir was killed at the Battle of Sit, his brother Iaroslav succeeded to his throne; their younger brothers, sons, and nephews assumed the thrones of other principalities—Suzdal, Starodub, Rostov, and Novgorod—in accordance with the dynastic rules of succession. In the south-western principalities the princes of Volhynia and Chernigov similarly resumed their former seats.

The distribution of lands and resources among the remaining princes facilitated effective defensive measures against other foes. As early as July 1240 Prince Alexander, son of Prince Iaroslav Vsevolodich, earned the epithet 'Nevsky' by defeating the Swedes in a battle on the Neva river, thereby repulsing their attempt to seize control over Novgorod's routes to the Gulf of Finland and the Baltic Sea. In another battle at Lake Peipus in 1242, he halted an eastward drive of the Teutonic Knights, who had been threatening the frontiers of Novgorod and Pskov.

When Batu returned to the steppe, he organized his realm as the Kipchak khanate or Desht-i-Kipchak, but commonly called the Golden Horde. It encompassed not only the Rus principalities but the steppe lands, extending from the Danube river in the west through the northern Caucasus and across the Volga river to the Sea of Aral. Its capital was Sarai, built on the lower Volga river. The Golden Horde constituted one component of the much larger Mongol Empire, which, at its peak, spanned an area stretching from Rus, Persia, and Iraq in the west to China and the Pacific Ocean in the east. The khans of the Golden Horde were subordinate to the great khan of the Mongol Empire (at least until the end of the thirteenth century), and their policies were shaped by imperial politics and their interactions with other components of the empire.

These factors influenced the nature of the khans' relationships with the Riurikid princes. The khans assumed the right to confirm the Riurikid princes' right to rule; to obtain a patent of authority (*iarlyk*), each prince had to present himself before the khan in symbolic recognition of his suzerainty. But to accomplish their broader goals, the khans also demanded from the Rus princes obedience and tribute—initially in the form of men, livestock, furs, and other valuable products, later in silver. The Church also recognized the khan as the supreme secular authority in Rus.

The practice of issuing patents reflected the new association of the Riurikid princes with the Mongol khans; that association gradually altered the political, especially dynastic, structures inherited from Kievan Rus. In 1243 Batu issued a patent to Iaroslav Vsevolodich to rule in Vladimir; similarly, *c.*1245, he confirmed Daniil Romanovich as prince of Galicia and Volhynia. Only Mikhail of Chernigov, the last of the Riurikids to go to the horde, met a different fate: when he refused to perform the rituals of obeisance, the khan had him executed (September 1246). The Riurikids confirmed in office, however, collaborated with the khan and his agents (*baskaki*) in the implementation of his orders and policies. And, when Riurikid princes competed for seniority, they appealed to the khan for arbitration and support. Thus, when Prince Alexander Nevsky's brother Andrei seized the throne of Vladimir from their uncle in 1248, and later conspired with Daniil of Galicia and Volhynia against the Mongols, Alexander turned to the Mongols for support. By placing Alexander (the elder of the two brothers) on the throne, the khan was upholding dynastic custom. Alexander subsequently obediently served the Mongol khan: he not only helped to remove his brother, but forced Novgorod in 1259 to submit to a Mongol census that then became the basis for tribute collection.

When Alexander Nevsky died in 1263, the khan passed over the rebellious Andrei (who had become prince of Suzdal), and conferred the office of grand prince on their younger brothers—first Iaroslav Iaroslavich (d. 1271/2), then Vasilii (d. 1277). When the throne passed to the next generation, however, Alexander Nevsky's sons competed to become grand prince of Vladimir. Like their father, they each appealed to the Mongols for help. But the horde itself was engaged in a power struggle that lasted through the 1280s and 1290s. As a result, Mongol support was divided: Alexander's eldest son and legitimate heir received a patent and military assistance from Nogai, a powerful Mongol chieftain in the western portion of the horde's lands, while his younger brother obtained the support of the khan at Sarai. The contest lasted until the elder brother died in 1294, and the younger legitimately succeeded to the throne. By 1299 the Mongols' internal dissension ended with the military triumph of Khan Tokhta, the death of Nogai, and reassertion of the khan's authority over the entire horde.

Even as Nevsky's two sons waged their battles, two other princes—their younger brother Daniil and their cousin Mikhail Iaroslavich of Tver—emerged as influential political figures in north-eastern Rus. With Daniil's death in 1303, followed by that of the grand prince in 1304, the throne of Vladimir passed with the approval of the khan to the next eligible member of their generation— Mikhail of Tver. But then a radically new situation arose. The princes of Moscow refused to recognize Mikhail. Under the leadership of Prince Iurii Daniilovich they went to war against him in 1305 and again in 1308. In 1313 Mikhail went to pay obeisance to the new Khan Uzbek. In his absence Iurii extended his own influence over Novgorod, whose commercial wealth was critical for satisfying the khan's demand for tribute. When summoned to appear before the khan and account for his behaviour, Iurii deftly used his new resources to outbid and outbribe Mikhail. He not only avoided punishment, but won the hand of Uzbek's sister in marriage as well as the patent for the throne of Vladimir. For his refusal to acquiesce Mikhail was recalled to the horde and in 1318 he was executed. Iurii held the throne of Vladimir until 1322.

According to dynastic rules, however, Prince Iurii of Moscow lacked legitimacy; his authority depended solely on the endorsement and military support of Uzbek. The khan's favour was contingent upon Iurii's ability to perform his functions as senior prince—to collect and deliver the tribute from Rus. But Iurii did not have the support of all the Riurikids; four times in as many years Uzbek had to dispatch military expeditions to assist his brother-in-law, and in 1322 he returned the throne of Vladimir to the legitimate heir, Alexander of Tver. Five years later an

Dominance over Novgorod and access to its wealth were factors in the political success of the Moscow princes. This sketch of one of the main streets of Novgorod is based on results of archaeological studies and represents the city's appearance in the fourteenth century.

anti-Mongol uprising in Tver forced Alexander to flee. In the aftermath Iurii's brother Ivan (known later as 'Ivan Kalita' or 'Money-bags') secured the Vladimir throne. With the exception of a few brief interludes later in the fourteenth century, the princes of Moscow retained the position of grand prince until their dynastic line expired at the end of the sixteenth century.

By the time the princes of Moscow had gained seniority in northern Rus, the south-western principalities were wholly detached. Like their northern neighbours, they too had recognized the suzerainty of the Golden Horde after the Mongol invasion. But by the middle of the fourteenth century, Galicia and Volhynia had been absorbed into the realms of Poland and Lithuania. During the following decades Lithuania added Kiev, Chernigov, and Smolensk to its domain as well. The lands of Rus lost their territorial integrity.

Simultaneously, the unity of the metropolitanate was also being threatened. Despite the broadening political gulf between the northern and south-western principalities, they had all continued to form a single ecclesiastical community. After Metropolitan Maxim moved from Kiev to the north-east in 1299, however, the unity of the see was repeatedly challenged. First, the prince of Galicia secured the establishment of a short-lived metropolitanate (c.1303–8); later, the rulers of Poland and Lithuania urged the creation of separate metropolitanates for the Orthodox inhabitants of the lands they had incorporated. Church patriarchs established a series of sees (c.1315–1340s), but under pressure from the metropolitans in north-eastern Rus, disbanded each of them.

Thus, a century after the Mongols destroyed Kiev, the institutions that had given cohesion both to Kievan Rus and to the post-invasion principalities were crumbling. The state had fragmented, and the unity of the Church was in jeopardy. Furthermore, the dynasty's complex rules of seniority and succession had been supplanted by the authority of the khans, who had begun to confer the throne of Vladimir not on the dynasty's legitimate heirs—the senior, eligible princes—but on the princes most likely to fulfil their demands: the Daniilovichi of Moscow.

The Foundations of Muscovy

Daniilovich rule was not automatically accepted by the rest of the dynasty. Although the legitimate heir, Alexander of Tver, had been soundly defeated, opponents of Daniilovich dominance surfaced repeatedly through the fourteenth century. Their pressure compelled the Muscovite princes to adopt policies aimed at retaining Mongol favour, neutralizing the dynastic opposition, and developing domestic sources of legitimacy. As a result of such efforts to stay in power, they also strengthened their own territorial, economic, and military base. The Daniilovichi thus transformed the distribution of power in the lands of northern Rus and laid the foundations for a new state—Muscovy.

The adversaries of the Daniilovichi were also Riurikids. Their domains, known as apanages (*udely*), had been carved out of older, larger principalities in accordance with a custom, dating from the Kievan Rus era, of subdividing the lands ruled by a dynastic branch to accommodate all its members and also to share the responsibilities for administration and defence. The practice was particularly pronounced among the Rostov clan, whose lands were carved into numerous apanages, including Iaroslavl, Beloozero, and Ustiug. The apanage princes of Rostov joined the various coalitions against the Daniilovichi and in support of the legitimate princes from the house of Tver.

Their protests, however, made virtually no impression on the Mongol khans, who maintained the Moscow princes—Ivan Daniilovich, then his sons Semen (ruled 1341–53) and Ivan II (ruled 1353–9)—in power. Only once did an anti-Daniilovich coalition achieve success: when Ivan II died and the Golden Horde itself entered a period of internal conflict, a coalition secured the confirmation of the prince of Suzdal as grand prince. Within three years, however, the Moscow line in the person of Dmitrii Ivanovich (later known as Dmitrii Donskoi) had recovered the Vladimir throne.

Although the Mongol khans paid little attention to them, the Daniilovichi themselves did respond to their dynastic opponents. One strategy they adopted to neutralize them was to form marital alliances. Ivan I arranged marriages for his daughters with the sons of two of his most vocal opponents, the princes of Beloozero and Iaroslavl; his niece became the wife of Prince Konstantin Mikhailovich of Tver, a champion of the anti-Daniilovich group. Ivan's son Semen married the daughter of the late Alexander of Tver despite the Church's disapproval of this, his third marriage. In 1366 Prince Dmitrii followed the pattern by marrying the daughter of his former rival, the prince of Suzdal. These marriages, all concluded with dynastic branches whose members had been reluctant to recognize the predominance of Moscow, created bonds of kinship and alliance. Although they could not transform the Daniilovichi into the senior dynastic line, they did have the effect of elevating the Daniilovichi's informal status with their in-laws and, thereby, helped to mute, if not completely neutralize, their opposition.

Another strategy adopted by the Daniilovichi was to subordinate princes from other branches of the dynasty and simultaneously to expand their own territorial domain. The Moscow princes ruled two sets of territories: lands that belonged to their patrimony (*otchina*) of Moscow and lands that were attached to the grand principality of Vladimir. Even before they became grand princes of Vladimir the princes of Moscow had extended their realm to include Serpukhov, Kolomna, and Mozhaisk; through the fourteenth century they continued to acquire new territories and add them to their patrimonial domain. Ivan Kalita is credited with aggressively expanding his family's domain and acquiring the principalities of Beloozero and Uglich (formerly Rostov apanages) and Galich. His grandson, Dmitrii Donskoi, consolidated control over

Galich, absorbed the principality of Starodub, and also brought the independent principality of Rostov under his influence.

Territorial expansion provided a variety of assets and advantages. One was
control over rivers, which had strategic as well as commercial value. By acquiring Serpukhov, Kolomna, and Mozhaisk, Muscovy encompassed the entire
length of the Moscow river as well as the segment of the Oka between Kolomna
and Serpukhov that formed the southern boundary of the principality. Dmitrii
Donskoi later sponsored the construction of walled monasteries at these towns
and, thereby, fortified the border. The Moscow princes also controlled a significant section of the Volga river from Kostroma (part of the grand principality of
Vladimir) to Nizhnii Novgorod. The principality of Uglich, located between
two of the remaining independent principalities, Iaroslavl and Tver, contained
another segment of the Volga. Remote from the main body of Moscow's holdings were Beloozero and the independent but subordinate principality of
Ustiug, which commanded the main trade routes that spanned the lands of the
north.

Territorial expansion also brought a larger populace under the direct rule of
the Muscovite princes. Moscow's economic and tax base was, correspondingly,
broadened. Retainers of subordinated princes, furthermore, were motivated to
transfer their allegiance to Moscow, whose own military force and administrative staffs were thereby enlarged and strengthened. The Muscovite princes were
able to collect transit and customs fees from the traffic and commercial trans-
actions conducted along their roads and rivers and in their towns. Their control
over segments of the Volga also gave them a greater role in the transport of
goods down that river to Bulgar and Sarai, hence in the Mongols' extensive trade
network.

Even though it was growing, Moscow's territory was divided into relatively
few apanages. During the reign of Dmitrii Donskoi (1362–89), only one
apanage principality (Serpukhov) was carved out of Muscovy's lands for his
cousin. After Dmitrii's death in 1389, his eldest son (Vasilii I) inherited the
throne; each of Dmitrii's other four sons then received an apanage principality.
But due to their failure to produce sons of their own, most of their lands eventually reverted to the grand prince. The only one to survive was the apanage
principality of Mozhaisk (later divided into two principalities, Mozhaisk and
Vereia). At least until the death of Vasilii I (1425), the few apanage princes of
Moscow as well as their senior advisers and military commanders (who held the
rank of boyar) were loyal supporters of the grand prince. This internal territorial and political cohesion provided a central, unified core for the expanding
state of Muscovy.

The wealth Moscow derived from its increased population, extended lands,
and commerce was reflected in the introduction of monumental stone buildings
into the wooden town. After the Mongol invasion the princes in north-eastern
Rus could not afford to construct major buildings. Tver was the first to

accumulate sufficient wealth (by the end of the thirteenth century) to resume the construction of stone cathedrals. Moscow followed: in 1326 its Prince Ivan (the future Grand Prince Ivan Kalita) and Metropolitan Peter co-sponsored the construction of the Church of the Dormition. Soon afterwards four more stone churches were built inside Moscow's kremlin. Prince Dmitrii rebuilt Moscow's kremlin fortifications in stone in 1367, fortified some towns and outposts on Muscovy's frontier, and also ordered the restoration of the Dormition Cathedral in Vladimir. In conjunction with the renewed construction activity, the arts of fresco- and icon-painting also revived. In the 1340s the walls of the kremlin churches were painted with frescos by Byzantine and Russian artists. Those of the Dormition Cathedral in Vladimir were painted with frescos at the commission of Vasilii I by Andrei Rublev, one of the greatest artists of the era.

Half a century after the Mongols set them on the throne of Vladimir, the princes of Moscow had transformed their realm. In addition to its visual signs, their growing power was manifested in Prince Dmitrii's military victories first over a challenger from Tver, and then over a general from the Golden Horde itself—Mamai. These confrontations occurred while the discord within the Golden Horde, begun concurrently with his own ascension to the throne,

A Lithuanian army assisting Tver appeared before Moscow in 1368, but was unable to breach the recently constructed Muscovite fortifications.

intensified. Dmitrii, indeed, had obtained his patent from Mamai, to whom he had pledged to deliver the tribute gathered from his lands. Yet Dmitrii found it increasingly difficult to make those tribute payments for at least two reasons. As the conflicts in the horde disrupted the Volga markets in the 1360s and 1370s, Moscow's revenue from commercial customs and transit fees collected from its Volga trade correspondingly declined. Secondly, Novgorod, whose commercial activities were responsible for importing silver into the Russian lands, was quarrelling with its Baltic Sea trading partners, who restricted the flow of silver to Novgorod and even temporarily suspended trade with Novgorod.

Mamai gambled on the supposition that he might receive larger tribute payments from another prince, and transferred the patent for the Vladimir throne twice, in 1370 and 1375, to the prince of Tver—Dmitrii's chief rival. These actions provoked open warfare between Moscow and Tver in 1371–2 and 1375. Despite the fact that Tver received support from Mamai as well as Lithuania, both outbursts of hostility ended in victory for Moscow. In 1375 the prince of Tver agreed to recognize Dmitrii as his 'elder brother' and as the legitimate grand prince of Vladimir; Mamai also returned the patent for the throne to Dmitrii.

Nevertheless, within a few years Dmitrii and his patron Mamai were at war. Because of the mounting discord in the horde and the seizure of Sarai by Tokhtamysh (a Mongol khan from the eastern half of the horde's territory), Mamai's own situation had become desperate. To defeat Tokhtamysh he had to obtain supplementary troops, his own forces having been weakened by a bout of bubonic plague. For that he required funds. Mamai, therefore, demanded that Dmitrii pay the tribute in full. But Dmitrii, whose revenues had been reduced, hesitated. Mamai raised an army and, with promises of assistance from Lithuania, advanced upon his former protégé. Dmitrii gathered an army drawn from the numerous principalities over which he and his forefathers had established ascendancy. On 8 September 1380 the two armies fought in the battle of Kulikovo; it was here Dmitrii earned the epithet 'Donskoi'. Dmitrii's armies were victorious over Mamai, whose Lithuanian allies failed to arrive. Mamai suffered another defeat in an encounter with Tokhtamysh the following year. Having restored order in the horde, Tokhtamysh launched his own campaign against Dmitrii and the other Russian princes in 1382. He laid siege to Moscow, which had been abandoned by Dmitrii, and restored Mongol authority over the Russian principalities. He reasserted the horde's demand for tribute and reconfirmed the Rus princes on their thrones.

The battle of Kulikovo did not terminate the Muscovite princes' subordination to the Mongol khans, but it did reduce their dependence upon them for legitimacy. The battle demonstrated Moscow's pre-eminence among the principalities of north-eastern Rus; no other branch of Riurikids ever again challenged the seniority of the Muscovite line and its claim to the position of grand prince of Vladimir. Although the princes of Moscow formally recognized the suzerainty of the khan of the Golden Horde, their practice, begun by Dmitrii Donskoi, of naming their own heirs implicitly minimized the significance of the khan's right to bestow the patent to rule.

The *Old Testament Trinity* exemplifies the work of Andrei Rublev, who produced it in the second or third decade of the fifteenth century for the Trinity–Sergius Monastery.

21

A sixteenth-century depiction of the battle of Kulikovo.

The Daniilovich success, however, was still incomplete. Although Dmitrii Donskoi had been able to mobilize a large number of north-eastern principalities to defeat Mamai in 1380, some important lands remained beyond the range of his authority. One was Nizhnii Novgorod, whose prince refused to place his retainers under Muscovite command at the battle of Kulikovo. Another was Tver; despite its prince's recent recognition of Dmitrii's seniority, its forces did not join Dmitrii's army. A third land, Novgorod, had similarly declined to participate.

Dmitrii's successors set about to remedy that situation. Vasilii I gained control over Nizhnii Novgorod and made a concerted, but less successful, effort to take control of parts of Novgorod's northern empire. Even before his reign, a monk, known as Stefan of Perm, had created a new bishopric for the far north-eastern portion of Novgorod's realm; the newly converted inhabitants (the Zyriane or Komi tribes) transferred their tribute payments from Novgorod to Moscow. Vasilii I attempted to gain control of another region subject to Novgorod—the Dvina land, rich in fish, fur, and other natural products that constituted major sources of Novgorod's wealth. Although his repeated efforts to annex the Dvina land failed, Vasilii did acquire Ustiug, which controlled access to both the Dvina and Vychegda rivers. Continuing pressure on its northern empire did, however, gradually undermine Novgorod's control over its economic resources; Vasilii II then defeated the weakened Novgorod militarily in 1456 and his successor Ivan III finally absorbed it into Muscovy in 1478. Ivan III continued the process by also annexing Tver in 1485.

The efforts of the Muscovite princes to consolidate their position within their growing realm benefited from the Church, which, already in the fourteenth century, was advocating unity and centralization. The Church's indirect endorsement of the Daniilovichi of Moscow provided a measure of domestically based legitimacy, which initially supplemented, but ultimately replaced Mongol favour as a justification for holding the throne of Vladimir.

Church support for the Daniilovichi was neither automatic nor explicit. Indeed, in the early fourteenth century Metropolitan Maxim (d. 1305) used his influence to discourage Iurii of Moscow from challenging the succession of Mikhail of Tver to the Vladimir throne. Although Metropolitan Peter, who succeeded Maxim, had sharp differences with Grand Prince Mikhail, he too did not unambiguously support Moscow. But he did co-sponsor the Church of the Dormition in Moscow, and when he died a few months after its construction had begun, he was buried in its walls; a shrine dedicated to him subsequently arose

The stone walls and towers of Novgorod's kremlin were Muscovite constructions, erected after Grand Prince Ivan III annexed Novgorod in 1478.

on the site. The association of Peter (who was canonized in 1339) with Moscow contributed to the city's growing reputation as an ecclesiastical centre.

For Metropolitan Peter and his successor Theognostus, however, the political fortunes of various princes were secondary to ecclesiastical concerns, the most pressing of which was maintaining the integrity of the metropolitanate of Kiev and all Rus. For the metropolitans of the second half of the fourteenth century, Alexis and Cyprian, that issue became a preoccupation. Just as Alexis became metropolitan in 1354, the Lithuanian prince Olgerd succeeded in establishing a metropolitanate over the Orthodox bishoprics in his realm, including Kiev and western Chernigov. The Lithuanian metropolitan was related to Olgerd's wife, a princess from the house of Tver. Alexis responded by formally transferring his seat from Kiev to Vladimir (a move made, *de facto*, by Maxim). Subsequent efforts to reunite his see took him to Constantinople, Sarai, and Kiev (where he was held in captivity from 1358 to 1360). Only in 1361, when the metropolitan of the Lithuanian see died, did he succeed in bringing the south-western Rus bishoprics back under his jurisdiction.

In 1375 the metropolitanate of Kiev and Lithuania was revived; its metropolitan, Cyprian, was expected to succeed Alexis and reunite the two sees. But when Alexis died in 1378 and Cyprian arrived in Moscow, he was humiliated and expelled by Prince Dmitrii. The prince gave his support to Pimen, who became metropolitan in 1380. Cyprian and Pimen competed for dominance within the Rus Church until the latter, as well as Prince Dmitrii, died in 1389. Cyprian was then able to return to Moscow; he led the Church until his own death in 1407.

Cyprian, supported by monastic spiritual leaders of north-eastern Rus, was an exponent of ecclesiastical unity. That theme was expressed in icons and frescos sponsored by the Church. It was also articulated in literature, which, like architecture and painting, was recovering from the decline it had suffered in the aftermath of the Mongol invasion. The Laurentian Chronicle, copied by the monk Lavrentii in 1377, for example, incorporated the Primary Chronicle and a second component covering events to the year 1305. Its broadly inclusive subject-matter and character, which drew upon sources from northern as well as southern Rus, affirmed the continuity and unity of the Orthodox community in all the lands of Rus.

Once Cyprian had become the unchallenged head of the Church, he placed even more emphasis on the themes of unity and continuity. His *Life of St Peter* (the former metropolitan) highlighted Peter's relationship with Prince Ivan Kalita, whom he praised specifically as the initiator of the process of 'gathering the Rus lands'. The Trinity Chronicle, compiled at his court, similarly praised Ivan Kalita and his grandson Dmitrii Donskoi. Its underlying premiss was that all the principalities of Rus formed a single ecclesiastical community and that Moscow had replaced Kiev as its centre. Although these themes were meant to relate to the Church, they implicitly promoted the concept of a politically unified secular state as well; such a state was envisioned as a necessary aid in the creation and protection of the ecclesiastical unity of the see.

By the mid-fifteenth century Church texts characterized Dmitrii Donskoi as the hero of Kulikovo and stressed his role as the prince who had gathered an army, drawn from many of the lands of Rus, to oppose the Tatars. They also likened his grandson Vasilii II to Vladimir; the latter had introduced Christianity to Rus and had subsequently been canonized as a saint, while the former was depicted as the protector of the Orthodox faith for rejecting a union with the Roman Church (1439) and supporting the Russian prelates' decision (1448) to name their own metropolitan without confirmation by the patriarch of Constantinople.

The deep concern of the Church to preserve the territorial and, after 1439, the spiritual integrity of the metropolitanate enhanced the prestige of the Muscovite princes, whose political policies were compatible with the causes of the Church. The Church, while pursuing and justifying its own ecclesiastical goals, furnished the Daniilovichi with ideological concepts that legitimized their rule.

By 1425 Muscovy had strengthened both its material and ideological foundations. The new domestic sources of legitimacy, however, remained secondary as long as the Golden Horde continued to be powerful and to support the Daniilovichi. Despite a devastating attack by Timur (Tamerlane) on Sarai and its other market centres in 1395, the horde was able to maintain its dominance over the Rus princes, to collect tribute from them, and even to launch a major campaign and besiege Moscow (1408). Lithuania similarly exerted a strong influence over the lands of Rus. It incorporated Smolensk (1395) and became increasingly involved in Novgorod, Tver, and Riazan. Vasilii I, who had married the daughter of Vitovt, the grand prince of Lithuania, not only met Lithuania's expansion with relative passivity, but named Vitovt one of the guardians of his son, Vasilii II.

Shortly after Vasilii I died in 1425, however, the balance of power in the region shifted. Muscovy's neighbours, Lithuania and the Golden Horde, had imposed internal order and external limits on the Rus lands. But in 1430 the Lithuanian grand prince died, and his realm fell into political disarray. At virtually the same time the Golden Horde, which had never fully recovered from the economic disruptions caused by Timur, began to disintegrate. During the next two decades the Golden Horde split into four divisions: the khanate of Kazan on the mid-Volga, the Crimean khanate, the khanate of Astrakhan, and the remnant core—the Great Horde.

Once Muscovy's neighbours had weakened, the Daniilovichi reverted to intradynastic warfare. At issue, as during the Kievan Rus era, was a principle of succession. In the second half of the fourteenth century the princes of Moscow (in the absence of living brothers and eligible cousins) had regularly named their eldest sons as their heirs. Although this practice established a vertical pattern of succession, it was adopted as a matter of necessity, not as a deliberate plan to replace the traditional lateral succession system. When Vasilii I died, however, he left not only his son Vasilii II, but four brothers. As long as his son's guardians (who included Vitovt of Lithuania and Metropolitan Photius) were alive, no one quarrelled with his succession.

But in 1430–1, within a year of one another, Vitovt and Photius both died. Shortly afterwards, the eldest of Vasilii II's uncles challenged his nephew for the throne of Vladimir. He and Vasilii each appealed to the Mongol Khan Ulu-Muhammed. Although Vasilii was awarded the patent, his uncle none the less contested the decision and seized Moscow in 1433. When he died in 1434, his sons continued the war even though, according to the principle of seniority their father had invoked, they had no claim to the throne. The prolonged war was both brutal and decisive. By the time it was concluded, Vasilii had blinded one cousin and had in turn been blinded by another; he had been captured and released by the Tatars of Ulu-Muhammed's horde (1445) as it migrated to the mid-Volga where it subsequently formed the khanate of Kazan; he had welcomed into his service two of the khan's sons who assisted him against his cousins; he had established Moscow's control over the vast majority of the northern Rus lands and increased its authority over Novgorod; and he had subdued his relatives—apanage princes in Muscovy—and restricted succession to his own direct heirs.

The triumph of Vasilii II over his uncle and cousins enabled him and his heirs to continue, virtually without restraint, the process of consolidating Muscovite authority over the northern Rus lands and forming a centralized, unified state to govern them. The principle of vertical succession, confirmed by the war, limited the division of lands to the formation of apanage principalities for the grand prince's immediate relatives. It correspondingly restricted the proliferation of large, competitive armies under the control of autonomous princes. In addition to subordinating most of the northern principalities to Moscow, the altered succession system served to unify and consolidate the Russian lands around Moscow. By the mid-fifteenth century the princes of Moscow had fashioned a new political structure, centred around their own enlarged hereditary domain and their dynastic line, within which eligibility for the post of grand prince had been narrowly defined. Built upon territorial, economic, military, and ideological foundations that displaced both the traditional heritage of Kievan Rus and Tatar authority, the new state of Muscovy was thus poised to exploit the disintegration of Golden Horde and the reduction of Lithuanian expansion and to become a mighty Eastern European power.

MUSCOVITE RUSSIA
1450–1598

NANCY SHIELDS KOLLMANN

Sixteenth-century Muscovy was a diverse ensemble of regions, ethnic groups, cultures, historical traditions, and geographic differences. To rule this expanding empire, Moscow's sovereigns devised strategies of governance that were flexible, integrating, and minimalist; they used coercion rarely, but ruthlessly. The result was a loosely centralized political system rich in ambition, poor in resources, and resilient in the face of crisis.

RUSSIA'S sixteenth century, like that of the Mediterranean in Fernand Braudel's eyes, was a 'long sixteenth century'. The hundred and fifty years from 1450 to the death of Tsar Fedor Ivanovich in 1598 was a cohesive era shaped by the tension between the interventionist policies of a state desperate to control its people and the nagging realities of geography, limited resources, and cultural diversity.

It was long-term geographical, institutional, and cultural realities that shaped Muscovy's drive to mobilize its human and natural resources. So we will try to see the realm as Moscow's rulers saw it, again evoking Braudel with a focus on long-term sources of change (geography, climate, settlement patterns, trade routes, and other aspects of Braudel's 'la longue durée') and middle-level ones (social and religious structures, ideational systems, etc.) in preference to individuals, wars, and events. But we need to start briefly with Braudel's 'histoire événementielle' to define the constantly expanding territory with which we will be concerned.

'Russia' constituted the realm of the grand princes (after 1547, the tsars) of Moscow, the Daniilovich line of the Riurikid dynasty that traced its descent to the rulers of Kievan Rus. Moscow amassed regional power starting in the fourteenth century; by 1450, after a decisive dynastic war, it embarked on expansion that continued unabated into the nineteenth century. Although much has been made of Moscow's relentless expansion, it was hardly unusual for the time. In Europe the Habsburgs and Jagiellonians were building empires, while England, France, and the Dutch were expanding overseas. They may have justified their expansion by the theory of mercantilism while Muscovy claimed to be restoring the 'patrimony' of Kievan Rus, but the motives—pursuit of resources, wealth, power—were the same.

Muscovy's expansion easily equalled that of other sixteenth-century empires. Russia expanded along lucrative trade routes, towards the Baltic, along the Volga, and into fertile steppe or the fur-bearing north and Siberia. Despite pious claims, much of what Muscovy won had not been part of Kievan Rus and Muscovy's expansionist zeal never turned to the Ukrainian heartland in the sixteenth century. Under Ivan III Moscow acquired, through marriage, inheritance, coercion, or conquest, contiguous territories that had once been sovereign principalities: Riazan, 1456–1521; Iaroslavl, 1463; Rostov, 1463, 1474; Tver, 1485. With the conquest in 1478 of the Baltic trading city of Novgorod came a rich hinterland stretching to the Urals. Since the conquest of Novgorod and of Pskov in 1510 under Vasilii III put Muscovy face to face with the grand duchy of Lithuania and Sweden, much of the sixteenth century was consumed with wars on the western border, including the draining and fruitless war for Livonia (1558–82). Under Ivan IV ('the Terrible') and Fedor Ivanovich Muscovy moved on several fronts, conquering Kazan in 1552 and Astrakhan at the Caspian Sea in 1556, thereby assuring Russian control of the Volga river route. The steppe

The interior of the Cathedral of the Nativity of the Virgin in Suzdal (its thirteenth-century ground floor was added to in 1528–30) served as the family church and mortuary of the Shuiskii princes, sovereigns of Suzdal before Moscow acquired the principality in the fifteenth century. The Shuiskie moved on to power as boyars in Moscow.

on either side became the next target of expansion in the second half of the century. Simultaneously, from the 1580s Muscovy was asserting political control into western Siberia, seeking the treasure of furs.

The only significant diversion that Moscow's rulers faced from these foreign policy goals was the era of the *oprichnina* (1564–72), a murky episode in which about half the tsardom (almost all the lucrative trading areas north and north-west of Moscow, stretching to the White Sea, plus several major towns in the centre) was designated as Ivan IV's personal realm. Parallel élites, armies, and bureaucracies were formed, with attendant confiscations of land and purges of individuals, clans, institutions, and regions deemed hostile to Ivan IV. The *oprichnina* might have been intended to consolidate central power, as some have argued, but more likely was the fruit of Ivan IV's own personal devils. Some, such as V. O. Kliuchevskii and S. B. Veselovskii, have argued that Ivan was insane or paranoid; Edward L. Keenan suggests that a debilitating spinal illness made Ivan create the *oprichnina* in an attempt to abdicate power, an argument made all the more persuasive by Ivan's later year-long abdication (1574/5) and by his erratic behaviour (he married several times, throwing clan-based court politics into disarray; even after 1572 he patronized a parallel élite of low-born families called the court [*dvor*]). Certainly some explanation in the psychological realm is required, since evidence shows that the *oprichnina* had no positive social or political consequences, devastating much of the centre of the realm and disrupting social and institutional structures.

The Span of the Russian Empire

We will begin by surveying the regions that made up Russia in the sixteenth century. There were three large divisions: the north, the centre, and the frontier, primarily a steppe frontier but also including the western border with the grand duchy of Lithuania. The north stretched from the Gulf of Finland in the west to beyond the Urals in the east and from the White Sea south to about 60° L. The north is a land of taiga, a largely coniferous forest turning into tundra and permafrost as one goes north; in addition to the taiga's acidic and leached soil, its marshiness and the brevity of the growing season (only three to four months, sufficient for only one crop) make it inhospitable to agriculture. This was an area of forest exploitation and trade.

The regions of the north from west to east included Karelia, centred around Lakes Onega and Ladoga and stretching north to the Kola peninsula; the Northern Dvina and Sukhona river basins (*Pomore*); the Mezen and Pechora river basins (home of the Komi-Zyriane); and the Perm and Viatka lands (key inland fur-trapping regions north-east of Moscow focused on the upper Viatka, Vychegda, and Kama rivers, also home to the Komi-Permians). The indigenous population here was Finno-Ugric speakers of the Uralic language family. Sparse Russian settlement hugged the rivers and shoreline, barely touching the far-eastern Viatka and Perm lands until late in the sixteenth century. Christianity came with Russian settlement but made few inroads among non-East Slavs throughout this time. In the tundra band lived nomadic reindeer herdsmen, fishermen, and hunters: the Finno-Ugric Lapps in Karelia and east of them the Nentsy (called in Russian *Samoedy*) who speak a Samoedic Uralic language. From the 1580s Muscovite expansion drove across the Urals, moving quickly up the Ob and Irtysh rivers and into the Enisei basin. Garrisons were founded at Tobolsk on the upper Irtysh river in 1587 and at Tomsk on the upper Ob in 1604. But Russian settlement in Siberia remained sparse indeed, save for the garrisons of musketeers and

The Church of Lazarus from near Lake Onega in the Novgorodian hinterland is dated as early as the fourteenth century and now resides at an open-air museum on the remote island of Kizhi in Lake Onega. Its simple structure—joined log chambers formed by walls of horizontal logs notched at the corners—is representative of the wooden village architecture that flourished in the forests of the far north.

Cossacks mustered from local populace or imported from the north, supported in turn by grain requisitions from Viatka, Perm, and other parts of the north. These garrisons collected tribute from the native peoples: farthest to the north were the Nentsy (*Samoedy*) living east of the Ob; south of them lived the Ostiaki (the *Khanty* in Russian) and inland to the west between the Permians and the Ob river lived the Voguly (*Mansy* to the Russians), also Finno-Ugric speakers.

Since Novgorodian times the dominant social and political organization among East Slavs and the Finno-Ugric population in the taiga lands from Karelia to Perm was the commune (*mir, volost*), composed of what contemporary sources call the 'black' or taxed peasants who were subject to the tsar directly and not subordinate to landlords as well. (Among native peoples of the Urals and western Siberia, however, Russia did not impose communal organization.) Northern communes differed from the nineteenth-century Russian peasant commune where land and labour were collectively shared. These were fiscal entities, territorial groupings of Slavs or non-Slavs for purposes of local administration and taxation. Nor is the term 'peasant' particularly appropriate for this populace. Members of communes were not primarily farmers, even the East Slavs among them, but were fishers, bee-keepers, traders, hunters, trappers, and artisans.

Straddling the border between the north and the centre were the Novgorod and Pskov lands to the north-west and the Beloozero and Vologda area north of Moscow. The north-west, including Novgorod and its five contiguous 'fifths' (*piatiny*), and Pskov and its environs, remained a centre of Baltic trade in the sixteenth century, and also supported at least a subsistence level of agriculture and relatively dense population. The Beloozero and Vologda areas lay on active trade routes to the White Sea and were productive centres for fish, salt, and furs. In these various lands the Russian population outnumbered Finno-Ugric speakers by the end of the century. Novgorod and Pskov had long been centres of Christianity and the Beloozero and Vologda areas became, from the mid-fifteenth century, magnets of energetic monastic colonization. Monasteries such as the St Cyril and Ferapontov monasteries near Beloozero, the Spaso-Prilutskii in Vologda, and the Solovetskii Monastery on the White Sea—expanded by taking over settled peasant lands and in the course of the sixteenth century became major local political and economic powers.

Although part of the Muscovite realm from the late 1400s, the north and north-west remained distinct as regions. When Moscow adopted at mid-century a new tax unit for arable land (the large *sokha*), for example, these areas retained the smaller, Novgorodian unit of measure. Similarly, surviving coin hoards from the second half of the century show a distinct split in the circulation of coinage between a north-west arena and a Moscow central one. Finally, gentry in the north-west were called upon to serve only within that region.

The centre, or 'Moscow region' (*Zamoskov'e*) in contemporary sources, differed from the north and the southern borderlands by its relative ethnic homogeneity, the economic primacy of agriculture, and the social power of landlords. By the early sixteenth century, the centre stretched from Beloozero and Vologda in the north to the Oka river and Riazan lands in the south; its western bounds were the upper Volga Tver lands and its eastern ones lay just beyond the lower Oka and its confluence with the Volga at Nizhnii Novgorod. An extension of the European plain that begins at the Atlantic, the region has a mixed deciduous–coniferous forest. It shares with Europe a continental climate, but its northerly latitude and distance from warming ocean currents made for harsher conditions. The winters are long (five months of snow cover) and cold (January mean temperature is −10.3 °C or 13.5 °F) and the growing season commensurately short (four to five months); because the soil was not particularly fertile, save for a triangle of loess north-west of Vladimir, yields were at subsistence level. Animal husbandry was limited by the sparseness of yields and the length of the winter which made provisioning large herds prohibitive; as a result natural fertilizer was inadequate. The populace supplemented its diet with food from the forests (hunting, fishing, berries, nuts, mushrooms) and income from artisan work.

The social structure in the centre was more complex than in the north. Settlement here was almost uniformly East Slavic, the indigenous Finno-Ugric peoples having been assimilated by the sixteenth century. Most of the populace, whether urban or rural, was taxed. Peasants lived in small hamlets (one to four households) and practised cultivation systems ranging from primitive slash-burn to three-field rotations depending upon population density, length of settlement in a region, and other factors. In 1450 most peasants were still free of landlord control, living in communes and paying taxes only to the tsar, but by the end of the sixteenth century virtually all of these 'black' peasants had been distributed to private landholders. Like the black peasants, artisans and petty merchants in towns were formed into urban communes (*posad*), which also paid taxes (here assessed not on arable land but as an annual rent or *obrok*), sales tax, customs, and other duties.

The non-taxpaying landholding strata were either military or ecclesiastical. The clerical populace was divided into 'black' (monks, nuns, and hierarchs—all celibate) and 'white' clergy (married parish priests). Church landholding increased at a phenomenal rate after 1450; particularly in the turbulent 1560s–70s landholders donated land in large amounts to monasteries, despite repeated legislation prohibiting such gifts (1551, 1572, 1580, 1584). But the Church's wealth was unevenly distributed: diocesan episcopates and a handful of major monasteries (for example, St Cyril-Beloozero, Simonov, Trinity–Sergius) had immense holdings by the end of the century, but one-fifth of the monasteries possessed no or fewer than five peasant households, and most parish churches possessed none at all.

Secular landholders were all obliged to serve the Moscow grand prince as a part of a cavalry army. A few select families lived in Moscow and enjoyed hereditary privileges to be boyars, that is, counsellors of the grand prince. The rest of the élite ranged from wealthy, large landholders to rank-and-file cavalrymen

This 1570 map of the city of Moscow from a foreign account depicts the Kremlin's origins as a fortress, ringed by bastions and walls and surrounded on three sides by rivers. The map represents Muscovy's social types with its berobed boyar and armed cavalrymen and oxen and docked ships allegorically representing the rural and urban economies.

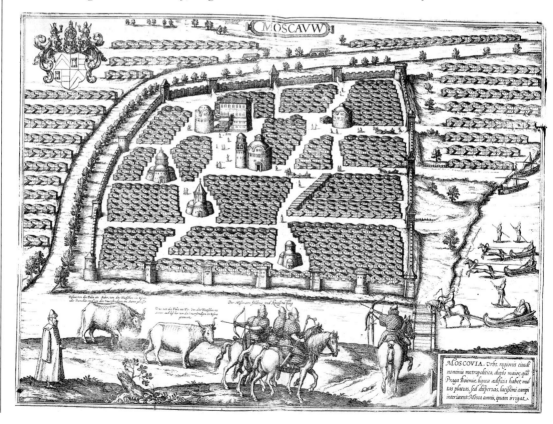

(called 'boyar's children' [*deti boiarskie*]). The landholding élite was not a corporate estate with juridical protection, but it did enjoy freedom from taxation,
an almost exclusive claim to landownership and high status.

Over the course of the sixteenth century other social groups developed, primarily in the centre. The tsar's élite merchants (*gosti*) were first mentioned in
the 1550s; by the 1590s two less prestigious associations of official merchants
(the *gostinnaia* and *sukonnaia* hundreds) were recorded. Merchants managed
the tsar's monopolies (salt, fur, vodka, and the like) or served as tax farmers, customs collectors, and entrepreneurs. In return they enjoyed the right to hold service tenure and hereditary land and to use the tsar's own courts instead of local
governors' courts. The highest ranks of the chancery secretaries (*d'iaki*) could
also hold hereditary or service tenure lands and utilize the tsar's courts. Most
worked in Moscow, but a few were stationed in the provinces (in 1611 the relative numbers were 55 and 17). In the second half of the sixteenth century most
secretaries came from the lesser cavalry ranks. Situated socially between the
taxed and non-taxed populations were non-cavalry army units, and of course
there were also people who did not fit in—those who refused to be caught in the
webs of landlord's control or urban taxation: vagrants (*guliashchie liudi*), minstrels (*skomorokhi*) so vilified by the Church, holy fools, unemployed sons of
priests, defrocked clergy, isolated hermits—in sum, the flotsam characteristic of
the social diversity of premodern societies.

Perhaps the most remarkable fact about the centre was its juridical diversity.
Much of this land was exempt from the grand prince's government and taxation, a situation that rulers not only tolerated but used to their advantage. Grand
princes countenanced areas that were virtually sovereign islands of political
independence—the old apanage (*udel*) principalities, granted to members of
the ruling dynasty and other notables. Apanages enjoyed autonomy from the
grand prince's taxation and judiciary and maintained small armies and boyar
élites of their own. They were enjoined only against conducting independent
foreign policy. From 1450 to 1550 apanages proliferated with the dynasty: Ivan
III and Vasilii III each had four brothers, and Ivan IV, one as well as two adult
sons. Each received lands with an apanage capital in towns such as Dmitrov,
Volok, Uglich, Vologda, Kaluga, and Staritsa.

Similar to dynastic apanages were the holdings of some high-ranking
princely families, called 'service princes'. The apanage rights of princes from
the upper Oka basin—the Mosal'skie, Mezetskie, Belevskie, Novosil'skie and
others—were extinguished in the early sixteenth century, but two such clans,
the Vorotynskie and Odoevskie princes, retained autonomy until 1573.
Similarly, descendants of the ruling dynasty of the grand duchy of Lithuania
long kept their rights: the Bel'skie until 1571, the Mstislavskie until 1585.
Descendants of the ruling lines of Suzdal, Rostov, and other principalities likewise kept some vestige of autonomous rights into the mid-sixteenth century.
The grand princes also actively created islands of autonomies as a political

strategy. In the mid-fifteenth century, for example, Vasilii II's government created a quasi-independent Tatar principality at Kasimov, designed as a refuge for a dissident line of the Kazan ruling dynasty and their Tatar retinues and thus as a focal point of opposition to the khanate of Kazan. It was located on the Oka river below Riazan and endured until the mid-seventeenth century. In the mid-sixteenth century an analogous apanage for a line of the Nogai Horde was created at Romanov, which lasted until 1620. In the Urals the Stroganov family acquired quasi-autonomous authority over vast tracts of lands in return for its colonization and trade activities.

Even more expansively the state accorded landlords judicial and administrative authority over their peasants except for major crimes. Ecclesiastical lands were particularly separate. By age-old statutes and tradition, the Orthodox Church had jurisdiction over all the Muscovite Orthodox populace in crimes declared church-related (such as heresy, sacrilege, inheritance, divorce, and adultery); it also exercised virtually total jurisdiction over the people living on its lands. Similarly, Muscovite towns, particularly in the centre, epitomized the patchwork quilt of administration and status that Russian society amounted to in the sixteenth century. Side by side with the taxpaying urban *posad* in most towns were privileged properties called 'white places' (i.e. untaxed), which competed with the trade of the *posad*. They could be enclaves of musketeers, postal workers, the tsar's artisans, Europeans, or Tatars; they could be urban courts of monasteries, great boyars, and large landholders. Such communities enjoyed preferential treatment in taxes, tolls, and customs, and immunities from the tsar's judiciary and administration.

It is important to recall, however, that the grand princes tolerated local autonomies as a quasi-bureaucratic convenience; they did not countenance political independence and they kept apanage princes and leading boyars and landholders on a tight rein. They often imposed surety bonds (*poruchnye zapisi*) on boyars or treaties on their kinsmen to guarantee their loyalty. The grand princes' closest kin were particularly distrusted, a bitter legacy of the dynastic war of the mid-fifteenth century, when the principle of linear dynastic succession triumphed over collateral succession but at the cost of bitter internecine battles. In succeeding generations uncles and cousins who loomed as potential rivals were closely controlled, forbidden to marry, imprisoned, or even executed. Within ten years of Ivan III's death in 1505 all collateral lines of the clan had died out, save the Staritsa line, which was finally extinguished in the *oprichnina* in 1569. The perils of this aggressive pruning of the family tree were exposed in 1598 when the dynasty itself died out, destabilizing the political system almost terminally.

Prince Dmitrii of Uglich, son of Ivan IV, depicted here in a seventeenth-century icon from Uglich, was the last apanage prince of the Moscow ruling dynasty. His death as a child in 1591 ended all realistic hope of continuing the line after Tsar Fedor Ivanovich (d. 1598). Canonized after his death, Prince Dmitrii became the focus of numerous pretenders to the throne in the subsequent Time of Troubles.

As diverse and dynamic as the centre was, even more volatile was the frontier on the west and south. In some ways calling this area the 'frontier' to the exclusion of the others is inaccurate. The north and centre were also riddled with 'frontiers'—between Slavs and non-Slavs, Orthodox and non-Christians, farmers and trappers, Muslims and 'pagans'. All these social interfaces generated tensions, synergies, and cross-cultural fertilization. But in the west and the south the classic meaning of 'frontier' as outposts of defence and conquest applies. In climate, precipitation, soil quality, and other key measures of agrarian fertility, these lands were far superior to those north of them and thus were coveted. On the west the frontier began with the Novgorod and Pskov lands south of the Gulf of Finland and extended south to the Smolensk area and south again to the upper Oka river region. This relatively narrow north–south strip, located between the sixtieth and fiftieth latitudes, moved from taiga at the Novgorod end through deciduous–coniferous mixed forest, approaching steppe in the south. These lands flanked the grand duchy of Lithuania and were hotly contested throughout the century; between 1491 and 1595 Muscovy spent a total of fifty years at war on the western front. After the rout of the Livonian War (1558–82) and the Time of Troubles (1598–1613) Muscovy yielded lands from Karelia to beyond Smolensk to Sweden (Treaty of Stolbovo, 1617) and the Commonwealth of Poland-Lithuania (Treaty of Deulino, 1618).

On the western frontier as in the centre Moscow tolerated administrative and social diversity. For example, when Smolensk was annexed in 1514, Vasilii III affirmed by charter the landholding and judicial rights historically granted to the region by the grand dukes of Lithuania. Similarly, as we have seen, princes from the upper Oka area retained autonomies as 'service princes' in Muscovy well into the sixteenth century.

On the south the frontier ran just south of the middle, west–east stretch of the Oka river, from around Tula across the Riazan lands to the border with the Kazan khanate in the east. Moving south from this forested zone one quickly encounters steppe (a prairie rich in grey and black soils), a line that moves roughly diagonally, south-west to north-east, from Kiev to Kazan. This south flank was exposed to raids and warfare: in the sixteenth century the Crimean Tatars made forty-three major attacks on the Muscovite lands, and the Kazan khanate forty. After Moscow conquered Kazan in 1552, the Nogai Horde of the lower Volga took its place as Moscow's steppe adversary. Already in the 1530s Muscovy fortified a line south of the Oka and at mid-century it conquered Kazan and Astrakhan (1552, 1556). A generally east–west line of fortifications pushed steadily southward from the 1550s; Muscovy also constructed a network of fortresses to fortify the Kazan heartland and Kama basin. In the 1580s Muscovy began to subjugate the Bashkirs, a Tatar nomadic people, on a southern tributary of the Kama, constructing a fort at Ufa in 1586; most of the Bashkirs remained subjects of the Siberian khan until Muscovy's final defeat of the khan in the late 1590s. A final stage of southern frontier fortification witnessed bold extensions of fortresses down the land and river routes used by the Nogais and Crimeans: Elets (1592), Belgorod, and Tsarev Borisov on the Donets river (1593, 1600).

The Kazan conquest added ethnically and religiously diverse lands to Russia: the élite was Tatar and Muslim, descended from the Golden Horde, but it presided over a variety of peoples who followed animistic cults. They included Finno-Ugric speakers (the Mari or Cheremisy and the Mordva) and Turkic speakers (the Chuvash, said to descend from the Volga Bulgars who had controlled the Volga before the Mongol invasion). The Chuvash and Mordva by and large inhabited the high, right bank of the Volga; the Tatars and Mari, the lowland left bank between the Volga and Kama rivers which had been the heartland of the Kazan khanate. Although fur-trapping, bee-keeping, and trade all engaged the populace, this was also an area of settled agriculture from the twelfth century: the land here was thinly forested or steppe, and the soil was the famous 'blackearth' topsoil, a thick layer rich in humus and nutrients.

With Russian conquest the Tatar populace was forcibly removed from the city of Kazan and those dwellings and shops were awarded to artisans, peasants, and lesser military servitors imported from the centre. The lands surrounding Kazan were distributed as service landholdings; there were no free peasant communes here as in the north and little hereditary land (*votchina*) save that granted to the newly founded archbishopric of Kazan (1555) and new monasteries. Christianization remained a minor goal for the Muscovite state here. Local élites were left relatively untouched as long as they remained loyal to the tsar; they collected the tribute (*iasak*) and administered communities according to local traditions. Muscovite governors were instructed to govern fairly without coercion. Nevertheless Muscovy was challenged repeatedly by uprisings of Cheremisy, Tatars, and Mari in the 1550s and thereafter.

Culture and Mentality

So diverse a populace cannot be said to have possessed a single mentality. Certainly sources on this for the non-Christian subjects of the tsar are lacking. But since clichés abound about the Russian character even for the Muscovite period, it is worth assessing sixteenth-century Orthodox East Slavs' attitudes towards the supernatural, community, and family, based on contemporary sources. (One should take with a grain of salt the reports of foreign travellers about popular culture since many were biased by Catholic and Protestant viewpoints, by a post-Reformation zeal for a more rational or more personal spirituality, or by a fascination with the 'exotic'.)

Sixteenth-century Russians were nominally Orthodox Christian, but that statement is as misleading as saying that most Europeans before the Reformation were Catholic. Just as in pre-Reformation Europe, sixteenth-century

Russian Orthodoxy combined Christian beliefs with practices drawn from the naturalist and animistic beliefs of the various Finno-Ugric peoples with whom the East Slavs came in contact. At the 1551 'Stoglav' Church Council (called 'Stoglav' or 'One Hundred chapters' after the document it issued), the hierarchy identified a wide incidence of improper religious practices, but apparently lacked the resources to change them. Parish schools or seminaries were non-existent; parish organization was weak; books, sermons, and learning were limited to ecclesiastical élites. The council had to content itself with establishing some mechanisms to supervise parish clergy but otherwise just exhort the faithful to avoid what it considered 'pagan' behaviour.

The opening chapter of a sixteenth-century manuscript copy of the protocols of the 1551 *Stoglav* Church Council, which grappled with reform in the administrative and spiritual life of the church.

By examining death rituals, marriage ceremonies, prayers, and a range of celebratory practices, one can discern a 'popular culture', that is, a range of beliefs and practices exhibited by the entire social range which was distinct from the prescriptions of the official Church. That culture featured a view of the world significantly different from the typical Christian one as Eve Levin points out. Rather than seeing the world as basically good, created by God and disrupted by the Devil, sixteenth-century Russians seem to have regarded it as a universe of powerful natural forces 'neither good nor evil but wilful and arbitrary'. They identified these forces in Christian terms (the Devil) or terms drawn from Finno-Ugric beliefs (*nezhit*, a force of evil in nature; bears and foxes were equated with evil). They summoned supernatural forces to protect themselves, drawing both on Christian intercessors (Jesus, Mary, and others) and Finno-Ugric (appealing to the power of ritual sites like bathhouses or trees and herbs imbued with supernatural powers). These customs showed no social distinctions: even the tsar's marriage ceremony shared folk customs associated with fertility; boyars are recorded consulting folk healers; wills with evocations of non-Christian attitudes stem from the landed class.

The Church in the sixteenth century railed against many of these practices, and had some success in asserting its presence and rituals at key moments such as death and marriage. It promoted a new vision of spirituality as well. Until the early 1500s, monasteries, monks, and an ascetic way of life had constituted the norm in church teaching about social and religious behaviour. But as monasteries became less exemplary with greater worldly success, the church hierarchy diversified the focus of spiritual life, offering saints' cults, sermons, other moralistic writings and teachings, and more ritual experiences to appeal more broadly. As Paul Bushkovitch has noted, official spirituality in the sixteenth century emphasized the collective, public experience of the faith, not the more inner-directed, personal piety that developed among the élite in the next century.

Attitudes towards daily life in the élite can be gleaned from a handbook of household management (the *Domostroi*), which was most probably based on a foreign secular model, but edited in an Orthodox Christian vein in Muscovy in the mid-sixteenth century. The *Domostroi* depicts the family as the structuring principle of the community and of the polity; the grand prince is portrayed as the head of the realm construed as a 'household', just as the father is the head of an extended household of wife, children, servants, and other dependents. Both patriarchs rule justly, but firmly; each demands obedience and responds with just and fair treatment. Women and children are to behave and

Although brewing beer was depicted as a man's job in this miniature from the mid-sixteenth-century Illustrated Nikon Chronicle, primary responsibility for the household economy was accorded to women in Muscovy.

obey; physical force is recommended to fathers to keep them in line. But women also have remarkably broad latitude and responsibility. Offsetting its otherwise more typical Muscovite misogynistic views of women is the *Domostroi*'s parallel depiction of them as capable household managers, empowered in the domestic realm. Theirs is the primary responsibility for leading the family to salvation by the example of virtue and piety; theirs is the responsibility of making the household economy and servants productive by skilful management. Christian values such as charity to the poor and just treatment of dependents are balanced by a keen attention to sexual probity, all of which values worked towards social stability as much as piety. The *Domostroi* did not circulate widely in the sixteenth century, but to some extent it did reach the landed gentry.

One can hardly argue that Russians were particularly spiritual or 'pagan' in the sixteenth century. This was a typically eclectic premodern Christian community. And, significantly, the church's *de facto* tolerance of syncretism, paralleled by the state's toleration of religious diversity (the Orthodox Church was specifically enjoined against aggressive missionary work in newly conquered areas such as Kazan and Siberia), helped ensure that the sixteenth century passed with remarkably little societal tension over matters of belief, a stark and oft-noted contrast to the turbulent sixteenth century of Reformation in Europe.

Administrative and Economic Strategies of Autocracy

A similar flexibility characterized the administrative, political, and fiscal strategies of the state: rather than trying to fit a uniform policy to lands of dazzling differences, the state modified policies to fit local needs, while never losing sight of its fundamental goals. Muscovite rulers were obsessed with the same issues as their European counterparts: bureaucracy, taxation, and the army. The goal has often been called 'absolutism', but the term is applicable only if it is redefined. Recent scholarship shows that in England and France as well as in Muscovy, 'absolute' authority was achieved by tolerating and co-opting traditional institutions and élites, rather than by replacing them with rational bureaucratic institutions. What resulted was not homogenization, 'centralization', or 'autocracy', but resource mobilization.

Muscovy's first concern in the sixteenth century was to expand its army. The army was primarily a cavalry, composed of a landed élite that served seasonally and provided its own equipment, horses, and training. Expansion was possible after Ivan III developed on a large scale the principle that servitors would be compensated with land given in conditional tenure (*pomest'e*). Until then hereditary landholding (*votchina*) had supported landowners and their retinues. The grand prince's role in recompense was presumably limited to booty and largesse. The large-scale use of service landholding began in

Novgorod: over 1,300 service estates were assigned to men transferred there from the centre, while Novgorodian deportees received lands in conditional tenure in the centre (Moscow, Vladimir, Murom, Nizhnii-Novgorod, Pereiaslavl-Zalesskii, Iurev-Polskoi, Rostov Velikii, Kostroma, and elsewhere). Recipients of service land were socially diverse: princes (mainly from Iaroslavl and Rostov), boyars and lesser non-princely families, and also clients (*posluzhil'tsy*) of such families (who constituted 20 per cent of service land recipients in Novgorod). Thus the service landholding system enriched and expanded the cavalry élite as a whole.

Muscovy found still other ways to expand the army. It recruited infantry militias from the peasants and townspeople by assessing a fixed number of recruits per unit of arable land or households in urban communes. In the north this system persisted through the sixteenth century for purposes of local defence; in areas where 'black' peasants were trans-

ferred to landlord control, landlords then recruited men according to a calculus issued in 1556—one man per every 100 *chetverti* of land. Richard Hellie estimates the resultant forces at 25,000 to 50,000 by the end of the century. But these forces were untrained and unspecialized. More valuable to the state were new formations of troops. Responding to the European 'military revolution', Russia began to develop regiments of artillery and musketeers (called collectively by the seventeenth century *sluzhilye liudi po priboru* or 'contract' servitors). In the mid-sixteenth century their numbers are estimated to have been around 30,000, thus outnumbering the cavalry servitors (approximately 21,000). By the end of the century there were about 30,000 cavalrymen, some 20,000 musketeers alone, significant numbers of artillery (3,500), as well as frontier Cossack and non-Russian troops (Bashkirs, Tatars).

Contract servitors were most probably recruited from the peasantry or impoverished landed élite; they did not enjoy the high social status or landholding privileges of the cavalry élite. They were garrisoned in towns throughout the

The social superiority of the landed cavalry class in Muscovy's traditional society is well illustrated by this ornamental saddle. Mounted in gold, studded with jewels, and embroidered with gold thread, it would have been used by a Kremlin boyar in ceremonial processions.

realm, but especially on the southern frontier. They stood as a middle social stratum between the taxpaying artisans of the *posad* and the landed gentry. They supported themselves from trade and farming their own plots; they paid no state tax (the *obrok* levied on *posad* people), but did pay tax on their sales.

These military innovations had tremendous impact on Muscovite social structure over the course of the sixteenth century, but differentially so. In the north, not including the Novgorod and Pskov areas, the land would not support nor local needs require the service landholding system and a landed cavalry élite. Garrisons manned by locally mustered Cossack, musketeers, and militia met the need for border defence. Conversely, the southern steppe frontier had a preponderance of contract servitors living in commune-type regiments. This area had relatively little hereditary landholding (secular or ecclesiastical), few enserfed peasants, few large landholders. What service landholding estates there were were small, farmed by poor cavalrymen with few peasants, making a lower cavalry class distinct from their relatively better-off counterparts in the centre. Social boundaries were fluid on the frontier. Here one finds such anomalies as musketeers holding service landholdings and cavalrymen serving as infantry and holding no land in conditional tenure; here all servitors, even gentry, were obligated to farm state properties and to provide grain reserves.

But in the centre and north-west the service landholding system had a great impact on social relations. By the end of the century service landholding dominated here, although in the centre a significant minority of land remained hereditary. Hereditary tenure was preferred because in theory service landholdings could not be transferred. But since many service tenure holders also held hereditary land, and since service holdings from the very beginning were treated *de facto* as transferable and heritable, and since hereditary landholders were also obliged to serve Moscow, hereditary owners (*votchinniki*) and service tenure holders (*pomeshchiki*) did not constitute separate social forces, as has traditionally been thought. The landholding élite constituted a consolidated élite, with divisions in power, wealth, and status based on regional association and family heritage, but not according to the type of landholding.

Muscovite grand princes used the system of service landholding to create stronger regional élites by resettlement. From the early sixteenth century they moved new settlers from the centre to areas previously conquered: Novgorod (1478), Viazma (1494), Toropets (1499), Pskov (1510), and Smolensk (1514). Later they continued to make grants of land in conditional tenure to populate newly conquered areas or to bolster frontier economies shattered by war. In the 1570s, for example, petty landholders from the Novgorod environs were moved to the western border (Velikie Luki, Toropets, Dorogobuzh, Smolensk, Viazma), while others were moved to recently captured territories in Livonia. When Russians were driven out of Livonia, they were resettled on the Novgorod frontier. These relocations severed original regional attachments but created new ones elsewhere, forging new regional élites and perhaps a more integrated centre.

Other policies also worked to create regional 'corporations' and a central élite. Laws from Ivan III's time forbade landholders in almost all regions, for example, to sell land to non-locals; parallel injunctions kept land within princely clans. Up until the mid-century Muscovy mustered the bulk of the army by region or princely clans; by the end of the sixteenth century it had developed a more differentiated system of regional gentry 'corporations' arranged around towns (*goroda*). At the social apex was the 'sovereign's court' (*gosudarev dvor*) with about 3,000 men at mid-century and set apart by privileges and largesse. In land, for example, by the end of the century the highest ranks received 3.5 times more service tenure land than the lowest. They also received largesse from the grand prince: after the victory of Kazan, Ivan IV is said to have distributed 48,000 roubles' worth of precious objects to his men in three days of feasting. The sovereign's court also had access to the Kremlin and the person of the ruler, attending daily and at ceremonial occasions and accompanying him on pilgrimages.

The grand princes also forged the metropolitan élite by bolstering the principle of clan. Access to boyar rank was hereditary within clans. Traditionally the number of clans with such access was small: from the 1300s to 1462 it stayed around ten. But with the influx of new servitor families, rulers added new clans to integrate and stabilize the élite. From 1462 to 1533, the number of boyar clans rose from around fifteen to twenty-four, and after the turbulence of Ivan IV's minority (1533–47) it nearly doubled to forty-six. Rulers used their own marriages to establish the political pecking order among the boyars: with his marriage in 1547 to a daughter of a leading faction (the Romanov clan), for example, Ivan IV resolved the struggles during the period of his minority. In 1555 he went a step further towards reconciliation in the élite by marrying off

Ambassadors, like these envoys to the court of Maximilian II in Vienna in 1576, were drawn from Moscow's élite boyar clans.

his distant cousin to a member of the boyar clan, the Bel'skie princes, who had been on the 'losing' side in the minority.

Rulers made clan the organizing principle of the sovereign's court below the boyar level as well. In the system of precedence (*mestnichestvo*) they offered protection to injured honour for servitors who alleged that their military assignments were beneath their clan's dignity, measured by genealogy and military service. To that end extensive official records of service and genealogies of the élite were compiled from Ivan III's time (*razriadnye* and *rodoslovnye knigi*).

The Moscow-based sovereign's court became increasingly high born in the aftermath of the *oprichnina* and Ivan IV's death when the many low-born families that Ivan IV had patronized in the *dvor* were relegated to provincial service, while the high-born families who had served in the *oprichnina* or the regular government (*zemshchina*) remained in Moscow. Socially, the impact of six-teenth-century policy was not to destroy a 'feudal' élite or raise up 'new men', as has been often held, but rather to consolidate the landed military élite in the centre into Moscow-based and regional 'corporations', divided by status, wealth, and duties.

One reason that the grand princes assiduously cultivated regional solidarities is that they came to use such communities for local administration. Traditionally, Muscovy had ruled through governors (*namestniki*) in the larger centres and local officials (*volosteli*) in smaller communities who collected taxes and administered the lands and, in return, received *kormlenie* ('feeding', i.e. material support) from the local populace. Starting in Ivan III's time, however, the state began to create specialized officers to collect specific taxes and duties—for example, officials to collect taxes for urban fortifications. In the late 1530s the state gave authority over local law and order to 'brigandage elders', who were elected by local communities; in the mid-1550s it gave tax-collection authority to boards of taxpayers—peasants or townsmen—elected by their communes. In the centre governors were in effect abolished. The result was not only better local government and higher revenues but also the strengthening of community solidarities in many parts of the realm. In the centre and north-west, landlords became a pillar of the tsar's administration. They ran the brig-andage system and oversaw tax-collection by peasant communes. In the north communal organization was the beneficiary; communes took on all these roles in the absence of gentry to do brigandage work. The work of overseeing was provided by chancery offices in Moscow. The *oprichnina* and other economic and political dislocations of the 1560s–80s, however, dealt a harsh blow to gen-try and to peasant communes in the centre and north-west, and going into the seventeenth century the principle of local representation in governance, except in the north, was severely compromised. A system of governors returned, but the social solidarity of regional gentry communities endured into the seven-teenth century.

Many places in the realm, however, stayed outside these administrative reforms and their attendant social impact. As we saw in the Smolensk lands, for example, the indigenous élite retained privileges and social structures of the grand duchy of Lithuania. In non-East Slav areas—western Siberia, the middle Volga, the tundra reaches of the Lapps and Nentsy—the Russians maintained a traditional tribute system (*iasak*), paid in furs, other goods, and some services and collected by local élites and communities. Where local forces were lacking, Moscow sent specially appointed officials (*danshchiki*) to collect the annual payment and otherwise left the status quo untouched. (The *iasak* was phased out as the basis of taxation in Siberia only between 1822 and 1917.) Similarly, in major cities on strategic borders (Novgorod, Pskov, Kazan, Astrakhan, Tomsk) governors exercised overall authority, since there was little social basis here for local fiscal or criminal administration. At the same time numerous servitor units stationed here, such as Cossacks, Streltsy (musketeers), and 'privileged hetman' (*belomestnye atamany*), enjoyed autonomies and communal landholdings as regimental units and ran their own affairs collectively.

Not surprisingly, Muscovy did not constitute a uniform legal community. Many legal codes served these various communities. Ecclesiastical law codes came to the Rus lands from Byzantium. The most significant compendium, known as the 'Rudder' (*kormchaia kniga*), was a collection of Byzantine secular and ecclesiastical codes. For day-to-day affairs communes and landlords apparently used the *Russkaia pravda*, a compendium of customary law from the Kievan era that still circulated in Muscovite lands (a new redaction was even compiled in the early seventeenth century). The grand princes and boyar council promulgated three law codes (1497, 1550, 1589) as procedural handbooks for judges. The 1589 edition was suited to the social structure and economic patterns of the north; contemporary sources also refer to separate law codes in use for the Perm lands (*zyrianskii sudebnik*).

Such administrative eclecticism strengthened the state, creating quasi-bureaucratic organs that freed grand princes to concentrate on those few issues they considered their own: supreme judicial authority, foreign policy, the army and defence, and above all the mobilization and exploitation of resources. It was a minimalist state, run by the ruler, his counsellors, and a household-based bureaucracy reminiscent of the Carolingian court. Until the mid-sixteenth century the work of the fisc, foreign policy, and the mustering of troops constituted the provenance of two general offices, the treasury and the court (in the sense of household, not judiciary). By the 1560s, the term *prikaz* (chancery) was used to denote the many new offices that were being established to meet new needs (the Brigandange, Slavery, and Streltsy Chanceries, for example) or to separate out specific functions (Military Service, Service Land, Foreign Affairs, Postal System Chanceries). By the end of the century there were approximately twenty-four chanceries, a system that was efficient but eclectic and irrational by modern, Weberian standards. No single principle governed the organization and

The Kremlin ensemble, showcasing the domes of the several churches and bell-tower complex constructed by rulers from Ivan III to Boris Godunov to show forth Moscow's power and eminence, was home to the tsar, church hierarchs, and boyars and also housed the growing chancery apparatus of governance.

jurisdiction of chanceries. Some had responsibility for a particular social group (the military élite, foreigners); others exercised one function over the entire realm (Fortifications, Slavery, Criminal Chanceries), or had total authority over a particular territory (the Kazan Chancery). Initially led by secretaries, from the time of Boris Godunov boyars ran more and more chanceries, presaging the transformation of the military élite into the 'noble official' class that has been chronicled for the seventeenth century.

No less important to the sixteenth-century state than the expansion of the army was the mobilization of wealth. That impelled a new fiscal strategy in 1551—elimination of the tax immunities traditionally enjoyed by lay and ecclesiastical landholders. But the government was inconsistent, issuing new immunities in times of political turbulence (1530s–40s, 1560s–70s, 1590s). At mid-century the state commuted taxes from payment in kind and services to cash, changed the tax assessment unit in the centre, raised existing taxes (especially for the postal system), and introduced new ones. The tribute-bearing peoples of Siberia and the middle Volga also filled Moscow's coffers, as did a tax on any furs brought to market from Siberia by Russian traders. Income from the tsar's monopolies such as salt and alcohol production (analogous to medieval European kings' monopolies or *regalia*) was also significant and the state aggressively patronized entrepreneurs, whether Russian (the Stroganovs) or

In conjunction with the dynastic struggle over Kiev the armies of Prince Andrei Bogoliubskii also attacked Novgorod, which supported his opponent Prince Mstislav Iziaslavich. The icon of the battle between the Novgorodians and the Suzdalians portrays Novgorod's miraculous victory in 1169. It became particularly popular in the fifteenth century during Novgorod's struggle with Moscow.

The Crown of Kazan, made in the mid-sixteenth century in honour of Ivan IV's conquest of Kazan, combines gold, jewels, engraving, neillo, and openwork; the precious fur trim recalls the strategic significance of Kazan and its hinterland as a hub of trade, including the export of furs.

foreign (the English Muscovy company received a charter of trade privileges c.1555). Trade through the White Sea with the British and Dutch grew to great proportions in the second half of the century.

But the government's drive to mobilize eventually blew up in its face. Taxes rose precipitously in the sixteenth century, exceeding the parallel inflationary rise of the century. It has been calculated that taxes rose 55 per cent from 1536 to 1545, another 286 per cent (with commutations to cash) from 1552 to 1556, another 60 per cent in the 1560s, and another 41 per cent in the 1570s before they began a steady decrease in the face of economic distress. At the same time in the 1560s and 1570s the north-west and centre experienced great disruptions from the *oprichnina*, Livonian War, and natural disasters that included plague, crop failure, and famine. Petty landlords responded by squeezing their peasants for more income, while larger landholders lured peasants to their lands with loans and tax breaks. They also began to consolidate their holdings into demesnes and to extract labour services, two to three days per week by the end of the century on much secular land. Trying to shelter the landed élite, the state ended taxation on landlord's demesne in the 1580s, shifting the tax burden all the more to peasants. In response the average peasant plot decreased: at the beginning of the century many peasant holdings were the equivalent of a mansus (in Russian, *vyt*, that is, the unit of land considered sufficient to support a peasant family). But from the 1570s most holdings ranged between just one-half to one-eighth of a *vyt*.

All this spelled disaster for peasants and petty gentry, especially in the north-west and centre. Thousands fled to new landlords in the centre or to the relative freedom of the Volga and Kama basins, the Dvina lands, or the southern border. Depopulation was acute: in the mid-1580s only 17 per cent of the land in the Moscow environs was being cultivated, while in the north-west 83 per cent of settlements were deserted. Towns suffered disproportionately: while the populations of urban communes had risen in the first half of the century, *posad* populations fell by 61 per cent in the 1550s–80s, and then another 45 per cent from the 1580s to the 1610s. In Novgorod in 1582, for example, a census recorded only 122 urban households as occupied and over 1,300 abandoned for such reasons as death of the family (in 76 per cent of the cases) and impoverishment (18 per cent). The economic situation stabilized in the late 1580s, but Russia was plunged again into turmoil by the turn of the century: not only foreign invasion, but crop failure and pestilence accompanied the end of the dynasty in 1598.

Having no other way to support its cavalry, and unwilling to transform this privileged estate into less prestigious contract servitors, the state endeavoured to secure peasant labour for landlords. In 1580 it forbade some peasants to change landlords and in 1592–3 made the ban universal, capping a legislative process that had commenced with restrictions on the peasant's right to move in the law codes of 1497 and 1550. These 'forbidden years' were perceived as temporary but, with the exception of 1601–2, endured thereafter. This incremental enserf-ment affected most directly the peasants of landlords in the centre, north-west, and steppe frontier, but it also had impact in the north and Siberia. Cadastres compiled throughout the realm in the 1580s and 1590s served as the basis for registering peasants in communes; they were then forbidden to leave, whether or not they were subject to landlords as well.

Sixteenth-century peasants faced with economic disaster and enserfment had two options. One was to flee to the frontier. Despite decrees beginning in the 1590s that steadily extended the statute of limitations on the recovery of run-away peasants, peasants with the means still had an opportunity to move. For most, however, the older option in hard times—debt slavery—was far more viable. Increasingly in the sixteenth century individuals sold themselves into a limited 'service-contract' (*kabal'noe*) slavery. Slavery offered them not only a loan but also refuge of a lord and freedom from the taxes and services due the state. Understandably, over the course of the sixteenth century, the government sought to regulate hereditary slavery and manumission, to forbid servitors to assume this status (1550), and to limit its duration (1586, 1597).

Mechanisms of Social Integration

The grand princes' primary goals in the sixteenth century may have been expanding their territory and extracting resources from it, but to do so they needed a minimal degree of social cohesion in the realm as a whole to ensure stability. Their major strategy in this regard, as we have suggested, was to toler-ate diversity. Even in contemporaneous Europe, where national realms were small and often ethnically cohesive and where dynasties worked assiduously to create a national unity, the reality was that stability was based not on the ruler's coercive power but on social traditions of deference to authority and loyalty to community and region. All the more so for Muscovite rulers. They had limited tools of integration and used them judiciously. As in other states, however, they relied on coercion and meted out harsh punishment to disloyal servitors, tax cheats, and rebellious subjects. They were particularly inclined to declare boyars to be in 'disgrace' (*opala*) for brief periods (often a few days) to chasten them and keep them in line. Frequently they tempered the punishments with last-minute reprieves, bestowing their benevolent 'mercy' and 'favour'. They also made abundant use of such harsh punishments as confiscation of property, demotion in rank, exile, imprisonment, and execution whenever their author-ity was challenged. But given the limits of central power in an early modern state, Muscovite tsars relied upon rewards, symbols, and ideas to inculcate loy-alty and to disseminate an image of a unified realm. And they put most of their energies into appealing to the élite since its loyalty was crucial to the state's goals.

Active techniques of integration that touched all society seem to have focused on the Orthodox population. The non-Orthodox (called 'tribute' people) generally were neither integrated into the élite (except for the highest clans among them) nor addressed by many of the less tangible institutions of integration. The Church was one of few institutions whose rituals and symbolism reached across the realm; conveniently, its teachings legitimated the secular government as appointed by God. The Church and State recognized local holy men as saints on the national or local levels and thus worked to integrate disparate parts of the realm into a putative Orthodox community. Rulers used ritual moments, such as pilgrimages and processions, to demonstrate the ruler's power, piety, and relationship to his men and people; such moments were often accompanied by the distribution of alms, the founding of new monasteries and chapels, and other overtures to the local community. Ivan IV participated almost incessantly in annual pilgrimages that traversed the centre of the realm; rulers' ceremonial entrances into conquered cities (see examples in chronicles *sub anno* 1478, 1552, and 1562) show the tsar both as humble penitent and powerful leader.

Rulers also used architecture as a symbolic statement. Ivan III reconstructed the Kremlin churches into a magnificent ensemble (including a family cathedral, the metropolitan's see, and a mortuary cathedral) that demonstrated not only his power and strength but, by incorporating architectural motifs from Novgorod and Pskov, the breadth of his conquests. Significantly, the centre-piece of the ensemble was the Dormition (*Uspenskii*) Cathedral, copied specifically from the metropolitan's see in Vladimir, not the Kiev example. Throughout the sixteenth century, this church was replicated—at the Trinity–Sergius Monastery, in Pereiaslavl-Zalesskii, Rostov, Vologda, Kazan, and elsewhere—stamping the landscape with a specifically Muscovite cultural idiom. Grand princes also left symbols of their authority in new churches and monasteries built to commemorate military victories (Sviazhsk, 1551; Kazan, 1552; the Church of the Intercession on the Moat or 'St Basil's' in Moscow, 1555–61; Narva, 1558; Velikie Luki, 1562) or to spread their patronage (Mozhaisk, 1563; Pereiaslavl, 1564).

The state also extended protection to all society for 'injured honour' (*beschest'e*), implicitly defining the state as a community

Built on the model of the Kremlin Dormition Cathedral but named after the Holy Sophia Cathedral in Novgorod and Kiev, this Vologda cathedral (1568–70) symbolized the interplay of northern traditions and Muscovite control. Claimed by Muscovy from the early fifteenth century, Vologda was the gateway from the centre to the great water route via the Sukhona and northern Dvina rivers to the White Sea.

unified by honour. Honour was defined as loyalty to the tsar, to the Church, to one's social rank, to family, and clan. Specifically excluded from the community of honour were 'thieves, criminals, arsonists, and notorious evil men', while even minstrels, bastards, and slaves were included (1589 law code). The state also appealed to all its inhabitants with a vision of community by according all subjects, even non-Orthodox, the right to petition the ruler. Individuals used formulae that accentuated their personal dependence on him: they referred to themselves with self-deprecating, although stylized, labels and beseeched the ruler for 'favour', be it a grant of land, release from service, or the resolution of litigation. Around 1550 a 'Petitions Chancery' was founded to encourage individuals to bring their grievances directly to the ruler.

Petitions, like the *Domostroi*, suggest symbolically that the ruler and his people were united in a patriarchal, personal family, that the realm constituted a single, homogeneous community. It has been noted that early seventeenth-century texts portray the tsardom as a 'God-dependent' community in which all, high and lowly, are personally dependent on the ruler and all equally share a responsibility to serve him loyally and offer him virtuous counsel when he errs. Sixteenth-century chronicle sources also strike these themes of consensus, unanimity, and patrimonial dependence, emphasizing the personal affection between grand princes and their boyars, or criticizing boyars for not giving the ruler counsel or for seeking 'personal power' (*samovlastie*). It is impossible to say how well these ideas were internalized by various strata of the population, but they were consistently and clearly articulated in the sources.

The central focus for building a cohesive state was the court, which sought to project a coherent public image of the realm and its relationship to the élite. Genealogies of the Daniilovich family traced its descent to the Vladimir-Suzdal principality (twelfth and thirteenth centuries), while panegyrics and hagiography created a pantheon of Muscovite heroes, most notably Grand Prince Dmitrii Donskoi (1359–89). The court also patronized cults of the 'Moscow miracle-workers', three fourteenth- and fifteenth-century metropolitans (Peter, Alexis, Iona) closely associated with the ruling dynasty. All these texts identified Moscow accurately with its fourteenth-century roots.

In the sixteenth century this vision became more universalist and less accurate. Genealogical tales of the Muscovite grand princes began to extend the family line through Kiev to ancient Rome in a typically Renaissance quest for a classical heritage. By the mid-century even more grandiose visions were constructed, with their roots firmly in the Orthodox past. Metropolitan Makarii's mid-century compilations of hagiography, chronicles, and didactic texts presented Muscovy as a holy kingdom, part of universal Christianity, linked through Kiev Rus to Byzantine Christianity and ultimately to God's creation of the earth. Icons such as 'Blessed is the Heavenly Host' (popularly known as the 'Church Militant'), new court ceremonies such as Epiphany and Palm Sunday processions, and fresco cycles that filled the interiors of the

Kremlin churches and palaces after the fires of 1547, all elaborated a 'Wisdom Theology' that immersed the reader or viewer in a biblical world. This vision was decidedly apocalyptic, lending great drama to the symbolic message and perhaps dispensing tension or exaltation among the viewers.

One should be quite clear about what Muscovite ideology was *not* saying in the sixteenth century. Moscow was not, for example, styling itself the 'Third Rome', heir to Rome and Byzantium and natural leader of the world. The 'Moscow, the Third Rome' text was a minor theme encountered in only a few ecclesiastical texts; it was originally used only to exhort the tsars to be just and humble, not to justify overweening power. It was most warmly embraced in the seventeenth century, and then by the schismatic Old Believers, at the same time that it was being discredited by the official Church. Nor did Muscovite ideology primarily exalt the tsar as next to God in power and as separate and above the common man. Although this viewpoint, associated with the Byzantine philosopher Agapetus, makes its appearance in mid-sixteenth-century texts, it was usually balanced with Agapetus' injunction to rulers to govern justly and with mercy. Nor did Muscovy see itself as a secular or pluralistic kingdom. There is

Ivan III, his son Vasilii and grandson Dmitrii and the court entourage — metropolitan, church hierarchs, and boyars—process through the Kremlin on Palm Sunday in an embroidery commissioned by Dmitrii's mother in 1498. Processions like these played a significant role in the symbolic representation of the political order, and they became more and more elaborate as the century went on.

no trace in sixteenth-century Muscovy of the keen debates over the *natio* that flourished in sixteenth-century England, France, Poland, and seventeenth-century Ukraine. Russia was outside that world of discourse; it defined itself in religious, not secular terms, as a family and community, not a state.

Much of this imagery directly appealed to the élite by making use of allegorical military themes. Moscow's boyars and élite, although illiterate, could absorb a consistent vision of the state and their place in it by gazing at the frescos, battle standards, and icons that decorated the churches and chambers where they attended the tsar. Allegorically these depicted the state as the Lord's heavenly army, a remarkably apt and probably compelling image for a state whose élite was defined by military service.

The image of the state as a Godly community of virtuous warriors and dependents of the tsar was acted out in collective meetings that first appeared in the mid-sixteenth century. Councils of the Land (*zemskie sobory*) were summoned at the initiative of the ruler; he set the agenda which usually concerned the issue of war and peace, but occasionally succession and taxation. Those present generally came from non-taxed social strata. The Councils were not parliamentary assemblies; they possessed neither legal definition, nor legislative initiative, nor decision-making power, nor consistent and representative composition. They seem to have fulfilled other functions than legislation; indeed, in the wake of the abolition of regional governors, they served as means of communication of state policy to the countryside to mobilize support for its military and fiscal policy. They also played an important symbolic role by physically creating a community of tsar and people in ritual fashion that may have worked cathartically, as Emile Durkheim described rituals working to energize the community, to build bonds, and to resolve tensions. Clearly these were the challenges that stood before Muscovite rulers in the sixteenth century as they sought to bolster stability in constantly growing and vastly diverse lands.

The Autocratic Project

They were not alone in facing such challenges. Religious, linguistic, cultural, and regional diversity was typical of premodern states across the European plain. French kings, for example, ruled over several language communities and had to contend with a basic division in legal relations between *pays d'état* (where estates negotiated laws and finances with the kings) and *pays d'élection* (where the king's officers had direct authority). French towns and rural communities used many different legal codes and fiscal systems; corporate groups— estates, guilds, municipalities, professions—enjoyed privileged status. Rulers tried to make diversity work for them, tolerating differences, co-opting élites, maintaining established customs and regional associations as a means to consolidate their own power in the long run.

At first glance Muscovy would seem to have been less successful at these 'absolutizing' goals than England or France in the sixteenth century. With the débâcles of the *oprichnina*, the Livonian Wars, exorbitant taxation, and peasant flight, Muscovy ended the sixteenth century impoverished and politically vulnerable. But if judged over the longer term, Muscovy had achieved a surprising degree of success. The course charted by Ivan III and Vasilii III endured. Ivan IV did not transform political relationships or institutions, nor create a new élite. Many boyar families who dominated politics from Ivan III's time survived the *oprichnina* and remained part of the élite into the next century; the new families that Ivan IV patronized by and large fell to provincial gentry status by the end of the century. Resource mobilization, development of a bureaucracy, military reform, and the consolidation of the élite survived the traumas of the 1560s–1580s, as did the march towards enserfment.

At this point it might be appropriate to reflect on the historical significance of Ivan IV 'the Terrible', whose enigmatic personality and actions have often been the main concern of narratives of Russia in the sixteenth century. His importance has been exaggerated in part because the *oprichnina* has long been considered Muscovy's equivalent to the great clashes of monarchy and nobility or Church and State that made sixteenth-century European politics so turbulent. In other words, Ivan was writ large for historiographical imperatives. But, as already suggested, the *oprichnina* had no discernible political programme and no lasting results. Ivan's significance has also been inflated because of the writings attributed to him, primarily a series of letters addressed to the *émigré* boyar, Prince A. M. Kurbskii, that articulated a claim to unlimited patrimonial power. But Edward L. Keenan has raised serious questions about the authenticity of Ivan's and Kurbskii's letters on the basis of manuscript history, content analysis, and linguistic style. Although most scholars have not accepted Keenan's arguments, many recognize as apocryphal some later pieces of the correspondence and some related texts; the debate and manuscript research on the question endures. Keenan's challenge sparked a fresh round of enquiry into the political and cultural world Ivan inhabited: was he literate, classically educated, and ahead of his time in political philosophy, or was he—like grand princes, tsars, and boyars before and after him to the mid-seventeenth century—cut from the same cloth as the Muscovite warrior élite, illiterate and little educated, but fiercely loyal to the ethos of Orthodox patrimonial authority? In any case, quandaries over Ivan's personality and motives pale in the face of Braudel's 'longue durée': Ivan IV did not divert,

Contemporary portraits of Russian rulers are rare before the mid-seventeenth century; this is a depiction of Ivan IV done in the style of an icon sometime after his death in 1584.

although he did disrupt, the Daniilovich project. His government, like that of his father and grandfather, made its main task the expansion of the tsardom, the consolidation of the élite, and the integration of a large and disparate realm.

Perhaps the best indicator that the Muscovite rulers had managed to increase cohesion in their realm by the end of the sixteenth century was the fact that disparate forces—service tenure landholders from the centre, Cossacks of the steppe frontier, communes of the north—mobilized in the Time of Troubles to rescue the state from foreign invasion. Moscow's rulers had at least consolidated an élite sufficiently cohesive to hold the state together. This achievement, done at the high human cost of enserfment, was possible because of the skilful use of coercion and co-option, but especially because of the state's minimalism. However autocratically they styled themselves, Moscow's rulers could exert their authority in only very narrow arenas. Sixteenth-century Russia is customarily called an 'autocracy', taking up the appellation (*samoderzhets*) that Boris Godunov introduced into the tsar's title. But if this was an autocracy, it was a pragmatically limited one.

From Muscovy towards St Petersburg
1598–1689

HANS-JOACHIM TORKE

From the time of Ivan the Terrible's oprichnina to the ascension of the Romanovs in 1613, Muscovy experienced uninterrupted crisis—extinction of a dynasty, foreign intervention, and tumultuous social and political upheaval. The seventeenth century witnessed a restless transition, as, amidst continuing upheaval at the dawn of modernity, Muscovy embarked on state-building, Westernization, and territorial expansion.

THE seventeenth century has long been a focus of historiographic debate. Impressed by the broad-ranging reforms of Peter the Great (1689–1725), most early historians tended to emphasize the 'break', juxtaposing a traditional Muscovy of the seventeenth century to a Westernizing state of the eighteenth. But for over a century specialists have realized that the Petrine reforms built upon changes initiated by his predecessors in the seventeenth century. The army, finances, state administration—favourite areas of Petrine reform—were also the subject of government reforms in the seventeenth century. While many of these reforms were driven by practical need, they reflected a desire not only to import Western technology and military experts, but also to reshape foreign and domestic policy in terms of Western ideas and theories.

Crisis: The Time of Troubles (1598–1613)

The age of transformation began with acute crisis—the 'Time of Troubles' (*smutnoe vremia*). This protracted crisis inaugurated a new period in Russian history, marked by fundamental changes that would culminate in the passing of 'Old Russia' and the onset of new 'troubles' in the 1680s. Perhaps the best schema for the Time of Troubles, devised over a century ago by the historian Sergei Platonov, divides this period into successive 'dynastic', 'social', and 'national' phases that followed upon one another but, to a significant degree, had some overlap.

The period begins with the extinction of the Riurikid line in 1598. The general crisis also had long-term social causes—in particular, the exhaustion of the land and its resources by the Livonian War and the *oprichnina* of Ivan the Terrible, which had devastated the boyars and triggered new restrictions on the peasants' freedom of movement. Without the trauma of 1598, however, the ensuing disorder would probably neither have been so intense nor have persisted for the entire seventeenth century, which contemporaries aptly called a 'rebellious age'. This first phase was portentous both because the only dynasty that had ever reigned in Russia suddenly vanished without issue, and because the ensuing events triggered the first assault on the autocracy. In the broadest sense, the old order lost a principal pillar—tradition (*starina*); nevertheless, there remained the spiritual support of the Orthodox Church (which held firm for several more decades) and the service nobility (which retained its resiliency until well into the eighteenth century). The year 1598 had one further consequence: a tradition-bound people could not believe that the dynasty had actually come to an end and therefore tended to support false pretenders claiming to be descendants of the Riurikids.

Muscovy responded to the extinction of its ruling dynasty by electing a new sovereign. Interestingly, no one as yet proposed to emulate other countries by electing someone from a foreign ruling house—a remarkable testament to the insularity of Muscovite society. Such a proposal, undoubtedly, faced an insuperable religious obstacle—obligatory conversion to Orthodoxy. In the end the choice fell on Boris Godunov—a Russian nobleman, though not from an élite family (i.e. descending from another Riurikid line or the Lithuanian grand princes). None the less, Boris had single-mindedly prepared his advancement under Tsars Ivan the Terrible (1533–84) and Fedor Ivanovich (1584–98): he himself married the daughter of a favourite in Ivan's court; his sister Irina married Ivan's successor, Fedor. Because the latter was personally incapable of exercising power, Godunov became regent and excluded all other competitors. After Fedor's death, on 17 February 1598 Boris was formally 'elected' as Tsar Boris by a council (*sobor*) of approximately 600 deputies drawn from the upper clergy, the boyar duma, and representatives of the service nobility who had gathered in Moscow. Although transparently stage-managed by Boris, the council seemed to confirm that the realm had 'found' the candidate chosen by God Himself.

The Church, which Boris had earlier helped to establish its own Patriarchate, supported his election. The new tsar could also count on the sympathy of the lower nobility. But Boris also had to use coercion to eliminate rivals among the boyars—such as Fedor Nikitich Romanov, the head of a family with marital ties to the Riurikids, who was banished in late 1600 and forced to take monastic vows in 1601 (with the name Filaret). That tonsure effectively eliminated him from contention for worldly offices.

Nevertheless, Boris's position was anything but secure. Apart from the fact that his government was beset with enormous burdens and problems, Boris himself failed to evoke veneration from his subjects. In part, that was because he had married the daughter of Grigorii (Maliuta) Skuratov—the *oprichnik* blamed for murdering Metropolitan Filipp of Novgorod in 1569. Moreover, his blatant efforts to ascend the throne lent credence to rumours that he had arranged the murder of Tsarevich Dmitrii, Ivan's last son, in 1591. Although an investigatory commission under Vasilii Shuiskii (a rival whom Boris had deftly appointed to lead the investigation) confirmed that the death was accidental, the death of the 9-year-old Tsarevich remains a mystery to this day. Indeed, it made no sense for Boris to kill the boy: at the time of Dmitrii's death, it was still conceivable that Fedor would father a son and avert the extinction of the Riurikid line. Nevertheless, Boris's adversaries exploited suspicions of regicide —a view which, because of Alexander Pushkin's play *Boris Godunov* (which Modest Mussorgsky later made into an opera), has persisted to the present.

Nor was Boris able to consolidate power after accession to the throne. His attempt to tighten control over administration failed—largely because of the traditional 'Muscovite procrastination' and corruption. His plan to reconstruct the towns also went awry, chiefly for want of a middle estate. Nor was he able to train better state servants: when, for the first time, Muscovy dispatched

Peasants. On this engraving peasants are shown in their typical clothes. Beards were a must, because according to the Orthodox faith humans were not allowed to change their natural outward appearances.

a contingent (eighteen men) to study in England, France, and Germany, not a single one returned. He recruited large numbers of European specialists (military officers, doctors, and artisans), but met with remonstrations from the Orthodox Church. Clearly, Boris had an open mind about the West: he not only solicited the support of ruling houses in the West, but also sought to consolidate his dynastic claims through attempts to marry his daughter Ksenia to Swedish (later Danish) princes, although such plans ultimately came to nought.

Boris attempted to establish order in noble–peasant relations, but nature herself interceded. From the early 1590s, in an attempt to protect petty nobles and to promote economic recovery, the government established the 'forbidden years', which—for the first time—imposed a blanket prohibition on peasant movement during the stipulated year. In autumn 1601, however, Boris's government had to retreat and reaffirm the peasants' right to movement: a catastrophic crop failure in the preceding summer caused massive famine that claimed hundreds of thousands of lives. The following year the government again had to rescind the 'forbidden year', a step that virtually legalized massive peasant flight. Moreover the government welcomed movement towards the southern border area (appropriately called the *dikoe pole*, or 'wild field'), where they helped to reinforce the Cossacks and the fortified towns recently established as a buffer between Muscovy and the Crimean Tatars. But many peasants sought new landowners in central Muscovy, adding to the social unrest. In fact, in 1603 the government had to use troops to suppress rebellious peasants, bondsmen (*kholopy*), and even *déclassé* petty nobles.

That uprising signalled the onset of phase two—the social crisis. This stage, however, overlapped with the dynastic crisis: as the general sense of catastrophe mounted, rumours suddenly spread that Tsarevich Dmitrii had not died at Uglich, but had miraculously survived in Poland-Lithuania. In 1601 a pretender surfaced in Poland, winning the support of adventurous magnates (in particular, the voevoda of Sandomierz, Jerzy Mniszech); he was actually a fugitive monk, Grigorii, who had fled from Chudov Monastery in Moscow and originally came from the petty nobility, bearing the name Iurii Otrepev before tonsure. That, at least, was the public claim of Boris Godunov, who himself had fallen ill and steadily lost the ability to rule. That declaration had no more effect than his representations to the Polish king, Zygmunt III, who remained officially uninvolved, but had secret assurances from the 'False Dmitrii' that Poland would receive Smolensk and other territories were he to succeed.

When the Polish nobles launched their campaign from Lvov in August 1604, their forces numbered only 2,200 cavalrymen. When they reached Moscow in June 1605, however, this army had grown tenfold, for many others—especially Cossacks—had joined the triumphal march to Moscow.

By the time they entered the Kremlin, Boris himself had already died (April 1605), and his 16-year-old son Fedor was promptly executed. Of Boris's reign, only the acquisition of western Siberia (with outposts as remote as the Enisei) and the expansion southward were achievements of enduring significance.

The pretender initially succeeded in persuading the populace that he was the real Dmitrii. The boyars were less credulous; several were judged guilty of a conspiracy under the leadership of Vasilii Shuiskii. But the pretender had the support of Boris's enemies (seeking personal advantage) and those who believed that the 'Pseudo-Dmitrii' (ostensibly a 'Riurikid') would restore the old order.

The first False Dmitrii, here in the armour of a Polish magnate, had his portrait as 'emperor' painted quite often in order to make himself known to foreign heads of states. In reality he was a run-away monk from a Moscow monastery whom the Polish-Lithuanian nobility used as a tool to conquer Muscovy.

Dmitrii, however, had secretly converted to Roman Catholicism, promised enormous territories to his Polish benefactors (especially Mniszech, whose daughter Maryna he had married), and even agreed to permit missionary activities by Catholic priests and to participate in a crusade against the Turks. Before fulfilling these commitments, he attempted to ensure the support of the petty nobility, for example, by issuing a decree in 1606 that re-established the five-year statute of limitations on the forcible return of fugitive peasants.

None the less, Dmitrii failed to consolidate his hold on power. Above all, the Polish presence exposed old Russian culture to massive Western influence and provoked a strong reaction, especially against the foreigners' behaviour—their clothing, customs, and contempt for Orthodox religious rites. Popular unrest reached its peak during the wedding ceremonies in May 1606 (intended to supplement Catholic rites conducted earlier in Cracow, though without formal marriage of the betrothed). Offended by the provocative behaviour of Polish aristocrats, Vasilii Shuiskii and fellow boyars organized a conspiracy that resulted in the overthrow and murder of the 'False Dmitrii'.

It is hardly surprising that Shuiskii himself mounted the throne—this time 'chosen' by fellow boyars, not a council of the realm. The scion of an old princely line and descendant of Alexander Nevsky, he represented the hope of aristocratic lines pushed into the background by Boris and Dmitrii. During the coronation ceremonies, Shuiskii openly paid homage to the boyars, not only promising to restore the right of the boyar duma to judge cases of capital punishment (denied by Ivan the Terrible), but also vowing neither to punish an entire family for the offence of a single member nor to subject their property to arbitrary confiscation. These concessions did not constitute an electoral capitulation for a limited monarchy, but were meant only to ensure a return to genuine autocracy.

Shuiskii immediately faced a serious challenge—the Bolotnikov rebellion, the first great peasant uprising in the history of Russia. To oppose the 'boyar tsar', Ivan Bolotnikov—himself a fugitive bondsman—mobilized a motley force of peasants and Cossacks from the south (who for several years had been fomenting disorder in the region), service nobles with military experience, and some well-born adversaries of Vasilii. The rebels did manage to encircle Moscow in October 1606, but their movement collapsed when petty nobles—alarmed by the insistent demand of peasants for freedom—abandoned Bolotnikov to join the other side. Bolotnikov, who had poor administrative skills, retreated to Tula; a year later, after months of siege by government troops, the town finally capitulated and turned Bolotnikov over for execution. In the interim, Vasilii cleverly attempted to win the nobility's allegiance by promulgating a peasant statute (9 March 1607) that extended the statute of limitations on the forcible recovery of fugitive peasants from five to fifteen years. The decree answered their primary demand: by tripling the period of the statute of limitations, his decree greatly increased the chances for finding and recovering fugitives. The statute also afforded some legal protection to the bondsmen: henceforth they might be held in bondage only on the basis of a written document (*kabala*).

Hardly had Vasilii eliminated the threat from peasants and Cossacks when he faced a new menace from the Poles: in late 1607 yet another pretender, likewise claiming to be Tsarevich Dmitrii, crossed the border with an army of Polish-Lithuanian warriors. The past of this second False Dmitrii is murky, but he apparently came from the milieu of the first. Although the Polish government and Catholic Church remained in the background, members of the Polish nobility under Jan Sapieha participated in his siege of Moscow in mid-1608. After establishing headquarters in the village of Tushino, he was joined by the wife of the first False Dmitrii, 'Tsarina Maryna', who 'recognized' the husband who had so miraculously survived. Filaret Romanov (whom the first False Dmitrii elevated to metropolitan, thereby facilitating a return to politics) also made his way to Tushino. As other adversaries of Vasilii also came, Tushino became the centre of a counter-government, with its own administration, and was recognized as the legitimate power by much of the realm.

Simultaneously, several towns along the upper Volga established their own army (the 'first contingent'), which proceeded to liberate Vladimir, Nizhnii Novgorod, and Kostroma. This army evidently had no ties with Vasilii, who was forced to accept the assistance of some 5,000 Swedish mercenaries.

Muscovy now entered phase three—the 'national crisis': in May 1609 the Polish Sejm approved a request by King Zygmunt III for funds to invade Russia—nominally under the pretext of repulsing a Swedish threat to Poland-Lithuania. Thus, by the autumn of 1609, two foreign armies—Swedish and Polish—were operating on Russian soil: the Poles concentrated on taking Smolensk, while the Swedes forced Vasilii to cede Korela and Livonia as compensation for their help. After some initial tensions, Moscow and Sweden soon enjoyed military success, overrunning the camp at Tushino at the end of 1609; a few months later the Swedish troops marched into Moscow. As most of the Poles retreated toward Smolensk, the second False Dmitrii settled down in Kaluga, but was slain by his own supporters at the end of 1610.

Nevertheless, Vasilii's hold on power steadily deteriorated, partly because of suspicions that the jealous tsar was responsible for the mysterious death of a popular commander, M. V. Skopin-Shuiskii. Vasilii's forces, moreover, had failed to liberate Smolensk from Polish control.

As Vasilii's power waned, in February 1610 his foes struck a deal with the king of Poland: his son Władysław, successor to the Polish throne, would become tsar on condition that he promise to uphold Orthodoxy and to allow the election of a monarch in accordance with Polish customs. He also had to guarantee current landholding relations and official ranks (*chiny*), the legislative power of the boyar duma and an imperial council (analogues to the Sejm and Senate), and the preservation of peasant dependence. The agreement also provided for a military alliance between the two states. Thus, for the first time in Russian history, élites set terms for accession to the throne. These conditions were reaffirmed in a new agreement on 17 August 1610, with the added proviso that the future tsar convert to Orthodoxy.

A month earlier, the conspirators (who evidently included Filaret) had already deposed Vasilii and forced him to take monastic vows. The Polish negotiator was hetman St Żółkiewski, who had conquered Moscow and, as commander of the Polish-Lithuanian occupation, held power in the capital. The agreement provided for a council of seven boyars (legitimized by an *ad hoc* council of the realm), which, with a changing composition, sought to govern during the interregnum. The boyars hoped to use the Polish tsar to overcome the internal strife, but their attempt would ultimately founder on the lesser nobility's fear of a boyar oligarchy.

That Muscovy obtained neither a Polish tsar nor a limited monarchy in 1610 was due to a surprising turn of events in Smolensk. There the Polish king received a 'great legation' from Moscow (with over 1,200 persons) to discuss the details of succession. Despite the mediation of Żółkiewski, the negotiations broke down as the two parties refused to compromise—chiefly over the demand by Russians (especially patriarch Germogen) that the future tsar convert to Orthodoxy, and over the Polish insistence that Moscow cede Smolensk. Zygmunt now announced that he himself wished to become tsar, which effectively eliminated any possibility of conversion to Orthodoxy. The tensions were soon apparent in Moscow, where the high-handed behaviour of the Poles and their Russian supporters triggered a popular uprising in February–March 1611. The leader of resistance was patriarch Germogen, who issued impassioned proclamations against the Poles before finally being interned. In April the king had members of the 'great legation' (including Metropolitan Filaret and the former Tsar Vasilii Shuiskii) deported to Poland and put on exhibition before the Sejm.

All this culminated in a great national uprising led by towns on the Volga. The provinces were still aflame with unrest and disorder: by mid-1611 eight pretenders claimed to be the 'true' Tsarevich Dmitrii; countless bands of peasants and Cossacks, purporting to fight for 'freedom', engulfed the land in conflict and plunder; Swedes tightened their hold on Novgorod (intended as a pawn to press other territorial demands) and ruled the entire north; and the Tatars invaded from the south.

In response Nizhnii Novgorod and Vologda raised the 'second levy', which united with the former supporters of the second False Dmitrii and advanced on Moscow. The army was led by P. Liapunov, the district governor (*voevoda*) of Riazan; like other district governors, he was originally a military commander, but had since become head of civil administration in his district. The supreme council of his army functioned as a government (for example, assessing taxes), but avoided any promise of freedom for fugitive peasants once the strife had ended. Despite written agreements, Liapunov's forces suffered from profound internal conflict, especially between peasants and petty nobles; Liapunov himself was murdered in the summer of 1611, marking an end to the 'second contingent'. The 'Council of Seven Boyars' in Moscow, meanwhile, continued to hope for the arrival of Władysław.

The 'third levy', though beset with internal differences, nevertheless liberated Moscow in October 1612. This army had been created a year earlier by K. Minin, the elected head of Nizhnii Novgorod, who persuaded the population to endorse a special tax amount (up to 30 per cent of their property). Many nobles joined this army, including its commander—Prince Dmitrii Pozharskii, who established headquarters in Iaroslavl. Minin and Pozharskii later became national heroes, memorialized to this day in a monument on Red Square. But the critical factor in their victory was the decision of Cossacks under Prince Trubetskoi to join their side in the midst of the battle.

The liberation of Moscow did not mean an end to the turbulent 'Time of Troubles': for years to come, large parts of the realm remained under Swedish and Polish occupation. But it was at least possible to elect a new tsar in 1613, a date traditionally accepted as the end to the Time of Troubles. Still, the ramifications of this era were momentous and enduring, especially the large-scale intrusion of the West, which generated much commentary—and controversy—among writers such as Ivan Timofeev, Avramii Palitsyn, Semen Shakhovskoi, and Ivan Khvorostinin. And, despite the election of a new tsar, society became more self-conscious as it entered upon decades of tumult in the 'rebellious century'.

New Beginnings: The First Romanov (1613–1645)

In 1613 Mikhail Fedorovich Romanov—Tsar Michael in popular literature—was only one of several candidates for the throne of Muscovy. Although not yet even 17 years of age, he had already been considered for this position three years earlier. But circumstances were now more complex: in contrast to Boris's election in 1598, this time some proposed to summon a foreigner—either Archduke Maximilian of Habsburg or the Swedish prince, Karl Phillip.

Because of the patriotic mood after the expulsion of Poles from the Kremlin, however, there was nevertheless a strong preference to choose a Russian candidate. Rivalry among candidates eventually eliminated all but one—the young Romanov, widely regarded as a surrogate for his father Filaret, still in Polish detention; the latter's martyr-like captivity, in fact, contributed to his son's election. Michael came from a relatively young boyar family, which first gained prominence when it provided the first wife of Ivan the Terrible. But the old boyar clans, given to bickering among themselves, savoured this humble background—and Michael's youth, which promised to make him easier to manipulate. The electoral assembly of 700 delegates was initially unable to reach a consensus, but on 21 February 1613 finally acceded to vigorous agitation from nearby towns that Michael be chosen as the compromise candidate. In the aftermath of the Time of Troubles, when the throne had changed hands so frequently, few could have foreseen that this dynasty would remain pure-blooded until 1762 and, with the infusion of some outside (mainly German) elements, retain the throne until 1917.

In contrast to Shuiskii, Michael made no concessions to obtain the throne. Indeed, the participants themselves wanted to restore the autocracy 'of the good old days' that had ensured order and stability. In foreign policy, restoration meant expulsion of foreign foes; in domestic policy, it meant resolving the conflict between landholders and peasants, which had disintegrated into virtual chaos. Despite this call for restoration, the election did not bring an end either to popular unrest or to the intrusion of Western culture.

The re-establishment of autocracy naturally did not mean that Michael—above all, given his youth—ruled alone. Initially, he was under the influence of powerful favourites from the Mstislavskii and Saltykov clans. After 1619, when peace with Poland brought an exchange of prisoners (including Filaret), the young tsar fell under the dominance of his father, who became a virtual co-ruler and even bore the tsarist title of 'Great Sovereign': in Muscovy it was simply inconceivable that a father might occupy a lower rank than his son. This paternal dominance also corresponded to their personalities, Filaret being energetic, his son meek and pious.

FOREIGN POLICY AND WAR

The accomplishments before Filaret's return, however, should not be underestimated. The primary task was to equip an army to fight the Swedes and Poles; because of the economic destruction and havoc wrought by marauding bands of peasants and Cossacks, however, it proved extremely difficult to raise the requisite funds. To obtain the needed levies, Michael summoned several 'councils of the realm' (*sobory*); although these could not issue binding resolutions (contrary to what historians once assumed), they provided the government with information about economic conditions in the provinces. The government used this information to levy special taxes—normally 5 per cent, sometimes up to 10 per cent, of the property value and the business turnover. In addition, it forced the richest merchants of the realm, the Stroganovs of Novgorod, to make contributions and loans. By 1618 the government had raised seven special levies to cut a budget deficit that, in 1616, had run to over 340,000 roubles.

Moscow finally concluded peace with its two adversaries. After Vasilii had been deposed, the Swedes remained ensconced in Novgorod and Ingermanland—perhaps with the intent of preventing an alliance between Muscovy and Poland. But Gustavus Adolphus decided to make peace, partly because the resistance of Novgorodians was so intense, partly because he needed Moscow as an ally in an impending conflict that would mushroom into the Thirty Years War. On 25 February 1617 the two sides signed the Treaty of Stolbovo, on terms favourable to Moscow: although the latter had to pay 20,000 silver roubles and to cede Ingermanland and eastern Karelia, in exchange it obtained the return of Novgorod and Swedish recognition of the tsarist title. Nevertheless, the agreement reaffirmed Swedish predominance on the Baltic Sea for another century.

Relations with Poland-Lithuania were more difficult. The Poles declined to recognize Michael; the Russians naturally refused to accept Władysław as tsar. After mediation efforts collapsed, the Poles launched a new military offensive in 1617 and were able to attack the city of Moscow in the autumn of 1618. That same year, however, the two sides agreed to an armistice of fourteen and a half years: both were exhausted from the conflict, the Polish Sejm (confronted with the outbreak of the Thirty Years War) denied more funds, and Moscow fervently wanted an exchange of prisoners. The armistice, signed in the village of Deulino (north of Moscow), compelled Moscow to renounce its claim to west Russian areas (Severia, Chernigov, and—with a heavy heart—Smolensk). The question of Smolensk, together with the Poles' refusal to renounce their claim to the throne of Moscow, carried the seeds of future conflict.

INTERNAL AFFAIRS AND THE SMOLENSK WAR

After his return in 1619, Filaret became the patriarch of Moscow (which, for the sake of propriety, was formally bestowed by the patriarch of Jerusalem). The world now seemed to be in order, even in the relations between father and son. Nevertheless, the government faced serious problems; in addition to seeking vengeance on Poland, Filaret had to address the question of tax reform. To finance the Streltsy (a semi-regular military unit of musketeers created to defend the court and borders), in 1614 the government already imposed some new special levies—'Streltsy money' from townspeople and 'Streltsy grain' from peasants. The government also increased the 'postal money', the largest regular tax. It assessed these levies on the basis of a land tax unit (*sokha*), which took soil quality into account, but was none the less so high that many commoners preferred to abandon their community and become indentured bondsmen of a secular lord, a monastery, or tax-free town. Because of the principle of collective responsibility (*krugovaia poruka*), those who remained behind had to assume the obligations of the bondsmen and thus pay even higher taxes. Ever since 1584 the government had periodically prohibited this form of tax evasion, but with scant effect. Filaret also failed to achieve a satisfactory solution, partly because he himself was an interested party: the Patriarchate owned approximately a thousand plots of land in Moscow, which were duly exempted from the ban. In effect, the government only forbade indentureship, not the acceptance of tax evaders. More successful in the long run was the gradual conversion of the tax base from land to household, a process that commenced in the 1620s but only reached completion in 1679.

Filaret's policy towards towns was still less successful. The basic problem was that, without a strong middle class, the towns did not constitute juridical entities. Filaret moved the rich merchants to Moscow to serve in central administrative offices (*prikazy*), but that policy only emptied towns at the provincial level. Moreover, the government put foreign policy over the interests of indigenous merchants: foreigners, especially British, engaged in retail trade throughout Muscovy, enjoyed exemption from most customs duties, and even had fishing rights in the White Sea. These privileges were the target of a collective petition from thirty-one Russian merchants in 1627—the first of numerous such complaints in the next decades. The townsmen of Moscow also complained of other burdens, such as billeting, in a collective petition of 1629.

In 1621–2 Filaret considered a new attempt to reconquer Smolensk and compel the Poles to recognize the Romanov dynasty. On the basis of information from a council of the realm, however, he realized that the country was simply unprepared for such an undertaking. But the Thirty Years War soon afforded an opportunity for vengeance; as an important ally of Sweden, Moscow was later named in the Peace of Westphalia in 1648. Although Moscow did not directly participate in the conflict, from 1628 it delivered commodities such as grain (which, as a state monopoly, yielded a huge profit) and, more important, in 1632–4 went to war with Poland, which was forced to divert forces to the east. Meanwhile, with Swedish aid, the Russians built their military force into a standing army with approximately 66,000 soldiers (the so-called 'Troops of the New Order'), which included approximately 2,500 Western officers under the Scottish colonel, Alexander Leslie. Nevertheless, Filaret, who died in 1633 in the midst of the war, had overestimated Moscow's power: the campaign proceeded so badly that the commander-in-chief, M. B. Shein, in the wake of mass desertion by his soldiers (which was hardly unusual at the time) and the futile siege of Smolensk, was found guilty of treason and executed. The two sides agreed to a new peace at Polianovka in 1634. Władysław did renounce his claim to the tsarist throne, but in exchange Moscow had to pay 20,000 roubles and to return all the areas that it had occupied.

THE FINAL YEARS

Nevertheless, the war drew Muscovy even closer to the West. Besides the Troops of the New Order (temporarily disbanded for lack of funds), the most tangible sign of Europeanization was the influx of Western merchants and entrepreneurs. Dominance shifted from the English to the Dutch: Andries Winius obtained monopoly rights to construct ironworks in the towns of Tula and Serpukhov (the first blast furnace began operations in 1637); the Walloon Coyet established the first glass plant in the environs of Moscow. The driving impulse, as in other spheres, was the demand for military armaments.

Lifting of a bell in the Kremlin. This is one of the rare pictures of a technical construction made by the Swedish traveller Palmquist. It took nine months to lift the bell in 1674 including many failures. The 'bell wall' no longer exists; neither does the building of the 'Foreign Office' which can be seen in the background to the right.

For the time being, the Orthodox Church was able to contain Western influence in cultural matters. The main spiritual influence, instead, came from Ukraine—for example, a proposal in 1640 by the metropolitan of Kiev, Petr Mohyla, to establish an ecclesiastical academy in Moscow, and the import of books with the 'Lithuanian imprint' (which, because of their Roman Catholic content, were prohibited). The Church also denounced as 'heresy' the correction of church books, which had commenced in 1618 (in conjunction with the development of printing) and sought to compare Russian liturgical texts with the Greek originals.

The religious tensions were also accompanied by increasing social conflict. In 1637 the tsar's service people filed their first collective petition and later persuaded him to reduce their service obligations by half. But as yet the government spurned their other demands—for a decentralization of the judicial system (to avoid expensive trials, corruption, and procrastination in Moscow) and for the total abolition of a statute of limitations on the return of runaway peasants. Michael did, however, extend the statute of limitations for the recovery of fugitives (from five to nine years). After another petition in 1641, he increased the term to ten years for the general fugitives and fifteen years for peasants who had been forcibly seized by other landowners.

In foreign affairs too the tsar had to make a difficult decision. In 1637 the Don Cossacks of Muscovy attacked the Turkish fortress of Azov and for four long years

Siberian sledge travel. In 1692 the mayor of Amsterdam, a friend of Peter the Great, published a book on Siberia for which he had collected information during a visit to Russia almost thirty years before. The picture from this account shows a very common vehicle in a region where the winters are long.

held out against the Ottoman army and fleet. A council of the realm in 1642, however, expressed deep reservations, and the tsar persuaded the Cossacks to abandon the fortress. War with Turkey would have certainly entailed immense losses, and the Sultan had already threatened to exterminate the entire Orthodox population of his empire. Similarly, Moscow continued to spurn the centuries-old urging of the West for a crusade against the Ottoman Empire.

By contrast, Muscovy's eastward expansion proved far more successful. After the first penetration into Siberia in the late sixteenth century, the government had sanctioned—sometimes *ex post facto*—the conquests of Cossack units acting on their own initiative: they thus founded Eniseisk in 1619 and Iakutsk in 1632, and reached the Pacific at the Sea of Okhotsk in 1639. To the south Moscow established timid contacts with China, sending its first envoy to Peking in 1619.

In general, the first Romanov tsar achieved a certain consolidation, but could not quell mounting social and spiritual ferment that would soon explode into major upheavals during the next reign.

The End of an Era: Tsar Alexis (1645–1676)

THE NEW TSAR

The new tsar—father of Peter the Great—embodied the cultural confrontation of the seventeenth century: devotion to old Russian tradition versus attraction to the achievements of West European civilization. Tsar Alexis (Aleksei Mikhailovich) overcame this cultural conflict, which proved profoundly disturbing in domestic life, through success in foreign affairs. His eventful reign was marked by a fierce battle between the old and the new, which indeed was reflected in the personality of the tsar himself. On the one hand, he took Ivan the Terrible as the ideal model and understood old Russian autocracy as rulership that was simultaneously gentle and harsh; on the other hand, he was the first tsar to sign laws on his own authority, to permit realistic portraits of his person, and to receive and write personal letters in the real meaning of the word. Throughout his lifetime he sought friendships—for example, with Patriarch Nikon and the head of the foreign office, A. L. Ordin-Nashchokin, whose human individuality (like that of the tsar) for the first time is reflected in contemporary sources. Indeed, the pre-revolutionary historian Platonov suggested that the individual personality made its first appearance in old Russia.

THE MOSCOW UPRISING OF 1648

The young tsar's first friend, brother-in-law, and former teacher, was B. I. Morozov. One of many 'powerful magnates' (*sil'nye liudi*), Morozov amassed enormous wealth by taking personal control of the most important and lucrative central offices (*prikazy*). By the time of his death, Morozov owned

9,100 peasant households (55,000 peasants) in nineteen districts—along with numerous manufactories, mills, and illicit distilleries. Tsar Alexis, following an order from his father, also empowered Morozov to investigate government administration and to conduct reforms to reduce social tensions. Morozov could in fact boast of certain achievements, but some of his measures aroused popular discontent. Thus, after being forced to cancel a new salt tax, in 1648 he attempted to collect arrears from the preceding two years—in effect tripling the tax burden for 1648.

This measure ignited a major uprising in June 1648, which together with the fires that swept through Moscow, cost approximately two thousand lives. Crowds murdered high-ranking, corrupt officials; with tears in his eyes, the tsar could do nothing more for Morozov than secure his banishment. By the end of July the rebellion generated more than seventy petitions that led to some concrete changes, including the cancellation of tax arrears as well as monetary levies for the tsar's bodyguards, the Streltsy. The latter, in fact, felt threatened by the new foreign troops and tended to support the rebels. Morozov did return in late October, but was never again to play a major role. The government faced the fearful spectre of a new Time of Troubles, especially when nobles and merchants aggressively pressed demands, sometimes even filing joint petitions. This solidarity, and the fact that Moscow itself was practically in rebel hands, forced the government in June 1648 to accede to an ultimatum that it convoke a council of the realm. The council, which convened that autumn, elected to compile a new law code (the *Ulozhenie*), which was promulgated on 29 January 1649 to replace the law code (*sudebnik*) of 1550.

At least 8.5 per cent of the 967 articles in this law code derived from initiatives of the population. It also drew upon earlier legislation and the Lithuanian Statute (from which came the first formal defence of the tsar and court). In general, it conceded many of the demands that had been raised during the preceding decades. The most famous was the establishment of serfdom, which at first only bound the peasant to the soil (i.e. restricted their mobility). The preparations for enserfment had been laid by earlier decrees extending the time-limit for the search and return of fugitive peasants; as early as February 1646, the government indicated its intention to issue a total ban on peasant movement. The law code thereby satisfied the nobility's demand to retrieve runaways without any time-limit. This initial bondage to the soil would evolve into a far more comprehensive 'serfdom' in the eighteenth century. Significantly, the prohibition on mobility also applied to the towns: anyone who owed taxes could not change their residence. The law code also forbade boyars to accept taxpayers as 'bondsmen' (*kholopy*); it also attacked the special interests of the Church by forbidding the clergy to accept landed estates and by reducing the competence of ecclesiastical courts. At the same time, however, the government still repulsed demands to decentralize the judicial system and to expand locally elected government.

Hence the victory of the petty nobility and townspeople did not mean a weakening of autocracy. On the contrary, the uprising impelled the tsar to take measures that had been long deferred and that served primarily to strengthen the bonds between autocracy and the lower nobility.

The law code itself did not address the long-standing grievances of the Russian merchants against foreign competition. But the government found a pretext to expel foreigners on 1 June 1649, when Alexis expressed his outrage over the execution of Charles I and banished the English from domestic trade in Muscovy. In 1654 he extended the prohibition to merchants from Holland and Hamburg. In general, the law code (published in a press run of 2,400 copies and distributed to all officials as the first law code) did more to bolster the old order than to build a new one. It was, consequently, already outdated by the time of Peter the Great. Remarkably enough, however, it officially remained in force until 1 January 1835, as Alexis's successors found themselves unable to compile a new code or even to issue a revised edition.

Continuing Instability

After the bitter experience of 1648, the tsar never again let the initiative slip from his grasp during subsequent urban uprisings. New disorders erupted three years later in Novgorod and Pskov; located on the western border, the two cities had always held a special status because of their commercial relations and were especially opposed to the competition of Western merchants. The discontent intensified because of the government's pro-Swedish policies, which, in accordance with the Peace of Stolbovo of 1617, required Muscovy to deliver grain to Sweden; that, however, caused higher grain prices at home and produced particular hardship for a grain-importing area like Pskov. The result was an uprising that erupted first in Pskov and soon spread to Novgorod. After Alexis's forces occupied the latter city and carried out several executions, the people of Pskov peacefully surrendered, bringing the rebellion to an end.

In 1662 the tsar faced far greater peril during the 'copper-coin uprising' in Moscow. The unrest itself was due to the war begun in 1654 against Poland-Lithuania: to finance the war, the government not only assessed special taxes and loans, but also minted copper coins that the people deemed to be worthless. Meanwhile, the owners of copper kitchenware bribed the mint masters to make coins from their copper pots; when the guilty officials were given only a light punishment, popular anger only intensified. The copper minting also caused inflation: whereas one copper rouble was equal to one silver rouble in 1658, this ratio rose to four to one by 1661, and then jumped to fifteen to one two years later. Compounded by other hardships, popular discontent in the summer of 1662 led to the formation of mobs, which demanded to speak to the tsar himself and moved *en masse* towards his summer residence in Kolomenskoe, south of Moscow. After Alexis promised to investigate the matter, the throng headed back towards Moscow. On the way, however, they came upon other rebels and decided to return to Kolomenskoe, which once again found itself in peril. This time the tsar ordered his Streltsy to disperse the crowd (now some nine thousand strong) with force; in the aftermath sixty-three rebels were executed, and many others sent into exile.

The 'rebellious century' was not limited to urban revolts: in 1670–1 peasants joined the greatest rebellion of the seventeenth century—a mass insurrection that began on the periphery under the leadership of Stepan ('Stenka') Razin. The rebellion sprang from the ranks of the Don Cossacks, who lived south of Muscovy's ever-expanding border and had their own autonomous military order (military council as well as the election of the ataman as chief and other officials). Through the influx of fugitive peasants, bondsmen, and petty townsmen, the Cossacks had multiplied to the point where they had their own 'proletariat'—some ten to twenty thousand Cossacks who could no longer support themselves by tilling the land. Their plight was aggravated by Moscow's decision to reduce its paid 'service Cossacks' to a mere 1,000 persons. War with Poland in 1654–67 increased the flight of people to the untamed southern steppes (*dikoe pole*). Although the government was not unhappy to see the strengthening of barriers against the Crimean Tatars, it promulgated a statute of limitations on fugitives and ordered the forcible return of 10,000 fugitives. Amidst this unrest, in 1667 Stepan Razin summoned Cossacks to join a traditional campaign of plunder and led some 2,000 Cossacks to the lower Volga, ultimately reaching the Persian coast in 1668–9. Over the next two years, however, the expedition turned into a popular rebellion against landowners and state authorities. With some 20,000 supporters, Razin prepared to strike at Moscow itself. Although he did establish a Cossack regime in Astrakhan and issued radical promises to divide all property equally, he had no coherent political programme and explicitly declared autocracy inviolable. In Simbirsk his forces attracted peasants, some non-Russian peoples, and petty townsmen and service people from the middle Volga. In the spring of 1671, however, Razin was betrayed by his own Cossack superiors: handed over to tsarist authorities, he was later executed in Moscow.

COSSACKS AND BORDERLAND POLITICS

Cossacks, certainly those on the Dnieper, exerted a major influence on Alexis's foreign policy. Indeed, together with the Moscow uprising, their actions made 1648 a watershed in Russian history: under the leadership of hetman Bohdan Khmelnitskii, they rebelled against their Polish-Lithuanian authorities. They had several main grievances: the oppression of Ukrainian peasants by Polish magnates and their Jewish stewards, discrimination against the Orthodox Church by Roman Catholicism, and a reduction in Cossack registration (i.e. the number of Cossacks in the paid service of the Polish king). Khmelnitskii hoped to achieve his goal—formation of a separate Cossack republic of nobles—with the aid of the Moscow tsar. The latter, while sympathetic to the idea of protect-

us Brother

Stepan Razin on the way to his execution. The leader of the greatest peasant uprising in the seventeenth century was executed, together with his brother Frol, in Moscow on 6 June 1671. Before the Don Cossack was captured he had led as many as 20,000 rebels up the Volga river to Simbirsk. The picture is from a travel account published by a British seaman in London in 1672.

ing his Orthodox brethren, was nevertheless exceedingly cautious: support for the Cossacks clearly meant war with Poland-Lithuania. Although Moscow yearned to settle old scores (dating back to its defeat in 1634 and above all the forfeiture of Smolensk), as yet it did not feel strong enough for such an undertaking. It was the Orthodox Church, particularly after Nikon's elevation to the Patriarchate in mid-1652, that induced Moscow to support the Cossacks in February 1653.

For Moscow, of course, this co-operation was conceivable only if it entailed Cossack recognition of the tsar's sovereignty, and Khmelnitskii duly complied, taking a unilateral vow of loyalty in Pereiaslavl on 8 January 1654. Russian and Soviet historians subsequently portrayed this oath as a merger of Ukraine with Muscovy, even a 'reunification' of Muscovy with Kiev Rus. By contrast, Ukrainian historiography depicts this oath as the beginning of an independent 'hetman state', which lasted until the time of Catherine the Great. In reality, however, the oath merely signified nominal subordination and guaranteed the hetman and his followers a social and legal order with a considerable autonomy, even in foreign affairs (except for relations with Poland and the Ottomans). Although Alexis henceforth proclaimed himself 'Autocrat of All Great and Little Rus', incorporation of Ukraine into the Russian Empire did not actually come until the eighteenth century.

The anticipated war, which commenced immediately in 1654 and lasted until 1667, was waged in western Russia. The very first year Moscow reconquered the long-sought Smolensk, and the next year its forces captured Minsk and Vilna as well. For Moscow, the only dark cloud was the fact that their quick victories had tempted the Swedes to intervene and attempt to seize the Polish ports in the Baltic. In 1656 Moscow opened hostilities against Sweden and by the following year had conquered most of Livonia. But Reval (Tallin) and Riga withstood the Russian siege; confronted with new military hostilities with Poland, Moscow concluded the Peace of Cardis with Sweden in 1661 on the basis of *status quo ante bellum*. In 1667 Moscow and Poland agreed to the armistice of Andrusovo, with a compromise partition of Ukraine: Poland renounced its west Russian gains of 1618, Moscow its claims to right-bank Ukraine (i.e. west of the Dnieper), with the exception of Kiev. The armistice was of considerable significance: it marked the beginning of the end for Poland's status as a great power in Eastern Europe but also brought an epoch-making reversal in Moscow's relationship to the Turks.

Initially, the driving force behind foreign policy was Ordin-Nashchokin, the Western-oriented 'foreign minister'. As the district governor (*voevoda*) of Pskov in the first half of the 1660s he had excelled in reducing social tensions, and he was also responsible for the 'New Commercial Statute' (1667), which strengthened the merchant class on the basis of mercantilistic ideas. His Western orientation contributed significantly to the Europeanization of Russia, which now became still more pronounced. In 1671 he was succeeded as head of the foreign chancellery by A. S. Matveev, who had married a Scottish woman (Lady Hamilton) and who was still more open-minded about the West. In contrast to Ordin-Nashchokin, who was interested chiefly in the Baltic Sea, Matveev was far more concerned about the southern border. In 1672, in the wake of Andrusovo, Moscow reversed a centuries-old tendency and now urged the West to support Poland against the Turks. The reason for this shift was simple: Moscow itself now shared a common border with the Ottoman Empire.

Western Influence and Church Schism

Acquisition of left-bank Ukraine was important for yet another reason: it brought an influx of learned men, and their new ideas, from that region. One was F. M. Rtishchev, who introduced polyphonic music, founded the first poorhouse and first hospital, and brought Ukrainian educational influence to Moscow (with the establishment of a school at Andreev Monastery). For the first time the state began to take up social tasks, in effect embarking on the path of Western absolutism. Similarly, it also began to require more education of those in civil service, created state economic monopolies, and established a 'Secret Chancellery' (originally just the tsar's private chancellery, but after 1663 a kind of economic administration that foreigners often regarded as a supervisory or police organ). Beginning in 1649 it refurbished its 'troops of the new order' and in 1668 even attempted to construct the first naval fleet (its five ships, however, being torched during the Razin rebellion in Astrakhan).

Alexis also behaved differently, especially after his marriage in 1671 to a woman who was more open-minded about the West. In 1672 the tsar and his family attended the first theatrical performance in Russia: the tragicomedy

Ahasuerus and Esther, composed by the Lutheran pastor Johann Gottfried Grigorii. The play, which lasted nine (!) hours and was staged at the family's summer residence in Preobrazhenskoe, marked the emergence of a 'court theatre'; the following year it staged the ballet *Orpheus und Eurydice* by Heinrich Schütz. And table music also became common at the court.

The Orthodox Church opposed the penetration of Western culture, but with declining effectiveness. However, its will did initially prevail: in 1652, for example, foreigners were forcibly resettled from Moscow to its environs—the North Europeans ('Germans') to the so-called 'new German suburb' (*novaia nemetskaia sloboda*) and the Poles to special districts. Subsequently, however, the influence of the Church steadily declined. One reason was the establishment of the 'Monastery Chancellery' in 1649, a secular body responsible for judicial matters involving both lay and ecclesiastical parties. Its creation was a distant analogue to the 'Church Regulatory Charters' in the West. Two other critical factors in the Church's decline were the 'Nikon affair' and the schism.

In the first half of the seventeenth century the Church had already split into opposing camps of reformers and conservatives, their position partly traceable to Ukrainian influences, but also to the practical problem of correcting liturgical books. With respect to the latter, the central question was whether to standardize texts on the basis of Greek originals presumed to be

Tsar Aleksei Mikhailovich receiving a foreign embassy (1674). Part of this stiff ceremony went back to the Byzantine court ritual, but the Mongol heritage was also present. The four persons with silver axes were chamberlains. To the right of the tsar is Prince Vorotynskii, the Keeper of the Exchequer, to his left Prince Dolgorukii, the Marshal of the Realm offering the tsar's hand to be kissed.

'Planting the Tree of the Russian Realm' (1668). In fact, Simon Ushakov's icon is dedicated only to the glorification of the city of Moscow, with its Holy Icon of the Virgin of Vladimir in the centre. At the bottom, behind the Kremlin wall and in front of the Cathedral of the Dormition, Ivan Kalita and Metropolitan Petr are planting the tree with its medallions of saints while the royal family is looking on in both corners.

uncorrupted (the opinion of patriarch Iosif), or concentrate on internal spiritual life (as demanded by a group of clergy under Vonifatev, the father-confessor of Tsar Alexis). The latter's circle of 'Friends of God' (subsequently known as the 'Zealots of Piety' in the literature) included the future Patriarch Nikon, who served as metropolitan of Novgorod for three years before his elevation to the Patriarchate in 1652. As patriarch he expanded the correction of texts into a fundamental reform of church ritual in 1653; the primary goal was to reverse the separate development of Russian Orthodoxy that had been in progress ever since the fall of Constantinople in the mid-fifteenth century. Moreover, by re-establishing ritual unity with the Kiev metropolitanate, such reform could also reinforce the political union with Ukraine.

These reforms, however, evoked fierce opposition from his former friends in the Zealots of Piety. Among them was the cathedral archpriest, Avvakum Petrovich, who became Nikon's intransigent adversary and leader of the 'old ritualists' or 'old believers'— that is, those who remained loyal to the old rites and defended the national religious idea against 're-Hellenization'. Nikon, however, enjoyed the support and friendship of the tsar; by 1653 Avvakum and his friends were already imprisoned, and two years later Avvakum himself was banished into exile, where he wrote his autobiography, the first in Russian history and justly famous for its literary and stylistic qualities. In 1667 a church council upheld Nikon's reforms and excommunicated its opponents, thereby formalizing the schism (*raskol*) in the Church.

Naturally, the causes of the schism went much deeper than a blind attachment to the old rites. Rather, the Old Belief represented a much broader social movement—a protest against enserfment, the centralizing activities of the government, and the intrusion of Western innovations. It also acquired apocalyptical expectations (especially in the north) and, after martyrdom of Bishop Pavel of Kolomna in 1657, claimed many more victims, Avvakum himself being burnt at the stake in 1682. The Old Believers also established a powerful centre at the Solovetskii Monastery on the White Sea, where the resistance of some 500 monks and fugitives from the Razin rebellion grew into

Patriarch Nikon teaches the clerics. Most scholars think that this picture was painted in 1667 by the Dutch painter Daniel Wuchters, because the composition and the power of expression are so unusual. If this is true, we would see Nikon at the time of his deposition from office by a church council.

an outright uprising. With a heavy heart Tsar Alexis used force to suppress the rebellion; the monastery, however, fiercely resisted and was finally taken only through betrayal.

The council of 1667 recognized the Nikonian reforms as valid, but also took measures against Nikon himself. At issue was his conception of the patriarch's power: this peasant's son stubbornly insisted that the tsar be subordinate to the patriarch—i.e. that they did not constitute a diarchy, the model that prevailed under Filaret and Michael. The tsar, favourably inclined towards Nikon, at first acquiesced and conferred the title 'Great Sovereign' on the patriarch in 1654, despite the absence of kinship (in contrast to Filaret's case). But Nikon later far exceeded the Byzantine conception of a 'symphony' between the secular and sacred domains and exploited the fact that the status of the tsar in the Russian Church had never been precisely formulated. Alexis cautiously expressed a different opinion in 1657–8, and it soon came to a personal confrontation between the two men. Nikon withdrew, but refused to resign from his office; according to canon law, only the Eastern patriarchs could order his removal. At the end of 1666 the tsar convened such a council, but with only the less important patriarchs of Antioch and Alexandria personally present. Not surprisingly, the latter—who were materially dependent upon Russian support—found Nikon guilty and even recommended expanding the tsar's power in the Church. After a few Russian bishops protested, the council settled on a compromise that ascribed worldly matters to the tsar, spiritual matters to the patriarch. Although this formula nominally preserved the status of the Church, it could not conceal the fact that the Church emerged from the schism and the Nikon affair deeply weakened. Thus the devastation that the Time of Troubles had dealt to tradition (*starina*) now extended to the Church, hitherto the sole spiritual power and a second pillar of autocracy. The reign of Alexis, so rich in rebellion, came to an end; the way was now free for a breakthrough to the modern era.

The Dawning of Modernity (1676–1689)

THE REIGN OF FEDOR (1676–1682)

Alexis's eldest son, who had received elaborate preparation to accede to the throne, died in 1670. Thus, when Alexis himself died six years later, the throne passed to his second eldest son, the sickly and bed-ridden Fedor, who was not quite 15 years old and had only another six years to live. Next in line included Ivan, who was mentally retarded, and then the 4-year-old Peter (Petr Alekseevich) from Alexis's second marriage, a strong and robust child who would go down in history as Peter the Great. Under the circumstances, the head of the foreign chancellery, A. S. Matveev, urged Peter's mother, Natalia Naryshkina, to speak out in favour of her son. But his suggestion ignited a power struggle between the Naryshkins and the family of Alexis's first marriage (the

СОБРАЗ ВЕЛИКАГѠ
ГДРА ЦРА ИВЕЛИКАГѠ
КНЗА・АЛЕѮ҃ЧА МІХА҆ИЛОВІЧА
ВЅЕА ВЕЛІКІА ІМА́ЛЬА
ІБ҃ѢЛЬА РОЅІІ САМОДЁРЖА.

Tsar Aleksei Mikhailovich. This official portrait is most likely only a posthumous copy from the 1680s while the original was lost. Though the picture contains some elements borrowed from contemporary Western style, e.g. the background drapery, the domineering impression is that of the traditional iconography of a ruler portrait including the deliberately archaic inscription.

This portrait of Peter Mikhailov as shipwright in Holland in 1697 reminds us of his artisan interests and talents. It also reveals his impressive physique, European style (no beard and simple clothing), and democratic or plebeian aspect.

Miloslavskiis, from which had come Fedor, Ivan, and their sister Sofia). Once the Miloslavskiis gained the upper hand, Matveev paid dearly for his initiative: dismissal and banishment into exile. The new tsar Fedor thus lost a Western-oriented statesman of great ability and a main conduit for West European cultural influence. It must have been a heavy blow to the tsar, who himself had been educated by Simeon Polotskii (a West Russian monk and poet), knew Polish, and wore Western clothing.

However, the West could hardly be ignored over the long term. That was clearly demonstrated by the 'Turkish question': after centuries of spurning appeals for an alliance against the Turks, Moscow now chose to confront the Ottoman Empire and waged its first war (from 1676 to 1681, virtually the entire reign of Fedor). The campaign, conducted without Western support, focused on Ukraine and hetman P. Doroshenko's attempt to unite both the right and left banks of the Dnieper. But the war ended inconclusively, as the Peace of Bakhchisarai (1681) simply reaffirmed the *status quo ante bellum* and hence Moscow's possession of left-bank (eastern) Ukraine.

Domestically, xenophobic measures (for example, closing the tsar's 'German' theatre) foundered on needs for systematic Europeanization. Thus, in contrast to the gradual military and economic policies of earlier decades, Moscow now began a conscious modernization of autocracy—amazingly enough, during

Tsar Fedor Alekseevich. This portrait on wood was painted in 1686 by Yelin and Smolianinov (aided by Saltanov), four years after the tsar's death, to be placed over his tomb. Therefore it is an idealized portrait which still bears many characteristics of icon-painting. The cartouches contain the Tsar's *vita*.

the 'weak' reign of Fedor. The changes occurred not merely because the time was 'ripe', but because of vigorous support from the tsar's favourites and advisers, especially V. V. Golitsyn.

The two most elemental reforms concerned taxation and the army—those spheres where the premodern state made the greatest demands on subjects. In 1679 the state completed a fiscal reform begun in the 1620s: it shifted the tax base from land to household, using a census of 1678–9 (which indicated an approximate population of 11.2 million subjects) and recorded in special 'revision books'. According to historian P. N. Miliukov, the new household-based tax produced revenues of 1.9 million roubles and enabled Moscow to abolish the 'Streltsy levies'. Altogether, the army consumed 62 per cent of state revenues (1.5 million roubles). The new standing army, which now essentially displaced the noble regiments, put at the tsar's disposal approximately 200,000 troops (including Ukrainian Cossacks). It was divided into eight military districts, which later formed the basis for Peter's division of the realm into eight administrative regions (*gubernii*).

Closely related to the military reform was the abolition of the 'system of precedence' (*mestnichestvo*). This system, which tied service position to birthright and the career of forefathers, was a serious problem: it blocked appointment on the basis of merit and ability and spawned endless litigious disputes. It was already subjected to some restrictions: in 1550 for wartime service and in 1621 for diplomatic missions. The well-born opposed these incursions, not only because they were so materially bound to service (in contrast to Western nobles), but also because they regarded precedence a matter of honour.

Nevertheless, in 1682 Fedor abolished precedence. Above all, his government understood that precedence must not be extended to the ever-expanding lower strata of servitors (chancellery secretaries; big merchants [*gosti*]), where individual merit was critical. Abolition of precedence actually formed part of a larger reform proposal prepared under Golitsyn's leadership and approved by the tsar. Abolition of precedence was also closely linked to military reform—the disbanding of military units called the 'hundreds' and the introduction of regiments, companies, and Western service ranks. Lineage books were still compiled (to determine claims to noble status), but they included the lower nobility and even non-noble ranks. The manifesto abolishing precedence is still more remarkable for its invocation of natural law—dramatic testimony to the declining influence of the Orthodox Church. Specifically, in justifying the reform, Fedor explained that he held the reins of power from God in order to govern and to issue laws for the 'general welfare' (*obshchee dobro*). Thus this manifesto, composed entirely in the spirit of European absolutism, marked the onset of modernity in Russia. The government now had philosophical support for borrowing from the West; the traditional touchstone—'as it was under earlier great sovereigns'—no longer prevailed. Although other reform plans did founder on the opposition of clergy and noble élites, Western rationality began to displace Orthodoxy, hitherto the sole authority.

Moreover, Fedor's reforms improved administration and, especially, finances. The government achieved a certain level of bureaucratization in Moscow, if not a general centralization. At the same time, it also strengthened its power at the provincial level, chiefly by investing more authority in the district governor (*voevoda*). The underlying dynamic was a pragmatic response to the shortage of competent people (a fundamental problem throughout Russian history), which was most apparent at the provincial level. The government also decided to conduct a land survey, which had long been demanded by the nobility and was finally undertaken after Fedor's death. But further discussions of tax reform and the convocation of townspeople and peasants under Golitsyn's leadership were interrupted by Fedor's death. These initiatives suggest a programme of reform that, had he lived longer, could have reached the scale it did under Peter the Great.

The reform, moreover, also included plans to establish the first institution of higher learning. The proposal originated with Simeon Polotskii: although Polotskii himself died in 1680, his pupil Silvestr Medvedev prepared the draft statute for a 'Slavic-Greek-Latin' school in 1682. Its programmatic introduction also invoked the concept of 'general welfare', thus reflecting the influence of the early Enlightenment; although still alluding to the sagacity of Solomon, the document also spoke of orderly justice and administration and adduced cameralist ideas of the well-ordered 'police state' (*Policeystaat*). Fedor, whose first wife was Polish, had a marked propensity for the Polish Latin world; as the historian V. O. Kliuchevskii observed, Russia would have obtained its Western culture from Rome, not Peter's Amsterdam, had Fedor reigned for ten to fifteen years and bequeathed a son as his successor.

STRUGGLE FOR SUCCESSION

Fedor's death in 1682 unleashed a new power struggle between the Miloslavskii and Naryshkin clans, each determined to resolve—to their own advantage—the succession claim of the two half-brothers, Ivan (a Miloslavskii) and Peter (a Naryshkin). Legally and especially theologically, precedence rested with the feeble-minded Ivan. Fearful that the Miloslavskiis would continue Fedor's 'Latinizing' tendencies, however, the patriarch himself interceded on behalf of the intelligent Peter: he convoked a council to proclaim the new ruler and annulled the exile of Matveev. But before the latter could return to Moscow, the situation had radically changed.

Whereas Peter's interests were represented by his mother Natalia Naryshkina, his half-sister Sofia became the leader of the Miloslavskiis. Her education marked by strong Ukrainian and Polish influences, Sofia herself symbolized the emancipation of élite women, who had been kept in the background in old Russia. During the next seven years she actually governed the country and thus became a precursor to the empresses who would rule in the eighteenth century. The pro-Petrine historiography has propagated a highly negative image of Sofia (including the insinuation that, from the outset, she conspired to seize power for herself). In fact, however, Sofia at first sought only to secure her family's position by ensuring the coronation of Ivan.

But she could hardly have succeeded had she not been able to exploit a simultaneous revolt of the Streltsy—élite troops created a century and a half earlier, but since subjected to a precipitous economic and social decline. Indeed, their salaries had fallen and at the very time that they were forbidden to supplement their income by plying a trade in Moscow. They especially resented the 'troops of new order' and felt themselves to be victims of discrimination. Hostility towards them was in fact widespread: the government distrusted the Streltsy because so many of them were Old Believers; the nobility despised them for

Terem Palace. The Terem—a word of Greek origin—was the residential area of the royal palace in the Kremlin containing the women's chambers. The picture shows the entrance gallery with its typical oriental ornaments. The Terem was built in 1635–7 by Ogurtsov and Sharutin and is considered the most important secular building of its time.

giving refuge to fugitive serfs; and taxpayers identified them with the loath-some 'Streltsy tax'. The Streltsy also complained that they were maltreated by their superiors and even used as unfree labour.

Although Peter had already ascended the throne, the Miloslavskiis conspired to exploit this discontent. They set 15 May 1682 (the anniversary of the suspicious death of the Tsarevich Dmitrii in Uglich) as the date for a massacre that, according to plans, was to take the lives of forty-six adversaries. To incite the mass of Streltsy, they spread false rumours that the Naryshkins had murdered Ivan; it did not help when the Streltsy who stormed the Kremlin were shown that Ivan was alive. For three days long they raged, killing some seventy victims, including Matveev (who had just returned from exile) and other high officials. The young Peter had to watch this bloodbath and suffered a nervous shock that had a profound impact on the rest of his life.

To Sofia's credit, she herself acted with moderation and persuaded the Streltsy to allow the mere banishment of many other boyars. She also reached a compromise agreement with I. A. Khovanskii (head of the Streltsy Chancellery and the rebels' leader) for the coronation of *both* tsareviches, as Ivan V and Peter I, on 26 May (using a specially constructed double throne). The manifesto justifying this diarchy cited precedents in world history but also practical advantages: one tsar could remain in the Kremlin while the other led military campaigns. More problematic was the regency of Sofia (which had been offered by the Streltsy): Ivan was already of age and Peter's mother could have been his regent.

As the rebels continued to indulge in a violent reign of terror (the 'Khovanshchina') and declared all bondsmen to be free, Sofia attempted to pacify them with gifts of money. But the Streltsy felt increasingly insecure. In early June they demanded that the government rename them 'court infantry' and also acknowledge the honourable goals of their rebellion—through a formal declaration and erection of a column on Red Square that would explain why so many famous men had to perish. Their political programme could have exerted considerable influence had the Streltsy themselves enjoyed the support of the general populace. But they had the support only of Old Believers, who—after Avvakum's immolation (on the eve of the rebellion)—regarded Khovanskii as their leader. At his insistence a debate over the true belief was staged in the Kremlin, with the participation of the patriarch and numerous high-ranking church officials. But the most sensational moment came when, contrary to tradition, Sofia herself intervened in the debate and, using deft arguments, dealt Khovanskii a defeat. She then put the rebels under pressure by announcing that the court was moving out of Moscow.

It did so that summer. Although élites usually went to Kolomenskoe to pass the summer, her real intent became apparent when the tsars failed to return to the Kremlin for new year celebrations on 1 September. The Streltsy were now blamed for having driven off the government. Shortly thereafter Sofia charged

Sofia. The so-called 'eagle' portrait is an unfinished anonymous oil-painting of 1689. Shortly before her overthrow the regent had herself depicted with orb and sceptre in a pose hitherto reserved for tsars.

Khovanskii with high treason and had him executed without trial. The government finally returned to Moscow in November, but only after the Streltsy had begged for forgiveness and removed their column from Red Square. Security for the Kremlin was now assigned to a noble regiment (a step that inadvertently laid the foundations for the recurring palace coups by guard regiments in the eighteenth century). The Streltsy threat neutralized, Sofia now assumed the reins of power, with the 'tsars' appearing only for Kremlin celebrations.

THE REGENCY OF SOFIA (1682–1689)

Her regency lasted just seven years, almost as brief as Fedor's reign. V. V. Golitsyn, her leading official and probably her lover, continued his predecessor's foreign policy and cultivated contacts with the West. However, reform initiatives were now rare; because plans for domestic reform were, unfortunately, poorly preserved, much about her reign must remain speculative. The tensions between the Miloslavskiis and the Naryshkins apparently hampered decision-making, but Sofia did tackle three problems: she finally began the long-awaited land survey, intensified the search for fugitives, and gave the conditional service estate (*pomest'e*) the same juridical status as the hereditary family estate (*votchina*). The last reform thus eliminated any distinction between the two forms of landholding—something that the service nobility had demanded. But this concession also served to level the nobility—something that the autocracy itself had wanted.

Golitsyn's tolerant attitude towards the West proved advantageous for the foreigners' suburb and even Jesuits. This was in marked contrast to the vigorous persecution of Old Believers, who were even burned at the stake if they refused to recant. Such harshness derived from the government's lingering fear of a new uprising of the Streltsy. But immolation failed to quell the religious dissenters and even impelled them to commit mass suicide—from apocalyptical fears that the Last Judgement was imminent, that they might somehow be ensnared in the service of Anti-Christ. As a result, some 2,700 Old Believers in Paleostrov Monastery and several thousand more in Berezov (on the Volok) burnt themselves alive in 1687–8 alone; after a year of siege another 1,500 in Paleostrov put themselves to the torch.

The infusion of Western culture also brought a major confrontation between

'Latinizers' and 'Hellenizers'. The two chief protagonists included a monk Evfimii (a collaborator of Patriarch Ioakim) and Silvestr Medvedev (the Polotskii pupil who drafted the charter for the Slavonic-Greek-Latin academy in 1682). Under the patriarch's direction, Evfimii revised that statute so as to replace Latin with Greek and to exclude teachers from Ukraine and Lithuania. The struggle, which lasted for several years, produced a number of learned treatises. When the academy finally opened in 1687 as the first school of higher learning in Russia, its curriculum nevertheless included Latin—as well as such subjects as grammar, poetics, rhetoric, didactics, and physics. Nevertheless, pressure against the 'Latinizer' Medvedev steadily mounted, for Sofia feared a new schism, particularly when many Old Believers—from anti-Hellenistic sentiments—expressed sympathy for the Latinizers.

By then Sofia had come to nourish her own ambitions. In 1685 she began to appear at public ceremonies that had traditionally been reserved for the tsar; in 1686 she affixed the title of 'Autocratrix' to her portrait. And, apparently, she sought formal coronation after signing the Eternal Peace with Poland in 1686, the greatest triumph of her regency. The agreement ratified the Armistice of Andrusovo (1667), for the Poles now realized the need to co-operate with Russia on the Ukrainian–Ottoman border. Therefore they now recognized the partition of Ukraine and approved Russia's entry into an anti-Turkish coalition that had been formed as the 'Holy League' (Habsburg, Poland, and Venetia) in 1684. In addition, the rulers recognized each other's title and granted freedom of confession to each other's fellow believers—the Orthodox in Poland-Lithuania, Catholics in Muscovy. This religious policy had been preceded by subordination of the Kievan metropolitanate to the Moscow Patriarchate in 1685, a long-cherished goal of the Russian Orthodox Church. Moscow also obtained a stronger claim to a protectorate over the Orthodox Christians under the Turkish yoke, something which it had already asserted for several decades. However, the tolerance promised to Catholics alienated the distrustful patriarch and impelled him to embrace Peter in the next coup of 1689.

PETER: SEIZURE OF POWER

This coup indirectly stemmed from the Eternal Peace itself. After the Poles and Habsburgs dealt a decisive defeat to the Turks at Vienna in 1683, the allies demanded that Russia launch an attack on the Crimea to ease the burden on the West. Under the supreme command of Golitsyn, Russian troops thereupon made two campaigns against the Crimean Tatars (in 1687 and 1689) and both times met with defeat. But in both cases Sofia—who needed success—suppressed the truth: to portray the military campaign as a victory, she lavished praise and gifts on Golitsyn and the returning troops. Her Eastern policy was no more successful: Russia established diplomatic relations with China (through the Treaty of Nerchinsk in 1689), but did so at the price of renouncing claims to the Amur region. The deception and disinformation generated growing

Novodevichii Convent. Vasilii III founded the monastery west of the centre of Moscow in 1524 in honour of the seizure of Smolensk, the oldest church on its compound being indeed the Smolensk Cathedral (1524–5). The other buildings date from the end of the seventeenth century. In this century the convent-fortress served as asylum for ousted female members of the royal family.

tensions between Sofia and Peter, even to mutual suspicions of murder. Fearing a new Streltsy uprising, in August 1689 Peter fled to the Trinity–Sergius Monastery north of Moscow. The turning-point came in September when the troops came over to his side, enabling Peter to claim power in his own right and to place his half-sister under house arrest in Novodevichii Convent.

Although Peter had seized power, for the moment he changed nothing in his own life, as he himself continued to take more interest in sea travel than in state affairs. Nevertheless, the rebellious turbulence of the seventeenth century had come to an end; the Streltsy mutiny in 1698 was merely an epilogue. If one looks at the government of the great tsar in the light of the seventeenth century, it is clear that his reforms—which made so great an impression in the West—emerged directly from the traditions of the seventeenth century and hardly constituted a 'revolution'. The seventeenth century had already signalled a major breakthrough—a self-conscious emancipation from the fetters of 'Old Russia'.

THE PETRINE ERA AND AFTER
1698–1740

JOHN T. ALEXANDER

*Peter inaugurated an imperial, radically Europeanized period
of Russian history. Building on seventeenth-century roots, he
broadened reform to include virtually every dimension of the
state and warfare, society, economy, and culture. His heirs,
invariably invoking Peter as a secular icon to legitimize power
and policies, continued (if less ambitiously) his efforts to remake
medieval Muscovy into modern Russia.*

The Streltsy Mutiny of 1682 and the murder of Artamon Matveev. Typical of the flat and wooden artistic style of late Muscovy, this print conveys the bloody violence that forced revision of young Peter's place in the succession to be co-tsar with his half-brother Ivan under the vague 'regency' of their sister Sofia.

PETER I is associated with many 'firsts' in Russian history. He was the first legitimate Muscovite ruler to have that name in Russian and European languages (Piter in Dutch), the first to use a Roman numeral after his name, the first to travel incessantly by land and water and to venture abroad, the first to be titled emperor and 'the Great, Most Wise Father of the Fatherland', the first to inspire radical change in diverse spheres of activity, the first to found urban sites sharing his name, the first to be buried in St Petersburg, and the first to imprint his name on an entire era encompassing the birth of modern Russia in an expanded, European context. His imperious personality impressed his world so emphatically that his impact remains vividly controversial even now. Inscribed 'Great Hope of the Future', the medal struck at his birth in the Kremlin on 30 May 1672 announced the dynastic sentiments vested in the huge baby, some thirty-three inches long. This label inaugurated a series pinned on Peter during his busy life (1672–1725) and long afterwards. Many lauded his personal attributes: warrior-tsar, artisan-tsar, tsar-transformer, Renaissance man, the great reformer who gave Russia a new 'body' primed for a new 'soul'. Others deplored negative qualities: Anti-Christ, the 'Bronze Horseman', first Bolshevik, brutal despot, cult figure and personification of a totalitarian-style dictatorship bent on forcible expansion—a ruthless ruler likened to such melancholy fanatics as Ivan the Terrible, Lenin, and Stalin. His towering physique—six feet seven inches tall as an adult—overshadowed contemporaries much as his historical shade dominates modern Russian political and cultural discourse. His physiognomy and figure have been depicted in many media and languages over three centuries. Both his fame and notoriety have assumed legendary stature.

It is amazing that the initial offspring of Tsar Alexis by his second wife should have been so precocious and so long-lived in contrast to the sickly sons and multiple daughters of his first marriage. Indeed, this novelty proved crucial in the selection of 9-year-old Peter by an impromptu assemblage to succeed his half-brother Fedor on 27 April 1682. A mere figurehead for a regime of his Naryshkin relatives, Peter's elevation evoked immediate resistance from his father's first family, the Miloslavskiis, led by Sofia in defence of the dynastic seniority of Ivan, aged 16. Sofia and her Miloslavskii relatives exploited dissension among the Streltsy to channel animosity towards the Naryshkins; the result was the riot in May 1682, described in the previous chapter, as also are the events of Sofia's regency.

Young Peter's marriage to Evdokiia Lopukhina on 27 January 1689 forecast imminent maturity. Although the marriage was unhappy (the groom soon departed for nautical diversions on Lake Pleshcheevo), Evdokiia gave birth to the future tsarevich Alexis in February 1690—another blow to the Miloslavskiis' dynastic interests. Sofia, though styled 'autocratrix' on a par with her brothers, was never crowned officially, her authority waning as Peter's partisans championed his cause anew. Who initiated the final showdown in August 1689 is uncertain, but Peter's 'party' quickly gained greater armed support in ostensibly forestalling a new Streltsy conspiracy while Sofia had to yield Fedor Shaklovityi—her new favourite and head of the Streltsy—for interrogation under torture and execution. At the end of September she entered the Novodevichii Convent as a lay person. After another abortive Streltsy mutiny in 1698 she accepted political extinction by taking monastic vows and died in monastic seclusion in 1704.

Early Travels and the Azov Campaigns

Peter did not, however, immediately assume Sofia's role in government, relinquishing the more prominent posts to his Naryshkin relatives and their friends, such as Boris Golitsyn, Tikhon Streshnev, and Fedor Romodanovskii. The tsar still resided at Preobrazhenskoe and in the autumn of 1690 participated in elaborate 'play' manœuvres featuring a scripted 'defeat' of the Streltsy by a combined force of noble cavalry, play regiments, and foreign-style troops. His shipbuilding and sailing on inland waters also continued, as did his fascination with fireworks in company with foreign mercenaries such as Franz Lefort and Patrick Gordon. He began to sign himself 'Petrus', to drink heavily, and to smoke tobacco. He ignored his deserted wife's letters and openly pursued Anna Mons, the daughter of a German wine merchant in the Foreign Suburb. When Peter suffered bloody diarrhoea for two weeks in December 1692, fears of Sofia's return to power fanned rampant rumours and, allegedly, plans for flight by Lefort and company.

Despite his mother's misgivings, Peter left Moscow in July 1693 with a substantial entourage to spend seven weeks at Archangel. He became the first Muscovite ruler to see the far north and to sail the open sea. He also helped lay down a seagoing vessel for future voyages. His horizons were widening by the hour. His mother's death in January 1694 only momentarily interrupted prepa-rations for a longer sojourn at Archangel, from 18 May to 5 September. He made extended voyages; during one he barely survived a storm by landing on the island of Solovki where he planted a cross with a Dutch inscription and European-style date, 'This Cross was made by Captain Piter anno Domini 1694'—evidence that he knew Dutch and already foresaw reforms in European terms. The budding fleet began using a white-blue-red flag based on the Dutch standard. Upon returning to Moscow, from 23 September to 18 October 1694 Peter organized grandiose military manœuvres involving over 7,000 men. A satirical pamphlet recorded the exercises along with exhibitions such as twenty-five dwarfs marching to military music. With the Streltsy again slated for defeat, 'bombardier Peter Alekseev' celebrated his last simulated engagement before real battle with Turks and Tatars. In concert with the Holy League of Austria, Poland-Lithuania, and Venice with financial backing from the papacy, the 22-year-old tsar aimed to mount the international stage by recouping Vasilii Golitsyn's losses.

Overweening ambition was apparent in Peter's choice of the primary target: the Ottoman fortress of Azov near the mouth of the Don river. A more difficult objective than the Crimea itself, Azov would require combined land and sea operations. Peter and his senior military advisers sought to avoid Golitsyn's error of marching across barren steppes by bringing most forces far south by boat. The main attack was also augmented by a thrust westward under the boyar Boris Sheremetev to divert Tatar forces and capture Turkish border forts. Though the siege of Azov began by early July 1695, lack of a flotilla precluded any naval blockade; while the Ottomans reinforced and resupplied their garri-son by sea, the attackers suffered great losses from Turkish sallies and the absence of unified command. Peter's insistence on a desperate storm on 5 August brought huge losses; a mining operation on 16 September harmed only the besiegers; another costly assault the next day barely failed. Lifting the siege on 20 October, the Muscovites sustained further losses—from exhaustion, frosts, and disease—during the retreat. The campaign taught the impatient tsar sev-eral harsh lessons, the whole campaign having been recorded in official journals (to be kept the rest of the reign). Retention of two Turkish watchtower forts (renamed Novosergeevsk) hinted at renewed efforts.

The new year began inauspiciously: Peter fell ill for nearly a month and his brother Ivan died suddenly on 29 January. Ivan's death formally ended the dynastic dualism, affirmed Peter's sole sovereignty, and cleared the way for an aggressively reformist militarist regime. Health restored, Peter hurried to Voronezh to assemble hundreds of barges and galleys for the new attack. If the first Azov campaign proved more difficult than anticipated, the second brought the fortress's capitulation with stunning ease on 19–20 July 1696. Austrian engi-neers assisted in supervising the siege-works. Command of the land forces was centralized under 'generalissimus' Aleksei Shein. Ironically, Muscovite sea-

power had predetermined the outcome by forestalling Ottoman relief efforts although Cossack boats did most of the fighting at close quarters—not the vessels built so feverishly at Voronezh. Sailing into the Sea of Azov, Peter sought out a site for a new naval station some leagues westward, at a point called Taganrog. Construction began at once as did rebuilding Azov itself; the Muscovites intended to stay permanently. Returning to Moscow in late September, Peter staged a Roman-style triumph with ceremonial gates—the first of many—decorated with Julius Caesar's aphorism: 'He came, he saw, he conquered'. A more menacing demonstration transpired at Preobrazhenskoe a week later: the Dutch deserter Jakob Jansen, whose betrayal had dearly cost the first Azov campaign, was broken on the wheel and then beheaded before a huge crowd.

Russian fleet at Archangel. Peter was the first Muscovite ruler to visit the realm's only seaport, to travel extensively by water at home and abroad, and to oversee the foundation of the Russian navy. The fleet defended St Petersburg and helped to assert Russian hegemony in the north-east Baltic.

The Grand Embassy to Europe

Amidst these celebrations Peter felt the fragility of Muscovite military and, especially, naval power. Even before returning from Azov he began to plan a large diplomatic and recruiting mission to the naval powers of Venice and Holland. This 'Grand Embassy' engaged as many as 270 persons (Peter himself incognito among many 'volunteers') and huge amounts of baggage, all estimated to have cost the stupendous sum of 200,000 roubles. The main mission spent sixteen months away from Moscow, 9 March 1697 to 25 August 1698, the longest and grandest Muscovite embassy ever. It was related to other missions such as sixty-one courtiers sent to study navigation; it was the first instalment of some twenty-six groups totalling more than a thousand 'volunteers' sent abroad systematically for study and training in the period 1697–1725 (other individuals went on their own). A parallel mission was undertaken by the eminent boyar Boris Sheremetev, who recruited foreign officers, lavished gifts wherever he went in Poland and Italy, and also visited the knights of Malta who awarded him the Order of Malta. The linguistically gifted Peter Postnikov, a recent graduate of the Slavonic-Greek-Latin Academy just completing MD and Ph.D. degrees at Padua's famed university, joined the Grand Embassy in Holland.

Peter tried to keep the Grand Embassy strictly secret at home and employed special invisible ink for sensitive communications. These precautions may have sprung from apprehensions that 'ill-intentioned' persons might exploit the tsar's absence, as earlier Streltsy had allegedly plotted to murder the tsar and restore Sofia and Vasilii Golitsyn. After an investigation by the Preobrazhenskii Bureau (the police organ given national jurisdiction over political crimes in late 1696), Colonel Ivan Tsykler and two supposed boyar accomplices were gruesomely beheaded over the exhumed corpse of Ivan Miloslavskii, dead since 1685. The incident occurred a week before Peter's departure abroad. The Preobrazhenskii Bureau had also investigated a 'Missive' by Abbot Avraamii criticizing state fiscal policies. Though absolved of malicious intent, Avraamii was banished to a provincial monastery and three minor officials accused of assisting him were sent into hard labour. All these punishments were obviously intended to intimidate potential opposition while Peter lingered abroad indefinitely.

In diplomatic terms the Grand Embassy largely failed because of Moscow's ignorance of current European politics and consequent poor timing. Efforts to buttress the anti-Ottoman alliance proved unavailing: Muscovy's allies made peace with the Turks at the congress of Karlowitz in January 1699, a step that left Peter livid at Austrian and Venetian perfidy, 'taking no more notice of him than a dog'. The embassy arrived too late to influence the Treaty of Ryswick of September 1697 ending the War of the League of Augsburg or the treaty between the Holy Roman Empire and France a month later. Still, Peter met several European counterparts, especially the military hero William of Orange (William III of England), Frederick III (elector of Brandenburg and soon to be king in Prussia), Emperor Leopold I, and Augustus II (elector of Saxony and newly elected king of Poland-Lithuania). Peter's instant friendship with the flamboyant Augustus II, together with Moscow's vigorous support of his election to the Polish throne, soon translated into an alliance aimed against Sweden. Moreover, the muddled Muscovite diplomacy showed that they must maintain permanent representation at the main European courts and provide longer training for those serving abroad. Dr Postnikov's linguistic facility and European experience, for example, resulted in appointment to the Muscovite delegation to the congress of Karlowitz and ultimately side-tracked his medical career in favour of diplomatic service in France, where he died in about 1709.

As regards recruitment of skilled manpower, intellectual and cultural broadening, the entire experience reaped manifold rewards and left vivid impressions. The host governments strove to impress the tirelessly inquisitive and shyly charming tsar. His portrait in armour was painted in Holland and England by Aert de Gelder and Godfrey Kneller. He saw all the local sights, from Antony van Leeuwenhoek's microscopic glasses and Fredrik Ruysch's anatomical museum to Dresden's famous Kunstkammer and Isaac Newton's English mint, hospitals, botanical gardens, theatres, industrial enterprises, government and church institutions. The German polymath Gottfried von Leibniz failed to win an audience, but transmitted ambitious proposals through Lefort's son. Peter observed mock naval engagements in Holland and England, spent much time in shipyards, drank prodigiously, and twice rammed other vessels while sailing an English yacht on the Thames. The versatile and extravagant Marquis of Carmarthen enthralled the tsar with his nautical innovations and helped obtain a monopoly on importing tobacco to Russia via financial machinations and the gift of the *Royal Transport*, the most modern experimental ship in the English navy. Furthermore, Carmarthen assisted in recruiting such English 'experts' as professor of mathematics Henry Farquharson, shipwrights Joseph Nye and John Deane, and engineer John Perry. All played crucial parts in building the new Russian navy.

Dr Bidloo's own drawing of the Moscow General Hospital and Surgical School, with part of Bidloo's decorative garden.

Peter's learned advisers, Jacob Bruce and Peter Postnikov, visited educational, medical, and scientific institutions, bought many books, medicaments, and instruments, and hired several hundred specialists including some sixty military surgeons. The embassy led directly to the hiring of Dr Nikolaas Bidloo, a Dutch physician, and Dr Robert Erskine, a Scotsman educated in London and on the continent. Both spent the rest of their lives in Russia, became close friends of Peter, and advised him on matters medical, scientific, and cultural. A Fellow of the Royal Society, Erskine served as the first imperial physician and head of the entire professional medical faculty; in 1707 Bidloo founded the first permanent hospital and surgical school in Moscow, equipped with an anatomical theatre and a large botanical garden. In preparation for further Europeanizing changes, Peter granted a fifteen-year monopoly on book imports to the Dutch printer Jan van Thessing. The bustling cities and harbours, merchant marines and fleets, armies and industries of Europe and England reinforced his determination to pursue change. While in Vienna in July 1698 Peter aborted plans for lengthy visits to Venice and Rome when he learned of the Streltsy mutiny and attempted march on Moscow.

Though quickly suppressed, the Streltsy mutiny afforded an ideal pretext to purge the despised 'janissaries' through ghastly tortures and massive public executions. Several victims were displayed outside Sofia's convent cell. The Streltsy constituted the first sizeable Muscovite institution that the tsar abolished; others such as the boyar duma, the council of the realm, and the *gosti* (privileged merchants and state fiscal agents) were already in eclipse or simply not summoned by the militarily preoccupied sovereign. He also divorced Evdokiia by incarceration in a monastery. After supervising almost a thousand Streltsy interrogations and executions, three weeks later Peter left for Voronezh. There he laid the specially designed keel of the 58-gun *Predestinatsiia*, a harbinger of his soaring ambitions while he privately vowed to dissipate his own 'dark cloud of doubt'.

His southern nautical ambitions inspired two more sojourns at Voronezh in the spring of 1699, interrupted only by Lefort's funeral in Moscow and the founding in March of the Order of the Apostle Andrew the First-Called, Muscovy's first knightly order. After launching the *Predestinatsiia* on 27 April amid great fanfare Peter reached the Sea of Azov with fourteen ships of the line by early June. Later that summer the tsar's squadron accompanied the 46-gun *Krepost'* (Fortress) to the straits of Kerch demanding passage for his envoy to Constantinople.

Peter soon refocused on the Baltic in anticipation of joining Denmark and Saxony to partition the sprawling Swedish Empire under its boy-king, Charles XII. The warrior-tsar's levy of recruits in November 1699 raised 32,000 men termed 'immortals' and destined for lifetime service. The new century was celebrated on 1 January 1700 by official adoption of the Julian calendar and twenty-four-hour day amid cannon-salutes, fireworks, and festive decorations.

Reforms for War

Eager for action in October 1700 Peter, at the death-bed of Patriarch Adrian, called for educated clergy, military, civil servants, architects, and those who knew 'the doctor's healing art'. German-speaking advisers such as Heinrich van Huyssen and the Livonian adventurer Johann Reinhold von Patkul were aware of cameralist notions of promoting prosperity through enlightened administration and good order ('Police', a term lacking in the Russian vocabulary). Peter's manifesto of April 1702 inviting foreigners—military officers, craftsmen, and merchants—to enter his service appeared in Patkul's German translation and adumbrated an emerging reform programme:

It has been Our foremost concern to govern Our lands in a manner that would bring home to Our subjects Our intention to ensure their welfare and increase. To this end We have endeavoured not only to promote trade, strengthen the internal security of the state and preserve it from all manner of dangers which might harm the common good, but also to institute good order [*Polizei*] and whatever else contributes to the improvement [*Cultur*] of a people in order that Our subjects may soon become fit to form all manner of associations and exercise various skills along with other Christian and civilized peoples.

With an artisan's eye and pragmatic mind, Peter envisioned the transformation of Russia into a great power, its state and society based on technology and an organization aimed at maximizing production. Its hallmarks would be a European-type army and navy (supported by heavy industry to produce arms), planned urban conglomerations after the model of St Petersburg, and large-scale public works, particularly canals linking the major waterways and productive centres into an integrated economic whole. Peter even commissioned Perry to oversee a canal connecting the Volga and the Don, an over-ambitious project not realized until the 1930s.

To supply the armed forces with skilled native personnel, Peter began founding makeshift educational institutions. He put Farquharson and two English students in charge of the Moscow School of Mathematics and Navigation (housed in the former quarters of a Streltsy regiment); its enrolments grew from 200 pupils in 1703 to over 500 by 1711. Farquharson assisted Leontii Magnitskii in compiling the encyclopaedic *Arifmetika* (1703), one of the first Russian books to use Arabic numerals, and fulfilled diverse duties. He copied out other textbooks for his students, wrote, translated, and edited scientific works, and supervised thirty-eight translations by others. He surveyed the Petersburg to Moscow road, charted the Caspian Sea, and went to Voronezh in 1709 to observe the solar eclipse. Transferred with 305 pupils to the St Petersburg Naval Academy in 1715, he rose to brigadier rank in 1737 and left a library of 600 books (half from the Naval Academy) upon his death. An artillery school was set up in Moscow in 1701, its 180 pupils increasing to 300 within three years, but it led a precarious existence until transferred to St Petersburg with 74 pupils in 1719. Private schools and tutoring continued as

A Moscow school in the seventeenth century. This woodcut depicts the rudimentary nature of home schooling in late Muscovy with emphasis on reading and writing, clergymen as teachers, and corporal punishment to deter the highjinks of adolescent males.

usual. Allowed back in 1698, the Jesuits had a boarding-school with about thirty boys until the order was expelled again in 1719. A German gymnasium opened under the Lutheran pastor Ernst Glück with state assistance in 1705; with seven teachers and seventy-seven pupils in 1711, it taught Greek and Latin, modern languages (including Swedish), geography, ethics, politics, rhetoric, arithmetic, deportment, and riding. It closed in 1715.

Little did Peter foresee that the apparently easy war against Sweden would burgeon into two decades of incessant campaigning over huge expanses of land and water between shifting coalitions of powers great and small. The Great Northern War (1700–21), so designated in retrospect, consumed the bulk of his life. His role as warrior-tsar was etched into the marrow of the Europeanizing empire and shaped virtually every institution and policy adopted over its tortuous course. The demands of long-term warfare, most notably during the first years, account for the peculiarly frenzied and economically wasteful character of the early Petrine reforms.

If Peter blithely entered the conflict, he was shocked by Charles XII's swift victory over Christian IV of Denmark and Augustus II's failure to seize Riga. The Swedes' decisive defeat of the Russian siege of Narva compelled the tsar to reconstitute and rearm the army almost overnight. Over the next eight years some 138,000 recruits were raised; the term *rekrut* began to be used in about 1705, one of some 3,500 foreign terms adopted in Petrine Russia. By the end of the reign twenty-one general and thirty-two partial levies conscripted over 300,000 men for the army and the fleet.

The armed forces became the model for the Europeanized society that Peter doggedly pursued. Utilizing European norms and Muscovite traditions, 'self-maintenance' first of all, he fitfully constructed an integrated force under uniform conditions of service, subject to discipline on hierarchical principles, the officer corps trained in military schools, and the whole managed by a centralized administration guided by written codes. The organization was constantly reshuffled as the ostensibly standing army and expensive fleet showed wanton ways of melting away (or rotting in the case of ships) from continuous mass desertion as well as shortfalls in recruitment and losses to disease and combat.

Despite constant losses from accident, inferior workmanship, poor maintenance, and difficult harbours, the navy grew swiftly, with 34 ships of the line mounting between 46 and 96 cannon, 15 frigates, 4 prams, 10 snows, and almost 100 smaller vessels and galleys deploying 2,226 cannon with crews and troops totalling 28,000 men by 1724. Ship names reflected victories and territorial gains: *Standart* (banner or rallying-point), *Kronshlot, Triumf, Derpt, Narva, Fligel'-de-Fam* (Dutch Flying Fame). The first ship of the line launched in 1710 was called *Vyborg*, and Alexander Menshikov presented Peter with the Dutch-built frigate *Sv. Samson* (St Samson) in honour of the Poltava victory. Peter personally launched the 54-gun *Poltava* at St Petersburg on 15 June 1712, while the Hangö victory of 1714 was celebrated in 1719 by the huge 96-gun *Gangut*.

Exceeding 174,000 men by 1711 and totalling almost 304,000 in 1725, the armed forces engulfed 90 per cent of the state budget in the former year and still 73 per cent in the latter, a time of peace. Service was essentially lifelong for officers and enlisted men alike. Military service enshrined the principle of merit as explicated in the Table of Ranks, the system of fourteen grades (thirteen in practice) applied to all three branches of state service—military, civil, and court. Military ranks enjoyed preference over civil, and all thirteen in the military conferred noble status as opposed to only the top eight in the civil service. Squabbles over precedence and place-seeking did not end, however; the concept of merit involved ambiguous notions of time in grade, individual achievement, education, and potential. Predictably, the great majority of officers came from noble backgrounds, and the two guards regiments constituted specially privileged preserves. An exception was Alexander Menshikov's Ingermanlandskii Regiment, a unit close in status to the two guards regiments with the highest proportion of non-noble officers (18 of 56). Menshikov, long-time crony of the tsar and energetic soldier-administrator-entrepreneur, came from dubious origins and fabricated a fanciful noble genealogy. Unable to write more than his name, he was promoted to aristocratic rank (Peter obtained for him the honorific title of prince of the Holy Roman Empire) and busily accumulated immense wealth. Having already abolished the rank of boyar and aware that Russian noble titles were devalued by the practice of equal inheritance, Peter introduced two European titles, count and baron, but conferred them infrequently and only for meritorious service. Baron Peter Shafirov, for example, gained his title in 1710; Baron Andrei Osterman obtained his in 1721 for negotiating peace with Sweden.

State service proved burdensome for nobles and their families, as Peter strove to ensure that military service take precedence over civil and that young noblemen fulfil their service obligations. When established in 1711, the Senate was ordered to hunt down and register noble boys as young as 10 so that they could be sent to school before beginning service at 15. Relatives were to denounce those in hiding; in 1722 such youths were outlawed as if bandits. But enforcing these prescriptions in distant provinces was problematical at best; towards the end of Peter's reign, Ivan Pososhkov decried the ease with which provincial nobles evaded service and concealed fugitives. Efforts to recover deserters oscillated between blandishments and threats, neither achieving much success.

The peasantry furnished the bulk of all recruits, whether for the armed forces, the 'manufactories', naval yards, or construction sites. They also provided most of the tax revenues. To guarantee the flow of revenue for the armed forces, the country was divided into huge provinces each of which was to support different regiments. Continual mobilization peaked in the Swedish invasion of 1708–9, by which time the central government had largely disintegrated. The country consisted of satrapies like Ingermanland presided over by Menshikov in St Petersburg; virtually all Peter's energies focused on the showdown with Sweden.

Prolonged war stimulated Muscovy's fledgling industry, especially iron and copper production, and to replace Sweden as a major supplier. In 1700 six iron smelters produced around 2,000 tons; by 1710 seventeen provided over 5,000 tons annually, the total redoubling in 1720. By 1725 twenty-four ironworks, eight operated by Tula merchant Nikita Demidov in the Urals, produced more than 14,000 tons: half from Demidov's plants, almost three-quarters from the Urals. The first silver mines began production at Nerchinsk in south-eastern Siberia. Most iron went to the armed forces as did the output of the other ninety or so manufactories founded in Petrine Russia. After 1715, however, Russian bar-iron and sailcloth became substantial exports. Nikita Demidov gained noble status and accumulated a huge fortune. Because Petrine statistics are so scanty, one cannot confidently assess costs or living standards. Agricultural prices may have more than doubled over 1701–30, whereas industrial employment reached 18,400 by 1725.

Baltic Expansion and Victory at Poltava

The Northern War's first years saw Peter and his generals gradually devise a strategy of nibbling away at Swedish dominion in the Baltic while Charles XII pursued Augustus II into Central Europe. Thus the Russians seized control of the Neva river by the spring of 1703, when the Peter and Paul Fortress was founded in the river's delta, the centre for a new frontier town and naval base. Further westward a fortress-battery called Kronshlot was hastily erected near the island of Kotlin, where the harbour of Kronstadt would soon be built. Peter and Menshikov personally led a boat attack on two Swedish warships at the mouth of the Neva in early May that brought Russia's first naval victory, celebrated by a medal inscribed 'The Unprecedented Has Happened'. Tsar and favourite were both made knights of the Order of Saint Andrew. In 1704 Dorpat and Narva fell to the Russians, as mounted forces ravaged Swedish Estland and Livland. Among the captives taken in Livland was a buxom young woman, Marta Skavronska, soon to become Russified as Catherine (Ekaterina Alekseevna). She enchanted Peter successively as mistress and common-law wife, confidante and soul-mate, empress and successor. Adept at calming his outbursts of rage, she matched his energy and bore him many children.

Peter certainly needed emotional comfort during these years of constant travels to the northern and western fronts, periodic illnesses, and the frazzling turnabouts of coalition warfare and civil war. His own role in government mushroomed so quickly that a personal *Kabinet* (chancery) was founded around 1704 under Aleksei Makarov whose clerk's rank soon evolved into cabinet secretary. While the Russians won localized victories in the north-west, exiled Streltsy suddenly seized Astrakhan in August 1705 and threatened to incite other Volga towns and the Don Cossacks. The rebels railed against shaving beards and wearing European clothing, endorsed the Old Belief, and massacred more than 300 persons and the local prefect. After Field Marshal Boris Sheremetev recaptured Astrakhan in March 1706, the Preobrazhenskii Bureau investigated more than 500 individuals (including 401 Streltsy), executed 314 of them, and banished the rest into hard labour. But tranquillity lasted barely a year: a similar outbreak led by the Don Cossack Kondratii Bulavin convulsed the lower Don in 1707–8—just as Charles XII invaded western Russia and Ukraine, where he was joined by Hetman Ivan Mazepa with a force of Ukrainian Cossacks. In the mean time Saxony had left the war, with Augustus II yielding the Polish throne to the Swedish-supported Stanislaus Leszczyński. Russia now faced Sweden alone.

Foreseeing prolonged conflict, Peter and his commanders had decided in December 1706 on 'scorched earth' tactics to sap the Swedes' strength and mobility while exploring a negotiated settlement. Peter fell ill several times amidst the constant tension. 'Severe fever' laid him low in Warsaw in July 1707, 'five feet from death' in delirium; another fever and mercurial medications confined him to bed in St Petersburg in May 1708, dissuading him from rushing to Azov against Bulavin. At Azov in April and May 1709, just before the climactic confrontation at Poltava, the tsar again took 'strong medicines' but after his chills and fever broke in August, still felt depressed and weak. A month later he boasted to Catherine of drinking bouts with his Polish allies.

The murderously frigid winter of 1708–9, together with epidemic disease, inadequate clothing, and short rations, conspired to divert the Swedes from Moscow, where earthworks had been thrown up around the Kremlin, and to

Peter at the battle of Poltava in 1709. The famous triumph was depicted in many media and often reproduced, portraying Peter's personal valour on the field of battle. Lomonosov's glassworks rendered it into mosaic form as part of a proposed Petrine monument that was never completed. It overlooks the main stairway of the original building of the Academy of Sciences in St Petersburg.

await supplies and link up with Mazepa in Ukraine. This detour allowed Peter's flying column to intercept the Swedish relief force at Lesnaia on 28 September 1708: day-long fighting ended in shattering defeat for the Swedes. By the end of the year several thousand Swedes had died from exposure.

The general engagement that Peter had so long postponed and Charles XII had so pursued came at Poltava on 27 June 1709. By then the Swedish army was no match, outnumbered almost two to one and outgunned seventy cannon to four. The predicament was symbolized by the king himself being shot in the foot ten days before (on his twenty-seventh birthday) so that he had to be carried about the field on a litter. He barely escaped capture after his army's demise. Although Sheremetev was the commander-in-chief, Peter took the field, his hat and saddle shot through. Within two hours the Swedish forces crumbled before the hail of Russian cannonfire, musketry, and Menshikov's slashing cavalry. The ensuing rout left some 9,000 Swedish dead on the field; 16,000 more surrendered three days later at nearby Perevolochna. Poltava placed a 'firm stone' in the foundation of St Petersburg, as the tsar expostulated in relief. Paintings and other artistic media quickly produced portrayals of Peter at Poltava, a favourite theme thenceforth.

100

The triumph was consolidated within eighteen months. The northern alliance was reconstituted with the addition of Prussia and the dethronement of Leszczyński in Poland. Sweden was offered peace on generous terms, but when the absent Charles XII refused to negotiate, Russian forces conquered the Baltic region in 1710 from Vyborg in the north to Reval and Riga in the west and south (despite a widespread plague epidemic that devastated Sweden but largely spared Russian territory). Incorporation of these non-Slavic territories led directly to the proclamation of Russia as a European-type empire. Indeed, Peter began using the designation *imperator vserossiiskii* ('emperor of all the Russias') as early as 31 May 1712 in a charter to his consul in Genoa while Sheremetev styled him 'Your Imperial Highness' in a petition of 1 August 1711 as did the merchants of Riga in a petition of 4 September 1712. Notifying Menshikov of his election as honorary fellow of the Royal Society in October 1714, Isaac Newton termed Peter 'your Emperor, His Caesarian Majesty'.

Peter's broadening political horizons also led him to arrange marriages of several relatives to foreign rulers. His niece Anna Ivanovna married the duke of Courland in late 1710 and his niece Ekaterina Ivanovna the duke of Mecklenburg-Schwerin in April 1716 in the presence of Peter, Catherine, and Augustus II. Neither marriage proved successful in personal terms; Anna was widowed almost immediately and Ekaterina returned to Russia with her young daughter in 1722. Tsarevich Alexis's marriage to Charlotte of Wolfenbüttel in October 1711 proved equally painful for the spouses although it did produce a granddaughter and grandson, the future Peter II. All these matches accented Russia's rising international stature and resolute entry into the European dynastic marriage market.

Cultural Revolution and Europeanizing Reforms

After 1711 Peter could devote more attention and longer consideration to a broader array of affairs. He pursued a number of initiatives that amounted to a 'Cultural Revolution' and accelerated the process of Europeanization by introducing the fruits of the Renaissance, the Reformation, the Age of Discovery, and the Scientific Revolution. Renaissance elements may be discerned in the new emphases on education, book-learning, and publishing. The number of presses, for instance, increased from three to ten by 1725, all under state control. Peter endorsed a simplified civil orthography in 1707, but presses and fonts remained so scarce that one-third of the secular titles before 1725 appeared in the old script. The annual number of titles rose from six or seven in the last decades of the seventeenth century to as many as forty-five per year in the first quarter of the eighteenth century. The content of printed material also changed, with government pronouncements, laws, and military writings constituting almost two-thirds of all publications in the period 1700–25. Many were translations from foreign publications; slightly less than one-quarter treated religion, Muscovy's traditional staple. Still, devotional writings were reprinted so frequently they comprised about 40 per cent of all books published in the Petrine era.

Russia's first periodical, *Vedomosti*, began appearing in late 1702 and offered an official selection of 'news', celebrating governmental authority and military victories more than general information or commercial reports. The number of issues per year varied wildly, dropping from fourteen annually in 1708–12 to seven in 1713–17 and only one in 1718. Print runs also oscillated oddly—from a high of 875 in 1709 (the year of Poltava) to only 205 in 1712. Readership was obviously small, perhaps declining, and minuscule compared to England or Holland.

Peter personally collected a library of 1,663 titles in manuscript and printed books in Russian and foreign languages. He also purchased the private collections of Dr Robert Erskine and others, which laid the basis for the Library of the Academy of Sciences and, by 1725, comprised some 11,000 volumes. Assisted by Erskine, Jacob Bruce, and other scholars, Peter founded the first public museum, the Kunst-Kamera in St Petersburg, and collected European paintings, chiefly of the Dutch and Flemish schools. Indeed, his picture gallery at Mon Plaisir in Peterhof was the first of its kind in Russia, with about 200 paintings by 1725. To encourage visitation, the Kunst-Kamera charged no entry fee and had a budget of 400 roubles for free refreshments (coffee, wine, vodka and the like). Renaissance notions likewise stimulated Petrine interest in secular history and the idea of Russia 'entering a new era'. Peter himself led the way, with a concern to document military affairs and travels, an interest that eventually supported the compilation of an official history of the Swedish War, not complete before his death and published only in 1770–2.

In another exhibition of Renaissance spirit Peter encouraged the liberation of élite women, his own female relatives in the first instance, and their attendance at public receptions called 'assemblies'. He authorized the first secular public theatre on Red Square in 1701. Opened in 1702 with elaborate sets and stage machinery, this 'comedy chamber' presented plays in German staged by a German company from Danzig. An abject failure crippled by a lack of Russian plays, a suitable literary language, and an audience, the theatre disbanded in 1706. Its sets, costumes, and scripts were handed over to Peter's sister Natalia, who established a court theatre at Preobrazhenskoe in 1707 that was soon transferred to St Petersburg and lasted until her death in 1716. It pioneered the presentation of European plays of chivalry and romance. In Kiev meanwhile Feofan Prokopovich, Ukrainian born and partly educated in Rome, composed the tragicomedy *Vladimir* while teaching at the Mohyla Academy. A historical drama focusing on Russia's conversion to Christianity and with many topical politico-cultural overtones, *Vladimir* was dedicated to Mazepa, who attended the first performance. This dedication had to be dropped after Mazepa's defection in 1708. Other plays were staged at Dr Bidloo's surgical school in Moscow including two by Fedor Zhurovskii, *Slava Rossiiskaia* (Russia's Glory) and *Slava pechal'naia* (Grieving Glory), which respectively commemorated Catherine I's coronation in 1724 and Peter's death in 1725.

The Reformation informed Petrine efforts to transform the Orthodox Church. In 1694 Peter discontinued the Palm Sunday practice of the tsar on foot leading the patriarch on horseback across Moscow's Red Square. In 1698 he criticized monks and monasticism, in 1700 reproved Patriarch Adrian for the Church's failure to educate the young, and in 1701 re-established the Monastery Bureau to manage church lands. Most striking was his radical decision to replace the Patriarchate with a council of hierarchs, the Holy Synod. He personally favoured Bible-reading; his library contained several copies of the New Testament but only one of the Old. Although Peter believed in justification by faith alone, he scorned superstition and discouraged the veneration of icons.

Peter's study in the Summer Palace in St Petersburg. The small room hints at Peter's spartan 'hands-on' style of rule and his interest in European-type book knowledge.

Peter's penchant for travel celebrated the Age of Discovery as did his absorption in naval and maritime affairs. The Persian Campaign of 1722–3 exemplified an urge for Oriental expansion, also revealed in an abortive secret mission to Madagascar in 1723–4. Themes of exploration and expansion stayed with Peter until the end of his life, when he commissioned the first Bering Expedition to investigate north-east Asia and North America for possible colonization.

The Scientific Revolution had enthralled Peter even before his first journey abroad, and his early acquaintance with foreign and native scholars reinforced ventures in the sciences, arts, and technology. Peter corresponded for more than twenty years with G. W. von Leibniz, whom he put on the payroll in 1711 and ultimately, in 1724, founded the Imperial Academy of Sciences and Arts in St Petersburg as the centre of state-organized research in the new Russian Empire. This multi-purpose institution combined research, teaching, and museum functions; it utilized a broad definition of 'sciences' encompassing secular knowledge that included arts and crafts, history and literature.

St Petersburg as the New Capital and Renewed Dynastic Disarray

As befitted a new European sovereign, Peter spent much time outside Muscovy's old borders: a total of almost nineteen months in the years 1711–13 that spanned the disastrous Pruth campaign, two extended visits to Carlsbad for water cures and to witness Alexis's wedding, and meetings with Leibniz at Torgau, Teplitz, and Carlsbad in 1711. The tsar's 'Paradise' at St Petersburg became the new capital in about 1713 with the transfer of the court and higher government.

In microcosm the city advertised many Petrine ideals. It was European in concept, name, and style—the style synonymous with the newly popular term *arkhitektura*. Its name and layout, the fortress and cathedral of Peter and Paul and the city crest all pointed to parallels with imperial Rome. Planned for commercial and economic efficiency (Peter even contemplated centring the city on the island of Kotlin in the Gulf of Finland!), security from fire (but not flood), and impressive splendour, the 'Residenz-Stadt' grew rapidly thanks to forced labour and forced resettlement in combination with vigorous state patronage and flourishing foreign trade carried in foreign vessels. With the arrival of the court and many state agencies, the state's presence in the guise of the huge Admiralty establishment, armoury facilities at nearby Sestroretsk, and the army and guards regiments fuelled a boom in local construction. Following the formation of the collegiate system of central administration after 1715, the city's chief architect, Domenico Trezzini, began in 1722 a huge unitary corpus for the eleven administrative colleges on Vasilevskii Island, a grandiose project only completed ten years later. By 1725 St Petersburg had a population of about 50,000 (with large seasonal fluctuations, as peasant labourers congregated during the spring-to-autumn shipping season), and featured several impressive palaces (Menshikov's in particular) with even more opulent estates flanking the approaches. The Summer Garden boasted abundant statuary and Peter's small Summer Palace, but his attempt to organize a zoo complete with elephant and polar bears faltered when the animals died.

Moscow remained the old capital and largest city, but after 1710 Peter visited it sparingly. Much of 1713–14 he passed on board ship co-ordinating the land and sea conquest of Finland, highlighted by the naval victory of Hangö—a nautical Poltava—on 27 July 1714. The European sojourns and campaigns culminated in a second triumphal tour, this time accompanied by Catherine except to France, for twenty months in 1716–17. Off Copenhagen in October 1716 Peter was named honorary admiral of the combined Danish, Dutch, English, and Russian fleets—pleasing recognition of Russia's new maritime might. Yet the ageing tsar was often mentally distraught, as hinted by twelve nocturnal dreams he recorded in 1714–16. Seriously ill in Holland for a month in early 1717, he later took the waters at Pyrmont and Spa. Both consorts grieved for the baby boy lost four hours after birth at Wesel in Holland on 2 January 1717.

St Petersburg. This modern photo captures the new capital's picturesque landscape of monumental European-style buildings overlooking watery expanses.

Dynastic distress ensued even earlier with the death of Alexis's wife in October 1715 shortly after having borne a son (and first grandson), Peter Alekseevich, followed soon by Catherine's delivery of a son, Peter Petrovich. Peter and Catherine had been privately married in Moscow in March 1711, a ceremony repeated publicly in St Petersburg on 19 February 1712, the tsar joking that 'it was a fruitful wedding, for they had already had five children'. This tardy marriage to a foreign commoner struck the English envoy as 'one of the surprising events of this wonderfull age'. Catherine quickly became the focus of a European-type court largely Germanic in cultural terms. At Moscow in February 1722 and St Petersburg the next year Catherine and her ladies donned Amazon costumes to celebrate Shrovetide.

Peter's relationship with Alexis, never close, became strained as his deteriorating health raised the succession issue. Alexis vowed to renounce the throne and enter a monastery, but did neither and suddenly fled abroad clandestinely—an acute embarrassment to his father. Enticed to return by the wily diplomat Peter Tolstoy, Alexis underwent intensive secret investigation that came to involve dozens of people, including Alexander Kikin (a former confidant of the tsar in disrepute for financial malfeasance), his mother, and Archpriest Iakov Ignatev (the tsarevich's father-confessor). Kikin was accused of inspiring

Tag for beard tax. Peter's decree against beards exemplified the campaign to alter Muscovite dress customs after current European fashion. The decree was widely ignored and tax payments evaded, but it was reissued several times and beards were not allowed in state service until the nineteenth century.

Alexis's flight abroad and the others of fostering hatred for his father. All were tortured; Kikin, the archpriest, and several others—including Elena's acknowledged lover—were all executed. After prolonged interrogation and torture Alexis himself was sentenced to death for treason in June 1718, perishing in prison in disputed circumstances. Although the investigation disclosed close contacts between the tsarevich and many prominent noblemen, the official version blamed Alexis's treasonous conspiracy on 'the long beards', that is, supposedly reactionary churchmen. In fact, many potential sympathizers did not wish to return to old Muscovy but disliked Peter's capricious despotism on behalf of breakneck change.

Alexis's demise complicated the succession: Peter Petrovich—the tsar's son by Catherine, not yet four but already three feet four inches tall—died on 25 April 1719, dealing another dynastic blow. 'The Czar took the loss of his only son so much at heart, that he run his head against the wall of the chamber and was seized with two convulsion fits', remarked the English envoy, who speculated that Catherine had passed childbearing age. She had one more daughter, Natalia, born in 1718 who died a month after her father in March 1725, and possibly two more still births. The Alexis affair, reminiscent of Ivan the Terrible's murder of his son, may have exacerbated Peter's tendency towards paranoia and alienation from former intimates such as Menshikov and, ultimately, Catherine herself. It also coincided with the formation of a hypercentralized and militarized police regime bent on resolute action dictated by an ageing autocrat disinclined to accept any counsel.

Outwardly the Petrine government went from triumph to triumph with the Peace of Nystadt ending the Great Northern War in 1721 and Peter proclaimed emperor of all the Russias and 'the Great, Most Wise Father of the Fatherland'. Prussia and Holland recognized the new title the very next year, Sweden and Denmark in 1723 and 1724, but Austria delayed until the early 1740s and Poland only conceded in 1764. Peter captained the triumphal Persian campaign in 1722 that added new territories along the Caspian Sea in emulation of Alexander the Great. A new succession law, announced in 1722, gave the reigning ruler the right to name whomever he chose to succeed him, and Catherine I was proclaimed empress and crowned in Moscow in May 1724.

Peter's death on 28 January 1725 happened so suddenly that he could not designate an heir. His health had long been in doubt despite visits to the mineral springs at Olonets. He travelled there in January 1719, for example, contracting 'a violent cold on the road'. He was also tormented by 'a weakness in his left arm, which was occasioned at first by his being let blood by an unskilful surgeon, who, missing the vein, made an incision in the nerve that lies by it'. Such pains led Peter to take the waters twice in 1724 in February and June. To Catherine he praised the curative qualities of the waters but complained of urinary difficulty and diminished appetite. In St Petersburg later that summer he

Burial of the cat by the mice. This famous engraving is often said to portray the Old Believers' negative attitudes towards Peter's death. But the subject was originally not so personalized and rather reflected a more generalized and less political example of late Muscovite popular culture: inoffensive clowning *not* seen as a parody of ruler or government.

was bedridden twice for almost two weeks between 16 August and 12 September 1724. He was one of those driven persons who cannot slow down, no matter what the doctors advised.

The condition that caused his death sparked controversy then and now, primarily whether it was venereal-related or not. Recent Russian scholars are split between gonorrhoea or uraemia. Considering the length and incredible tempo of his life, the cause of death may be less significant than the superhuman achievements of the 'body' and 'soul' involved. After the traditional forty days of mourning Peter's body was interred in a magnificent casket in a small temporary wooden church amid the still uncompleted Peter and Paul Cathedral— the first Russian ruler to be buried outside Moscow. Feofan Prokopovich pronounced a brief grandiloquent funeral oration that was widely distributed and translated and that compared the late tsar to biblical prophets and kings— Samson, Japhet, Moses, David, Solomon, and Constantine.

Russia without Peter

Catherine succeeded Peter the day of his death via a bloodless palace coup master-minded by Menshikov and backed by the guards' military muscle. The coup pre-empted the claims of Peter's grandson, Peter Alekseevich, but Catherine endorsed the traditional right of male succession as personified in the 9-year-old boy. Menshikov and the other Petrine 'principals' had apparently talked Catherine out of becoming regent for Peter on grounds that such an arrangement would foster division and discord. Just before his death Peter I had approved the marriage of his eldest daughter, Anna Petrovna, to Karl Frederick, duke of Holstein-Gottorp, a secret article of the contract providing that the

Russian ruler might bring back Anna's male issue as successor to the Russian throne. Considering the late great tsar's estrangement from Catherine during the final three months of his life (because of a scandal involving William Mons), her actual succession entailed abundant surprise and irony. Most amazingly, Catherine I inaugurated virtually continuous female rule in Russia for almost seventy years. Paradox also abounded in the efforts exerted over her reign of barely twenty-six months to undo several Petrine policies.

Some reaction against the imperious Petrine legacy was probably inevitable. Three decades of unremitting mobilization had engendered widespread crisis in much of the expanded empire, troubles lately compounded by harvest failures, massive peasant flight, and near bankruptcy. Hence Catherine's first steps included reduction of the poll-tax (from 74 to 70 copecks) and withdrawal of the army from the provinces. Her government also strove to economize the workings of the inflated Petrine administration by abolishing many offices and dispensing with salaries for low-ranking civil servants in favour of restoring the customary practice of charging petitioners for official services. Much wrangling raged over bloated military expenditures in particular.

Though empress and autocratrix in name, Catherine I was so tired and sickly that her reign looked to be short. A new era of 'clique government' ensued much like that which had prevailed for almost a quarter century after Alexis's death in 1676. This oligarchy assumed institutional shape on 8 February 1726 under a new governmental body, the Supreme Privy Council, a six-man council empowered to advise the empress and headed by the masterful Menshikov. But he was ageing and so uncertain of his future that he vainly attempted to become duke of Courland. As Catherine's demise approached in the spring of 1727, Menshikov endeavoured to safeguard his future by purging two rivals, Count Peter Tolstoy and his brother-in-law Policemaster-General Anton Devier, who were sentenced to death for conspiracy and treason before banishment to remote regions. Just prior to Catherine's death on 7 May 1727 Menshikov oversaw the compilation of her 'Testament', which named Peter Alekseevich 'suktsessor' under a joint regency of nine persons. With a minor on the throne, Menshikov's dominance seemed assured. He sought to conciliate young Peter by freeing his grandmother, the nun Elena, and arranged his daughter Maria's betrothal to the future tsar on 25 May 1727. Barely a month later Duke Karl Frederick of Holstein and his wife Anna left for Kiel, removing two more political rivals from the scene. Even so, prolonged illness in the summer of 1727 enabled Menshikov's rivals led by Ivan Dolgorukii and the crafty Andrei Osterman to rally the Supreme Privy Council against Menshikov's 'tyranny', so the 'semi-sovereign despot' was placed under house-arrest on 8 September 1727. Stripped of his honours, jewels, and multiple estates, Menshikov was exiled with his family to Berezov in Siberia, where he died in 1729.

Peter II's reign proved as brief and uneventful as Catherine I's. He hardly 'reigned', for actual power rested with the Supreme Privy Council until he

Catherine I, born Marta Skavronska of Germanic, Protestant, and non-noble background, was crowned Russia's first empress in 1724 and became the new empire's first female ruler in 1725. She personified the accelerated Europeanization of the Romanov dynasty.

suddenly died of smallpox as an unmarried minor on 18/19 January 1730. The general domestic tranquillity was underlined by abolition of the Preobrazhenskii Bureau in 1729. Peter II moved the court and several offices to Moscow, where he spent the last two years of his life mainly hunting in silent protest against the rigours of Petersburg life.

Peter II died without issue and without designating a successor, thereby precipitating renewed political crisis. The Supreme Privy Council, now expanded to eight aristocrat-officials—four Dolgorukiis and two Golitsyns—endeavoured to resolve the dynastic dilemma by secretly offering the throne on restrictive conditions to Anna Ivanovna, the widowed duchess of Courland and childless niece of Peter the Great. This move inadvertently inaugurated a month of intense political manœuvring. Led by the widely experienced Prince Dmitrii Golitsyn, the privy councillors sought to establish an oligarchical constitution that would limit monocratic arbitrary rule (autocracy) by making the council permanent and hedging Anna's sovereignty with restrictions. Failure to publicize the council's 'Conditions' (*Konditsii*)—a new term in Russian political discourse—and its other proposals for reform fanned rumours of an aristocratic grab for supreme power, inflaming immediate opposition and alternative platforms backed by several hundred aristocrats and lesser nobles in some cases. When the 'Conditions' were finally announced at a meeting of about eighty dignitaries on 2 February 1730, additional projects had been put forward, one signed by 361 persons, and Anna had already arrived in Moscow and become the focus of a loose coalition suspicious of the oligarchs and of the effort to abridge the autocrat's authority. Osterman and Feofan Prokopovich contacted confederates in the guards and even released broadsides attacking the Supreme Privy Council with the spectre of disunity and chaos. Within a few weeks the competing groups had neutralized each other, so that Anna tore up the 'Conditions' and proclaimed herself 'Empress and Self-upholder of All Russia'. She abolished the Supreme Privy Council and gradually dispatched all the Dolgorukiis into exile. Dmitrii Golitsyn remained free, albeit largely silent, until imprisoned in 1737, a year before his death. He accepted responsibility for the constitutional fiasco, remarking: 'The banquet was ready, but the guests were unworthy'.

From this tumultuous inception, Anna's reign exhibited familiar elements of 'clique government' along with a confusing mix of conservative restoration, continuity with Petrine policies, and occasional reform. Her reign has endured a generally bad press, mostly Petrine in perspective but also animated by antipathy to female rule and Germans. She has often been viewed as a puppet controlled by her 'German' favourite, Ernst Johann Biron, her reign later derided as the notorious time of 'Bironovshchina' ('Biron's repressive regime'). Such crude indictments have recently receded in favour of renewed attention to important continuities in the ruler's role, foreign policy and territorial expansion, economic development, and institutional change. Whatever Anna's intimate relationship with Biron, who was named count and senior chamberlain in 1730 and by whom she may have had a son, he held no significant independent status until elected duke of Courland in 1737 and named regent upon Anna's death. His fragile regency lasted barely three weeks until overthrown by Field Marshal Burkhard von Münnich. Biron's presumed role behind the scenes and attempt to marry a son to the empress's niece provoked accusations of dynastic ambitions, like a new Godunov or Menshikov, whereas his love of horses, cards, and theatrical troupes fostered charges of talking to people as if they were horses and to horses as if they were people. In fact, his influence on high policy appears to have been minimal, and the Chancery of Secret Investigative Affairs, as the secret police was renamed in 1730, handled no more than 2,000 cases as compared to 2,478 during Elizabeth's first decade of rule and about the same number during her second. Foreigners did not enjoy undue preference during Biron's alleged hegemony, and he had little to do with the persecution of Old Believers, some twenty thousand of whom are supposed to have been exiled during Anna's reign (a patently inflated statistic). Besides, Anna's regime was dominated by Russian aristocrats: Chancellor Gavriil Golovkin, Vice-Chancellor Andrei Osterman, Prince Aleksei Cherkasskii, and later Pavel Iaguzhinskii and his successor Artemii Volynskii. The execution of Volynskii on 27 June 1740 on charges of treasonous conspiracy has often been blamed on Biron, though the court that condemned him consisted solely of Russian magnates.

Like her predecessors, the widowed and (officially) childless Anna confronted succession problems throughout her reign. She kept a sharp eye on the orphaned Karl Peter Ulrich in Holstein, Peter the Great's sole surviving grandson, and on the vivacious Elizabeth and her small 'Young Court'. To reinforce the dynastic line of her Miloslavskii relatives, she adopted her half-German, half-Russian niece, daughter of the duke and duchess of Mecklenburg and russified as Anna Leopoldovna, upon the death of the latter's mother in 1733. This princess was converted to Russian Orthodoxy, given a European-style education, and reluctantly married Duke Anton Ulrich of Braunschweig-Wolfenbüttel-Bevern in July 1739. They promptly sired a son, Ivan Antonovich, the future Ivan VI, born on 12 August 1740, just two months before the empress's own sudden death on 17 October. Regent for her infant son after Biron's overthrow, Anna Leopoldovna showed little interest in ruling and was easily deposed by the competing dynastic line personified by Elizabeth as the old Miloslavskii–Naryshkin rivalry reappeared.

Anna Ivanovna's government had adopted several policy changes bruited during the constitutional crisis of her accession. The unpopular Petrine law on single inheritance was abrogated, for instance, and the Noble Cadet Corps was founded in St Petersburg, its graduates entering the military as officers. Officers' pay was made equal to that of foreigners, and the lifetime service requirement was shortened to twenty-five years with one son entirely exempted. The court returned to St Petersburg in January 1733 amid great ceremony. Links to the interior were improved by completion of the Ladoga Canal, a showpiece supervised by the German military engineer Burkhard von Münnich, whom Anna richly rewarded and promoted to field marshal. He gained a chequered military reputation in leading the Russian armies to victory in the War of the Polish Succession in 1733–5 and the related Russo-Turkish War of 1736–9. Both conflicts involved allied coalitions and gained some success, especially Münnich's multiple invasions of the Crimea despite substantial Russian losses partly because of a large outbreak of plague. Russia defeated the Turks and the Crimean Tatars, but Austria's sudden withdrawal limited territorial gains to so-called New Serbia and Azov without the right to fortify the latter. These were Russia's first triumph over the Turks since Peter the Great's second Azov campaign and first successful invasion of the Crimea. Another major gain of territory came via the Orenburg expedition, a state-sponsored venture led by Vasilii Tatishchev and others that pushed the Russian frontier into the southern Urals, opening abundant lands to cultivation and mining. The huge Bashkir revolts that greeted this Russian invasion lasted from 1735 to 1740 and resulted in the extermination or resettlement of almost one-third of the Bashkir population. This rich new territory accelerated the economic boom begun in Petrine times and compensated for the loss of the Caspian lands returned to Persia in 1735.

Economic and Cultural Continuities

Indeed, Russian ironworks and copperworks multiplied in the post-Petrine decades, twenty of the former being built in the Urals from 1726 to 1733, thirteen of the latter from 1726 to 1737. Russian exports of iron to England presented serious competition to Sweden and were only one of many commodities regulated by the new Anglo-Russian trade treaty of 1734. St Petersburg blossomed as a major seaport, especially for exports, but Archangel was revived by the fairer tariff of 1731. Most of Russian iron and copper production went to the armed forces, the mint, or for export. The fleet was somewhat revived as the *Anna*, a huge ship of the line with 140 guns, was launched by the English shipwright Richard Brown in June 1737 with a ball and a banquet.

Post-Petrine Russia also manifested many continuities in cultural affairs. The Imperial Academy of Sciences and Arts, planned by Peter and endorsed by the Senate, officially opened in December 1725 under the presidency of Dr Laurentius Blumentrost, Moscow-born and European educated. On 27 December 1725 Georg Bülffinger, professor of physics at the academy, delivered a speech in Latin (111 pages!) on the value of such institutions and studies, especially on the means of determining longitudes. A copy was sent to the Cambridge University Library. Catherine I's son-in-law, Duke Karl Frederick of Holstein, attended the session. Another speech was given on 1 August 1726 by Jakob Hermann on the history of geometry and the perfection of telescopes with a reply by Christian Goldbach. The audience included Catherine I herself, but the preface of the published speech (Petropoli, 1727) explained that most of Hermann's address was not delivered, while the empress actually heard a German panegyric by Georg Bayer praising her and the origins of the Russian people.

To ensure international recognition, the academy's protocols were published in Latin until 1734, German until 1741. All the academicians were foreigners, perhaps the most eminent being the mathematician Leonhard Euler who worked in Russia 1727–41 and again from 1766 until his death in 1783. Though the academy developed slowly and unevenly, it attracted some gifted individuals, notably Mikhail Lomonosov, the great polymath from provincial origins, who as a mature student absorbed the best of Muscovite education in Moscow and Kiev before attending St Petersburg's academic university and then advanced study abroad. In literary affairs Antiokh Kantemir and Vasilii Trediakovskii began to make their mark. Foreign scholars such as G. F. Müller accompanied the Bering expeditions, collected many sources on the history of Siberia, and collaborated in a variety of publications. Outside the academy the versatile engineer and administrator Vasilii Tatishchev began compiling a monumental history of Russia—and in Russian—that was only published decades after his death in 1750. Ballet was initiated under Anna with the work of Jean-Baptiste Landé and the arrival of several foreign theatrical troupes.

If Catherine the Great is usually credited with infusing Russia with 'soul', Peter the Great's earlier efforts merit mention. In 1718 the poet Aaron Hill lauded 'this *giant-genius* sent; | Divinely siz'd—to suit his crown's extent!' To our late twentieth-century ears Hill's encomium rings ominously:

> He breath'd prolific *soul*, inspir'd the land,
> And call'd forth *order*, with directive hand.
> *Then*, pour's whole energy, at once spread wide,
> And old obstruction *sunk*, beneath its tide.
> Then, shad'wing all, the dread dominion rose,
> Which, late, no *hope*, and now, no danger knows.

THE AGE OF ENLIGHTENMENT
1740–1801

GARY MARKER

*These decades witnessed a flourishing Empire—with
ever-expanding borders, demographic and economic growth,
and a blossoming in aristocratic arts and culture. But it was no
golden age for commoners: townsmen suffered from crippling
restrictions, serfs became mere chattels, and minorities underwent administrative Russification. The result was widespread
unrest and, most dramatically, the Pugachev Rebellion of
1773–75.*

AFTER Peter's death in 1725 and another fifteen years of troubled and ill-defined rule, the next six decades witnessed a self-conscious reassertion of the Petrine legacy. For the remainder of the century, indeed of the old regime, legitimacy was linked to the name and achievements of Peter, officially canonized both as the founder of the All-Russian Empire and its great Europeanizer. Ironically, this epitome of masculine authority, this father of the fatherland, was enshrined and succeeded by strong female rulers, first his daughter Elizabeth (1741–61) and, after the brief reign of Peter III (1761–2), Catherine the Great (1762–96).

The paradox of strong female rule in a patriarchal system of authority added yet another riddle to the enigmas of Russian politics. What did sovereignty and 'autocracy' really mean, especially in so vast a realm with so primitive a bureaucracy? What was the relationship between the absolute authority of the ruler and the everyday power of clan patronage? In a country without a fixed law of succession, where the death of every ruler evoked a political crisis that invited court circles and guards regiments to intercede in the choice of a new ruler, it is indeed surprising that 'autocracy' should have remained firmly entrenched.

Yet it did, accompanied by a fascination with the precedent of the Roman Empire that reshaped the regime's own sense of identity. The classical influence found ubiquitous expression—medals and coins depicting Catherine as a Roman centurion, the statue of Minin and Pozharskii (the national heroes of the Time of Troubles) draped in Roman togas, the classical columns on St Isaac's Cathedral and numerous governmental buildings in St Petersburg, and the odes and panegyrics celebrating Catherine the Great. An exemplar of the latter is an ode by Mikhail Lomonosov, the prominent scholar and patriotic thinker, who sought to pay homage to the new empress: 'Sciences, celebrate now: Minerva has Ascended the Throne.'

These classical images not only linked Russia to contemporary Europe (where a revival of classical antiquity was in full swing), but also suggested ties to the accepted fount of imperial authority—ancient Greece and Rome. Significantly, classicism functioned to separate Russia's 'imperiia' from the lineage of the contiguous Byzantine and Mongol Empires, which it had traditionally invoked to legitimize territorial claims and even validate the mantle of rulership. But eighteenth-century expansion to the east, south, and west had little to do with the Byzantine and Mongol

The Bronze Horseman, statue overlooking the Neva river, next to the Winter Palace in St Petersburg, built by Falconet in 1782, and commissioned by Catherine the Great to pay homage to Peter and to link her name with his. The inscription reads 'Petro primo, Catharina secunda'.

legacies; hence the soaring leap across space and time to establish cultural ties with classical empires—which had made similar grandiose claims—became an ideological imperative. That impulse lay behind the proclamation in 1721 that Russia was an empire, a claim embraced by Peter's successors and integral to the new state identity.

However imposing the classical representations of power may have been, they were meaningless if people refused to submit to its will. And in Russia, more so than in many other states, the theatricality of imperial and autocratic power had little relevance to the everyday life of people remote from court and capital. As the historian Marc Raeff has observed, the rulers of eighteenth-century Russia attempted to graft the cameralist order of Central Europe's 'well-ordered police state' onto the apparent sprawling disorder of the empire's multiple populations. Although the police state could not create social order by itself, it did articulate an institutional and conceptual framework that allowed state institutions to proclaim their sovereignty.

Expansion and Foreign Policy

The navy and the standing army had deteriorated severely in the decade after Peter's death, but they none the less remained a powerful force and consumed most of the state's revenues—approximately 70 to 90 per cent in any given year during the eighteenth century. Russia concentrated most of its forces along the southern waterways and the borders of the Ottoman Empire, but major resources had to be diverted to deal with other conflicts—for example, those that ended in the defeat of Sweden (1743) and the annexation of the Crimean peninsula (1783).

Of particular import was Russia's involvement in the Seven Years War (1755–62). Initially, Russia interceded as an ally of Austria and France against Prussia; despite the expense and losses, the campaigns were advancing successfully and, during the final months of Elizabeth's reign, Russian troops were making steady progress towards Berlin. Peter III, however, suddenly terminated Russia's participation (whether from blind admiration for things Prussian or from an awareness that the state coffers were empty) and switched sides, to the outrage of his erstwhile allies. Catherine initially repudiated this volte-face in policy, but in a few years took a similar tack—chiefly because the new alignment (including Austria as well as Prussia) provided the only way to secure Russia's growing interest in Poland.

Prior to the outbreak of war with revolutionary France in the 1790s, however, Russia's foreign policy focused primarily on the Black Sea. The old chestnut of a primeval Russian 'urge to the sea' has long since faded into well-deserved oblivion, but the Black Sea did affect vital national interests—as an outlet to international waters and especially international markets. Although Peter the

Engraving by
G. F Schmidt (1761)
from a portrait by
Toke (1758) of
Elizabeth Petrovna,
daughter of Peter the
Great and Empress
of Russia, 1741–61,
shown here as
imperial mother, with
orb and sceptre and
silhouetted by Roman
columns. Notice the
virtual absence of
religious imagery.

Great gained a foothold on the Baltic (through the acquisition of Livland and Estonia in 1721), he had had much less success against the Ottoman Empire, leaving the Black Sea out of reach. Thus the strategic waterways that connected the Black Sea with the eastern Mediterranean still traversed territories under Ottoman control. Obviously, any attempt to satisfy these territorial ambitions meant long-term enmity between the Ottoman and Russian Empires. But Catherine did nourish such far-reaching ambitions; at one point, she embraced the vision of southern dominion articulated by her favourite, Prince Grigorii Potemkin, and even spoke of 'liberating' Constantinople in the 1780s and making it her new capital.

Fortunately for Russia, however, cooler heads prevailed. Turkish miscalculations helped: when the Grand Vizier declared war on Russia in 1768, he assumed that other European powers would come to his aid. When this assistance failed to materialize and the Porte was left to face Russia on its own, the two powers waged a bloody and exhausting war for six full years. In the end, Russia prevailed and forced the Ottomans to sue for peace at the village of Kuchuk Kainarji on 10 July 1774. The treaty forced Turkey to cede Azov and a small strip of land on the Black Sea to Russia, to recognize the independence of the Crimean peninsula, and to grant passage to Russian merchant ships (but not warships) through the Dardanelle straits. It also empowered Russia to construct a Black Sea war fleet, a concession that greatly enhanced its military firepower on the southern border. The treaty also authorized the Russian ambassador to make representations on behalf of a newly established Orthodox Church in Constantinople, a somewhat vague concession, but one that would loom large in nineteenth-century diplomacy.

Given this sea access to the West both on the Baltic and in the Black Sea, Russian interest in the three partitions of Poland had little to do with sea-power. Rather, it was a reaction to the precipitous decline of a major power, where the domestic political order had been so subverted by external influence that it ceased to be a viable independent state. The decline invited the first partition—

'An Imperial Stride', caricature by Thomas Rowlandson, 1791. Catherine holding orb and sword, steps over the other European powers to extend Russia's sway across the Black Sea and all the way to Constantinople, a frightening spectre for the rest of Europe after the Treaty of Kuchuk Kainarji.

by Russia, Prussia, and Austria—in July 1772: Russia obtained mainly what is now Belarus, while Austria and Prussia annexed Galicia and West Prussia respectively, effectively denying sea access for the rump Polish state. The catalyst for the second partition (by Russia and Prussia in January 1793) was a Polish constitution of 1791, which created a hereditary (as opposed to the traditionally elected) Polish monarchy, established an elected legislature, and abolished the *liberum veto* that had been so destabilizing. After this partition ignited a Polish uprising (led by the hero of the American War of Independence, Tadeusz Kościuszko), Russia and its allies signed a new series of agreements in 1795 that expunged Poland from the map of Europe.

Population and Social Order

The Russian Empire experienced enormous growth not only in territory, but also in population during the eighteenth century. Natural growth alone accounted for much of this growth—from about ten or eleven million inhabitants in 1700 to about twenty-eight million by the end of the century. The annexation of new territories added greatly to this amount, increasing the total population to over forty million in the 1790s. It was, moreover, an overwhelmingly rural empire: although some estimates run higher, the government's own censuses consistently show that over 90 per cent of the population belonged to the peasantry and still more lived in rural areas.

These subjects bore multiple identities. All belonged to a specific legal estate (noble, serf, state, peasant, and numerous lesser ones); virtually everyone (the élite excepted) was also attached to a specific location. These social categories, in turn, belonged to one of two large aggregate categories—the *podatnye* (those disprivileged groups liable for the poll-tax) and the *nepodatnye* (those exempt). Much more was at stake than the poll-tax: registration in the poll-tax population carried onerous obligations like conscription and corporal punishment that, taken together, formed *the* great divide in the social order. Women were identified, if at all, by the standing of their fathers or husbands. These identities proliferated unsystematically during the eighteenth century, often leaving little correlation between legal status, wealth, and occupation. Many nobles had neither land nor serfs; most 'merchants' neither traded nor produced commodities; and most 'traders', juridically, were not merchants.

Indicative of the incongruity between juridical status and human activity was the special category of *raznochintsy*, which literally designated people who fitted none of the accepted ranks or grades. The state employed the category in so many mutually exclusive ways that it was virtually devoid of any coherent meaning; the status, which few voluntarily espoused, was essentially an *ad hoc* juridical trope that the state invoked when its usual categories, themselves highly artificial, were found to be wanting or inappropriate. In the end, the categories that the state used to classify its population were overlapping, contradictory, often incoherent. Still, these juridical categories provide a useful (if crude) map to the social order, helping to identify groups in terms of their relative rights and obligations.

TOWNSPEOPLE AND MERCHANTS

Russia's urban population was, as already suggested, exceedingly small—some 3 per cent according to the official census of the 1760s, slightly more by the end of the century. The overwhelming majority of urban residents belonged to the legal status of townspeople (*meshchane*), inscribed in the poll-tax (1.24 roubles—almost twice that of peasants) and liable for the attendant disabilities—most notably, conscription and corporal punishment. The term 'townsman' itself was misleading; although many engaged in artisan crafts or petty trades, they also supported themselves through agriculture by tilling garden plots, tending orchards, and raising various kinds of livestock.

The élite in urban society held the rank of merchants (*kuptsy*), the subject of much legislation in the eighteenth century (which culminated in the 'Charter to the Towns' in 1785). It was chiefly for purposes of taxation, not economic regulation, that the state divided merchants into three 'guilds' (*gil'dy*). According to the system in place before 1775, merchants had to have disposable capital of over 100 roubles to register in the first guild, 50 roubles for the second, and 10 roubles for the third. The guild status, in fact, said nothing about the volume or form of their commercial activities; once all internal tariffs were abolished in 1754, merchants—regardless of guild—could engage in whatever trade they chose, with few restraints. Indeed, 'merchants' did not necessarily even engage in commerce; by some estimates, 80 per cent of the Moscow merchants registered in the third guild in 1766 did not engage in trade.

The guild status, however, played a critical role for determining status and obligations. Each guild bore specific responsibilities and had to bear a tax based on their declared *kapital*. The primary urban service was to participate in the urban magistrate (*magistrat*), the elected (and mostly unpaid) councils obligated to collect (but not levy) taxes, to keep population records, to oversee town services (for example, fire-fighting, public health, and road construction), and to maintain law and order. Given the relative frequency and popularity of drunken mêlées (*kulachnye boi*), this last responsibility was important. The magistrates also had to deal with major crises like food shortages and epidemics, as in the Moscow plague riots of 1771. In return, guild members had certain privileges—the right to engage in certain types of commerce, display their wares, hang signs, and a few other modest advantages.

Their status was anything but secure, however. If a merchant's declared capital fell below the specified minimum, he was obliged either to register in the next lowest guild or even to drop from merchant status into the ranks of the common townspeople. Such downward mobility was exceedingly common. As has been recently demonstrated, only a fraction of merchant families in Moscow and provincial towns remained in the first and second guilds for more than a generation; although a few connived to be elevated into the nobility, the great majority dropped into the third guild or the common townspeople.

Catherine clarified the legal standing of merchants after 1775 and, in the process, significantly raised the minimum requirements for guild registration. In contrast to the small sums required earlier, merchants now had to declare 10,000 roubles of capital for the first guild, 5,000 for the second, and 1,000 for the third. Those who lacked such capital had to register either in artisanal guilds or in the general pool of urban commoners. Predictably, the new standard caused the massive demotion of merchants unable to meet the new property qualifications: the number of registered merchants plummeted from over 213,053 in 1772 to 24,562 in 1775, a decline of 88 per cent. However, those excluded from guilds could still trade, since the correlation between legal and commercial status was minimal. Still, those who lost guild status became ordinary members of the poll-tax population, with all the attendant disabilities— taxation, conscription, labour, and hindrances to travel.

The few who remained in the merchant guilds, however, enjoyed important new privileges. One was formal exclusion from the poll-tax rolls, although at the price of paying an annual 1 per cent levy on their capital. Moreover, members of the first and second guilds were exempt from the degradation of corporal punishment, could not be consigned to work in onerous places (such as salt mines), and enjoyed important symbols of social status (for example, the privilege of riding in carriages). And they could buy themselves out of military and civil recruitment. Catherine's legislation also defined their privileged spheres of commercial activity: the first guild could engage in foreign trade, the second in national trade, and the third in local and regional trade.

Catherine also created a further élite category that included trained professionals, businessmen with capital over 50,000 roubles, wholesalers, shipbuilders, and people deemed 'eminent citizens' (*imianitye grazhdane*, i.e. wealthy merchants who had been elected to serve in an official post). This élite, in recognition of their service, enjoyed a host of privileges that ranked them near the nobility in standing, except for the fact that their titles were not hereditary and they could not own serfs. As one might expect, many of these eminent citizens ultimately obtained those privileges by successfully petitioning for elevation into the ranks of nobility.

STATE PEASANTS AND INTERSTITIAL CATEGORIES

The category of state peasants was a catch-all term to identify those living on state lands and owing dues to the state rather than to private landlords. Most state peasants lived in agricultural settlements as members of a repartitional commune, but some, like the *odnodvortsy* (homesteaders) in the south, functioned as family units. As for economic activity, most were primarily engaged in agriculture. In the north, working in heavily wooded territory and handicapped with poor soil and extensive frost, state peasants supplemented—and even replaced—agriculture with other activities, such as fishing, trapping, bee-keeping, and logging. In the case of those who lived near waterways and canals, many worked on barges, hauling them downstream with teams of rope-pullers working each side of the river. And state 'peasants' living along the White Sea worked mainly as commercial fishermen and whalers. In areas where the state sought to foster industrial growth it assigned some state peasants to factories and plants, where, as 'ascribed' (*pripisnye*) peasants, they had to supply a stipulated amount of labour each year. In short, the umbrella category of 'state peasant' was primarily a definition of tax and other obligations, not a coherent economic or social classification.

One important subgroup of state peasants had formerly belonged to the Russian Orthodox Church—primarily monasteries, occasionally to parish churches. Despite recurrent attempts by Peter the Great and his successors to sequester or at least exploit this population, the Church succeeded in retaining ownership and limiting any exactions by the state. In 1762, however, Peter III secularized the Church's landed estates and transferred its peasants to state jurisdiction. Although Catherine temporarily rescinded that edict, in 1764 she confiscated these lands and peasants once again. She then converted this popu-lation into a special category called 'economic peasants' (named after the 'College of the Economy' established to administer them), essentially just another of the myriad subgroups within the larger aggregate of state peasants.

The peasant population also included a congeries of other smaller social units. One category, bridging the status of state and seigneurial peasant, was the 'crown' (*dvortsovye*) peasants, who lived on crown land, held this hereditary sta-tus, and owed dues to the imperial family. A substantial population (over half a million males, or 5 per cent of the peasantry), these peasants were administered by a governmental agency and hence were more approximate to state than seigneurial peasants. Yet another special category was the 'possessionary' (*pos-sessionnye*) peasant, who was 'possessed' by a factory or plant: declining to extend the noble privilege of owning serfs to other social groups, the govern-ment permitted industrial enterprises (not their owners) to purchase unfree labour.

Regardless of juridical status, most peasants did not occupy themselves exclu-sively, or sometimes even primarily, with field work. Even in agricultural com-munities, peasant households spent the long winter months indoors, repairing tools, tending animals, and threshing or milling grain. A substantial proportion of peasants hired themselves out for seasonable labour and participated actively in rural fairs. So many peasants engaged in the local and regional markets that the law designated them as 'trading peasants', who legally remained members of the peasantry, but whose long-term presence in commerce had become a recognized fact.

SERFS

If any population did roughly corre-
spond to our conception of the pri-
mordial peasant wedded to the land,
it was the serfs. According to the poll-
tax census of the 1760s, Russia had
5.6 million male serfs (56.2 per cent
of the peasant population). For all
practical purposes, Russian serfs
were invisible to Russian law and
justice: subject to their squires (who
collected dues, designated recruits,
and meted out punishment), the serf
had virtually no identifiable status in
the imperial system. It is, in that
sense, ironic that the Russian term

Baba Iaga fights the crocodile. Baba Iaga was a familiar figure in the lore and folk life of Russia, a supernatural and frequently witch-like figure in fairy-tales and popular prints. Here she appears in a famous wood-block print (*lubok*) of the mid-eighteenth century.

for serfdom—'serf law' (*krepostnoe pravo*)—was distinctive precisely for the
absence of 'law' to regulate the mutual relations between squire and serf. In this
legal vacuum nobles could—and did—modify the obligations of serfs at will,
not to mention sell and relocate them. By the late eighteenth century Russian
'serfdom' bore less in common with Old World serfdom than with New World
slavery.

Some developments did, however, work in the serfs' favour. In purely economic terms, the poll-tax (set at 70 copecks per male soul in the first half of the
century) remained at the same level—notwithstanding the sharp inflation of
succeeding decades. In real terms, then, the material burden of the poll-tax
declined substantially. In addition, the natural growth of the population diminished the per capita burden of other obligations, especially recruitment, but also
such duties as portage and temporary road work. And, given the exigencies
of state service, many nobles had little opportunity to meddle in the daily lives
of their peasants. If a recent historian's findings for the village of Petrovskoe in
Tambov province are typical, or even widespread, some serfs exercised considerable collective control over their working and life routines.

Still, the second half of the eighteenth century marked a major deterioration
in serfs' legal status. Many squires, as we shall see, had strong incentives and
new opportunities to intercede in village life, encroach on its quotidian autonomy and assert new powers of regulation and control. Peasant communities,
moreover, had few legal mechanisms of resistance; no longer full-fledged subjects (ceasing, after 1741, to take an oath of allegiance to the sovereign), serfs—
in contrast to state peasants—did not even have the right to petition the
emperor. Except for serious crimes or disputes involving other estates, the landlord exercised virtual private-law authority on his estate. He had final authority over serf marriages, although as a practical matter these were typically

arranged by the peasant families and councils of elders. When an important piece of legislation filtered down to the locality it was often the landlord's responsibility to have it read aloud by the local priest, bailiff, or scribe. And, in moments of 'disobedience' and rebellion, the landlord could summon governmental authorities to send police or troops to restore order and punish the intransigent.

How did the serfs respond to all these changes? At one level, it seems unlikely that serfs were well informed about the law and its impact on what they deemed to be tradition. After all, serf communities had few contacts with anyone from the government and conducted their day-to-day relations mostly within their own institutions—the household and commune. Nor did they have much opportunity to become more familiar with the law: they could not legally file petitions and—in contrast to state peasants—did not participate in the Legislative Commission of 1767–8 (an experience that, especially through the preparation of 'instructions', raised the legal consciousness of other groups). Nevertheless, as the ethnographer M. M. Gromyko has argued, serfs probably had some familiarity with law and, with time, increasingly invoked decrees (real or bogus) in the defence of their rights and justice. A higher awareness of the outside world was particularly likely given the peasants' non-agrarian activities (especially for those who travelled regularly to towns to trade or work) and the geographic dispersion and intermixture of social categories, whereby the most diverse status groups—from serf to state peasant—lived in close proximity. It was, in short, no accident that in the 1770s and subsequent decades, serfs became increasingly restive and exhibited their own judgement on this consummately 'immoral economy'.

NOBILITY

Although the nobility stood at the apex of the social pyramid, with claims to pedigree and precedence, its status was uncertain and ambiguous. Significantly, the collective term for nobility, *dvorianstvo*, did not prevail until the mid-century and lacked precise meaning, much less a clear English-language equivalent. The Petrine Table of Ranks of 1722 compounded this confusion by creating a mechanism to elevate the meritorious to personal nobility and, if they rose high enough, to hereditary nobility. Whether of ancient lineage or parvenu, nobles enjoyed important and distinctive privileges, including exclusion from the onerous poll-tax and its attendant disabilities.

Nevertheless, until 1762 the nobility still owed service to the state, ordinarily in the military. As a practical matter, however, many evaded this obligation, a nonfeasance that actually increased—partly because of the quantum increase in service demands under Peter, partly because of the state's transparent inability to coerce compliance. Moreover, lifetime service took nobles away from their estates, transforming them into absentee landlords who were obliged to depend upon stewards (often peasant-born estate managers) to oversee day-to-day operations and to mediate social and economic relations with the peasants. Such management was not only expensive (diverting scarce labour from the field) but extremely inefficient and unreliable, riddled with graft and deception. Finally, service was financially onerous, even for middling and élite strata—especially the requirement that they maintain two or more residences (for which they received no specific compensation), including one in St Petersburg for the most successful.

Still, for the ambitious and well connected, cosmopolitan service was an absolute necessity, bringing not only status and power, but wealth as well. The nominal salaries, though niggardly for the lower and middle range of servitors, were quite substantial for the upper range of the Table of Ranks. And to that must be added the spoils of service, which, in this venality-ridden order, often far exceeded any legal income. Servitors could always dream of special imperial grants, and in fact rulers transferred over 100,000 peasants and millions of acres of arable land to private hands during the last half of the eighteenth century.

Such largesse was not only desirable but essential, for few nobles found their landed estates to be a source of substantial income. Above all, agricultural productivity lagged far behind that in Western Europe and showed little trace of the concurrent 'agricultural revolution'. Moreover, most nobles belonged to the category of petty landowners, with scanty resources and meagre incomes. The truly rich with more than 1,000 male souls comprised only about 1 per cent of the hereditary nobility; another 17 per cent (the 'middling nobility') owned between 100 and 1,000 male souls. Four out of five noble households owned fewer than 100 male souls, most having fewer than twenty, or even none at all.

Even for those with substantial numbers of serfs, the net return on their estates was uncertain and paltry. Above all, Russian agriculture—with its three-field system, primitive technology, and unfavourable climate—produced far less than the modernizing estates in the West. Peasants consumed the bulk of this scant output (with a diet exceeding 3,000 calories per day, including much protein, according to some research); and another 10 per cent of that was lost through spillage and spoilage. The net yield left little for squire and state.

Compounding agricultural inefficiency was the system of partible inheritance that negated 'economies of size'. Peter had attempted to impose a system of single inheritance in 1714, but the adverse reaction among nobles ultimately impelled Anna to rescind the law in 1731. Restored in full force, partible inheritance guaranteed real estate to all heirs, including widows, but doomed noble estates to endless division to the point where they ceased to be economically viable. Unless new resources could be secured, this system inevitably reduced a noble family to penury and virtual landlessness within a few generations. Moreover, even in the best of circumstances, estates were fragmented, with individual villages, meadows, lakes, and forests parcelled among several owners. This land 'system' gave rise to endless disputes and litigation (lasting decades, sometimes more than a century) over boundaries and ownership. Even when service (whether through grants or purchase) brought new property, the new lands were usually remote from the family estate and gave no opportunity to form a single, large estate.

Given this economy, families that had already achieved hereditary nobiliary status recognized the importance of retaining high standing on the Table of Ranks. Historians have demonstrated that, during the first four or five decades of its existence, old aristocratic families dominated the upper levels of the Table of Ranks and collectively prevented large numbers of parvenus from achieving hereditary noble status. A manifesto by Peter III on 18 February 1762, however, freed the nobility from obligatory service and significantly reshaped service patterns for the nobility. This famous decree, interestingly, has confounded historians as much as it did contemporaries: why did Peter III choose to 'emancipate' the nobles from service? After all, the fundamental pre-miss of the imperial system was an implicit social contract based on universal service: serfs toiled for nobles so that the latter could serve the state. Did the manifesto not nullify one of the principal moral foundations of serfdom? Where indeed was the state to recruit for civil servants and military officers if not from the nobility? And how, without service, were noble clans to remain economi-cally viable?

Although historians have not reached a consensus on these questions, most reject the old canard that the nobility collectively demanded its 'freedom' and that this 'concession' marked the beginning of a noble oligarchy. Nobles needed service, and service needed nobles—a fundamental symbiosis not to be changed by a mere paper manifesto. It is by no means clear that most nobles welcomed the change. Contemporary tales may have portrayed the roads from St Petersburg as clogged with nobles departing for their family estates, but—according to the few scholarly studies on the subject—most nobles still chose to serve, thereby avoiding the inevitable decline in their family fortunes.

Nevertheless, the manifesto did contribute to the formation of a new noble consciousness of its station in Russian society. The fact that the decision to serve now rested with them ('unto eternity and to all generations to come'), not with the monarch, seemed to reconstitute the hereditary nobility as a corporate body endowed, in the words of the manifesto, with 'freedom and liberty'.

But why did the state abolish the service requirement? Contemporary gossips speculated that the manifesto was merely concocted to cover a nocturnal dal-liance of Peter III and his mistress. More likely, the manifesto came from the emperor's personal secretary, D. V. Volkov, who wanted the Table of Ranks to serve state interests, not the nobility. In Volkov's view, the old élite clans had transformed the service ranks into a facsimile of the medieval system of prece-dence (*mestnichestvo*) based on birthright, thereby denying the state an oppor-tunity to recruit, promote, and reward the meritorious with rank, pay, ennoblement, and political influence. Thus the manifesto of 1762 endeavoured to separate service rank from social status, at once enabling the state to replenish its service class with outsiders and to accord a respectable alternative for those who chose not to serve.

State policy for the next two decades, which culminated in the Charter to the Nobility in 1785, sharpened the distinction between service (as a *voluntary* attribute of nobility) and privilege (as the temporal reward for this historic service). In the event, nobles obtained important and exclusive privileges: to own serfs, to register family patents and heraldry books with local governments, to convene provincial assemblies (which were to provide officials for local government), to appoint local judges, to be exempt from corporal punishment, to travel at home and abroad without special permission, and to ride about in carriages (a symbolic, but important gesture). Most concessions emphasized the provincial locus of noble status; they also provided symbolic and material venues outside the capital and the service system onto which the meaning of nobility could be inscribed.

Nobles also acquired new and weighty economic advantages. Above all, they had a legal monopoly on the ownership of servile labour: they alone could buy and sell serfs, with or without land; they could even break up serf families, send the unruly into hard labour (while deducting the deportees from recruit quotas), and wilfully increase feudal dues (as quitrent, corvée, or both). They could engage in any occupation or trade, and could also open manufactories to exploit the free labour of their serfs. For all these ventures they had exclusive access to cheap credit: they also had special access to the country's sparse credit reserves through long-term, low-interest (5–6 per cent) loans from the Noble Land Bank established in 1754.

The consequences of the new distinction between service and status were simultaneously momentous and disorienting. From the perspective of the 'police state', corporate privilege whetted the aspirations of an élite 'estate' now distinguished by its inalienable rights, not its duty to serve. Moreover, with the expansion of state administration, especially at the provincial level, nobles could now retire from the capitals, yet retain the trappings of privilege. Thus many were able to flaunt their status, indulge in conspicuous consumption beyond their means, and open clubs and lodges for their amusement and, on rare occasions, for the discussion of more serious matters.

Some, however, did devote themselves to the development of their estates. At a minimum, they sought to reorganize and manage their estates personally and more effectively—no small task given the diffuse landholding. An audacious few attempted to redesign rural life according to the latest 'scientific' methods, even issuing learned 'instructions' to their bailiffs on how to run their estates. Some also carried the injunction 'to administer justice to the peasants without prejudice or oppression' (in the words of a Soviet historian), but the main impulse was to regulate social and economic life on the estate—not unlike what the enlightened absolutist was attempting to do at a macro level.

Others, however, were only interested in their estate's output, not its operation, and preferred to give free rein to their poetic imaginations—organizing serf theatres or choruses, constructing English gardens or French waterfalls, and inventing local family festivals to celebrate the virtue and *bonhomie* of their enlightened paternal vision. Of course, many of these same people remained in service; their periodic visit to the family estate, now inscribed with a poetics of permanence and heritage (which belied the fluid, transitory realities of noble landownership), represented a naïve return to innocence.

Not without cause has Catherine's era been dubbed the 'golden age of the Russian nobility'. Never had they been so privileged, so economically advantaged, and so handsomely rewarded for doing so little. In exchange, however, they abdicated nearly all political pretensions. Although they might act on behalf of clan and patronage network, they did not mount a defence of their social estate. In part, that is because they had no need to be institutionally or politically active: they had done quite well *vis-à-vis* other groups—and without involving themselves collectively in politics or raising an ideological challenge to the autocracy. Hence the vaunted palace coups—which not only installed individual rulers but also resulted in the murder of two sitting monarchs (Peter III in 1762 and Paul I in 1801) and one former monarch (Ivan VI)—did not precipitate a constitutional crisis. At issue was only the person of the nominally all-powerful autocrat, not the system itself. As a result, the aggressive intrigue, the discourse about good rulers and polities, and the 'legislomania' of the second half of the eighteenth century rarely proceeded very far towards imposing formal limitations on rulership. Increasingly, the succession crisis of 1730 appeared as an aberration, not to be revisited until the Decembrist revolt of 1825.

All of these material advantages coexisted uneasily with a deepening moral discomfort among the service nobility over the legitimacy of their special privilege. Although most still served, they were no longer bound to do so. Educated and literary nobles freely invoked the language of freedom, rights, and virtue at the very moment when they legally became the sole group in Russian society with the right to hold fellow subjects in virtual slavery. The embryonic provincial assemblies and noble courts were a far cry from French *parlements* or the manor-based authority of the English peerage. Increasingly, the edifice of hereditary nobility rested upon the precarious

The domed ceiling in the hall of Tavrichesky (or Tauride) Palace, which Catherine the Great had built in St Petersburg for Grigorii Potemkin, her one-time lover and leading adviser on foreign policy.

Engraving of Ivan Antonovich (Ivan VI), the infant tsar who 'reigned' in 1740–1 until he was overthrown by a coup that brought Elizabeth to the throne. Blessed by God, enveloped by majesty and authority, and nurtured by maternal care, he nevertheless spent most of his life locked away in a tower.

claim of historic, ancestral service. This malaise did not, however, precipitate a full-fledged identity crisis during the eighteenth century; most nobles were anything but rootless and alienated. But the discomfort was real and unresolved, evoking a rare but important *cri de cœur* in the final decades of the century.

A Multinational Empire

From its very outset Russia had included diverse peoples and, as the boundaries of the state expanded, this multi-ethnic character became more pronounced. Coming to terms with these newly acquired ethnicities, cultures, and religions took on both administrative and symbolic importance for Elizabeth, Peter III, and Catherine II. Much of this expansion had been accomplished during the seventeenth century, with the incorporation of the vast Siberian expanses and much of Ukraine, followed by territorial gains in the Baltics and elsewhere during the reign of Peter the Great. But expansion was particularly marked during the reign of Catherine the Great, as the Russian Empire annexed most of Poland (through the three partitions), the Crimea and the northern Caucasus. In the process, the empire came to include large numbers of Poles, Jews, Tatars, and Caucasian peoples.

Recently, the demographic historian V. M. Kabuzan produced estimates of the ethnic distribution of the Russian Empire during the eighteenth century shown in the table.

ETHNIC GROUPINGS IN THE RUSSIAN EMPIRE, 1760s–1790s (IN MILLIONS)

	1760s	1780s	1790s
Total Population	23.55	36.59	41.17
Russian	14.67	18.08	20.12
Ukrainian	3.38	7.06	8.16
Belorussian	1.57	3.18	3.40
Poles	0.57	2.21	2.53
Lithuanians	0.0	0.54	0.82
Latvians	0.31	0.68	0.72
Moldavians	0.11	0.18	0.21
Germans	0.04	0.21	0.24
Jews	0.05	0.55	0.58
Estonians	0.39	0.47	0.48
Udmurts	0.09	0.11	0.13
Karelians	0.11	0.14	0.14
Komi	0.04	0.05	0.05
Mordvinians	0.22	0.28	0.35
Mari	0.01	0.12	0.15
Tatars	0.77	0.76	0.80
Bashkirs	0.14	0.15	0.19
Chuvash	0.28	0.33	0.35
Finns	0.63	0.78	0.90
Kalmyks	0.07	0.08	0.09
Swedes	0.08	0.11	0.13
Others	0.43	0.52	0.63

Source: V. M. Kabuzan, *Narody Rossii v XVIII veke. Chislennost'i etnicheskii sostav* (Moscow: Nauka, 1990), 230.

Although the government was committed to a model (perhaps 'illusion' is a more accurate description) of administrative uniformity, relations between St Petersburg and the outlying non-Russian populations varied considerably. In the case where local élites accommodated themselves to Russian rule, willingly swore allegiance to the monarch, and demonstrated their ability to run their territories by keeping order and supplying labour and revenue, these peoples retained considerable autonomy and saw their separate traditions, institutions, and social organizations remain largely intact. Unfortunately, most of the new subjects proved troublesome, either because they believed fiercely in their right to independence (as was true with Poland and the Crimean Tatars) or because they were deemed to be too alien to be trusted (as was the case with Jews in the former Polish territories).

Money, Finances, and Markets

Historians customarily portray the Russian economy as eternally backward, technologically primitive, and fundamentally unproductive. Although these characterizations are not entirely off the mark, they do not accurately characterize the Russian economy in the second half of the eighteenth century. On the contrary, the growth rates in Russia were then comparable to those in England—a remarkable fact given England's technical superiority and the onset of

Kalmuk housewife and girl. Tatar and Nagay Musicians. Two views of 'exotica'. These two pictures are drawings made for Peter Pallas, the German scientist and ethnographer, during his travels through the Russian Empire, undertaken on behalf of the Imperial Academy of Sciences in the 1770s. Several of these drawings were included in the published account of his travels, and they displayed for learned audiences in Russia and elsewhere, his impressions of the colourful ethnic varieties that he encountered.

its industrial expansion. Russia was a net exporter of numerous raw materials, not only the traditional forest products like timber and furs, but also such agricultural products as hemp, rye, and tallow (and—by some accounts—silver).

The domestic market also became more active and complex. Apart from the seasonal flow of peasants to towns (bringing wares, trade, and food), some areas of the empire provided a ready market for agricultural goods. That was true of cities in general, but especially the newly built capital, St Petersburg, which expanded from nothing to over a quarter of a million inhabitants by the end of the century. Because the surrounding soil was so marshy and infertile, St Petersburg had to plunge its supply lines deep into the empire, with the requisite network of canals and roads. Similar conditions obtained in the dense forest territories of northern Russia, where poor soil and adverse climate made agriculture marginally productive; as a result, the local population had to import food from the south, providing yet another stimulus to internal trade. The robust trade in agricultural products also fostered a proliferation in rural fairs, which expanded in number (from 383 per year in the 1750s to 3,180 in the 1790s), geographic breadth, and commodities exchanged. Although most fairs were seasonal and lasted only a few days, they had nevertheless become a mainstay of the rural economy.

The primary beneficiaries of expansion were the state and landlords, not the serfs. The former profited directly from a profound eighteenth-century 'price revolution', which, coming much later than similar inflation in Western Europe, brought a fourfold increase in the price of grain, hemp, flax, and textiles. This price revolution, moreover, impelled many landlords to transfer their serfs from quitrent to corvée dues. Whereas quitrent provided a regular monetary sum, corvée labour enabled the squire to increase the volume of his own production and hence profit from the rising prices on agricultural commodities. As a result, a historic shift took place in serfdom wherein peasants from the central black earth regions, heretofore working the land mostly on quitrent, were consigned increasingly to corvée, much to their dismay and resentment.

QUITRENT AND CORVÉE: SERF DUES

Years	Total seigneurial serfs (in millions)	Quitrent (%)	Corvée (%)
1701–10	2.9	55	45
1751–60	4.1	50	50
1791–1800	5.6	44	56

Source: B. N. Mironov, 'Vliianie revoliutsii tsen v Rossii XVIII veka na ee ekonomicheskoe i sotsial'no-politicheskoe razvitie', *Istoriia SSSR*, no. 1 (1991), 95.

An additional measure which greatly advantaged landlords was colonization. Catherine believed firmly in the mercantilist notion that population equalled wealth. She did all in her power to promote immigration to the empire, including inviting whole communities of religious dissenters, mostly Mennonites, to resettle from southern Germany to southern Russia. She also opened border-lands in the south-east (near Ufa and Orenburg) and south-west (in the territories north of the Black Sea known officially as 'New Russia') to nobles, granting vast tracts of land to those who resettled their serfs there. Apart from mercantilism, here the empress was also motivated by concerns of security: by settling large Russian populations on borderlands historically populated by Turkish peoples (mostly Bashkirs and Kalmyks), Tatars, and Cossacks, she hoped to domesticate these peoples and integrate them into the empire. Catherine further believed that the borderlands were ripe for agricultural exploitation. Endowed with fertile soil and favourable climate, this underpopu-lated region had remained untapped for centuries because their open plains made them difficult to defend and vulnerable to incursions from without.

By the late eighteenth century, however, the balance of power in the south had shifted from the indigenous populations in favour of the Russian state. Cossack hosts and tribal populations retained considerable autonomy and, in most instances, enjoyed exemption from conscription and the poll tax. But their service obligations as subject peoples were now firmly inscribed in law and prac-tice. None of them favoured the influx of Russian nobles and serfs, but, beyond verbal protests and occasional disturbances, they were powerless to resist. As a result, the vast rich expanse of the Black Sea basin was now opened for cultiva-tion. These lands generated higher yield, with seed grain ratios of 4:1 to 5:1 rather than the usual 3:1 in central Russia. A large portion of this output went to market and, because of the proximity to the Black Sea, for export. To handle this burgeoning trade, in 1794 Catherine founded the port city of Odessa, which within a few decades would become one of the largest cities in the empire.

These developments—the price revolution, the expansion of rural markets, the export of grain, and the increasing control over serf labour—proved a verit-able windfall for those nobles able to take advantage of them. According to one estimate, their profit from corvée rose from 36 copecks per male serf in 1710 to 10 roubles in 1800, a rate that far exceeded by sevenfold the general inflation rate. In practice, only a relatively large estate was able to exploit this opportu-nity, and that required a noble family to remain visible and acquire enough land so as to counteract the downward pressure of partible inheritance. Although some nobles succeeded, many others did not, widening further the stratification along the continuum of poor and rich noble.

Taken as a whole, Russia's eighteenth-century economy presented quite a paradox. On one hand, it could boast of burgeoning trade and markets, increased exports, rapid expansion of paper money, and very healthy growth rates. On the other hand, all of this led somehow to a wealthier and more priv-ileged nobility alongside a weaker, smaller, and less secure merchant status. The centre of gravity for wealth, social power, and even population stood far more firmly in the countryside in 1800 than it had a century earlier.

The Pugachev Rebellion

Probably the single greatest blow to the moral foundations of the existing order was the fateful decision by Peter III to free the nobility from service. The reciprocal principle of universal service—serfs serve the noble, the nobles serve the state—had provided the primary justification for serfdom; Peter the Great had said as much, as had every one of his successors. It was the tsar's will; and, as the Orthodox Church taught, God Himself demanded obedience to the tsar's will. But 'freeing' the nobles had abrogated this reciprocity. Here and there serfs circulated rumours that this was just the first step, that soon the tsar would free them as well. When this did not happen, and when Peter III was deposed shortly afterwards, these rumours were transmuted into a variant of the familiar pretender myth: Catherine II and her cohort were illegitimate (indeed, German!) usurpers, Peter III was not dead but had taken refuge with loyal Orthodox peasants until he could return triumphantly, reclaim his throne, and complete his emancipatory project. This myth spawned numerous pretenders during the 1760s and 1770s, some as far away as Silesia, Hungary, and the Urals, all claiming to be the true Peter.

The greatest challenge, however, came from a rebellion led by a fugitive Don Cossack, Emelian Pugachev, who waged intermittent campaigns against the state between 1772 and 1774. Like previous rebellions, this one drew principally on disaffected frontier Cossacks—in this case the Iaik Cossacks north of the Caspian Sea, who were fighting a lengthy and losing struggle to maintain autonomy from the imperial state. But the rebellion eventually attracted many other disaffected elements, producing the bloody *Pugachevshchina* that could only be suppressed by a full-scale military expedition.

Pugachev began to proclaim himself the avenging Peter III sometime in 1772 and assembled his own 'court', surrounding himself with confederates who renamed themselves after leading figures in the capital. This cadre of impersonators gathered a small contingent of Cossacks and fugitive 'possessionary' factory serfs and next proceeded to lay siege to Kazan and Orenburg. Success increased credibility and garnered new support; soon some of the Turkic peoples of the southern Volga (Kalmyks, Bashkirs, Kazakhs, and Tatars) joined the rebellion. In 1774 the conflagration spread to the mining settlements at the foot of the Urals, and Ekaterinburg found itself besieged.

Once the Russo-Turkish War ended in 1774, Catherine could now redeploy the returning regiments to deal with Pugachev. His forces were on the run, losing control of most of the towns they had earlier overwhelmed. But in midsummer of 1774 they crossed the Volga into territories populated mostly by Russian serfs. At one point Pugachev acquired a printing press and began to issue manifestos and decrees declaring the serfs free and ordering them to wreak vengeance against their 'former' masters. To the dismay of nobles and state officials, such radical appeals struck a sympathetic chord with many serfs, who seized lands, pillaged granaries and warehouses, and torched numerous manor-houses. Over 1,500 landlords were reported killed before the wave of violence was suppressed. What began as a frontier rebellion had turned into a dangerous peasant jacquerie.

Despite widespread support, Pugachev's forces were no match for the experienced military and suffered a decisive defeat in August 1774. A month later Pugachev was delivered to the authorities by erstwhile followers in the town of Iaitskii gorodok. At last the rebellion was over, and the perpetrators were shipped to Moscow where they were paraded in the streets in cages before being interrogated, tried, and executed. But troubling questions lingered. Never before had a Cossack revolt succeeded in rousing so many peasants. Did the serfs really believe that Pugachev was Peter, and did they genuinely think themselves free and empowered to act violently? Certainly this was their defence once the rebellion was crushed, but such claims were made by peasants desperately trying to minimize the state's retribution against them. Whatever the peasants actually thought, the whole episode showed that the myth of freedom 'in the name of the tsar' was sufficient to mobilize serfs for organized violence. Whether or not serfs looked upon their bondage as unjust in the wake of the 1762 manifesto is a matter of conjecture, but the mere fact that they acted as if they did introduced a new element into the political cosmology of the countryside: the incompatibility of justice and serfdom now that universal service was no more.

Emelian Pugachev, leader of the rebellion of 1771–4, being led away in a cage after his capture. This print was one of several circulated widely to show Pugachev as little more than an animal, subdued and captured by the power of the state.

From Rebellion to Reform

Although the *Pugachevshchina* was the last great Cossack-led rebellion, it forced Catherine to recognize the dangers of 'under-government' at the provincial level. Leaving administration largely to local landlords may have sufficed in peaceful times, but Pugachev's activities coincided with a war that forced many landlords to resume their careers in uniform and thus leave provincial service. In the absence of full-time civil administrations, whole regions found themselves virtually bereft of governmental personnel, a vacuum that allowed the popular violence to spread uncontrolled. In response, Catherine decided upon a major restructuring of provincial government, a process that culminated in the Statute on Provincial Administration in 1775 and the Law on Provincial Police (*blagochinie*) in 1782.

These two reforms expanded the number of provincial governments from eight to thirty-five (later the number rose to fifty), each having a population between 300,000 and 400,000 souls. Each provincial capital had a full-time and salaried civil staff headed by a governor, who was appointed personally by the sovereign and given a large salary and high grade on the Table of Ranks. In addition, there was to be a commander-in-chief, appointed by the Senate, with responsibility for maintaining order. Courts and judgeships were established, and responsibility for staffing them was shared by the central authorities and the local nobility. Charity, education, wardship, and the like fell under the aegis of a newly established body called the Board of Public Welfare, an agency headed by the governor but managed by representatives from the local élites.

The Law on Provincial Police nominally established local police offices and empowered them to maintain order, keep track of religious minorities and schismatics, and oversee local publishing. But in practice these responsibilities, like many of the provisions in the 1775 Statute, were honoured mostly in the breach, at least during the eighteenth century; hence serious investigations typically had to be handled by other agencies. Nevertheless, the two statutes had the combined effect of establishing a civil presence sufficient to prevent local disturbances from getting out of control. By the minimalist standards of Russian government in the eighteenth century, this was one definition of success.

The Church, Dissenters, and Popular Religion

With the sequestration of church lands and peasants in 1764, Catherine severely limited the Church's resources and capacity to address its various problems. However, the 'Common on Church Properties' provided a modest budget for ecclesiastical administration and some funds for monasteries (many of which, however, were abolished as redundant and 'useless'). But that budget contained no funds to provide proper support for the parish churches and their staffs. Given the lack of endowments, benefices, or tithes, parish clergy had to support themselves primarily by cultivating the plot of parish church land and by exacting gratuities for various religious rites (for example, baptism, weddings, and burials). Significantly, the parish as an institution was also losing its centrality in daily life: it did not form a lower unit of civil administration, had indeed no juridical status in state law, and even lost some of its traditional functions as the commercial and cultural vortex of the community.

At the same time, parish clergy underwent far-reaching changes in their status and training. The Spiritual Regulations of 1721 had required them to be educated, to know Feofan Prokopovich's catechism, to read laws and important notices to the parishioners, and to maintain accurate parish registries of births, deaths, and marriages. As ever, imperial fiat was slow to become everyday fact, but in the second half of the century parish clergy did in fact find it necessary to fulfil these various mandates. Perhaps the most significant change pertained to formal education: from the 1740s the Church gradually erected a network of diocesan seminaries where, increasingly, the clergy's sons were forced to enroll—on pain of exclusion from the clergy and even conscription into the army. It took time, of course, to construct a seminary system based on the Latin curriculum of Jesuit schools, but by the mid-1780s nearly every diocese had established such a seminary, with advanced classes in philosophy and theology. Few students completed the course of study, however, and most departed at the first opportunity to fill a vacant clerical position in their home region. Nevertheless, ecclesiastical élites—above all, the 'learned episcopate' and isolated members of the parish clergy—did master the curriculum and, on the basis of their education, held the top positions in church administration.

For most rural clergy, however, a schooling based on rote memory and Latin curriculum was irrelevant to the service in a village church. Although church leaders recognized the shortcomings of the new seminary, they remained staunch adherents of the classical curriculum, chiefly because it provided a symbolic link to a sacred antiquity and placed the clerical élite on the same level as learned savants in the West. But the classical curriculum crowded out instruction in subjects essential for rural clergy, such as homiletics, the teachings of church fathers, and dogmatic theology. Equally startling was the scanty instruction in civil Russian. In the wake of Peter the Great's language reforms, Church Slavonic was increasingly remote from the civil Russian of official documents and cosmopolitan society—a significant handicap in the light of the extensive secular duties ascribed to parish priests. Not until the 1780s did the Church attempt to rectify the deficiency by introducing parallel literacy instruction in Slavonic and civil Russian, and by offering specifically 'Russian classes' (*russkie shkoly*) in the seminaries.

Hamstrung by these material and cultural deficiencies, the Church found itself ill-equipped to combat the spiritual deficiencies of its flock. Despite the claims to be 'Holy Rus', the clergy knew that they faced formidable problems among the nominally Orthodox. These included not only simple superstition and ignorance, but far more deep-rooted problems—such as shamanism, worship of nature or ancestors, and deviant interpretations of basic Orthodox doctrines (for example, the Trinity, the resurrection, and the annunciation). The line between popular Orthodoxy and heresy remained blurry and shifting; its rank-and-file parish clergy had neither the training, nor the independence, nor the incentive to make the mass of illiterate peasants into self-conscious Orthodox believers.

Moreover, the Church faced a formidable adversary in the 'Old Belief'. Indeed, the threat of dissent increased, not least because the state had assumed a far more tolerant attitude towards Old Believer communities. The new policy permitted many Old Believers to return from distant borderlands to central Russia, even within a relatively short distance from Moscow itself. More distant Old Believer strongholds, such as those of Vyg and Klintsy, maintained close contact with their brethren across the realm, often circulating manuscripts and printed books to sustain the Old Belief. Compared to most peasants, the Old Believers could boast of a higher rate of literacy and also had a sharper grasp of their basic beliefs. They were thus a serious threat to the Church and its uncertain flock of believers.

Enlightenment and Élite Culture

Compared to the problems of the Old Belief and popular religion, the cosmopolitan Enlightenment represented a matter of relatively minor concern for Church and State. Indeed, Catherine the Great herself was a principal progenitor and propagandist of Enlightenment ideas. Drawing upon the Petrine tradition, but also relying almost verbatim on the works of contemporary European writers, Catherine adumbrated a full-blown theory of enlightened absolutism, one which combined a faith in reason and reform with a recognition of the absolute authority of the monarch. These principles reached their apotheosis in the 'Great Instruction' (*Bol'shoi nakaz*) that she prepared in advance for the Legislative Commission (1767–8). It was a most remarkable document, one that began by proclaiming Russia to be both a European and absolutist state, but followed with prolix chapters replete with references to reason, rights, tolerance, and happiness.

Her 'Great Instruction' was not, of course, the only product of the Russian Enlightenment. Indeed, such sentiments and values came to pervade the service élite—newly educated, mostly noble in origin, who imagined themselves to be European gentlemen (and women), moral, fashionable, and literary. Their new cultural world conferred great privilege and honour on the printed word, reading, and writing. It identified France's 'Republic of Letters' as the model of choice, the *philosophe* as the preferred (if postured) identity.

The first secular men of letters—Vasilii Trediakovskii, Antiokh Kantemir, Alexander Sumarokov, and Mikhail Lomonosov—received their education before mid-century, either at the newly established academies for military cadets or at seminaries for prospective priests. Each proved to be a prolific essayist, poet, and translator; each endeavoured to preside over the emergent secular print culture housed at the Academy of Sciences. During the 1750s, however, élite secondary education underwent a significant transformation; it now placed far greater emphasis on modern languages, *belles-lettres*, and gentlemanly pursuits (fencing, dancing, parade-ground assembly)—all at the expense of narrowly technical subjects. Equally important was the establishment of Moscow University in 1755 (Russia's first), with its affiliated secondary boarding-schools (*pansiony*) in Moscow and Kazan.

For the next two generations Moscow University and, especially, its two boarding-schools, would train cohorts of literati who would subsequently establish the main translation societies, journals, and printing presses. Although they received little or no income for their literary endeavours, these first intellectuals devoted at least as much time to their cultural activities as to service and, indeed, saw these activities as a proper extension of their official duties. Their cultural engagement was facilitated by the reduced demands of state service: commissioned officers had few daily responsibilities in peacetime, those in administration rarely had to work more than three or four mornings a week. Favoured with such leisure, the young literati embraced the world of letters, expanding the annual number of publications from under 100 in the 1740s to about 500 in the late 1780s. They created a new genre of literary and polemical journalism, an enterprise that, by the 1770s, was producing two or three new periodicals a year. Most literary journals had tiny press runs (rarely more than a few hundred copies per issue) and often failed after just a few issues. Nevertheless, others quickly took their place, keeping the spirit of creation and engagement alive.

Indeed, journals and publishing circles were the principal foci of secular intellectual activity. As such, they were decidedly noble (dominated by service nobles) and cosmopolitan, housed either in Moscow or St Petersburg. Their audiences, predictably, were also urban and noble; for example, over three-quarters of all subscribers to journals were members of the hereditary nobility. Book readers were less likely to subscribe (hence register their status), but here too the vast majority came from the nobility.

Significantly, the new cultural activity gradually moved intellectual life towards autonomy from state and monarch. Court patronage did remain as an essential feature of literary and cultural life; until 1783, for instance, nearly all secular publications came from institutional presses, mainly the typographies at the Academy of Sciences and Moscow University. Increasingly, however, these presses left editorial decisions to the literati themselves, for they printed most manuscripts with few changes, especially if the author or translator helped pay the bill. Even this modicum of control vanished in 1783, when Catherine gave private individuals the right to own presses without prior approval.

That decree effectively neutralized the monarch's ability to direct and control literature, not because of any ideological conflict, but because writers could now pursue literature independently of the government. In large measure the literati gained this autonomy precisely because they had not posed a threat to

Medal commemorating Catherine the Great being innoculated against smallpox, 1768. Catherine had several such medals disseminated in order to convince others to follow her example. Notice the blending of imperial and maternal imagery in these coins.

the existing structures of authority, whether formal or informal. In fact, the vast majority of writers shared Catherine's enlightenment vision of the state as the principal agent of improvement and moral direction; few raised basic questions about the existing social order. All concurred with the empress that Russia was part of Europe, that reinforcing this affinity served the best interests of the fatherland and individual. Some dissented, it is true. Most notably, the great journalist and publisher Nikolai Novikov railed against mindless slavishness towards French fashion ('Voltairianism') and launched major publication ventures, such as the *Drevniaia rossiiskaia vivliofika* ('Ancient Russian Library') in twenty volumes, to celebrate Russia's own antiquity and traditional culture. But even he devoted immense attention to translations and adaptations from contemporary French and English letters. For example, the so-called satirical journals of 1769–74 (*The Painter, The Drone, Bits of This and That*, and others) included pieces purloined directly from Joseph Addison's *Spectator*.

During the 1770s and 1780s, however, the initial concord between writers and empress gradually deteriorated, largely over such issues as French influence and political virtue. Some traditionalist voices, such as M. M. Shcherbatov's *On the Corruption of Morals in Russia*, castigated a purported decline of public virtue and respect for fatherland. Others, as in Denis Fonvizin's play *The Minor*, raised subtle questions about the erosion of virtue in political leadership. This critical strain reached its most radical expression in the—legal—printing of Alexander Radishchev's *Journey From St Petersburg to Moscow* (1790), a scathing attack on Catherine and the Russian social order, serfdom included. The tome outraged the empress, who penned furious rebukes in the margins of her copy, ordered all available copies destroyed, and subjected the author to trial and banishment into Siberian exile.

Radishchev's views were quite exceptional, however. Far more common were the moral and spiritualist misgivings that pulsated in the Masonic lodges, especially those of the Moscow Rosicrucians around Novikov and his spiritual overseer, Johann Schwartz, a Rosicrucian from Berlin. During the 1780s the Moscow Rosicrucians grew increasingly distressed over the spiritual and religious decline of cosmopolitan Russia, the soulless fashionability, and the frivolity that (in their view) permeated élite society. Novikov himself was a major purveyor of the Encyclopaedist Enlightenment and entertaining literature, but his lodge steadily moved away from the celebration of amusement. Even signs of political engagement can be discerned; in 1785, for example, some Rosicrucians developed connections to the court 'party' around the Tsarevich Paul; some even entertained the idea of making him emperor before his mother's death—apparently on the basis of (false) rumours that Paul was more sympathetic to their moral agenda. Whatever the case, the affinity between Rosicrucianism, Paul, free publishing, and geographic distance aroused growing distrust among Catherine's officials, with a steady chilling in the relations between ruler and writers.

The chill had consequences. In 1785, because of the flirtation with Paul and the publication of religious materials (still a monopoly of the Orthodox Church), the state launched a formal investigation of Novikov's publications that ended in a mild reprimand. Two years later Catherine ordered an empire-wide raid of book stores to impound dangerous, seditious titles. By the early 1790s, once the violent anti-monarchism of the French Revolution had become a disturbing reality, Catherine (and later her successor, Paul) erected a harsh and repressive censorship, greatly restricting the import of foreign books (banned entirely for a few months in 1800), imprisoning eminent figures such as Novikov, and ultimately closing most private presses. By 1800 publishing had declined to a trickle; literary journalism had all but disappeared; and the international book trade was virtually nil. Although recovery came quickly after the new Emperor Alexander I (1801–25) eased restrictions, state and letters now constituted two separate spheres, with only coercive censorship—not common values—providing the old link between them.

Reign of Paul (1796–1801)

Catherine the Great succumbed to a stroke on 17 November 1796. Her final years were marked by bitterness and political repression, but without any fundamental retreat from the tenets of enlightened absolutism. Her love-affairs, always semi-public, took on the aura of scandal, while unpopular favourites such as Platon Zubov garnered unwonted influence on public policy. The legislative fervour of her earlier reign was gone, and Catherine's self-construction as a reforming ruler could not adjust to the new political antinomies of revolution and legitimacy. Her son, Paul I, shared none of her commitments to reform and progress; indeed, most accounts describe him as being openly hostile to his mother and everything that she stood for. His five-year reign saw the enactment of numerous decrees that distanced Paul from the powerful families at court, and ultimately turned them against him. His most noteworthy act was to decree, in 1797, that serfs could be forced to work no more than three days per week of corvée—a nominal attempt to curb abuses that had seen some landlords forcing their peasants to work five or six days on estate lands, leaving very little time for them to work on their own fields. This decree apparently had little effect on actual practice, but it deepened the gulf between Paul and his magnates. The unpopular repression of literati and some political figures, as well as the less than successful direction of Russia's initial clashes with Napoleon, convinced leading court parties that Paul had to be removed. With the tacit agreement of his son and successor, the future Alexander I, a small conspiracy of military leaders and Masonic lodge members arrested and quickly murdered Paul in the bedroom of the newly constructed Michael Castle, on the night of 11 March 1801.

In many respects, the preceding decades had fulfilled the agenda of the Petrine era and set a new one for the nineteenth century. Thus Peter still cast a long shadow over the entire eighteenth century: so much that Peter had decreed but had been unable to implement actually came into existence in the decades that followed his reign. In that sense, his successors not only claimed lineage to Peter to legitimize their power, but also attempted to realize (if in modified form) his ambitions. Much else, however, was new—the changes in noble status, the territorial gains in the south, and the far-reaching acculturation of élites in the two capitals. At the same time, many other issues were still unresolved, most notably the powder keg of serfdom and the role of the Westernized nobility. These and other problems would be the centre of attention in the coming decades of the nineteenth century.

PRE-REFORM RUSSIA
1801–1855

DAVID L. RANSEL

The regime began the century in a reformist spirit and met the challenge of the Napoleonic invasion, but thereafter abjured far-reaching reform and, especially, the emulation of Western models. By the 1850s it faced a disaffected élite at home and, as the Crimean War demonstrated, could no longer compete militarily with the European great powers.

IF the murder of Tsar Paul in 1801 brought instant relief to the political élite of Russia, it did not have the same healthy effect on the new ruler, Alexander I, son of the murdered tsar. Alexander was himself a conspirator, for he had authorized the overthrow of his father, if not his assassination, and the new tsar initially expressed despair about the killing, feelings of incompetence about ruling, and stark fear that he too might be killed. The recent series of executions and overturns of European rulers had made royalty insecure everywhere in Europe. And Russia had its own tradition of rebellion, including at least nine violent changes of regime in the preceding 120 years. Alexander was understandably concerned not to offend powerful persons at court or in the armed forces. His fears may have deterred him from articulating any plan of political action other than a vague promise to rule in the manner of his grandmother Catherine the Great, whom most nobles remembered fondly for her readiness to protect their interests. The new ruler's failure to establish a clear political or social programme encouraged groups within the political élite to work out their own proposals for change.

Early Efforts at Reform

The first concern of governing élites was to establish a framework of legality, by which they meant protection of the person and property of nobles. Tsar Paul had assaulted their security time and again. Beyond this, the leadership understood that Russia's administrative and social institutions needed reform. During the eighteenth century, most Russian nobles had become Europeanized and the best educated among them regarded themselves as members of a wider European society. They could not remain unaffected by the revolutionary changes occurring in Europe and the challenge these changes presented to the dynastic and feudalist regime that they led. Opinions about how best to meet that challenge coalesced in three groups at court.

Initially the most important was the group near Alexander who had plotted and carried out the overthrow and assassination of Tsar Paul. The principal leaders were a military man Count Peter Pahlen and a civil servant Nikita Panin. They hoped to impose constitutional limitations on tsarist power and may even have obtained Alexander's agreement to such a reform before the *coup d'état*. Their aim was to prevent a recurrence of the despotism that they had just ended. At first, Alexander appeared to be frightened of these men, fearful perhaps that if he did not do their bidding, they would turn on him as they had on his father. To counter their influence he summoned to St Petersburg friends from his youth in whom he had more confidence. This group of advisers became known as Alexander's 'young friends' or 'the unofficial committee'.

The young friends included men who had grown up with Alexander, or associates of these men. Unlike Alexander, all of them had spent time abroad and acquired a comparative measure of Russia's development. They were well aware of Russia's need for administrative and social reform if the country were to compete successfully with the Western powers. Among the young friends were Adam Czartoryski, a Polish aristocrat and later acting Minister of Foreign Affairs for Alexander, Pavel Stroganov, a mathematician who had studied in Switzerland and in France and had joined a Jacobin club in Paris, Viktor Kochubei, another well-educated member of the Russian upper class and for most of the 1790s Russian envoy to the Ottoman government, and Nikolai Novosiltsev, at 40 the oldest of the 'young friends', scion of a large landholding family, and a cousin of Pavel Stroganov. In contrast to the other political groupings, these men were not interested in placing restrictions on the power of the monarch but in using his supreme authority to bring Russia closer, socially and economically, to the West. This meant promoting economic development under an enterprising middle class and doing something about serfdom, which these men considered a disgrace and an anachronism. Such aims prompted worried conservatives to refer to these advisers as the 'Jacobin gang'.

With the support of his 'young friends' and his increasing popularity with the public (the result of a series of decrees overturning his father's despotic rules affecting the nobility and the armed forces) Alexander soon began to feel more secure on the throne, sufficiently so to dispatch the assassins. Within two months of the *coup d'état*, he forced Pahlen to retire to his estates in the Baltic region and, a few months later, ordered Panin into internal exile as well.

A third group with which the new ruler had to contend was the 'old men' of the Senate. The Senate was Russia's highest administrative and judicial institution and the seat of the leading noble families. During the reign of Catherine II, senators had opposed constitutional projects and relied upon the favour of the empress and their own command of slow-acting collegial institutions to keep policy under their control and to protect their interests. In not following the constitutionalists of their own time, they sacrificed the opportunity to institutionalize the legislative process and thus lost the chance to make law something other than the mere declaration of the monarch's will, whether expressed orally or in writing. This choice left them defenceless against Paul, who saw the leading institutions as an obstacle to Russia's moral and social regeneration. Now the old men of the Senate at last understood the importance of constitutionalism and proposed new powers for the Senate, including rights to represent the public, propose taxes, nominate candidates for high administrative posts, co-opt new members of the Senate, and to question tsarist decrees not in conformity with established law or practice (a right of remonstrance similar to that of the French *parlement*). This programme of conservative constitutionalism, which aimed at limiting abuse of power by the sovereign and protecting the political and economic position of the high nobility, encountered stiff opposition from both the 'young friends' (who saw it as a barrier to social reforms)

Those who met Alexander I commented on his charm and handsomeness. Here is a well-known portrait of him, executed by Baron Gérard.

and the bureaucratic conservatives (who regarded it as a recipe for governmental paralysis of the kind that led to the revolution in France).

The best that the 'old men' of the Senate could obtain was the right to receive reports from top government departments and the right of remonstrance, both of which were announced in a decree on the reform of the Senate in September 1802. The more important, at least potentially, was the right of remonstrance; but it proved hollow: the first time the senators invoked this right, Alexander berated them for their effrontery and abruptly withdrew it. At issue was a decree about military service that violated earlier pronouncements about the nobility's freedom from required service (first issued in 1762 and renewed in 1785). The Senate initially agreed to the decree but then impulsively decided to oppose it. The procurator general (administrative head of the Senate), though favouring a larger constitutional role for that body, disagreed with its action and urged Alexander to reject it. Alexander himself treated the whole process with contempt. One might well ask what kind of basic rights the tsar would recognize if he was willing to grant and withdraw them on a whim. As for the rest, no one seemed to be aware that an important principle of government was at stake; this episode seemed to show that Russian leaders had no understanding of what legal order was.

The rejection of the Senate's demands was a sign that constitutional reform was not on the agenda, despite the rhetoric of the emperor and his associates. The Senate would have had to be a key institution in such a reform but, instead of gaining in stature, it quickly descended to an institution of secondary importance. Its administrative leadership was supplanted by government ministries, established in 1802 to replace Peter's collegial boards. The Senate was left as merely the highest appellate court of the land.

If reform was to occur, it had to be limited to changes in social and economic relationships and not touch the political order. Here the role of the 'young friends' was important. Above all, they wanted change in Russian serfdom. The impulse was not new with them: Catherine the Great had intimated eventual abolition of the serf order in Russia thirty-five years earlier in her 'Instruction to the Legislative Commission of 1767'. Her son Paul took the first step towards regulating relations between serfs and masters in an edict limiting corvée labour (*barshchina*) to three days a week (1797). Alexander and his young friends supported such reform, spoke of the need to abolish serfdom, but in the final analysis proposed small changes that did not threaten the established social order. They imposed a ban on the advertisement of serfs for sale and issued a law on Free Cultivators (1803), whereby landlords—with the approval of the emperor—could free whole villages of serfs on the basis of agreements negotiated with the peasants. But this transaction, which required the voluntary participation of the landlord and payments on the part of the peasants, resulted in fewer than 50,000 manumissions by the end of the reign—an infinitesimal percentage of the tens of millions of serfs. Somewhat greater progress was made in the Baltic provinces of Estland, Lifland, and Kurland, where local nobles agreed to regulate serf obligations and grant the peasants rights to their lands. These were steps towards what would be a full-scale emancipation of the serfs in the Baltic provinces in the years 1816–18.

An important initiative early in Alexander's reign came in the field of higher education. Although the Russian Empire boasted universities at Moscow, Dorpat, and Vilnius, only the first of these educated predominantly Russian students (the other two served, respectively, German and Polish constituencies). To these, Alexander added three new universities (Kharkov, Kazan, and St Petersburg, the founding of the last delayed until 1819) on the basis of equality of admissions without regard to class status. It was hoped that the universities would train the public servants so badly needed by the Russian government. A continuing concern of the ruling élite throughout the first half of the nineteenth century was the inadequate supply of talented administrators and consequent frustration of government action either by an absence of qualified personnel or by corrupt practices of ill-educated and undisciplined officials. The educational institutions founded by Alexander and their expansion during subsequent reigns went far towards supplying trained people for administration.

Missing from the court and high politics of Alexander's reign was the participation of women, a dimension of Russian politics prominent in the eighteenth century. The sole exception was imperial charity, which included the largest foundling homes in Europe, hospitals, schools, huge manufacturing operations and banking institutions—all were managed efficiently and lovingly by Paul's wife, Empress Maria Fedorovna, until her death in the late 1820s. Except for this traditional female concern, women lost their former prominent place in government; Paul's succession law of 1797 specifically excluded women from rulership until all male heirs from all collateral lines of the imperial family had died off. The change coincided with a shift in the mores of the society and court towards a reinforcement of the domesticity of élite women, stressing their role in early child-rearing and intimate family social life, in contrast to politics and court entertainment. Princess Ekaterina Dashkova, who served during Catherine II's reign as director of both the Russian Academy and the Imperial Academy of Sciences, justifiably complained of the misogyny of Alexander's court and the diminished place of women in Russian society more generally. Henceforth, the importance of women in Russian politics, apart from the symbolic roles of women in the imperial family, would be in individual acts of protest and in movements of opposition to the established order.

International Affairs

Although the reforming impulse at the Russian court did not die out after 1803, it had to give way for a time to the government's concern with international affairs. Peter the Great's conquests in the early eighteenth century had brought Russia into the European state system; the ensuing wars and alliances showed Russia to be an intimate partner in the balances and conflicts of the system. The country could not stand apart from the upheaval now being caused in the European state system by Napoleonic France's wide-ranging conquests, re-arrangements of national borders, and dominance of continental policy.

At first, Alexander merely put a close to the wildly fluctuating policies of his father, who had begun his reign as an enemy of France and ended it as France's ally against England. Alexander recalled an expeditionary force his father had

This contemporary English cartoon captures the spirit of the Treaties of Tilsit. Napoleon's aggressive move into East Central Europe reduced Prussia to a fraction of its previous size and forced on Russia a revived Poland, known as the Duchy of Warsaw, recognition of Napoleon's new order in Europe, and support for the Continental Blockade against England. Europeans could well imagine the crowns falling from the heads of the continent's dynastic rulers.

THE IMPERIAL EMBRACE on the _ Raft _ or Boneys New Drop.

sent to conquer British territories in India and composed other differences with Great Britain so that the mutually beneficial trade between the two countries could resume. In 1803, when hostilities reignited between France and Great Britain, Alexander hoped to be able to act as a peacemaker and tried above all to restrain Napoleon's expansionist policies. Relations between Russia and France took a sharp turn for the worse in 1804 when Napoleon seized the duc d'Enghien from a neighbouring neutral country and had him summarily executed for plotting the overthrow of the French government. Alexander's protest at the execution was met with contempt from Napoleon. Soon after, Russia joined a new coalition against Napoleonic France, which led to war the following year and a major defeat of Austrian and Russian forces at Austerlitz. After further defeats in 1806, abandonment by his allies, and the opening of hostilities between Russia and the Ottoman Empire, Alexander saw no option but withdrawal from the war largely on terms dictated from Napoleon in the summer of 1807 at Tilsit, a town on the Niemen river in Poland. The famous accords signed at Tilsit had the practical effect of dividing Europe between France and Russia and also committed Russia to adhere to the continental blockade through which France hoped to undermine British commerce and finances.

Mikhail Speranskii's Reforms

Concern about the inadequacies of the Russian political order continued. Alexander seemed to see the problem as essentially one of personnel, a shortage of honest and effective administrators. Others, however, recognized the need as well for structural changes. One of these was Mikhail Speranskii, a priest's son, who rose from humble origins to the pinnacle of Russian government. A brilliant seminary student and teacher, he became secretary to a highly placed aristocrat, served in the Ministry of Internal Affairs early in Alexander's reign, and by 1808 had risen to the position of State Secretary, the leading official for domestic affairs. No less than Alexander, Speranskii lamented the deficiencies of Russian officials and convinced the tsar to introduce exams for promotion to senior government ranks, a step that did not endear him to the many noble officials who had gained their positions through patronage and without the necessary educational and technical qualifications. Speranskii also proposed legal and financial reforms and achieved some success in stabilizing the currency and increasing tax revenues. His financial measures included a temporary tax on the nobility, which, again, won him no friends among that important class.

The most sweeping changes proposed by Speranskii touched political and administrative organization and included a plan for the separation of powers patterned on Montesquieu's ideas. He proposed to divide the Senate into separate administrative and judicial hierarchies and to create a third branch of government, the legislative, with an assembly elected on a narrow franchise. The entire system was to be capped by a cabinet headed by the emperor and called the State Council. Although Speranskii undoubtedly had won the emperor's agreement to pursue such a project, Alexander ultimately refused to approve major changes and implemented only the plan for the State Council, which was established in 1810 together with a reorganization of government ministries. By this time, the clouds of war were again gathering as Napoleon prepared the invasion of Russia. Whether or not Alexander was inclined to additional government reforms, this was not the time to launch a political experiment that could have compromised lines of authority. Moreover, Speranskii was unpopular with the nobility because of his crack-down on incompetence and support of financial policies harmful to noble interests. The nobility supplied Russia's military leadership and officer corps, and to solidify support for the regime in the face of the impending challenge, Alexander sacrificed Speranskii's policies and indeed Speranskii himself, whom he exiled to Siberia on trumped-up charges just before the invasion by Napoleon's armies.

Napoleon's Invasion

Napoleon's *Grande Armée* entered Russia in June 1812. Its forces numbered nearly half a million, almost twice the strength of the Russian army. However, only half the invading army was French, the rest being composed of troops from countries conquered by Napoleon, which were less than reliable instruments for the pursuit of French aims. The size of Napoleon's army also presented grave problems of supply, especially after the Russian generals decided to withdraw deep into the country while stripping away supplies and housing in the path of Napoleon's advance. Napoleon had hoped to destroy the Russian army in the western borderlands or, if they chose not to fight near the border, to corner them at the first great fortress city of Smolensk, where he was certain they would make a stand. He miscalculated. The Russians mounted a spirited but brief defence of Smolensk, withdrawing after just two days and burning the city as they left. Russian generals, particularly Mikhail Kutuzov, to whom Alexander gave command after the fall of Smolensk, had learned in earlier encounters with the French that they could not expect to win a pitched battle against Napoleon's superior leadership and disciplined troops. Their hope lay in the exhaustion of the *Grande Armée* as failing supplies and disease steadily reduced its numbers, morale, and fitness. Alexander courageously supported this strategy despite its unpopularity with a large segment of influential opinion and mounting, sometimes vicious, criticism of his national leadership.

The Russians could not surrender Moscow without a fight and decided to make a stand at Borodino, a village in the western reaches of Moscow province. This epochal battle proved costly for both sides, but especially so for the French, who could not replace their losses at Borodino—nearly one-third of the remain-

ing able-bodied men. Although the Russians pulled back (to save what remained of their army) and left open the road to Moscow, Napoleon's occupation of the ancient capital brought no resolution to the conflict. Moreover, as Napoleon reached the heights above the city's western outskirts and waited for the 'boyars' to greet him in submission, he saw not a delegation of the defeated but ominous veins of smoke rising from many points in the city, signs of the fires set by retreating Muscovites that would rage for nearly a week and leave much of the capital in ruins. It was the middle of September by the time Napoleon entered Moscow, a devastated city without adequate shelter for his troops; foraging parties sent out of the town encountered fire from Russian troops, and the Russian winter was soon to close in. Alexander steadfastly refused to negotiate. The hopelessness of the French position was apparent.

The Approach to Borodino.

151

Louis Lejeune (1775–1848), who travelled with the French army during its invasion of Russia, produced this panoramic view of the great battle of Borodino. Though technically a French victory (the Russian army withdrew), Borodino is regarded as a turning point in the war. The Russians delivered a crippling blow to the *Grand Armée*.

A month after its arrival, the *Grande Armée* departed from Moscow, moving out towards the south in the hopes of retreating through a region untouched by the Russian scorched-earth policy. But Russian forces met the invaders at Maloiaroslavets and forced them back onto the path of destruction by which they had entered the country, helping to turn what might have been an orderly withdrawal into an increasingly desperate and disorganized flight. Russian partisans harried Napoleonic forces and picked off stragglers the entire way. Napoleon himself abandoned the army to its fate and made a dash for France to raise new forces. Only about 10 per cent of the original invading army was able to escape from Russia in good order. The end of the Napoleonic empire in Europe was in sight. Alexander, emotionally lifted by the great victory and inspired by a wartime religious conversion, prepared to play a leading role in creating a new order for Europe.

A view of Moscow ablaze in the first week of the French occupation. The picture, an engraving based on a painting by d'Oldendorf, shows French soldiers moving along the Moscow river embankment toward the Kremlin.

After the War

The post-Napoleonic settlement for the European world associated with the name of the Congress of Vienna created a long period of general peace for the continent despite continuing stormy calls for democracy and national self-determination and the occasional limited conflicts they generated. The new state system, often mistakenly labelled a balance of power, was in reality a set of interlocking hegemonies exercised by Russia, Great Britain, and Austria. As long as the governments of these countries were able to maintain amicable relations, no major conflicts arose in Europe or its dependencies. Towards the end of Alexander's reign, the principles of the system—the legitimacy of established governments and territorial integrity of existing countries—were tested by the rebellion of Greeks within the Ottoman Empire. Many Russians were sympathetic to the Greek cause. Catherine the Great had even worked out a plan in her time to resurrect Greece under the rulership of her grandson Constantine (named purposely after the last Byzantine emperor). But Alexander did not succumb to calls for Russian intervention on the side of the Greeks, and he held to the ideas of legitimacy and stability of established relations. Russia played a larger role in the Greek conflict after Alexander's death, when a part of Greece became independent. Conflicts in this region ultimately destroyed the Congress of Vienna settlement, but during Alexander's reign, Russia supported the conservative European regimes in resisting popular aspirations throughout the continent for greater political participation and national expression.

In Russia itself, the same conflict being played out on the European stage between dynastic (and in some cases still feudalistic) regimes and the proponents of democratic nationalism was repeated on a smaller scale. The stunning victory over Napoleonic France resolved the earlier doubts on the part of most of Russia's leaders about the country's administration and social system. The autocrat had held firm, the nobility had served and led the conquering army, the common people had remained loyal and even fought partisan campaigns against the invader. The victory strengthened the ruling groups' belief in the system such that they no longer saw the necessity for fundamental reform. The mood had begun to shift in favour of the conservative voices in high politics. This mood accompanied a European-wide change in political thinking away from the rationalist, mechanistic ideas of the eighteenth century towards organic theories of society on the model enunciated by Edmund Burke, Joseph de Maistre, and Friedrich Karl von Savigny. De Maistre, a refugee from Napoleonic Europe who spent many years in Russia, was able to exert a direct personal influence on Russian statesmen.

Until recently, historians have seen the post-Napoleonic period (or final ten years) of Alexander's reign as a single piece characterized by a sharp turn away from the reform policies of the previous era. In terms of the outcomes, this view may still be justified. Yet recent research has made a strong case for dividing the period into two five-year segments, in which the first witnessed a continuing sympathy on the part of the tsar and some of his close advisers for the reform ideas of the early reign. Alexander continued as late as 1818 to speak publicly of his wish to establish a constitutional order for Russia, and privately he was still expressing such hopes in 1820. Work on a draft constitution was apparently also in progress as late as 1820. Nor had Alexander given up on making a start towards emancipating serfs from bondage to private landlords despite opposition from most of the nobles in high government. In 1818 he instructed one of his closest aides, General Aleksei Arakcheev, to design a project for emancipation and the following year ordered his minister of finance to work out the fiscal problems associated with a possible emancipation. Finding no support for a broad project of reform in 1820, Alexander proposed at least to bar the sale of serfs separate from their families and without land. But this proposal too met near unanimous opposition from the members of the State Council.

The reform impulse died after 1820. Vigorous opposition from the nobility finally convinced the tsar of the hopelessness of attempting a change in the status of the serfs. The courts, dominated by the nobility, were even proving reluctant to enforce laws for the protection of serfs already on the books. Since ideas of constitutional order were linked in the minds of reformers with the necessity for emancipation of the serfs, opposition to serf reform doubled as opposition to constitutionalism. It seems, moreover, that Alexander had lost interest in the idea of a constitution for Russia after dealing with the increasingly refractory Polish diet (Sejm). In 1821 he told a French envoy that constitutional government may be appropriate for enlightened nations, but would be unworkable in the less educated societies of Europe. No more was heard about a constitution for Russia, and, indeed, the government now turned to repression of any voices that echoed the tsar's earlier promises of a constitutional order.

Some reforms were implemented in the post-war period of Alexander's reign, but they were of an entirely different kind; they represented an accommodation and adaptation to the given political and social system. The most prominent such reform was the creation of military settlements, frontier colonies for the maintenance of army units in peacetime. Since it was impossible to demobilize an army of former serfs and send them back to their estates and yet too expensive to keep them continually under arms, the government settled them on lands occupied by state peasants near the frontier and set them to producing their own maintenance through farming. The reform included some enlightened features such as subsidies to families, government-sponsored health care and birthing services, and regulation of community hygiene. Even so, the settlements were not popular with either the peasants or the soldiers on whom they were imposed. They joined the hard labour of peasant farming and a highly regimented military life in a combination so odious that it frequently sparked mutinies. Surprisingly, in view of the poor record of the settlements in saving on military expenditures and the easy target they made for opponents of the regime, this reform was the most enduring of Alexander's reign. Military settlements lasted until the Great Reforms of the 1860s.

This period also brought conservative reform to Russian universities. Under the influence of a religious revival following the victory over Napoleon and Alexander's own spiritual conversion during the war, the Ministry of Education was combined in a dual government department with the Directorate of Spiritual Affairs (the former Holy Synod). In 1819 a member of this institution's governing committee, Mikhail Magnitskii, visited Kazan University and discovered to his horror that professors were teaching about the rights of citizens and the violence of warfare. Although Magnitskii could think of no better recommendation than closing down the university, Alexander decided instead to appoint him rector with powers to reform the institution. Magnitskii promptly dismissed eleven professors and shifted the curriculum towards heavy doses of religion and the classics, a direction that was subsequently followed at St Petersburg University and others.

Decembrist Rebellion

The shift to conservatism was not shared by all of Russia's élite. Many of the young men who had fought in the campaigns against Napoleonic France returned home with a different spirit. They had liberated Europeans from French domination and brought their own country to the first rank among

On December 14, 1825, the military leaders of a secret revolutionary society, later known as 'Decembrists' after the month of their insurrection, brought troops under their command on to Senate Square in the heart of St Petersburg to demand a new ruler and a constitution. A standoff lasted much of the day as the new emperor, Nicholas I, searched for a peaceful solution to the crisis. In the end, he ordered loyal troops to fire on the rebels and followed this bloody climax with arrests of all those even remotely associated with the insurrectionists.

European nations. Proud of Russia's leadership, they yearned to make their country the equal of Europe in other respects: to end serfdom at home and to enjoy there the kind of constitutional order that existed in France, the United States of America, and other enlightened states. In other words, they combined ideas of liberalism and constitutionalism with elements of modern, romantic nationalism. They met to discuss their hopes and dreams in private clubs, successors of the Masonic lodges to which their fathers and grandfathers had belonged.

At first, they thought that Alexander shared their beliefs and hopes. His postwar pronouncements about a constitution for Russia encouraged this belief, just as the tsar's conservative advisers had warned him it would. But increasing repression at home, the reform of the universities, Alexander's opposition to movements for national independence in Greece and elsewhere soon disillusioned those hoping for a continuation of the liberal reform plans of the early reign. When Alexander reinstituted a secret police regime in 1821 following a rebellion in one of the élite regiments of the capital cities, the young dissidents formed secret societies and prepared for revolution. Although the leaders were divided on their ultimate aims—some preferring a federated system, others a unified state; some preferring a constitutional monarchy, others a republic—they held together long enough to attempt a *putsch* during an interregnum in December 1825 caused by the sudden death of Alexander on a tour of the south of the country. The tsar died childless, and confusion about which of his two brothers was supposed to succeed to the throne gave the insurgents an opportunity to strike. The rebellion had two phases, the first in the capital St Petersburg and the second two weeks later in the Ukraine; both were quickly defeated. Five leaders were hanged, and 284 other participants, many from the most prominent families of the nobility, were imprisoned or exiled to Siberia. This insurgency, known to history as the Decembrist Rebellion, exhibited features of both a palace guards coup of the eighteenth century and a modern revolution in the name of popular sovereignty. However, by virtue of a rich legacy of memoirs, poetry, art, and historical reconstruction, the event shed its archaic features and became semioticized into the first act of the Russian Revolution. An important element of its appeal was the role of the wives of the Decembrists, many of whom left comfortable upper-class homes and followed their convicted husbands into Siberian exile. Although women had made such sacrifices earlier, the Decembrists' wives were the first to be inscribed as a literary model and hence the first to provide a script for Russian women's selfless devotion to the cause of resistance to autocracy.

Nicholas I: The Early Years

The new tsar, Nicholas I, had not expected to become ruler and had prepared for a military career. Historians have been inclined to interpret his policies and behaviour as those of a militarist martinet. If Alexander has been known for his earnest planning for political and social reform (and even perhaps excused, because of the epic struggle with France, for not having carried it through), Nicholas has usually been described as a ruler lacking in vision, a thoroughgoing conservative who sought only to hold back change. This contrast is misleading. Alexander was ultimately far more committed to the rhetoric of reform than its substance, and Nicholas's actual accomplishments surpassed those of his older brother. Indeed, both regimes shared central values and goals, including most prominently a dedication to the notion of disciplined administration, legality in governance, and the role of the tsar as benevolent overseer of this legal order (however imperfectly these ideas may have been realized in practice). The misleading contrast in the popular picture of the two regimes may stem from the sharply differing reform methods of the two rulers. Alexander and his 'friends' adopted a deductive approach to reform typical of the age of rationalism in which they were nurtured, whereas Nicholas preferred an inductive approach of investigating issues exhaustively before implementing changes. Moreover, having learned from the Decembrist revolt the dangers of encouraging hopes of reform, Nicholas insisted on the strictest secrecy in the consideration and formulation of plans for change. The reforms that he introduced were carefully thought through and implemented under controlled conditions. Though intended to strengthen the given system of authority and property relations, Nicholas's reforms laid an essential foundation for the momentous social, economic, and legal transformations of the next reign.

The first months of Nicholas's reign were taken up with the investigation and prosecution of the Decembrist rebels, a task that the new ruler delegated to Mikhail Speranskii, the reformist state secretary of the previous reign who had been exiled to Siberia in 1812. After this, Speranskii and a former member of Alexander I's 'committee of friends', Viktor Kochubei, were put in charge of a commission to look into government operations and recommend changes where needed. The commission's broad mandate advised it to discover: what is good now, what cannot be left as it stands, and what should replace it. The commission sat for several years and produced a shelf of reports. Its final recommendations proposed incremental improvements in established institutions and policies rather than fundamental reforms. In regard to serfdom, the commissioners advised against allowing the transfer of serfs from field work to the squire's household (to allay fears caused by an increasing number of landless peasants); it also proposed to improve the situation of state peasants in ways that would create a model for emulation by private landlords. In regard to the upper class, the commission wanted to restrict the flow of new entrants to the nobility through the Table of Ranks and instead to reward deserving non-nobles with privileges not tied to hereditary status. Concern for the preservation of the nobility found expression in a recommendation to establish entail and thereby prevent the fragmentation of noble landed estates. The commission also took up some of Speranskii's favourite ideas about the division of the Senate into separate administrative and judicial bodies.

But before reforms could proceed, a number of challenges rocked the regime at the start of the 1830s, a circumstance that strengthened the hand of those who favoured repression over reform. After three decades of the Russian army's steady, successful penetration of the Caucasus Mountains and subjection of its peoples, a reaction occurred. Native peoples overcame their differences and united in a resistance that threatened to disrupt Russia's near-eastern policies. Second, the Russian home front was stricken by a devastating cholera epidemic, the first in a series of outbreaks that recurred in the nineteenth century. Initially, the hardest hit was the south-central agricultural province of Tambov, where terrified peasants rioted and in some instances were joined by the soldiers dispatched to bring them under control. When the epidemic spread to the capital cities, disturbances erupted there as well. In one case, Tsar Nicholas himself, no coward, rode on horseback into a panicked and rioting crowd on Haymarket Square in St Petersburg, scolded them, and sent them home. The third and most disturbing event, however, was a national rebellion in Poland towards the end of 1830. Sparked by the overthrow of the restored Bourbon monarch Charles X in France earlier that year, which provided a stimulus for rebellion in Italy, Germany, and elsewhere, the Polish insurgency lasted through much of 1831 and brought an end to the Poles' autonomy in internal affairs. The constitution granted Poland by Alexander I was replaced by an Organic Statute, making Poland an integral or 'organic' part of the Russian Empire.

In response to these crises and the continuing challenge of liberal ideas and national aspirations, Russian leaders devised a new ideological formula (later dubbed 'Official Nationality') that sought to co-opt the spirit of romantic nationalism and put it to the service of fortifying a dynastic, imperialist regime. The new formula, first enunciated in 1832 by the deputy minister of education, Sergei Uvarov, exalted the principles of Orthodoxy, Autocracy, and Nationality. The first implied a rejection of the Voltairian scepticism of the eighteenth-century court and likewise an end to the experiments with biblical fundamentalism sponsored by Alexander I. The principle of Autocracy was meant to reinforce the notion of a personal rule sanctioned by divine right, which was necessarily incompatible with either enlightened absolutism (and its appeal to Reason), conservative constitutionalism (as proposed in the reform projects of Nikita Panin, Alexander Bezborodko, and Mikhail Speranskii), or the radicalism of the Decembrists. The murky principle of Nationality (*narodnost'*) stressed the unique character (*samobytnost'*) of the Russians as a people and therefore the inappropriateness of foreign political and social institutions for Russia. Thus Uvarov's new formula sought to replace the universalistic assumptions of the Enlightenment by asserting the distinctive character of Russia and its political and social systems. But, unlike modern cultural relativism, it conferred a higher value on Russian ideas, institutions, and especially on the Russian people, who were celebrated as trusting, faithful, and pure of heart.

Reforms of the Mature Years

However delusory the new ideology of Official Nationality, a number of significant reforms were carried out by the regime that fostered it. One of the most important of these reforms was the creation of a comprehensive law code, the first since 1649. Again, the tsar turned to Mikhail Speranskii and asked him to direct the work. Speranskii departed from the previous generation's (and his own earlier) method of designing reforms on general principles and borrowing directly from foreign models; in line with the new notions about the organic nature of society, he assembled past law, beginning with the Code of 1649 and including the thousands of statutes enacted in the intervening 180 years (omitting some, such as those related to government crises); the *Complete Collection of Laws of the Russian Empire* was published between 1828 and 1830 in 45 volumes and has been an invaluable tool for historians ever since. He then distilled from this compendium a thematically organized fifteen-volume codex of living, currently applicable law called the *Digest of Laws*, which went into effect in 1835. Though not systematic and normative, the new code addressed the contradictions and chaos of the accumulated statutes and presented law in a usable form, accessible to courts throughout the land. Yet, as government officials understood, a country without a corps of jurists knowledgeable about and committed to a legal system was a country in which laws remained vulnerable to manipulation in courts influenced by bribery and clientelism. Here, too, Nicholas's government made a valuable contribution, opening a School of Jurisprudence in 1835 to train sons of élite families in modern legal practice. The graduates of this institution played an indispensable role in the creation and widely acknowledged success of the sweeping juridical reforms of the 1860s, which adopted such key features of Anglo-American practice as justices of the peace, trial by jury, and life tenure for judges.

Important changes were also made in state financial policy. Half a century of war and administrative expansion paid for by increasingly inflated paper money (*assignats*) had wreaked havoc on state finances. Building on ideas initially sketched by Speranskii during Alexander I's reign, the Minister of Finance, Egor Kankrin, succeeded in bringing inflation under control by tying the value of *assignats* to that of the silver rouble and thereby laid a solid foundation for economic growth. The Crimean War at the close of the reign, it is true, undid much of this work and left Russia poorly prepared to manage the costs of the reforms of the 1860s, but matters would have been far worse without Kankrin's policies.

Nicholas should be given credit for preparing the ground for the reform of serfdom, even if during his reign little change occurred in the actual status of the serfs. At best, a law passed in 1842 allowed landlords to manumit with land serfs who were able to come up with a high buy-out price. But this option, dependent as it was on the acquiescence of the landlord, resulted in few manumissions. The law nevertheless underlined the government's insistence that freed serfs be provided with land, an ominous sign for noble landlords who hoped that emancipation would recognize their title to all the lands currently in their possession. More significant was a reform of state peasants carried through by the Ministry of State Domains under the leadership of Count P. D. Kiselev. This reform, introduced in the late 1830s and early 1840s, granted state peasants a measure of self-government, village schools, public-health facilities, and agricultural extension services; it also shifted the method of taxation from an assessment on individuals to an assessment on the amount of cultivable soil, a fairer measure because of its link to potential productivity. This reform, though affecting only peasants under state supervision, bore unmistakable implications for the eventual abolition of serfdom. Indeed, during the latter half of Nicholas's reign secret committees were already at work designing such a reform.

Lest there be any doubt about the government's willingness to infringe on the nobility's rights and privileges, Nicholas also enacted a reform of the nobility itself, a remarkable and revealing act in European affairs, demonstrating that the Russian upper class was not a self-governing social estate of the European type that had evolved ahead of or in tandem with the monarchy but rather a creation of the monarchy, its place and privileges subject to definition by the ruler. The reform was occasioned by a growing division in the nobility between

those who built their economic livelihood and status on the management of their serf estates and those who did so primarily on positions in the state administration. Many of the second group had acquired patents of nobility by education and advancement through the Table of Ranks, and these new arrivals did not share the values of the established landed nobility. In response to pressure from the hereditary landed nobility to restrict entry to the class, Nicholas's reform commission proposed to create new status designations to reward persons who advanced through merit to high government office. But Nicholas, no doubt rightly, feared that such a change would impede the government's efforts to recruit capable men for government service; he did not agree to end ennoblement through the Table of Ranks but only to stiffen requirements for attaining personal nobility and hereditary nobility (qualification for individual nobility for life being raised from the 14th to the 9th rank, that for hereditary from the 8th to the 5th rank). The principal effect of this change was to speed up promotion through the ranks.

At the same time, Nicholas made other changes in the status of the nobles. He raised property qualifications for voting in local assemblies of the nobility, reduced the length of legal foreign residence for nobles from five years to three, pressured nobles to serve in provincial government before applying for posts at

This romanticized image of peasant life, 'The Threshing Floor' (1821) by Aleksei Venetsianov, was one of the first genre paintings by a leading Russian artist and helped set the course of Russian art toward the realism of the second half of the century.

the centre, and limited their rights of buying and selling serfs. Given the division within the noble estate, these measures might be opposed or favoured by one or the other constituency. The important point is that they all violated the Charter to the Nobility granted by Catherine II in 1785 and demonstrated the ruler's determination not to be bound by fundamental rights supposedly adhering to the nobility. The reform of the nobility prefigured the far-reaching assault on noble privilege that occurred in the following reign.

Intellectual and Cultural Life

The intellectual life of Nicholas I's Russia developed in the shadow of the Decembrist revolt and was therefore constrained in its public expression by tough, if flexible, government censorship. Many accounts of this era, especially those by Western visitors and critics such as the Marquis de Custine, describe Nicholas's Russia as a night-time of repression. It needs to be kept in mind that most educated Russians, including the brilliant and much-admired Alexander Pushkin, agreed on the necessity of censorship, however much they may have chafed at its limits. It is also important to recall that this was a period of extraordinary cultural creativity, the golden age of Russian letters. Not only was it the era of Pushkin, perhaps the greatest poet in all of Russian history (and whose government censor was, interestingly, Tsar Nicholas himself!), but it was also the time when Russian high culture broke free of its former imitation of Western arts and produced works that themselves reshaped the contours of world culture. In the novels and verse of Pushkin and Mikhail Lermontov appeared the 'superfluous man', the hero turned anti-hero. The work of Nikolai Gogol contained at once biting satires on the human failings of his own time and fantastical characters and plot turns that anticipated the post-modernist writings of our own age. These writers and the novelist Ivan Turgenev, whose *Sportsman's Sketches* for the first time portrayed Russian serfs as fully formed human actors, paved the way from Romanticism to realism in European literature.

The usual picture of the intellectual life of this time derives from the narrative constructed by the victorious revolutionary leaders of our own century and focuses on the few oppositional figures whom later revolutionaries counted as their inspiration. The story begins with Peter Chaadaev, a thoughtful and conscience-stricken military officer who left the army after Alexander I's brutal repression of the Semenovskii guards regiment. His writings criticized the idealism of the Decembrists and their futile attempt to impose foreign political institutions on Russia, but he is best known for his ringing indictment of government propagandists and the self-congratulatory stance of Official Nationality. The only one of his 'philosophical letters' to be published during Nicholas's reign inveighed against the sterility and backwardness of every aspect of Russian life, beginning with the empty ritualism of the Orthodox religion and continuing on to the country's intellectual poverty and useless veneer of Western institutions devoid of the true spirit of the Western political order. The outburst—the later revolutionary Alexander Herzen called it 'a shot resounding through a dark night'—was so unimaginable in the highly censored press of the era that when it appeared in a prominent magazine in 1836, Nicholas pronounced its author a madman and subjected him to regular medical examinations. The unfortunate publisher suffered a worse fate—exile to Siberia. Chaadaev was aberrant, however, only in having the courage to speak out. Others were writing and saying similar things in private. Educated Russians had no wish to leave the definition of Russia's proper purpose and destiny to government propagandists.

Even before the publication of Chaadaev's letter, young Russians had been coming together in small groups, 'circles' as they were called, at regular weekly meetings to discuss literature, philosophy, and national purpose, but Chaadaev's letter crystallized many issues and forced the young thinkers to define their stance towards Russia's development. Some accepted the position that Russia was a European country whose social evolution lagged behind the rest of Europe and whose political institutions had been deformed by the unbridled power of autocracy. These 'Westernizers' saw Russia's proper course in liberalism, constitutionalism, the rule of law, and Western enlightenment. Others adopted a nativist position that superficially resembled the government's programme of Official Nationality. However, these thinkers, known as Slavophiles, regarded the government as an alien institution imposed by Peter the Great and responsible for breaking Russia's natural evolution from the seventeenth-century tsardom, which the Slavophiles believed was characterized by a familial attachment of the people to their tsar, by Orthodox piety and a sense of community among the people and between the people and the ruler. Like the Westernizers, the Slavophiles were opposed to serfdom, bureaucratic supervision of social and intellectual life, and the militarism of Nicholas's regime. In other words, the famous debate of the 1840s between the Westernizers and Slavophiles was a contest over the meaning of Russia's past and Russia's future. Both sides opposed the Russian present.

Despite the severity of the political regime, intellectual life was vibrant during the 1830s and 1840s. Small groups of writers and their friends met in private homes and intensely debated issues of national identity, social justice, and aesthetics. Here we see one such gathering, a housewarming arranged on the occasion of the opening of a bookshop by Alexander Smirdin, a publisher and bookseller. Among the guests are Ivan Krylov, Vasilii Zhukovsky, and Alexander Pushkin, the greatest poet of the time.

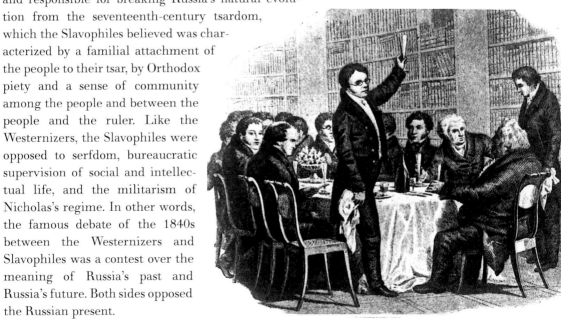

Our inherited narrative ends the era of more or less open discussion of these matters with a celebrated exchange in 1847 between Nikolai Gogol and the literary critic Vissarion Belinskii. In a work titled *Selected Correspondence with Friends*, Gogol gave a ringing endorsement to key propositions of Official Nationality, advising Russians to love their ruler, accept their station in life, and spend more time in prayer. Belinskii, though unable to reply in print, responded with a letter that enjoyed wide circulation in manuscript copy. He lambasted Gogol for his obscurantism and betrayal of his own earlier writings, which had held government administrators up to ridicule and demonstrated the absurdity of serfdom. This exchange, plus the departure of Alexander Herzen (a major figure in the intellectual circles of the time) for Europe in 1847, marked the close of this period, except for a final act—the suppression of the Petrashevskii circle amidst a ferocious government crack-down provoked by the European revolutions of 1848. Although the members of this circle did little more than read forbidden writings and discuss socialist ideas, the government's fears of sedition were so deep that twenty-one of the members of the circle received death sentences, which, however, were commuted to Siberian exile minutes before the executions were to be carried out. Among those made to suffer this death watch and personal psychological trauma was the later literary giant Fedor Dostoevsky.

This story of the intellectual life of the era as a struggle between a severely repressive government and an increasingly alienated educated public, though enshrined in the literature by later revolutionaries, does not paint an accurate picture. The dissidents were a small minority. Most educated Russians took pride in the knowledge that their country was the strongest land power in the world and a respected member of the European concert of nations. They felt secure from outside threats and were enjoying a period of relative economic prosperity. Although the few dissidents and some foreign visitors lamented government supervision of intellectual life, most Russians recognized the need for censorship and were able to create and consume a rich and varied cultural life within its bounds. Over 200 new periodical publications were begun in Nicholas's reign, and several dozen were on the market at any one time. The creative arts flourished; the Russian opera came into its own in the works of Mikhail Glinka and Alexander Dargomyzhsky, the paintings of Karl Briullov, Alexander Ivanov, and Ivan Aivazovskii shifted artistic style away from classicism to romanticism, while the genre painting of Pavel Fedotov and others captured characteristic moments of Russian life. A rapid growth of scientific literature and scientific investigation was evident. Official Nationality and Slavophilism were symptoms of educated Russians' need for a clearer sense of national identity and their place in the world; the result was plans for historical and ethnographic museums to house representations of the people and culture of Russia. This was the period of the founding of the Imperial Russian Geographic Society, which set out to map literally and figuratively the physical

A favourite Russian winter pastime was sledding down high ramps covered with ice. Even Empress Catherine the Great had sledding ramps built at her suburban palaces for the entertainment of her court and guests. Here, in a lithograph by Beggrov, we see such ice 'mountains', as they were called, constructed for public amusement on the frozen Neva river at St Petersburg.

and cultural boundaries of the nation. Its establishment in early 1845 was followed by a major ethnographic research programme to discover the folklore, material life, and practices of the Russian and other peoples inhabiting the empire. Nicholas's reign also saw an increasing effort by the Orthodox Church to raise the educational, religious, and moral level of the common people through a rapid growth of local schooling and printings of inexpensive editions of didactic literature. The Church likewise launched new efforts in the missionary field, including work in the Altai Mountain region, eastern Siberia, and Alaska that led to linguistic and ethnographic reports that corresponded to the work of the Geographic Society. Indeed, the Geographic Society could well stand as a symbol for an age whose leaders were intent on recording the economic, topographical, and human conditions of the empire. This process reflected Nicholas's inductive approach to reform, the exhaustive study of conditions before acting, an impulse that helped prepare the Great Reforms of the 1860s while encouraging educated Russians to find a personal and national identity in service to the common people.

Close of the Reign

The final years of Nicholas's reign effaced many of its most important achievements. The success with which a flexible censorship had allowed for important scientific and cultural growth while checking dissident opinion was lost in the orgy of repression that followed the news of revolution in Europe in 1848. The continuing expansion and democratization of the educational system and the opportunities for Russians to continue higher studies abroad succumbed to the same crack-down when, in the wake of the Petrashevskii circle's arrest, Nicholas slashed university enrolments by two-thirds and ordered all Russians

We normally hear only about the defeats of Russia in the Crimean War. Russians were apt to emphasize their victories, as is done here in a broadsheet showing in the points of a Greek star scenes of Russian victories and acts of heroism in the early months of the conflict. The text invokes the help of God in the war. St George the dragon slayer is pictured at the centre.

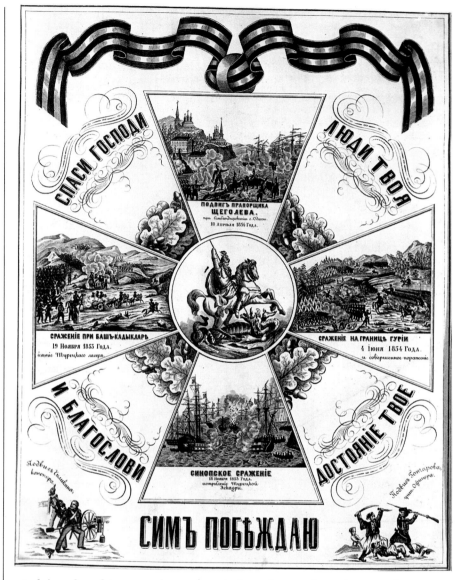

studying abroad to return home (unwisely, as it turned out, because the return-ing students brought with them detailed and accurate information about the upheavals occurring in their places of study). The progress being made on peas-ant reform came to a halt, as the tsar feared further social change of any kind. Even the success of the government in stabilizing the currency and promoting economic development was harmed by the expensive and futile war in the Crimea.

The outbreak of this war nullified one of Nicholas's greatest achievements: his reversal of the constant warfare of the previous two reigns and maintenance of a long period of peace and security for his country. Armed conflict occurred during his reign, but it involved pacification of the borderlands of the Caucasus and Poland and did not threaten the security or livelihoods of most Russians. When Russian troops did venture abroad, they stayed close to their borders, for example, brief sorties into Persia and the Danubian principalities early in the reign and an expedition to Hungary in 1849 to suppress a nationalist insurgency. Even the Crimean War at the end of his reign was not a conflict Nicholas consciously sought out for the aggrandizement of Russia or himself. Indeed, he very much wished to avoid a war provoked by an assertive French government claiming rights over sacred institutions in Palestine. These demands raised questions about Russia's protectorate over Christians in the Ottoman Empire, a position affirmed in the peace treaty of Kuchuk-Kainardji (1774) but disputed by the Turks. As the diplomatic conflict escalated in early 1853, the Russian government counted on the support of Austria (which it had rescued from dismemberment four years before) and Britain (which had recently been in conflict with France over their respective positions in the Middle East). But Nicholas badly miscalculated. Austria threatened to join the Ottomans if Russia attacked through the Balkans; Britain played a double game, urging the Ottomans to avoid war but also indicating that they could expect British support if war broke out. With Russia seemingly isolated but still making stiff demands for the right to protect Ottoman Christians, the Turks decided to resist and force an armed conflict.

For want of a better place to engage (Austria blocked an invasion of the Balkans and Russia could not challenge the allies at sea), the two sides fought the decisive battles in the Crimea and nearby port cities on Russia's Black Sea coastline. Though a strong force on paper, the army on which Nicholas had lavished much of his attention was no match for the allies. Much of its strength had to be deployed elsewhere to protect against possible attacks on other borders, the forces sent to the Crimea were supplied by ox cart because of Russia's late start into railway building, Russian weapons (not upgraded since earlier wars) had far shorter effective range than the enemy's, sanitary conditions were appalling, and disease claimed far more men than did battle. The result was demoralization and defeat. In the midst of this ruin of his diplomacy, army, finances, and record of peace and security, Nicholas took ill and died of pneumonia in early February 1855.

Conclusions

During the first half of the nineteenth century, Russian government and society changed in a number of important respects. Though threatened by French power at the beginning of this era, Russians met the challenge of an invading force much superior in numbers to their own and went on to conquer and occupy Napoleonic France. For the next forty years, Europeans regarded Russia

Russia was late in entering the railroad age and suffered for it. Poor transport to the south hindered the government's prosecution of the Crimean War. This picture sketches the opening of the first railway between Moscow and St Petersburg in 1851. The sketch underlines that troop transport was an important function of this new method of conveyance.

as the continent's most formidable power. But as often happens, victory brought complacency. Russian leaders failed to recognize the need for technological development and left the country poorly prepared for the next great struggle. Russia lagged in weapons development, logistical support, education, and industry—all the things that constitute the strength of a state. It is enough to observe that on the eve of the Crimean War, when railways had already spread their tentacles through much of Western Europe, Russia was just completing its first major line between Moscow and St Petersburg. Russia's military in the century before 1850 had defeated Prussia and France when each was at the height of its power; for nearly another century Russians would prove incapable of defeating any country but Ottoman Turkey. Japan defeated the Russians in 1904–5, Germany in 1914–18, and Poland in 1920; and even little Finland in 1939–40 held off an immeasurably superior Soviet force for more time than anyone could have believed possible. A decisive shift in Russia's international position had occurred in the reign of Nicholas I.

Domestic affairs proved more successful. Although the nineteenth century began with promises of constitutional government and serf emancipation, these goals were incompatible and unrealizable. Constitutional government would have turned legislative power over to the very landed élite who opposed the reform of serfdom. This élite resisted even the timid reform initiatives that the autocrats were ultimately able to enact. Substantive change in the serf order required the co-operation of the landed nobility, and this was not forthcoming until the shock of defeat in the Crimean War caused the élite to recognize the need to end agrarian bondage and move towards a modern economy capable of meeting the challenge of Western power. The government did nevertheless make important improvements that prepared the ground for the revolutionary changes of the next era. Among these improvements were the growth and differentiation of government administration, creation of a law code and regulation of legal practice, a disciplined economic policy and stable currency, and the expansion of educational opportunity.

The growth of education, so necessary for the building of economic and military strength, also brought two developments that threatened the imperial state: nationalism and the desire for political participation. Both of these impulses found powerful expression in the Decembrist rebellion of 1825. Despite the government's attempt to co-opt the nationalist spirit through the imperialist doctrine of Official Nationality, a specific Russian nationalism continued to evolve in the writings of Chaadaev, the Slavophiles, and even the Westernizers. Soon it was joined by other nationalist programmes emerging first in Poland, Ukraine, and Finland, an impulse that by the twentieth century spread to other non-Russian peoples of the empire and destroyed the hold of a centralizing imperial ideology. The desire for political participation and its frustration by periodic government repression drove a wedge between government and some members of educated society as early as the 1820s. Thereafter the divide widened. The dissidents, though few at first and never a threat to the government in this period, exercised great symbolic force by challenging a fundamental tenet of tsarist ideology: the notion that the ruler was a good father who cared for and was at one with his children, the people of Russia. When many of the nation's most talented sons and daughters were being repressed by the regime and half the tsar's 'children', the peasant serfs, continued in bondage, the dissidents could well ask what kind of fatherly care was the ruler providing? The failure of the regime to draw many of the country's best people into its service or to provide them with a national mission they could support augured ill for the future.

REFORM AND COUNTER REFORM
1855–1890

GREGORY L. FREEZE

Stunned by the Crimean War débâcle, Russian statesmen rebuilt basic institutions and even abolished the linchpin of the old order, serfdom. But these 'Great Reforms' had serious shortcomings, generated widespread discontent, and ignited an organized revolutionary movement. By the 1880s the regime embarked on 'counter-reforms' to rebuild a powerful state based on autocratic state power.

THE period 1855–90 marks Russia's transition from counter-revolution to revolution—from the 'Gendarme of Europe' to the bastion of revolutionary forces. That transition reflected the profound impact of the 'Great Reforms', which brought not only far-reaching changes (the emancipation of serfs and a host of other Westernizing, modernizing reforms), but also a new kind of politics and relationship between state and society. In so many respects, the epoch of reform and counter-reform encapsulated the fundamental processes at work in the history of Russia: the dangerous and unpredictable consequences of reform, the awakening of unfulfilled expectations, the unleashing of liberal and revolutionary movements, and the powerful, implosive impact of borderland minorities on politics in the central heartland.

Why Reform?

Despite its odious reputation as the bulwark of brutal reaction, the Russia of Nicholas I had incessantly, if clandestinely, pondered the prospects and process of reform. From the very first years of his reign, and partly in response to the Decembrist uprising, Nicholas I (1825–55) did not fail to discern the fundamental problems afflicting his land—from its corrupt bureaucracy to the serfdom that seemed so similar to slavery. Although the state under Nicholas recognized the need for reform, even in the case of serfdom, it had resisted taking decisive and especially public measures and, instead, contented itself primarily with cautious and (above all) secret reforms. Fear of uncontrolled social disorders, an unquestioning belief in the power and omniscience of bureaucracy, a smug assurance of Russia's military prowess despite its markedly un-Western system and economic backwardness—all this encouraged the conceit that Russia could be a great power *and* maintain its traditional social and political order. That order alone seemed immune to the revolutionary bacillus that had infected the rest of Europe in 1830 and 1848; Russia's very distinctiveness (*samobytnost'*) seemed responsible for its unparalleled stability at home and its military power abroad.

With Nicholas's death, however, the regime soon embarked on wide-ranging reform, including the Gordian knot of serf emancipation. To explain why the Russian state finally embarked on reform, historians have advanced a number of theories. One explanation, popular among pre-revolutionary and Western historians, emphasized the triumph of liberal humanitarian ideas within the higher ranks of state and society: imbued with Western values and culture, these élites could not fail to recognize the contradiction to their own status as serf-owners. While the influence of Western ideas can hardly be denied for some parts of the élite, it certainly did not extend to the nobility as a whole; most, in fact, vehemently opposed emancipation. Some Marxist historians, chiefly Soviet, have emphasized the economic factor: as the nobility found their estates becoming less productive, as their debts and the spectre of bankruptcy increased, the serf-owners themselves supposedly came to recognize the inefficiency of serfdom and the validity of criticism by Western liberal economists. Again, although isolated expressions of these views can be found, such sentiments were hardly prevalent among most members of the government or the nobility. A third interpretation stresses fear of peasant unrest: cognizant of the statistics on murder and the incidence of peasant rebellion (which swelled from 990 disorders in 1796–1826 to 1,799 disorders in 1826–56), nobles and bureaucrats purportedly came to realize that emancipation alone, not procrastination, could ensure social stability in the countryside. While fear certainly did grip many members of the provincial nobility, it did not figure significantly in the calculations of the high-ranking state officials who actually engineered emancipation. The latter, the emperor included, were indeed wont to exploit noble fears, but they themselves did not evince real concern for their own safety.

Why, then, did the regime finally take the fateful step towards emancipation? Although the factors cited above to some degree did abet the process, the key linchpin in fact was the débâcle of the Crimean War. That foreign fiasco led to domestic reconstruction, for it exposed the real backwardness and weakness of the old servile order and all that it connoted. The Crimean War not only exacted a high cost in lives, resources, and prestige, but also vitiated the main impediment to reform—the belief that the existing order was consonant with stability and power. As a liberal Slavophile Iurii Samarin wrote in 1856: 'We were vanquished not by the foreign armies of the Western alliances, but by our own internal weaknesses'. The same year a liberal Westernizer Boris Chicherin wrote that, without the abolition of serfdom, 'no questions can be resolved—whether political, administrative, or social'. Even before the war had been irrevocably lost, conservatives as well as liberals had come to much the same conclusion.

Emancipation of the Serfs

The critical question became not whether, but how the serfs were to be emancipated. In part that 'how' concerned the terms of emancipation—whether they would receive land (in what quantities and at what price) and whether they would become full-fledged citizens. These two issues became the central focus of the reform debates inside and outside the government. But emancipation also raised a further question: how was reform to be designed and implemented, what indeed were to be the politics of reform? Was the state simply to promulgate emancipation (perhaps with the assistance of secret committees, to use the previous tsar's methods) or was society itself somehow to be involved in this process? The politics of reform were as important as the terms of emancipation, for they were fraught with long-term implications about the relationship between state and society and, especially, the status and role of old élites.

The 'reform party' was a coalition of different interests with a common objective. It was, in any event, not the mere handiwork of a reformist monarch. Although the traditional historiography inclined to personalize politics and ascribe much to the emperor himself, and although Alexander II (1855–81) acquired an official accolade as 'Tsar-Liberator', he was in fact highly conservative and a deeply ambivalent reformer. Far more important was the constellation of what W. Bruce Lincoln has called the 'enlightened bureaucrats', the *gosudarstvenniki* (state servitors) who identified more with the interests of the state than those of their own noble estate. Indispensable because of their superior education and practical experience, the enlightened bureaucrats (such as Nikolai Miliutin and Ia. S. Solovev) played a critical role in the reform process. Another influential party of reformers was to be found in the military; generals such as Mikhail Gorchakov concurred that 'the first thing is to emancipate the serfs, because that is the evil which binds together all the things that are evil in Russia'. And some members of the imperial family (especially the tsar's brother, Konstantin, and his aunt Grand Duchess Elena Pavlovna) were also instrumental in the reform process. Although the reformers encountered significant resistance (above all, from the nobility, certain segments of the bureaucratic élites, and the police), the catastrophe in the Crimea had made the argument for reform, including emancipation, irresistible.

The process of emancipation, however, was by no means unilinear: it was only gradually, through trial and error, that the regime finally formulated the specific terms of the Emancipation Statutes in 1861. In his first year, in fact, Alexander deliberately tried to discourage the wild expectations that traditionally accompanied each new accession to the throne and often ignited a wave of rumours and peasant disorders: he replaced reputed reformers (such as the Minister of Interior, D. G. Bibikov, and the Minister of State Domains, P. D. Kiselev) with men known for their arch-conservative opinions.

By 1856, however, the defeat in the Crimea was not to be denied and neither could the exigency of fundamental reform. In a famous speech to the nobility of Moscow on 30 March 1856, Alexander ostensibly endeavoured to reassure the serf-owners, but ended his comments with a clear intimation of the imperative need for reform 'from above':

Rumours have spread among you of my intention to abolish serfdom. To refute any groundless gossip on so important a subject, I consider it necessary to inform you that I have no intention of doing so immediately. But, of course, you yourselves realize that the existing system of serf-owning cannot remain unchanged. It is better to begin abolishing serfdom from above than to wait for it to begin to abolish itself from below.

Although Alexander may have hoped that the nobility, mindful of its traditional 'service ethos' would take its own initiative, nothing of the sort transpired. As the Third Section (secret police) was well aware, 'the majority of the nobility believe that our peasant is too uncultured to comprehend civil law; that, in a state of freedom, he would be more vicious than any wild beast; that disorders, plundering, and murder are almost inevitable'.

On 1 January 1857 Alexander resorted to the favourite device of his father: he appointed a secret commission with the charge of designing the reform of serfdom. The commission was, however, dominated by old-regime officials, most of whom were adamantly opposed to reform; moderates were a distinct minority. Over the next several months the commission slowly worked out an extremely conservative reform project whereby peasants were to compensate the squire for their homestead, to receive no arable land, and to obtain freedom, but only through an extremely protracted process. A vexed emperor, dismayed by the snail's pace of work, castigated the commission for lethargy and procrastination: 'I desire and demand that your commission produce a general conclusion as to how [emancipation] is to be undertaken, instead of burying it in the files under various pretexts'. Coming under the influence of Western advisers, who warned of the dire social consequences of a landless emancipation, Alexander reiterated that his 'main anxiety is that the matter will begin of itself, from below'.

A major turning-point came on 20 November 1857, when the government issued a directive to the governor-general of Vilna that became the famous 'Nazimov Rescript'. The directive (which shortly afterwards was also sent to all other governors) instructed the governor to organize provincial assemblies of the nobility to discuss the terms of emancipation most suitable for their own region. However, the rescript did not give the nobles *carte blanche*, but set the basic parameters of reform: the landlord was to retain the land and police powers, but some provision was also to be made for peasant land purchases and self-administration. The underlying strategy was to shift the reform process from the pettifogging bureaucracy to society and to propel reform forward by mobilizing the support of the nobility itself. The Minister of Interior made it perfectly clear that local officials were to engineer assent: '[The serf-owner] must be brought to his senses and persuaded that at this point there is no turning back, and that the nobility is *obligated* to execute the will of the Sovereign, who summons them to co-operate in the amelioration of peasant life' (a euphemism for serfdom). Shortly afterwards, Alexander established the 'Chief Committee on Peasant Affairs' to oversee the reform process. At the same time, the government significantly relaxed censorship (the word *glasnost'* for the first time, in fact, coming into vogue). A dramatic break with the reform politics of Nicholas I, this very publicity made reform appear all the more irrevocable and inevitable.

To the government's dismay, however, virtually the entire nobility either opposed emancipation or demanded that its terms be cast to serve their own selfish interests. The Third Section reported that 'most of the nobles are dissatisfied [with plans for emancipation]', and explained that 'all their grumbling derives from the fear that their income will diminish or even vanish altogether'. Resistance was especially strong in the blackearth areas, where land was valu-

The imperial palace at Petrodvorets (formerly Peterhof), initiated by Peter the Great and substantially expanded and rebuilt (with the aid of such famed architects as B. F. Rastrelli) by his eighteenth-century successors, became a monument to the splendour and wealth of the Romanovs. The Great Cascade in the foreground consists of 3 cascades, 64 fountains, and 37 statues; its centrepiece is the gilded Sampson Fountain, built to commemorate the victory at Poltava on St Sampson's Day in 1709.

Catherine the Great, a portrait by Andrei Ivanovich Chernyi. A cameo designed to convey Catherine's purity (cherubs, austere gaze), military authority (swords, drums, trumpets, breast-plate) and maternal connection to the bounty of nature.

(below) This famous painting by Ilia Repin, 'Religious Procession in Kursk Province' (1880–3), captures the motley composition of the participants (priests, ordinary believers, and the throngs of disabled and diseased) as well as the semi-official character of the procession (under strict supervision of the police, who do not even shun the use of force to maintain order).

able and nobles fiercely opposed any scheme for compulsory alienation of their property. In special cases (for example, where land was poor in quality) some nobles were more inclined to support emancipation, but only on condition that they be compensated for the person of the serf, not just the land itself.

Distressed by this response, persuaded of the perils of a landless emancipation (which threatened to create a 'rural proletariat'), the emperor was persuaded to resume 'emancipation from above'—by the state, with only nominal participation of the nobility. By December 1858 a liberal majority had come to prevail on the Main Committee. It shared a consensus on two critical points: the peasantry must become a free rural class (with the commune replacing the squires' police powers), and must have the right to purchase an adequate land allotment. Although the government retained the fiction of noble participation (a special 'editorial commission' was to rework the recommendations of provincial noble assemblies), in fact the liberal majority now proceeded to design a reform that would deprive the nobility not only of their police powers but also of a substantial portion of their land.

Without the police powers to coerce peasants to work their lands, without a complete monopoly on land, many nobles feared total ruin. As a ranking member of the ministry wrote, 'the landlords fear both the government and the peasantry'. To consult and ostensibly to mollify, the government invited representatives of the nobility to come to St Petersburg and express their views in August 1859 (from the non-blackearth provinces) and January 1860 (from the blackearth provinces). On both occasions the government encountered fierce criticism and, more shocking still, even audacious demands for political reform. Although the tsar officially rebuked such demands and protests, the Editorial Commission none the less made some gratuitous attempts to represent emancipation as an expression of the nobility's collective will. The commission had completed the main work by October 1860; after a final review by the State Council (an extremely conservative body that inserted some last-minute, pro-noble provisions), Alexander signed the statute into law on 19 February 1861. Fearful of peasant protests, public announcement was delayed for another two weeks—when the onset of Lent (and the end of the merry-making of Shrovetide was past) promised to produce a more sober and docile peasantry.

The government had good reason for anxiety: the 360-page statute was mind-boggling in its complexity, but one thing was clear—it corresponded little to the expectations of the peasantry. Although they were granted 'the status of free rural inhabitants' (with the right to marry, acquire property, conduct trade, and the like), they were still second-class citizens. Emancipation did foresee a gradual integration of peasants into society, but for the present they remained separate, bound to their own local (*volost'*) administration and courts. To ensure police power over the former serfs, the government shifted authority from the squire to the commune and resorted to the traditional principle of 'collective responsibility' (*krugovaia poruka*), which made the ex-serfs collectively

Reading the
Regulations;
peasants on the
Prozerov estate near
Moscow hear the
1861 statute.

accountable for taxes or indeed all other social and financial responsibilities. For
the next decades the peasantry were to be the subject of special disabilities and
obligations—such as the poll-tax (until 1885), corporal punishment (until
1904), and passports to restrict movement (until 1906).

For the peasants, however, the most shocking part of their 'emancipation' was
the land settlement. In the first place, it was not even immediate; for the next
two years peasants were to continue their old obligations to the squire as the
government compiled inventories on landholdings and the peasants' obligations
as serfs. Thereafter these 'temporary obligations' were to remain in force until
both sides agreed to a final settlement, whereupon the peasants would acquire
a portion of the land through government-financed redemption payments.
Peasants who had customarily assumed that the land was theirs now discovered
that they would have to make immense redemption payments over a forty-nine-
year term. The redemption payments were, moreover, increased by inflated
evaluations of the land (up to twice its market value before emancipation). And
worst of all, the emancipation settlement had special provisions to ensure that
the nobility retained at least a minimum part of their estate; as a result of
'emancipation', peasants suffered a loss of land that they had utilized before
emancipation—from 10 per cent in the non-blackearth provinces to 26 per cent
in the blackearth provinces.

The government itself wondered, with deep anxiety, 'what will happen when
the people's expectations concerning freedom are not realized?' The answer was
not long in coming. Whereas the number of disorders had been low on the eve
of emancipation (just 91 incidents in 1859 and 126 in 1860), the announcement
of emancipation ignited a veritable explosion of discontent in 1861—some
1,889 disorders. The most serious confrontations took place in the blackearth

provinces (about half of the disorders were concentrated in ten provinces) and, especially, on the larger estates. In many villages peasants—incredulous that these could have been the terms of the 'tsar's' emancipation—adamantly refused to co-operate in compiling inventories. As a peasant in Vladimir province explained, 'I will not sign the inventory, because soon there will be another manifesto—all the land and forests will be given to the peasantry; but if we sign this inventory, then the tsar will see this signature and say: "they're satisfied, so let it be"'. In many cases military troops had to be summoned to pacify the unruly peasants; among the worst incidents was the bloody confrontation in a village called Bezdna in Kazan province, where the troops panicked and started to shoot, killing and wounding hundreds of unarmed peasants. Although the number of disorders gradually declined (849 in 1862, 509 in 1863, 156 in 1864), the village continued to seethe with resentment and discontent.

Not only peasants, however, would have cause to bemoan emancipation: the former serf-owners were also appalled by its terms. They lost all their police powers, effectively depriving them of any opportunity to force their former serfs to fulfil their old obligations. Nor could squires be certain that they would be able to secure, at reasonable prices, what had earlier been 'free' serf labour to cultivate their lands. Most important, the nobles lost a substantial portion of their land; although in theory they received compensation, much of this went to pay off old debts and mortgages (62 per cent of all serfs had already been mortgaged before emancipation). In short, nobles found themselves short of capital and uncertain of labour, hardly a formula for success in the coming decades. Not surprisingly, emancipation provided a new fillip for gentry liberalism and, especially, demands for the formation of a national assembly of notables to serve as a counterweight to the 'reds' in the state bureaucracy. In 1862, for example, the nobility of Tver issued an address to the emperor: 'The convocation of delegates of all Russia is the sole means for achieving a satisfactory solution to the problems that the [emancipation] statutes of 19 February have posed but not resolved.' Dismayed by the terms of emancipation and by their *de facto* exclusion from the decision-making process, even the socially conservative among the nobility could give their assent to the political programme of 'gentry liberalism'.

The Other Great Reforms

Although emancipation was the most explosive and significant reform, the government also undertook to carry out reforms on many of the other fundamental institutions of the realm. In part, this reformist zeal derived from the general 'Crimean syndrome', which had seemed to demonstrate not only the evil consequences of serfdom, but the general bankruptcy of the old administrative and social order. In addition, many of the reforms derived from the consensus of liberal officials that not only serfs, but society more generally must be 'emancipated' from the shackles of state tutelage, that only this emancipation could liberate the vital forces of self-development and progress. The centralized state had clearly failed to ensure development; freedom thus must be accorded to society. But emancipation itself mandated some changes: abolition of serfdom had eliminated the squire's authority (which had been virtually the only administrative and police organ in the countryside) and hence required the construction of new institutions.

One was a new set of local organs of self-government called the zemstvo. Because the pre-reform regime had been so heavily concentrated in the major cities (with only nominal representation in rural areas) and plainly lacked the human and material resources to construct an elaborate system of local administration, in 1864 the government elected to confer primary responsibility on society itself by establishing a new organ of local self-government, the zemstvo. The reform statute provided for the creation of elected assemblies at the district and provincial level; chosen from separate curiae (peasants, townspeople, and private landowners), the assemblies bore primary responsibility for the social and cultural development of society's infrastructure. Specifically, by exercising powers of self-taxation of the zemstvo, 'society' in each province was to build and maintain key elements of the infrastructure (such as roads, bridges, hospitals, schools, asylums, and prisons), to provide essential social services (public health, poor relief, and assistance during famines), and to promote industry, commerce, and agriculture.

A second major sphere of reform was education, both at the elementary and higher levels. Of particular urgency was the need for elementary schooling: if the former serfs were to become part of the body politic and good citizens, it was essential that the massive illiteracy be overcome. First through the initiative of the Orthodox Church, later the Ministry of Education and the zemstvo, a host of schools sprang up across the countryside. In contrast to the clandestine reformism under Nicholas I, the liberal bureaucrats not only drafted legislation but also published these plans to solicit comment at home and abroad; they then drew heavily on these critical comments as they prepared the final statutes on schools and universities. The Elementary School Statute of 1864 provided the legal framework for this multi-tier system but left financing as the legal responsibility of the local community. A parallel statute sought to regulate and promote the growth of secondary schools. More complex, and political, was reform at the university level, which had been shaken by student unrest and appeared to be a hotbed of radicalism. None the less, the University Statute of 1863 generally dismantled the crippling restrictions of Nicholas I's rule and transformed the university into a self-governing corporation, with far greater rights for its teaching staff and even some recognition of student rights.

The third (and arguably most liberal) reform was the judicial statute of 1864.

Russian courts had been notorious for their corruption, inefficiency, and rank injustice; indeed, so notorious were they that Nicholas had initiated reform by establishing a commission in 1850 to rebuild the court system. But that commission had been dominated by old-regime bureaucrats who lacked formal legal training; in 1861 Alexander, persuaded of their incompetence, abolished that commission and established an entirely new committee, which was dominated by liberal *gosudarstvenniki* (civil servants devoted to the state and its interests). Drawing heavily upon European models, the commission adumbrated the following 'fundamental principles' of the new order: equality of all before the law; separation of the judiciary from administration; jury trial by propertied peers; publicity of proceedings; establishment of a legal profession and bar; and security of judicial tenure. As in the educational reform, the commission published its basic principles and invited commentary by the public and legal specialists. It then reviewed these comments (summarized in six published volumes) and made appropriate adjustments before the statute was finally promulgated in November 1864.

A fourth important focus of reform was the military, which had acquitted itself so badly during the Crimean War and was plainly in need of thoroughgoing reconstruction. The military leaders, indeed, proved to be energetic reformers, eager to rebuild the army and to borrow freely on Western models. The result was a protracted and far-reaching set of reforms—measures for technological rearmament, administrative reorganization, professionalization of military schools. But one essential reform—replacement of a huge standing army without reserves by universal military training—proved politically difficult, chiefly because the reform abrogated the nobility's right *not* to serve (conferred in 1762 and deemed a fundamental privilege). None the less, military reforms prevailed: the Universal Military Training Act of 1874 established all-class conscription, with the terms of service determined solely by education, not social origin or rank. The statute inadvertently had the effect of strengthening peasant interest in popular education, since a two-year elementary schooling could reduce the term of service from six to two years.

A fifth reform was the reform of city government in 1870. The main problem with the existing urban system was that it excluded important residential categories (above all, the nobility) from tax and other obligations, thereby weakening the social and fiscal basis of city government. A commission established in 1862 first conducted a massive survey of public opinion (obtaining formal reports from commissions in 509 cities and towns) and then designed a new self-governing order based on the election of a city council (with curiae weighted according to property ownership). Like the zemstvo, the city council was to provide basic social services, promote commerce and industry, and generally assume responsibility for the development of its own city.

A sixth reform was censorship, which had exercised so notorious and pernicious an influence in pre-reform Russia. The late 1850s had already witnessed a gradual relaxation of censorship (as the regime tolerated public comment on serf emancipation and other reform plans), but the pressure for reform accelerated with the proliferation of journals and newspapers in the 1860s. To a considerable degree, the government found it practically impossible to engage in pre-censorship. It therefore issued the 'Temporary Regulations' of 1865, which abolished most pre-censorship in favour of punitive measures (involving suspensions or closing). Although censorship was by no means eliminated, the new regulations significantly enhanced the ability of the press to publish quickly and, within limits, to exercise some freedom of expression.

The seventh reform concerned the Russian Orthodox Church, which had internalized many norms, structures—and problems—of state and society. Critics emphasized the deplorable condition of seminaries, the caste-like profile of the parish clergy (who had to marry and whose own sons replaced them), the corrupt and inefficient condition of ecclesiastical administration and courts, and the poor support accorded most parish clergy. Special commissions designed a broad range of reforms, including the establishment of parish councils in 1864 (to raise funds for local needs), the reform of ecclesiastical schools in 1867 (modernizing curriculum and opening the schools to youths from all social classes), the formal abolition of the clerical caste in 1867, and a radical reorganization of parishes in 1869 (essentially combining small, uneconomic parishes into larger units). Still more reforms were in preparation, including a liberalization of ecclesiastical courts and censorship.

These Great Reforms thus affected a broad set of social, administrative, and cultural institutions. Most reflected a common set of principles—*vsesoslovnost'* ('all-estateness', i.e. all estates were to participate), *glasnost* ('publicity', i.e. with societal participation in planning and implementing reform), and clear willingness to draw upon Western models. Moreover, most reforms aspired to shift power—and responsibility—from the state to society or particular social groups. Aware that the state lacked the capability or even financial means to modernize, the reformers endeavoured to liberate society's own vital forces and to create structures (from the zemstvo to parish councils) where local initiative could sponsor development.

Economic Development

Although the government appeared to have won the political struggle, in fact deep structural changes were dramatically reshaping society and economy—and not necessarily in the direction of stability or controllable change. By the late 1890s the realm would be shaken by profound unrest—from the factory to the village—that ultimately derived from the pattern of economic and social change in the preceding decades. The key dynamic here was the explosive combination of agricultural crisis and industrialization.

The roots of the agricultural crisis clearly go back to the very terms of emancipation: emancipation transferred the land to the peasant commune, not the individual peasant. The system was partly designed so as to ensure payment, for communal ownership also meant communal (not individual) responsibility for tax and redemption payments. This arrangement greatly facilitated tax-collection (sparing the state the onus of tracking down individual defaulters); given collective accountability, the commune had a powerful motive for ensuring that land was apportioned according to the ability to use it (i.e. according to the number of able-bodied workers in a family). Since family composition naturally changed over time (through births, marriages, and deaths), the commune periodically redistributed land to take these changes into account. Communal landownership also had another appealing feature: it guaranteed each peasant the right to a fair share of land and therefore served to avoid creating a landless proletariat. Indeed, the statute made it virtually impossible for a peasant to alienate his land even if he so wished.

While this arrangement ensured tax-collection and averted the formation of a rural proletariat, it was nevertheless fraught with significant long-term consequences. First, it tied the peasant to the village: since he could not alienate the land, he could not relocate permanently to the city (but, at most, obtain seasonal passports from his commune). Because of this impediment to migration to the

The traditional fair, held on religious holidays and in the close proximity of the church, persisted into modern times. This photograph shows an annual fair from 1875 in the Cossack settlement of Zymlianskii.

city and because of the high rate of demographic growth (the population nearly doubled between 1863 and 1913), the inevitable result was the shrinking average size of peasant allotments—from 5.1 dessiatines (1860) to 2.7 (1900). Although the peasantry did purchase and lease private lands, such acquisitions failed to compensate for the steady demographic growth in the peasantry. The result, heard all across the empire by the late nineteenth century, was the central battle-cry of rebellious peasants—'Land! Land! Land!'

Apart from encouraging peasants to eye jealously the huge fields of the nobility, the individual utilization of small allotments meant that the peasantry (despite their aggregate holdings) could not take advantage of economies of size and afford new technology. Moreover, communal landholding also proved highly inefficient: to ensure that each peasant had a share of the different kinds and quality of communal land, to link land allotment with a family's labour resources, the Russian commune divided its fields into tiny strips (sometimes a yard wide) and periodically redistributed these (taking strips from families with fewer workers and giving them to families with more). This system of land utilization may have been socially just, but it was also economically regressive: it wasted much land on pathways, discouraged individual peasants from improving their strips (which were only temporary allotments), and forced all the peasants to observe the traditional three-field system (to avoid cross-fertilization, no peasant could violate communal practices).

The nobility, at least in theory, were far more advantageously positioned: they retained at least one-third of their entire arable land and obtained capital as compensation for the land redeemed by peasants. While many did seek to modernize and rationalize their estates, they soon encountered serious problems. One was a dearth of investment capital: much of the compensation vanished to cover old debts, and venture capital was as yet difficult to obtain. Labour constituted an additional problem; emancipation had taken away the 'free' corvée and obliged landowners to hire peasant workers, who were exceedingly expensive and notoriously unproductive. Nor were most estates easily linked to the domestic or foreign grain markets; until the railway knitted the empire together and cut transportation costs, many landowners had little incentive to modernize their estates in hopes of increasing productivity and output.

Saddled with all these disadvantages, peasant and gentry agriculture were soon to experience the most devastating factor of all: the collapse of the world grain markets in the 1870s and 1880s. The key was a steady increase in supply, as the railway and new oceanic shipping enabled a massive influx of

Women provided essential labour, not only at home, but in the field, where work remained largely unmechanized right into the twentieth century. The undated photograph from the late nineteenth century shows women threshing.

Industrialization and economic development penetrated not only the major cities of central Russia, but also the periphery. Oil production, illustrated in this photograph from Baku on the Caspian Sea in 1890, was a major growth industry that attracted domestic and foreign capital.

grain from North American and other grain-producing areas outside Europe. The result was a sharp drop in grain prices between 1870 and 1890—about 38 per cent for wheat, 29 per cent for rye, and 41 per cent for barley. By the late 1870s a noble official in the blackearth province of Orel wrote that 'anyone who looks at [this district] might well think that it has been ravaged by a hostile army—so pitiful has its position become'. The steady rise in peasant arrears (overdue tax and redemption payments) and a sharp increase in noble bankruptcies signalled the emergence of a full-scale agrarian crisis.

Industrialization, which had been so retarded and even discouraged by the pre-reform regime, faced considerable obstacles. The country still lacked a proper institutional infrastructure; its regressive business law made it possible to establish a mere thirty-two corporations by 1855. Nor was it easy to mobilize and attract venture capital, either from domestic or foreign sources, because of the lack of a domestic banking network and Russia's low credibility on international money markets. Transportation, especially the virtual non-existence of railways (the only line before 1855 ran between the two capitals), meant that key resources (such as iron ore and coal) and markets could not be easily and economically linked. Russia was also technologically backward; it still imported 70 per cent of all machinery and relied heavily upon outmoded technology. And labour, whether under serfdom or emancipation (which deliberately restricted mobility), was problematic in terms of quantity, skills, and cost.

As in agriculture, emancipation did not primarily seek to serve economic needs or to foster development. Indeed, its initial impact on industrial production proved negative: emancipation of factory serfs brought production at many plants to a standstill, especially in the important metallurgical plants in the

Urals. Still, the regime now had a new and deeper appreciation for the importance of industrialization, especially in the wake of the débâcle of the Crimean War. As one highranking official explained: 'Russia is not Egypt or the Papal States—to be content to purchase materials for her entire army from abroad; we must build our own factories to make arms in the future.' Supported by the military lobby and a small but influential corps of economists, the government was far more sensitive to the needs of industrial and commercial development.

Although the aggregate growth was relatively modest (especially in the 1860s and 1870s), by the mid-1880s the country embarked on an extraordinarily high rate of growth. A considerable part of the growth was concentrated in the vital area of transportation; the total of railway lines increased nearly thirteenfold (from 2,238 versts in 1861 to 28,240 versts in 1887). Simultaneously, the industrial base grew substantially: from 15,000 to 38,000 enterprises (with a corresponding increase in fixed capital, labour force, and output). The corporate structure also expanded substantially; during the years 1861–73 alone, the number of joint-stock companies increased from 78 (with capital of 72 million roubles) to 357 (with 1.1 billion roubles capital). Altogether, industrial production roughly doubled in the quarter-century after emancipation.

Nevertheless, the 'take-off' was yet to come. If 1913 industrial production was 100, by 1885 the empire had only achieved 21 per cent of that output. Despite the growth, Russian industry still suffered from such perennial problems as the lack of venture capital and low labour productivity. Both the heavy and light industrial branches relied heavily upon old technology, had a low level of mechanization, and made only limited use of steam power. Russia still had to import

Off-season handicrafts provided a major source of income for many peasant families, who could use the long winter months to earn a substantial supplement to their agricultural income. This photograph depicts the production of samovars in central Russia in the 1880s.

much of its machinery and even a substantial proportion of its iron and steel from abroad. Moreover, for the first time, the industrial sector was now becoming vulnerable to international business cycles; the economic depression in the empire in the 1870s coincided closely with that in Western Europe. Finally, industrialists also faced a remarkably soft domestic market; the mounting economic woes of the countryside—whether in peasant communes or on gentry manors—limited demand for the goods of the factory.

Despite the weakness of the countryside and gains in the factory, the country grew even more dependent upon grain exports. These had already risen from 16 to 31 per cent in the pre-reform period (1801–60); over the next three decades grain rose to represent 47 per cent of all exports, thereby constituting the backbone of foreign trade and the vital linchpin in the balance of payments. Like the rest of Europe, Russia also gravitated from free trade to protectionism, with an inexorable rise from the low tariffs of the 1850s and 1860s—first to a 10 per cent tariff in 1881, then 20 per cent in 1885, and finally to a prohibitive tariff of 33 per cent in 1891.

Society

The Great Reforms sought to permit *some* social change, but it also endeavoured to ensure that it was slow and gradual. Hence many of the reforms were consciously 'all-estate' (*vsesoslovnyi*), not 'non-estate' (*vnesoslovnyi*); that is, they deliberately sought to include all estates, but to include people *qua* members of the estate, not to disregard estates altogether. Hence the zemstvo included nobles, peasants, and townspeople, but segregated them in separate electoral curiae. And, as a famous contemporary painting by one of the 'itinerants' (*peredvizhniki*) showed, the social distances remained great indeed.

The nobility itself underwent profound change in the wake of emancipation. Juridically, it not only lost the right to own serfs but also surrendered important privileges and perquisites, especially those pertaining to its special access to civil and military service. The new legislation opened schools, including the élite military officer schools, to non-nobles; the inexorable result was a steady influx of non-nobles into institutions of higher learning and, subsequently, into the military and civil service. The change was most dramatic in that old bastion of noble privilege, the officer corps, where the proportion of hereditary nobles shrank from 81 per cent in the 1860s to a mere 12 per cent by the end of the century. The nobles not only forfeited old privileges but also had to bear new responsibilities and burdens. Most notable was the retraction of their right *not* to serve by the Universal Military Training Act of 1874. Economically, as already pointed out, many nobles fared badly under the conditions of post-emancipation agriculture; especially once the international grain crisis descended on Russia, their debts mounted rapidly, leading to a sharp increase in

185

bankruptcies (from a handful in the 1870s to 2,237 in 1893) and in land sales (by 1905 nobles had sold over 40 per cent of their land held at emancipation). Little wonder that, amidst such distress, the nobility proved such fertile ground for opposition in the zemstvo and, from the 1890s, would spearhead the first phase of the 'liberation movement'.

A second component of the élite was the 'nobility of the pen'—the bureaucracy. Although it had early on become differentiated from the landholding nobility (and, especially at the provincial level, had been recruited from non-nobles), this 'democratization' accelerated sharply after 1855 and inexorably recast officialdom, even the élite bureaucracy in the two capitals. Although the very top rungs of the civil service remained the purview of blue-blooded nobles, the middling and lower ranks now drew primarily on other groups, especially the offspring of clergy, townsmen, and the educated professions. But even more remarkable than the change in social composition was the enormous growth in aggregate size of the civil service, which swelled from just 112,000 in 1857 to 524,000 in 1900 in the Table of Ranks (plus many others in lower positions). The 'state', which in pre-reform Russia had been chiefly myth, was rapidly being reified, even in the countryside, where the bureaucracy was gradually coming face to face with the peasantry.

A third component of élite society consisted of men of means—the old merchants but also the new stratum of rich industrialists and bankers. A relatively thin stratum of society, this 'bourgeoisie' actually consisted of several different groups. One important component included Muscovite industrialists and merchants, whose roots went back to the period of Nicholas I and who derived their wealth chiefly from the production and sale of consumer goods (especially textiles) on the domestic market. By all accounts they tended to be more conservative, even in religious matters (with a disproportionate share of Old Believers). Another group was quite different—the St Petersburg industrialists and financiers, who were active in banking and heavy industry. Since much of their activity depended on good relations with the government, they tended to be very conservative politically. The third, highly visible, group consisted of non-Russians, both those from minority groups (especially Jews) and from foreigners (like the Nobel family). In relative terms, this commercial-industrial élite remained very small and, for the most part, remote from politics.

The 'semi-privileged' social orders included the clergy of the Orthodox Church—the parish clergy as well as those serving in monasteries and convents. Although the Great Reforms had endeavoured to improve their status and material condition (indeed, publicists spoke of an 'emancipation' of the clergy, not unlike that of the serfs), in fact the reforms had catastrophic consequences. Above all, the reforms failed to improve the material condition of clergy, for neither the state nor the people proved willing to change the form or amount of material support. The parish statute of 1869, which proposed to amalgamate parishes into larger and more viable economic units, likewise proved a dismal

failure: while it did reduce the number of clerical positions and hence increase the ratio of parishioners to priests, it failed to generate greater income, as parishioners pronounced traditional sums sacred or even reduced them. The seminary reform of 1867 may have improved the curriculum, but it also shifted much of the financial burden of seminaries to the parish clergy. At the same time, the reform gave the clergy's sons new opportunities to *leave* the clerical estate, and they did so in vast numbers (comprising 35 per cent of university students in 1875, for example). As this mass 'flight of the seminarians' gained momentum, the Church suddenly encountered an acute shortage of candidates and had to ordain men of inferior education. By the 1880s observers could already discern an absolute decline in the educational level of the clergy, a process that would continue unabated until the end of the *ancien régime* and indeed beyond.

Another semi-privileged stratum consisted of the new professions, which gained markedly in numbers, status, and self-awareness in the decades after 1855. Previously, most professions had not even enjoyed legal recognition or, at most, simply comprised a subordinate unit of the civil service (for example, doctors and surveyors). After 1855 their number rapidly proliferated, in no small measure because of the rapid expansion of institutions of higher learning and specialized training. As a result, between 1860 and the end of the century, the total number of university and technical-school graduates increased from 20,000 to 85,000; beyond these graduates were many more who failed to graduate or who had an élite secondary-school education. Many of these discovered greatly expanded opportunities for employment not only in state service and the private sector, but also in the new organs of local self-government—the zemstvo and city council, which became a major employer for teachers, doctors, statisticians, agronomists, and the like. By the 1880s, for example, the zemstvo employed some 23,000 white-collar professionals, including 15,000 teachers, 1,300 doctors, and 5,000 registered ill-trained medical practitioners (*fel'dshery*). Some, most notably lawyers and doctors, raised their corporate juridical status by establishing a professional organization, with the right not only to regulate but also to represent their profession. Because of their growing size, importance, and organization, the new professional intelligentsia was rapidly becoming a major force in Russian society and politics. It would play a central role in the liberation movement from the 1890s.

The rank-and-file 'burghers' (*meshchane*) constituted a highly variegated group in the towns, ranging from petty merchants and skilled artisans to the unemployed, unskilled, and unwanted. Certainly their number was increasing sharply, as the cities themselves grew rapidly in size, even more rapidly than the population as a whole. It remained more protean than powerful; while wielding little influence in state and society, it did absorb the steady influx of migrants from the countryside and also became a major source of the upwardly mobile into the new semi-professions and civil service.

The largest, and most disprivileged, segment of society was of course the peasantry. Apart from the economic problems bequeathed by emancipation, the peasants also suffered from legal discrimination (special obligations like the poll-tax, for example) and subordination to the commune. Despite the reformers' attempt to inhibit a sudden social transformation of the traditional village, the peasantry none the less did undergo some far-reaching changes. One was a gradual stratification; despite the levelling effect of the commune, the village came to have its own 'have-much' and 'have-nothing' families, along with the mass of 'have-littles'. And the families themselves began to change, with the gradual breakup of the patriarchal, extended family and formation of smaller, independent family units. Peasant society also came inexorably to reflect changes in urban culture, as increased contact with the city (especially through seasonal labour) helped to disseminate a new material culture, attitudes, and values to the countryside. Partly because of such changes, but also because of the Universal Military Training Act (which reduced service on the basis of education) and the opportunities open to the literate and schooled, the peasantry began to abandon its traditional antipathy towards the school as a useless luxury. Although the reduction of illiteracy was an enormous task, the new schools did have a distinct impact.

Another group, the workers, had antecedents in the pre-reform era, with some forebears going back to the metallurgical and textile plants of the eighteenth century. The steady, if modest, industrial growth from the 1850s to the 1880s brought a substantial increase in the number of workers, from roughly 700,000 in 1865 to 1,432,000 in 1890. While many of these were seasonal

(returning part of the year to cultivate their communal plot of land), a small but growing number had been born in the city or had permanently relocated there. The workers also displayed the explosive volatility for which they would later become so renowned; the St Petersburg textile strike of 1870, a watershed in Russian labour history, heralded the onset of a new era of spontaneous outbursts and, ultimately, more conscious and organized strikes.

The condition and consciousness of women, more generally, underwent a significant transformation during these decades. From the mid-1850s the impact of the women's movement in the West gradually became apparent, especially among those in élite status groups. By 1866 the first women's journal appeared, followed shortly after by a 'Proclamation' (admittedly penned by a man) and the major infusion of radical women into the revolutionary movement. Still more important was the emergence of female professionals; though banned from the civil service, they appeared in increasing numbers in certain professions (especially teaching), sometimes acquired a Western medical degree, or turned to a popular female career equally popular in the West—monasticism and church service. But all this change had to overcome the opposition of society and regime, which still excluded women from the university and resisted proposals to improve their civil rights. Typical was the failure to reform the laws

The petty towns-people—small shopkeepers, merchants, and artisans—provided essential services to the city. The photograph depicts the 'butchers' (*miasniki*) working for family shops at a meat market in the late nineteenth century.

A famous painting from the 1870s by Ilia Repin depicted the 'barge haulers'—the men ashore who helped pull the heavy barges on the Volga river. But women too worked as barge haulers; the photograph shows women pulling a barge on the Oka river (undated).

on divorce and separation, which were highly restrictive and left many women defenceless against abusive spouses and loveless marriages.

The empire's numerous minorities had long been a subject of intense concern. Although the 'Great Russians' comprised a majority (and, together with Ukrainians and Belorussians, nearly three-quarters of the population in European Russia), the empire had a huge and highly differentiated bloc of minorities. Some, like the Ukrainians and Belorussians, were Orthodox by faith and, despite some stirrings in a tiny nationalist intelligentsia, as yet did not pose a serious threat to the territorial integrity of the realm or its internal political stability. And many of the 'internal' minorities, located within Russian-dominated areas, had already been Russified to a considerable degree. The government also sought to suppress neo-Slavophile chauvinism, especially demands for repressive measures against various minorities; typical was Alexander's sharp rebuke in 1869 to Iurii Samarin for his inflammatory book, *The Borderlands of Russia*.

Indeed, in some regions the government launched far-reaching reforms to ameliorate the condition of selected minorities. Certainly the most remarkable beneficiaries were Jews, who, ever since the establishment of the Pale of Settlement in the late eighteenth century, had suffered from a crescendo of disabilities and discriminatory laws, especially in the reign of Nicholas I. In 1856, shortly after coming to the throne, Alexander II vowed 'to review all the existing decrees on the Jews with the general goal of fusing this people with the indigenous population', and in fact did approve a series of important reforms. That same year his government abolished the discriminatory rules on military conscription, which had drafted Jewish youths not only at a higher rate but also at a younger age, as part of a deliberate strategy to subject the 'cantonists' to forcible conversion. From the mid-1850s the government even began to dismantle the restrictions of the Pale of Settlement—although only for selected, valuable members of the Jewish community: first-guild merchants (1859), certain categories of artisans (1865), and finally all Jews with a university degree (1879). Similar concessions were extended to certain other minorities. For example, in the grand duchy of Finland, where a Swedish élite held sway, Finnish was adopted for use in provincial government and courts (1856), later in customs and schools; in 1863 it was formally recognized, along with Swedish, as one of the two official languages.

But the era of Great Reforms included repression as well as concession, especially when the government encountered overt opposition and organized resistance. By far the most volatile area was Congress Poland: long a hotbed of open discontent and the site of a major rebellion in 1830–1, the Poles had jubilantly celebrated news of Russia's defeats in the Crimean War and, despite state attempts at conciliation, became still more rebellious in the first years of the new regime. Tensions steadily mounted in the area and finally exploded in the Polish rebellion of 1863. Although this insurrection was more easily suppressed than that of 1830–1, it none the less precipitated a systematic campaign of repression: abolition of the Polish governmental councils (1867), reorganization of the area into ten Russian administrative provinces (1868), conversion of Warsaw University into a Russian institution (1869), and introduction of the Russian judicial system (1876). Blaming the Catholic Church for fanning anti-Russian and anti-Orthodox sentiments, the government took steps to neutralize this threat by confiscating Catholic property and imposing new controls on its administration (1864–5). The area continued to seethe with discontent and remained a constant source of instability and ferment. The state also resorted to force in the Caucasus, which had been annexed decades earlier, but remained a cauldron of unrest and armed resistance. Although a military campaign in 1857–62 achieved a modicum of control, Russian power remained tentative and vulnerable.

The 1860s and 1870s also marked the expansion of Russian rule into Central Asia, which had long been subject to Russian influence and pressure, but only now came firmly into its orbit of control. Although the motive may have been partly commercial (an interest in its capacity for cotton production), far more important was the need to establish a firm and reliable border in the area. Whatever the motive, between 1864 and 1873 Russia gradually reduced the three khanates (Khiva, Bukhara, and Kokand) to a protectorate status, with unmistakable Russian predominance.

The Revolutionary Movement

Even as the government embarked on the Great Reforms, it encountered not only dissatisfaction among peasants and nobles, but also opposition from an important new force in society—radical youth who collectively came to be called the 'intelligentsia'. Although Russia had had its share of radicals before, they had not constituted a self-conscious social group, with a distinctive identity and subculture. By the 1860s, however, they had gained sufficient critical mass and developed a new social identity, first as 'the new people' (from N. G. Chernyshevskii's novel, *What is to be Done?* [1863]) and eventually as the 'intelligentsia'. Set apart by a special subculture (with distinctive dress, speech, mores, and values), still drawn disproportionately from the upper reaches of society, the intelligentsia none the less conceived of itself as a supraclass force and charged with representing the interests of 'society', especially its lower orders. Sharing a common *Weltanschauung* (which provocatively abjured their fathers' idealism and romanticism in the name of science and materialism), they believed that they could escape the elusive, ethereal forces of history and, with the aid of science and rational planning, construct society and state along entirely new lines. The model for young radicals was skilfully etched in Ivan S. Turgenev's famous novel, *Fathers and Sons* (1862), with the sharp contrast between the older generation and the archetypical lower-class antithesis, Bazarov.

The radicals of the 1860s, still few in number but concentrated in the capitals, marked the first real effluence of an organized revolutionary movement. For the most part these early radicals waged the fight with proclamations, like that of *Young Russia* in 1862: 'With full faith in ourselves and our strength, in the people's sympathy for us, in the glorious future of Russia (to whose lot it has fallen to be the first country to achieve the glorious work of socialism), we will utter a single cry: "To the axe!!" and then strike the imperial party without restraint ... in the city squares ... in the narrow streets of the cities, in the broad avenues of the capital, in the villages and in the small towns'. These early revolutionaries, however, also established the first conspiratorial organizations to wage a battle against autocracy in the name of the people. Alarmed by the upsurge of student disorders, revolutionary proclamations, scattered acts of random violence (from the fires of St Petersburg in 1862 to the failed assassination of Alexander II in 1866), the government grew increasingly repressive in seeking to contain this new and growing wave of radicalism.

The 1860s were only a pallid harbinger of what would come in the 1870s. In contrast to the 1860s, this next stage was marked by an idealization of the peasantry and, especially, hopes that they were on the verge of a bloody Jacquerie against the nobility and autocracy. Later encapsulated in the term 'populism' (*narodnichestvo*), the movement of the 1870s emphasized both the significance of the peasant commune (as an embryonic unit of communism), but also the moral and spiritual strength of the people. The movement indeed affected a whole generation of intellectuals, from writers wont to celebrate the peasantry to zemstvo statisticians intent upon demonstrating the economic superiority of communal agriculture. But for the populist radicals eager to demolish autocracy and truly emancipate the people, it was axiomatic that the peasantry itself was a vital revolutionary force that at most required the co-ordination of the intelligentsia.

In the first phase the radicals were deeply influenced by the teaching of Peter Lavrov, whose *Historical Letters* (1869) emphasized the duty of the intelligentsia—who had acquired their culture and education at the expense of the common folk—to repay their enormous debt by bringing culture and education to the folk. Although Lavrov's challenge to 'repentant noblemen' initially encouraged attempts to disseminate books and literacy, it eventually mushroomed into a more radical campaign of 'going to the people' in 1874–6. That new phase drew less from Lavrov than from the anarchist teachings of M. Bakunin and P. Kropotkin, who believed that the peasantry was innately revolutionary and needed only encouragement. As a result, several thousand members of the urban intelligentsia flooded into the countryside—as teachers, blacksmiths, and the like—for the purpose of fusing with the people. Despite some positive response by the peasantry, the police easily identified and arrested most of these urban misfits and effectively decimated the rank-and-file activists. Though nominally still espousing confidence that revolution could still come from below, the intelligentsia now turned to terrorism—violent attacks on high-ranking officials, the emperor included—in a vain, but desperate attempt to ignite popular revolt and obtain vengeance for the uncompromising violence and repression of the state. Organized in a conspiratorial organization called 'Land and Freedom' (*Zemlia i volia*), the terrorists waged war on the autocracy and bureaucracy even as some of their number continued attempts to ignite a popular Jacquerie from below.

By 1879, however, revolutionary populists turned increasingly to terrorism and, for all practical purposes, abandoned hope of popular insurrection. As the organization's very name 'the People's Will' (*Narodnaia volia*) suggested, the revolutionaries now envisioned themselves as the agents of revolution acting on behalf of the peasantry. This phase of the populist movement drew on the teachings of P. Tkachev, who emphasized that Russia's very backwardness meant the lack of a strong bourgeoisie or nobility and hence the lack of a real social base for autocracy. 'In reality', he wrote, 'the [state's] power is only apparent and imagined; it has no roots in the economic life of the people, and it does not embody the interests of any class'. But this desperate paroxysm of violent terrorism also derived from fear: their encounter with the village (reinforced by the vignettes of populist writers and the numbers of the zemstvo statisticians) revealed that the commune was beginning to dissolve, that the collective was giving way to the kulak. Russia's very development posed the danger that the commune, its special path to the future, was heading unmistakably towards disintegration. It was thus becoming increasingly urgent, the populists believed, that they strike down the very embodiment of the hateful state—the emperor himself.

Counter-Revolution and Counter-Reform

Although the crescendo of revolutionary violence provided one major reason for the government's retreat from the liberal reformism of the 1860s, it was not the only or even the primary reason. No less important was the simple fact that the liberal reforms had failed to work as anticipated or, indeed, had sometimes created new problems while aggravating old ones. Moralizing historians have long been wont to blame the revolutionary intelligentsia for Russia's failure to tread the Western liberal path, but in fact the reforms—themselves deeply influenced by Western models—proved highly dysfunctional and destructive.

The zemstvo reform that established elected bodies of self-government is a case in point. In part, the government was dismayed to find that these organs promptly proceeded to raise political demands—above all, that the edifice be crowned by a national zemstvo. Although the government for the moment was able to stifle such pretensions, in moments of crisis—as in the late 1870s—the zemstvo liberals seized upon the government's weakness and vulnerability to renew their demand for political, not mere administrative, reform. No less important, the zemstvo failed to exercise its authority and in fact proved highly lethargic, falling far short of expectations. While most nobles had little interest in levying local property-based taxes to build schools for peasants, the latter lacked the means to build schools that seemed to offer no immediate material benefit.

Judicial reform proved equally dismaying. In part, contemporaries were deeply alarmed by an apparent explosion in the crime rate, a perception magnified in turn by lurid reporting in the press. Apart from the dissolution of the squire's police powers over the peasantry, some contemporaries were wont to blame the judicial system itself, especially the purported (but exaggerated) leniency of the jury system. More worrisome for the government was the apparent inability of the judicial system to combat political crime and revolutionary terrorism; as a result, the government transferred crimes against the state to a government body (1872) and erected military tribunals to deal with terrorists (1878). When the revolutionaries used public trials as a political stage, when a jury acquitted a female terrorist who had shot and wounded the governor of St Petersburg, the government became still more disenchanted with its system of Western justice. That disillusionment extended to virtually all the other reforms as well—the liberal censorship that tolerated attacks on the government, the universities that produced so many radical revolutionaries, the church reform that left priests in even worse straits than before, and the emancipation that appeared responsible for the plight of both nobles and peasants.

All this served to erode the reform ethos of the 1860s, even among those who had participated in designing the reforms. A former Minister of Interior, P. A. Valuev, was now more sensitive to the dilemmas of stimulating social initiative from below: 'The Russian people, for centuries, have been accustomed to strong authority and its uniform application everywhere. Only government authority, balanced in its weight and with equal, forceful influence on all the far-flung parts of our state, will be able to guide society to its further development on a true and lawful path'. Even more radical was the shift in sentiment of K. P. Pobedonostsev, who had helped design the liberal judicial reform of 1864 but within a few years had become the chief spokesman for conservative retrenchment.

Hard labour and exile were long a preferred device for dealing with political dissenters and ordinary criminals. This photograph from the early 1890s shows the attachment of chains to prisoners in Sakhalin.

Although the government had begun to revise and repair the Great Reforms earlier, the watershed came in the acute political crisis of the late 1870s. The regime found itself now confronted not only by a relentless political terrorism but also by growing restiveness in educated society—at least partly because of yet another débâcle in foreign affairs, the Russo-Turkish war of 1877–8. The conflict had promised to protect Russia's co-religionists from persecution in the Ottoman Empire, and restore Russia's place as a great power; despite the high costs incurred, however, all these gains were undone at the congress of Berlin. By 1879 educated society (which included conservative, not just liberal elements in the nobility) were adamantly demanding political reforms like a constitution and a national assembly. Pobedonostsev, the arch-enemy of such demands, wrote to the emperor's heir that 'what I hear [in St Petersburg] from high-placed and learned men makes me sick, as if I were in the company of half-wits and perverted apes. I hear everywhere the trite, deceitful, and accursed word—constitution'. Indeed, some of the more liberal segments (headed by nobles from Tver) had even entered into clandestine contact with the revolutionary populists.

When repression alone failed to stifle the revolutionary movement, in February 1880 Alexander II appointed a new Minister of Interior, M. T. Loris-Melikov, to deal with the crisis. His tactic, known as the 'dictatorship of the heart', continued the war against revolutionaries but also made a calculated attempt to solicit the support of Russia's more conservative, propertied elements in society. Although wrongly described as a parliamentary reform, his plan essentially foresaw a series of consultative commissions (not unlike those that preceded emancipation) to help advise the government on the proper course of action. Both the preparatory and general commissions would include regular state officials and members elected by the zemstvo and city councils; their task was to make a systematic review of the Great Reforms. This scheme was not, however, intended as a permanent institution; as Loris-Melikov himself explained, 'it would be unthinkable for Russia to have any form of popular representation based on Western models'. Reassured, Alexander II approved the proposal on 1 March 1881.

That same day the terrorists finally got their quarry: a bomb mortally wounded the emperor, who died a few hours later. Although his successor, Alexander III (1881–94), at first hesitated, he was eventually persuaded by Pobedonostsev to reaffirm the fundamental principles of autocracy in a manifesto of 29 April 1881. The manifesto, implicitly a repudiation of Loris-Melikov's plan and indeed of the Great Reforms, led immediately to the resignation of the liberal ministers and to the formation of a far more conservative government. The path was now open for a far-reaching revision of the earlier legislation.

Although contemporaries (especially liberals) characterized the new measures as a 'reaction', they did not constitute a 'restoration' of the old order. It was, of course, plain to all that neither serfdom nor the order it sustained could be re-established. What the new government did seek to do, however, was to reassert the primacy of dynamic state leadership and autocracy. The 'counter-reforms' in censorship (1882) and education (1884), for example, specifically sought to emphasize the state's power and dispensed with earlier hopes that society would show initiative and responsibility. Particularly important on the agenda was the re-establishment of firm police power; the 'temporary regulations of 14 August 1881' created 'extraordinary' security powers which, in fact, were renewed every three years and expanded to a growing list of areas until the regime finally fell in 1917. Indeed, the regime of Alexander III was wont to cultivate and reward *proizvol*—the gratuitous display of arbitrariness and power—among its officials. Reassertion of the autocratic principle had increasingly assumed the form of a counter-*Rechtsstaat*, a volte-face in policy that was all the more anathema and provocative for liberal, educated society.

The 1880s also signalled an important new era in state policy towards national minorities. Although Alexander II had dealt brutally with the rebellious Poles, he had not engaged in systematic, coercive Russification and even made significant concessions in some instances. His son's government, by contrast, launched a far more aggressive campaign, one that crossed the divide from administrative to cultural Russification. Perhaps the most striking example of the change in policy concerned the Baltic Germans, an élite that had served the empire loyally and that had enjoyed the special confidence and protection

For all the state's attempts to control population movements, with stringent passport regulations, the countryside was nevertheless alive with a floating population of private traders, vagabonds, and beggars. This photo from the end of the century depicts a 'typical indigent'.

of Alexander III's predecessors. From the mid-1880s, however, St Petersburg took vigorous measures to 'Russify' the area, requiring that Russian be used in state offices (1885–9) and elementary and secondary schools (1887–90), that the imperial police and judicial system be adopted (1889), and that the German university of Dorpat be Russified as Iurev University (1889–93). Simultaneously, the government reversed its earlier concessions to Jews. The most important repressive measures included the 1887 quotas limiting the number of Jewish students in secondary schools and universities (10 per cent in the Pale, 5 per cent outside, and 3 per cent in the two capitals). Later measures included rules to exclude Jews from the bar (1889), zemstvo (1890), and city councils (1892). Similar encroachments were made on other groups, even those like the Finns, who had hitherto enjoyed special protection, but now were exposed to a gradual Russification that would reach a crescendo in the late 1890s.

But paternalistic autocracy also made concessions, at least for its putative base of 'loyal subjects'. For the nobles it created a new Noble Bank (with special low-interest rates) and, in an imperial manifesto of 1885, made new promises of a greater role: 'The Russian nobles [will] preserve their preponderance in the military command, local governments, courts, and in the dissemination (through example) of the precepts of faith and fidelity'. The government also made concessions to the lower social groups as well—such as the Peasant Bank (1883) to assist in land purchases and the abolition of the poll-tax (1885). Disturbed by unrest among factory workers and influenced by the social policy in Bismarckian Germany, the government also adopted a number of far-reaching laws to restrict child labour and other labour abuses in 1882–6. By 1890 repression, moderated by such social concessions, appeared to have restored stability to the realm: disorders in the factory and village were at a nadir, even the revolutionary movement appeared to constitute no real match for the regime's police forces.

But the dominant element, especially in contemporary perception, was 'reaction'—blind attempts to repress and refasten the shackles of the old order. This reversion was all the more intolerable because it seemed to reverse the gains of the 1860s and 1870s. It was, indeed, in many instances outright counter-productive. While seeking to reconstruct the multinational empire into a homogeneous state, with uniform Russian culture and administration from border to border, the government was merely succeeding in accelerating the development of national consciousness and revolutionary sentiments, even among the most

A group photograph of metalworkers, who quickly shed their peasant dress and in time became a critical driving force in the working-class movement.

loyal minorities in the empire. To a very considerable degree, the geographic periphery was becoming the political centre: the rebellious sentiments, combined with weakness of state control, was turning the borderlands into the staging-ground and bastion of revolution. The revolutionary movement would recruit heavily from these borderlands as the *ancien régime* gradually slid towards the abyss of 1917.

REVOLUTIONARY RUSSIA
1890–1914

REGINALD E. ZELNIK

*Rapid industrialization, though vital for military power abroad,
ignited deep-rooted unrest in both town and country. By 1905
this 'modernizing autocracy' suffered humiliating defeat in the
East and revolutionary upheaval at home. In the aftermath,
despite grudging if important concessions, the regime failed to
establish the social solidarity—or submission—needed to
survive the onslaught of modern warfare.*

ANY analysis of imperial Russia at the end of the nineteenth century and beginning of the twentieth must include the obvious but essential reminder that Russia was still an autocracy (*samoderzhavie*). This was not simply a garden-variety old regime, with a divinely anointed absolute monarch at the top and a system of legally defined social estates (*sosloviia* = *Stände*), headed by the nobility, defining its social hierarchy. It was also an old regime whose sovereigns, even the most 'liberal' (Alexander II), self-consciously resisted the dilution of their sovereign power, the delegation of that power to intermediary institutions, and its limitation by any constitutional mechanism. Although laws abounded, and had even been codified, until 1906 Russia's rulers refused to recognize as definitive any body of law that could not be subordinated to or reversed by the autocratic will, as it often was. There was, again until 1906, no equivalent of a Reichstag, no universal manhood suffrage (indeed no suffrage of any sort at the national level), no legal parties to outlaw (as German Social Democracy had been outlawed in 1878), no labour unions or other free associations of workers to persecute and harass.

It was also a regime that deeply distrusted and only grudgingly tolerated any kind of independent civic association organized from below, not only by the lower classes, but even by society's élites. It was still more distrustful of organizational activity that brought those élites into contact with 'the people' in social contexts free from state supervision or that seemed likely to escape the reach of government oversight and control. It was, in short, a polity in which invisible mechanisms of cultural hegemony, civic normalization, *embourgeoisement*, positive or negative integration—or whatever other metaphor one chooses to suggest the idea of social control without flagrant resort to *force majeure*—were neither readily available nor easily deployed.

The Great Reforms of the 1860s and 1870s did, however, represent a significant change in the mode of government, marking Russia's entry into a new era. During this period the serfs were freed, the zemstvo was introduced as an element of civil society at the local level, trial by jury and a relatively independent judiciary and bar were authorized, and the free professions were permitted to begin an open if vexed existence, with their own professional associations. It was also a period when some branches of government attracted a new breed of enlightened bureaucrat, less reluctant to open his mind to new ways and ideas, even while forced to submit to the domination of officials of an earlier stamp.

All these developments seemed to contradict the principle of unbridled autocracy, while a (more or less) capitalist industrialization, first in the 1870s and 1880s, then more intensively in the 1890s, moved powerfully, if never decisively, against the grain of old status-based hierarchies. Nevertheless, notwithstanding all these dramatic (and to important elements of the government) disturbing changes, indeed in part *because* of them, there was enormous reluctance to allowing the winds of change to blow in the direction of a liberalized political system, where society might seek to fulfil its aspirations independently of the state.

This is not to say that the state could snuff out all the ventures of society, of unofficial Russia acting in an organized capacity and a 'civilizing spirit'. For with the slow but continuing development of Russia's public sphere (in a word, of *glasnost'*), each decade from the 1870s—even the 'reactionary' 1880s and 1890s—witnessed the appearance, sometimes even with official approval, of new initiatives from below. They came mainly from members of the educated élite (less often from peasants or workers), many of them openly dedicated to high-minded public causes, to social progress, and to forging positive links between the 'people' (*narod*) and 'society'. As long as such activity respected certain limits, even if never fully trusted by the government, it was tolerated to some extent, even during the so-called era of 'counter-reforms' of the late 1880s and 1890s.

The traditional version of the story of late imperial Russia, one that highlights the promise of the Great Reforms, but then goes on to recount the erosion of that promise in the age of 'reaction', is not without its virtues: the Great Reforms did promise constructive and enlightened (if not necessarily liberal) change, and the decades of the 1880s–1890s did witness a reversal of certain reforms of the previous reign, especially in the areas of local self-government and higher education.

Yet some important qualifications must be added to this seductively clear picture. From the very outset the Great Reforms were beset by serious contradictions: the coexistence of peasant courts and special administrative punishment with a new, Western-model jury system; abolition of serfdom but preservation of special disabilities for peasants—an internal passport system, compulsory redemption payments, and obligatory membership in communes; acceptance of a new property-based franchise as the foundation of local government, but reaffirmation of institutions based on the traditional juridical estates (not to mention the *de facto* dominance of the hereditary gentry, barely 1 per cent of the population). At the same time, even during counter-reforms and reaction, radical changes overtook society, economy, and government policy and continued to move the country in a more Westerly, 'progressive', modern (if not truly liberal) direction. In sum, at almost every point between the emperors' most dramatic manifestos—the Emancipation manifesto of 1861 and the October manifesto of 1905—Russian society was in a state of tension, with multiple protagonists and antagonists, some of them seeking a radical reconfiguration of power and policy.

Industrial Progress and Rural Hunger

Around the time of the 'counter-reform' of 1890, the revised zemstvo statute, the tensions in Russian society became increasingly apparent. The 'Witte era' (1892–1903) was about to begin. These were the years marked by the influence, if not full political dominance, of the controversial but eminent Minister of Finance, Sergei Witte (Vitte), the former railway executive whose provocative developmental economic policies raised the ire of so many gentry and caused so much friction within the government itself. The policies of his predecessor, Ivan Vyshnegradskii (1887–92), anticipated those of Witte and also exposed their problematic consequences. Among the most important policy initiatives launched by Vyshnegradskii and continued by Witte was the pressure, applied through taxation, to force peasants to market grain at low prices. These ministers of finance also imposed a high protective tariff, which grew with time and made it increasingly difficult for market-oriented grain producers to purchase much-needed machinery and chemical fertilizers abroad. The 'modernizing' purpose here was to further economic progress by improving Russia's balance of trade and by promoting domestic industries. But the consequence was to alienate both gentry and peasantry, the tsar's élite servitors and his poorest subjects, respectively. Though often in conflict with each other over such issues as land use, both groups felt squeezed by the ministry's developmental policies (a situation, *grosso modo*, that could be traced back to Peter the Great). And as always, the image of poor peasants victimized by government policy provided grist to the mill of the liberal and radical intelligentsia, with their keenly felt obligation to the people and reluctance to equate 'progress' with capitalist development (the populist writer Nikolai Mikhailovskii being a good case in point). In this instance, however, the criticism of modernizing 'bureaucracy', from both the right and the left, conservatives and liberal alike, did not mean that the state was walking sensibly down the middle of the road. It was not.

Maria Iakunchikova (née Mamontova), wealthy patron of the arts, and artist Natalia Davydova, both members of the cultural intelligentsia, exemplified the desire of that élite to identify with Russia's common people in general, peasants and rural artisans in particular. Here the two very dedicated women are seen in the early 1880s wearing peasant dress.

Tolstoy, in what had become a characteristic pose, sharing his simple wisdom with his grandchildren. The death of this 'evil genius' (words of Nicholas II) in 1910 was a major event in Russia's cultural and political history.

The accumulating resentments multiplied in 1891–2, when large parts of the Russian countryside, some twenty provinces in all, experienced this period's greatest famine (followed by devastating cholera and typhus epidemics), a human catastrophe with casualties in the hundreds of thousands. Historians still argue about responsibility—whether famine was the product of government policies or the deeper cyclical malfunction of a backward agrarian structure. Apart from the famine as such, they argue about whether the peasants' lot was actually worsening by 'objective' measurements (for example, caloric intake), about the meaning of rural overpopulation (was demographic growth a sign of 'progress'—a reflection of declining mortality?), and even about the best methods for measuring such assessments. This debate will continue, a scholarly controversy that echoes England's classic 'standard-of-living' debate. But whatever the truth about 'objective' conditions, there can be no doubt that contemporaries were deeply alarmed about the famine and its aftermath, or that their 'subjective' perception fuelled resentment against state programmes that seemed inherently harmful to society in general and to 'the people', especially the peasants (over 80 per cent of the population), in particular. The Ministry of Finance won few friends with its programme for economic progress.

This negative assessment of state policy in the 1890s readily reinforced existing attitudes of the educated public. Russia's radical intellectuals (best typified by the sometime liberal, sometime radical, N. K. Mikhailovskii), but even many moderates (not to mention the eccentric, politically enigmatic figure of Leo Tolstoy), generally placed a low premium on economic development, widely viewed as attainable only at the common people's expense. Less surprising but no less important was the low value placed on economic progress by conservative intellectuals, whose fear of what today is called the evils of modernization or Westernization—Alexander Solzhenitsyn comes readily to mind—sometimes made them odd allies with people who otherwise stood far to their left.

From a political perspective, the most important result of the famine was revitalization of the zemstvo, earlier a locus of non-governmental public activity and liberal aspirations, but in the 1880s restricting itself to 'small deeds'. Ineffective in efforts to combat famine when utilizing only its own resources, by late 1891 the government was once again driven to encourage the very kind of grass-roots, voluntary social action that it normally distrusted—from the relief work of district zemstvos and university students to the charitable efforts of national cultural figures such as Tolstoy and Anton Chekhov. Society was summoned back to life to take part in a national war on poverty.

Throughout the most hard-hit areas of Russia, the hungry blackearth and Volga provinces, the zemstvos took the lead (although, as Richard Robbins has argued, the degree of successful co-operation between zemstvo and central government is often underestimated). The point, however, is not that the zemstvos' efforts were universally successful (far from it), but that their self-confidence, self-assertion, and self-importance were given an enormous boost, so much so that in the immediate post-famine years, some zemstvos again challenged the central government.

The advent of Nicholas II to the throne in 1894 encouraged zemstvos and other civic bodies to convert their newly acquired prestige into a political force. In keeping with their as yet modest goals, perhaps encouraged by the recent flashes of co-operation with the government, their approach—except for the aggressive Tver zemstvo—was the traditional supplication: a hopeful request to the new, little-known young monarch to include them in his policy deliberations. His notorious response in January 1895 rejected such aspirations as 'senseless dreams' and reaffirmed the autocratic principles of his beloved father, Alexander III. This insensitive response was only the first of several dramatic moments (the 1896 Khodynka Field tragedy, when hundreds of spectators were trampled to death at the Moscow coronation ceremonies, was the next) that disrupted constructive dialogue between state and society in the first ten years of Nicholas's rule.

Revival of the Left

The events of 1891–2, with the continued rigidity of autocratic governance in the years that followed, helped to revive the radical left, which, like the more moderate zemstvo movement, had been licking its wounds in the 1880s. True, the People's Will and other like-minded, terror-oriented grouplets (including a short-lived conspiratorial student band in 1887 dominated by Alexander Ulianov, Lenin's elder brother) had never entirely ceased their plotting. But until the new mood of the 1890s, they had entertained precious little hope, certainly less than in the 1870s, of effective contact with the 'people' (whether peasants or workers) on the one hand, or with zemstvos and other moderates or liberals on the other. From the mid-1890s, however, radicals saw new opportunities: alliances, however uneasy, with increasingly disaffected liberals to their right; contact, however awkward, with the 'people', especially the growing numbers of factory workers in and near the rapidly industrializing larger cities.

Except for the earlier stages of the 1905 Revolution, co-operation between liberals and socialist radicals never seemed brighter than in the early 1890s. The so-called 'People's Rights Party' (1893–4), a populist-oriented organization that jettisoned terrorism, stressed the importance of political freedom and welcomed both radicals and moderates to join its ranks. Although that party was short-lived, the entire period from 1892 to early 1905 saw on-again-off-again efforts of the more flexible radicals, both populist and Marxist, and the more daring liberals to find common ground. At the same time, more cautious liberals courted the more enlightened members of the bureaucracy, who in turn were willing to co-operate with 'trustworthy' leaders of the zemstvo movement, especially the so-called neo-Slavophiles. It was as if every point on the Russian political spectrum, save the most extreme ones, was occupied by someone desperately seeking to hold hands with allies to the right and to the left.

Labour Unrest

Thanks to Witte's initial success, in the 1890s Russia experienced a rate of industrial growth never to recur until the 1930s. Indeed, industrial production increased at an average of 8 per cent per annum, higher even than that of the USA. Did this rapid growth augur progress or conflict? As in other countries, the answer was *both*: 'progress', as Russia's national economy closed the gap somewhat with other European countries, but also 'conflict' as Russian cities experienced the tell-tale warning signs of urban blight, working-class dissatisfaction, and gathering social tensions.

The renewed labour unrest that erupted in some of the factories of central Russia, including Moscow, in the mid-1890s, was dwarfed by a succession of city-wide strikes in St Petersburg's textile industry in 1896–7. Never before had

Drawn by Isaak Brodsky and entitled 'Tired', this picture expresses the bitter despair and fatigue of some parts of the Russian Left in the wake of the suppression of the 1905 Revolution.

The intense gaze of socialist realism can already be seen in this poster commemorating International Women's Day, 8 March, the anniversary of the original demonstrations that launched Russia's Democratic Revolution in February 1917 (the calendar of course was 13 days behind that of the West until the Bolsheviks adopted the Gregorian calendar in early 1918). Women's liberation remained high on the agenda of the young Soviet state.

labour unrest been so widespread and so well co-ordinated in a single Russian city, indeed, not in just any city but in the imperial capital, seat of royal authority and centre of imperial administration.

But were these strikes of great political significance? Historians have debated this point, opinions ranging from those who see them as spontaneous and purely economic, to those who read them as early successes of a young Russian Marxism. Although the Russian Social Democratic Workers' Party (RSDWP) was not officially founded until 1898, Marxist circles were already in full flower in the capital by mid-decade. While the influence of early Russian Marxism should not be exaggerated, Allan Wildman has clearly demonstrated that the spontaneous labour movement was aided, abetted, and to some degree even inspired by Marxist agitators, some of whom had been closely connected with the young Marxist Vladimir Ilyich Ulianov.

But of still greater historical importance was the strikes' *indirect* political significance: Russians of all persuasions saw them as a major historical moment,

As the labour movement gained momentum, factory owners, often with government support, tried to inculcate conservative religious notions into their workers, as illustrated by this shop-floor Orthodox service at a plant in the Urals at the turn of the century.

pregnant with either promise or peril, depending on the observer's politics. Not that these perceptions were always consistent or predictable. In government circles, for example, some interpreted the strikes as a 'wake-up call', warning of the dire consequences of continuing Witte's policies, while others saw them as evidence of the need for enlightened labour legislation to meet the needs of a modern industrializing society. A few officials, at times including Witte himself, went so far as to contemplate the legalization of labour unions, while the Minister of Interior proposed to shorten the working day (a logical extension of labour legislation on women and minors promulgated in the 1880s). A limit on the working day was introduced in 1897; (partial) legalization of unions did not come until 1906, however, and then in a very different context.

In the wake of the Petersburg strikes of 1896–7, even conservative officials who loathed Witte's industrialization schemes recognized the need to contain working-class unrest. As often happened, such awareness was motivated by a mixture of direct Russian and vicarious European experience. Just as the Paris Commune of 1871 had precociously alerted Russians to potential dangers in their own urban centres, the spread of social democracy and labour militancy among 'disloyal' German workers, when added to such events as the Petersburg strikes, convinced conservatives in the Ministry of Interior, most notably the notorious Sergei Zubatov, that police-supervised associations were needed to stem the tide of unrest. To men like Witte, however, the very idea of placing the fate of industrial labour in the hands of the police (later described by critics as 'police socialism') was a foolish provocation. Moreover, such approaches seemed like yet another expression of gentry hostility to Witte's policies, so rampant in the Ministry of Interior. Lacking a clear alternative, the Witte faction vacillated between advocacy of simple repression and of such daring moves as the legalization of unions. The tension between Witte and Zubatov over labour policy was emblematic of a larger tension between the Ministry of Interior and the Finance Ministry, with the basic direction of social and economic policy at issue.

The Role of Foreign Policy

Given the social and political strains produced by Witte's policies, historians have asked whether they were necessary. Might an alternative path have been followed? Even if one forgoes foreign-policy determinism (*Primat der Außenpolitik*), one must still concede that Russia's relations with the outside world, and especially with the European powers, configured the context for the policies of the Finance Minister, sometimes in the foreground, sometimes at a further remove. Russia's frail finances severely restricted the risks that the government could assume in foreign policy, especially with respect to the critical areas of the Balkans and the Black Sea, but also with respect to expansion in the Far East. At the same time, Russia's presumptive but precarious position as a 'great power' provided an underlying motivation for the pursuit of economic development, industrial strength, and financial independence.

To be sure, Russia's rulers always had the theoretical option of abdicating their great-power aspirations. But to do so would have threatened to undermine the entire regime, dynasty and all. It is hard to imagine a Romanov ruler openly agreeing to renunciation of great-power status, which would have entailed the closing of the Black Sea to Russian shipping, the resurrection of an independent Poland, perhaps even the abandonment of Peter the Great's Baltic conquests and withdrawal from Central Asia. It took little imagination to itemize the potential losses from such an abdication—not to mention the symbolic significance of the forswearing of Russia's traditional role, ever since the eighteenth century, as protector of Christian minorities from their Ottoman oppressors. A Russian ruler who openly repudiated these ambitions effectively abandoned his claim to be emperor, and to rule—and, quite conceivably, the moral and political support of the gentry élite.

Such considerations belie the historical possibility of a very different course. There were indeed real choices to be made, but they were between a bold, adventuristic, risk-taking policy that courted the twin dangers of humiliation and bankruptcy, and a more cautious, conservative policy that postponed immediate gratification and gambled on economic development as the key to future claims to power. The latter policy underlay Witte's domestic programme, though a cautious posture was increasingly difficult to maintain as Russia became entangled in Asian adventures.

The successful pursuit of a cautious foreign policy also required stable relations with Germany. Yet those relations were strained by the Russo-German tariff war, already under way when Vyshnegradskii took office in 1887, at a time when there was little reason to be sanguine about Russia's international position. A war scare with England two years earlier had added yet another chapter to the story of Russian humiliations in Paris in 1856 and Berlin in 1878. By the time Witte succeeded Vyshnegradskii, the Russian military—despite the misgivings of political conservatives and enemies of republicanism—had begun its turn to France, a move long favoured by Pan-Slavs and liberals alike. In 1892, even a cautious Foreign Ministry (still ever mindful of the need to get on well with Germany) concluded its first, quite limited *entente* with Paris. By the end of the decade Russian economic as well as foreign policy were more oriented towards France than ever, with French bankers, businessmen, and government officials filling gaps created by the withdrawal of Germans. This of course meant more potential conflict with Austria-Hungary, the Ottoman Empire, and—though there were temporary respites in the tariff wars from 1894 to 1901—ultimately with Germany itself, thereby creating a vicious circle that made loans from France all the more imperative. But until the turn of the century, it was still too early to foresee the potential conflict brewing with Japan over the two countries' competing ambitions in the Far East.

Revolutionary 'Parties'

In the 1890s these foreign-policy issues were of little concern to the Russian left. As was their wont, radicals were more attentive to the fate of peasants and workers, with workers attracting an ever-greater share of their attention. If labour policy and attitudes towards workers exposed and intensified divisions in the government, they also produced divisions on the left, which had never been without its internal conflicts over how best to relate to the people that it aspired to lead or represent. Even in the 1870s, when revolutionaries envisioned the peasantry as the repository of their 'Utopian' dreams, they had already become heavily involved in the lives of urban workers, especially those in St Petersburg. This involvement entailed closer and closer contacts in that city between a marginalized group of young factory workers and a *self*-marginalized group of student intelligentsia, with the two groups interacting within the confines of the clandestine 'circle' (*kruzhok*), meeting in the overcrowded apartment of some of the members. These gatherings were the spiritual descendants of the intelligentsia circles of the age of Nicholas I, yet differed to the extent that they now drew many genuine plebeians into their orbit. Though the strategies and tactics varied over time (for example, armed rebellion vied with peaceful propaganda, tight conspiracy with openness), the circles had a powerful, persistent institutional presence right up to the revolutionary events of 1905, and to some extent beyond. Often heterogeneous in its class composition, the 'all-class' circle or 'mixed-class' circle soon gave birth to an illegitimate offspring—the circle composed exclusively of workers, who often struggled to define themselves in opposition to the intelligentsia-dominated, socially mixed groups that had spawned them.

By increasing the size and concentration of the working class, Witte's policies expanded the arena of radical activity and opened the door to a Marxist perspective on the left. By the eve of 1905 the left included competing revolutionary strategies, each eventually embodied in a 'party': the Party of Socialist Revolutionaries (PSR, or simply the SRs, formally constituted in 1901) and two rival factions of the Russian Social Democratic Workers' Party (RSDWP), the Bolsheviks and Mensheviks (products of the party's schism in 1903). 'Party' is placed in quotation marks to emphasize that none was a party in the traditional West European political sense, that is, an organization that existed for the competitive pursuit of national elective office: there *was* no such office before 1906. Instead, these parties were underground organizations, seeking to overthrow the existing system and—here came some monumental disagreements—replace it either *temporarily*, with a liberal-democratic, constitutional polity and market economy (a 'bourgeois phase'), or *permanently*, with a 'socialist' order (in any case a clearly non-capitalist socio-economic system). Among European Marxists, nowhere was the issue of the succession of revolutionary 'phases' more hotly debated than in Russia, yet another expression of the reworking of West European experience into a relatively backward socio-economic context.

The SRs, identifying strongly with populist traditions of the 1870s and the terrorism of People's Will, welcomed signs of worker rebelliousness, but treated workers as but another component part of the larger 'people', whose centre of gravity remained in the huge peasant majority. Both workers and peasants, from the SR perspective, were victims of state-sponsored capitalism, a system that lacked a broad social base or other redeeming feature and could still be short-circuited either by revolutionary action or reversal of government policy. Most SRs were of the ultra-revolutionary persuasion. They were often high-energy revolutionary performers, and their patience with any schemes for a 'transitional' or temporary phase, postponing socialism to some more distant point in time, was, for the moment, very thin. There was, to be sure, a handful of populist-oriented publicists in the 1890s who believed in peaceful persuasion and other lawful means, but these 'Legal Populists' had lost much of their influence by the end of the century.

Some Marxists, those who became the Mensheviks, did not believe Russia ready for 'proletarian' or 'socialist' revolution and set as their proximate goal a 'bourgeois' revolution, whereby not workers—their ostensible constituency—but the enemy camp of capitalists would be the immediate beneficiary. Strictly speaking, the Mensheviks were following the logic of Orthodox Marxism, or that, at least, was their own perception. Capitalism was evil, of course, but a necessary evil, which carried the seeds of a socialist future in its womb. Rapid economic growth was therefore a sign of progress, auguring a liberal, bourgeois revolution (though one that the working class might have to lead!) in the near term, a proletarian revolution sometime thereafter. This complex analysis led some 'Legal Marxists' (Peter Struve, despite his early misgivings about the 'cowardice' of the Russian bourgeoisie, is the most illustrious example) away from socialism and all the way into the liberal, non-revolutionary camp. It was an analysis, however, that would not necessarily appeal to workers, even those who eschewed revolutionary rhetoric and practice.

Finally, there were the Bolsheviks, who, like the Mensheviks, claimed to spurn much of the populist legacy—glorification of the commune, rejection of a capitalist phase, terrorism. But the Bolsheviks shared the populists' thoroughgoing impatience with intermediary, liberal-type solutions, their almost personal contempt for liberals, and even for revolutionaries who tolerated them (Lenin best embodied this contempt), and their furious rejection of any form of *attentisme*. As Marxists they had no choice but to share the Menshevik belief that the growth of capitalism in Russia was secure and augured progress; this indeed had been the central argument in Lenin's huge, statistically burdened book *The Development of Capitalism in Russia* (1899). But as Russian revolutionary maximalists they would seek every possible way to drive their insurrectionary train past the capitalist station with, at most, the shortest of stops.

None of the revolutionaries, and least of all the future SRs, could openly endorse Witte's policies. But the two main groups of Marxists (there were still others, the most vital of which was the Jewish Social Democratic 'Bund') did greet the spread of capitalist industry as evidence of the predictive power and dialectical astuteness of their Marxist 'science' and welcomed the appearance of both industrial bourgeoisie and industrial proletariat as positive omens of impending class struggle. New labour unrest provided them with further evidence: the militant 'Obukhov defence' in St Petersburg in 1901 and general strikes in Rostov-on-the-Don and Odessa in 1903, Russia's greatest year of labour unrest before 1905. Predictably, the industrial recession that set in around 1900, discrediting the Witte system in the eyes of many, was viewed by most Marxists not as a sign of the weakness of Russia's economy (and its dependence on foreign capital), but as further evidence that a capitalist Russia was now enmeshed in the international business cycle. It was.

Militant Moderates: 1900–1904

The years 1900–4, while displaying great continuity with the 1890s, also witnessed some important new lines of development. One was a burgeoning aggressiveness and self-assertion on the part of liberal constitutionalists. Their centres of gravity were both the zemstvos (including zemstvo employees, generally more radical than their gentry employers) and the thriving professional associations of lawyers, doctors, academics, and journalists, all of them inspired by resurgent unrest among university students (which, after all, most professional intelligentsia had been). At the same time, these years also witnessed the revival of revolutionary terrorism. Usually conducted by a conspiratorial section of the PSR, this terrorism evoked unexpected sympathy among other, less radical members of educated society, many of whom were increasingly alienated from the autocratic state. And, perhaps most important, during these years Russia's Asian policy became increasingly expansionist and aggressive, culminating in a fateful war with Japan in 1904–5. That war, and especially its glaringly unsuccessful conduct and the resulting national humiliation, served to raise the level of political unrest in almost every layer of society and within every political grouping, pushing Russian political dialogue several degrees to the left.

The immediate political beneficiary was the movement of liberal constitutionalists. Having started to stir again in the 1890s, they now came to life as never before and, I would argue, never again. By 1902 zemstvo activists—including zemstvo agronomists and other employees, the so-called 'Third Element'—joined together with urban professionals and even some former Marxists to organize their own illegal, left-liberal paper (*Liberation*, published in Stuttgart under the editorial leadership of Struve). In one respect, namely

A 1904 propaganda postcard representing the Russian navy defeating the Japanese navy in the Russo-Japanese war. The picture is unrealistic in more ways than one.

their conception of a newspaper as 'political organ' and organizing centre for their movement, the 'Liberationists' were not very different from Lenin, who in his famous 1902 tract *What is to be Done?* treated the SD paper *Iskra* (the Spark) with the same tender adulation as Struve and his colleagues soon were treating *Osvobozhdenie* (Liberation).

Liberals also turned out to be ingenious at developing their own non-revolutionary yet militant tactics, of which the most effective was the 'banquet campaign' of November–December 1904 (inspired by a similar campaign before the French Revolution of 1848). They used the pretence of every plausible anniversary celebration—from the Emancipation to the 1864 judicial reforms—to assemble, in defiance of government restrictions, and draw society's attention to the need for constitutional reform. Unsuccessful war had been a major catalyst for change half a century earlier, a lesson not lost on the constitutionalists of 1904–5. And whereas the assassination of Alexander II had purportedly thwarted reform, the new wave of assassinations (which included three imperial ministers and a grand duke and culminated in the SR murder of Plehve, the hated Minister of Interior, in July 1904) actually served to debase the government's credit and quicken the winds of change. That even liberals like Pavel Miliukov seemed to welcome news of Plehve's assassination was a sure sign of trouble ahead for the state.

The tsar's decision to replace Plehve with a moderate, Peter Sviatopolk-Mirskii (already known for his willingness to appease radical students), as the new Minister of Interior was less a reflection of the tsar's enlightenment and flexibility than of his vacillation and despair. And it was interpreted as such by contemporaries. After a brief optimistic 'spring' based on a false hope that the new minister would be allowed to bring about some fundamental change, the process of political polarization resumed. The contentiousness of autocracy's enemies now grew apace, as even moderates waited impatiently for the moment that would advance their cause.

Enter Father Gapon: A Road to Bloody Sunday

That moment was soon provided by St Petersburg's industrial workers. In 1904, in what seemed like a reprise of the Zubatov experiment (defunct since the summer of 1903) without Zubatov, the charismatic Orthodox priest Georgii Gapon had succeeded in mobilizing thousands of members into his 'Assembly of Russian Factory Workers'. Originally approved and even financed by the police (with the goal of weaning workers away from the radicals and bolstering their commitment to autocracy by providing safe outlets such as tea-rooms and public lectures), Gapon's organization soon took on a life of its own. On the one hand, some of his most trusted aides turned out to be former Marxists who, though no longer very revolutionary, still provided workers with intense exposure to the Western model of a legal labour movement and notions of civil rights and constitutional order. On the other hand, the grass-roots movement— and in this respect *gaponovshchina* recapitulated the story of *zubatovshchina*— developed its own dynamic as defender of the interests of its worker-members.

Both worker militancy and the mood of the former Marxists could not fail to be influenced by society's leftward swing, especially in the hothouse atmosphere of the capital. When in December 1904 some workers at the giant Putilov factory, members of Gapon's Assembly, were dismissed, with little justification, in what appeared to be an effort to reduce the Assembly's influence, the organization could not maintain its credibility unless it rose to the defence of the injured parties. In a sense, everything that had happened to the Assembly over the past year—its organization into neighbourhood branches, the swelling of its ranks, its members' exposure to liberal and worker-centred political discourse— had conspired to prepare it for this moment of truth. To this concoction must be added the charismatic and sympathetic personality of Gapon himself, who came to embody all the workers' conflicting and confusing aspirations, lending them palpable personification at a moment when the workers might otherwise have lacked unity and direction.

The outcome was a city-wide general strike in January 1905 and a dramatic decision, taken almost simultaneously at the grass-roots and upper levels of Gapon's organization, to organize a mass march on the Winter Palace with a petition for Tsar Nicholas, 'our father'. Undoubtedly drafted in large part by the workers' ex-Marxist intellectual advisers, but also with ample feedback from many workers, the petition combined class-centred demands for higher wages and shorter hours (the eight-hour day, an 'economic' demand with special political resonance) with a liberal political programme that included a constitution and free elections based on direct, universal manhood suffrage.

The decision of the emperor was no less dramatic. It was to disregard the petitioners by failing to appear at the palace to receive the petition. Even more fateful was the decision to authorize military units to fire on advancing petitioners. Since the procession—which included women and children—not only was unarmed but carried Orthodox crosses and icons (Sergei Eisenstein's filmed depiction of marchers carrying red flags and likenesses of Marx should be ignored) and sang patriotic songs, the order to shoot to kill proved particularly repulsive. Indeed, it turned public opinion against the tsar almost as soon as word got out that well over a hundred were dead and many more were wounded on this 'Bloody Sunday' (9 January 1905).

The 1905 Revolution

The year 1905 defies succinct summary, in part because the situation changed so radically from month to month, even week to week, in part because each of the various historical actors—workers, peasants, soldiers, liberal intelligentsia, radical political parties, national minorities, students, even clergy—followed a distinct trajectory, even if at times displaying a modicum of co-ordination. Still, whatever its vicissitudes, 1905 was a watershed in the history of late imperial Russia. By early 1906 these varied movements had driven their common enemy to grant a quasi-constitutional political order, based in principle on the rule of law and in some respects comparable to the troubled constitutional order in Germany. Hence it would not be amiss—though the point should not be overstated—to treat pre- and post-1905 Russia as having discrete historical characteristics.

What happened in 1905 to prepare Russia for change and what accounts for the limits of the change that occurred? Let us begin with the workers, whose January procession had transformed a liberal protest movement (which rarely transgressed the boundaries of civil disobedience) into outright acts of revolution. At issue is not who deserves more credit (or blame) for launching the revolution, workers or liberal professionals: each played an indispensable role and each encouraged the other. Rather, the task is to understand how labour's clashes with the state drove the revolution in an ever more bellicose direction, forcing the authorities into moderate concessions such as creation of the 'Shidlovskii Commission' to hear the grievances of the workers' elected representatives. In this classic example of 'too little too late', elections were held but the elected body never convened. As a result, the government not only augmented the frustration and anger of already embittered workers but also inadvertently provided them with their first large-scale experience of electoral activity (though a small number of factories had held elections in compliance

Large street demonstrations and processions were an important feature of the 1905 Revolution in Russian cities. Here the lead banner in the middle of the photograph reads 'Proletarians of All Countries, Unite!' Other slogans, only partially visible, include: 'We Demand a Constituent Assembly!', 'Down with Autocracy!', and 'Russian Social Democratic Workers' Party'.

with a 1903 law on factory elders). This electoral experience subsequently helped workers select and shape their own leadership and prepared them in the autumn for elections to the Petersburg 'soviet' (Russian for 'council'). The latter was an extraordinary assembly of workers' representatives, initially a city-wide strike committee, but soon evolving into what was virtually a shadow government, led for a while by the militant Marxist Leon Trotsky.

The fact that the soviet began as a strike committee shows that it was the strike movement above all that catapulted workers into the forefront in 1905. September was the key month, for it witnessed a nation-wide general strike, originating with Moscow printers but forming its central nervous system along the railway lines of which Witte had been so justly proud, with the old Moscow–St Petersburg line as the network's spinal column. The strike gave birth to the Petersburg soviet in October, with other towns soon following the capital's model. Although the term *dvoevlastie* was not used until 1917, the transformation of such soviets from strike committees into revolutionary governing bodies represented Russia's first portentous experiment with 'dual power'.

Although a Peasant Union had already been formed in July, September was also a pivotal month for the peasant phase of 1905. In general terms, it was the absence of government troops—off fighting the Japanese on Russia's eastern frontiers until the war ended in August, then slowly returning to central Russia on the politically inflamed railways—and the example of unpunished worker defiance that facilitated the appearance of peasant unrest. But more specifically, it was the end of the harvest season that triggered September's intense wave of rural upheaval, including the widespread theft and destruction of gentry property. The confluence of these two great streams—peasant rebellion and working-class militance—drove the government to make concessions sufficiently meaningful to split the liberation movement.

Here the role of the liberal professionals becomes all-important. Their movement, first represented by the Union of Liberation, was transformed into that organization's militant successor, the 'Kadet' or Constitutional Democratic Party (which also absorbed the organization of zemstvo constitutionalists). If the defiance of professionals and liberal zemstvo men in late 1904 had emboldened the labour movement, the militancy of workers and peasants later gave wavering liberals the courage to defy the government and form their own party. Although the movements of workers, peasants, and professionals remained distinct, in the autumn of 1905 they came close to walking hand in hand, however briefly, a co-operation already anticipated earlier in May by the creation of the 'Union of Unions', a coalition of organizations headed by Miliukov. That Union was more an association of professionals than of blue-collar workers, but it had a broad range of member organizations, and its inclusion of railwaymen gave the coalition not only symbolic but real material power.

Faced with these adverse circumstances, coupled with a resounding military defeat (though the peace with Japan signed in Portsmouth in August proved less humiliating than expected) and the painfully slow return from the front of reliable troops (some of whom were in a mutinous mood), the tsar now pledged the biggest concessions to society he had ever made. Earlier, even as recently as August, reform proposals by his government had consistently lagged behind society's leftward-moving curve. Various configurations of advisory and consultative bodies had been discussed (most notably the so-called Bulygin Duma in August), but none granted genuine legislative independence, let alone election by anything resembling a democratic franchise. On 17 October, however, Nicholas issued a manifesto containing a vague promise to grant an elected legislative body (elected not directly or equally, however, but at least on the basis of near universal male suffrage) as well as civil and religious liberties and—for the first time in Russian history—the right to organize unions and political parties. When the detailed electoral law was issued in December, it clearly favoured Russia's already privileged classes, but was surprisingly generous to peasants, at least in comparison to workers.

Here at last was a document, the 'October Manifesto', with enough substance to divide the opposition. Because it fell far short of the full-fledged Constituent Assembly (in effect the end of the autocratic system) demanded by most of the left, including Kadets, the Manifesto failed to put an immediate end to the re-volution. But because it went as far as it did, it proved satisfactory to the regime's more moderate critics, including many zemstvo constitutionalists who, having now grown wary of the destructive force unleashed by the popular classes in Russia's city streets and villages, organized a political party called the Union of 17 October; its members ('Octobrists') vowed to co-operate with the government as long as it held to the Manifesto's promises.

Although the government still faced a bloody struggle, it soon was able to recoup its forces sufficiently to arrest the Petersburg soviet and to suppress the December uprising of workers and revolutionaries in Moscow. Thanks in part to continuing upheaval among ethnic minorities and peasants, calm would not be fully restored for another year and a half, and then only with the aid of field courts martial and other draconian measures. But the back of the revolution had been broken, especially in the capital cities, and the army, despite some flashes of rebelliousness, was now obeying orders.

National Minorities

This account of 1905 would be incomplete without a word about the national minorities. Russia's previous expansion had extended Romanov rule into Ukraine, Poland, Bessarabia, the Baltics, Finland, Crimea, the Caucasus, Siberia, and Central Asia (the last two regions being special targets of internal peasant migration during this period). Like Austria-Hungary, Russia was truly a multinational empire, though one in which the dominant nation held a much greater numerical preponderance than did Germans in the Habsburg lands (according to Russia's census of 1897, the population of 125 million included some 57 million 'Great Russians', plus another 22 million Ukrainians and 6 million Belorussians). At varying rates and intensity, minority discontent (in some cases reflected in massive emigration to America and elsewhere) was steadily mounting, especially once Alexander III had made coerced assimilation, though unevenly applied, official policy. Particularly aggrieved were Poles (whose rights were sharply curtailed after the 1863 uprising), Finns (whose status as a semi-independent grand duchy was subjected to major encroachments), and Jews (who though always subject to official discrimination, fell victim to a series of bloody pogroms in 1881–2 and most notoriously in Kishinev in 1903, and were exposed to a new series of discriminatory measures beginning with the infamous 'May Laws' of 1882). Poles, Finns, and Jews played particularly active roles in 1905, but other minorities, especially in Transcaucasia and the Baltic region (most notably the Latvians), also had significant nationalist, socialist, and liberal (sometimes all three simultaneously) movements. In the autumn of 1905 Jews were again the victims of pogroms (though the degree of govern-ment connivance remains uncertain).

As this photo of the victims of the 1905 pogroms in Ekaterinoslav illustrates, Jews were often the victims of the violence unleashed in Russia that year. Similar pictures from Odessa and other towns could have been shown.

Within certain limits, many Russian political groups, including liberals and Marxists, sympathized with the national and religious minorities and incorporated defence of their rights in their platforms, including in some cases the right to national autonomy and even independence. Marxists defended the right of nations to self-determination in principle (though just what constituted a viable 'nation' was always a thorny question), while urging their comrades among the national minorities to work for proletarian unity rather than secession and independence. SRs, because they tended to favour a loosely organized, federal political system, found it easy to co-operate with the minorities. Kadets, however, increasingly vulnerable to the currents of Russian nationalism and generally wedded to the goal of a liberal but unitary state, tempered their sympathy for minorities with an uneasy hostility to the more radical demands, especially in the case of Poles and Ukrainians. Octobrists, whose statist nationalism was much more brazen than that of Kadets, were firmly opposed to most minority aspirations; that chauvinist spirit was increasingly apparent in the Octobrist-dominated Third Duma, especially in its measures to reduce Finland to the status of a mere province.

Constitutional Russia?

The apparent defeat of the revolution at the end of 1905 (in fact still far from a total rout) did not mean that the government felt sufficiently confident to risk rescinding its October promises. To do so, in any case, was to hazard the loss of the still less than solid support of Octobrists, many of whom were uneasy about becoming identified as a government party. In 1906 the government therefore kept its promise to hold elections for the lower house (the State Duma), to grant

The Emperor and Empress wished to project their children with lovely Victorian images of tranquillity and innocence, as seen in this carefully posed photograph. The picture dates from *c*.1900.

broader (though by no means unrestricted) rights of free expression and assembly, to allow workers to form unions, and to confer various other rights. The old State Council, formerly appointed by the tsar, was transformed into an upper house; one half was still appointed by the tsar, the balance elected from mostly conservative institutions on a very restricted and undemocratic franchise. Although imperial ministers were still appointed by the tsar, they were now allowed to function as a cabinet, with a chairman (in effect, a Prime Minister) whose power derived, personality aside, from his critical position between the other ministers and the sovereign.

Did all this mean that Russia now had a 'constitution'? Historians who have argued over this word have really been arguing about something else: the likelihood of Russia's non-violent evolution into a liberal polity between 1906 and 1914 (when the disruptions of war thoroughly changed the terms of debate), a question to which we will return. For brevity's sake, Western historians sometimes subsume this debate under the catch-phrase 'optimism' (no revolution) versus 'pessimism' (inevitability of revolution). Suffice it to say that, insofar as 'constitution' means a set of fundamental laws that are meant to be binding on the government as well as the people, Russia formally acquired such a system on 23 April 1906. But the more important issue is not the formal definition of this system but its durability, stability, and capacity to function.

One source of instability *was* formal: the infamous Article 87, which empowered the tsar to dissolve the Duma and promulgate new laws in the interval between elections. Because the same article also required that, for such laws to be valid, the next Duma must approve them within two months, Article 87 by itself did not directly undermine the new order, but it did create a situation where an insecure or embattled regime could promulgate a law to change the Fundamental Laws themselves, and thereby alter the composition of the next Duma. Such an action was illegal, tantamount to a *coup d'état*, which was precisely the term employed when the 'Prime Minister', Peter Stolypin, did just that on 3 June 1907. There was yet another formal source of instability; the Fundamental Laws invested the tsar (still called 'autocrat') and his appointed ministers with what appeared to be full power over diplomacy and war, but made any increase in the military budget contingent on the approval of the Duma.

The Stolypin Reform

No less important than the contradictions inherent in the Fundamental Laws were the political and social challenges that brought these problems to the surface. Foreign policy questions had saturated domestic politics from 1890 to 1905, and they continued to do so in the post-revolutionary years. Despite or perhaps because of Russia's recent military defeat, the aspiration to renewed great-power status and to participation in *Weltpolitik* continued unabated. Russia's military position, however, was weaker than ever, especially in the light of losses suffered in the Russo-Japanese War. The consequent growth of the deficit made the costs of rearmament very difficult to meet. If this deficit was ever to be overcome, the economy had to recover and social stability had to be restored.

First and foremost this meant seeking a fresh solution to the peasant land problem. The question, in the new post-1905 context, was whether the solution to land hunger, so vehemently expressed by peasant insurgency in 1905 (and there was much more to come in 1906), should be attained by the compulsory redistribution of gentry land, and if so, whether with compensation (the liberal or Kadet position) or without (the radical position).

No one, whether in or out of government, could fail to see that the agrarian status quo was no longer tenable, as the termination of redemption payments even before 1905 bears witness. But the post-1905 government, and the extremely astute Stolypin in particular (first as head of the Ministry of Interior, but soon thereafter as Russia's third 'Prime Minister'—following Witte and the less than competent Ivan Goremykin)—had a solution, indeed one that Witte himself had advocated earlier. The central idea was to reallocate not gentry lands but *communal* lands, and to transfer them to individual peasant proprietors in the form of compact, enclosed, self-standing farmsteads. The reform was promulgated without Duma approval in November 1906, but was later approved and extended by the conservative Third Duma. This complex approach, Stolypin's so-called 'wager on the strong', was intended to create a productive class of hard-working, individualistic, free farmers ('yeomen' if one likes them, 'kulaks' if one does not), a new class of property owners with a strong stake in the existing system, men whose legal personalities and citizenship status—in contrast to the peasants emancipated in the 1860s and their descendants—would cease to differ from those of other landowners.

This was, in the jargon of the Russian left, a 'bourgeois' reform, sponsored and supervised by the state, but with powerful implications for a Russian future where social position would derive from capital and labour, not from the status ascribed by birth. It was, in a sense, the belated fulfilment of the original promise of 1861, a promise that the government had feared to fulfil lest disruption of the communal structure foster proletarianization, unrest, even rebellion. But now that serious unrest and rebellion had been taking place even in the *presence* of the communal order, a major rationale for the status quo had been eliminated, at least in the eyes of many conservatives.

Who, then, was left to support the 'anachronistic' commune? A surprisingly broad range of groups, from the PSR on the left to anti-individualist conservatives on the right. Almost every political programme that called for confiscation of gentry lands, whether with or without compensation, entailed the transfer of those lands to village communes (or to larger townships consisting of communes), not to individual peasants. Even liberals who looked forward to a system of individual proprietorship saw this as the result of a natural evolutionary process, not aggressive state measures (though it should be noted that the Stolypin programme was based, in part, on voluntary compliance). Peasants themselves were no doubt torn, but to the extent that they were represented in the first two Dumas by the new 'Trudovik' (Labour) Party and by large numbers of peasant and peasant-oriented independents, they often resisted both the spirit and the letter of Stolypin's master plan.

Village and county elders, headmen, and scribes gathered at a peasant assembly (*skhod*) in 1910, at the height of the Stolypin reforms. Their power over other peasants was extensive, but state officials had enormous power over them.

It was this resistance—dramatized by the failure of the government's efforts to seek collaboration with some Kadets and other moderates—that impelled Stolypin to carry out his 'coup', that is, to dissolve the Second Duma (more radical than the First) and revise the electoral law to ensure a more conservative composition. Peasants had once been the regime's golden hope; but having demonstrated that, be they monarchist or otherwise, they could not be relied on to vote with the government, they were now deprived of much of their electoral weight. The same fate befell the rebellious minorities. The landed gentry, who were never fully trusted by the state, but who now exhibited signs of disillusionment with the Kadets (for example, by routing Kadet candidates in zemstvo elections) and a greater readiness to rally to their tsar, gained vastly disproportionate electoral rights. The change in franchise redounded to the benefit of the Octobrists and parties to their right. The new law was complex, but the result was a 'loyal' Duma, with moderate Octobrists (fortified by the adherence of many industrialists) and conservative Nationalists providing Stolypin with a safe majority, at least for the moment. Kadets were now reduced in number, subdued in spirit, and internally divided; SDs and SRs, though fielding candidates, elected too few delegates to give them an effective voice.

The Period of the Third Duma: 1907–1912

Despite strict limitations on its competence (military matters as such were excluded), serious policy issues were discussed in the halls of the Third Duma (1907–12), the only one to survive for its full five-year term (the Fourth came close). But some of these issues led to serious conflict, demonstrating the fragility of the government's relationship with even a conservative Duma. Three particularly controversial issues were: (1) control over budgetary matters, especially the debate over the naval budget in 1909, which raised the issue of the Duma's competence more than issues of substance (though the navy's desire to sponge up resources badly needed by the army was a perennial source of strife); (2) the so-called Western zemstvo crisis of 1911, where the Council of State sought, successfully at first, to thwart Stolypin's plan, which was to extend elected zemstvos to six Western border provinces, but without enhancing the power of Polish Catholic noble landowners; (3) Stolypin's and the Duma's long efforts, also thwarted by the State Council, to extend the zemstvos to the lower township (*volost'*) level. Without engaging the complex details of these divisive issues, suffice it to say that each revealed the lack of a clear consensus that could unite the upper and lower houses with each other or with Stolypin's cabinet (itself very divided), or any of these institutions with the tsar, given the strange vagaries of mood at the imperial court. At the same time, it must be granted that agreement was possible on some important matters, including the agrarian reform and (during the Fourth Duma) a progressive workers' insurance law, partially modelled on the programmes of Bismarck.

If the situation is addressed more generally, it makes sense to say that the politics of the Third (and Fourth) Duma regularly presented the Octobrists, now the pivotal party in the Duma, with the same choice: either to turn rightward to co-operate with the Nationalists (essentially a pro-government and Stolypin-oriented coalition), or to turn leftward to the Kadets (essentially an oppositionist coalition, though moderate in tone and 'loyal' in content). In most respects the Duma's extreme right and extreme left were irrelevant to these coalitions, neither being truly committed to the compromise politics of a parliament, preferring the direct-action politics of the street. As a result, the other major players in this political drama were the government (Stolypin's, and later Kokovtsev's, cabinet) and the State Council, consistently dominated by a conservative-to-reactionary majority that either favoured the government or criticized its policies from the perspective of the respectable right. Since all laws had to be approved by both houses, the State Council could sabotage any serious liberal legislative initiative that the Duma promoted (as it did on occasion).

Problems of the Pre-War Period: 1912–1914

By the time the Fourth Duma was elected in 1912, some evidence had accumulated that the system erected by Stolypin was starting to work, but there also was plenty of evidence that it could not—hence the unending historiographical debate between 'optimists' and 'pessimists'. For the latter, the most dramatic evidence was the assassination of Stolypin himself in September 1911 by an SR, probably one of Russia's ubiquitous double agents. Although none of Stolypin's successors had comparable abilities, historians have suggested that even had Stolypin lived he was well on his way to dismissal. Relations with his erstwhile Octobrist allies had hit an all-time low, almost driving the Octobrist leader Alexander Guchkov (sometime chairman of the Duma and in a sense the first of the 'pessimists') to despair. Stolypin's Duma calculus had shifted from Octobrists to the more narrowly based Nationalists. Stolypin was distrusted by the State Council's conservative majority, his own cabinet, and courtiers close to the very tsar who had appointed him. Other 'pessimist' evidence may be adduced, including renewed unrest in the universities: by 1910–11, especially in Moscow, professors and students (among them, since 1905, a substantial number of women) protested against government efforts to rescind the concessions made to them in 1905; they were now in a virtual state of war with the Minister of Education, Lev Kasso.

Even before the Fourth Duma had convened, Stolypin's successors faced yet another alarming problem: the resuscitation of a militant labour movement in the capital and elsewhere. The trigger was news that government troops had massacred over a hundred striking miners at the Lena goldfields in March 1912. The explosion of strikes and demonstrations led to stunning Bolshevik victories, at the expense of the more moderate Mensheviks, in elections to the Duma, union governing boards, and newly organized workers' insurance boards. This revitalized unrest continued to intensify right up to the outbreak of war in 1914, providing the most persuasive evidence for the pessimist school.

On the 'positive' side of the ledger, optimists can cite evidence, if not of great achievements, then at least of some stabilization in the political and social status quo. Duma factionalism and wrangling had failed to pose a successful challenge to government authority; the opposition parties were bitterly divided and in disarray; revolutionary activity was virtually dormant for several years; even some of the radical intelligentsia questioned their own past values; and the Third Duma had made some progress in certain areas, especially in elementary education. Most tellingly, the agrarian reform, if by no means a proven success at this early stage, had finally received the Duma's blessing and was in the process of being implemented without provoking significant peasant unrest (for a while turning even Lenin, in a peculiar sense, into an unwilling 'optimist').

On the international scene, as on the domestic, evidence could be cited of both success and failure. The greatest failure had come in 1908, when a series of diplomatic misunderstandings left Russia helplessly embarrassed when Vienna unilaterally annexed the disputed Balkan provinces of Bosnia and Herzegovina. Competition between the army and the navy, often attaining a high degree of rancour (contributing to the divisiveness of Duma politics), was depleting the budget and demoralizing the military. (Military historians generally agree that the navy's demands were particularly unrealistic.) Earlier plans for establishing Russian hegemony over Mongolia and Manchuria were forcibly scaled down. Key Russian decision-makers were bitterly divided over how far to the west Russia should commit itself to a fortified defensive perimeter against Germany and Austria.

On the other hand, important diplomatic problems appeared to be resolved. Beginning in 1907 relations with Japan and England had significantly improved, and in 1909 Paris, though still a wary ally (witness France's restraint at the time of the 1908 annexation crisis), agreed to advance Russia a generous five-year loan. This was an enormous boost to Russia's economy, facilitating several successive years of industrial recovery (though even that recovery, because industrialists were reluctant to share its rewards with their workers, contributed to the militancy of the strike movement that destabilized urban Russia a few years later). Finally, the Balkan Wars of 1912–13, while in some ways frightening to Russian military planners, had the consequence of committing them to a 'Western'-oriented strategy and, for better or worse, a readiness for full rather than partial mobilization in the event of a major international crisis.

Literature and the Arts

Perhaps the most difficult spheres of Russian life to place squarely in the framework of the optimist–pessimist debate are literature and the arts. Without doubt, the reign of Nicholas II (and especially its last decade or so) witnessed extraordinary artistic creativity, so much so that cultural historians routinely use such terms as 'silver age', 'second golden age', and 'cultural renaissance'. In poetry in particular, but also in fiction, theatre, music, and the plastic arts (characteristically, the walls between these fields were often scaled), new 'modernist' modes of expression, with Symbolism in the lead, asserted themselves among the cultural élite. Modernism boldly challenged the hegemony of realism, positivism, and a socially oriented and utilitarian civic art that had dominated Russian aesthetics for decades. As part of this challenge, modernists introduced religious, metaphysical, and philosophically idealist perspectives into artistic and intellectual discourse (as, for example, in the collection of essays published in 1902 entitled *Problems of Idealism*). It should be said, however, that such intellectual experimentation had little effect on the taste of a new mass reading public, a group that expanded rapidly with the growth of primary education and the popular press.

As this advertisement shows, by the end of the first decade of the twentieth century, whatever her relative social 'backwardness' *vis-à-vis* the rest of Europe, Russia was entering the motorized age of automobiles, aeroplanes, and speedboats. This poster promotes gas, grease, and oil for cars, boats, and planes.

If the first essential steps in a modernist direction preceded the 1905 Revolution, the years that followed were particularly creative, with avant-garde writers such as Andrei Bely, Zinaida Gippius, Dmitrii Merezhkovskii, Valerii Briusov, Alexander Blok, and Vasilii Rozanov producing some of their most creative (and controversial) work. The Symbolist perspective that now dominated soon spawned a series of competing, often polemicizing movements (Acmeism, Futurism, and others), but all purportedly rejected what they viewed as the prosaic civic-mindedness of nineteenth-century Russian writers. Not surprisingly, many readers, including members of the political intelligentsia, were hostile to the modernists, viewing their artistic products as esoteric, self-indulgent, and out of touch with popular needs (not to mention popular tastes).

Related to, if distanced from, the modernist rejection of traditional Russian aesthetics was a concurrent rebellion against the traditional assumptions of the left and liberal intelligentsia. Because it originated within the intelligentsia itself, that rebellion sometimes took the form of severe self-criticism. In 1909 a group of prominent intellectuals—among them Struve, Sergei Bulgakov, and other veteran leftists who now harboured painful second thoughts—published *Vekhi* (Signposts), a symposium that repudiated their past commitment to Marxism and atheism, their lack of national spirit, and their former narrowly political aesthetics; the collection unleashed a stormy backlash, not only from the far left, but also from the likes of Miliukov.

The affinity between the modernists and their civic-minded cultural rivals may have been greater than either side cared to admit. They not only had similar backgrounds, they shared the typically Russian notion that art and literature must perform a specially high moral mission for the nation. Though their solutions differed, they assumed that the writer was duty-bound and able to resolve the apparent antagonism between life and art. And, notwithstanding their programmatic differences, they all tended to view the existing order, and especially the governing bureaucracy, with some contempt. By no means did Russia's Bloks and Maiakovskiis serve as props of the old regime. In sum, neither the splits in the ranks of the cultural intelligentsia nor the defensive postures adopted by liberal and radical people of letters in the face of the modernist challenge were necessarily good news for the government.

In the last analysis, the optimist–pessimist debate, though perhaps unavoidable, is a thought-experiment, a kind of metaphysical sparring match inseparable from counter-factual speculation about Russia's likely fate in the absence of world war. It must be pointed out, however, that a serious ambiguity, even confusion, is often found in how the optimists pose the question. Is proof for their position to be found in the trajectory of economic, social, and political progress that was followed from 1907 to 1914? If so, the evidence, on balance, is rather thin. Their case is strongest in the economic realm (especially if one concentrates on heavy industry and ignores the

This intense 'man of God', as Nicholas II called Rasputin, exercised an enormous influence on the Emperor and Empress, in large part because of his apparent ability to suppress the bleeding of their haemophiliac son, the Tsarevich Alexis.

Leonid Pasternak's famous poster soliciting donations to aid the soldier-victims of the First World War was first displayed shortly after the war began. Although many posters of this period were heroic and up-beat in tone, this picture of war-weariness was easily transformed into an anti-war poster in 1917.

explosive issue of dependency on foreign investment) and in the visible signs of a vibrant, modern urban culture—advertisement, commercial press, cinemas. But the optimists have greater difficulty when they try to build their case on the government's capacity to ensure social peace and on the political stability brought about by the *coup d'état* of 3 June 1907. Here the point is not simply that urban social stability lasted only until 1912 or that the rift between privileged society and court (thanks to the influence of Rasputin and the empress) was growing wider. For even if we granted the government's capacity, prior to the war, for maintaining a precarious social peace (for upholding order, if not law), this would not serve as evidence that problems were being solved or progress was being made. Indeed, it was precisely the government's ability to maintain order through coercion, while restricting progress and upholding autocratic rule, that allowed so many social and political sores to fester, thereby promoting maximalist visions of social and political change.

It was a sign of weakness, then, not strength, that the Russian regime that went to war in the summer of 1914 had successfully resisted becoming a functioning constitutional monarchy. Nicholas II may have succeeded in achieving his goal of January 1895, not only to retain but even to invigorate the symbols and rituals of monarchy that adorned his English cousin; he also retained, while wielding it ineptly, much of the power of personal rule. Despite a promising beginning in 1906, the symbolic and the substantive spheres of authority were never fully separated in Russia, neither in real life nor in the fantasy-life of a monarch who in June 1914, contemplating yet another coup, came close to abrogating the legislative powers of the Duma, just as the nation was poised to join in a momentous struggle for its very survival.

RUSSIA IN WAR AND REVOLUTION
1914–1921

DANIEL ORLOVSKY

*The thunder of artillery shells signalled the onset of
uninterrupted war, revolution, and civil war. These years
brought massive destruction; not only a dynasty, but vast
numbers of people, resources, and territories vanished in the
conflagration. Amidst these ruins, the Bolsheviks—inspired as
much by old social hatreds as new revolutionary visions—
attempted to build a new proletarian order.*

THE years separating the outbreak of war in 1914 and the announcement of the 'New Economic Policy' in 1921 form a critical watershed in modern Russian history. The revolutions of 1917, while not an unbridgeable caesura, fundamentally transformed the polity and social order. This era also had a profound impact on the 'bourgeois' West, which in the coming decades had to contend with the spectre of a socialist Prometheus in the East.

The First World War

In a memorandum of February 1914 P. N. Durnovo, a former Minister of Internal Affairs, implored the emperor to avoid war with Germany. The Kaiserreich, he argued, was a natural ally, joined by imperial ties of blood and by conservative principles and institutions; it was the alliance with democratic Britain and France that was unnatural. Moreover, the strains of war might topple the fragile order reconstructed from the shambles of 1905. But Durnovo was more prescient than persuasive: within months the government found itself helplessly sucked into the whirlpool of war.

Above all, it feared another diplomatic defeat in the Balkans, not simply out of sympathy for Balkan nationalism, but because of the volatile domestic situation. After decades of high-stakes gambling, in 1908 Russia had suffered a humiliating defeat when Austria annexed Bosnia-Herzegovina and then reneged on a promised quid pro quo. Russia seemed to be losing its long quest to dominate the Ottoman Empire and Black Sea. Russian policy was also driven by its desire to recover great-power status, by its fear of Germany's growing economic and military might, and by its strategic and diplomatic commitments to France and Britain. And, like the other powers, Russia was unduly deferential towards strategic planning and the general staffs, the ideology of the offensive, and the illusion that war could be localized and won quickly. None imagined the trench warfare, the carnage, the destruction of élites and empires, or the profound domestic upheavals that the 'Great War' would bring.

Declaration of war in Russia evoked a moment of 'patriotic union', symbolically captured on film that showed Nicholas bowing before several hundred thousand loyal subjects who had massed to sing 'God Save the Tsar'. Unity proved ephemeral: military defeats and domestic strains rekindled the smouldering social and political conflict. Although Russia did not fare badly against Austria and Turkey, by early 1915 German divisions had dealt a string of shattering defeats. Russia's stock of ammunition and weapons was perilously low; neither domestic production nor imports could satisfy the gargantuan demand of this first modern war. As morale plummeted, the army replaced a decimated officer corps with young officers from lower social ranks—non-aristocrats who had minimal training and little authority over peasant soldiers. By early 1915

Communal or public baths were an old Russian tradition that has persisted across the revolutionary divide and still exists today. The baths existed for people of all social classes though urban baths for the middle and higher social groups included elaborate steam rooms, pools of cold water, the customary birch branches for stimulating the circulation as well as various forms of food and drink.

one high official declared that Russia could only pray to her patron saints and rely upon her vast spaces and the spring mud to slow the relentless German advance. Failing the divine intercession of saints and mud, Russia needed 'total war'—a complete mobilization of resources, human and material.

War, however, proved particularly difficult for Russia, one reason being that the 'crisis was at the top'—a mutual alienation that divided state and 'Society' (professional and economic élites), which had rejected state tutelage and demanded a role in running the country. The war gave centrist parties a splendid opportunity to demonstrate their patriotism and, simultaneously, to exploit the alliance with democratic France and Britain and the wartime crisis in order to extort concessions from the state. Such ambitions reinforced Nicholas's tendency to distrust 'Society', to select weak ministers, to heed his wife's inept advice, and to reassert the inviolability of autocratic power. Within a few months the 'patriotic union' had dissipated; the rancour of pre-war politics and recrimination resumed in full force.

To mollify the opposition, however, in mid-1915 Nicholas agreed to replace the most odious ministers with men enjoying the confidence of 'Society'. These gestures, together with new military débâcles, only redoubled the Duma's determination to extract political concessions: in August 1915 centrist Duma parties formed the 'Progressive Bloc' to press long-standing demands—above all, for a government 'responsible' to the Duma. Confronted by a hostile majority in the Duma, appalled by his ministers' readiness to compromise, Nicholas prorogued the Duma and assumed personal command of the army, relinquishing power to chosen viziers, his unstable wife, and an unsavoury entourage that included the dissolute 'Grishka' Rasputin. Military defeat, political incompetence, personal stubbornness, and an adamant refusal to share political power or even consider the question negotiable—all this gradually dispelled the mystique of the Romanov dynasty and even fuelled suspicions that Nicholas and Alexandra were themselves traitors.

Nicholas did, however, accord 'Society' a greater practical role in the war by establishing new institutions outside the Duma. Most important were 'the Union of Zemstvos' and 'Union of Municipalities' (with a joint co-ordinating body called 'Zemgor'), but these too were rooted in bastions of liberalism—the zemstvo and municipal Duma. Their charge was to organize refugee relief, food supply, and even industrial production and distribution. Another important institution was the War Industries Committee; established on the initiative of Moscow industrialists, its network of local committees mobilized medium and small-scale industry to produce military equipment and ammunition.

The war economy inexorably increased bureaucratic intervention in the economy, if in partnership with the private sector. This co-operation included special councils (on defence, food supply, fuel, and transport), with a mixed membership and a monopoly over vital materials like sugar, leather, and metals. This process (which emulated the policy of other belligerents) enhanced the power of the responsible branches of the bureaucracy and set them against the more traditional ministries still closely tied to the court and nobility. As the lines between 'public' and 'private' blurred, three competing centres of economic and political power emerged: the state bureaucracy, private industry and capital, and public organizations (with a mixed composition, strong ethos of public service, and moral opposition to vested political and economic interests).

Although the military record improved in 1916 (partly because of the contribution of public organizations), the war also had profound repercussions for the lower social orders. Mobilization of manpower, industries, and transportation inevitably caused disruptions in the production and distribution of food, with dire consequences at the front and at home. Increasingly, the state lost the capacity to requisition food, fuel, and manpower, reflecting the decline in its moral authority or sheer capacity to coerce. Those close to the front suffered most: Russia's scorched-earth policy denied Germany the spoils of victory, but also unleashed a tidal wave of refugees that overwhelmed the administration and economy of interior provinces. Still more dangerous were the labour and agrarian questions, raised but not resolved by the Revolution of 1905; as inflation and food shortages ravaged the home front, disaffection also spread rapidly among the soldiers and sailors. Unrest also simmered among the lower-middle class and white-collar 'labourers', of unpredictable political behaviour, but deeply affected by the privations of war. A state at war also found it increasingly difficult to cow, let alone control, its national minorities; even 'backward minorities' grew rebellious—the largest insurrection of 1916, claiming thousands of lives, erupted in Turkestan in response to a new conscription drive. And, as inflation and food shortages reached critical levels at home, disaffection also spread rapidly among the soldiers. By the autumn of 1916 discontent was so intense that the police were issuing dire warnings that the regime's very existence was in jeopardy. And the government itself, paralysed by 'ministerial leapfrog' and the tsar's absence from the capital (to direct the war effort from military head-quarters), was steadily losing control of the situation.

The February Revolution

Few contemporaries imagined that, after three centuries of rule, the Romanov dynasty could vanish in several days. Even fewer could have predicted that, within months, a moderate regime of liberals and socialists would disintegrate and in October surrender power to Bolsheviks marching under the banner of 'All Power to the Soviets'.

The February Revolution began with street demonstrations in Petrograd to protest against food shortages, a direct consequence of wartime privation and the regime's inability to provision even the volatile capital. For months police officials had issued dire warnings and taken preventive measures (arresting, for example, worker representatives to the Central War Industries Committee). On 23 February (8 March NS) a crowd of women seized the occasion of International Women's Day to demonstrate against the high bread prices and food shortages. Their march coincided with calls by the revolutionary under-ground (from Bolsheviks and others) to resume the demonstrations of December and January. The next day crowds of strikers and demonstrators took to the streets, some reaching the centre of Petrograd. When the regular police failed to disperse the crowds, local authorities called out the troops, but again without effect. The next day Petrograd was virtually paralysed by a general strike. Desperate to regain control, on 26 February the authorities resorted to firearms: the Volhynian regiment opened fire, killing several dozen demonstra-tors. This volley proved suicidal: the next day the same Volhynian unit (joined by several guards regiments) took sides with the crowds. The insurgents then seized arsenals, emptied the gaols, and burnt the central headquarters of the hated political police. By 28 February the tsarist ministers were under arrest; the police itself had discreetly vanished.

As the government in Petrograd disintegrated, Nicholas desperately strug-gled to retain power. He formally dissolved the State Duma, attempted to return to the capital, but soon found himself stranded in a provincial town. There, at the urging of his own generals and Duma politicians, he agreed to abdicate for the sake of domestic tranquillity and the war effort. Ironically, his final act as emperor was characteristically illegal: in contravention of the 1797 Law of Succession, Nicholas abdicated not only for himself but also for his son.

The February Revolution began on International Women's Day with women taking to forming bread lines in response to ongoing shortages brought on by the war. The cold winter and prolonged hardships resulting from the First World War were made worse by inadequate supply policies and the capacity of peasants to hold grain off the market and away from the state procurement agencies. All this prepared the way for a revolution in which women would have a prominent role from beginning to end.

His abdication, compounded by the dissolution of the Duma, raised the question of legitimacy that would bedevil the Provisional Government throughout its brief existence. The designated heir, Nicholas's brother Michael, declined the throne until a constituent assembly had defined the nature of the Russian state. Michael probably had no inkling that his decision would bring the monarchy to an end and dramatically accelerate the revolutionary process.

Still earlier, two contenders for power had already emerged in Petrograd. One was the State Duma, which the tsar had dissolved on 27 February and hence had no legal right to rule. None the less, the Duma deputies convened in Tauride Palace and created a 'Provisional Duma Committee' that included members from conservative, liberal, and even socialist parties. In essence, the Duma represented 'propertied society' (*tsensovoe obshchestvo*), which received a preponderant share of power in the Duma under the 1907 electoral law. The Duma Committee took steps to claim power, restore order, and establish contact with the leading public organizations. They also dispatched 'commissars' to take command of key ministries, including the Ministry of Communications that controlled the all-important railways. Implicitly acknowledging a lack of legitimacy, the Duma members called its committee 'provisional' as would the 'Provisional Government'. Until conditions permitted a constituent assembly to convene, however, it claimed the right to rule.

The Duma deputies, however, were not the only claimants to power: a *mélange* of intellectuals, party operatives, and trade-union leaders simultaneously convened in another wing of the same Tauride Palace. Drawing on the experience of 1905, they re-established the famous 'soviet' and summoned workers and soldiers to send elected representatives. The result was the Petrograd Soviet of Workers and Soldiers Deputies, led by an Executive Committee composed mostly of moderate socialist intellectuals. Curiously, the soviet leaders made no claim to rule: scarred by the failure of 1905, they intended to observe the 'iron laws' of a two-stage revolution, whereby a 'bourgeois' revolution would beget a 'bourgeois' government to rule for a discrete interval before a second, socialist revolution. Because the tsarist police left revolutionary parties in disarray (with ranking members in prison or in exile), the soviet leaders also felt unqualified to seize the reins of power and deemed the 'bourgeoisie' better suited for this historic task. Some were also overawed by the myth of counter-revolution, which seemed less likely if Russia were ruled by a bourgeois government.

The year 1917 was a complex story of 'dual power', the Provisional Government representing 'Society', the soviet representing workers, peasants, and soldiers. With the approval of the soviet, the Duma Committee established a 'Provisional' Government, its cabinet drawn largely from liberal Duma circles. Thus the 'bourgeois' government required by socialist theory had finally emerged. It vowed to hold free elections for a Constituent Assembly and, in the interim, was to exercise the plenitude of executive, legislative, and even judicial power of the *ancien régime*. From the outset the Provisional Government had an uncertain status: the Duma committee had simply usurped power, and the soviet agreed to give its support 'only in so far as' the government followed the 'democratic' script for the Revolution.

Provisional Government

History has judged the Provisional Government harshly, but one must remember that it ruled during a raging war and profound social cataclysm. Eight months afforded little time to build a new state, wage war, and resolve acute social and political questions that had accumulated over many decades.

Its ministers included the leading figures in the Progressive Bloc and public organizations. Most prominent were the Kadet Party leader, P. N. Miliukov (Minister of Foreign Affairs) and the Octobrist leader, A. I. Guchkov (Minister of War). Other appointments proved fateful—in particular, the choice of Prince Georgii Lvov as Minister-President and Minister of Internal Affairs. Although Lvov distinguished himself as head of the All-Russian Union of Zemstvos and Towns, he was a weak leader and ill-equipped to lead a democratic revolutionary state. At best he exuded a dreamy Slavophile faith in 'the people' (*narod*); at worst he refused to use the instruments of power to restore public order or instil respect for the rule of law that he so cherished. Some appointments were surprising, especially the choice of A. I. Konovalov (a Moscow industrialist) as Minister of Finance and an obscure Kievan sugar magnate, M. I. Tereshchenko, as Minister of Trade and Industry. Although socialists in the Petrograd Soviet declined to join the cabinet, one did agree to serve: Alexander Kerensky, a radical SR and Duma deputy, became Minister of Justice.

On 8 March the Provisional Government announced its 'Programme' of democratic principles and goals, which envisioned a revolutionary transformation on liberal principles, with appropriate guarantees of civil rights and more autonomy for minorities. The government also vowed to establish the rule of law and later appointed a juridical commission to give counsel on legislation and inculcate respect for the judicial order. But the most far-reaching plank in this Programme was its promise to end bureaucratic hegemony over political life and to create self-government at every level, down to the township (*volost'*) level. In effect, the government refashioned the pre-revolutionary structure (provincial administration, zemstvos, and town dumas) into a new system of zemstvos and town dumas now elected on the basis of democratic suffrage. The new bodies were to assume the powers of police and administration that had long been identified with autocracy itself. The Programme promised to convoke a constituent assembly, 'democratically' elected and empowered to resolve the questions of legitimacy and to determine the form of the new Russian state. It was a heady agenda, one not easily realized, especially in the throes of war and social upheaval.

The February Revolution produced not only a liberal, reformist government, but also the soviets, supported by popular forces committed to 'democracy'. The Petrograd soviet formally recognized the Provisional Government, but immediately began to encroach on its authority. The most famous instance was 'Order No. 1': a harbinger of social revolution in the army, it established the soviet's authority over army units and created soldiers' committees to check the regular command hierarchy, thereby unleashing a radical 'democratization' in the army itself. The military committees, nominally obliged to maintain order, fanned revolutionary and anti-war sentiments among soldiers and officers.

In the provinces the revolution was greeted with jubilation and a replication of 'dual power'. As word spread from Petrograd, local activists seized power from tsarist administrators and police, who silently melted away. The new structure emerged with astonishing rapidity. Committees of Public Organizations, usually centrist, took formal authority. Chairmen of the old zemstvo boards briefly replaced tsarist governors until 'commissars' were sent. Simultaneously, workers and soldiers created soviets in towns, while peasants formed their own village organs—*volost* committees, peasant unions, and even peasant soviets.

Iconoclasm was a powerful force in 1917 (and later during the civil war), but eventually it was a force to be channelled and even co-opted for political ends. Here the crumbled remains of a statue of Alexander III remind onlookers of the destruction of the 'old' order and the openings or possibilities of the 'new' in 1917.

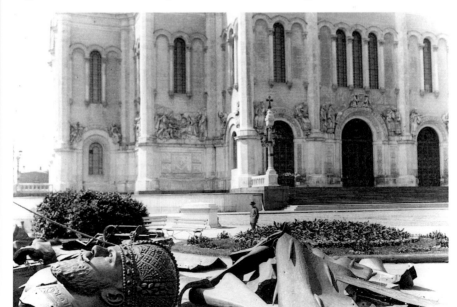

'Democratization' extended to the grass roots, blanketing the Russian land-scape with township and village committees, factory committees, and every imaginable variety of soviet, union, and professional organization. These organs—manned sometimes by plebeians, but often by white-collar workers— filled the power vacuum left by the *ancien régime*. As the revolution unfolded, better organized, often antagonistic social groups emerged as the main actors.

Amidst this 'democratization', the Provisional Government endeavoured to rule and reform. It granted virtual independence to Poland (in any event, under occupation by the Central Powers) and autonomy to Finland, freed political prisoners, drafted legislation on self-government, made plans for judicial reform, and established countless committees to consider other critical issues. Indeed, the government contemplated or initiated reform in virtually every imaginable sphere—in education (democratization of access and administra-tion), labour relations (the eight-hour day and arbitration chambers), corporate law, and religion (secularization of schools, liberalization of divorce, and sepa-ration of Church and State).

It proved far easier, however, to appoint committees than to reform. Apart from the magnitude of its agenda, the government had to rely on the old tsarist bureaucracy and to operate in the absence of an elected, authoritative legisla-ture. Typically, the government established a committee, with great fanfare, col-lected data and drafted laws, but inevitably elected to defer the main issues for resolution by the constituent assembly. Still, given its narrow timeframe, the government addressed a broad range of critical issues.

Meanwhile, the revolution did not stand still. Within a few weeks, it was clear that the Provisional Government must immediately address new problems (especially food shortages and greater industrial production) as well as old ones (such as land and labour reform). Ultimately, the government was driven to nul-lify its liberal Programme and adopt very different social and economic policies, essentially more corporatist and socialist than liberal. On 25 March, for ex-ample, the government established a grain monopoly to regulate prices for cer-eals and mandate deliveries to the state—in effect, declaring all grain to be state property. To manage this monopoly, it created a new hierarchy of provisioning committees and ultimately a Ministry of Food Supply. When the government entrusted provisioning (and much of consumer supply) to co-operatives, it undermined not only the market for foodstuffs but also the established com-mercial infrastructure of the empire. Thus a regime professing liberalism and tarred as 'bourgeois' asserted state authority over the economy, shoving aside entire business firms and an entire class. But in the case of land reform the gov-ernment acted with less abandon: consigning this matter to resolution by the constituent assembly, it merely created a Main Land Committee to 'study' the issue and directed local land committees to gather information and adjudicate land disputes over such matters as rents and competing land claims.

In the interim, the question of war eroded the foundations of 'dual power'. At issue were war aims and hence the terms for stopping the carnage. On 14 March the Petrograd Soviet issued an 'Appeal to All the Peoples of the World', repudiating expansionist war aims and espousing instead 'revolutionary defencism', i.e. to prosecute the war only in defence of Russia and its revolution against German authoritarianism and imperialism. It became clear, however, that the government had not abandoned the tantalizing gains promised by its allies. To allay soviet apprehensions, on 28 March the Provisional Government issued a 'Declaration on War Aims' renouncing territorial claims, but on condition that peace cause neither humiliation nor the deprivation of 'vital forces'. In fact, the government retained its original war aims: in a note to the allies on 18 April, the Foreign Minister (Miliukov) ascribed the government's Declaration to domestic politics and reaffirmed its determination to observe all treaty obligations, with the implication that the allies must also honour their promises, especially on Constantinople and the Straits.

News of this note ignited a new political crisis in Petrograd, with mass demonstrations on 23–4 April protesting against the government's foreign policy. The worker and soldier demonstrators carried banners demanding peace and 'Down with the Bourgeois Government', and 'Down with Miliukov and Guchkov'. The Provisional Government refused to deploy troops and use force to restore order. After the two most unpopular ministers (Guchkov and Miliukov) resigned, the government invited the Petrograd soviet to help form a coalition. The soviet leaders reluctantly agreed, a decision that instantly blurred the lines of dual power and made them culpable for the policies of the Provisional Government. This first coalition, which included six socialist ministers (including Viktor Chernov as Minister of Agriculture), avowed a commitment to 'revolutionary defencism' in foreign policy, state regulation of the economy, new taxes on the propertied classes, radical land reform, and further democratization of the army.

Lenin and the Bolsheviks

Prior to Vladimir Lenin's return in the famous 'sealed train' in early April, the Bolsheviks had already undergone a radical shift in party policy. At the outbreak of the February Revolution, the radical underground activists who dominated the Petrograd apparatus rejected the 'bourgeois Provisional Government' and demanded a revolutionary soviet government. But the ranking Bolshevik leaders (including Iosif Stalin) who returned to the capital in early March overruled the radicals and not only joined other socialists in supporting bourgeois rule, but even sought reconciliation with the Mensheviks. This initial crisis revealed deep internal differences that would persist throughout 1917 and beyond.

The differences emerged again in the 'April crisis' following Lenin's return on 3 April. Such divisions made Lenin's role decisive: his powerful drive, and obsessive belief in revolution overcame the internal party fissures and gave the Bolsheviks a decisive edge over moderate socialists and the Provisional Government. Lenin's 'April Theses' promised peace, bread, land, and workers' control—that is, not only to end the unpopular war and food shortages, but also to satisfy long-standing grievances. Most controversial of all, he demanded the elimination of dual power and transfer of 'all power to the soviets'. The 'professional revolutionaries' in the party were aghast; it took all Lenin's energy and personal authority to overcome their caution and to unite the party behind his vision.

His vision drew on mass radicalism and his own ideological utopianism. It also offered a strategic alternative to the discredited ideologies of autocracy and liberalism, which were splintered, politically ineffective, and without a deep social base. The language of socialism and class conflict became the idiom of public discourse for the press, rally, public meeting, and all manner of political propaganda. Lenin projected a strong vision of transforming through technocratic change, of reshaping consciousness, and of making the proletariat a true universal class—for itself and, if need be, in spite of itself.

The All-Russian Crisis

The first coalition quickly exposed the gulf between liberalism and socialism—and the government's inability to bridge that chasm. The conflicts in the coalition correlated directly with the declining authority of the Provisional Government (and, by contrast, to the surge in Bolshevik influence). On a whole range of issues the coalition could neither agree internally nor satisfy the spiralling expectations of various social groups.

Disagreement in the coalition was profound, especially on central questions like economic regulation, labour, and land. Liberal and socialist ministers agreed on the need for government regulation of the economy, but for radically different ends: liberals sought to preserve the market in wartime, socialists imagined the beginnings of socialist planning. The two sides also differed on the land question: liberals wanted to uphold private property and legality, whereas the left sought to sanction peasant land seizures and local 'initiative' regardless of legal niceties. As to workers' demands (for higher wages, shorter hours, and worker control), the liberal ministers supported factory owners in the patriotic production for the war. Socialists were in a quandary: as state officials supporting labour discipline and resumption of work, they risked appearing as capitalist stooges and becoming easy targets for Bolshevik attacks.

The war itself was divisive. It made liberals illiberal, disposed to defer elections and constituent assembly until more propitious times; they were also under pressure from the allies to keep fighting. The war also invited attacks from the left; neither 'revolutionary defencism' nor the 'renunciation of territorial claims' stopped the carnage or defused popular discontent. The fact that non-Bolshevik socialists actively supported the war effort (even the June offensive) was grist for Bolshevik propagandists, who identified their own anti-war stance with popular will and tarred all war advocates, especially socialists, as enemies of the people. The disastrous June offensive had no effect on German lines and only hastened the demise of the Russian army, shattering the fragile truce between officers and soldiers and unleashing a wave of mass insubordination and desertion.

Equally explosive was the nationality question. The revolution was a powerful catalyst for the development of national consciousness, encouraging entire peoples to demand autonomy and independence and calling into question the very existence of the Russian Empire. Although national movements varied

In the era of Nicholas and the gendarmes, the Finnish lion exemplified unexceptional docility …

… and how quickly the character of that animal (mistakenly thought of as grateful) changed when the democracy began to converse with it.

considerably, most demanded democratization and self-government and drew their leadership from the intelligentsia and 'semi-professions'—white-collar personnel employed by the co-operatives, zemstvos, schools, and the like. In Finland and Ukraine, for example, activists created national equivalents of the class-based soviets that became centres of growing national consciousness and power. Even the 'backward' Muslims organized a Muslim Congress in May to proclaim their hostility to Russian colonialism and to demand autonomy.

Shaken by these anti-Russian movements, neither socialists nor liberals were prepared to comprehend, let alone control, the national revolutions of 1917. In essence, their term 'imperial' (*vserossiiskii*, 'all-Russian-empire') connoted 'Russian' (*russkii*), denying any special status for non-Russian peoples; their term 'statehood' (*gosudarstvennost'*) subsumed empire, not just state. Believing that the revolution and new state were a 'democratic' antithesis to tsarism, the Provisional Government naïvely assumed that by definition this state could not oppress minority nationalities, that their programme of self-government and democratization would satisfy the aspirations of national minorities, that the latter would be only too grateful. They thus tended to hypostatize the Russian state and to insist that national groups support the democratic revolution and its government. The ministers dimly understood modern nationalism, perhaps because it was so flaccid among Russians themselves. They failed to anticipate that national strivings would quickly escalate into demands for autonomy and independence, and that as minority and Russian interests diverged, the government inevitably would tread in the footsteps of the tsars. Surprised and dismayed, the Provisional Government and much of Russian public opinion accused the minorities of stabbing Russia in the back and undercutting its democratic revolution.

Still more menacing was the threat from lower classes in the Russian heartland—above all, the workers. Some historians have revived an earlier tendency to denigrate the workers' role in the revolution and even discount it altogether. Recent works by Richard Pipes and Martin Malia, for example, deny that the revolution had any significant social dimension and claim that the prime mover was ideology, the intelligentsia, or some primal Russian obsession with power and authoritarianism. While this 'un-revisionism' rightly suggests that the revolution involved more than working-class aspirations, it revives the anti-Bolshevik stereotypes of 'working-class backwardness'—hence Bolshevik manipulation, hence the illegitimacy and 'un-Marxian' character of the 1917 Revolution. Ironically, this conservative view derives from Menshevik sour grapes: to account for their own failure to attract workers, Mensheviks claimed that the workers were just green peasants easily seduced by cunning Bolsheviks.

Beyond the Mensheviks' confession of their own political ineptness, this thesis has little to commend it: collective action of workers profoundly shaped the politics of 1917. Indeed, the aggressive measures of factory owners and the government's inability to mediate or satisfy minimal demands contributed to the steady radicalization of the workers. The result, as S. A. Smith has shown, was the growing importance of organizations such as factory committees, as a powerful force for 'democratization' demanding workers' control and self-management and as hotbeds of Bolshevik activism. These organizations enabled Bolsheviks to offer an alternative to the trade unions and to outflank their Menshevik rivals. Nor can any serious account of 1917 ignore strikes and their impact. According to Diane Koenker and William Rosenberg, the eight months of revolution in 1917 witnessed 1,019 strikes involving 2,441,850 workers and employees, led by metal and textile workers (as before), but reinforced by printers and service personnel. It was all a clear expression of dissatisfaction with the Provisional Government and moderate socialists.

Revolution also swept across the countryside, where peasants now found little to prevent the realization of long-standing claims and aspirations. Their maximalist expectations were evident early, as in a resolution from Riazan: 'The revolution is already three weeks old and nothing has happened yet'—a transparent allusion to the all-important land question. Although the government initially dampened expectations of immediate repartition of land, by early summer the peasant movement had gathered a full head of steam, with a steady increase in disorder, violence, and collective seizure of land. The peasants shared a fundamentally revolutionary, not liberal, conception of law and justice: land should belong to those who actually cultivate it, not the landlords and speculators who merely prevented this rational distribution of land. The war redoubled their feeling of injustice: while city folk obtained draft exemptions and special concessions, the long-suffering village sacrificed its men for slaughter at the front.

The agrarian question deepened the rift within the coalition. The Main Land Committee and Chernov's Ministry of Agriculture became bastions of SR influence and, contrary to the express wishes of the Provisional Government, proposed the 'socialization' of land—that is, the abolition of private property and transfer of ownership to peasant communes. The Ministry believed that, in the midst of revolution, just demands took precedence over the laws of a defunct regime. But liberal ministers saw only a crass violation of the rule of law and resigned from the coalition. Significantly, the socialists themselves were divided on this issue. Whereas Chernov fanned the flames of peasant revolution, the Menshevik Minister of Internal Affairs ordered his apparatus to combat peasant lawlessness and to assert control over the land committees. Such fissures, along ideological and class lines, paralleled and deepened the divisions in society at large.

By early summer the coalition was in a shambles, its popularity waning. The First All-Russian Congress of Soviets in June exposed deep rifts on the left and subjected the coalition to withering criticism. To stave off a Bolshevik challenge, the soviet leadership cancelled anti-government demonstrations on 10 June and ordered its own march a week later. It proved a stunning fiasco, as soldiers and workers carried Bolshevik banners: 'Down with the Capitalist Ministers', 'Peace', and 'Down with the Bourgeoisie'. The rhetoric of class war prevailed: conciliation, appeals to unity and 'nation', in fact any appeals not based squarely on 'class' and 'class conflict' fell on deaf ears.

The crisis culminated in the famous 'July Days', when soldiers and workers (with the aid of lower-echelon Bolshevik organs) staged an abortive insurrection. The July days bequeathed unforgettable visual images—the populace scattering under rifle fire in Petrograd's main squares, angry crowds attacking soviet leaders ('Why haven't you bastards taken power?'). The government blamed the Bolsheviks, arrested several key leaders, and accused Lenin himself of 'treason' (claiming that he had taken German money to subvert the democratic revolution). As Alexander Rabinowitch has shown, however, the Bolshevik leaders did less to lead than to follow popular radicalism. Troops loyal to the Provi-

sional Government suppressed the disorders, but the crisis reinforced the rhetoric of violence, the sense of insurmountable problems, and lack of confidence in the government's ability to deal with them. For the short term, however, the combination of force and anti-Bolshevik propaganda restored some semblance of authority.

But in fact state authority continued to disintegrate. The government now operated under the cloud of military catastrophe, even the threat that Germans would occupy Petrograd itself. And on the domestic front its problems were legion: land seizures and pogroms, strikes and demonstrations by workers, massive breakdowns in supply and transport, and the strident demands of nationalities. In early July the first coalition finally collapsed from disagreements over Ukrainian autonomy (which, to the liberals' dismay, the socialists proposed to acknowledge) and Chernov's agrarian policies (which the liberals saw as sanctioning illegal peasant actions). Once Prince Lvov and the Kadet ministers resigned, only a rump cabinet of socialists remained in charge.

That government now became the personal instrument of Kerensky, who succeeded Lvov as Prime Minister. Kerensky was vain, egotistical, and poorly versed in the left-wing ideologies that he would have to combat. A consummately inept politician, he became a caricature of the strong executive he pretended to be. By late July he had fashioned a second coalition, which called for state intervention in the economy and peace without indemnities or annexations.

Alexander Feodorovich Kerensky (1881–1970) came to power in 1917 as a young radical lawyer and Duma Deputy and nominal member of the SR Party. The first and only socialist member (as Minister of Justice) of the original Provisional Government, Kerensky moved on to the posts of War Minister and finally Minister-President where he presided over the summer offensive and eventually the demise of the government itself. He came to symbolize both the democratic promise and failures of the February Revolution.

245

But this coalition was new in another sense: responsible neither to parties nor the soviet, it steadily abandoned a commitment to parliamentary democracy and, instead, sought legitimacy in pseudo-parliamentary assemblies. Thus in mid-August, amidst much pomp and ceremony, Kerensky convoked the so-called 'State Conference' in Moscow. It included representatives of traditional corporate interests (government ministries, the Academy of Sciences, and social estates), as well as delegates from the 'democratic' institutions (self-government, co-operatives, the 'labouring' intelligentsia, and the like). While the left declaration of 14 August reaffirmed the commitments of July, the centre and right catalogued the horrors of the deepening revolution. Ministers spoke candidly about the enormous problems facing the regime. All felt the drama, the sense that things could not go on, that new upheavals were imminent, either from a German attack or a coup from the left or right. Public voices were already warning that either Kornilov or Lenin would sunder this Gordian knot.

The Kornilov Affair

General Lavr Kornilov, a war hero of modest origins, became a key public figure in 1917 because of his principles and his determination to suppress disorder during the April crisis. When Kerensky appointed the general as commander-in-chief after the summer offensive, he implicitly sanctioned Kornilov's plan to restore the army's fighting capacity by restoring discipline and the death penalty (though without dismantling the army's democratic committees). But Kornilov had broader political ambitions, for he doubted that the coalition had the will either to win the war or to stabilize the domestic front. Regarding the government as a soviet hostage, he concluded that a true patriot must put an end to dual power. This judgement coincided with that of many landowners, industrialists, and political figures on the centre and right: only suppression of 'democracy run amok' could save Russia. In late August Kornilov led loyal troops on a march towards Petrograd to restore order.

Much ink has been spilled on the Kornilov affair, mostly along predictable political lines, with the left accusing the general of an attempted coup (Kornilov did order the march on Petrograd to destroy the soviet and install himself as a Napoleonic strongman) and the right and centre (who accuse Kerensky of goading Kornilov to act and then perfidiously betraying him). Both accounts are true: the general did attempt a coup, believing that he had Kerensky's support; and Kerensky did lose his nerve and renege, sacrificing the general in a desperate effort to regain popular support. Workers and paramilitary units known as Red Guards were mobilized quickly to repulse 'counter-revolution' and, without much bloodshed, arrested Kornilov and disarmed his troops. Kerensky dissolved the second coalition and declared himself head of a new government, a five-man 'Directory'.

Armed detachments of Red Guards and militant soldiers and sailors patrolled the Petrograd streets in 1917, providing an edge for militant workers as well as expressing their own discontents. The Provisional Government was incapable of disarming such groups, whose existence lent credence to the idea of government weakness and alternatives to its legitimacy.

The Kornilov affair had enormous repercussions. Kerensky's machinations soon became public, severely damaging his personal authority. It also lent new credibility to the spectre of counter-revolution—a myth that greatly exaggerated the power of conservative forces, but none the less impelled workers, soldiers, and activists to organize militias, Red Guards, and *ad hoc* committees to defend the revolution. Even when the Kornilov threat had passed, these armed forces refused to disband and became a powerful threat to the government itself. Thus the Kornilov affair, though a farce and fiasco, further eroded support for Kerensky's government and facilitated the Bolshevik seizure of power, without, however, in any way pre-ordaining the methods or timing of the October Revolution.

The Coming of October

As Kerensky's authority faded, the strikes reached a new crescendo in September. They revealed that the workers no longer believed in the capacity of the government to honour its pledges or in the willingness of factory owners to negotiate in good faith. The collapse of production, lock-outs, unemployment, violence, and social polarization profoundly changed the scale and tenor of the strikes. For three days in September, a strike by 700,000 railway workers paralysed transportation; in mid-October 300,000 workers struck at textile factories in Ivanovo and nearby communities; 'workers' included pharmacists as well as oil workers. Mood, not just numbers, is critical: the strikes often culminated in violent confrontations that accelerated the breakdown of law and order

The fiery orator and revolutionary leader Trotsky returned to Russia from exile in New York to eventually join in the Bolshevik enterprise. Here he addresses a crowd that included members of the middle and professional classes. He would prove to be Lenin's crucial ally in forcing the issue of revolution upon a sometimes recalcitrant and divided party leadership and structure and would go on to a leading role in Party affairs including organization of the Red Army after October. Later Stalin completely outmanoeuvred him in the struggles for succession.

(already marked by a rise in looting, physical violence, and vigilante street justice). Koenker and Rosenberg point out that the strikes became the workers' main 'form of participatory politics', 'the central conduit of labour mobilization and, to a large extent, of management mobilization as well'. The workers' animosities and aspirations provided the primary drive and justification for early Soviet power—even if, ultimately, the Bolsheviks were to subvert the workers' democratic impulses and to transform their institutions (soviets, factory committees, trade unions, co-operatives) into instruments of mobilization, hierarchy, and control.

In a desperate bid to stabilize the situation, Kerensky manœuvred to form yet another coalition cabinet. To offset popular radicalism, he wanted representatives of 'propertied' society—the same circles of the Kadet Party and Moscow business circles discredited in the popular mind as Kornilov's accomplices. In mid-September, the soviet and democratic circles sponsored a Democratic Conference to unite the representatives of 'democracy' and to guide Kerensky in forming a stable government. Rather than enhance the regime's stability and legitimacy, the meeting proved a disaster: the delegates at first voted in favour of a coalition, but *without* the Kadets—an absurd proposition, since the Kadets were the only 'bourgeois' party disposed to ally with 'democracy'. Later, despite Bolshevik opposition, on 25 September the conference voted for a coalition and thus paved the way for Kerensky's final cabinet. The moderate left and centre thereby sacrificed their last opportunity to seize power or at least form a 'unified socialist government'. Desperately seeking to end the crisis, the conference voted to summon another gathering—the Council of the Republic, or so-called 'pre-parliament'. Intended as a surrogate for the constituent assembly and

boycotted by the Bolsheviks, this weak body convened in October to hear gloomy ministerial and committee reports about the deepening crisis; it was the final sounding-board for the aspirations of Russia's democratic revolution and its Provisional Government.

The Bolshevik Party, meanwhile, debated the prospects of this 'revolutionary situation'. The Kornilov episode had unleashed a new wave of radicalism, which was reflected not only in an upsurge of agrarian disorders and urban strikes, but also in pro-Bolshevik votes and elections in the soviets. Encouraged by this remarkable shift in mood, Lenin now revived the slogan 'all power to the soviets' abandoned after the July Days.

But internal dissension also rent the Bolsheviks. From various hiding-places Lenin bombarded the Central Committee with letters demanding that the party seize power in the name of the working class. His 'Letters from Afar' were a forceful blend of theory and practice, dogma and power. No blind believer in an 'inevitable' Bolshevik victory, Lenin insisted that the moment be seized, lest the Germans invade or strike a deal with Kerensky. Confronted with Lenin's demand for an immediate armed uprising, party members revealed

Strikes and street demonstrations ebbed and flowed during 1917 and provided an accurate measure of the revolutionary tide in 1917 Petrograd. Here the crowd surges forward under the banner of 'Communism' expressing its various dissatis-factions on the eve of October. The visual presence of the 'masses' played upon the psychology of ordinary citizens and government members alike.

deep differences in their assessment of the situation. Two 'Old Bolsheviks', L. B. Kamenev and G. E. Zinoviev, believed that a broad-based socialist coalition, not the Bolsheviks alone, should take power. But the majority (including Trotsky and Stalin) acquiesced in Lenin's demand: on 10 October, by a 10–2 vote, the Central Committee secretly endorsed Lenin's theses on seizing power. But it hedged this decision: without setting a timetable, it called for patient work among the troops and proposed to await the Second All-Russian Congress of Soviets later in October to legitimize a seizure of power in the name of the soviets. Meanwhile, the Petrograd soviet made a tactical decision of great practical significance when it established the 'Military Revolutionary Committee'. Ostensibly created to defend Petrograd against the Germans, this Bolshevik-dominated body, working under the cover of soviet legitimacy, became the Bolshevik command centre during the October Revolution.

The Bolsheviks brilliantly exploited the situation, but owed much to 'objective conditions'—the ongoing war and economic collapse, the weakness of the government, the fissures within possible rival parties, and the inability of interest groups and democratic organizations to mobilize public opinion. The Bolsheviks exploited Kerensky's ill-timed counter-assaults to evoke the spectre of 'counter-revolution' and, on the night of 24 October, began seizing key centres of power in Petrograd (the Winter Palace itself, of little strategic value, was seized only the next evening). The Bolsheviks then informed the assembled soviet congress that they had taken power in the name of the soviets and were creating a temporary Workers' and Peasants' Government. The frustrated SR and Menshevik delegates could only denounce the action and stalk out of the assembly. As Kerensky fled Petrograd in a vain search for support, the Bolsheviks set about constructing a new state order.

Rebuilding the State

October signified much, but huge questions remained—how to extend and consolidate soviet power over the vast empire, and how to build the world's first socialist state and society. Bolsheviks had to address these problems under conditions of war, not only the ongoing Great War but a violent civil war implicit in Bolshevik ideology and the process by which they had come to power.

These first years were, in Merle Fainsod's felicitous phrase, 'the crucible of communism'—an attempt to create a socialist state, economy, society, and culture later known as 'war communism'. The latter phrase signifies much, not only the wartime conditions, but also a violent militancy that informed Bolshevik measures. Historians have passionately debated the regime's intentions, the coherence of its war communist programme, the relative weight of civil war and ideology as causal factors, and the role of Lenin. Estimates of Lenin vary wildly, from that of malevolent ideologue and precursor of Stalin to that of a moderate pragmatist opposed to utopian leaps. Some see the 'seeds of totalitarianism' (to use an outmoded term) in Bolshevism itself; others blame the crescendo of authoritarianism and violence on the civil war alone.

Such one-sided interpretations obscure the ambiguities, alternatives, and texture of early Soviet history. October most certainly did not mark the end of the revolution; the new Bolshevik regime had to surmount the same social and national movements that destroyed its predecessors. But the Bolsheviks approached these issues in their own inimitable way. In particular, they attached great significance to ideology—hence the obsessive determination to build socialism as the historical antithesis of capitalism. Regarding 'class war' as the dominant reality, they ruthlessly sought to abolish the market and associated 'bourgeois' institutions, cultural values and ethical norms. Still, Bolshevik behaviour cannot be reduced to ideology: they also drew—sometimes unconsciously, sometimes reluctantly, sometimes enthusiastically—on traditional political culture and bureaucratic power. It was not the contradictions between these different impulses but their fusion that led to the great successes—and excesses—of the early Soviet regime.

The Bolsheviks used the cover of the Second All-Russian Congress of Soviets to legitimize the seizure of power and formation of a workers' and peasants' government. But they made haste not only to consolidate power but to *use* it. That meant a torrent of decrees—like the land decree, which formally nationalized land but in reality empowered peasants to complete the agrarian revolution on their own terms. The Bolsheviks also demolished symbols of the old regime—its ranks, titles, and traditional social estates. They also sought to establish a monopoly on political discourse, re-establishing censorship and banning 'bourgeois' and 'counter-revolutionary' newspapers. Given the disintegration of administration and law in 1917, early Bolshevik rule (as Peter Kenez has suggested) was largely 'rule by decree' using threat, exhortation, and propaganda.

Constructing power—not only in Petrograd and Moscow, but in the interior and borderlands—was the primary concern. This process replicated the seizure of power itself, as so-called 'military-revolutionary committees' and garrison troops seized power in the name of the 'soviet'. But Lenin sought to monopolize power, not just construct it—hence his fierce opposition to the idea of a coalition with other socialists. Although his first government was eventually forced to include some left SRs, the coalition lasted only a few brief months. Important too was Lenin's decision to retain the ministerial bureaucracy and cabinet executive: rather than destroy these creatures of the tsarist regime (as recently envisioned in his *State and Revolution*), he simply relabelled ministries 'commissariats' and the cabinet 'Council of People's Commissars'. With this legerdemain he rebaptized these bodies as qualitatively different, purportedly because they were now part of a workers' and peasants' state and presumably staffed by proletarians.

That was a masterful illusion: few proletarians were prepared for such service. It created, however, a golden opportunity for the white-collar employees of the tsarist and provisional governments, not only the army of petty clerks and provincial officials, but also mid-level technical and administrative personnel in the capitals. They found the transition easy, for example, from local War Industries Committees and zemstvo economic organs into 'proletarian' institutions like the Supreme Council of the National Economy (*Vesenkha*) and its local 'economic councils' (*Sovnarkhozy*). War Communism spawned a fantastic profusion of economic bureaucracies, including vertical industry monopolies called 'Main Committees' (*Glavki*) that were direct heirs of the earlier administration. Thousands of employees and technical personnel, economists, statisticians, agronomists, and middle- and lower-ranking managers, specialists with higher education, university graduates, and sundry other professionals poured into these organizations. Typical was the case of doctors and lesser medical personnel, who quickly found a home in revolutionary projects for public health. Similarly, scientists and engineers eager to remake the world after technocratic visions eagerly joined in 'building socialism'. Hence the Bolshevik triumph was a triumph of the lower-middle strata providing the very infrastructure of the Soviet state. In this sense the white-collar engagement was as important as the workers' and peasants' movements lionized in official discourse and mythology.

But the most unique—and devastatingly efficient—innovation of these early years was the creation of the hybrid 'party-state'. Membership in the party itself grew exponentially, from a mere 23,600 members in January 1917 to 750,000 four years later. The party gradually metamorphosed into a hierarchically organized bureaucracy, with the discipline mandated in Lenin's 'democratic centralism'. At the apex the Central Committee began to specialize in function and policy area to become a shadow cabinet exercising real power. At all levels this party-state system had overlapping competence, with party functionaries in a 'Bolshevik faction' making decisions and ensuring implementation. Local party secretaries were plenipotentiaries, directing state institutions and soviets. To control key management positions, the party created the famous *nomenklatura* system for assigning reliable party members to these posts. The Bolshevik organs gradually marginalized the 'soviets' in whose name the revolution had been made; they also eliminated any corporate bodies and social organizations that might temper ministerial power. Hence the key revolutionary institutions of 1917—soviets, factory committees, trade unions, co-operatives, professional associations, and the like—were gradually subsumed into the new bureaucracy or extinguished outright.

This party apparatus became Stalin's institutional base in the struggle for power. When the Central Committee created the 'Orgburo' (Organizational Bureau) to manage this apparatus in 1919, it was under Stalin's command. Hence, even before becoming General Secretary in 1922, Stalin controlled major appointments, including those of provincial party secretaries; he thereby shaped the composition of party conferences and congresses, a critical asset in the power struggles of the 1920s. Stalin also was the first head of the Workers' and Peasants' Inspectorate (*Rabkrin*), another organ of paramount influence.

Others, however, discerned here a mortal danger to the proletarian state. Many protested against the privileges of 'bourgeois specialists' and their prominent role in the new state. Lenin himself rejected such 'specialist-baiting', dismissing fears of bourgeois contamination on the grounds that these people now worked for a socialist state and the working class. Bureaucratization was another cause of concern; 'Democratic Centralists', a faction at the Eighth Party Congress in March 1919, demanded decentralization and shift of power from party *apparatchiki* to soviet democracy. Another group, the 'Workers' Opposition', defended the autonomy of trade unions and the principle of workers' control. Predictably, the party hierarchy denounced such dissenters and reasserted 'democratic centralism' to command obedience and submission.

In December 1917, faced with what seemed to be regime-threatening opposition, Lenin created a supreme political police—the 'Extraordinary Commission to Combat Counter-Revolution and Sabotage', known by its Russian acronym Cheka. At its head was a Polish Bolshevik, Feliks Dzerzhinskii, charged with becoming the 'sword of the revolution' against 'class' enemies, real and imagined. He rapidly made the Cheka a state within a state, arbitrarily meting out revolutionary justice and terror. His empire constructed a network of prisons and labour camps that later became the world's first concentration camp system.

A critical turning-point came in January 1918, when the long-awaited Constituent Assembly finally convened in Petrograd. Lenin had permitted elections to the Constituent Assembly, something that the socialists and liberals had endlessly promised but endlessly deferred. Bolsheviks garnered only a quarter of the votes, the PSR emerging the clear victor—but only, the Bolsheviks argued, because the ballot failed to distinguish between left SRs (who supported October) and right SRs (who did not). Well before the Assembly convened, Lenin made clear his hostility towards a 'bourgeois' (hence irrelevant) parliament. The result was a single, seventeen-hour session on 15–16 January: after passionate SR and Menshevik fulminations against the Bolsheviks, Lenin simply dissolved the Assembly and forbade further sessions.

Civil War

By the spring of 1918, the Bolsheviks had extended soviet authority to the Russian heartland but could hardly claim to have a firm grasp on power. For the next three years they would combat and defeat an incredible array of adversaries: White armies of patriots and anti-communists, liberals and SRs, peasant rebels ('greens') and urban anarchists, and minority movements spread along the borderlands and inside Russia proper itself. The regime would also combat interventionist forces from Britain, France, the United States, and Japan, and in 1920 became embroiled in a bitter war with Poland. By early 1921, however, the regime had vanquished adversaries, signed treaties with its neighbours, and turned its attention to reintegration and rebuilding.

The civil war began in the winter of 1917/18. Apart from small bands of patriotic officers (interested more in continuing the war against Germany than in defeating Bolsheviks), the first important 'White' leader was General M. V. Alekseev. Together with General Kornilov, in January 1918 he created the Volunteer Army in the Don region: its goal was to cast off the German-Bolshevik yoke and reconvene the Constituent Assembly. Throughout its existence, this army operated within the territory of the Don and Kuban Cossacks—a serious handicap, since the Cossacks had their own agenda independent of saving the Great Russian state. The Don Cossack ataman, General A. M. Kaledin, did offer his services to the White generals, but he was unceremoniously abandoned by the Cossacks when a Red force invaded and elicited popular support. After Kornilov himself fell in battle at Ekaterinodar, command passed to General Anton Denikin—an uncharismatic, but intelligent commander of great personal integrity.

Other White forces gathered along the Volga and in Siberia. Perhaps most significant was the Czech Legion, tsarist POWs scheduled for repatriation; ordered to disarm, they resisted and soon found themselves at war with the Bolsheviks. In Siberia (with its strong tradition of autonomous regionalism and great ethnic diversity), moderate SRs and Kadets created the 'Siberian Regional Council' at Omsk. On the Volga, radical SRs under Chernov established the 'Committee to Save the Constituent Assembly' (*Komuch*). These SRs evoked little popular support and deemed White generals a greater menace than the Bolsheviks—a sentiment reciprocated by the military. In September 1918 they met at Ufa in a lame attempt to re-establish the Provisional Government (as a 'Directory'), but it lacked even a programme, much less an apparatus to implement it. In November 1918 the military ousted the radicals (in a coup marked by executions and brutality that were becoming the norm) and installed Admiral A. Kolchak as military dictator and 'Supreme Ruler'. Kolchak was emblematic of White leadership: a man of deep personal integrity, courage, and patriotism, but a taciturn and erratic personality completely lost in the world of politics. His forces never mounted a sustained threat; he even failed to obtain diplomatic recognition from the allies (at the instigation of Woodrow Wilson, who heeded Kerensky's advice). He was finally captured and executed by the Cheka in early 1920.

The previous year had already marked the high point of the White assault, mounted from the south by A. I. Denikin's Volunteer Army. He launched the offensive in the spring of 1919, but made the fatal blunder of splitting his army into two units: a smaller force under Baron P. N. Wrangel (which captured Tsaritsyn on 30 June), a larger formation advancing into the Donbas. In the 'Moscow Directive' of 3 July Denikin ordered an assault on the capital along a very broad front stretching from Samara to Kursk. It was an all-or-nothing gamble, for Denikin realized that the Red Army was growing more powerful by the hour, and that further Allied support was dubious. He counted on enthusiasm from the momentary flush of victory, as his armies rapidly captured Kursk, Voronezh, Chernigov, and (on 13–14 October) Orel—a town just 300 kilometres from Moscow. Simultaneously, White forces under N. N. Iudenich advanced on Petrograd. But White fortunes soon changed: on 18–19 October Semen Budennyi's Red Cavalry counter-attacked and smashed the White army advancing on Tula; it was only a matter of time before victory followed in the north, the Crimea, and Ukraine. The final denouement came in 1920, as the remaining White forces, under General Wrangel, were evacuated to Constantinople.

Bolshevik victories, which seemed unlikely, were due to several factors. Geography afforded great strategic advantage: the Bolshevik hold on the central provinces permitted shorter lines of supply and communications, whereas White forces were stretched out along the periphery—in the south, along the Volga, in Siberia, western borderlands, and Ukraine. Moreover, Bolsheviks were better prepared to mobilize human and material resources, for their state administration capitalized on the personnel and organizations of preceding regimes. Whites, by contrast, were inept administrators; their camp was a mobile army engaged in field operations, with neither the skill nor the inclination to put down administrative roots.

Ideology was also important in the Bolshevik victory. The socialist vision had not lost its lustre for many workers, peasants, and white-collar workers. Although Bolshevik social and economic polices unquestionably provoked considerable opposition, the government at least had policies and, more important, provided a public discourse to rationalize these as essential for plebeian victory in a class war. By contrast, the Whites symbolized property and privilege; they utterly failed to articulate an alternative vision acceptable to workers, peasants, and other plebeians caught up in the revolutionary storm.

Bolshevik nationality policy also contributed to their success. Whereas most (especially patriotic Whites) sought to re-establish the empire, the Bolsheviks recognized the volatility of the nationality question and promised national self-determination—albeit, with the proviso that self-determination be subordinate to the interests of the proletariat. Despite the activities of the Commissariat of Nationalities (led by Stalin), the Bolsheviks actually could only abide and applaud the breakup of the empire. By mid-1918 independent states had arisen in Georgia, Armenia, Azerbaijan, Ukraine, Finland, and Belorussia; a powerful pan-Islamic movement was sweeping through the Muslim peoples of Central Asia. However much Lenin wished to reconquer the lost territories, this consummate *Realpolitiker* accepted the status quo, if only temporarily. He also

Bringing art (and propaganda) to the people, instructing them, merging art and life in a practical way—these were traditional nineteenth-century concerns that appeared quickly in new guises during the revolution and civil war. Here a decorated agitational train plies the rails along the shifting fronts of the civil war.

wrapped policy in a theory of 'federalism', which granted nationalities the trappings of statehood but within the framework of a Russian socialist state.

The Bolshevik cause also benefited from the fractious disunity of their adversaries. They were indeed a motley group—radical socialists, anarchist peasants, moderate Kadets and Octobrists, and of course arch-conservative officers from the gentry. Ultimately the main adversary was the White officer corps, which tended to replicate the politics—and mistakes—of 1917. Thus they plainly despised moderate socialists, even in the cause against Bolsheviks. Moreover, White generals such as Kolchak, Iudenich, and Wrangel were miserable administrators and even worse politicians. That was particularly evident in the nationality question: though fighting amidst non-Russian peoples on the periphery, the Whites loudly proclaimed their goal of resurrecting 'Great Russia', with all the minority territories. Such nationalistic views, while typical of the officer corps (and indeed the centre and moderate parties in the Dumas and Provisional Government), were naturally opprobrious to aspiring national groups like the Cossacks.

Intervention by the allies, however much they might have loathed Bolshevism, had little military effect. It could hardly be otherwise: a momentous revolution in the vast Russian spaces could not be channelled, let alone halted or reversed, by the tiny tactical forces of the allied powers. Exhausted by four years of total war, fearful of domestic unrest, the allies provided some men and equipment, but lacked the clear purpose and persistence necessary to stay the course. Nor did they even share common goals. Under Winston Churchill's leadership,

Britain supplied the most money and equipment; its primary aim was to contain German power (and avert a German–Russian alliance) and to prevent Russian advances in Asia and the Near East. For its part, Japan landed troops for the simple purpose of acquiring territory in the eastern maritime provinces. Wilson dispatched American soldiers but eagerly seized on Soviet peace feelers, first at an abortive conference in Prinkipo in late 1918, later in a mission by William Bullitt and the writer Lincoln Steffens to Moscow in early 1919. In the end the allies, having denied unconditional support to the Whites, gradually withdrew from the conflict, having done little more than to reify the myth of hostile 'imperialist aggression' against the young socialist state.

War Communism

The civil war left a deep imprint on Bolshevik political culture. War made the Red Army the largest, most important institution in the new state: it absorbed vast resources and, to ensure political reliability, deliberately conscripted the most 'class-conscious' elements of the working class and party. As a result, the army not only represented a military force but also provided the formative experience for the first generation of Bolsheviks. Not surprisingly, Soviet Russia developed as a military-administrative state, the military idiom and norm permeating government, economy, and society. Civil war reinforced the ideology of class conflict that informed Bolshevik policy, not just propaganda, during these early years.

Of course, the party still embraced a broad spectrum of opinion and interests. Its radical, impatient wing demanded that socialism be constructed immediately, in a militant fashion. At the time of the Brest-Litovsk Treaty (March 1918), 'left-wing communists' also hoped to ride the wave of history and export the revolution beyond Soviet borders. L. Kritsman, in an influential tract written during the civil war, codified the notion of militant and heroic communist state-building and adumbrated a coherent policy agenda of 'War Communism'—proletarian and collectivist. Lewis Siegelbaum has demonstrated that this famous term has been used without analytical precision, and that a heady mixture of realism and utopian ideology actually shaped Bolshevik policy from mid-1918 to early 1921.

Lenin himself reflected this mix of fantasy and common sense. On many issues he was pragmatic and at odds with the radicals—as, for example, in the bitter controversy over the Brest-Litovsk Treaty, where he dismissed left-wing communism as an 'infantile disorder'. Pragmatism likewise informed his concessions to bourgeois specialists (whom he consistently shielded) and his view on trade unions (where he opposed Trotsky's militant plans to conscript labour). Lenin was also cautious about nationalizing industry in late 1917 and early 1918; his 'state socialism', modelled on the German wartime economy, did not entail state take-over of economic life until much later. All this has inclined some historians to distance Lenin from the radicals and to depict his pragmatism as a clear antecedent for the evolutionary, gradualist plan of socialist development known as the New Economic Policy in the 1920s. Indeed, Lenin himself introduced the term 'war communism' in 1921 to discredit his opponents.

Nevertheless, Lenin had not shorn all the radical impulses that brought him power. He was instrumental in establishing the Communist International and pressing its revolutionary mission abroad. He also introduced radical agrarian and food-supply policies. In the spring of 1918, for example, when the new regime faced the perennial grain crisis that bedevilled both the tsarist and provisional governments, Lenin expanded the latter's 'grain monopoly' into a full-scale food supply dictatorship. Similarly, Lenin was never comfortable with the original land decree, which closely echoed the SR 'socialization of the land'— all the more since the countryside was teeming with SR agronomists and surveyors, intent on realizing their own, not the Bolshevik, vision of land reform. Theirs was profoundly non-Marxist, insensitive to 'class' or aims of radical transformation.

That vision, which placed so much faith in the peasantry, was anathema to Lenin. Instead, he propagated a scheme of collectivized agriculture and established some prototype large-scale collective farms, appropriately aimed at the 'poor and landless peasantry'. Although the chaos of the civil war permitted few such experiments, they provided the precedent and rationale for more Promethean efforts in Stalin's 'Great Turn' of 1929–30. More telling still was Lenin's attempt to foment class war in the villages. At bottom he applied a crude Marxist sociology of village society that divided the peasants into a small class of rich exploiters (the infamous *kulaki*, often simply the most competent farmers), self-sufficient 'middle peasants' (*seredniaki*), and the revolutionary and exploited 'poor peasants' (*bedniaki*). To stoke the fires of intra-village revolution, the Bolsheviks created 'Committees of Poor Peasants' (*kombedy*) to implement Soviet decrees and to drive the wealthier from power. This policy pitted neighbour against neighbour; it often fostered violence and the settling of old scores that had nothing to do with 'class struggle'. Moreover, in many blackearth regions peasants viewed Bolshevik commissars, grain detachments, army draft apparatus and the like as worse than any conceivable class enemy. The result was a fierce civil war between organized peasant bands, sometimes called 'greens', and Bolshevik forces. Recent research has revealed the extraordinary intensity of this brutal conflict in Tambov and other grain-producing regions as Red Army detachments came to pacify the village. Here civil war persisted long after the Whites had been crushed, providing a primary impulse for the 'New Economic Policy' in early 1921.

War communism also informed the construction of social orders, with appropriate status and disabilities. In the first constitution (July 1918), labour was a universal duty and defined social status. To the toiling classes of workers and

Folk and cubo-futurist themes merge in this 1920 ROSTA poster calling on peasants to give up their grain to feed the Red Army defenders of their freedom and land lest they wind up once again in the subservient position of feeding the landlords.

peasants were juxtaposed the 'formers' (*byvshie*), i.e. members of the former exploiting class—nobility, bourgeoisie, clergy, and the like. All these 'exploiters' were deprived of civil rights and legally classified as the 'disenfranchised' (*lishentsy*). They had no right to work, but could be mobilized for menial labour or public works. Not all the social terror came from above: murderous pogroms against Jews and spontaneous assaults on clergy and other 'formers' were also a regular part of daily life during these violent years.

These years of terror and discrimination also brought incredible hardship and privation. Under the banner of progress historical progress appeared to have reversed course, with a return to a natural economy, barter, wages in kind, and 'currency' in the form of eggs, clothing, and other basic necessities. It was the era of the 'bagmen' (*meshchochniki*), petty traders who plied the black market in grain and other goods. The state summarily and sporadically punished the black marketeers, but in fact had to tolerate a sector that still supplied much of the food and basic commodities.

Revolutionary Culture

Besides the market-place, culture was another key battleground. Under the Provisional Government, cultural leaders organized unions and demanded the creation of a Ministry of Culture to replace the traditional state and court patronage of the arts. As important as cultural creation was cultural destruction (the iconoclastic demolition of symbols from the *ancien régime*) and the search for new symbols and festivals.

Here too the party divided into radical and conservative camps, reflected in the debate between A. A. Bogdanov and Lenin over the historical meaning of culture and its place in a proletarian state. Both recognized the importance of culture for revolutionary transformation, but had long disagreed on fundamental principles of Marxism and culture. Lenin (the more orthodox Marxist) saw culture as pure superstructure, subordinate to class conflict and the task of seizing and rebuilding power. Culture (from literacy campaigns to university learning) was crucial, yet secondary; it was just another component of the superstructure. Lenin's conservative tastes carried an aversion to utopian experiments, an affinity for classical Russian culture, and a desire to integrate artists and writers into well-defined hierarchies under party control. His tool was A. V. Lunacharskii's bailiwick, the Commissariat of Enlightenment, the very 'Ministry of Culture' that intellectuals and artists had proposed in 1917. This new patron of the arts sponsored a full range of artistic activities (including the feeding, shelter, and clothing of the intelligentsia); it also attempted to create a new educational system based on such radical doctrines as the Unified Labour School, which jettisoned traditional disciplines and substituted practical work and learning through labour.

Bogdanov's vision, similar to that of the Italian Marxist Antonio Gramsci, could hardly have been more different. It posited the defining role of culture—i.e. cultural transformation was the pre-condition of social and political transformation. To complete the revolution, argued Bogdanov, it was vital to have 'new people' mastering the dominant forces of technocracy and technology, information and language. The new people had to create their own culture and hence create themselves. Bogdanov was a true radical, rejecting the traditional high culture as the product of old élites and hence antithetical to the needs of the proletariat. To help fashion proletarian culture (therefore its own essence or being), Bogdanov created the 'Proletarian Culture Movement' (*proletkul´t*), a fusion of organization and theory at the grass-roots level all across the country. It enabled 'workers' (broadly defined to include not only factory workers, but also white-collar employees, peasants, and others) to produce their own cultural artifacts, from literature to stage performances, from *belles-lettres* to literary readings. Although the movement was for a time exceedingly popular, that very popularity sealed its doom: proletcult was culture 'from below', inevitably representing an alternative to party dogma and inviting different readings of Marxism itself. In addition, the 'cultural front' (a military metaphor typical of the time) had too many players (not only the Commissariat of Enlightenment, but the trade unions and party itself), all competing for scarce resources. By the early 1920s, in short, proletarian culture faced a phalanx of determined foes in this 'proletarian' state.

A memorable expression of constructivism and revolutionary 'modernism' was Vladimir Tatlin's model of a tower to commemorate the Third International. Full of resonance to the Eiffel Tower and other monuments of industrialism and urbanism, this icon of revolutionary creativity was never built.

Revolutionary enthusiasm pervaded culture and society at many other levels. It was a driving force in high culture—fine arts, literature, architecture, which reflected powerful modernist currents, buttressed by aggressively anti-bourgeois and apocalyptic topoi. 'Non-objective' movements like suprematism, as well as constructivism and futurism, flourished in the heady atmosphere of revolution. The same spirit penetrated daily life, most dramatically in the question of the family and women's status. After secularizing marriage and radically liberalizing divorce, the party sought to address these questions by creating the Women's Section (Zhenotdel), an apparatus summoned to fashion a new Soviet woman—proudly proletarian, independent, an activist in the vanguard of the party as a leader and builder of consciousness. This vision, like revolutionary culture itself, would arouse rising hostility and suspicion from state and society alike in the 1920s.

In these years, however, the Bolsheviks were cultural revolutionaries, particularly in their feverish attempt to construct a new symbolic world—with new icons, new language, new monuments, new festivals— to bestow legitimacy on the new order. Suggestive of this campaign was the attempt, in early 1918, to sponsor a competition for the design of monuments to commemorate the great deeds of the Russian Socialist Revolution. Lenin himself issued a 'plan' for legitimate festivals and for rewriting the past (especially the 'history' of the still ongoing revolution itself). The use of festivals for education, socialization, and morale was quickly apparent—in the well-orchestrated celebrations of May Day, the first anniversary of the Revolution in 1918, and later in the public participatory spectacle to re-enact the October Revolution in 1920. Of course there were glitches and crudities (for example, offering special rations and luxury goods to arouse 'enthusiasm'), and this political theatre allowed variant decodings. The regime also adopted the Gregorian calendar, modernized the alphabet, and expropriated urban space (by renaming streets and squares). Finally, Bolshevik 'God Builders' (i.e. those who saw Bolshevism as a new religion with the proletariat as deity) began to foster a cult of Lenin, especially after an SR terrorist critically wounded Lenin in 1918. Party intellectuals then made haste to foster the idea of his immortality and to promote the public worship of this new saint, casting the die for the far more ominous elaborations in later years.

THE NEW ECONOMIC POLICY (NEP) AND THE REVOLUTIONARY EXPERIMENT

1921–1929

WILLIAM B. HUSBAND

With NEP, the new Bolshevik regime pragmatically sought to consolidate power and rebuild a shattered economy. But these were also years of insoluble economic problems, fierce social tensions, and deep divisions in the party. Ultimately, NEP did more to exacerbate than solve fundamental problems; it was a critical prelude to Stalin's 'great turn' in the late 1920s.

ONCE the Bolsheviks had consolidated their victory in the Russian civil war, the revolutionary experiment in socialism could begin in earnest. The defeat of principal military enemies in conjunction with the use of mass mobilization and repressive force seriously impaired those rivals not completely driven from the political arena. By that time, the Bolsheviks had already undertaken a broad programme of social and economic change. They attempted to co-ordinate all economic life by creating the Supreme Council of the National Economy in 1917, soon thereafter nationalized factories, and outlawed private trade. Their endorsement of workers' control aspired to establish innovative management and labour relations, and the collapse of the national currency appeared to hasten the transition to a barter economy. New laws attacked social institutions and practices that reflected the values of the former regime. And in both city and village, workers and peasants implemented their own agendas, beginning with the appropriation of property belonging to élites of the old order.

Only revolutionary maximalists could have equated these early measures with socialism: by the early 1920s building a new society was still a task for the future. Despite the bold language of revolutionary pronouncements, years of 'government by decree' in 1917–20 had given the Communist Party only a paper hold on most spheres of life, while seven years of warfare had reduced the national economy to ruin. During the closing months of the civil war, the population increasingly demanded that the state produce tangible improvements to justify the sacrifices made in the name of revolution. As public tolerance of grain requisitioning and other emergency measures reached its limit, workers and peasants openly defied Soviet power. Even the most ideological Bolshevik could not deny the gravity of the situation. In March 1921— on the eve of the important Tenth Party Congress—the state had to use force to repress an anti-Bolshevik uprising at the Kronstadt Naval Base, a bastion of revolutionary radicalism in 1917.

Both in response to public pressure and in keeping with their own ideological predilections, in 1921–9 the Bolsheviks pursued what would be the most open and experimental phase of Russian commu-

State propaganda showed healthy, energetic workers setting about the task of building socialism. Such representations clashed with the harsh realities of life in the first years of NEP. 'With Arms We Have Defeated the Enemy, With Labour We Will Get Bread. Everyone Get Down To Work, Comrades!' reads this 1921 poster.

nism. The turning-point came in 1921 when the Tenth Congress endorsed the controversial New Economic Policy (NEP). Its aims were many: to ease public resentment against the emergency measures of the civil war; to regularize supply and production through a limited reintroduction of the market; to invigorate the grass-roots economy and generate investment capital for industrialization; and, in general, to lay the foundation for the transition to socialism at some unspecified but inevitable future date. At the same time, the political and military victory demanded that revolutionaries fulfil their promise of a more equitable social and economic order. In that sense, the extensive destruction of the pre-revolutionary system in 1917–20 provided a mandate for broad reconstruction and social transformation.

With opportunity, however, came responsibility; the real tasks of a ruling party soon brought the limitations of Bolshevism into sharp focus. The political leaders were divided; their control of the country was largely illusory. The international proletarian revolution that the Party had confidently predicted failed to materialize, and Soviet Russia found itself the steady object of international suspicion and antagonism. Ongoing economic problems threatened the survival of the regime, forcing compromises on the state that engendered widespread resentment. Social and artistic innovations produced genuine improvements, but their unanticipated results frequently offended public sensibilities. In the end, NEP promoted at once conservative and revolutionary sentiments. Paradoxically, enthusiasm for experimentation and for Stalinist regimentation sprang from the same source.

The Politics of Revolutionary Consolidation

The Communist Party faced a pressing need in 1921 to transform itself from a revolutionary cadre into an effective ruling institution. Early in the year, the Bolsheviks continued to increase repression and centralization despite popular discontent; only in the face of the Kronstadt revolt did the awareness of the need to retreat strike root. The leadership also faced challenges within the party. One faction advocated the reinstitution of greater internal democracy; another sought to restore the independence of trade unions; and a third complained that the party had lost its revolutionary vision. Faced with such contradictory pressures, the Tenth Party Congress did not rush into political reform. It did endorse NEP—a market, an end to grain requisitioning, a tax on harvests, and denationalization of small-scale enterprises—but not before the Bolsheviks had outlawed opposing political parties and banned party factions.

In the politics of the 1920s, the Bolsheviks were neither omnipotent nor single-minded. As before, their policy reflected as much mass pressure as Marxist ideology; the problem of discipline was as great as ever. Regional and local institutions were weak, unreliable, even non-existent; considerable segments of intermediate and lower officials resisted central authority and opposed the NEP. When Lenin declared that the party would pursue NEP 'seriously and for a long time', he tacitly admitted that Bolshevism had failed to establish a dictatorship of workers and poorer peasants. Rather, Lenin admitted, Soviet power had produced a burgeoning bureaucracy that was staffed largely by officials from the old regime and by opportunists, especially in the local areas.

The Eleventh Party Congress (March–April 1922) specifically addressed this issue. Lenin himself complained that communists frequently adopted the ways of the pre-revolutionary ministries and thus launched the attack on bureaucratism. The delegates resolved to tighten discipline in lower organs and to combat the internal factionalism that had earlier been outlawed but by no means eradicated. Partly in an effort to reach these objectives, the Central Committee elected I. V. Stalin as General Secretary—i.e. head of the Secretariat, a post with extensive appointment powers. Although he would use these prerogatives for his own political advancement, the initial intent was to reform the personnel apparatus of the party.

Lenin's partial incapacitation by a cerebral haemorrhage in May 1922 seriously altered the dynamics of Soviet politics, however, and the reformism adopted at the Eleventh Congress never ran its intended course. Lenin's deteriorating health—he suffered additional strokes in December 1922 and March 1923—triggered a succession crisis and exacerbated factional conflict that lasted well beyond his death in January 1924. Uncertainty and instability prevailed at the top. Lenin's authority, unparalleled if not always unchallenged, was personal rather than institutional. His dominance derived from his experience, intellect, and political acumen, not any title or office. To replace Lenin, it was necessary not just to name a successor, but to reconsider the very concept of leadership in the party.

Lenin himself contributed to the contentiousness when he dictated his so-called 'testament' in December 1922, emphasizing the shortcomings of all major political figures. It declared that Nikolai Bukharin was 'the favourite of the whole party' and its 'most significant theoretician', but weak on dialectics and somewhat scholastic. Lenin noted that Grigorii Zinoviev and Lev Kamenev had wavered at the time of the October Revolution—which was 'not, of course, accidental'. Of the younger Bolsheviks, G. L. Piatakov was too preoccupied with administration 'to be relied on in a serious political situation'. And Lenin especially feared that a rivalry between Stalin and Leon Trotsky might split the party. Although Trotsky was 'certainly the most able man in the present Central Committee', he was given to 'excessive self-confidence' and an exaggerated concern with 'the administrative aspect of affairs'. Stalin as General Secretary 'had concentrated boundless power in his hands', and Lenin worried whether Stalin would 'always know how to use this power with sufficient caution'. In a postscript he added that 'Stalin is too rude' to be General Secretary and recommended that 'the comrades consider removing Stalin from this post'.

The succession struggle commenced even before Lenin died. In 1923 and despite a pledge of collective leadership, a triumvirate of Stalin, Zinoviev, and Kamenev accused Trotsky of Bonapartist aspirations. At the same time, Lenin launched his own assault against Stalin: he strongly criticized Stalin's treatment of minority nationalities and threatened to sever relations for Stalin's insulting behaviour towards Nadezhda Krupskaia, Lenin's wife. Lenin also asked Trotsky, Stalin's most bitter rival, to represent his views at the forthcoming Twelfth Party Congress of April 1923. But Trotsky, for reasons still unclear, chose not to present Lenin's case against Stalin and thereby squandered a unique opportunity to use Lenin's authority against Stalin. By December 1923 the triumvirs had prevailed in party infighting and put Trotsky and his followers on the defensive.

Lenin's death in January 1924 had a mixed impact. Publicly, it signalled the beginning of a cult of Lenin: thousands viewed the open coffin, Petrograd became Leningrad, and quasi-religious symbolism of Russian Orthodoxy crept into the funeral. And over the objections of Krupskaia, the Central Committee placed the embalmed body on permanent display in Red Square. Behind the scenes, however, Lenin's death—long anticipated—did not interrupt adversarial high politics. In February 1924 the Central Committee launched a recruitment campaign, the Lenin Enrolment, to 'proletarianize' the party by

A cult of Lenin, which he undoubtedly would have opposed, arose immediately following his death in January 1924. Later that year, this bust of Lenin occupied a prominent place in the May Day parade in newly renamed Leningrad.

admitting more actual industrial workers. Although this step would ultimately erode the meaning and significance of party membership, in the short term it added primarily to the numerical strength of Stalin's supporters. By the time the Thirteenth Party Congress opened at the end of May 1924, over 128,000 new candidates had joined. That number would soon surpass 240,000, thus increasing the size of the party by more than half. The triumvirate also fortified itself in other ways. Krupskaia pressed the leadership to make public the criticisms in Lenin's testament, which had been kept secret (even from the party members for over a year), but was rebuffed. When Trotsky attacked Zinoviev and Kamenev in his *Lessons of October*, published for the anniversary of the revolution, he succeeded only in driving them back into a closer alliance with Stalin. And in December 1924 Stalin cast down an ideological challenge to Trotsky, counterposing his own idea of 'socialism in one country' to Trotsky's concept of 'permanent revolution'. Stalin's argument—that the Soviet Union could create a socialist state without an international proletarian revolution—directly controverted Trotsky's belief that the final victory of socialism depended on successful revolutions in the West. With the prospects of international revolution clearly receding (especially after the Ruhr débâcle of 1923), Stalin's view resonated strongly with the rank and file.

With Trotsky weakened, the struggle entered a second phase in early 1925 when the triumvirs turned against one another. In 1924 Stalin had already begun to use his appointment powers as General Secretary to replace followers of Zinoviev and Kamenev with his own. This rivalry now intensified, just as the character of NEP itself became the central public issue. Indeed, 1925 would prove to be the apogee of private economic initiative during NEP. Zinoviev, ostensibly alarmed at capitalist 'excesses' in a socialist state, went on the attack. That impelled Bukharin, NEP's strongest advocate in the top leadership, to join forces with Stalin. Ultimately, however, this phase of the struggle was decided more along factional than policy lines. At the Central Committee meeting of October 1925 and again at the Fourteenth Party Congress in December, the more numerous Stalin–Bukharin bloc simply ran roughshod over the Zinoviev–Kamenev group.

The third phase of the succession produced an unlikely alliance: the 'united opposition' of Trotsky, Zinoviev, and Kamenev in 1926–7. Seeking to offset the support for Stalin (and, to a lesser degree, Bukharin) in the rank and file, these former foes resorted to direct action to achieve what they had been unable to gain in internal party politics. This strategy unravelled even before it was implemented. When one of the opposition's conspiratorial meetings was easily uncovered in mid-1926, the Central Committee charged Zinoviev with violating the party ban on factions and removed him from the Politburo. In late September, the 'united opposition' took their case directly to the factories by staging public demonstrations, but without success. As the party press mobilized its full wrath against them, in early October 1926 the trio capitulated and publicly recanted. Trotsky was removed from the Politburo, and Kamenev lost his place as candidate member. After further machinations and conflicts, in October 1927 the trio was dropped from the Central Committee, followed by the expulsion of Trotsky and Zinoviev from the party itself in November. One month later, the Fifteenth Congress revoked the party membership of Kamenev. Zinoviev and Kamenev would be readmitted in 1928 following a humiliating recantation, but Trotsky was first exiled and then forcibly deported in 1929.

Hostile as the factional struggle thus far had been, nothing prepared—or could prepare—the country for its final act. In 1928–9, Stalin moved against what he labelled the 'right opposition' led by Bukharin, Aleksei Rykov (head of the Council of People's Commissars, Sovnarkom), and the trade unionist Mikhail Tomskii. Neither the party nor the public had reason to expect this offensive. Certainly the Fifteenth Party Congress in December 1927 had endorsed nothing

This 1927 political cartoon ridicules the united opposition: Trotsky, the organ grinder; Zinoviev, the singer; Kamenev, the parrot. 'We play and play, but no one comes to us,' reads the caption.

stronger than greater restrictions on the most prosperous peasants, the gradual and voluntary collectivization of agriculture, and an increased effort to develop heavy industry. The congress gave no strong signal that the party was about to scuttle NEP. Yet when this final phase concluded, NEP had ended and the USSR was engulfed in class warfare.

Stalin proceeded cautiously, but as always with a strong sensitivity to the prevailing political opinion. By the late 1920s the belief that the revolution had failed to fulfil expectations of 1917 became widespread in Soviet society; a renewed socialist radicalism pervaded the Central Committee and many rank-and-file communists as well. The population outside the party deeply resented the privileges still accorded to managers, engineers, and technical personnel a full decade after Red October. The fact that such a large proportion of state officials were neither workers nor peasants provided an additional irritant. Many also believed that kulaks (the pejorative term for the most prosperous peasants) were withholding their grain from the market in an economy of scarcity. And everywhere one encountered bitterness and jealousy towards those who had used NEP to enrich themselves.

Stalin did not create this mood or control it, but he knew how to exploit it. His first target was a shortage of grain. Marketings by the end of 1927 were down 20 per cent from the previous year. Due to low prices being paid by the state, peasants with a surplus simply held it back in the hope of better terms, used it to fatten livestock for slaughter, diverted it to the illegal production of grain alcohol, or in some cases shifted to planting more profitable industrial crops. These factors, compounded by poor harvests in several areas, accounted for the drop. Stalin, however, placed the blame elsewhere. On a three-week tour of Siberia that began in mid-January 1928, he repeatedly declared the same culprits to be greedy kulaks and local officials too lenient in dealing with them.

He also fanned class hostilities in industry. In March 1928, at Stalin's personal invitation, the state initiated a show trial of fifty engineers, the first of several against the 'bourgeois specialists'. Stalin made the class underpinnings of this Shakhty affair, as it became known, the main theme in a speech to the party in April 1928. The defendants, primarily men who had held responsible posts under tsarism and three Germans working under state contracts, were charged with sabotaging coal-mining in the vital Donets basin and conspiring with foreign capitalists. The Shakhty Trial, held in May–July, became a mass spectacle. Newspapers prominently featured the proceedings and sought to intensify class antagonisms.

The General Secretary broadened his assault on the right opposition. In the second half of 1928, Bukharin worried that Stalin would use the power of the Secretariat to replace the editorial staffs of important national publications with his own appointees. And that is precisely what he did. By the end of the year he had also replaced the leading officials in the Moscow branch of the party and in the national trade-union organizations, both of which had previously eluded his control. In February 1929, Stalin led a Politburo attack on Bukharin, Rykov, and Tomskii for factionalism; the denunciation came into full public view in August. Bukharin was removed from the Politburo in November 1929; Rykov and Tomskii would suffer the same fate in 1930.

This was not, however, merely an exercise in power politics: vital policy issues played a significant role in the outcome. When he made public the specific charges against the 'right deviation' in 1929, Stalin accused his rivals of an excessive and non-socialist sympathy for independent economic development. His own formula therefore called for a more rapid, centrally planned, and avowedly ideological transformation to pure socialism. Against detractors who considered its high quotas and objectives unrealistic, Stalin sponsored the First Five-Year Plan in April 1929 (declared retroactively to have begun in October 1928). Its emphasis on accelerated development of heavy industry was the direct converse of Bukharin's call for a gradual transition and non-centralized endeavours. With his role as party leader secure, in late 1929 Stalin pressed for the immediate collectivization of agriculture and liquidation of the kulaks as a class.

Stalin had read the national mood correctly. His campaign against gradualists and bourgeois specialists was replicated in practically every administrative and professional institution in the country as impatient radicals attacked their more cautious colleagues and those who remained from the tsarist period. The state taxed the private economic sector out of existence, ended the market

Private traders provided goods and services the state could not. The level of activity at Moscow's largest outdoor market, the Sukharevka, suggests both the degree to which the public depended on it and the reasons why it symbolized everything the opponents of NEP found galling.

experiment, and dispossessed even small-scale entrepreneurs. Workers and peasants received preferential treatment in spheres such as education, and NEP's permissive social and artistic experiments came under full-scale attack. The succession to Lenin was over, NEP was abandoned, and a cultural revolution had begun.

But consolidating the revolution entailed more than seizing the commanding heights of politics. Better than any other high-ranking Bolshevik, Stalin had understood the significance of the changing size and character of the party in the 1920s. From 23,600 in January 1917 it had expanded to 750,000 at the beginning of NEP. This number contracted to fewer than 500,000 at the time the Lenin Enrolment began in 1924, but by the end of the decade total membership had climbed to 1.5 million (including candidate members). In general, the new recruits were young, urban, male, and poorly educated.

Numbers alone, however, do not tell the full story. The All-Union Communist Party (Bolshevik)—the party's official name until 1952—differed significantly from pre-revolutionary Bolshevism. Whereas participation in an illegal, underground cadre required a special revolutionary dedication, the new circumstances demanded other things of those who joined after 1921. Whereas the pre-revolutionary party put a premium on loyalty and proficiency in ideological matters (with sophistication in Marxist theory a prerequisite for a leading position), NEP required different criteria, not always appreciated by the old guard. An ability to carry out assignments, even a certain ruthlessness, proved more important once the party was in power. Indeed, Stalin's dubious credentials as a theorist, which had first caused experienced Bolsheviks to underestimate him, were not nearly as important to the new recruits. Moreover, Stalin appealed to the idealism that appeared, especially among the young, in the last years of NEP. Appointment powers and the ferocity of Soviet politics notwith-standing, Stalin could not have triumphed had he been supported only by ideo-logues, cynics, and opportunists. His supporters also included many idealists who believed that measures like the Five-Year Plan, collectivization of agricul-ture, and cultural revolution held the key to the transition to genuine socialism. For the young radicals attracted by Stalin's opposition to NEP, the policy had never been a pragmatic retreat, but a betrayal of the basic ideals and goals of the revolution.

Harnessing such idealism was important. While it is true that party members now held key positions in most institutions and enterprises, this alone did not ensure total control or total obedience. Throughout the decade local officials continued to ignore central directives, formulate policy on their own, behave dishonestly and immorally, and in general to comport themselves in ways that reflected badly on Soviet power. And as late as 1929, the Soviet administrative apparatus barely existed in the countryside. In sum, by 1929 the politics of con-solidating Red October and Stalin's emergence as leader had led to a redefini-tion of leadership and, by extension, of the party itself. All this provided the immediate background for the different kind of revolution that would com-mence with the 'Great Turn' of 1929–30.

Foreign Policy of an Internationalist State

International politics presented a special challenge for the Soviet state. In the Marxist schema, the Russian Revolution was but the first of a forthcoming wave of proletarian uprisings that the communists would lead and support. In the conditions of 1921–9, however, the Bolsheviks could furnish little more than encouragement and example; Soviet Russia during NEP needed not the rapid exportation of revolution, but above all time to heal its wounds and strengthen itself militarily. Thus, while by no means abandoning the Marxist vision of the future, the immediate focus of Soviet foreign policy was survival and state interest. Not surprisingly, Bolshevik international behaviour was also entwined with Soviet domestic politics.

The Comintern (Communist International) was founded in 1919 and served as the co-ordinating centre of the world workers' movement. Although it was based in Moscow, the Soviet state maintained the fiction that the Comintern was an independent body without government ties. The fact that no less a fig-ure than Zinoviev served as its head—from its founding until his disgrace in 1926—belied such claims, however. The Bolsheviks attempted to co-ordinate Comintern activities with the national priorities of the Soviet state, and by the early 1920s it was clear that Moscow was dictating Comintern policy. When, for example, the country needed a breathing spell in 1921, fiery rhetoric from the Comintern gave way to a more diplomatic posture towards Europe. The open promotion of revolution was redirected almost exclusively towards Asia. In 1924 the emergence of Stalin's 'socialism in one country' further curbed the language of international proletarian revolution. In addition, Zinoviev's replacement by Bukharin as Comintern head in 1926 was clearly a by-product of Soviet internal politics, as was Bukharin's replacement with Stalin's protégé Viacheslav Molotov in July 1929.

The Comintern also tried to define the correct relationship towards right-wing groups and non-communist socialists. In 1928 the Sixth Comintern Congress aroused considerable dismay in foreign ranks by forbidding alliances between revolutionary Marxists and moderate socialists. It asserted that the greatest danger came not from the many emerging fascist groups in Europe, but from the moderate parties on the left. This led to key defections, notably but not exclusively among French communists, who felt that *Realpolitik* dictated a common cause with other leftist elements in their own countries against the increasingly menacing right. This policy also hampered the German Communist Party by channelling its energy against socialists rather than the Nazis. Thus, by the end of the decade, Bolsheviks had made the Comintern centralized and subservient, but at the cost of reducing its effectiveness abroad.

In its foreign policy, a pragmatic internal logic governed Soviet behaviour. Revolutionary Russia faced a hostile international community in 1921: the overthrow of tsarism by a mass movement had alarmed the ruling élites in the West, giving rise to the Red Scare. The Bolshevik state compounded such fears when it nationalized industry, including foreign-owned enterprises, and repudiated the pre-1917 national debt (much of which was held by foreign creditors).

As Russia entered NEP, Lenin adumbrated the concept of peaceful coexistence. He argued that the capitalist and socialist camps could both compete and co-operate, and that military conflict between them was not necessarily inevitable. Socialist states could interact, especially economically, with the capitalist world because in any long-term competition socialism would ultimately prevail. Such thinking fitted the circumstances of the early 1920s. In the absence of the Western assistance that was to have come from the international proletarian revolution, it was vital that the Soviet republic end its diplomatic isolation and, if possible, attract financial help. This would not be easy. As the decade opened, no major industrial nation had yet given the revolutionaries diplomatic recognition, nor was there any sign of support for providing significant investment.

Pragmatism, within limits dictated by the internationalist element of Marxism, therefore shaped Bolshevik foreign relations. Soviet Russia's unalloyed hostility to the League of Nations before 1927 contained elements of both. But it was surely economics, not ideology, that led to the Anglo-Russian Trade Agreement (March 1921), and to Bolshevik participation in the Genoa Conference (April 1922). The latter, organized by the major industrial powers to discuss the reconstruction of the European economy, produced a rude shock: Germany and Russia, the two pariah states of Europe, independently unveiled their own Treaty of Rapallo, which officially renounced mutual claims and foresaw closer economic ties between the two. The treaty also gave Germany and Russia diplomatic leverage to play England and France off against one another. Perhaps most important of all, it laid the grounds for secret German–Soviet military co-operation: Germany could conduct training and weapons testing (forbidden by the Treaty of Versailles) on Soviet soil, and in return the Russians benefited significantly from the exposure to German military expertise. Rapallo was partially undone in 1925 when the Western powers included Germany in the Locarno Pact, which sought to stabilize European politics by achieving an agreement on permanent borders. The blow of being excluded from Locarno was softened only partially for the Soviets when Germany and the USSR reaffirmed Rapallo in 1926 with the Treaty of Berlin.

Russian relations with the West were mercurial. Britain's first Labour government granted diplomatic recognition to the USSR in early 1924, and Italy and France—although not the United States—soon followed. By October, however, relations already became strained when the 'Zinoviev letter' caused a scandal during British elections. Allegedly a directive on tactics from the Comintern to the British Communist Party, the publication of this forgery played a role in the Conservative victory. By May 1927 matters deteriorated to the point that Britain severed diplomatic ties, and France demanded in October that the Soviet Union recall its ambassador. Stalin capitalized on the furore: although legitimately concerned, he publicly exaggerated the imminent danger of military conflict and deftly exploited the 'war scare' against the Trotsky–Zinoviev–Kamenev bloc in the politics of succession.

In the end, the Soviet state achieved little in foreign relations during NEP: nor was it able to ignite international revolution to improve appreciably its standing in Europe. When Stalin ascended to top leadership, he replaced Lenin's policy of 'peaceful coexistence' with a philosophy that emphasized the link between internal mobilization and foreign threats: the concept of hostile capitalist encirclement. But behaving as if surrounded by enemies bent on the destruction of the country only served further to estrange the USSR. Hence Soviet Russia ended the 1920s much as it had begun the decade—without reliable allies and widely distrusted.

'Building Socialism with Capitalist Hands'

Economic life in 1921–9 reflected the full measure of the national crisis the Bolsheviks inherited, the consequences of party political struggles, and the limitations that ideology imposed on proposed courses of action. The problems were fundamental and ubiquitous; conflict over the correct policy of industrialization left the party deeply divided. An incomplete and inconsistent commitment to NEP both nationally and locally undermined its effectiveness. Ongoing economic chaos and recurrent crises continued to plague the grass roots.

In terms of national development, the leadership felt an acute need for a strategy of industrialization. By 1921 the economy certainly had to be resuscitated for practical reasons, but other important considerations also played a part. Above all, orthodox Marxism had posited that socialism could come into being only in a fully industrialized economy. That was hardly the case in Russia: the Bolsheviks had made a 'proletarian revolution' in an overwhelmingly agrarian country. To square the circle, all party leaders accepted as axiomatic that Soviet Russia must industrialize to continue on the road to socialism. But that left the door open for fundamental disagreements over the tempo and short-term priorities. In the event, implementing NEP as a step in this long-term undertaking (what Lenin called 'building socialism with capitalist hands') in no way ensured unity even at the highest levels.

The Soviet state hoped that projects like the electrification of the country would improve the quality of life and increase public support for the regime. An elderly peasant couple have their first opportunity to examine an electric lamp in 1926.

There were more pressing matters, however, before industrialization reached the top of the agenda. By 1921 the country faced almost total economic collapse: gross industrial output had fallen to less than one-fifth of the level before the First World War, production in some industries such as textiles was a mere one-tenth. Matters were hardly less catastrophic in agriculture: when the 1921 harvest produced significantly less than half the pre-war average, famine and epidemics ensued, claiming millions of lives. By 1922 hyper-inflation had driven prices, particularly those for agricultural products, to astronomical heights. In response, the government created a new currency backed by gold, the *chervonets*. This tight-money policy, however, caused difficulties in wage payments at many factories, triggering strikes and disorders.

The year 1923 witnessed the famous 'scissors crisis', a complete reversal of the price relationships of the previous year. In essence, agriculture had now begun to recover more quickly than industry. Although food was still not abundant, the shortage was no longer desperate. The supply of agricultural products thus outstripped the production of manufactured goods; as a result the index for industrial prices in 1923 rose to a level three times higher than agricultural prices. When plotted on a graph, these price indices—industrial prices rising, agricultural prices falling—resembled scissors, hence the name. In response, peasants resorted to grain-hoarding and a low level of marketing in the subsequent two years; that caused agricultural prices to recover in 1924–5, although obviously not in the way the state desired. As a result, the scissors crisis further

Millions lost their lives in the famine of 1921–2, which overwhelmed the resources of the revolutionary state. Bodies of famine victims lie unburied in a cemetery in 1921.

exposed the fragility of NEP, suggested an incompatibility of private agricultural and industrial sectors, and—perhaps of greater long-term significance—reinforced the chronic fears of the kulak.

Nevertheless by 1924 the national economy began a recovery of sorts. Industrial reconstruction proved deceptively rapid: restarting factories closed during the civil war caused a sharp rise in manufacturing output. Supply networks also began to function once again: the workers who had fled during the civil war and famine made their way back to the plants. As a result, the output of large-scale industry reached nearly half its pre-war scale in 1924 and 75 per cent a year later. Industrial exports rose to nine times what they had been at the beginning of the decade, even if still but a third of pre-war figures. Recovery was still more marked in agriculture: by 1924 the cultivation of arable land approached 1913 levels, and marketable output in agriculture increased 64 per cent between 1922 and 1925.

But this was recovery, not expansion of the pre-war base. And industry, in particular, soon reached a point of diminishing returns. Seven years of warfare, followed by new hardships in the early 1920s, had destroyed a significant portion of the industrial base. There had been virtually no renewal of the capital stock since before the First World War; what the Russian civil war had not destroyed was badly worn or outmoded. Restarts could increase output, but without significant new investment it could never reach the pre-war standard. But that was precisely the Bolsheviks' charge: to create the industrial foundation for socialism. And trade and foreign investment, although up considerably after 1921, fell far short of underwriting a venture of such magnitude.

This was the context of the party debate over industrialization. All leading protagonists agreed that the transformation was necessary and that the peasantry would absorb the chief cost. But they disagreed on three main issues: (1) tempo; (2) whether short-term development would centre first in heavy or light industry; and, (3) the degree of peasant entrepreneurship the state would tolerate during the process. Simply put, all sides agreed that capital investment would be generated in agriculture and 'pumped over', as the communists phrased it, to the industrial sector. The left—Trotsky and the economist Evgenii Preobrazhenskii, joined later by Zinoviev and Kamenev—favoured the rapid development of heavy industry and the substitution of centralized planning for the market. The right—Bukharin, Rykov, and Tomskii—championed a gradual tempo, the development of consumer goods manufacturing, and above all an alliance (*smychka*) with the peasantry. In their view, a tax on peasant profits could generate the needed investment capital. Scholars frequently present

Stalin's position as simply opportunistic. In one popular scenario, he first cynically sides with the right; then, after the left was politically defeated in 1927, he shifts maliciously to a position even more radical than that of Trotsky–Preobrazhenskii in order to attack the right.

In reality, the politics was more subtle and complex. It began in 1924, when Preobrazhenskii addressed the Bolsheviks' need to create the material pre-conditions for socialism in Russia. Marx had written that in the early stages of Western industrialization, entrepreneurs practised 'primitive capitalist accumulation' by denying workers the full value of their labour and by reinvesting a significant portion of the surplus profit. Preobrazhenskii called for something analogous in the USSR. Since, however, the majority of toilers were not factory workers, but peasants, Preobrazhenskii proposed a 'primitive *socialist* accumulation' by turning the terms of trade against the peasantry. By setting state prices for agricultural produce artificially low but artificially high for industrial goods, the state could create the analogue of profit to be reinvested. This position, with its hostility towards peasant prosperity and to market economics, signalled a fundamental attack on NEP.

Bukharin countered in 1925. He argued that the Preobrazhenskii plan risked alienating the peasants, and he reiterated the logic of the *smychka*. Not exploiting but taxing a prosperous peasantry made more economic and political sense. For Bukharin, industrialization would best result from a healthy economy that was reinvigorating itself in stages from the bottom upward. In this spirit he borrowed a phrase attributed to François Guizot that would haunt him politically: hoping to drive home the importance of grass-roots prosperity for long-term economic growth, Bukharin encouraged the peasants to 'enrich yourselves'. He warned that investment in heavy industry, as Preobrazhenskii proposed, was suicidal: such ventures required several years to produce a return, and in the interim the Soviet economy would collapse. Investment in the production of consumer goods, he reasoned, was more rational in an impoverished country that needed a rapid return on its limited capital. Preobrazhenskii replied that Bukharin's more gradual tempo posed the larger danger. What was left of the national economy would erode while implementing it.

Stalin was not simply opportunistic: he too was a proponent of heavy industrialization in 1924–5, but in his own way. At that time Stalin was politically aligned with Bukharin, and he allowed Bukharin the main role in articulating their public position against the opposition. It is doubly significant, however, that Stalin's formula of 'socialism in one country' in December 1924 ascribed primary importance to the development of heavy industry. Of even greater importance, before 1925 had ended, Stalin took special care to distance himself publicly from Bukharin's slogan 'enrich yourselves', which opponents of Bukharin denounced as excessively sympathetic to the kulaks.

It is, of course, beyond question that Stalin wanted fervently to become party leader in the 1920s, but this does not mean that he desired *only* power, free of ideological or policy preferences. Something far more complex guided his behaviour. Stalin adjusted his short-term course of action several times during the decade in response to manifold crises, but the same can be said of all party leaders. More significant is his unwavering commitment to certain ideas— above all, an ongoing preference for heavy industry and an abiding fear that kulaks withholding grain from the market could undermine the state and its programmes. Equally consistent was his antidote of using state power to deal with recalcitrant social elements. Thus, when Stalin attacked the right opposition in late 1927–early 1928, this marked an assault on his remaining political rivals *and* an intensification of a position he had defined by mid-decade. In early 1928, when he blamed the kulaks for the grain shortage (and, by extension, for jeopardizing the industrialization programme) he certainly brought his ideas more clearly into public view, but they were nothing new. The Stalinist tempo of industrialization and collectivization would later outstrip anything Trotsky and Preobrazhenskii had envisioned, but it was foreshadowed in the positions he established earlier against gradualism in industrialization and against NEP agriculture.

The full scope of economics, however, reached far beyond policy-making at the national level. Local considerations loomed large, for NEP pulled the state and society in contradictory and frequently conflicting directions. It ended outright starvation, but not hard times. It also renewed social antagonisms: most Russians still struggled to subsist, while private traders—the Nepmen—often made exorbitant profits and enjoyed a life-style of conspicuous consumption.

The petulance of lower officials, in combination with a limited enthusiasm at the top, produced an inconsistent implementation of NEP in various regions of the country. Private trade was legal but not secure. Some local officials disobeyed national directives and arrested Nepmen on the basis of laws already repealed, or simply on their own whim. In 1923–4, as Lenin lay dying, the national leadership responded to public resentment against Nepmen by arbitrarily closing 300,000 private enterprises. This proved short-sighted: by late 1924 it was clear that the state itself could not provide many of the services it had eliminated. In some locales, driving out the private traders had closed up *all* supplies; areas called 'trade deserts' sprang up where Nepmen had previously operated. But the period 1925–7—not coincidentally, the high point of Bukharin's influence—brought a policy reversal; it was during these years that the Soviet state showed its greatest tolerance of private enterprise under NEP. Understandably sceptical of resuming business at first, many Nepmen had to be reconvinced of the state's sincerity, but by the end of 1927 the market was in full swing again.

The following year, however, brought yet another change of course. In early 1928 Stalin's rhetoric against the 'right deviation' began to include talk of a showdown with both kulaks and Nepmen. The state used administrative measures to crack down on private entrepreneurs, and it increased business taxes exponentially. If a Nepman somehow scraped together enough to pay an initial levy, the tax-collector doubled the bill on his next visit. The state even applied a retroactive tax to those who had already gone out of business. Those who could not pay had their possessions seized and were thrown into the street; they lost access to ration cards, housing, and other public services. The entire process could take as little as three days.

Their fate as *lishentsy* aroused scant sympathy. NEP had brought back not only the market, but also prostitution, gambling, drugs, and other affronts to public morality. The fact that many Nepmen flaunted their wealth caused deep anger. Moreover, the preferential treatment the state gave the trained specialists, engineers, and factory managers from the old regime, who were technically not Nepmen *per se*, did nothing to make NEP more popular with the masses. In a different vein, a large number of Russians distrusted the profit motive and operated from the belief that personal enrichment can

СЕГОДНЯ И ЕЖЕДНЕВНО
ГОСЦИРКЕ

НЕГРО-ОПЕРЕТТА

Popular culture during NEP embraced the permissive attitudes and tastes that arose in the West after the First World War. This 1928 poster for the second State Circus advertises 'Negro Operetta'.

come only at the expense of another. The prevailing prices beyond the means of most citizens certainly reinforced this view. In the end, Nepmen became the focus of all these resentments.

The lowest level of the economy experienced additional problems. Stricter cost-accounting in reopened factories and the demobilization of six million Red Army soldiers increased unemployment from 640,000 in 1923 to more than 1.3 million in 1929. In addition, rural poverty drove the desperate into the cities despite the shortage of jobs. Moscow, for example, gained 100,000 new residents per year. Not surprisingly, the major urban centres experienced acute housing problems: not enough spaces and chronic disrepair in overcrowded, occupied units. The homeless population overwhelmed urban social services. Gangs of homeless orphans, the *besprizorniki*, in combination with the unemployed, contributed to a serious rise in crime as both groups fed an expanding corps of thieves, petty hoodlums, and prostitutes.

The situation, however, was not universally bleak. Workers' real wages rose steadily, albeit slowly, throughout the decade. By the late 1920s the shortages of goods and services were far less serious than at the beginning of NEP. The Soviet state could point to legitimate improvements in public health, working conditions, and infant mortality rates. And if workers still devoted too much of their income and energy to acquiring housing, food, and clothing, the standard of living stood well above that of 1918–21.

The village underwent its own transformation. By 1921 millions had acquired private holdings from the seizure of land belonging to the nobility, Church, crown, and richer peasants. As a result, the number of farms rose sharply, but the average size fell. In addition, the peasant commune—subjected to a frontal assault in the Stolypin reforms—reappeared. And when the commune reinstituted traditional, collective modes of cultivation, agriculture regressed technologically. Inefficient strip-farming, along with the primitive three-field system of crop rotation, once again predominated. In 1928 more than five million households utilized the traditional wooden plough, the *sokha*; the scythe and sickle still reaped half the annual harvest. Such backwardness of technique meant a low yield per acre, which in turn aggravated the long-standing peasant 'land hunger'. With more mouths to feed than such agriculture could support, the village had to push its marginal elements towards the city.

This village economics both influenced and was influenced by other realities. Social differentiation in the rural areas narrowed; as extremes of income closed, categories such as kulak, middle peasant, and poor peasant became blurred. Moreover, the Soviet state had only a minimal administrative presence in the countryside. After grain requisitioning ended in 1921, the villages had recouped much of their pre-revolutionary insularity and control over internal affairs. Although rural soviets formally held power, the peasant commune actually exercised the principal authority over day-to-day economics and law. And it was not until 1925 that the Communist Party made a serious attempt to increase membership in its rural organizations. In short, the Russian village—historically separated from and suspicious of the towns—closed ranks. In 1921–9, it identified with its own past and its own interests, not with Bolshevik visions of a revolutionary transformation.

'The New Soviet Man'

Despite upheavals, the Bolsheviks did not narrow their social vision, which went far beyond the transfer of political authority, reassessment of foreign relations, and redistribution of goods and services discussed thus far. While that political and economic reorientation was a mandatory first step, the Bolsheviks understood 'revolution' more broadly: it must also encompass a fundamental transformation of not only social institutions, but also values, myths, norms, mores, aesthetics, popular images, and traditions. Ultimately, the result would be not only a citizen of a new type (known in Bolshevik parlance as 'the new Soviet man') but nothing less than the recasting of the human condition for the better.

In 1921–9, therefore, a central element in the process the Bolsheviks called 'building socialism' was the inculcation of a new world-view. Bolshevism held that if Russia were to progress from its present condition through socialism to communism, society would have to understand its collective experience in a new way, that is, in terms of the rational application of scientific principles to human development. As Marxists, the Bolsheviks believed this would promote a more objective understanding of social existence that would, in turn, achieve greater mass co-operation and co-ordination among citizens. As Russian revolutionaries, they also intended that it would enable science and technology to help overcome economic and material backwardness.

Such an undertaking presented a multi-faceted challenge. At the very least it required extensive utilization of state power, and central authorities initiated ambitious projects—ranging from the eradication of illiteracy to the electrification of the whole country. By the end of NEP, the regime would ultimately use its administrative power to attempt to reconceptualize law, eliminate religious superstitions, recast education, and in general construct a proletarian culture in both the aesthetic and sociological sense. But wielding power was not enough: the Bolsheviks recognized that they could not simply *impose* new modes of thinking on society. Laws and decrees alone, even when backed by repression, could not automatically alter popular consciousness. They therefore also launched an unprecedented effort to educate and indoctrinate the masses.

Some campaigns to create the 'new Soviet man' addressed specific audiences. Party organizations such as the Zhenotdel (Women's Department) and the Komsomol (Young Communist League) concentrated on distinct groups, but suffered from the fact that—as in politics and economics—the party did not speak with a single voice. Even before the announcement in early 1930 that the Zhenotdel would be disbanded, for example, tepid support from the party leadership and open hostility from local officials undercut agitational and instructional work among women. For its part, the Komsomol instructed adolescents on topics as diverse as basic politics and sexual morality, but was frequently criticized for accomplishing little.

The campaign to eliminate illiteracy attempted to target women and national minorities. This ethnically mixed group of women in the Caucasus study together in a literacy circle.

Other messages focused on correcting specific problems and were aimed at society as a whole. To deal with the problem of chronic alcohol abuse, for example, the Bolsheviks initially continued the prohibition policy adopted by the tsarist state in 1914. When this failed to stem the widespread production of illegal spirits, the government conceded defeat and in 1925 reintroduced the state production of vodka. In a different instance, until conservatives finally prevailed in mid-1929, reformers sought to improve criminal justice by making penalties more lenient and taking into account the circumstances surrounding crime. To cite a third case, the state took steps to improve public health and sanitation. Building on reforms initiated in the last decades of imperial Russia, the People's Commissariat of Health raised the level of professionalism in health care markedly after 1921; preventive medicine and the curtailment of infectious diseases subsequently made impressive strides. But inadequate funding impeded additional plans to improve sanitation, and the reluctance of doctors to take rural posts left medicine in the countryside largely in its pre-revolutionary condition.

In their effort to create a new social ethos, the Bolsheviks also devoted special energy to redefining the family and the individual. Perceiving the patriarchal, religiously sanctioned family as tsarist society in microcosm, Soviet state legislation in 1918 gave official recognition only to civil marriages, made divorce readily available, declared the legal equality of women, and granted full rights to children born out of wedlock. Subsequent decrees stripped fathers of their extensive legal and proprietary authority over wives and children and dropped adultery from the list of criminal offences. Easing the divorce law had particularly rapid and widespread ramifications. Under tsarism, civil and church law made divorce impossible except for a few, and then only after lengthy proceedings. Allowing Soviet citizens to dissolve marriages easily produced a true social revolution. In addition to contributing to a general atmosphere of emancipation for all citizens, liberalizing divorce assaulted patriarchal authority, provided women with new social latitude, and co-opted a valued prerogative of the Russian Orthodox Church.

But these innovations also led to family instability and astronomical rates of family dissolution. The 1918 provisions also made it difficult to collect alimony and support for children; by the time of NEP a significant portion of married women equated easy divorce with desertion. In theory, the emerging socialist society was to assume greater responsibility for child-rearing and for social welfare; in reality, however, such plans were no more than declarations of intent, for the state simply lacked the resources to implement them. It was not the state but individual women—whose wages rose but still lagged behind pay for males and who endured higher rates of unemployment—who bore the brunt. Thus, while the new family law seemed to enhance the legal position of women, it also subverted the males' traditional responsibilities towards wives and children.

The issue of divorce was closely tied to an emotional exchange taking place at the same time over public morality. One side attacked traditional standards of sexual conduct as arbitrary bourgeois restraints on the individual, and there was no shortage of young men in particular who rallied to the philosophy of free love. Those less sanguine about discarding existing conventions too quickly, however, emphasized the already familiar issues of social stability, male accountability, and economic plight of the female. In the second half of the 1920s, these champions of collective responsibility prevailed over the proponents of individual choice—or, to view matters from another perspective, social conservatives defeated supporters of sexual liberation. In any event, both the party and Komsomol began to take a more direct interest in the personal lives of members, strenuously to oppose promiscuity, and to uphold heterosexual marriage as the social norm.

The introduction of legalized abortion produced additional tension. On the eve of NEP, the state reacted to a spate of illegal abortions by allowing doctors to terminate pregnancies in state hospitals without charge. This decision, although expedient, complicated the issue of building a new society. Indeed, according to prevailing wisdom among state officials, neither abortions nor the rights of the individual over society were being condoned. Rather, the argument ran, in the more prosperous times that lay in the future, once an adequate child-care system was in place, and when better-educated women achieved a higher socialist consciousness, Soviet female citizens would recognize the social obligation of child-bearing. This did not occur in the 1920s. By the middle of the decade, registered abortions climbed to more than 55 per 100 births. Evidence also indicates that in the countryside the travel and paperwork involved in a hospital abortion caused rural women to continue to rely on illegal practitioners and folk remedies.

The state, therefore, moderated some of its early enthusiasms with the Family Code of 1926. This new legislation addressed the issue of desertion by extending official sanction—and with it the right to alimony and child support—to unregistered unions, and it established joint ownership of property acquired during the marriage. But it also relaxed divorce requirements further by transferring jurisdiction from the courts to a simple procedure at a government office, with notification of the other spouse sometimes only by postcard. By the end of the 1920s the urban Soviet divorce rate was the highest in the world.

In the countryside the impact was less. Church weddings were sustained far more strongly in rural areas, where marriage and birth-rates remained high. Divorces, although more numerous than previously, never approached city levels; peasants proved less eager to dissolve marital unions than their urban counterparts. Also, when the reassertion of communal authority once again made the peasant household the predominant social unit, the prospect of dividing joint property was a legal nightmare. As a result, traditional rather than Soviet legality continued to prevail in the village.

Soviet youth, the citizens of the future, also occupied a central place in revolutionary thinking, and here the Bolsheviks faced an especially difficult situation: juvenile 'hooliganism' and homeless orphans had already emerged under tsarism, and the years of world war, revolution, and civil war had greatly exacerbated the problems. Thus the first years of NEP reduced the early Soviet declaration that 'there will be no courts or prisons for children' to a pious wish. By 1921 the *besprizorniki* had not only proliferated in numbers, but exhibited behaviour indicating that many were beyond the reach of any attempt to reintegrate them. As a result, in the 1920s far more *besprizorniki* encountered the criminal justice system than experimental rehabilitation programmes. Especially in the first half of the decade, homeless children became a fixture of the Soviet social landscape, wreaking havoc that caused all of society to demand action.

Concern for the young, however, was not limited to dealing with juvenile miscreants. Creating the 'new Soviet man' also demanded a revolution in education, seen as the engine of social change. Narkompros (the People's Commissariat of Enlightenment) was called upon simultaneously to expurgate the social residue of bourgeois society, produce proletarian citizens, and cope with a dearth of economic resources. Ideally, Soviet education would transcend the narrowness (deemed characteristic of the tsarist approach), enhance the substance of instruction, and also eradicate élitism by providing free public education for all. Innovators in Narkompros devised a new pedagogy, the 'Complex Method', which would not teach just academic subjects, but life itself. The Complex Method would integrate the study of nature, society, and labour in order to prepare graduates for successful entry into both the labour force and society. In addition, the new pedagogy would promote secularism by teaching materialist, scientific values.

There were successes as well as problems. The retention rate of girls enrolled in elementary schools in urban areas, but not total enrolment of girls, rose in the 1920s. Workers and peasants received increased access to higher education. A special institution for workers, the *rabfak*, provided an equivalent of secondary education; by 1928 *rabfak* graduates constituted a full third of entrants to institutions of higher learning. Night courses were added, and there was an aggressive national campaign to end illiteracy. Also, by 1921 the newly founded Communist Academy and the Institute of Red Professors were training Marxist scholars for careers in the social sciences.

But failure was also common. Shortages of funds plagued all facets of education, and schools were forced to supplement their meagre budgets by reintroducing student fees. In addition, Narkompros encountered sharp internal divisions over the wisdom of the Complex Method; resistance was even greater in the schools. Most experienced teachers ignored the new curriculum and continued to teach traditional subjects. Moreover, classroom instructors greeted secularism with little enthusiasm, especially in the numerous instances when rural

Seven years of warfare brought about a sharp rise in the number of homeless orphans, *besprizorniki*, who became a common part of the urban landscape in the 1920s. Frequently seen loitering in public spaces, they survived by begging and stealing. Gangs of *besprizorniki* terrorized citizens on public conveyances and presented a general threat to public security.

teachers were also wives of priests. Finally, the preferential enrolment of more workers and peasants in universities—where males still outnumbered females by a margin of three to one—fostered a lowering of standards, and charges of faulty preparation also haunted the graduates of the Institute of Red Professors.

No Bolshevik assault on tradition could overlook religion. Existence, Marx taught, determines consciousness, and only knowledge derived from observed reality, without the intercession of any external force or mover, is valid. Therefore, if religion had been 'the opiate of the masses' under the old order, religious belief in the new world constituted superstition and, as such, an impediment to creating a progressive, scientific society. In 1918, therefore, the Soviet state decreed a separation of Church and State that nationalized church land and property without compensation. Outside the law, anti-religious militants desecrated churches and monasteries in the atmosphere of atrocity during the Russian civil war, and a significant number of bishops and priests died violently before 1921.

Given the party's implacable hostility, it might appear incongruous to describe NEP as a period when the persecution of religion was relaxed, but compared to 1918–21, this was in fact the case. Not wanting to alienate the peasants further, the government softened its attack between 1921 and the onset of the forced collectivization of agriculture in 1929. Thus the state allowed both religious and anti-religious propaganda, and its Commission on Religious Questions advocated the eradication of religion only through agitation and education. The commission restrained rather than incited anti-religious violence and regularly ruled in favour of groups of believers against local officials. The

Union of Militant Atheists did not hold its founding congress until 1925; it began serious work only following its second gathering three years later. Anti-religious propaganda was therefore the responsibility of all party organs, which in practice meant that it was conducted *ad hoc* and at most incorporated within its general advocacy of secularism. Even in national publications such as *Bezbozhnik* (The Godless), anti-religious tracts and caricatures of priests shared space with articles on popular science, public health, the eradication of illiteracy, the evils of anti-Semitism, and even the improvement of personal hygiene.

State and Church of course remained foes. In this regard, the Russian Orthodox Church was vulnerable, for it entered the revolutionary era divided and demoralized. Its leadership was ill-prepared to resist the surrender of sacrosanct valuables to the state, ostensibly for famine relief in 1921–2. The fact that liberal offshoots of the main Church were often more accommodating to state power undercut Orthodoxy further, as did the rising number of conversions to other denominations, especially the Baptist Church. Moreover, official disapproval by no means halted illegal assaults on churches and clergy; local soviets utilized existing laws to confiscate places of worship for use as workers' clubs, cinemas, and libraries. Finally, as NEP came to an end, the state enacted a new law on religious associations in 1929 that restricted religious activity only to registered congregations, banned all religious instruction and proselytizing, and presaged the still more brutal assault on the Church soon to come.

To what degree did this mixture of repression and education produce the desired result? On the one hand, church and state sources of the period both reported a sharp decline of religiosity in the cities, especially among the young. There was also no shortage of testimony from the countryside that pre-revolutionary peasant anticlericalism had grown into religious indifference during NEP, among village males in particular. Frequently, the mock processions staged by the Komsomol to parody Easter and Christmas worship bitterly split villages along generational lines. On the other hand, the Church and State regarded peasant women as consistently devout. And in the realm of religion-as-social-ritual, some who ceased observing (including party members) nevertheless hedged their bets by baptizing their children or undergoing a second, church wedding. Soviet attempts to raise labour productivity by eliminating the numerous rural religious holidays were unqualified failures, while at the same time traditional apocalyptic formulas—including the coming of the Antichrist—entered the world of peasant rumour when the threat of collectivization grew. In the end, it is not possible to quantify the level of religious belief in the 1920s since the 1926 census contained no query about it, but in 1937 57 per cent of the population still identified themselves as believers (45 per cent of those in their twenties, but 78 per cent of those in their fifties). In sum, formal religion loosened its hold on Soviet society during NEP, especially among the younger and urban segments. Since this drop was both incomplete and not accompanied by the eradication of Russian belief in supernatural

Facing: Soviet anti-religious campaigns employed measures of both propaganda and repression. In 1927, this nationalization of a monastery degenerated into its looting by soldiers of the Red Army.

The severe housing shortage meshed with innovation in architecture to produce the symmetrical high-rise apartment complexes that dominated residential design to the end of the Soviet period.

intervention in human affairs, however, the official state position by 1929 was that the most important anti-religious work still lay ahead.

All dimensions of the new world view converged in high and popular art. As NEP opened, the revolutionary society was already embroiled in controversy over how best to reconstruct culture. Could a proletarian culture evolve organically, or must the new society first master bourgeois elements and build further? Opinions differed. Revolutionary intellectuals in an aggressive institution called 'Proletkult' (Proletarian Cultural-Educational Institutions) wanted to create an entirely new culture to operate independently of government institutions (especially Narkompros), and to receive extensive state support. In addition, artists working both inside and outside the Proletkult championed a number of movements—Futurism, Constructivism, Objectivism, Acmeism, Cubism, and others—rooted in pre-revolutionary radical expression that was now liberated. And among the intelligentsia that comprised much of the party leadership, many agreed with Lenin and Trotsky that Soviet society must make bourgeois aesthetics the basis of proletarian culture. In 1921–9, all these views reached the public.

It was no coincidence that in a country battling against illiteracy, the Bolsheviks placed special emphasis on the visual arts. The party had been an innovator in the political applications of poster art in its rise to power, and it continued to rely on this powerful means for influencing mass attitudes. The revolutionaries placed strong faith in other visual media as well. The cinematic and thematic innovations of directors such as Sergei Eisenstein, Alexander Dovzhenko, and Vsevelod Pudovkin put the Soviets in the front rank of world film in the 1920s. They and others combined the art of political persuasion with imagery and techniques unprecedented in the medium. Frequently they succeeded too well, however, and their sophisticated presentations baffled their intended audience, who in the 1920s continued to prefer escapist American and German adventure films to those designed for their edification.

Painting and sculpture entered the process in a related way. Simply put, pre-revolutionary experimental artists such as Kazimir Malevich and Vasilii Kandinskii viewed art as an essentially spiritual activity free of ideological or other restraints, and they and like-minded others continued to produce prolifically during the 1920s. But their view collided with the conception of art advanced by the likes of Vladimir Tatlin and Alexander Rodchenko—that the artist was essentially an engineer in the service of proletarian society, that his art must not only be beautiful, but useful. Acting on slogans like 'art into life' and 'art is as dangerous as religion as an escapist activity', these Constructivists produced works that not only celebrated the mechanistic, materialist worldview, but demonstrated how to implement it. Such thinking inspired art, not all of it strictly Constructivist, that ranged from the idealization of ordinary objects to a more noble representation of labourers.

The artistic currents also influenced architecture. One did not have to be a communist to envision a future world of skyscrapers and rationally designed, utilitarian working and living spaces. In the first half of the 1920s, economic scarcity largely limited innovation to the realm of conceptualization, but the ideas were imaginative and diverse—garden cities, symmetrical urban utopias, and high-rise apartment dwellings. After 1925, however, it became possible actually to carry out designs that fostered additional creativity. Everything from the redesign of household furniture to workers' clubs and massive public buildings became the object of architectural scrutiny, and the Soviet pavilion was by far the most radical at the 1925 Paris Exhibition of Decorative Arts.

NEP influenced the non-visual arts as well. In music, important emigrations weakened the ranks of classical composers, despite the emergence of Dmitrii Shostakovich in the mid-1920s. In popular culture, while Nepmen supported pre-revolutionary forms, jazz made its first inroads, but met with a mixed review from the party. In literature, the situation was different. A variety of poets and satirists—Vladimir Mayakovsky, Sergei Esenin, Boris Pasternak, Osip Mandelshtam, Anna Akhmatova, Marina Tsvetaeva, Mikhail Zoshchenko—evoked every emotion, from shocking society out of its bourgeois complacency to scoring the foibles of the new regime. Fedor Gladkov's *Cement* was the first proletarian novel, but many others soon delved into the revolutionary experience. New works recounted heroic events and employed the genre of science fiction to put forward utopian and dystopian visions.

Redesigned furniture for peasant dwellings blended message with medium.

289

By the late 1920s, however, eclecticism in the arts came under as much fire as did gradualism in other spheres. Militants in the Komsomol, Institute of Red Professors, and a number of organizations such as RAPP (Russian Association of Proletarian Writers) grew impatient and pressed for a more rapid adoption of proletarian values. Youthful exuberance, idealism, and the results of protracted exposure to state propaganda inspired confrontations over a correct social politics and led to the removal of gradualists and the former bourgeoisie from positions of influence. In short, the pre-conditions of Stalinism that had emerged in politics and economics converged with a predisposition towards cultural revolution. At the end of the decade, the strategy of creating a new worldview shifted from inculcation to imposition.

Conclusion

NEP, a period of experimentation, taught valuable lessons. When the Bolsheviks came to power, they understood more clearly what they opposed than how to implement a singular conception of the future. And while the decade of the 1920s produced a wide range of innovation, it also tapped a strong reservoir of traditionalism. By the mid 1920s experimentation was under fire from within. Revolutionary ardour in politics, economics, and society did not diminish, but life itself forced a serious reassessment of what was both possible and desirable. By 1928–9, therefore, Bolshevik rule had given rise to widespread sentiment for realizing the promise of the proletarian revolution more rapidly, and it had also spawned a backlash against the results of ill-conceived programmes. Ironically, these sentiments were as much complementary as conflicting. And both would play a central role in the Stalinist upheavals about to begin.

BUILDING STALINISM
1929–1941

LEWIS SIEGELBAUM

*The 1930s brought monumental change—reflected most
dramatically in the 'great purges and terror', most
fundamentally in the campaign to collectivize agriculture and
build a modern industrial economy. The regime expended,
prodigiously and wastefully, human capital in what was
advertised as the building of socialism, but what can better
be described as the building of Stalinism.*

THE 1930s have long represented a watershed in the grand narratives of Soviet history. According to the Marxist-Leninist version, *de rigueur* in the Soviet Union until the late 1980s, it was the decade of 'socialist construction'. Under the leadership of I. V. Stalin (or in the post-1956 de-Stalinized variant, the Communist Party), the Soviet people confounded sceptics, both domestic and foreign, by rapidly and enthusiastically constructing gigantic factories and dams, transforming backward villages into collective farms, and in the process becoming citizens of a genuinely socialist society. Their achievement was celebrated and formalized in the 'Stalin Constitution' of 1936, which guaranteed civil rights and equality among all the peoples of the USSR. But hectic industrialization and collectivization were not simply functions of ideological correctness. The threat of imperialist aggression that loomed throughout the period further justified this tremendous effort. Industrialization thus guaranteed survival of the nation and the cause of socialism that it represented.

Diametrically opposed is a version more familiar to Western scholars. It holds that in the 1930s the Soviet Union became a full-blown 'totalitarian' society in which formal legality—including the 1936 Constitution—was a mere smokescreen for the dictatorship of the Communist Party and the caprice of its General Secretary, Stalin. The labour camps that dotted the outer reaches of the nation represented one manifestation of the regime's repressiveness; the collective farms, supposedly an advancement on small-scale private agriculture, were also a form of incarceration, a 'second serfdom' for the peasantry. Industrial workers, ostensibly the ruling class, found themselves subjected to a harsh regimen of speed-ups and without recourse to independent representation or organized protest, while the intelligentsia was cowed into silence or conformity.

As different as are these two renditions of the Soviet 1930s, they exhibit two common qualities. One is the emphasis on transformation. That is, both acknowledge that between 1929 and 1941 the Soviet Union changed dramatically and, so it seemed, irrevocably. The other is that they absolutize the transformations they register—categorically positive in the Marxist-Leninist version and no less categorically negative in the Western view.

Obviously, both cannot be right. Even in the heyday of the Cold War, when scholarship was at its most polarized, one could find formulations that fell somewhere between the two poles. On the left, non-Soviet Marxists posited a 'state capitalist' social formation in which the bureaucracy functioned as the ruling class. Others stressed the neo-traditionalist elements of Stalinism, perceiving a 'Great Retreat' to traditional Russian (Orthodox) values, while still others argued for a more polymorphic understanding of power and its exercise.

Only in the 1970s, however, did professional historians begin to contribute to the scholarly discourse, offering treatments more subtle than those available in earlier accounts. This new work, often social historical in nature, made a conceptual shift from preoccupation with the state to a focus on society.

Combining two key themes of the Soviet industrialization drive—youthful athleticism and giganticism—a Komsomol stands astride a machine for converting cellulose into paper (Balakhna, 1931).

Consequently, the totalitarian model of Soviet politics, which depicted the state as the absolute arbiter of people's fortunes, began to yield to an understanding of how different social groups—workers and managers on the shop-floor, peasants on state and collective farms, and the non-Russian peoples—employed techniques of resistance and accommodation to 'negotiate' their relationship with party and state officials. Excursions into cultural history and anthropology have since deepened this understanding through the inclusion of such cultural practices as anniversary celebrations, polar expeditions, aviation, music, film, the theatre, and literature.

Ironically but understandably, the collapse of the Soviet Union and the annihilation of its Communist Party has led to the revival of the totalitarian model, especially within the Russian scholarly community. This is not necessarily a bad thing: 'revisionist' scholarship tended to obscure the total claim of the regime on its population, a claim that demanded acclamatory participation and was sanctioned by coercive, even arbitrary, forms of rule. Even if this claim was mythic and unrealizable, its very aspiration was of fundamental importance, for it shaped—or at least affected—social and personal lives in the 1930s, 1940s, and for some time thereafter. None the less, this 'totalitarian' state was rife with turbulence in the formal institutions of state and society in the 1930s; indeed, this instability was inherent in the Stalinist articulation of a totalistic agenda. In seeking to actualize its total claim on society, the Stalinist regime unleashed social mobility and flux; the lethal politics of implementation and a political culture of grandiosity and conformity masked an inherent unpredictability in political and social life.

'There is no fortress the Bolsheviks cannot take'

After the confusion of NEP, a policy that purported to build socialism through capitalist practices but appeared to many communists to build capitalism through socialist retreat, the Stalinist initiatives—the 'Great Turn'—appeared to set priorities right. Instead of letting the market mediate in relations between state-owned industry and peasant agriculture, the state would centrally allocate resources and assign prices according to its own determination of rationality and need. Instead of 25 million peasant households producing agricultural goods on small plots with primitive methods and inadequate machinery, the state would assist peasants to establish collective farms, practise scientific farming, and remit their surpluses as partial payment for the equipment they leased. And in contrast to high levels of industrial unemployment endemic to NEP, investment in construction and industrial expansion would provide millions of new jobs and expand the size of the proletariat.

This programme was nothing if not ambitious. Devised and advertised as the 'Five-Year Plan for Industrialization and Socialist Construction', it represented

The construction of the Turkestan–Siberian (Turksib) Railway began in 1926 and was completed in 1930, one year ahead of schedule. Extending some 1,500 km. from Frunze in Kirgizia to Semipalatinsk in northern Kazakhstan and thence to the Trans-Siberian line, it was designed to link the cotton-growing areas of Central Asia with the rest of the Soviet Union. It also facilitated Russian and Ukrainian migration to these sparsely settled areas.

a radical break with previous economic policy and previous understanding of economic laws—now condemned as 'bourgeois'. For the first time, the state would not only intervene in economic relations but actually serve as the chief, even sole, manager of the economy. In its 'optimal' version, the Five-Year Plan aimed to increase investment by 228 per cent, industrial production by 180 per cent, electrical generation by 335 per cent, and the industrial labour force by 39 per cent. But even these levels were deemed too modest by the regime: by the end of 1929 'Five in Four'—that is, the fulfilment of the Plan in four years— became official policy.

How is this 'riotous optimism', in Alec Nove's phrase, to be explained? Was it designed to mobilize available human resources—heedless of the real capabilities for reaching targets? This is an intriguing possibility, but not yet substantiated by concrete evidence. Or was this a political plan to provoke and discredit 'Right Oppositionists' (Nikolai Bukharin and others), who sought to scale down targets? It can be argued that Stalin exploited the 'politics' of the plan, but that the process of target inflation goes beyond such tactical manœuvres. The circumstantial should not be overlooked: with the onset of the Great Depression, the Five-Year Plan had tremendous propagandistic value. Indeed, the Soviet regime expended much effort to demonstrate the contrast between general economic crisis in the capitalist world and the extraordinary feats of construction and industrial expansion in the Soviet Union. Technomania was a further impulse: the introduction of new mechanized technology, much of it imported from the West, promised bountiful, even unimaginable returns.

But the 'over-ambitious' Five-Year Plan (Holland Hunter), and in a larger sense the entire Stalin revolution, derived from the merger of two hitherto discrete elements within Bolshevism. One was Prometheanism, the belief that collective human effort could accomplish transformative miracles. The other was revolutionary maximalism, a psychology of egalitarianism, expropriation, even a belief in the creative role of violence. The former had its roots in nineteenth-century machine worship; the latter in the voluntarist strain of populists of the 1870s and Bolsheviks (in contrast to Mensheviks) after the turn of the century. Together, they comprised a new political culture, one that sought to 'catch up to and overtake' the advanced capitalist countries but, in its very haste, reproduced some elements of backward Russia.

Promoted from the top and exalted by the emerging cult of Stalin, the new political culture set the tone for industrialization and a good deal else. As Moshe Lewin has noted, 'the readiness not to bother about cost, not being too squeamish about means, the ability to press hard on institutions and people—this was the style and the temperament of those Stalinists, for whom most old guard Bolsheviks were by now too European and too "liberal"'. Pressed by V. M. Molotov, G. K. Ordzhonikidze, L. M. Kaganovich, and other Politburo members who fanned out across the country on trouble-shooting missions, the directors of industrial enterprises and far-flung construction sites resorted to all manner of stratagems in their dealings with supply agencies and in turn pressed hard on their subordinates. Provincial (*obkom*) party secretaries experienced the same sort of pressure and likewise learned to deflect it downwards. As a result, Stalin concentrated power at the top even as he diffused responsibility downward through thousands of *vintiki* (little screws) who had their own strategies for survival.

Industrialization was analogous to a gigantic military campaign—with recruitment levies, mobilizations, 'fronts' (Donbas coal, the Dneprstroi dam, Magnitogorsk, the Stalingrad Tractor Factory), 'light cavalry raids' of the Komsomol against bureaucratic practices, heroic 'shock troops of labour' thrown into the breach, and victories (mostly symbolic) and frequent set-backs. In this frenzied atmosphere, replete with threats, verbal abuse, and recrimination, *Angst* was combined with enthusiasm, individual opportunism with collective effort. The result was a constant state of emergency, ubiquitous shortage, and near total chaos.

Yet, by 1932 the regime could boast of some real achievements. Gross industrial production, measured in 1926–7 roubles, rose from 18.3 milliards to 43.3 milliards, actually surpassing the optimal plan. Producers' goods, valued at 6.0 milliards in 1927–8, reached 23.1 milliards in 1932 compared to a projected 18.1 milliards, and within that category, the value of machinery more than quadrupled. Even taking into account considerable statistical inflation (i.e. the overpricing of machinery), these were impressive results. Less impressive were the rise in consumer goods production—from 12.3 milliard to 20.2 milliard roubles—and significant shortfalls in the output of coal, electricity, and steel. Total employment in construction, transportation, and industry did surpass the plan, increasing from 11.3 million to 22.8 million people.

The War against the Peasants

Simultaneously, Stalin launched an assault on the final bastion of the old order—the hinterlands that encompassed the predominantly grain-growing provinces of Russia and Ukraine, the arid steppes of Central Asia, and the hunting and fishing preserves of the far north and Siberia. Here, according to the census of 1926, lived nearly 80 per cent of the Soviet Union's 142 million people. Here too was the greatest challenge to the Communist Party leadership and its ambitions for socialist construction. Communists were few and far between in the Soviet countryside: in July 1928 they numbered 317,000 (22.7 per cent of the party's total membership)—one communist for every 336 rural dwellers. Most were recent recruits with only the most tenuous grasp of communist ideology. Although teachers, agronomists, and other white-collar professionals represented the state and could propagandize the fruits of Soviet rule, the peasant masses generally were distrustful of 'their' village soviets and the Soviet government at large, a wariness borne of a history of endless depredations by outsiders.

This attitude was mutual. Notwithstanding the rhetoric of 'alliance' (*smychka*) or rather because prosperous peasants (kulaks, literally 'the tightfisted') seemed to profit from the concessions associated with NEP, Soviet authorities regarded the peasantry as a petty bourgeois mass of small property-holders and

The members of a village soviet 'vote' to form a collective farm in 1929. Such rituals enacted throughout the length and breadth of the USSR belied the coercive measures (punitive taxation, seizures of livestock, arrests, etc.) brought to bear against recalcitrant peasants.

a major barrier to the building of socialism. By all accounts, the grain procurement crisis of 1927–8 was the turning-point in this conflictual relationship. Having personally supervised the campaign to seize grain and other foodstuffs in the Urals and western Siberia, Stalin hit on the idea of organizing collective and state farms to pump out surpluses. These rural production units, fitfully and ineffectually sponsored in the past, henceforth became the regime's formula for socialist construction in the countryside that was to serve the over-arching goal of industrialization.

The industrialization drive itself was suffused with military metaphors, but collectivization was the real thing, a genuine war against the peasants. The 'fortresses' in this war were the peasants' 'material values'—their land, livestock, draught animals, and implements, all of which were to be confiscated and pooled as collective property. Party propagandists characterized mass collectivization as a 'rural October', analogous to the Bolsheviks' seizure of power in Petrograd in 1917. But collectivization and the resistance it provoked among the peasants cost vastly more in lives than the October Revolution or even the ensuing civil war.

Not all peasants opposed collectivization. The poorest elements in the villages (the *bedniak* families without land or the means to work it) probably welcomed the prospect of gaining access to the property of their better-off neighbours. But the mass of 'middle peasants' (*seredniaki*) was not swayed by promises of tractors and credits. As a peasant told Maurice Hindus (a Russian-Jewish *émigré* who visited his native village), 'Hoodlums and loafers ... might readily join a *kolkhoz*. What have they to lose? But decent people? They are *khoziaeva* [independent producers and householders], masters, with an eye for order, for results. But what could they say in a *kolkhoz*? What could they do except carry out the orders of someone else. That's the way I look at it'.

The way Stalin looked at it, as he made clear at a party conference in April 1929, was that the kulaks were fomenting opposition to collectivization. This *ad hoc* 'theory' of the 'intensification of the class struggle' henceforth guided party policy as if it were a universal truth. Over the ensuing months, the party sought to accelerate the formation of collective farms. By June, one million—out of some 25 million—peasant households had enrolled in 57,000 collectives. Obviously, though, the vast majority still held back. Regional party *apparatchiki*, spurred on by directives and plenipotentiaries from the centre, pleaded with and cajoled village assemblies. 'Tell me, you wretched people, what hope is there for you if you remain on individual pieces of land?' an agitator shouted at the peasants in Hindus's village. 'You will have to work in your own old way and stew in your old misery. Don't you see that under the present system there is nothing ahead of you but ruin and starvation?' 'We never starved before you wise men of the party appeared here,' was the reply.

The rhythm of collectivization, like much else during the First Five-Year Plan, proceeded in fits and starts. During the summer and autumn of 1929, the rate accelerated largely due to two initiatives: the enactment by local officials of 'wholescale' (*sploshnaia*) collectivization in certain grain-growing areas of the North Caucasus and lower Volga; and the establishment of giant collectives absorbing whole groups of villages. Most were of the relatively loose kind (i.e. *tozy* rather than *arteli* or *kommuny*), whereby households retained ownership of seed, machinery, and draught animals. Meanwhile, the administrative infrastructure for collective farming began to take shape with the formation of an all-Union *Kolkhoztsentr* for channelling credits and equipment, and a *Traktortsentr* (Tractor Centre) for overseeing the establishment of machine tractor stations (MTS).

The most intense phase occurred during the winter of 1929/30. The signal was Stalin's article in *Pravda*, published on the thirteenth anniversary of the October Revolution. Entitled 'The Great Turn', it claimed that the 'middle peasant'—that 80 per cent mass of the village—'is joining the collective'. On the basis of recommendations produced by a special Politburo commission under A. Iakovlev, the Commissar of Agriculture, the party's Central Committee issued its fateful decree, 'On the Tempo of Collectivization', on 5 January 1930. The decree called for collectivizing not merely the 20 per cent of arable land envisioned by the First Five-Year Plan, but 'the huge majority of peasant farms' in the most important grain regions by the autumn of 1930. It also rejected the *toz* in favour of the more 'advanced' *arteli*.

The question of what to do with the kulaks was finally resolved in a Central Committee decree of February 1930. They were to be expropriated—'liquidated as a class'—and subjected to one of three fates: (1) resettled on inferior land out-side the kolkhoz; (2) deported and resettled on land in other districts; or (3) arrested and sent to prisons or labour camps in remote parts of the country. By 1933 approximately 1.5 million people had been subjected to the second form of dekulakization and 850,000–900,000 to the third. That almost any peasant who agitated against collectivization could be labelled a kulak (or 'subkulak' a kulak sympathizer) was the key point: 'dekulakization' was as much a weapon of intimidation against non-kulaks as it was a sledge-hammer against the well-to-do peasants.

By March 1930 an estimated 55 per cent of peasant households at least nom-inally had enrolled in collective farms. At this point, however, Stalin decried the excesses of local officials, claiming that they were 'dizzy with success'. This admonition let loose the floodgates holding peasants within the kolkhoz and, as recently declassified archival documents testify, caused acute consternation among provincial agents of collectivization who feared 're-kulakization'. By June only 23 per cent of households remained within collective farms. The reversal was short-lived, however. Fines and compulsory sales of property for peasants unable (or unwilling) to meet delivery quotas drove many back into the kolkhoz system; by July 1931 the proportion of households had risen to 53 per cent, and a year later to 61.5 per cent. This included the pastoral Kazakhs who were subjected to 'denomadization', a process that virtually wiped out their sheep herds and, in conjunction with a typhus epidemic, led to the death of approximately 40 per cent of the population between 1931 and 1933. Throughout the Soviet Union, the losses of livestock due to slaughter and neglect were enormous: by 1933 the numbers of cattle, pigs, and sheep were less than half what they had been in 1928.

The peasants' traditional strategies in this war of survival—prevarication, dissimulation, and other 'weapons of the weak'—were of limited utility. They also resorted to more direct forms of resistance—theft of kolkhoz property, the slaughter of livestock, women's riots, and murder of collective farm officials (including workers dispatched to the countryside as 'Twenty-Five Thousanders' to assist in the collectivization drive). All this suggests the scale of peasant des-peration. As if calculated to intensify the apocalyptic mood, the authorities intensified anti-religious campaigns, including pogroms against priests and church property. Thousands of churches, synagogues, and mosques were closed or converted into meeting-halls, cinemas, cowsheds, and the like. The exact number of peasants executed, killed in skirmishes, or dead from malnutrition and overwork in the labour camps defies precise determination, but undoubt-edly ran into millions.

Peasant resistance to collectivization also spawned opposition, if less dra-matic, in the party itself. Some who had supported Stalin against Bukharin and the 'Right Opposition' began to have second thoughts in the wake of the collec-tivization drive. By late 1930 several prominent party members of the RSFSR and Transcaucasian governments expressed misgivings that Stalin construed as factionalism and opposition ('the Syrtsov–Lominadze Right-Left Bloc'). Retribution did not prevent the formation of other groups in 1932, most notably the conspiratorial circle of M. N. Riutin and the group of A. P. Smirnov, G. G. Tolmachev, and N. B. Eismont. Even loyal Stalinists such as S. V. Kosior, I. M. Vareikis, K. Ia. Bauman, and M. A. Skrypnyk began to question the growing centrism of power as well as Stalin's pro-Russian nationality policy.

In sum, the state won only a partial victory over the peasantry. True, it did bring the peasants under its administrative control and, through the machine tractor stations, made them technologically dependent. The kulaks and the clergy, rival élites in the village, had been annihilated. But peasant resistance extracted certain concessions, such as the legalization of private plots and the exclusion of domestic animals from the collective. In the longer term, a combination of administrative incompetence, under-investment, and peasant alienation led to extremely low levels of productivity and thus an agricultural sector that, rather than providing resources and capital investment for industrial development, became a net drain on economic growth.

A Nation on the Move

Not unlike the enclosures at the dawn of the English Industrial Revolution, collectivization 'freed' peasants to work and live elsewhere. Of course, there was nothing new about peasant seasonal out-migration (*otkhod*), particularly from villages in the 'land-hungry' provinces of central Russia. But during the First Five-Year Plan, the number of peasant departures increased dramatically, in 1931–2 reaching an all-time high. Between 1928 and 1932, according to a recent estimate, at least ten million peasants joined the urban work-force as wage or salary earners.

In general, departures took three forms: involuntary deportations (through dekulakization); relocation through agreements between collective farms and individual industrial enterprises (a process known euphemistically as *orgnabor* or 'organized recruitment'); and voluntary independent movement officially labelled *samotek* or 'drifting'. These distinctions are analytically useful but hardly capture the scale or complexity of population movement in the 1930s. There was much 'push' (to leave the village), but also much 'pull' (demand for labour at the other end). Such was the competition among recruiters that train-loads of recruits were waylaid and rerouted to other destinations. In other cases, recruits upon arrival found working or living conditions so unappealing that they soon moved on—via *samotek*—to places where conditions were reportedly better. As Stephen Kotkin has noted, 'The train, that ally of the Bolshevik leadership and its bureaucrats and planners, was being used against them: construction workers were using the trains to tour the country'.

How the steel was tempered—Blast Furnace no. 2 at Magnitogorsk. Arising on the western Siberian steppe, Magnitogorsk, the 'socialist city of steel', was populated by workers 'mobilized' by their trade unions, peasant recruits, ex-kulak deportees, and substantial contingents of engineers, state and party officials, and foreign workers. Many succumbed to industrial accidents, the harshness of the climate, and primitiveness of living conditions, but many others became true Soviet patriots.

The growth of Magnitogorsk, the celebrated socialist 'planned' city built on the steppe behind the Urals, was spectacular: from 25 inhabitants in March 1929 to 250,000 by the autumn of 1932. But older cities swelled too. Moscow's population increased from 2.2 million in 1929 to 3.6 million by 1936; Leningrad's rose from 1.6 million in 1926 to 3.5 million by the end of the 1930s. Regional centres, particularly in the industrial heartland, were also inundated by newcomers. Stalino (Donetsk), a coal and steel town in the Donbas, doubled its population between 1926 and 1937, reaching 246,000 by the latter year.

This phenomenal growth in urban population did not in itself constitute urbanization, a process that normally suggests qualitative as well as quantitative change. Indeed Moshe Lewin's neologism, 'ruralization'—the squeezing of the village into the city and the subjection of urban spaces to rural ways—is more accurate. Railway stations became temporary shelters, clearing-houses of information, informal labour exchanges, and (illicit) bazaars. Factories took on many of the same functions, as did parks.

Housing construction could not possibly keep pace with the population increase. At Magnitogorsk and other construction sites, newcomers were 'housed' in tents and hastily constructed dormitories where bedspace was often assigned in shifts. To accommodate the in-migrants, in 1931 municipal authorities in Leningrad deported thousands of 'parasites and other non-working elements'—i.e. the pre-revolutionary nobility, the clergy, youths expelled from the student body because of their 'old regime' backgrounds, and those who had been purged from the Soviet apparatus. This social cleansing freed some

'Uprising', 1923, by Kliment Redko. Originally titled 'Revolution', this painting combines a pantheon of Party leaders with a representation of the rank-and-file against a symbolic geometric backdrop.

Worker and kolkhoz woman (Vera Mukhina, 1937). This sculpture in stainless steel, standing 24 metres high, originally stood on top of the Soviet pavilion at the 1937 Paris Exposition. In 1939 it was placed at the entrance to the Moscow Agricultural Exhibition (renamed in 1958 the Exhibition of Achievements of the National Economy—VDNKh). Symbolizing the determination and confidence attributed to Soviet working people and typifying the gendered depiction of workers and peasants, it is a prime example of socialist realist art.

200,000 sq. m. of living space, mostly in the form of communal apartments where several families shared a kitchen, bathroom, and toilet. Global statistics for per capita living space in the entire USSR show a decline from a crowded 5.65 sq. m. in 1928 to an even more crowded 4.66 sq. m. by 1932.

The 'harvest of sorrow' in Ukraine. One of the more horrendous consequences of the collectivization of agriculture was mass starvation among peasants. Long denied by Soviet authorities, the famine of 1932–3 claimed upwards of four million victims, the majority of whom lived in Ukraine.

Food too was in short supply. The shortages were due not only to disruptions caused by collectivization and increased urban demand (from the influx of peasants), but also because of the low priority given to food-processing in the First Five-Year Plan. The state imposed a ration on most foodstuffs in 1929, whereby urban residents exchanged their coupons at Workers' Co-operative stores. They also relied on cafeterias and other communal dining facilities, government stores (where the quality—and prices—of food was higher), or, if they could afford it, the peasant markets.

In December 1932 the state introduced internal passports for urban dwellers, thereby making flight to the cities more difficult for the dispossessed and hungry in the villages. This measure, which remained in effect for decades, closely followed a decree denying ration cards to those guilty of absenteeism from work. Their combined effect was to put a temporary halt to in-migration and to trigger the deportation or 'voluntary' exodus of several hundred thousand people from the cities. The timing of the passport law was all-important. Harsh climate, primitive technology, and the necessity of marketing or turning over a substantial proportion of the crop had left peasant producers without a margin to build up reserves. After three years of borrowing from the previous year's seed grain to deliver to an expanding urban population, the Red Army, and foreign consumers, there was no margin left.

The resulting famine of 1933 has been described by both Western and Russian scholars as 'man-made' or 'artificial' on the grounds that its primary cause was the excessively high procurement quotas set by the state. Some note the disproportionate effect on Ukrainian peasants and claim that the famine was deliberate and genocidal. But recent analyses of the data on the 1932 harvest have shown that, contrary to the official yield of 69.9 million metric tons (which approximated the grain harvests for preceding and successive years), the real output was well below 50 million tons. If so, the famine was precipitated by an absolute shortage of grain. That the rural population (not only in Ukraine) suffered disproportionately and that this deprivation was due to a political decision are not in question: procurements displaced famine from the city to the village. Altogether, it is estimated that the famine took 2.9 million lives in Ukraine and 4.2 million throughout the USSR in 1933.

Cultural Revolution

In addition to industrialization and agricultural transformation, the 1930s witnessed a third revolution—in culture. This 'cultural revolution' signified not only the overturning of previously existing scientific standards and aesthetic values, but full-scale assaults against their bearers—the technical and cultural intelligentsia—and their replacement by workers from the bench as well as (often self-designated) representatives of the proletariat. In retrospect, the cultural revolution underscores the instability and provisionality of the *modus vivendi* between the intelligentsia (the sole collective survivor among the pre-revolutionary élites) and the Communist Party. Lenin's conception of cultural revolution —essentially, raising the masses to the level of the bourgeoisie by enlisting the aid of 'bourgeois specialists'—was pursued more or less faithfully by his lieutenants who came from relatively cultured backgrounds, relied on the expertise of such specialists, and rewarded them accordingly. But to many party militants, such dependence merely perpetuated the cultural dominance of a group that displayed haughtiness and condescension towards the masses (and, not incidentally, party members) and dubious loyalty to the ideals of communism.

Tensions exploded in the spring of 1928 when fifty-three mining engineers were charged with wrecking and sabotage of mining installations in the Shakhty district of the North Caucasus. What set off the explosion was not so much the trial itself, as the 'lessons' that Stalin drew from the affair. In contrast to other high-ranking officials, who warned of the economically disruptive consequences of igniting mass resentment against specialists and therefore sought to play down the case, Stalin invoked 'class vigilance', warned that 'Shakhtyites are now ensconced in every branch of our industry', and demanded extensive purges not only of industrial administration, but throughout the Soviet, trade-union, and party apparatuses, educational institutions, and central economic organs.

The purges were essentially of two kinds, each extensive and feeding off the other. 'Social purging' (i.e. the exclusion of individuals from privileged backgrounds from institutions of higher education) was most pronounced in 1928–9. Usually carried out by Komsomol and local party committees, this type of purge was often spontaneous, irritated authorities in the affected commissariats, and ultimately provoked resolutions of condemnation. The second, more formal, purge was conducted by special commissions of Rabkrin (the Workers' and Peasants' Inspectorate) and the party's Central Committee. With a mandate from the Sixteenth Party Conference, Rabkrin removed some 164,000 Soviet employees in the course of 1929–30. The purge in the party, which removed about 11 per cent of its members in 1929, sought primarily to expel careerists, corrupt elements, and those guilty of criminal offences, but it also took into account political criteria, such as the failure to carry out the party line in the countryside.

Purges constituted one aspect of the cultural revolution: no less important was the intensification and politicization of struggles within the professions. These conflicts generally pitted the pre-revolutionary (predominantly non-Marxist) intelligentsia against the new Soviet intelligentsia (overwhelmingly communist). What the former interpreted as a full-scale assault against culture itself, the latter saw only as its 'proletarianization'. The former expected intellectuals to set an example for the masses or to take them under their wing; the latter advocated subordination to and learning from the masses. This reversal of valorization prematurely terminated many careers and led to the temporary abolition of secondary-school education. Not for nothing did the Marx–Engels metaphor of 'withering away' of school and law appeal to cultural revolutionaries.

Perhaps the best-documented struggle of the cultural revolution was in literature. Thus, writers and critics affiliated with the Russian Association of Proletarian Writers (with the Russian acronym RAPP) fought bitterly against their Marxist rivals in the 'Literary Front' (*Litfront*). And both stridently attacked the political aloofness of 'fellow travellers', as well as the decadent individualism of the literary avant-garde. The former Komsomol activist, L. L. Averbakh, helped RAPP to establish, if only briefly, 'proletarian hegemony' (typified by its cult of the 'little man') over literature. *Time Forward!*, Valentin Kataev's novel of 1932 about a record-breaking shift at Magnitogorsk, represented its apotheosis. But what has been called a 'wave of reaction' against this ethos of the First Five-Year Plan was apparent even before the end of the Plan. 'It was as if', writes Katerina Clark, 'everyone had tired of the "little man", of sober reality and efficiency; they looked for something "higher".' This yearning corresponded to Stalin's own impatience with the turbulence of literary politics. On 23 April 1932 a Central Committee resolution 'On the Reformation of Literary-Artistic Organizations' formally abolished RAPP and called for the creation of a 'single Union of Soviet Writers with a communist fraction in it'.

The 'proletarian episode' in Soviet literature had its analogues in other fields such as legal theory, pedagogy, and architecture. In each case, rival claimants to the correct interpretation of Marxism battled it out, employing such terms of abuse as 'bourgeois pseudo-science', 'Menshevizing idealism', and 'right deviationism'. As in literary criticism, the iconoclastic and even nihilistic tendencies of the cultural revolutionaries (E. B. Pashukanis's 'commodity exchange' theory of the law; V. N. Shulgin's notion of the 'withering away of the school'; anti-urbanism among town planners) ran their course until the Central Committee—or, in the case of historical writing, Stalin himself—intervened to restore order if not the status quo ante.

The third dimension of the cultural revolution, which has received much attention from historians, was the rapid and systematic promotion of workers into white-collar positions, either directly from 'the bench' or after crash-course training programmes at institutions of higher education. As Sheila Fitzpatrick

Vsevolod Meyerhold, shown here signing a copy of Griboedov's nineteenth-century play, *Woe from Wit* (which he adapted in a 1928 production titled *Woe to Wit*) was the Soviet Union's premier theatrical director throughout the 1920s and 1930s. Arrested in June 1939, he was tortured in prison before being executed.

has shown, this programme of proletarian 'advancement' (*vydvizhenie*) represented 'the positive corollary of the campaign against the "bourgeois" intelligentsia and the social purging of the bureaucracy'. In time, the beneficiaries of this process (the *vydvizhentsy*), formed the new Soviet intelligentsia, which was more numerous, plebeian, and (befitting an industrializing nation) technically oriented than its bourgeois predecessor. And it was also more beholden to the political leadership.

Two themes thus dominate most accounts of the cultural revolution. One was its anti-intellectualism, tinged with a certain xenophobic colouring. The other was its social radicalism, rendered as 'revolution from below', where 'below' signified three distinct phenomena: the spontaneous actions of lower-level party committees and the Komsomol, the revolt of younger and previously marginal elements within the professions, and the promotion of proletarians. But one should not overlook the degree to which the cultural revolution was coded as a male pursuit and the advantage that proletarianism gave to ethnic Russians at the expense of peoples in less industrialized areas. Dissolution of both the party's women's department (Zhenotdel) and Jewish section (*Evsektsiia*) in 1930 may well have reflected these biases.

Communist Neo-Traditionalism

In 1933, after several years of almost unceasing tumult, the Soviet Union embarked on the Second Five-Year Plan. Early drafts of the Plan exhibited the same 'great leap forward' psychology that had characterized its predecessor. But by late 1932, when it became clear that the economy was overstrained, the key indices were scaled back. Instead of the 100 billion kilowatt-hours of electricity originally projected for 1937, the revised version (adopted by the Seventeenth Party Congress in February 1934) called for 38 billion; the target for pig iron was cut from 22 million to 14.5 million tons, and so forth. Referring to the famine, Alec Nove observes: 'The terrible events of 1933 may have had their influence, by a kind of shock therapy.' The plan, still ambitious if scaled back, shifted the emphasis from ever-increasing inputs of labour, punctuated by occasional bouts of shock work (now deprecated as 'storming'), and towards the assimilation and mastery of technology. As Stalin told a plenary session of the Central Committee in January 1933, the 'passion for construction' of the First Five-Year Plan had to be replaced by the passion for mastering technology. That required more vocational training, but also more labour discipline.

Few terms appeared more frequently in Bolshevik discourse in the early 1930s than 'labour discipline'. Precisely because the industrial labour force had absorbed millions of male peasants and unskilled urban women, the demands for increasing labour discipline became ever shriller, the measures to combat violations ever harsher. Stricter control over the organization of production led to the abrogation of several First Five-Year Plan innovations: the 'continuous work week' (*nepreryvka*, a staggered schedule of four days on and one day off); the 'functional system of management' (a Taylorist approach that in its Soviet application encouraged parallel lines of authority and avoidance of personal responsibility); and production collectives and communes (shop-floor units that workers organized to protect themselves from the fluctuations in wages and the general disorganization of production).

The restoration of a more hierarchical approach to management entailed an expansion of the responsibilities, prestige, and privileges of managerial and technical personnel. 'The ground should shake when the director goes around the factory,' declared M. M. Kaganovich in a pep talk to managers, adding that 'workers like a powerful leader'. Successful directors had to do more than shake the ground. Presiding over vast complexes with tens of thousands of workers, they learned how to wheel and deal for scarce resources, establish cosy relations with local party and NKVD officials, read the signals emanating from Moscow, and above all fulfil—or at least appear to fulfil—the quantitative targets of the plan. As a veteran journalist later recalled, 'it was during those years that the names of metallurgical factory directors became known, not only to a narrow circle of economic officials, but broad sections of the Soviet public. For their work, for their successes, the country celebrated them as in wartime it had followed the successes of military leaders.'

Engineers were also celebrated. Stalin had already signalled the official rehabilitation of the old technical intelligentsia in 1931, but no less important was a parallel and longer-lasting phenomenon—the rehabilitation of engineering as a profession. Symbolic of the engineers' new stature was the injunction to writers at the founding congress of the Writers' Union in 1934 that they become 'engineers of human souls'. It has been pointed out that the engineer-designer, icon of technical mastery and order, began to supplant the production worker as the main protagonist in contemporary novels and films.

These changes in industrialization and labour policies constituted part of a larger process: consolidation of a system that was generally known, though not officially acknowledged, as Stalinism. If the Stalin revolution was more or less coterminal with the First Five-Year Plan, then Stalinism—the repudiation of egalitarianism and collectivist 'excesses' of that revolution—was its outcome.

Retaining the ideological prop of a dogmatized Marxism (officially renamed 'Marxism-Leninism'), Stalinism identified the political legitimacy of the regime not only in the October Revolution, but also in pro-Russian nationalism and glorification of state power. It thus incorporated a conservative and restorative dimension, emphasizing hierarchy, patriotism, and patriarchy.

The Stalinist system depended on an extensive network of officials, the upper echelons of whom were included in the party's list of key appointments (*nomenklatura*). Wielding vast and often arbitrary power, these officials ruled over their territories and enterprises as personal fiefs and were not above—or below—developing their own cults of personality. Leon Trotsky, one of the earliest and most trenchant critics of the Stalinist system, regarded it as essentially counter-revolutionary ('Thermidorist'), a product of the international isolation of the Bolshevik Revolution, Russian backwardness, and the political expropriation of the Soviet working class by the bureaucracy. But unlike many others who followed him down the path of communist apostasy, Trotsky did not consider the bureaucracy a ruling *class*. Bureaucrats, after all, were constrained from accumulating much in the way of personal property and, as the periodic purges of the decade demonstrated, lacked security of tenure. This was why Trotsky wrote that 'the question of the character of the Soviet Union is not yet decided by history'. It was, rather, a 'contradictory society halfway between capitalism and socialism'.

Notwithstanding its exercise of terror and monopolistic control of the means of communication, the bureaucratic apparatus alone could not sustain the Stalinist system. Another dimension of Stalinism, which has only recently received attention from historians, was its assiduous cultivation of mass support and participation—through education and propaganda, leadership cults, election campaigns, broad national discussions (for example, of the constitution, the Comintern's Popular Front strategy, and the ban on abortions), public celebrations (such as the Pushkin centennial of 1937), show trials, and other political rituals. The system, then, was more than a set of formal political institutions and 'transmission belts'. In addition to forging a new political culture, it also fostered and was sustained by a particular kind of mass culture.

James van Geldern has characterized this culture in spatial terms as 'the consolidation of the centre', a consolidation that 'did not exclude those outside, [but] aided their integration'. The centre was Moscow, the rebuilding of which constituted one of the major projects of these years. Moscow came to represent 'the visible face of the Soviet Union ... a model for the state, where power radiated out from the centre to the periphery'. Corresponding to a shift in investment priorities, the heightened cultural significance of the capital 'signalled a new hierarchy of values, by which society's attention shifted from the many to the one outstanding representative'. The Moscow Metro, a massive engineering project that 'mocked utility with its stations clad in semi-precious stone', became an object of not only Muscovite but national pride. The towering Palace of Soviets (the excavation for which involved the razing of the great gold-domed Church of Christ the Saviour) would have been the source of even greater pride had the project not been abandoned and the pit turned into a large outdoor swimming pool.

The periphery was integrated not only through a vicarious identification with the centre but by being recast as an asset. Taming the vast wild spaces of the USSR (for example, through industrial projects such as Magnitogorsk or the settlement of nomads on collective farms) transformed them into both economic and cultural resources. Folklorism, characterized by Richard Stites as 'politicized folk adaptation', made a strong comeback via Igor Moiseev's Theatre of Folk Art, founded in 1936, and a national network of amateur folk choirs and dance ensembles. These 'prettified and theatricalized Stalinist ensembles ... [promoted] images of national solidarity, reverence for the past, and happy peasants', images that were reinforced by highly publicized photographs of smiling peasants, decked out in 'ethnic' or folk garb, meeting Stalin in the Kremlin.

The imagined harmony of the mid-1930s went beyond folk ensembles and photo opportunities. At the Seventeenth Party Congress in 1934, Zinoviev, Kamenev, Bukharin, Rykov, and Tomskii—all vanquished political enemies of Stalin—repudiated their previous positions and heaped praise on Stalin's wise leadership. The congress, in a show of reconciliation, applauded their speeches. The Kolkhoz Congress of 1935, where Stalin announced that 'socialism' had been achieved in the countryside, represented another type of reconciliation: shortly afterwards the government issued a kolkhoz statute (conferring certain guarantees and concessions) and dropped legal proscriptions against former kulaks.

'Life has become more joyous,' Stalin exulted in November 1935. Endlessly repeated and even set to song, the 'life is joyous' theme—the myth of a joyful people achieving great feats and adoring their genial leader (*vozhd'*)—was woven into the fabric of Soviet life. If previously life's satisfactions were derived from the knowledge that one's work was contributing to the building of socialism, now the formula was reversed: the achievement of socialism, officially proclaimed in the 1936 Constitution, was responsible for life's joyfulness which in turn made work go well. It suddenly became important to demonstrate the prowess of outstanding individuals in a variety of fields: Soviet aviators, dubbed 'Stalin's falcons', took to the skies to set new records; arctic explorers trekked to the North Pole in record time; mountain climbers scaled new peaks; the pianist Emil Gilels and the violinist David Oistrakh won international competitions. All covered the Soviet Union with national glory.

But the most celebrated individual feat of the decade was fittingly in the field of material production. On the night of 30 August 1935, Aleksei Stakhanov, a

Begun in 1932, the construction of the Moscow Metro was one of the 'heroic' projects of the decade. The first line was opened on 15 May 1935 to a great fanfare. A source of national pride, the Metro contained stations with decorative mosaics, each with a particular theme. The one shown here, depicting a woman operating a threshing combine, characteristically coded collectivized agriculture as feminine.

'Ever Higher, Ever Farther!' Photographed in front of their plane, Motherland, are three female pilots who set a record in September 1938 for non-stop flight by women, travelling 6,000 kilometres from Moscow to Komsomol'sk-na-Amure. Such flights, the forerunners of the Soviet space achievements in the 1950s and 1960s, were celebrated officially and entered into popular literature and song.

30-year-old Donbas coalminer, hewed 102 tons of coal—more than fourteen times the norm for a six-hour shift. Stakhanov achieved his record thanks to a new division of labour that enabled him to concentrate on coal-cutting while others cleared debris, installed props, and performed other auxiliary tasks. Within days of the record, which *Pravda* had rather perfunctorily reported, other miners were surpassing it. But only after some prompting from the People's Commissar of Heavy Industry, 'Sergo' Ordzhonikidze, did the Stakhanovite movement take off, spreading rapidly to other industries and to agriculture.

Stakhanovism was a complex phenomenon, both something more and something less than what higher political authorities intended. Idiomatically, it encompassed such a broad range of themes—mastery of technology, the creation of the New Soviet Man, the cultured working-class family, role reversal (the Stakhanovite was the expert; the expert became student of the Stakhanovite), upward social mobility—that internal contradictions were bound to occur. It tapped into popular desires for public recognition, adequate conditions of work, and consumer goods that at least some Stakhanovites enjoyed. At the same time, it raised these same expectations among workers who either could not become Stakhanovites or, having achieved that status, did not receive commensurate rewards. Resentment also increased as Stakhanovite records inexorably led to higher output norms for rank-and-file workers.

Moreover, expectations of political leaders that Stakhanovites' innovations and production records would raise labour productivity all around were largely unfulfilled. Indeed, in some measure Stakhanovism was dysfunctional, as managers concentrated on supplying workers in the 'leading' professions, machinery became overstrained, and inter-shop deliveries broke down. Just three months into the 'Stakhanovite year' of 1936, speeches of political leaders and the press began to use words like 'saboteur' and 'wrecker' to describe managers and engineers who had ostensibly blocked the application of Stakhanovites' methods or whose enterprises had failed to meet their targets. It was all Ordzhonikidze could do to deflect these charges and prevent the demoralization of industrial cadres in the face of what looked like a revival of cultural revolution specialist-baiting. In fact, something far more lethal was in store not only for enterprise directors, but also for Soviet officials, political functionaries, and military officers.

The Great Purges

The subject of harrowing memoirs and painstakingly researched academic studies, of folk legend and official investigations, the Great Purges continue to fascinate and appal. Emblematic of Stalinism, the 'repressions'—to employ the term more common in Russian parlance—of 1936–8 seem to have been so arbitrary in victimization, so elusive in motivation as to defy explanation. Access to long-closed archives of the NKVD, while clarifying some issues, has not yet yielded a satisfactory explanation. Indeed, even what hitherto were assumed to be incontrovertible, basic facts are now in question.

According to the once standard version, Stalin initiated the Great Purges by arranging the assassination of the Leningrad Party boss, Sergei Kirov, in December 1934. Stalin's purpose here was twofold. First, he sought to eliminate a potential rival. Reputedly the leader of a 'moderate' faction within the Politburo, Kirov had also received more votes than Stalin himself in the elections to the Politburo at the Seventeenth Party Congress. Second, by claiming that the assassination was the work of 'Zinovievists' and ultimately inspired by Zinoviev and Kamenev, Stalin could legitimize the physical annihilation of former leaders of the opposition, their retinues, and eventually anyone else on whom he chose to pin the label 'enemy of the people'. This grand scheme for mounting a campaign of terror included the verification of party documents in 1935, the three public show trials of former oppositionists (Zinoviev and Kamenev in August 1936; Piatakov and Radek in January 1937; and Bukharin and Rykov in March 1938), the execution of Marshal Tukhachevskii and most of the Red Army general staff in June 1937, the elimination of nearly the entire regional leadership of the party later that year, and the arrest and disappearance of prominent persons from a wide variety of fields. The NKVD and its commissar, N. I. Ezhov, were the ruthless executors of Stalin's designs, and indeed the entire period is sometimes referred to as the 'Ezhovshchina' (the evil epoch of Ezhov).

Treating these events as instances of a single phenomenon, most scholars assumed that Stalin was intent on eliminating any potential source of opposition, beginning with past opponents but eventually including any who might appear to be unreliable in the future. Some have suggested that the Nazis' assumption of power in Germany and the increasing prospect of international war provided the impetus—or at least pretext—for Stalin's actions. Other accounts have emphasized the pathological nature of Stalin's suspiciousness and his psycho-dramatic replay of Ivan the Terrible's elimination of the boyars. Still others stress an inherent imperative of the totalitarian system: not only to atomize and terrorize society, but to achieve a turnover of cadres. Another interpretation derives the Great Terror from the bureaucratic imperatives associated with the NKVD's aggrandizement of power and its supervision of the GULAG. Whatever the dynamics, the traditional historiography shared a consensus that the Great Terror and purges represented a unitary process and that they served some rational function.

J. Arch Getty was the first to challenge the prevailing consensus. He noted the heavy reliance on rumour and gossip in memoirs, questioned the existence of a Stalin–Kirov rivalry or a moderate faction in the Politburo, and denied the existence of a master plot concocted by Stalin. Basing his analysis primarily on materials in the Smolensk Party Archive (seized first by the German army in the Second World War, then taken by American forces from the Germans) he argued that the party apparatus was hardly an efficient machine implementing the dictates of its leader, but a 'petrified bureaucracy' incapable even of keeping track of its members. According to Getty, the Great Purges actually derived from the failure of two campaigns to renovate the party: a series of operations to purge passive and degenerate members, and the initiatives spearheaded by Andrei Zhdanov to give party cadres a political education and to introduce 'party democracy' through contested secret ballot elections. The anti-bureaucratic impulse here struck a responsive chord with lower-ranking party members, but aroused resistance from regional party secretaries. As Ezhov undertook a search for enemies, which had extended from former oppositionists to regional military commanders, such resistance took on a sinister colouring. 'Anti-bureaucratic populism and police terror' created a vicious cycle of accusation, denunciations, and arrests that decimated the ranks of the party and certain high profile professions.

When Getty recently revisited the 'politics of repression', he concluded that 'glasnost' and the collapse of the Communist Party have put the secretive history of Stalinism on a more evidentially sound footing'. He notes that the investigation of a Politburo commission found no evidence of Stalin's participation in Kirov's assassination or the prior or subsequent existence of a moderate bloc; he therefore reiterates his scepticism about the planned nature of the terror. 'Indecision and chaos', he argues, were more evident in the evolution of repression before mid-1937. Thereafter, it is at least as plausible that Ezhov was pursuing his own agenda, which may—or may not—have coincided with Stalin's. Not that, in Getty's view, this exonerates Stalin from responsibility; on the contrary, Stalin was an active participant, personally edited lists of defendants and their statements for the 1936 and 1937 show trials, signed tens of thousands of death sentences, and established target figures for executions in each province. But some scholars remain dissatisfied with Getty's interpretation and even assert that Getty glossed over 'one of the darkest and most tragic episodes in Soviet history'.

As in the historiographical controversy among Germanists over 'intentionalist' vs. 'function-structuralist' interpretations of the Holocaust, this debate raises some complex and profound issues: the process of decision-making at the highest levels, the role of Stalin himself, popular attitudes and participation, the actual quantitative scale of the repression, and its immediate and longer-term psychic effects. Neither orthodox nor revisionist, Moshe Lewin suggests that the terror was a function of Stalin's unwillingness to be bound by the system he himself had built and presided over. This system had brought to the fore new social groups, especially state functionaries, who though powerful, lacked security of office and sought it in greater social stability and 'socialist legality'. It was just this craving that threatened Stalin's role as unfettered autocrat. Thus, two models coexisted uneasily and at some point collided. In the long run, the bureaucratic model, relying on the nomenklatura, would prevail; but during 1936–8, the autocratic model, consisting of the cult, the police, and a demonological mentality, was in ascendance.

That mentality was not Stalin's alone. Gabor Rittersporn has argued that attributing political conflict and the shortcomings of daily life to 'plots', 'wrecking', and the 'intensification of the class struggle' was not simply a matter of scapegoating, but reflected real belief. Subjected to a public discourse that postulated the achievement of socialism and the ubiquity of subversion, many people understood irregularities, shortages, or other deviations from what was supposed to happen in Manichean terms. They knew that they were not enemies or conspirators, but had no way of being sure about their bosses, colleagues,

The Moscow–Volga Canal, 128 km. in length, was built between 1932 and 1937. Inspecting the newly opened waterway were (from left to right) K. I. Voroshilov, V. M. Molotov, Stalin, and N. I. Ezhov. The latter was then at the height of his power as Commissar of the NKVD.

neighbours, even friends and relatives. Bukharin, who believed the accusations against Kamenev, was no different from Lev Kopelev and other 'true believers' convinced of the need for unrelenting cruelty to deal with enemies. Those lower down the social hierarchy, including many workers with grievances against their bosses and peasants still angry over collectivization, evidently considered the reprisals against party and state functionaries to be just retribution.

Even those who knew that innocent people had been arrested recoiled from the idea that Stalin condoned such action. 'We thought (perhaps we wanted to think) that Stalin knew nothing about the senseless violence committed against the communists, against the Soviet intelligentsia', the novelist and journalist Ilia Ehrenburg recalled. Many blamed Ezhov, whose removal as People's Commissar for Internal Affairs in December 1938 prompted one self-described 'ordinary citizen of the USSR' to write to the Central Committee urging it to 'correct the Ezhovite mistakes so that the NKVD will really begin to fight against elements hostile to Soviet power, and honest working people will be guaranteed normal and peaceful work'.

Such letters—and there are many in recently opened archives—should not be construed as prima facie evidence of popular support for the terror. But they do suggest that the machinations in the Kremlin were not the whole story. In Belyi *raion* of the Smolensk district, the defining political issues were not 'Trotskyite and fascist wrecking', but the crop failure of 1936, shortfalls in procurement targets, admission of former kulaks into collective farms, and other local issues. But at a certain point in 1937 local élites responsible for economic failures or bossism could find themselves so labelled.

As to the number of people arrested and shot by the NKVD, research by Russian and Western scholars in recently opened archives has produced estimates that are considerably lower than those previously posited. According to Viktor Zemskov, slightly less than one million people were confined in NKVD-run camps on 1 January 1937, a number that rose to 1.3 million by 1939; another 315,000 people were in 'corrective labour colonies' in 1940. These figures are a good deal lower than earlier estimates (for example, Robert Conquest's number of seven million in the camps by 1938), but they do not include people incarcerated in prisons, special resettlements, or other places of detention. It also remains unclear how many were 'politicals', convicted of engaging in 'propaganda or agitation' against the Soviet state, a crime punishable by five to eight years in a camp; an archival document indicates that the GULAG population sentenced for 'counter-revolutionary offences' was 12.6 per cent in 1936 and 33.1 per cent in 1940. As for executions by order of military tribunals, 'troikas', and other special bodies, official figures show 1,118 executions in 1936, 353,074 in 1937, 328,618 in 1938, and 2,552 in 1939. According to information released by the KGB in 1990, the total executed in 1937–8 represented 86.7 per cent of all death sentences carried out 'for counter-revolutionary and state crimes' between 1930 and 1953. Mass burial sites, recently uncovered at Kuropaty in Belarus and elsewhere in the former Soviet Union, constitute one of the most horrifying relics of the Stalin era.

Sic transit gloria mundi. Airbrushing photographs was one of the more crude techniques for revising the past to safeguard the future. Like many once-prominent Bolsheviks including some of his more famous victims, Ezhov became an 'unperson' after his fall from grace. Ironically, he served briefly as Commissar of Waterworks after his removal as head of the NKVD.

Who were the victims? We have long known about the prominent party officials, military officers, and members of the scientific and cultural élites. The publications of Conquest and Roy Medvedev in the early 1970s added more names, notably from the non-Russian republics. More recently, thanks to greater archival access and innovative research, the sociology of victimization has become more precise. It now seems clear that the most vulnerable groups were the party élite, former oppositionists, high-ranking economic officials, and military officers. Contrary to earlier assumptions, Old Bolsheviks—those who joined the party before the October Revolution—and members of the intelligentsia were not disproportionately repressed.

Several conclusions are in order here. First, vulnerability or risk must be correlated with proportionality: even if the majority of camp inmates were peasants and workers, those in élite positions were at greater risk if the data are compared to their numbers in the population at large. Second, the tragic fate of family members—vividly and movingly described in the memoirs of Nadezhda Mandelstam, Anna Larina (wife of Bukharin), and others—must be taken into account in any overall assessment of the purges. Notwithstanding Stalin's earlier injunction ('sins of the fathers should not be visited upon their sons'), said in reference to the offspring of dekulakized peasants, family members—sons, daughters, wives, and even more distant relatives—were frequently subjected to interrogation and incarceration in orphanages and camps. Third, no amount of statistical work is likely to explain why so many individuals were summarily executed in 1937–8 and why this 'ultimate sentence' was prescribed more sparingly after Lavrentii Beria became the NKVD's commissar. Finally, to comprehend the repression of these years, use of a term like 'the Terror', with its implication of unitariness, tends to obfuscate the overlapping patterns and cross-currents of repression.

The Enemy Without/The Enemy Within

Corresponding to the Great Turn of the late 1920s, the Comintern directed communist parties to expel 'Right opportunists' from their ranks and abandon tactical alliances with Social Democrats, henceforth labelled 'social fascists'. This 'class war' strategy, which persisted until the mid-1930s, disorganized working-class opposition to fascism and proved particularly disastrous in Germany. The call by the Commissariat of Foreign Affairs (Narkomindel) for total disarmament evoked nothing but scepticism in European capitals, but the Soviet Union did succeed in normalizing relations with neighbouring countries and establishing full diplomatic relations with the United States in 1933.

The triumph of the Nazis in Germany and the consolidation of a Japanese puppet state (Manchukuo) on the Soviet Union's eastern borders precipitated the Comintern strategy of Popular Fronts with all 'progressive forces' and an intensification of Soviet efforts to achieve collective security with the European democracies. These policies bore fruit in the form of mutual assistance pacts with France and Czechoslovakia (in 1935) and the election of a Popular Front government in France (in 1936). But the great test of the European commitment to contain fascism—the chief aim of the popular fronts—was the Spanish Civil War. Despite Soviet assistance to the Republic—or perhaps because European statesmen feared a 'red' Spain more than one ruled by Franco—the Western powers failed the test. The betrayal of Czechoslovakia at Munich (September 1938) confirmed Soviet suspicions that neither Britain nor France were unduly concerned about Nazi expansion to the East.

For the Soviet Union, the decade of the 1930s lasted until the Nazi invasion of 22 June 1941. The increasing likelihood of war in Europe precipitated a radical shift in foreign policy away from seeking collective security with the Western democracies and towards an accommodation with Hitler. Acting on secret provisions of the Soviet–German Non-Aggression Pact of August 1939, Soviet armed forces occupied eastern Poland, the three Baltic republics, and the Romanian province of Bessarabia. Finland resisted territorial concessions along its eastern border; in the ensuing 'Winter War' (1939–40) the Red Army triumphed, but with difficulty and only because of superior numbers.

In the mean time, the regime moved to restore the authority, if not security, of cadres in state and industrial management—badly shaken by the Great Purges and wary of denunciations from below. Laws stipulating a longer working day and draconian punishment for tardiness and absenteeism put teeth into demands for labour discipline. The Stakhanovite movement continued to celebrate high achievers among workers; but as the regime sought to close ranks with managerial and technical personnel, it now tended to attribute innovations to engineers. A steady diet of Soviet patriotism—psychological preparation for war—accompanied a massive build-up of the armed forces and defence industries.

Ten years earlier, in the midst of the First Five-Year Plan, Stalin told a conference of economic officials that they could not afford to slacken the pace of industrialization because to do so 'would mean falling behind. And those who fall behind get beaten'. He thereupon recited all the beatings 'backward' Russia had suffered—by 'Mongol khans', 'Turkish beys', Swedish feudal lords, the Polish and Lithuanian gentry, British and French capitalists, and Japanese 'barons'. 'All beat her—because of her backwardness … military backwardness, cultural backwardness, political backwardness, industrial backwardness, agricultural backwardness'. But, he added, correlating gender with political transformation, 'Mother Russia' has since become the socialist fatherland. 'Do you want our socialist fatherland to be beaten and to lose its independence? … We are fifty or a hundred years behind the advanced countries. We must make good this distance in ten years. Either we do it, or we shall go under'.

Stalin's forced-pace industrialization undoubtedly contributed mightily to the Soviet victory in the Great Patriotic War. The tempo of industrialization was literally killing and extremely wasteful, but by 1941 the USSR had closed the gap, militarily and industrially. The greatest spurt occurred during the 'three good years' of industrialization (1934–6). By 1937 steel output was nearly three times greater than in 1932, coal production had doubled, and electricity

Cotton cultivation in Uzbekistan required the diversion of scarce water resources. Among the projects that eventually would result in the ecologically catastrophic depletion of the Aral Sea was the construction of the Fergana Grand Canal (1939–41) which drew on the headwaters of the Syr Darya river. Note the absence of mechanized equipment.

generation had risen by 250 per cent. Thereafter, the Great Purges and the channelling of investments into armaments—defence expenditure quadrupled between 1936 and 1940—caused growth rates in these and other branches of industry to subside. But on the eve of the war, Soviet industry was producing 230 tanks, 700 military aircraft, and more than 100,000 rifles every month. However, agriculture still lagged. A major crop failure in 1936—a yield even smaller than the official harvest for 1932—strained the state's reserves and distribution network; it has even been argued that this crisis contributed to the political events of 1937. Because of increased military expenditure, investments in the collective and state farm system remained woefully minuscule.

But 'backwardness' is qualitative, not merely quantitative. In cultural and political terms, the USSR's backwardness was perpetuated, even intensified, not because party and state officials tried to do too little, but because they tried to do too much. Browbeating the nation into modernity and socialism—the two were deemed to be synonymous—Stalin and his lieutenants provoked much resistance, but also conjured up demons of their own Manichean imaginings. These they combated with cults, reliance on miracles, and a great deal of force. They thus conformed to what Moshe Lewin has called 'the contamination effect', whereby radical and rapid transformation in fact ensures the survival of fundamental continuities, especially in social behaviour and political culture. Hence, the methods employed in 'building socialism', derived from previous centuries and combined with twentieth-century technology, actually built something called Stalinism.

THE GREAT FATHERLAND
WAR AND LATE STALINISM
1941–1953

WILLIAM C. FULLER, JR

*Few events loom larger in Russian historical memory than the
'Great Fatherland War'. Why was Stalin's Soviet Union so
ill-prepared for the conflict and how did it nevertheless manage
to prevail? In the aftermath of victory, heedless of the threat of
a cold or even thermonuclear war, the ageing tyrant rebuilt
Stalinism at home and expanded its reach abroad.*

An index of the initial success of Operation Barbarossa was the enormous number of prisoners that fell into the Germans' hands. By the end of 1941 three million Red Army soldiers were German captives. Denied adequate food, shelter, and medicine, Soviet POWs died by the hundreds of thousands.

At four a.m. (Moscow time) on 22 June 1941, several thousand pieces of German ordnance simultaneously thundered into Soviet territory. Operation Barbarossa had begun, initiating four years of the most brutal and destructive war in history. From the very beginning the Soviet–German conflict was waged with a ferocity and savagery that was unparalleled in modern times. When Hitler announced his move against Russia to his highest officers (30 March 1941), he made it absolutely clear that he expected his troops to discard every principle of humanity, chivalry, or international law. This was, he said, to be a war 'of extermination'.

The 153 divisions of the invasion force formed three army groups—north, centre, and south. Army Group North was to punch through the Baltic republics in the direction of Leningrad. Army Group Centre was supposed to entrap and destroy Soviet units in the western expanses of the country. And, the third force—Army Group South—to drive south-east of the Pripet marshes and slice Ukraine off from the rest of the Soviet state.

It was obviously impossible to mask the colossal military preparations for Barbarossa. Since February, Germany had been concentrating forces on the Soviet frontier, 'explaining' this as a defence against British air raids. In the months, weeks, and days prior to 22 June, the Soviet government received over *eighty* discrete warnings of German attack. None the less, the surprise was virtually total. Though aware of the massing of German forces but unwilling to accept the truth, at 1 a.m. Stalin issued orders to Soviet military commanders not to shoot even if the Germans penetrated Soviet territory so as to avoid 'dangerous provocations'.

It was in part this ill-conceived order that enabled the *Wehrmacht* to achieve astonishing results on the very first day of the invasion. By 23 June, for example, elements of

Army Group Centre had already advanced sixty miles. Directives from Moscow, commanding Soviet units to launch vigorous counter-attacks, only played into German hands. Since most of the Soviet air force had been destroyed on the ground, and since Soviet formations were poorly organized and undermanned, the abortive counter-attacks tore even larger holes in Soviet defensive lines. By mid-July the Germans had conquered Latvia, Lithuania, Belorussia, and most of right-bank Ukraine. By August Army Group North had put Leningrad under siege, Centre had captured Smolensk, and South was investing Odessa on the shores of the Black Sea.

At this point Hitler intervened, redirecting offensive operations to achieve the rapid capture of Leningrad and Ukraine. Although Kiev fell in mid-September, Leningrad continued to resist. Hitler changed his strategic emphasis once again, this time detaching over 1.8 million men for 'Operation Typhoon'—an assault on Moscow. By mid-October the German army was within sixty miles of the capital.

During these first few dreadful months of war, Germany and her allies—Hungary, Slovakia, Romania, and Finland—had overrun territory larger than France. They took two-thirds of the pre-war Soviet industries and lands that produced one-third of the country's total agricultural output. By the end of 1941 the invaders had destroyed almost 84 per cent of the pre-war active Soviet armed forces: 1.5 million Soviet troops were dead while another 3 million were German POWs. Two million of the latter would perish by February.

Soviet Weakness in 1941

What accounted for Soviet weakness in June 1941? It clearly did not stem from a neglect of defences. By the late 1930s the Soviet Union was a thoroughly militarized state; Soviet defence outlays in 1941 amounted to over 43 per cent of the country's GNP. Nor was there a gross imbalance in numbers or technology: in the immediate invasion zone roughly 2.8 million Soviet soldiers confronted about 3 million Germans, supported by twelve Finnish and six Romanian divisions. Similarly, whereas Germany and her allies attacked with 3,600 tanks and 2,500 planes, the Soviet armed forces disposed of over 20,000 tanks (of which 1,862 were modern T-34s or KVs) and at least 10,000 combat aircraft.

What then were the reasons behind Russia's dismal military performance that summer? One reason was clearly the quality and skill of its enemy. At the operational and tactical levels of war the German *Wehrmacht* was then the finest army in the world. Other reasons, however, inhered in a series of self-inflicted wounds—a bitter legacy of the 1930s.

One of the gravest was the political purge of the Soviet military. It began in June 1937 with the announcement that Marshal Mikhail Tukhachevskii and seven other prominent Soviet soldiers had been convicted of treason and executed. At the same time Stalin delivered a speech in which he called for the discharge of 'all vacillating army men' from their posts—a statement taken by the Soviet political police, the NKVD, as a direct order for comprehensive terror against the Soviet officer corps. The pretext here was the putative existence of a 'Trotskyite conspiracy' within the Red Army that was scheming to stage a coup and install a military dictator. Although accurate statistics are still lacking, it would appear that some 35,000–40,000 officers were removed from their commands (many of them shot or condemned to hard labour in the camps). In other words, at least 35 per cent of the officer corps was purged. The eliminated included three of the five Soviet marshals, thirteen of the fifteen army commanders, fifty-seven of the eighty-seven corps commanders, 110 of the 195 divisional commanders, and all but one fleet commander in the navy.

The impact of this repression upon the Soviet armed forces cannot be exaggerated. It served to demoralize the Red Army, not only because of the arrests and executions, but also because Stalin upgraded the role of the political commissars and reinstituted dual command. However, those removed possessed invaluable technical knowledge. Tukhachevskii, for example, had been the prophet of mechanization and motorization; yet the purges eliminated not only Tukhachevskii but also some of his closest associates. Repression was a never-ending spiral: arrest was followed by interrogation and torture, which did not end until the accused confessed and named 'accomplices'. To be minimally plausible, such accusations typically implicated immediate associates; as a result, the purges were most destructive to the more technical branches, especially armour.

The military purges must be distinguished from other forms of political terror in the 1930s: an investigation by the Party in the Khrushchev era established that the order for the military repression came from the top and used patently fabricated evidence. To this day, the rationale for the military purges remains a mystery. One theory holds that Stalin—misled by what had happened in the Spanish Civil War—had come to believe that Tukhachevskii's expertise was dispensable. Another is that Stalin sought to check signs of excessive independence within the military, signs that had become visible as far back as the ill-fated Seventeenth Party Congress in 1934. And some believe that Stalin feared Tukhachevskii's popularity, seeing him as a potential rival. In any event, the purges slowed down when the 'Winter War' of 1939–40 with Finland exposed the weaknesses of the Red Army. Certain officers (including such gifted leaders as K. K. Rokossovskii) were released from the camps and reinstated. None the less, on the very eve of the war, three-quarters of Soviet commanders had been in their posts for less than a year. And at the highest echelons, the Red Army was led by talentless sycophants and overrated cavalry men from the civil war era.

Another weakness had to do with doctrine and planning. For a variety of reasons, the Soviet leadership believed that a war with Germany would most likely start after an extended period of crisis, which would give the Red Army time to mobilize. Thus a formal declaration of war would be followed by a brief defensive phase, in which Soviet forces would check and repel the invader near the frontier; the Red Army would then open an offensive into Central Europe. Thus, Soviet military and political élites presupposed a short war, largely fought on the enemy's soil; they paid little attention to the possibility that the war might become protracted, that it might require the USSR to organize a defence in depth.

The relative de-emphasis on defence also had implications for frontier fortifications. Whereas the Soviet Union possessed a considerable network of these in 1939, expansion by 1941 (as a result of the annexation of the Baltics, eastern Poland, and Bessarabia) had pushed the frontier 150 to 300 kilometres to the west. Work on new lines commenced in 1940, but procrastination and disorganization slowed progress. In February and March 1941 the Soviet command decided to cannibalize existing fortifications in order to build the new ones. The result was that *neither* set was operational when the war came: only a quarter of the new fortifications had been built on the new borders, while the pillboxes of the 1939 Stalin line were useless, semi-demolished and stripped of their weapons and ammunition.

Finally, the greatest blame for the ruinous start to the war must rest with Stalin himself. After the signing of the Ribbentrop–Molotov Pact in 1939, Stalin had constructed a foreign policy based on co-operation and collusion with the Nazis, evidently hoping that they would exhaust themselves in a lengthy war of attrition against the French and British. This delusion vanished with the fall of France in 1940. Although Stalin thereafter came to believe that an armed confrontation with Germany was unavoidable, he none the less supposed that Moscow—not Berlin—would determine its timing. After all, it was unlikely that Hitler would turn east while Britain remained unsubdued. In the spring of 1941, although Stalin permitted the mobilization of some of the reserves, he insisted that war with Germany would not come until the following May at the earliest. He therefore saw Hitler's massive military build-up of 1941 as the prelude to negotiations, not war. From Stalin's perspective, the only real danger was that war might break out accidentally; it was to guard against this contingency that Stalin was so determined to avoid 'provoking' Hitler. That is why Stalin disregarded G. K. Zhukov's advice (May 1941) to launch an immediate preventive attack to disrupt the concentration of the German army, as well as that of S. K. Timoshenko, whose frantic request to transfer forces from the interior to the border was not approved until June. In a very real sense, Stalin's miscalculations foreordained the military surprise and devastating consequence of the invasion.

Once the fact of German invasion was beyond dispute, the authoritarianism and centralization of Stalin's regime showed only torpidity and inertia in the face of military emergency. For example, Moscow's order in the evening of 22 June for the west front to destroy the German concentration at Suvalki was useless: the advancing enemy was no longer there. When Stalin personally began to direct the war effort, his command that the Red Army cede no territory and

his refusal to countenance withdrawal squandered tons of equipment and material and consigned hundreds of thousands of troops to death or captivity. Fifty-
six per cent of all military casualties suffered by the Soviet Union during the
Second World War occurred during the first eighteen of its forty-seven months.
The Red Army paid dearly for Stalin's errors in dealing with Hitler.

Phases of the War

By early autumn, despite a succession of military disasters, morale in the Red
Army had stiffened. Party officials reported to Stalin that 'flights of military
units [from the battlefield] have become rarer', and wounded soldiers were
observed bearing their arms with them to the field hospitals, rather than toss-
ing them away, as formerly. As a result of this, as well as better organization and
better generalship, Germany's string of triumphs in Russia came to an abrupt
end with the battle of Moscow. The failure of the second German assault on the
city in November enabled Zhukov to counter-attack in early December, forcing
the Germans to fall back between 100 and 250 kilometres.

At this point Stalin ordered the Red Army to attack, not along one or two axes
of advance, but along the entire two thousand kilometres of front from the
Black Sea to the Baltic. This over-ambitious offensive had largely spent itself by
April 1942. The Soviet General Staff thereupon recommended a strategic
defence in order to reinforce the army and build up stocks of equipment. Stalin
agreed at first, but then authorized an attack in May designed to liberate

Workers digging anti-
tank traps, Moscow
1941. The Soviet
Union mobilized its
entire population for
the war effort. In the
autumn of 1941 over
five hundred thousand
civilians took part in
constructing forti-
fications for the city
of Moscow. Civilian
labourers dug over
thirty kilometres of
anti-tank ditches and
strung forty-six kilo-
metres of barbed wire.

Kharkov. It disastrously misfired. The Russians retired behind the northern Donets and the Germans occupied the Crimean peninsula.

Hitler had a new plan: a south-east advance into the Don, Kuban, and Volga regions as a first step towards the conquest of oil-rich Transcaucasia. Operation Blue began in the spring of 1942. By mid-July 1942 it was evident that the Germans were driving for Stalingrad on the lower reaches of the Volga. In late August, General Friedrich von Paulus's forces had crossed the Don and attacked Stalingrad. After two weeks of shelling, bombing, and bloody street fighting, the Germans were in possession of most of the city. The Soviets, however, had no intention of capitulating; on 19 November they counter-attacked ('Operation Uranus'), penetrating and encircling Paulus's army from both north and south. Now Paulus himself was besieged.

Time was not on the side of the Germans at Stalingrad. Hitler flatly forbade any attempt at a break-out, even though the Soviets succeeded in stalling F. E. Manstein's relief columns. As the temperature fell, so too did reserves of food and ammunition; the Luftwaffe's attempt to supply Paulus's forces by air failed. Finally, at the end of January and in early February 1943, Paulus and the remnants of his sixth army surrendered. One hundred and fifty thousand of his men were casualties; another hundred thousand were prisoners of war. Although the battle of Stalingrad did not predetermine German defeat in the war, it made a total German victory extremely improbable.

Emboldened by success at Stalingrad, the Red Army launched a series of offensives in the early months of 1943. These had three important results. First,

The battle of Stalingrad began in July 1942 and ended with the surrender of the German forces by Field Marshal Friedrich von Paulus in February 1943. Much of the battle was characterized by desperate fighting in the rubble of destroyed homes and factories. The two Soviet soldiers in the photograph carry weapons particularly suitable for this type of combat: the PPSh sub-machine-gun and the ROKS–2 flamethrower.

the Soviets managed to cut a corridor through German lines to relieve belea-
guered Leningrad. Second, by April they had effectively demolished Germany's
positions in the northern Caucasus. Finally, by February the Red Army had
defeated the German second army near Voronezh, forcing it to retreat two hundred miles, creating a bulge in the German lines known as the Kursk salient.

Hitler saw this salient as a major opportunity: a decisive blow there might
shatter Russia's defences and allow him to regain the initiative. The German
plan for 'Operation Citadel' entailed two simultaneous thrusts towards Kursk,
one south from Orel, the second north from Kharkov. However, Hitler decided
to stockpile still more military equipment and postponed Operation Citadel
from the spring until the summer of 1943. This delay enabled Soviet intelligence to discover the time and place of the attack and also permitted a massive
reinforcement and fortification of the battlefield.

The German preliminary bombardment that began on 5 July was answered
by an even more intense counter-bombardment, indicating just how ready the
Soviets were. The battle of Kursk was the largest tank battle in world history,
with six thousand vehicles engaged on each side. It was also distinguished by an
unprecedented scale of carnage and slaughter, even on the eastern front. The
upshot was a Soviet victory; by the end of July, Germany had lost half a million
soldiers and was forced to retreat another two hundred miles. This battle was a
true turning-point in the Second World War, for henceforth the Germans would
be largely on the defensive in the east.

By January 1944 the Red Army had raised the siege of Leningrad and had
crossed the old 1939 border. In May it had liberated Ukraine and was driving
deep into Poland and Romania. The most significant event of the year, however,
was 'Operation Bagration', the Russian attack on Army Group Centre, which
held a salient in Lithuania and Belorussia that protruded into Soviet lines. At
the end of June the Soviets struck into the salient with a series of co-ordinated
thrusts, even one staged through the Pripet marshes. Offensive operations continued until the end of the summer, utterly destroying seventeen German divisions, and reducing the combat strength of another fifty divisions by half.

By the end of 1944, Soviet armies had already overrun Romania and were
swinging north towards Budapest. The central group of Soviet fronts were
poised to clear Poland of the enemy, before invading Germany itself. The first
step in this process was the Vilna–Oder operation in January and February 1945,
where the Red Army used its superior numbers and firepower to smash into
East Prussia. Indeed, certain units under Zhukov's command had crossed the
Oder and were but forty miles from Berlin. But because Zhukov's forces were
exhausted and had outrun their supply lines, the Soviet High Command
decided to defer the battle for Berlin until the spring. In mid-April 1945, some
2.5 million Soviet troops squared off against 1 million Germans, many of them
young boys, cripples, or old men. There was little doubt about the outcome. By
25 April Berlin was encircled; two days later Soviet troops had shot their way

Signal flares light the way for a night advance of Soviet IS–2 heavy tanks during the battle of Kursk (July–August 1943). The combined total of Soviet and German tanks engaged at Kursk exceeded 6,100, making Kursk the largest tank battle in history. Hitler's defeat at Kursk gave the Red Army the strategic initiative for the remainder of the war.

into the centre of the city; two days after that Adolf Hitler killed himself. The German government's emissaries travelled to Zhukov's headquarters and signed the act of unconditional surrender on 9 May 1945.

With Germany now defeated, Stalin honoured his pledge to the British and American allies to enter the war against Japan. Over the next three months tens of thousands of Soviet soldiers entrained for the Far East. On 9 August (the very day that the atomic bomb fell on Nagasaki) Stalin's forces erupted into Manchuria and rapidly pulverized the Japanese Kwantung army. Within days Tokyo had decided to treat with its enemies. On 2 September 1945 Soviet representatives were present to witness the Japanese surrender on the deck of the American battleship *Missouri*.

How the Soviets Won the War

To understand how the Soviet Union managed to prevail in its war with Nazi Germany, it is no less important to consider the reasons for German failure as the reasons for Soviet success. In key respects, the Germans undermined their own war effort.

In the first place, German strategy for the invasion of the Soviet Union was based on entirely erroneous intelligence. For example, prior to the war the Germans had calculated that the Red Army had only 200 divisions; by early August 1941 they had identified 360. The German intelligence services also undercounted the Soviet tank park (by at least 50 per cent) and grossly underestimated the scale, and productivity of the Soviet war economy. Nazi racist ideology also contributed to this depreciation of the enemy. Regarding the Russian as an *Untermensch*, Hitler was supremely confident that the Germans could conquer the Soviet Union to the Urals in three months, for the entire rotten structure of the Soviet state would surely collapse 'as soon as we kick the door in'. The battle of Moscow, however, soon demonstrated that the war was not going to be brief. And Hitler had given no thought to a protracted war in the east, specifically to its economic and logistical dimensions.

Ideology also dictated German aims in Russia, and this had major implications for the conduct of the war. With one lightning summer campaign, Hitler aimed to reverse thousands of years of Eastern European history: to overthrow the Soviet government, eradicate communism, and annex Soviet territory as far east as the Urals. This newly acquired *Lebensraum* could then be used to support a population of some 100 million additional Germans or Germanized Scandinavians. In the course of this process, 'racially undesirable populations', especially Jews and Gypsies, were to be systematically exterminated. The fate of the Slavs, and the Russians in particular, was not merely slavery but *tribalism*: denied any future possibility of a state of their own, they were to be confined to squalid villages and maintained in filth and ignorance.

But the Nazis' genocidal policies in the occupation zone ultimately detracted from the prosecution of the war, diverting thousands of troops, as well as hundreds of locomotives and wagons, from military operations. The Nazis' bestial treatment of the Slavs was also ultimately self-defeating, since it alienated them by the millions. Hence the German side failed to capitalize on the anti-communist sentiments of the peasants; not until the very end of the war (and even then with reluctance) did the Nazis authorize the raising of entire Russian military units to fight Stalin. Confiscations of food, fuel, tools, and clothing as well as rape, torture, and shootings undercut German efforts to extract economic benefits from occupied territories. After the harvest of 1942, for instance, the Germans permitted peasants to retain only enough grain for two-thirds of a pound of bread a day. These starvation rations depopulated the countryside and engendered flight or sullen non-co-operation among the survivors. The deportation of almost five million people for work in Germany further exacerbated the labour shortage in the occupied zone. Agricultural output fell by 50 per cent in the areas under Hitler's control: although his armies in the east could be fed locally, very little in the way of a surplus remained for shipment back to the Reich.

The Nazi leadership was slow to grasp that the economy of its eastern conquests had to be rebuilt and managed, not merely plundered. By the time it finally did, the expropriations and atrocities had hardened resistance to German rule and fuelled the growth of the partisan movement, which may have enrolled as many as 200,000 people by 1943.

None the less the Germans were defeated not only by themselves but by their Soviet enemies. Paradoxically, the USSR won the war both because of *and* despite the Stalinist system.

Although the blunders of the Soviet leadership had enabled a surprise attack and a summer of catastrophic defeat, certain characteristics of the regime helped the country weather those initial shocks. Stalin himself observed in November that 'any other country that had lost as much as we have would have collapsed', and there was some truth in his remarks. The upheavals and turbulence of the 1930s had taught the mass of Soviet citizens a healthy respect for the power of the state and had inspired belief in its solidity and permanence. This psychic capital, combined with an immediate tightening of the monopoly on information (all radios in the country were confiscated at the end of June)

On 24 June 1945, four years and two days after the German invasion, the Soviet Union staged a triumphal victory parade in Red Square. At the climax of the parade, two hundred German military banners were thrown into a heap at the base of the Lenin mausoleum.

enabled the regime to insulate the population from knowledge of the military débâcle and to combat rumour and panic.

Second, the extreme centralization of the Soviet dictatorship, so cumbrous in the opening phase of the war, eventually proved to be an asset; this authoritarianism permitted the state to mobilize the people and the resources necessary to prosecute total war. Mobilization entailed conscripting millions as soldiers, and millions more as labourers. On the very first day of the war Moscow called up almost all classes of reservists born after 1905. At the same time, it issued a new labour law that compelled vast numbers of Soviet civilians, both men and women, to take up war-related work. Industrial absenteeism was soon declared a felony; railways, waterways, and even many factories were placed under martial law. The State Defence Committee (GKO), created in June 1941 to unify the direction of the war effort, accelerated the evacuation of industrial enterprises from the western borderlands to the Urals, Siberia, and Central Asia. By November of that year the regime had dismantled and shipped 1,523 plants east; roughly 1,200 of them were up and operating by mid-1942.

The management of the Soviet war economy was no easy task, especially in view of the army's ravenous appetite for fresh manpower. The Soviet Union would eventually draft 16 per cent of its population into the armed forces during the war, thus permitting the Red Army at its height to maintain 11.2 million people under arms. Such unprecedented military conscription stripped the factories and farms of able-bodied men, thereby creating a labour shortage of staggering proportions. The release of prisoners from GULAG (the net outflow was 1.1 million people during the war) provided scant relief. Women, children, and the elderly had to substitute for the absent soldiers. By the end of the summer of 1941 women comprised 70 per cent of the industrial labour force in Moscow.

Matters were still worse in the countryside, as agriculture was feminized, demechanized, and deprived of draft animals. The proportion of women in the rural labour force increased from 40 per cent on the eve of the war to 70 per cent in 1943 and 82 per cent in 1944. The Red Army also requisitioned machines and horses in vast numbers—some 400,000 by the end of 1942, and almost half the horses from the collective farms by the end of the war. Peasant women experimented with harnessing cows to till the fields; others pulled the ploughs themselves. All of this had dire implications for food production, as agricultural yields in the uninvaded zone plummeted in 1943 to less than 50 per cent of the pre-war level. And this paltry stock of food had to sustain a population swollen by twenty-five million refugees.

Despite the severity of the labour and food problems, and despite clumsy inefficiencies in balancing the needs of the army and the needs of the economy, the Soviet Union was clearly winning the industrial war against Nazi Germany even as early as 1942. Although in that year Russia's supply of steel and coal was only one-third that of Germany, it nevertheless manufactured twice the num-

Soviet industrial production was an indispensable element in USSR's victory over Germany. By transferring factories to the Urals, militarizing labour, and shifting resources to war industries, the Soviet Union was able to achieve astonishing increases in its output of arms. Between 1943 and 1945 the USSR manufactured over 82,000 aircraft, 73,000 tanks, and 324,000 pieces of artillery. In the photograph, workers assemble ZIS–3 76 mm. guns.

ber of weapons. Simply put, the Soviets outproduced the Germans. All types of new armaments from aircraft and tanks down to automatic pistols were designed, machined, and delivered to the front. New industrial plants were built from scratch and operated twenty-four hours a day. Some of them were gigantic, such as the tank factory in Cheliabinsk, which boasted sixty-four separate assembly lines. Between 1943 and 1945 Soviet factories turned out over 73,000 tanks and self-propelled guns, 82,000 aircraft, and 324,000 artillery pieces.

The USSR thus acquired the wherewithal to fight, and the government deserves some credit for this achievement. Munitions do not, however, win wars all by themselves: skilful generalship is also necessary. Once the rank incompetence of figures such as S. M. Budennyi and K. E. Voroshilov had been amply demonstrated, Stalin's regime was in fact successful in identifying and promoting dozens of talented commanders; G. K. Zhukov, I. S. Konev, K. K. Rokossovskii, N. F. Vatutin, A. M. Vasilevskii, and B. M. Shaposhnikov—to name but a few—were instrumental in planning campaigns and leading Soviet armies to victory. The Soviet High Command improved throughout the war and in its later phases Soviet generals were responsible for numerous advances in tactics and operational art. Soviet generals also became adept at 'combined arms' warfare—that is, the integrated and mutually supportive employment of artillery, armour, infantry, and air power. They evinced brilliance in the use of reconnaissance, camouflage, and deception. And they perfected the mobile force structure that was the hallmark of Soviet offensives from 1943–5.

We come to Stalin himself. What role did his leadership play in the Soviet war effort? That Stalin was a despotic butcher is beyond dispute; he also bears direct responsibility for the catastrophic losses in the first months of the war. Deceived by Hitler, guilty of issuing the inept orders that disorganized the Red Army's defences, Stalin also sought to divert blame from himself by executing scapegoats. When the western front crumbled under the German onslaught, its commander—General D. G. Pavlov—was arrested in July and shot for treason. (His real crime, it now appears, was to have courageously protested against the military purges in 1938.) Firing-squads claimed the lives of twenty-nine other Soviet generals in 1941 and 1942; Stalin personally signed many of the death warrants.

Nevertheless, one cannot disregard Stalin's positive contributions. First, for many Soviet citizens, he became a symbol of national unity, an embodiment of the spirit of resistance. Certain of his speeches and writings, such as his first wartime address (3 July 1941) and the famous 'not one step back' order-of-the-day (29 July 1942) are said to have rallied the people and given invaluable boosts to their morale. Second, so great was the terror that he inspired at the highest echelons of party and state that a rebuke from him, let alone a threat, could elicit impressive performances from factory managers and generals alike. Finally, although Stalin committed military blunders throughout the war, he improved as a strategist—not least because he became aware of his own professional limitations. Unlike Hitler, he encouraged strategic debate and did not hesitate to solicit or accept advice. Zhukov praised his accomplishments in the strategic arena, as did several allied generals.

The Stalinist system then did help the USSR win the war. But without the contribution of the Western allies, victory would not have been achieved as quickly as it was. Without the contribution of the peoples of the Soviet Union, victory would not have been achieved at all.

The Second World War was a war of coalitions, and coalitional warfare typically leads to friction among the alliance partners. Russia's relationship with her British and American allies was no exception. Thus Stalin held that Roosevelt and Churchill—as leaders of capitalist, imperialist states—were by definition hostile to Soviet interests. The Soviet tyrant worried lest Washington and London collude against him, particularly over the question of the second front. Moscow had been appealing for the opening of a second front to draw German forces away from Russia since late 1941; indeed, Stalin courted his allies with such gestures as abolition of the Communist International in the hope of speeding up their invasion of the continent. Owing to the Pacific war and operations in Africa and Italy, however, D-Day did not come until June 1944. Stalin regarded this as a 'treacherous delay', since he had been led to believe that the attack would occur a year earlier. Indeed, his frustration apparently induced him to extend peace feelers to the Germans in 1943.

From the standpoint of London and Washington, Stalin's evasiveness and penchant for secrecy were irritants. The spectre of a separate Soviet–German peace was, however, truly petrifying: the Western allies were well aware that the Soviet Union bore the brunt of the struggle with Hitler's legions. Until the Normandy landing, Germany never deployed less than 90 per cent of her best combat troops against the Soviet Union. In the end, 80 per cent of all German casualties in the war would be inflicted on the eastern front. Franklin Roosevelt and Churchill also believed that Soviet participation would be essential for the rapid defeat of Japan. Both of these considerations militated in favour of concessions to Stalin in the interest of keeping the coalition together.

One such concession was the delivery of crucial supplies to Russia with no strings attached. The British and Americans shipped these stocks to Pacific and White Sea ports, or conveyed them overland through occupied Iran. Ten per cent of all Soviet tanks and 12 per cent of all Soviet combat aircraft came from Stalin's Western allies. American Lend-Lease also furnished 427,000 motor vehicles, one million miles of telephone wire, a quarter of a million field telephones, and fifteen million pairs of boots. The allies also provided aircraft steel, petroleum, zinc, copper, aluminium, and chemicals. Especially important, given the Soviet food crisis, was the transfer of comestibles. The United States alone gave enough concentrated food to the Soviet Union to have supplied twelve million soldiers with half a pound for every day of the war. The total value of British aid came to £420 million; that of the United States to almost $11 billion.

Although the Soviet Union could have won the war without allied supplies, their delivery none the less shortened the war. Allied trucks, jeeps, aircraft fuel, and communications equipment made possible the enormous mobile offensives of 1943–5. Western assistance also allowed the Soviet Union to keep millions of people in uniform (eight million by one calculation) whom it otherwise would have had to withdraw from the front to prevent a collapse of the economy.

In the strictly military arena, the Western allies rendered valuable services to the Soviet Union even before the break-out from Normandy pinned down 105 German divisions. Operations in the Middle East, Sicily, and Italy drained Axis resources. The Anglo-American bombing campaign against Germany was so massive that, in the judgement of some scholars, it constituted a second front all by itself. At the very least, since the German anti-tank gun doubled as an anti-aircraft gun, thousands of these weapons were kept trained on British and American aeroplanes, not Soviet tanks. Finally, after November 1943 Hitler's strategy in Europe was to de-emphasize the Eastern Front and to build up strength to repel the allied invasion that he anticipated in France or Norway. This decision also alleviated the pressure on the USSR.

None the less the greatest credit for victory in the war surely belongs to the Soviet population itself. It was Soviet men and women who sowed the fields, operated the lathes, stormed enemy positions, and survived siege and occupation. They often did so with signal heroism under conditions of unspeakable deprivation.

The war exacted appalling sacrifices from Soviet citizens. The USSR lost more soldiers than did any other belligerent. Nor was the civilian population spared. One million people succumbed to famine or disease during the siege of Leningrad alone—more than all combat deaths sustained by the British, Commonwealth, and American armed forces put together. In the urban areas of the country factory labourers put in twelve- to sixteen-hour working days and achieved record outputs. And they did so despite malnutrition: by 1942 official rations provided a caloric consumption nearly a quarter less than the pre-war norm. This led to an explosion in black marketeering and grotesquely inflated prices; in 1945 a kilo of butter in Rostov-on-the-Don cost 1,000 roubles. Rural Russia felt hunger and want too. The government's official rationing system deliberately excluded peasants, and left them to their own provisions. Consumption of bread (the chief staple in the peasant diet) declined to 40 per cent of pre-war levels. Manufactured goods, including such necessities as clothing and medicine, were virtually unavailable.

What sustained the people through these trials? What kept them working and fighting? Revulsion from the barbarism of the Nazis was certainly one motivation. On a deeper level, however, there was a sense that the war was a national struggle. For millions of people the war was for the survival of Russia, not necessarily for the defence of communism. No doubt for that reason the regime itself chose to sell the war to the population by using symbols and images from pre-revolutionary Russian history, not socialist bromides. Stalin relaxed ideological controls: the poems, novels, and journalism of the early war years were remarkably free from cant. He also initially put some restraints on the activities of the secret police, and in 1943 permitted the Orthodox Church to re-establish the Patriarchate. Such measures of liberalization encouraged the belief that victory would bring still more substantive reforms. Agents in occupied territories fed these expectations by apparently spreading the rumour that Stalin intended to de-collectivize agriculture as soon as Hitler had been beaten. Nevertheless, millions of ardent communists marched off to war; millions more joined the Communist Party during the war. But most of those who waged war did so not because they wanted to preserve the Soviet Union as it was, but in the hope that it would soon evolve into something better. This is yet another sense in which the war was won despite the Soviet regime.

The Costs of the War

By the time the war was over 8.6 million Soviet troops and at least 17 million civilians had been killed. Twenty-five million survivors were homeless; *zemlianki*, or earthen huts, provided the only shelter for hundreds of thousands. The war had destroyed 1,700 towns, 70,000 villages, 30,000 factories, and 65,000 kilometres of railway. It has been estimated that one-third of the national wealth had been obliterated. The gross yield of all foodstuffs produced in the country in 1945 was only 60 per cent of what it had been in 1940. Still worse,

In 1945–53 the Stalin cult was at its apogee. Stalin's image was ubiquitous as were articles glorifying his genius. This poster of 1950 celebrates Soviet achievements in developing hydroelectric power. Although the poster quotes Lenin's old slogan ('Communism is Soviet power plus the electrification of the entire country') and although it asserts that 'we are advancing towards Communism on the Leninist path', the representation of Stalin leaves no doubt that he, more than anyone else, deserves credit for Soviet economic recovery.

Despite a vigorous anti-religious campaign under Khrushchev and continual persecution over the next two decades, the Orthodox Church continued to draw support and attract large crowds of believers, especially on the high religious holidays. Under perestroika, it enjoyed an extraordinary renaissance, reopened numerous churches and monasteries, and came to occupy a significant public role in the new order.

Coup 1991. People standing on tanks: the euphoria of victory. By midday on Wednesday 21 August it was clear that the tide was turning against the plotters who had attempted to remove President Mikhail Gorbachev in favour of hard-line Gennady Ynnaev, the Vice-President. The pro-democracy forces, led by Russian President Boris Yeltsin, carry the day. By late afternoon the army tank columns begin to leave Moscow.

Conflict in Nagorny Karabakh. Nagorny Karabakh was an enclave, populated overwhelmingly by Armenians, in Azerbaijan which wished to amalgamate with Armenia. On 13 February 1988 the first riots occurred in Nagorny Karabakh, followed by a pogrom of Armenians in Sumgait, Azerbaijan. Moscow imposed special rule but the conflict was not resolved before the collapse of the USSR.

The war devastated Soviet cities, towns, and farms and left the country swarming with millions of homeless refugees. The picture shows Kreshchatyk Street in the centre of Kiev as it appeared in 1943 when the Red Army liberated the Ukrainian capital.

severe drought would visit the harvest of 1946, bringing famine and typhus in its train.

Nevertheless, the Soviet Union had gained power and prestige from the war. Battered at it was, the USSR was the strongest land power left standing on the continent of Europe. In the post-war era, the Soviet Union had to rebuild its economy, while coping with unique opportunities (and dangers) abroad.

Soviet Domestic Policies after the War

First on the agenda was economic reconstruction. Rapid demobilization was essential: the armed forces had to release soldiers, sailors, and airmen for work in the factories and farms. Over 11 million men strong in late 1945, the Red (now Soviet) Army numbered just under three million three years later.

Labour was but one of the factors of production. Another was capital. The state raised money by manipulating its currency, slashing interest rates, and reducing the face value of war bonds. It also showed considerable interest in foreign economic transfers through the continuation of American Lend-Lease, reparations, and exploitation of any territories occupied by the Red Army. In August 1945, however, the Truman administration suspended unconditional Lend-Lease assistance to Russia. Russian expectations for a considerable share of reparations from the western zones of occupied Germany were similarly frustrated (despite the promises that the Soviets felt had been made during the Potsdam Conference in June 1945). In Soviet-held territories matters were

There was a dramatic increase in the population of the Soviet Union's forced labour camps after the war. Perhaps the most brutal camps in the entire system were clustered around the Kolyma river in northeastern Siberia, where hundreds of thousands of prisoners mined gold under conditions of scarcely imaginable horror. Some sense of the suffering of the inmates there can be obtained from the *Kolyma Tales* of Varlaam Shalamov, a survivor. The photograph, taken in 1956, shows the men's camp of Nizhnii Seimchan, no. 6 in Kolyma.

different: Soviet authorities openly looted eastern Germany, Austria, Bulgaria, Romania, and Hungary for machinery and equipment (even entire industrial plants were dismantled and shipped back to the Soviet Union). Indeed, self-collected Soviet reparations are estimated to have provided 3 to 4 per cent of total Soviet budgetary receipts. With regard to Eastern Europe (and eventually Manchuria), the Soviet Union established theoretically 'bilateral joint-stock companies', which provided raw materials, machines, and finished goods at rock-bottom prices.

Because, however, such methods were insufficient to defray the total bill for the recovery, the government resorted to a traditional expedient—squeezing rural society to finance economic expansion. In September 1946 Stalin signed a decree on the 'liquidation of the abuses of the statute of the agricultural artel and collective farm'. This and supplemental laws reduced the size of private plots and levelled confiscatory taxes on the income that they were supposed to generate. Cash payments for daily labour on the collective farms dwindled; in 1952 collective farmers in Tula earned just one kopeck a day. At the same time, the regime burdened the rural population with enormous state delivery quotas for agricultural goods. Compulsory deliveries amounted to at least half the collective farm output of grain, meat, and milk from 1945 to 1948; the prices that the state deigned to pay were actually less than production costs. These extortionate policies led in the short term to the famine of 1946 and to the impoverishment and immiseration of the villages. The result was a new exodus from country to town that, by Stalin's death in 1953, had involved nine million people.

The goal was of course to rebuild the country's industrial base. The Fourth Five-Year Plan (adopted in March 1946) set the target of matching and exceeding pre-war levels of production by the end of 1950. In fact, the Soviet Union fulfilled this plan in most significant sectors; by 1950 gross industrial output exceeded that of 1940 by 40 per cent.

If reconstruction of the economy was a matter of the highest importance, the imposition of stricter domestic political controls was also a priority. Indeed, the screws began to tighten in the last years of the war. One major sign of this was the mass deportation of over a million indigenous people of the Crimea, Caucasus, and Caspian steppe to Kazakhstan and Siberia, ostensibly for collaboration with the Nazis or 'objective characteristics' that predisposed them to do so.

336

The repression might at first seem to make no sense: after all, the war probably expanded the regime's base of popular support. At the very least, the Soviet government could legitimize its claim on power by pointing to its military victory over Nazism. Certainly the Communist Party had never been healthier. The war years also witnessed an explosion in party recruitment—from 3.8 million members in 1941 to 5.7 million by May 1945. By the war's end, 69 per cent of party members had joined since 1942.

But these statistics had to trouble Stalin: the party was his instrument of personal rule. How trustworthy could it be when diluted by hundreds of thousands of new communists admitted under the lax rules and perfunctory screening of wartime? Clearly it would be necessary to purge the party of its slackers and opportunists. Then there was the Soviet military, whose profile at the end of the war was a bit too high for Stalin's taste. To guard against potential 'Bonapartism', Stalin reorganized the High Command, personally assumed the portfolio of Minister of Defence, and conducted a 'purge of the victors', i.e. the arrest or demotion of many prominent officers. Insecurity about the reliability of party and army was therefore one reason behind the political and ideological crack-down.

Another was the civil war on the westernmost borders of the Soviet state. In Ukraine, the Organization of Ukrainian Nationalists and the Ukrainian Insurrectionary Army were conducting full-blown military operations to prevent the reintegration of Ukraine into the USSR. The scale of the problem was immense: at the end of 1945 the Red Army had deployed over half a million troops against the Ukrainian partisans. This armed resistance in Ukraine persisted until well into the 1950s.

Anti-Soviet guerrillas were also active in Estonia, Latvia, and particularly Lithuania. Annexed by Moscow in 1940 and occupied by Germany during the war, the Baltic republics wanted independence, not Soviet communism. Stalin pacified the Baltics by a tradition hallowed in Muscovite history—the forcible exchange of populations. As a result, by 1949 a quarter of the inhabitants of the Baltic states had been 'resettled' to the RSFSR, replaced by ethnic Russians.

In the aftermath of the war, Ukrainian partisans waged a full-blown guerrilla campaign to prevent the reincorporation of Ukraine into the Soviet Union. In this anti-Soviet postcard of 1949, Ukrainian partisans bearing a banner with the slogans 'Freedom to the Peoples! Human Freedom!' trample the Soviet flag and break down the door to the cell in which 'Ukraine' is imprisoned. The device on the building reads: 'The Soviet Union is the prison of the peoples'.

Finally, reconstruction on the scale and at the tempo envisioned by Stalin would have been impossible without the reinstitution of the strict pre-war discipline and police controls. The population had to be mobilized, prepared for additional suffering, and shielded from corrupting Western influence. The imperative for stern internal political control produced a massive propaganda campaign, emphasizing sacrifice and vigilance. It was also expressed in the adoption of internal policies of extraordinary and stunning brutality.

In February 1946 Stalin gave his much quoted 'electoral speech'. This address, which reiterated the old formula that the internal contradictions of capitalism inevitably gave rise to war, baffled those Western politicians who had predicted an era of cordiality with Russia. For Soviet citizens, however, the speech was an unmistakable signal that good relations with the Western allies would not continue in the post-war era, that they were not to expect cultural or political liberalization.

One telling indicator of the retrenchment was the labour-camp population, which swelled by millions after the war. The regime imprisoned hundreds of thousands of displaced persons and so-called 'enemy elements' from the Eastern European and Baltic countries. Axis POWs comprised another major source of prisoners, of whom many remained in captivity until the mid-1950s. German POWs played a conspicuous role in the construction of 'Stalinist teeth'—the ghastly skyscrapers that blighted the Moscow skyline after the war, including the new building of Moscow State University.

The fate of Soviet POWs and slave labourers held by the Nazis was particularly cruel. Approximately a million Soviet prisoners survived the final collapse of Hitler's Reich. Millions of other Soviet citizens, many of them women, were sent to Germany as *Ostarbeiter*. Many of these people were recaptured by the Red Army; the Western allies deported hundreds of thousands of others back to the Soviet Union. There execution or lengthy terms in the camps typically awaited them.

Why did they meet such savage treatment? The repatriated did indeed include some collaborators; between five hundred thousand and one million Soviet citizens, including some POWs, had actually served in the *Wehrmacht*, or in auxiliary or support formations in 1944 and 1945. But Stalin's definition of guilt was capacious enough to include those whose only crime had been to be taken alive: his Order No. 270 early in the war branded any soldiers who surrendered as traitors. Even before the war was over, the Soviet government sent liberated Russian POWs to special camps for 'verification'—which usually ended in consignment to the GULAG. As for the *Ostarbeiter*, Stalin evidently suspected spies to be among them. Even involuntary residence abroad might have left favourable impressions of the West, dangerous if disseminated in Soviet society.

In the cultural sphere, the Central Committee's decision of August 1946 on the journals *Zvezda* and *Leningrad* marked the beginning of the

In the post-war period, Stalin's government changed the urban landscape of Moscow by building a series of 'wedding cake' skyscrapers throughout the city. The new building of Moscow State University, depicted here, was constructed between 1949 and 1953. The central tower is twenty-eight storeys high.

Zhdanovshchina—a xenophobic campaign to purify Soviet intellectual life of Western, bourgeois influences. The campaign derived its name from its organizer, A. A. Zhdanov, one of Stalin's most prominent lieutenants. Making examples of the poet Anna Akhmatova and the satirist Mikhail Zoshchenko, Zhdanov insisted that formalism, political neutrality, and aestheticism had no place in Soviet literature. The literary establishment scampered to conform with the new party line. Scores of dreary novels celebrated the party's victory in the Great Patriotic War, taught hostility to the West, and promoted the materialist and professional values that ostensibly appealed to the mid-level managers, engineers, and technicians who were the essential personnel in rebuilding the country. The purpose of fiction and *belles-lettres* was education and indoctrination, the provision of what Zhdanov woodenly called 'genuine ideological armament'.

Andrei Zhdanov, the party boss of Leningrad, spearheaded Stalin's campaign against Western influences in Soviet culture. In 1946 his attacks on the short-story writer Mikhail Zoshchenko and the poet Anna Akhmatova initiated a period of repression known as the Zhdanovshchina.

It was shortly the turn of the cinema industry. In September 1946 the Central Committee attacked several recent films, including those by the highly regarded directors V. I. Pudovkin and S. M. Eisenstein. The film that brought Eisenstein to grief was his historical epic *Ivan the Terrible, part II*. Stalin had greatly enjoyed the first part in 1944; he may even have identified with its depiction of Ivan IV as a fearless nationalist and decisive leader surrounded by traitorous boyars. But the second part, which showed a doubting, half-crazed tsar unleashing a reign of terror, was too much for the Soviet despot. Eisenstein was compelled publicly to apologize for his mistakes.

Other spheres of thought and culture also underwent ideological purification in the post-war years, from theatre and art to philosophy and economics. Nor was music spared; in February 1948 the party censured such distinguished composers as D. D. Shostakovich, S. S. Prokofiev, and A. I. Khachaturian for 'formalism' and insufficient use of folk themes. Even the natural sciences were not immune from persecution. Thus the expulsion of twelve persons from the Academy of Agricultural Sciences in August 1948 confirmed the triumph of the quack agronomist T. D. Lysenko, whose bizarre theory—that characteristics acquired by an organism in one generation could be genetically transmitted to the next—was utterly incompatible with modern biology and genetics. But the regime embraced Lysenko, whose 'discoveries' held the promise of limitless human power over nature. Soviet agriculture and biological science were to bear the scars of Lysenkoism for years.

Zhdanov died in the summer of 1948, but the cultural repression persisted. In early 1949 the press exposed an 'unpatriotic group of drama critics'. And at the Nineteenth Congress of the Party in 1952, G. M. Malenkov was still insisting that the typicality of a novel's characters bore witness to the correctness of the author's ideological attitude.

Foreign Policy and the Cold War

Wartime alliances almost never persist once the threat that brought them into existence disappears. It is hardly surprising, therefore that the bonds of the Grand Alliance predictably weakened in the aftermath of the war. The deteriorating relationship between the Soviet Union and its former allies soon gave way to the overt hostility of the Cold War. From Washington, it appeared that Stalin was orchestrating a world-wide campaign of aggression against the West. The year 1946 saw Soviet pressure on Turkey over the Dardanelles, a communist insurrection in Greece, and the establishment of Soviet-backed Azeri and Kurdish regimes in northern Iran. Simultaneously the communization of Eastern Europe proceeded apace, culminating in the dramatic Czechoslovak coup of February 1948. Later that same summer, Stalin blockaded the western zones of occupied Berlin. The following year Mao Tse-tung defeated his nationalist enemies and proclaimed the People's Republic of China. And in 1950 Kim Il Sung's forces swarmed across the 38th parallel, touching off the Korean War.

There are, of course, many theories about the origins of the Cold War. Some of the more fanciful blossomed precisely because the dearth of reliable information about the Soviet side made it impossible ultimately to disprove them. Thus while some works argued that Stalin initially sought accommodation with the West and only took the path of confrontation in 1948, others argued the exact reverse—that Stalin was harshest towards the West prior to that date and at his most conciliatory thereafter. Still other studies concluded that Stalin was weaker after the Second World War than before, and accounted for the evolution of Soviet foreign policy largely in terms of domestic politics or the clashing preferences of his subordinates.

With the partial opening of Soviet archives, we now have more evidence than before. The data are, however, far from complete; no definitive interpretation of Soviet foreign relations has yet emerged. The discussion that follows is based on three premises: that Stalin was firmly in charge of international affairs; that he was both an ideologue and a geopolitician; and that two signal post-war objectives were to avoid war while strengthening Soviet control over foreign communist parties.

Stalin was not, in principle, averse to war. In fact, his Marxist *Weltanschauung* predisposed him to believe inevitable armed conflict between the Soviet Union and the capitalist world. In the spring of 1945, as Soviet tanks rolled towards Berlin, he informed a horrified delegation of Yugoslavian communists that 'the war will soon be over. We shall recover in fifteen or twenty years and then we will have another go at it.'

As that comment suggests, Stalin was aware that the Soviet Union was too devastated to wage war in the near future. Then, too, the United States had emerged from the Second World War with greatly increased relative strength and with the atomic bomb. But here was the rub: Soviet ideology made all capitalist regimes *ipso facto* anti-communist. What then would prevent a great capitalist coalition, led by the United States, from exploiting the Soviet Union's temporary debility to launch an annihilating attack? How was Stalin to shield the USSR from such a blow?

The answer was to bluff—to project an exaggerated image of Soviet military might. This entailed denying the West accurate knowledge about the true situation within the Soviet Union by waging a massive counter-intelligence campaign, by prohibiting even the most mundane contacts between Soviet citizens and foreigners, and by severely curtailing the movements and activities of Western diplomats, attachés, journalists, even tourists. Swathed in an impermeable miasma, thought to be possessed of overwhelming military power, the Soviet Union would buy the time necessary to rebuild, rearm, and acquire nuclear weapons. Thus, paradoxically and counter-intuitively, the best way to avoid war was to pretend that the USSR was in fact ready to risk one.

Simultaneously, Stalin had to avoid unnecessarily provoking the West or arousing Western suspicions, but to take a hard line against the plots that the imperialists would surely concoct against the USSR. In 1946, for instance, he backed the Azeri and Kurdish separatists in northern Iran (in response to what he saw as British oil intrigues). His government condemned the Marshall Plan in 1947 and ordered the French and Italian communists to sabotage it. And in June 1948, he retaliated to a Western currency reform (which he thought prefigured the establishment of a capitalist West Germany) by imposing the Berlin blockade.

Yet Stalin was willing to retreat when the price of confrontation grew too high or threatened war. For example, he pulled out of northern Iran, informing the Azeri communists that he did not want to give Britain an excuse to remain in Egypt, Syria, and Indonesia. And after eight months of tension he lifted the blockade of Berlin.

Stalin thus attempted to strike an extremely delicate balance in the conduct of foreign relations, but if successful the Soviet Union might benefit in both the long and short term. After all, Soviet truculence might persuade Western governments that the USSR was too hard a nut to crack. In that event, capitalist states might soon revert to their usual rapacious competition for markets. With any luck, such commercial rivalry might produce internecine wars among the capitalist states, which could debilitate them all, thereby advantageously positioning the USSR for the eventual day of military reckoning.

Another important objective for Stalin was to reimpose discipline and centralized control over the international communist movement. There were several considerations operating here. First, Stalin believed that he alone could formulate the correct strategy and tactics, which should be binding on communists everywhere. His leadership was particularly necessary to prevent headstrong foreign communists from unduly alarming the Western powers. Second, if directed by Moscow, non-ruling communist parties and front groups might pressure Western governments to act in ways favourable to Soviet interests. Third, the maximum economic exploitation of Central, Eastern, and Southeastern Europe would only be possible if communist governments were installed there. Although Stalin might have been delighted by the prospect of further acquisitions in Europe and Asia, these could be forgone. But Eastern Europe was non-negotiable; it was the great prize the Soviet Union had won in the Second World War. The East European countries were to be Sovietized; as Stalin put it, 'whoever occupies a territory also imposes on it his own social system. Everyone imposes his own system as far as his army can reach. It cannot be otherwise.' It goes without saying that Stalin expected the Eastern European communists to submit obediently to his dictation.

The problem, however, was that many foreign communists exhibited an annoying independence. Non-ruling parties were eager to make gains; communists who had seized power in Eastern Europe were often too ideologically fervid to heed Stalin's cautionary advice. The Chinese communists are a good example: despite Stalin's suggestion that they form a coalition with the nationalists, they made a hard push for military victory in the immediate aftermath of the Second World War. Similarly, Stalin opposed the Greek communist insurrection of 1946–8 as premature. The Czechoslovakian coup of February 1948—an event usually interpreted as awakening even the most generous Western observers to Stalin's ambitions—was very likely launched by the Czech communists themselves, not at Moscow's behest. Finally, the Soviet–Yugoslavian rupture of 1948 originated in Stalin's inability to moderate Tito's recklessness either at home or abroad.

Stalin sought to impose his will on the Eastern European communists by a variety of means. One was territorial expansion. A series of post-war treaties annexed large parts of eastern Prussia, eastern Poland, Bessarabia, and Ruthenia to the Soviet state. This westward expansion gave the Soviet Union a common border with its Czechoslovak and Hungarian client states. Another instrument was the Cominform (Communist Information Bureau), established in 1948, specifically to ensure Soviet dominance in Eastern Europe. Finally, after the break with Tito, Stalin resorted to an 'anti-nationalism' campaign of terror and purges. Important communist leaders such as R. Slansky

After his victory over the nationalists in 1949, Mao Tse Tung travelled to Moscow for consultations with J. V. Stalin, the leader of the Communist world. Here Mao attends a reception in honour of Stalin's seventieth birthday. Despite such posed testimonials to Sino-Soviet friendship and despite the conclusion of a treaty of alliance between China and the USSR in February 1950 Stalin and Mao actually disliked and mistrusted each other.

(Czechoslovakia), T. Kostov (Bulgaria), W. Gomulka (Poland), and L. Rajk (Hungary) were imprisoned or executed, as were thousands of others.

Certain elements of Stalin's post-war domestic and foreign agendas were closely interrelated. The key imperatives—war avoidance and economic reconstruction—were obviously congruent. The explosion in the labour camp population also served to fulfil several of Stalin's goals; it mobilized forced labour to rebuild the country and insulated Soviet society from first-hand testimony about the West. And, significantly, Stalin did achieve several key objectives. A robust Soviet economy rose out of the rubble of war; the USSR enhanced its military power. Stalin's regime made significant investments in military research and development, developed a plan to modernize its military hardware, and broke the American nuclear monopoly by acquiring its own atomic bomb in 1949.

Yet it is also obvious that other components in Stalin's programme were contradictory. Bellicose rhetoric, if essential to justify the demands on the Soviet population, invalidated both the Soviet peace offensives as well as efforts to confuse the West about Soviet intentions. The same point applies to efforts to control Eastern Europe. Since Stalin's authority over the foreign communists was at first imperfect, he could not prevent such events as the Greek civil war from frightening Western statesmen. But his own territorial expansion and political terror, used to solidify his power in Eastern Europe, tended to confirm, rather than allay, Western suspicions. The most important contradictions lay in the irreconcilability among Stalin's domestic and foreign objectives. In 1945 Stalin had expected a rapid American withdrawal from a weakened, squabbling Europe. By 1949, largely because of his own policies, he found himself confronting European states that were reacquiring confidence and repairing the damage of war. NATO was cementing Western unity and the United States had extended an open-ended political commitment to the new alliance. After Stalin authorized the Korean War (partially as a subtle bid to enhance his influence with Mao Tse-tung) that American commitment became much more military.

Stalin's Last Years

In December 1949 Stalin celebrated his seventieth birthday. It was an occasion of national jubilation. The price of many consumer goods was lowered. Party and state organizations all over the country vied with each other in tendering gifts and extravagant professions of loyalty to the great leader. A special exhibition—'J. V. Stalin in Representational Art'—opened, featuring scores of paintings and sculptures to glorify every phase of his life. The official review of the exhibition bore the title: 'An Inexhaustible Source of Creative Inspiration'.

The post-war era was the apogee of Stalin's cult of personality. Stalin was accorded god-like veneration: he was the hero of plays and the subject of folk-songs; symphonies and odes were composed in his honour; canals and dams were dedicated to his name. Statues of gypsum, concrete, granite, and marble were erected in his image. Orators praised him as 'the father of the peoples', 'the coryphaeus of all sciences', the 'highest genius of mankind', and 'the best friend of all children'. Rapturous enthusiasm greeted his every pronouncement. When he took it into his head to author a treatise on linguistics, learned philologists wrote letters to the newspapers humbly thanking the leader for setting them straight.

However gratifying, universal adulation did not relax Stalin's vigilant concern for his personal power. In the last years of his reign the tyrant took pains to keep his closest associates in a constant state of poisonous antagonism and mutual suspicion. It is not known whether his motivation was authentic fear of conspiracy, belief in the efficacy of *divide et impera*, or mere perversity. Immediately after the war, Stalin elevated Zhdanov as a counterweight to Malenkov. Upon the former's death, Stalin permitted Malenkov and the chief of the secret police, Beria, to purge Zhdanov's old power base in Leningrad on the charge of 'anti-party activity'. This 'Leningrad affair' resulted in the expulsion of two thousand communists from party and state jobs and two hundred executions, including that of N. A. Voznesenskii, a member of the Politburo. Stalin then summoned N. S. Khrushchev from Ukraine to Moscow as a counterweight to Malenkov. As for Beria, the Georgian purges of 1951 exterminated many of his staunchest supporters and political clients.

The most ominous manifestation of Stalin's mistrust of his subordinates occurred in the very last months of his life. In January 1953 the press announced the arrest of nine physicians for conspiring to assassinate the top Soviet leadership with toxic medical treatments. Anti-Semitism, on the ascent in the USSR since the end of the war, figured prominently in the 'doctor's plot'—seven of the accused were Jewish. The 'plot', it has been speculated, was the first step in a campaign of terror against Jews. In any event, Stalin most probably instigated the affair of the 'doctor murderers' to serve as a pretext for the elimination of Beria, and perhaps other high figures in the regime.

Before any of this could happen, on 5 March 1953 Stalin finally died of a stroke. The official announcement of his passing evoked shock and then grief from millions. The dictator's body reposed in state within the Kremlin, and columns of mourners paid their last respects. Even as a corpse Stalin brought calamity: five hundred people were trampled to death in Moscow because of poor security on the day of his funeral. Stalin was gone, but Stalinism remained. There would ensue a struggle for the succession. And when this was over, Stalin's heirs would undertake the reconstruction and reform of the system he had bequeathed them.

FROM STALINISM TO
STAGNATION
1953–1985

GREGORY L. FREEZE

After 1953, as the structural faults became increasingly
apparent, Stalin's successors applied various panaceas to repair
or conceal the fissures. But neither the spasmodic reformism of
Khrushchev nor the systematic stand-pattism of Brezhnev had
much effect. Despite superpower status abroad and repression at
home, by the early 1980s the USSR—like its leadership—was
tottering on the verge of collapse.

AFTER decades of personalized tyranny, news of Stalin's illness had a traumatic impact on the population. Recalling the recent 'doctors' plot' (with transparent anti-Semitic overtones), some contemporaries suspected that 'the doctors are involved in this. If that is confirmed, then the people will be still more outraged against the Jews.' Many found the idea of life without the all-knowing *Vozhd'* (Leader) unthinkable. Hope of instantaneous justice was gone. As one letter to the Central Committee put it: once Stalin is dead, 'there won't be anyone to complain to. If something happens now, people say: "We'll complain to Comrade Stalin", but now there won't be anyone'.

But there was 'someone', in fact several of them, all fighting to succeed the Leader. That successor, however, would inherit not only the panoply of power but also the other legacy of Stalinist rule: a host of critical problems. These problems unleashed a torrent of letters to newspapers, government organs, and especially the Central Committee.

The problems were daunting in their complexity and gravity. One was power itself: Stalin himself had so personalized power, leaving the lines of institutional authority so amorphous and confused, that many key organs (even the Central Committee) had atrophied and virtually disappeared. To re-establish regular governance, it was essential to rebuild the institutions of party and state administration. Related to this was another grisly legacy—the victims and survivors of the purge and terror. Apart from posthumous rehabilitation, the most urgent question concerned the two million politicals and common criminals currently in the GULAG and still larger numbers in exile and banishment. Stalin's heirs also had to resolve critical economic questions—above all, whether to continue Stalin's one-sided industrialization (which emphasized heavy industry) or to develop agriculture and light industry. The Stalinist model, as one acerbic letter to the Central Committee noted, had produced not communism but 'deficit-ism'. N. S. Khrushchev admitted that 'there is little milk or meat' and asked: 'What kind of communism is this if there are no sweets or butter?' That 'deficitism' exacerbated social tensions, for it did not apply to everyone. Stalinist social policy had vigorously combatted 'levelling' (*uranilovka*) in favour of sharp wage differentials and a highly stratified social order, with scarce resources being diverted to political élites and the scientific-technical intelligentsia. A letter to the Central Committee complained bitterly that 'of late our country has simply forgotten the simple person—the worker, the kolkhoznik. All that the press and radio talk about is the academicians, scholars, agronomists, engineers'. Another critical domestic issue was minority tensions, especially in the newly annexed territories of the West. As authorities confirmed, 'in many districts [of western Ukraine] an anti-Soviet nationalist underground still exists and is actively operating as armed bands that commit sabotage, plunder, and terrorize the population and party-Soviet activists'.

In foreign policy Stalin's heirs faced another knot of difficult questions—

from the Korean War and Maoist pretensions to the infernal 'German Question' and Tito's challenge in Yugoslavia. Resolutions of these problems also had major domestic implications, above all for the military budget, which consumed an inordinate share of national income. Even the 'official' military budget of 1952 (a pale reflection of reality) revealed a 45 per cent increase since 1950. Clearly, a regime seeking to modernize its economy could ill afford to divert so many resources—capital, labour—to so unproductive a sector.

Historical scholarship on the post-Stalinist period is still in its infancy. Until recently most literature belonged to the genre of 'Kremlinology'—a mélange of inferences and wild guesses based on party propaganda, diplomatic gossip, distorted statistics, and symbolic gestures. Recently, however, Russian authorities have declassified materials from the super-secret 'Kremlin Archive' (renamed 'Presidential Archive') and from the operational files of the Central Committee. This chapter draws heavily upon these materials. It aims to present a fresh portrait of the Khrushchev and Brezhnev eras—named after two men who symbolize two different approaches to salvaging Stalin's legacy: reform and retrenchment. By the early 1980s, however, it was obvious that neither had worked.

Perils of Reform

The first decade after Stalin's death was marked by change so profound that perceptive observers began to question the static 'totalitarian' model that still shaped Cold War policy towards the Soviet Union. That decade was an era of frenetic reformism not only in the political system but also in society, economy, culture, and nationality policy. It was also a time of excesses and errors, which Khrushchev's critics attributed to his boorishness, his penchant for 'harebrained schemes', and his reckless search for panaceas. The ill-repute of the Khrushchev era was so intense that, in the days of perestroika, even reformers were loath to invoke his name or reconsider his strategies. In that sense, perhaps the worst legacy of Khrushchevism was not that reform failed, but that it deterred new attempts until it was too late.

THE STRUGGLE FOR SUCCESSION

On the evening of 5 March, two hours before Stalin's death, his heirs met in the Kremlin to assign spheres of power. The most prominent appointments included Georgii Malenkov (Stalin's heir apparent) as chairman of the Council of Ministers, Lavrentii Beria as head of the Ministry of Interior (reorganized to include the Ministry of State Security), and Viacheslav Molotov as Foreign Minister. After a bizarre incident involving *Pravda* (which published a self-serving photomontage of Malenkov, ostensibly without his knowledge), on 14 March Malenkov resigned as ranking secretary in the Central Committee and assumed leadership of the state apparatus. Power in the Central Committee now devolved on Khrushchev, who eventually (September 1953) assumed the title of 'First Secretary'.

Initially, at least, Khrushchev seemed an unlikely pretender for power: he did not even speak at Stalin's funeral, an honour reserved for the big three—Malenkov, Beria, and Molotov. None the less, Khrushchev was the consummate party functionary, bore the imprimatur of a top-ranking Stalin aide, and had close ties throughout the party apparatus. He also had extraordinary sang-froid and the capacity to speak effectively; his role at the Central Committee plenums, in particular, shows a self-confident *'apparatchik's apparatchik'*. But he also knew how to relate to the common folk; an incorrigible populist, he loved to visit factories and kolkhozy to see conditions for himself. Khrushchev had a genuine concern for popular welfare. As Ukrainian party secretary, in 1947 he had even had the temerity to resist Stalin's unreasonable demands for grain deliveries that ignored crop failure and famine—an act of defiance that earned a furious Stalinist epithet of 'populist' and temporary replacement by L. M. Kaganovich. By the end of the year, however, Khrushchev was reinstated as Ukrainian First Secretary and subsequently, in December 1949, summoned to Moscow as a secretary of the Central Committee and First Secretary of the Moscow party committee.

Beria, with the vast forces of the Interior Ministry and secret police at his command, was the most formidable contender. Recent archival disclosures have shown that, whether from conviction or cunning, Beria suddenly struck the pose of 'liberal' reformer. Within days of Stalin's death, he not only spoke of the need to protect civil rights but even arranged an amnesty on 27 March that released many prisoners (too many common criminals, in Khrushchev's view), including some people associated with the élite (for example, Molotov's wife, Mikoyan's son, and Khrushchev's own daughter-in-law). Beria also shifted the GULAG from his own domain and later proposed that it be liquidated 'in view of its economic inefficiency and lack of prospects'. He also exposed some major fabrications in late Stalinism, most notably the 'doctors' plot' (4 April) and also proposed to release 58,000 former 'counter-revolutionaries' from permanent exile. The security chief even challenged the policy of Russian predominance in non-Russian republics; heeding Beria's recommendation, on 12 June 1953 the party leadership agreed to condemn various 'distortions', to replace officials who did not speak the local language, and to require the use of the local language in republican communications. Beria also took an interest in foreign affairs, proposing to allow a unified (but neutral) Germany and to seek a *rapprochement* with Yugoslavia.

United by fear if not principle, Beria's adversaries called a meeting of the Presidium on 26 June 1953 and, in his presence, voted unanimously for his immediate dismissal and arrest. Shortly afterwards they convened a plenum of the Central Committee to discuss the 'criminal anti-party and anti-state activities of

Beria'. An opening address by Malenkov gave a vivid description of how Beria 'put the Ministry of Interior above the party and government', with the result that the ministry 'acquired too great an influence and was no longer under the control of the party'. Malenkov also castigated Beria's new-found liberalism (in particular, his mass amnesty of criminals and proposals for a radical change in policy towards Germany and Yugoslavia) and denounced his maladroit attempts to gather information on 'shortcomings in the work of party organs' and even to maintain surveillance on members of the Presidium. The second main address was delivered by Khrushchev, who reiterated the attack on Beria's belated liberalism and bluntly accused the police of fabricating 'many falsified cases'. Six months later Beria and five of his close associates were tried, pronounced guilty, and shot.

The principal threat eliminated, the main contenders were the two main speakers at the July plenum—Malenkov and Khrushchev. At one level, the two simply manœuvred to broaden their respective political bases—Malenkov in the state apparatus, Khrushchev in the party. But they also raised important issues, especially questions of economic development and agricultural policy. Malenkov proposed a 'liberal' policy giving greater emphasis to light industry, chiefly by diverting resources from agriculture; in his view, the regime had 'solved' the production problem and could rely on an intensification of production (i.e. mechanization, electrification, and increased use of mineral fertilizers). In response Khrushchev challenged the emphasis on consumer goods and,

Khrushchev never tired of personal visits to collective farms and plants to meet the people and see things for himself. Here he is shown visiting the I. Pavlov State Farm in Kazakhstan (part of the Virgin Lands campaign) in 1956.

To commemorate the tricentenary of the 'reunification' of Ukraine and Russia in 1954, Moscow transferred the Crimea from the Russian Federation to the Ukrainian SSR. This photograph shows the holiday demonstration in Voroshilovgrad on 23 May 1954. Interestingly, notwithstanding Khrushchev's early attempts to dismantle the 'cult of personality', the demonstrators carried prominent photographs of not only Lenin, but also Stalin.

especially, Malenkov's cheerful assumption that the agricultural question was 'solved'. Khrushchev proposed to increase, not cut, investment in the agricultural sector, above all through the 'Virgin Lands' programme—an ambitious scheme to convert huge tracts of pastureland in southern Siberia and Kazakhstan to arable land. By shifting wheat production to the Virgin Lands, the Ukraine could grow the corn needed to provide fodder for greater meat and milk production.

Khrushchev's programme, however, proved a hard sell in the party. Investment in agriculture (a radical break from Stalin's utter neglect) encountered stiff opposition from conservatives in the centre, especially the 'metal-eaters' in heavy industry; it also elicited opposition from Central Asians, who feared wind erosion, Moscow's intervention and control, and a mass influx of Russians. By August 1954, however, the First Secretary had prevailed: a joint party-government decree endorsed the Virgin Lands programme and raised the target for newly cultivated land from 13 million to 30 million hectares by 1956. Blessed with unusually good weather, the Virgin Lands programme initially brought huge increases in agricultural output (a 35.3 per cent increase between 1954 and 1958), causing the ebullient Khrushchev to make the foolhardy prediction that in two or three years the Soviet Union could satisfy all its food needs.

Simultaneously, Khrushchev declared war on 'bureaucracy'. In part, he was seeking to undermine Malenkov's power base—the state apparatus, which was indeed bloated (with 6.5 million employees by 1954). But Khrushchev, the former provincial party chief, also recognized the need to decentralize and shift power and responsibility to the republic level. As a result, by 1955 he had cut the number of Union-level ministries in half (from 55 to 25) and state employees (by 11.5 per cent). This decentralization significantly enhanced the authority of national republics; for example, enterprises under republic control rose from one-third of total industrial output (1950) to 56 per cent (1956). The shift was especially marked in Ukraine, where the republic-controlled output rose from 36 to 76 per cent.

By late 1954 Khrushchev's programme, and its main architect, had triumphed over Malenkov. The latter, defeated on policy issues and confronted with ominous references to his 'complicity' in fabricating the 'Leningrad affair', resigned in December 1954. Two months later, he was formally replaced by N. Bulganin as premier, Khrushchev's nominal co-equal in the leadership.

CULTURAL 'THAW' AND DE-STALINIZATION

Amid the struggle over power and policy, the regime cautiously began to dismantle the Stalinist system of repression and secrecy. Symbolically, in late 1953 it opened the Kremlin itself to visitors; during the next three years, eight million citizens would visit this inner sanctum of communist power. Openness also extended to culture, hitherto strait-jacketed by censorship and ideology. The change was heralded in V. Pomerantsev's essay 'On Sincerity in Literature' (December 1953), which assailed the Stalinist canons of socialist realism that had prevailed since the 1930s. Thus began a cautious liberalization that took its name from Ilia Ehrenburg's novel *The Thaw* (1954), and that extended to many spheres of cultural and intellectual life. It even applied to religion—long a favourite target of persecution; a party edict of 10 November 1954, responding to complaints about illegal church closings, admonished party zealots to avoid 'offensive attacks against clergy and believers participating in religious observances'.

The most important change, however, was crypto-de-Stalinization—a cautious repudiation of the 'cult of personality' that commenced immediately after Stalin's death. The initiative came from above, not below. Not that all in the leadership supported such measures; Stalin's henchmen, such as Voroshilov and Kaganovich, themselves deeply implicated, remained inveterate foes of de-Stalinization. Apart from some early veiled critiques (for example, Malenkov's comment about 'massive disorders' under the 'cult of personality'), the principal sign of Stalin's 'disgrace' was sheer silence about the leader. For example, the regime declined to 'immemorialize' Stalin by renaming the Komsomol in his honour, dropped plans to transform Stalin's 'near dacha' into a museum, and let 1953 pass without mention of the 'Stalin prizes' or the customary celebration of his birthday. Servile quotations from Stalin quietly disappeared; authors who persisted were roundly criticized for ignoring Marx and Lenin. The silence did not go unnoticed; in July a party secretary in Moscow wrote to Khrushchev to enquire 'Why have editorials in *Pravda* recently ceased to include quotations and extracts from the speeches and works of I. V. Stalin?'

Why did Stalin's closest associates decide to demote the Leader to a Non-person? Apart from a desire to distance themselves from Stalin's (and their own) crimes, de-Stalinizers had several motives. Zealous 'de-Stalinizers' (including Khrushchev) were zealous communists: they denounced the cult for its voluntarism and for crediting Stalin, not the party or people, for the great achievements of industrialization and victory over fascism. That is why, for example, authorities decided to interdict a poem by A. Markov that failed to show the people as the 'creative force in history' and assigned 'the main place in the poem' to Stalin, who is 'shown in the spirit of the cult of personality'. In a memorandum of 27 April 1953 the philosopher G. A. Aleksandrov denounced the cult and opposed reprinting the Stalin biography—partly because of its 'many factual inaccuracies and editorial mistakes', but mainly because of its 'populist-subjectivist view on the role of the individual and especially of leaders in history' and because of its failure 'to elucidate sufficiently the role of the Central Committee of the Communist Party in the struggle of the Soviet people for socialism and communism'. Khrushchev similarly complained that Stalin had been 'a demigod', who 'was credited with all accomplishments, as if all blessings came from him'.

Zealous de-Stalinizers, moreover, had personally experienced Stalin's fearsome tyranny. Close family members of Stalin's top associates were counted among his victims—kinsmen, even immediate family members, of members in the Politburo. Post-war campaigns like the 'Leningrad affair' swept away top figures in the party, leaving many others feeling profoundly vulnerable. The philosopher Aleksandrov himself had been a victim of the 'anti-cosmopolitan' campaign: after A. A. Zhdanov denounced his history of Western philosophy (for exaggerating West European influence on Marxism) in June 1947, Aleksandrov was replaced as ideological watchdog by M. A. Suslov. In Stalin's final years top aides grew fearful that the dictator had new designs on them; according to Khrushchev, only the dictator's death prevented him from carrying out plans to arrest Molotov and Mikoyan.

Khrushchev himself had reason to fear the ageing tyrant. The most dramatic incident involved Khrushchev's proposal to increase agricultural output by merging kolkhozy into larger 'agrocities'. He advertised this idea in a *Pravda* article on 4 March 1951, but without first obtaining Stalin's endorsement—probably because Stalin no longer read many documents. After Stalin subjected the article to devastating criticism, a terror-stricken Khrushchev hastily sent Stalin a letter of abject self-abasement and pleaded for the opportunity to denounce himself: 'Profoundly distraught by the mistake I committed, I have been thinking how this could best be corrected. I decided to ask you to let me correct this mistake myself. I am prepared to publish in the press and to criticize my own article, published on 4 March, examining its false theses in detail'.

Khrushchev and his supporters also addressed the question of the cult's victims and initiated a cautious rehabilitation, beginning first with élite figures. A typical early case involved I. M. Gronskii, a former editor of *Izvestiia*; sentenced to fifteen years in prison for 'wrecking', in June 1953 he petitioned the Central Committee to review his case. An investigation confirmed that his 'confession' was obtained through coercion and that he was innocent. In May 1954 the party established special commissions to review the cases; during the first year, these cautious commissions rehabilitated 4,620 individuals, leaving the mass of politicals—and ordinary criminals—in the maws of GULAG.

Apart from appeals for rehabilitation, the regime had other reasons for concern about GULAG. Above all, this prison empire became increasingly volatile, with frequent and violent disorders. The most famous, at 'Gorlag' (Norilsk) in 1953, required a military assault that left more than a thousand prisoners dead. Insurrections also exploded at Steplag (1954), Kolyma (1955), and Ozerlag (1956). More important, the 'corrective labour' system was anything but corrective: rates of recidivism were shockingly high. According to one study (April 1956), 25 per cent of current prisoners were former inmates. But such results were inevitable for a system manned by people with abysmally low professional standards: three-quarters of the camp administrators did not even have a secondary education. The size and complexity of GULAG also militated against better results. The population of camps and prisons (2,472,247 on 1 January 1953) declined after the Beria amnesty, but then increased sharply. On 1 January 1956 the prisons held 1.6 million inmates (with another 150,000 in transit or under investigation); GULAG's 46 corrective labour camps and 524 labour colonies held another 940,880 people (including 113,739 guilty of 'counter-revolutionary activity'). In short, initial measures had barely altered the Stalinist prison-camp system; it was the Twentieth Party Congress that would open the floodgates for rehabilitation and reform.

TWENTIETH PARTY CONGRESS (1956)

The first such assembly since Stalin's death, the Twentieth Party Congress was a watershed in the political history of modern Russia. It sought to revitalize the party by including many new faces, not only among the 1,349 voting delegates, but also in the leadership: roughly half of the *oblast* and regional secretaries, even the Central Committee, were new. That turnover reflected Khrushchev's campaign to consolidate power: one-third of the members of the Central Committee came from Khrushchev's Moscow and Ukrainian 'tail' or entourage. The congress began in humdrum fashion, with little hint of the coming fireworks; Khrushchev's report as First Secretary made only passing reference to Stalin. Critical tones, however, reverberated in the speeches of M. Suslov (about the 'cult of the individual') and Anastas Mikoyan (who attacked the cult and Stalin's last opus, *The Economic Problems of Socialism in the USSR*).

But the bombshell exploded unexpectedly on 24 February, when delegates were summoned to an unscheduled, late-night speech by Khrushchev behind closed doors. His speech on 'the cult of the personality and its consequences', a text of 26,000 words requiring four hours for delivery, offered a devastating account of Stalin's crimes after Kirov's murder in December 1934. It presented shocking statistics on the number of party members, congress delegates, and military leaders who perished in the 1930s amid 'mass violations of socialist legality'. The report also blamed Stalin for catastrophic mistakes in the Second World War, for the mass deportation of entire peoples, and for other crimes after the war. By suggesting that the cult appeared after collectivization and industrialization (which were thus not called into question), Khrushchev sought to distinguish between Stalin's crimes and Soviet achievements and to uphold the principle that 'the true creators of the new life are the popular masses led by the Communist Party'. The main thrust of the speech was incorporated in a Central Committee resolution of 30 June 1956 'On Overcoming the Cult of the Individual and its Consequences'.

By then the rehabilitation process was already in high gear. The regime advised investigatory commissions that many convictions were based on unproven accusations or 'confessions obtained through the use of illegal methods of investigation'. Nevertheless, it exempted whole categories from rehabilitation: 'nationalists' in Ukraine, Byelorussia, and the Baltics who had fought against the Soviet Union during the war as well as those 'who were really exposed as traitors, terrorists, saboteurs, spies and wreckers'. To accelerate the process, a party commission was sent to interview political prisoners and judge whether they should be released. The undertaking was enormous, involving more than one hundred thousand 'counter-revolutionaries'. According to a report from 15 June 1956, authorities had already released 51,439 prisoners (including 26,155 politicals) and reduced the sentences for another 19,093. Although restricted to cases initiated after 1935 (on the specious grounds that 'mass violation of individual rights' commenced only then), by 1961 rehabilitation gradually enveloped a large number of Stalin's victims, including half of the politicals who had been executed.

De-Stalinization was also fraught with foreign repercussions. Khrushchev's secret speech, leaked by a Polish communist, quickly found its way into print (with the assistance of the American CIA). It had an extraordinary impact on foreign communists—many of whose comrades-in-arms had perished in the Stalinist repressions. In April 1956 the *Pravda* correspondent in Bonn reported that West German communists reacted favourably to the speech, yet wanted to know why the CPSU had failed to stop Stalin and, more important, 'where is the guarantee that the Soviet comrades will not again make mistakes and bring harm to the fraternal parties through their new mistakes?' Khrushchev personally had to fend off similar questioning from Italian communists. The attack on Stalin also contributed to the rebellious mood in Poland, where demonstrations in Poznan ended in bloodshed and brought a change in party leadership.

The main explosion came in Hungary: in late April 1956 the Soviet ambassador, Iurii Andropov, warned Moscow that de-Stalinization had exacerbated internal tensions and provoked criticism from Stalinists in the Hungarian Politburo. By September Andropov's dispatches became increasingly alarmist, with warnings about an anti-communist movement and disintegration of the Hungarian Communist Party. The popular movement culminated in street demonstrations on 23 October, when angry crowds smashed Stalinist statues and shouted demands for democratization and the withdrawal of Soviet troops. The next day the Hungarian party elected Imre Nagy as its chief, and he promptly summoned Andropov to ask about Soviet troop movements in eastern Hungary. The denouement came soon: after Hungary declared itself a neutral state, on 4 November the Russian army invaded and suppressed the popular insurrection with raw force. A week later the KGB chief reported that Soviet forces had arrested 3,773 'counter-revolutionaries' and seized 90,000 firearms.

The attack on Stalin also had reverberations inside the USSR. Rehabilitation involved such vast numbers that even Khrushchev became anxious. Thus, to protect 'state interests' and understate the scale of repression, the KGB falsely informed relatives that many of the executed had received sentences of hard labour and died of natural causes. More problematic was the fate of entire peoples deported to Siberia and Central Asia for alleged collaboration—such as the Karachai, Chechens, Ingushi, Kabardinians, and Balkars. Although the government began in April 1956 to allow certain groups (the main exceptions being the Volga Germans and Crimean Tatars) to return home, repatriation created new problems of its own when returnees demanded restitution of property. The result was fierce ethnic conflict, such as the four-day riot in August 1958 that involved Russians, Chechens, and Ingushi.

But the political resonance from de-Stalinization was muted in Russia. A KGB report on 'anti-Soviet' activities during celebrations for the October Revolution in 1956 cited only minor incidents—for example, 'hooligans' demolished two sculptures of Stalin in Kherson, shredded photographs of party leaders in Sevastopol, defaced a portrait of Khrushchev in Serpukhov, and disseminated anti-Soviet leaflets in Batumi. The action of a tenth-grade student in Iaroslavl (who marched past the tribune with a banner that read: 'We demand the removal of Soviet troops from Hungary') was as unique as it was courageous. Nevertheless, the 'vigilant' leaders became anxious and on 14 December 1956 approved the proposals of a special commission (chaired by L. I. Brezhnev) to combat the growth of anti-Soviet sentiments and activities. The next year the KGB crushed a student democratic movement at Moscow State University that, under the leadership of L. Krasnopevtsev, had distributed leaflets and agitated in favour of full-scale democratization. In Archangel the police uncovered a tiny group that categorically repudiated the Stalinist legacy: 'Stalin, having destroyed his personal adversaries, established a fascist autocratic regime in the USSR, the brutality of which has no equals in history'.

All this galvanized Stalinists to oppose Khrushchev and his policies. Although Khrushchev later claimed to have broad support in the party, many party members—including several members of the Politburo—opposed de-Stalinization. Stalwarts like A. M. Peterson of Riga openly challenged the new policy: 'Comrades in the Central Committee, do you really not feel that the party expects from you a rehabilitation of Stalin?' Pro-Stalinist sentiments were particularly strong in Stalin's home republic of Georgia; news of Khrushchev's secret speech had even ignited street demonstrations in Tbilisi.

The foreign and domestic turbulence impelled Khrushchev to retreat from a public campaign against Stalin, with the rationalization that the 'people' were not yet ready for the new line. Although individual rehabilitations continued, the regime took steps to curtail debate and criticism of Stalin. A telling sign of the change was the famous 'Burdzhalov' affair in October 1956 involving a historical journal (*Voprosy istorii*), which had published revelations about Stalin's role in 1917 and subsequent falsification in Soviet historiography. By reprimanding the chief editor and cashiering the assistant editor (E. N. Burdzhalov, the principal culprit), the regime made clear that it would not tolerate anything that might delegitimize the revolution and its own claims to power.

The zig-zags in policy aroused confusion and criticism from below. Local party officials quoted one member as complaining that 'the leaders of party and state have become muddled in criticizing the cult of personality of Stalin: at first they condemned him, but now they have started to praise him again'. In January 1957 an engineer wrote to the Central Committee to complain that 'there are two N. S. Khrushchevs in the Central Committee of CPSU: the first N. S. Khrushchev with complete [adherence to] Leninist principles directly exposes and wages battle against the personality of Stalin; the second N. S. Khrushchev defends the actions of Stalin that he personally perpetrated against the people and party during his twenty years of personal dictatorship'. Individual rehabilitation continued, but Khrushchev now turned his attention from de-Stalinization to political and administrative reform.

DEMOCRATIZATION AND DECENTRALIZATION

The years 1957–61 marked the apogee of Khrushchev's attempt at structural reform along two main lines. One was 'democratization', a campaign to dislodge an entrenched bureaucracy and to shift responsibility directly to 'the people'. Khrushchev was the consummate populist, fond of hobnobbing with workers and peasants and flaunting his closeness to the people. He was also profoundly suspicious of 'bureaucrats' and 'partocrats' (party functionaries). And their numbers were legion; as a Central Committee resolution (21 May 1957) acidly observed, since 1940 primary party organizations had increased twofold, but their number of salaried functionaries had grown fivefold. To combat bureau-cratization and ensure 'fresh forces', Khrushchev applied term limits not only to regional and *oblast* secretaries (two-thirds of whom were replaced between 1955 and 1960), but even to those in élite organs: two-thirds of the Council of Ministers and one-half of the Central Committee changed between 1956 and 1961. The objective, as a party resolution explained in 1957, was to eradicate the cult of personality and 'ensure the broad participation of the working masses in the management of the state'. This also meant an expansion of party member-ship, which increased from 6.9 million to 11.0 million members between 1954 and 1964 (60 per cent of whom were listed as workers and peasants in 1964). Khrushchev also sought to expand the people's role in running the state—for example, by increasing the authority of organs of 'popular control' and reviving 'comrade courts' to handle minor offences and misdemeanours.

The second, related thrust of reform was decentralization—a perennial Russian panacea for solving problems and inciting initiative at the grass roots. By 1955 Khrushchev had already transferred 11,000 enterprises (along with planning and financial decisions) from central to republican control. Moscow went further in May 1956, reassigning the plants of twelve ministries to republic jurisdiction. The capstone to decentralization came in 1957 with the establishment of sovnarkhozy—105 regional economic councils given compre-hensive authority over economic development. Republican authorities gained so much power that their prime ministers became ex officio members of the USSR Council of Ministers. Khrushchev also dismantled much of the old bureaucracy (including 140 ministries at the republic, union-republic, and union levels). The underlying idea was to bring decision-making closer to the enterprise to ensure better management and greater productivity.

Decentralization, together with resentment over de-Stalinization, fuelled growing opposition to Khrushchev. Although Khrushchev had strong support in the Central Committee (where republic and provincial secretaries—the main beneficiaries of reform—dominated), he faced stiff opposition in the ruling Presidium. The latter represented old party élites and entrenched officialdom in Moscow, who not only watched their empires shrivel or disappear, but some-times had to relocate to a provincial site. When, for example, Khrushchev relo-cated the main offices of the Ministry of Agriculture 100 km. from Moscow (to be closer to the fields!), top officials had a daily commute of two to three hours in each direction.

One month after the sovnarkhoz reform was promulgated, Khrushchev faced a full-blown revolt in the Presidium. On 18 June his nominal co-equal, Bulganin, asked Khrushchev to convene a meeting of the Presidium, where a majority was prepared to vote his dismissal. Khrushchev, however, insisted that only the body that elected him—the Central Committee—could authorize his dismissal; with the assistance of military aircraft (supplied by his ally, Marshal Zhukov), Khrushchev flew Central Committee members from their provincial posts to Moscow. His adversaries in the Presidium finally agreed to convene a special plenum of the Central Committee. The result was a complete rout of Khrushchev's opponents, who were denounced as 'the Anti-Party Group' and their leaders (Malenkov, Kaganovich, and Molotov) expelled from the Central Committee. The new Presidium included critical supporters, such as Marshal Zhukov, and high-level functionaries like L. I. Brezhnev and A. I. Kosygin who would later have Khrushchev himself removed. Although, for the sake of appearances, Bulganin was allowed temporarily to remain head of the state, in March 1958 Khrushchev assumed his post as chief of state.

Having tamed the opposition, Khrushchev next dealt with his key supporter—Marshal Zhukov. The latter had begun to voice the military's dissatisfaction with Khrushchev's decision to scale down the army (from 5.8 million in 1950 to 3.6 million in 1960) and to deny costly weapons systems (cutting the military's share of the budget in 1956 from 19.9 per cent to 18.2 per cent). On 29 October 1957, just a few weeks after the spectacular launch of the world's first artificial satellite *Sputnik* (4 October), a party resolution denounced Zhukov for restricting its role in the army (thereby 'violating Leninist party principles') and for propagating 'a cult of Comrade G. K. Zhukov ... with his personal complicity'. The last major political counterpoint to Khrushchev appeared to have been removed.

ECONOMY, SOCIETY, AND CULTURE

The late 1950s represented the golden age for the Khrushchev economy, which boasted extraordinarily high rates of growth in the industrial and agricultural sectors. Altogether, the annual rate of growth in the GNP increased from 5.0 per cent in 1951–5 to 5.9 per cent in 1956–60 (the Fifth Five-Year Plan). The most spectacular progress was to be found in the industrial sector: the total growth (80 per cent) even exceeded the ambitious plan target (65 per cent). In 1987 Soviet analysts revealed that this was by far the most successful industrial growth of the whole post-Stalinist era. With labour productivity rising by 62 per cent and the return on assets ('profit') amounting to 17 per cent, the Soviet economy made enormous strides. The launching of the satellite *Sputnik* seemed to demonstrate the might, if not superiority, of the Soviet system. As Soviet industrial production increased from 30 to 55 per cent of American output between 1950 and 1960, Khrushchev seemed to have good ground for his bravado about 'overtaking and surpassing' America.

Agriculture, the unloved stepchild of Stalinist economics, became a new focus of development. The policy yielded immediate results, as output increased 35.3 per cent (1954–8); the 'Virgin Lands' programme opened up an additional 41.8 million hectares of arable land, which produced high yields and a spectacular bumper crop in 1958. Altogether, the average annual output between 1949–53 and 1959–63 increased by 43.8 million tons (28.9 million tons of which came from the virgin lands). Not only gross output but productivity was higher:

the yield per hectare rose from 7.7 centners (100 kg.) per hectare (1949–53) to 9.1 (1954–8). Encouraged by this success, Khrushchev cut back the investment in agriculture (its share of investment falling from 12.8 per cent in 1958 to 2.4 per cent in 1960), on the assumption that the virgin lands would sustain large harvests. He also forced kolkhozniki to grow more maize, though at the expense of other grains (oats production, for example, fell by two-thirds). And he applied decentralization to agriculture, chiefly by liquidating 'machine tractor stations' (January 1958) and undercutting the power of party bureaucrats.

'Democratization' also meant a higher standard of living for ordinary citizens—a rather unexpected policy, given Khrushchev's earlier criticism of Malenkov for 'consumerism'. There was much social inequity to overcome: because of Stalinist wage differentials, the 'decile coefficient' (the official standard for income distribution, measured as the difference between the ninth and first deciles) was 7.2 in 1946—far higher than that in capitalist countries (the comparable figure for Great Britain in the 1960s was 3.6). Resentment against the privileged informed this anonymous letter to the Komsomol in December 1956: 'Please explain why they babble (if one may so speak) about the well-being of the people, but there is really nothing of the sort; things are getting worse—and worse for us than in any capitalist country'. The letter derided the endless radio propaganda about progress towards communism: 'You [party élites] of course have communism; we have starvationism, inflationism, and exploitationism of the simple working people'. A letter from eleven workers in Lithuania ridiculed state propaganda 'that people live badly under the capitalists' and declared that the common people live worse in the USSR, that 'this is not socialism, but just a bordello (*bardak*) and hard labour'.

Khrushchev took important steps to improve popular well-being. One was a revolution in labour policy: he decriminalized absenteeism and turnover, made drastic reductions in wage differentials, and established a minimum wage. After fixing a 'poverty line', the regime reduced the number below this limit from 100 million in 1958 to only 30 million a decade later. As a result, the decile coefficient dropped from the Stalinist 7.2 (1946) to 4.9 (1956) and then to 3.3 (1964). Considerable improvements were made among the lowest-paid segments of society—rural labour: between 1960 and 1965, the average income of kolkhozniki rose from 70 to 80 per cent of the average-paid state employees. Although the kolkhoznik remained a second-class citizen (without pensions, sickness benefits, or even a passport), his material condition had improved significantly.

Khrushchev also increased social services, housing, and educational opportunities. Expenditure on social services increased by only 3 per cent in 1950–5, but rose by 8 per cent in 1956–65. As a result, the housing stock doubled between 1955 and 1964; although built mostly as the notorious 'Khrushchev barracks' (with low ceilings, tiny rooms, and shoddy construction), it was a serious response to the housing shortage and rapid urbanization. Notwithstanding

The rapid pace of housing construction, together with the strong penchant for shoddy workmanship (*khaltura*), led to poor quality that became standard fare for the leading journal of caricature, *Krokodil*. When one speaker observes that 'this building looks as though it has never been renovated', the other replies that 'this is absolutely correct—it was just built'.

the ideological antipathy towards 'private ownership', in 1955 the regime launched a programme to construct privately owned flats from personal savings (with a down-payment of 15–30 per cent and a mortgage with 0.5 per cent interest rate). The Khrushchev regime also 'democratized' the educational system: dismayed that 80 per cent of all university students were coming from the intelligentsia, in 1958 Khrushchev abolished school and university tuition fees and dramatically restructured secondary schooling to force all children into the labour force for two years to learn a trade.

Although decentralization abetted the special interests of individual nationalities, Khrushchev detested 'petty-bourgeois nationalism'. That attitude clearly informed school language policy, where Moscow took steps to promote Russian language instruction. This policy elicited considerable opposition from minority nationalities; a Belorussian complained in 1956 that his 'language has now been expelled from all state and Soviet institutions and institutions of higher learning in the republic'. The main objective was not simply closer ties (*sblizhenie*), but the assimilation (*sliianie*) of small nations into Soviet Russian culture.

TWENTY-SECOND PARTY CONGRESS (OCTOBER 1961)

The 'extraordinary' Twenty-First Party Congress of 1959 dealt with primarily economic questions (including a scheme to restructure the five-year plan into a seven-year plan), but otherwise did not mark a significant event. That could hardly be said of the Twenty-Second Party Congress, attended by some 4,400 voting delegates. Above all, it signalled a new and open offensive against Stalinism. Khrushchev himself implicated Stalin in Kirov's murder and suggested that several leading cadres (Kaganovich, Molotov, and Voroshilov) personally abetted Stalin in perpetrating the crimes. The Congress also raised the question of Stalin's mummified corpse, which since 1953 had rested alongside Lenin in the Mausoleum. This time the party was blessed with instructions from the next world, kindly transmitted by a deputy from Leningrad, D. A. Lazurkina: 'Yesterday I asked Ilich [Lenin] for advice and it was as if he stood before me alive and said, "I do not like being beside Stalin, who inflicted so much harm on the party".' The congress resolved to remove Stalin because of his 'serious violations of Leninist precepts, his abuse of power, his mass repressions of honest Soviet people, and his other actions during the cult of personality'. The former dictator was reburied in an unmarked grave along the Kremlin wall.

The congress also adopted a new party programme, the first since 1919. It included brash predictions that the Soviet Union would surpass the United States by 1970 and complete the construction of communism by 1980. It also included new rules to ensure 'democratization' in the party and preclude the formation of a vested bureaucratic class. It also called for 'the active participation of all citizens in the administration of the state, in the management of economic and cultural development, in the improvement of the government apparatus, and in supervision over its activity'. To ensure popular participation, the new party rules set term limits on officials at all levels—from a maximum of sixteen years for Central Committee members to four years for local officials. The goal was to ensure constant renewal of party leadership and the infusion of fresh forces—even at the top, where a quarter of the Central Committee and Presidium were to be replaced every four years. However, the rules had an escape clause for 'especially important' functionaries (such as Khrushchev himself, presumably). Finally, the programme sought to replace full-time functionaries with volunteers and part-time staff, thereby reducing the number of paid functionaries and ensuring more involvement by the rank and file. The new programme, understandably, was the kind that would not do much to raise Khrushchev's popularity among the 'partocrats'.

FROM CRISIS TO CONSPIRACY

Despite Khrushchev's apparent triumph at the party congress in 1961, within three years the very men who led the 'prolonged, thunderous ovations' were feverishly conspiring to drive him from power. The populist was becoming unpopular, not only in the party, but among the broad mass of the population. Several factors help to account for his fall from power.

One was a string of humiliating reverses in foreign affairs. Khrushchev, for example, took the blame for the Sino-Soviet split: although relations were already strained (because of Chinese resentment over insufficient assistance and respect), the tensions escalated into an open split under Khrushchev. De-Stalinization was partly at issue, but still more divisive was Khrushchev's 'revisionist' theory of peaceful coexistence and his refusal to assist the Chinese in acquiring a nuclear capability. Next came the Berlin crisis of 1961; although provoked by the East German leadership (as is now known), at that time the crisis was blamed on Khrushchev, who appeared to have fecklessly brought Soviet–American relations to the brink of war. That débâcle was soon followed by the Cuban missile crisis. After publicly denying the presence of missiles, the Soviet Union was embarrassed by clear CIA aerial photographs, prominently displayed at a stormy session of the United Nations Security Council. Confronted by an American 'quarantine' of Cuba, Khrushchev was forced to back down; although he obtained important concessions in secret negotiations, the public impression was one of total Soviet capitulation. Khrushchev suffered another fiasco in India, the recipient of massive economic and military aid, but an unreliable ally—a 'neutral' that did not hesitate to criticize the Soviet Union or its surrogate Communist Party in India. But India was hardly the only recipient; by 1964, for example, the USSR had given 821 million dollars to Egypt, 500 million to Afghanistan, and 1.5 billion to Indonesia (which became pro-Chinese in 1963). Such foreign aid brought scant political return and became increasingly unpopular at home, especially amid the food shortages and sputtering economy. Finally, party élites were embarrassed by Khrushchev's penchant for vulgar jokes and crude behaviour—as in the infamous 'shoe-pounding' escapade during Harold Macmillan's speech at the United Nations session in 1960.

A second factor in Khrushchev's demise was his cultural policy, which gradually alienated both the intelligentsia and general population. Even earlier, as in the 1958 campaign of vilification against Boris Pasternak (whose *Doctor Zhivago*—illegally published abroad—had won a Nobel Prize), Khrushchev made clear that the 'thaw' did not mean artistic freedom. Nor was he even consistent: one month after authorizing publication of Aleksander Solzhenitsyn's *One Day in the Life of Ivan Denisovich* he publicly castigated modern art at the 'Thirty Years of Moscow Art' exhibition. He was also increasingly distrustful of writers; as he declared in 1962, 'Do you know how things began in Hungary? It all began with the Union of Writers'. In December 1962 and March 1963 Khrushchev and party ideologues convened special meetings with writers to reaffirm the limits on literary freedom. One early victim was the future Nobel prize-winning poet, Joseph Brodsky, who did not belong to the official Writers' Union and was therefore convicted of 'parasitism' in February 1964. The intelligentsia was not the only victim: in 1961 Khrushchev launched a vigorous anti-religious campaign, ending nearly a decade of qualified tolerance. The campaign affected all religious confessions, but was particularly devastating for the Russian Orthodox Church: over the next four years, the regime closed 59 of its 69 monasteries, 5 of its 8 seminaries, and 13,500 of its 22,000 parish churches.

A third reason for Khrushchev's downfall was economic, as his policies and panaceas began to go awry. As a Soviet economist Abel Aganbegian demonstrated, the growth rate in the early 1960s declined by a factor of three—the result of systemic inefficiency, waste, and backwardness permeating every sector of the economy. And, despite official claims of 'full employment', the real unemployment rate was 8 per cent nationally and as high as 30 per cent in small towns. Aganbegian identified three main causes: (1) massive defence allocations, which diverted 30 to 40 per cent of the work-force into primary or secondary defence plants; (2) failure to modernize and automate production; and, (3) 'extreme centralism and lack of democracy in economic matters', compounded by a primitive planning apparatus that lacked computers or even reliable economic data. 'We obtain many figures', he noted, 'from American journals sooner than they are released by the Central Statistical Administration'. The result was hoarding, low labour productivity, shoddy quality, forced savings, and the omnipresent *defitsity* (goods shortages) that fed inflation and a booming black market. Recent data confirm Aganbegian's analysis, showing a sharp drop in the growth indicators for the gross domestic product (from 5.9 per cent in 1956–60 to 5.0 per cent in 1961–5) and investment (from 16 per cent in 1958 to 4 per cent in 1961–3).

But economic problems were most apparent in agriculture: although average grain output rose from 98.8 million tons in 1953–6 to 132.1 in 1961–4, that yield fell short of expectations and demand. According to one calculation, the grain output needed to satisfy demand in 1955 was 160 tonnes; that was about 20 per cent more than average output in 1961–4. Moreover, output fell behind increases in personal income: although per capita agricultural production increased slightly during 1959–65, disposable money income rose dramatically (48 per cent in 1958–64). The increased demand was also due to population growth (33 per cent) and urbanization (250 per cent), leaving more and more people dependent on the agricultural sector. In short, Khrushchev had severely underestimated demand and overestimated output.

The miscalculation had several causes. One was just bad luck: the drought of 1963 caused an abysmal harvest of 107 million tonnes—larger than a Stalin harvest, but only 61 per cent of plan targets. The low harvest forced the Soviet Union, which had recently boasted of overtaking America, to take the ignominious step of purchasing twelve million tonnes of grain abroad. But it was not only bad luck and bad weather: Khrushchev himself contributed to the failure in agriculture. He was blindly devoted to maize; apart from climactic and technological problems, its cultivation met with adamant peasant resistance, duly reported by the KGB: 'We don't need to sow corn; it will just cause a lot of trouble and bring little use'. But the First Secretary, sullied as the *kukuruznik* ('maize-man'), was determined, especially after his visit to the United States in 1959, to grow maize. By 1962 he had forced peasants to plant 37 million hectares of maize, of which only 7 million ripened in time for harvest. Nor did his panacea—the Virgin Lands programme—work the expected miracle. As a result of drought, erosion, and weed infestation, the output from the virgin lands fell far short of plan expectations. After the first bumper harvests, output steadily declined in the late 1950s, partly for want of grass covers and fertilizers to renew the soil. Worse still was the irreversible damage caused by feckless cultivation of areas unsuited for grain production: in 1960–5 wind erosion ruined twelve million hectares of land (four million in Kazakhstan alone)—roughly half of the virgin lands.

Moreover, Khrushchev's 'decentralizing' strategy weakened administrative control, inviting evasion, resistance, and malfeasance. The most famous case involved the party secretary of Riazan, A. N. Larionov, who 'over-fulfilled' the meat quota in 1959 threefold, but by illicit means—by slaughtering dairy as well as beef cattle and by purchasing meat from neighbouring provinces. His miraculous achievements were loudly celebrated in *Pravda*, but the next year the newly minted 'Hero of Socialist labour' committed suicide to avoid the awful day of reckoning. His case was hardly exceptional. An official investigation revealed that party secretaries in Tiumen *oblast* 'engaged in all kinds of machinations to deceive the government, included reports on unproduced and unsold production to the state, thereby creating an apparent prosperity in agriculture in the *oblast* and inflicted great harm to the state, kolkhoz, and sovkhoz'. The problem was bad policy, not just bad people. After years of massive allocations to agriculture, Khrushchev suddenly reduced the flow of investment. Difficulties for this sector were further compounded by the decision in 1958 to abolish machine tractor stations, forcing collective farms to purchase this equipment and divert scarce resources into capital goods. Moreover, Khrushchev ambitiously pursued his earlier fetish for merging collective farms into ever larger units, their total number falling by nearly a third in 1953–8 (from 91,200 to 67,700); such mergers, however, failed to bring 'economies of size' and eroded effective administration. It also reinforced the kolkhoznik's devotion to his individual plot, which yielded over half their income in 1960 (with even higher proportions in some areas—for example, 75 per cent in Lithuania). When Khrushchev urged collective farmers to abandon their monomaniacal cultivation of private plots, one peasant in Kursk eloquently summarized popular sentiment in an encounter with the First Secretary: 'Nikita, what's got into you, have you gone off your rocker?'

Although the regime took special measures to provide cities with basic necessities, it also attempted to dampen demand in June 1962 by raising prices—38 per cent on meat and 25 per cent on butter. The price increases aroused intense popular discontent and even disorders. To quote a KGB report from June 1962: 'In recent years some cities in our country have experienced mass disorders, accompanied by pogroms of administrative buildings, destruction of public property, and attacks on representatives of authority and other disorderly behaviour'. Although police tried to blame 'hooligan' elements (including people so diverse as former 'Nazi collaborators, clergy, and sectarians'), the root cause of course lay much deeper.

Those causes were clearly visible in the most famous disorder of all—in Novocherskassk in June 1962. It began at a locomotive plant, where workers rebelled against rising food prices, wage cuts (30 per cent), and a backlog of unresolved grievances (housing shortages, work safety, and even food-poisoning of 200 workers). The workers quickly won the support of local townspeople; as the KGB later reported, the 'man-in-the-street' believed that 'prices should have been left as they were, that the salaries of highly paid people should be reduced, [and] that aid to underdeveloped socialist countries should cease'. When the striking workers marched into the centre of Novocherkassk, they attracted a crowd of some 4,000 people and managed to repulse the assault of local police and, later, even armoured units. 'Mass disorders' continued the next day, as the

insurgents seized the offices of the city party committee and tried to storm the KGB and militia headquarters. Moscow hastily dispatched a key Khrushchev aide, F. R. Kozlov, who denounced the 'instigators' as 'hooligan elements', defended the price rise, but promised to improve the food supply. Troops were eventually able to restore order, but not before taking scores of civilian lives.

But Khrushchev's fatal error was to attack the 'partocracy'—the central and local élites who comprised the only real organized political force. His attempt to democratize and ensure renewal, especially through 'term limits', posed a direct threat to career officials, from highest to lowest echelons. Decentralization itself was anathema to *apparatchiki*, especially those holding power in Moscow. His original scheme of sovnarkhozy not only reduced the power of Moscow functionaries, but also forced many to depart for provincial posts—'I myself had to work in a sovnarkhoz', a high-ranking functionary later complained. In 1962 Khrushchev undermined his base of support even among provincial officialdom through his scheme to divide the party into industrial and agricultural branches at the regional and *oblast* levels, thereby undercutting the power of local potentates. And, for all the pain, decentralization seemed only to beget

Although private plots comprised only a tiny portion of the Soviet Union's vast expanse of arable land, they produced a huge proportion of the foodstuffs, which the peasants sold legally at the collective farm markets (such as this one in Kiev in the mid-1970s).

corruption, falsified reports, and non-compliance. In response, Khrushchev was forced to build a new layer of intermediate bodies and central organs to co-ordinate—and control—the sovnarkhozy. The drift towards recentralization culminated in a decision of March 1963 to establish the 'Supreme Economic Council of the USSR'—in essence, an attempt to reassert central control over the lower economic councils.

Finally, Khrushchev's colleagues came to feel that he had begun to rule imperiously and, at the time of his removal, denounced him for taking decisions impetuously and ignoring collective opinion. Although Khrushchev gamely responded ('But you, who are present here, never spoke to me openly and candidly about my shortcomings—you always nodded in agreement and expressed support!'), the critique was not amiss. As a high-ranking functionary A. Shelepin observed, Stalin—but not the cult—had expired: '[Khrushchev] was also a *vozhd'* [Leader]. And the same psychology of the *vozhd'* remained. And in the subordinates' relationship to the *vozhd'*. No one had the courage to speak out against him'. The fact that Khrushchev had assumed both party leadership and the top position in the state—because it was too much work, because it centralized too much power—also elicited criticism. There was keen resentment too over his tendency to promote family members, such as his son-in-law Aleksei Adzhubei, who was made editor of *Izvestiia* and recipient of undeserved awards and privileges.

The plot to depose Khrushchev evidently commenced as early as February 1964, led primarily by Nikolai Podgornyi and Brezhnev. Khrushchev did receive some prior warnings, but did not take them seriously. The opportunity came in October, as Khrushchev was vacationing at his Crimean dacha: the conspirators summoned him back to Moscow for an extraordinary session of the Central Committee and subjected him to devastating criticism. In his defence Khrushchev emphasized that he had 'worked all the time', but professed to greet his removal, through democratic means, as a 'victory of the party' over Stalinist illegalities. The public announcement of his 'retirement' castigated the former First Secretary for 'crudeness', 'bombastic phrases and braggadocio', and 'overhasty conclusions and hare-brained schemes divorced from reality'. Granted a 'personal pension', Khrushchev lived in obscurity until his death on 11 September 1971.

Perils of Restoration

With Khrushchev's removal, the 'old guard'—most of whom had served under Stalin—sought to restore stability and order to the political system. Although initially evincing interest in economic reform, this 'new old régime' became increasingly restorationist, even with respect to the persona of Stalin, and averse to extensive change in policies or personnel. Subsequently castigated as the 'era of stagnation', the two decades after Khrushchev's removal were a marvel of contradictions—economic decline amid apparent prosperity, détente and confrontation, harsh repression and a burgeoning human rights movement. By the early 1980s, however, restoration had plainly failed, stagnation devolving into the systemic crisis that would trigger the frenetic reformism of perestroika and final demise of the Soviet Union in 1991.

FROM REFORM TO RESTORATION

The regime made the dismantling of Khrushchev's unpopular reforms its first priority. It abolished the 1961 rules on 'term limits' (in favour of 'stability' in party leadership) and reasserted the principle of centralization—and, by extension, the power and prerogatives of the Moscow partocracy. The new regime quickly abolished Khrushchev's sovnarkhozy and re-established 'all-union' ministries in Moscow, with a corresponding reduction of authority at the republic and *oblast* levels. It also scrapped Khrushchev's educational reform, which had proven immensely unpopular. Restoration was the principal theme of the Twenty-Third Party Congress in March 1966, which reinstated old terms like 'Politburo' (for 'Presidium') and 'General Secretary' (for 'First Secretary').

Initially, at least, the regime professed an interest in economic reform. Responding to earlier proposals (most notably, a famous article in 1962 by Evsei Liberman entitled 'The Plan, Profit and Bonus') and current assessments of the Soviet economy, the government—under the leadership of Aleksei Kosygin—sought to change the economy itself, not simply the way it was administered. Although favourably disposed towards recentralization, the reforms attempted to overcome the crude quantitative criteria of gross output that purported to show plan fulfilment but actually produced mountains of low-quality output. The reform proposed to measure (and reward) real economic success by placing more emphasis on sales and profits; it also assessed a small charge on capital to ensure efficiency and to limit production costs. In September 1965 the regime adopted plans to rationalize planning and introduce computers, to enhance the power of plant managers, to merge plants into larger production units (*ob"edi-nenie*), and—most important—to replace gross outputs with gross sales. The new strategy also included tighter controls, a stress on automation, and the purchase of advanced technology from the West (for example, the 1966 contract with Fiat to build a plant in Stavropol *oblast* called Togliatti).

The reforms yielded short-term gains (especially in labour productivity), but soon foundered on several major obstacles. First, despite the incentives for productivity (e.g. penalties for excessive production costs), it was the State Price Committee, not the market, that set prices and therefore determined costs, value, and 'profitability'. Second, managers lacked the authority to discharge unproductive or redundant workers—a legacy of caution after events in Novocherkassk. Third, despite lip-service to technological innovation, 'success' meant fulfilling quarterly and annual production plans; that low time horizon effectively militated against long-range strategies and drove managers to focus on short-term results. Recentralization meant tighter control by the Moscow partocracy, a major impediment to innovation and change. And despite the fanfare about 'automation' and 'cybernetics', the Soviet Union missed the computer revolution: the number of computers per capita in the United States was seventeen times higher and at least a full generation ahead. By the late 1960s the Soviet leadership abandoned the pretence of economic reform and settled into an unruffled commitment to the status quo.

As reform at home stalled, the regime intervened to suppress change elsewhere in the Soviet bloc—above all, the famous 'Prague Spring' of 1968. After the Czech 'Action Programme' of April 1968 proclaimed the right of each nation to follow its 'own separate road to socialism', the country was engulfed by autonomous movements demanding not only economic efficiency, but fundamental changes in the social and political order. On 10 August the Communist Party itself drafted new party statutes to require secret balloting, set term limits, and permit intra-party factions. Although the party chief Alexander Dubček promised to stay in the Warsaw Pact (seeking to avoid Hungary's provocative mistake in 1956), Soviet leaders found the experiment of 'socialism with a human face' too threatening and led a Warsaw Bloc invasion on 21 August to restore hardliners to power.

The regime also had to suppress dissent at home. It had grounds for concern: the KGB reported that 1,292 authors in 1965 had composed and disseminated 9,697 'anti-Soviet' documents (mostly posters and leaflets). It identified about two-thirds of the authors—a motley array that included workers (206), schoolchildren (189), university students (36), state employees (169), pensioners (95),

Andrei Siniavskii (bearded) and Iulii Daniel on trial in Moscow in 1965 for publishing anti-Soviet works secretly in the West. The trial lasted four days; both the accused pleaded not guilty, an almost unheard-of defiance in such a trial. Above all, the trial signalled the determination of the new Brezhnev regime to crack down on dissent.

collective farmers (61), and even party members (111). Protest also became public for the first time in decades, as some two hundred dissidents held a demonstration on Pushkin Square, with one demonstrator bearing the sign, 'Respect the Constitution'.

Although most dissenters were dealt with 'prophylactically' (a KGB euphemism for intimidation), the Kremlin leadership decided to send a clear message to dissidents. In February 1966 it staged the famous show trial of two dissident writers, Andrei Siniavskii and Iulii Daniel, who had published satirical works abroad and, of course, without official permission. The court predictably found them guilty of 'anti-Soviet' activity and meted out harsh sentences (seven years of hard labour for Siniavskii, five for Daniel). The KGB boasted that the trial not only evoked an outpouring of popular demands that the 'slanderers' be severely punished, but also that it had intimidated the intelligentsia. Simultaneously, authorities launched an attack on Alexander Nekrich's historical monograph, *22 June 1941*, which blamed Stalin personally for the Nazis' initial success in the war and thus contravened official plans to rehabilitate Stalin. In response, party functionaries campaigned against Nekrich's study as allegedly based on 'the military-historical sources of capitalist countries'.

The repression was harsh but ineffective. When, for example, the regime organized a public discussion of Nekrich's work at the Institute of Marxism-Leninism in February 1966, the audience openly supported Nekrich and subjected a 'loyal' party hack to humiliating insults and censure. Sixty-three Moscow writers signed an open letter of protest against the Siniavskii–Daniel trial, and another two hundred prominent intellectuals sent a letter to the Twenty-Third Party Congress demanding that the case be reviewed. Nor did the demonstrative repression intimidate the intelligentsia or even end public demonstrations: a few days after the invasion of Czechoslovakia dissidents staged a short demonstration on Red Square, carrying placards that read 'Hands off the ČSSR', 'For Your and Our Freedom!' and 'Down with the Occupiers!' Dissent was particularly animated among national minorities. For example, the Crimean Tatars—still denied repatriation and restitution—organized a demonstration in April 1968 that culminated in hundreds of arrests. The Muslim peoples of Central Asia also became increasingly restive; as the KGB reported (after a fierce mêlée at Semipalatinsk in June 1965), Kazakhs resented the fact that Russian was the official language and that ethnic Russians monopolized the best positions in the army, state, and administration.

YEARS OF STAGNATION

Amid all this turbulence, Brezhnev steadily consolidated his power. An associate observed that, in contrast to Khrushchev, 'Brezhnev never read anything except *Krokodil*', a lightweight satirical magazine that he even brought to meetings of the Politburo. As the years passed Brezhnev also grew increasingly vain,

At the Kremlin Palace of Congresses, N. V. Podgornyi opens the 24th Party Congress on 30 March 1971. In the waning phase of the 'triumvirate', Brezhnev sits to his right and Kosygin to his left. Directly behind Podgornyi is Iurii Andropov, then head of the KGB and later the General Secretary in his own right.

fond of medals and praise. He encouraged fawning and toadying, like that in a 1973 report by the KGB head, Iurii Andropov, claiming that people regarded Brezhnev's recent speech as 'a new creative contribution to the theory of Marxism-Leninism', that it 'brilliantly reveals the paths and prospects of communist construction in the USSR and inspires new heroic feats of labour in the name of strengthening our multinational state, the unity and solidarity of the Soviet people'. Three years later Brezhnev was awarded the rank of 'marshal of the Soviet Union', his *fifth* medal for the 'Order of Lenin', and his second medal as 'Hero of the Soviet Union'. (Satirists later speculated that he died from a chest operation, undertaken to broaden his chest to hold more medals.) The same year he 'won' a Lenin Prize for his memoirs, with this explanation: 'For their popularity and their educational influence on the mass of readers, the books of Leonid Ilich are unrivalled.' Popular demand, however, was less than insatiable: after his death, a report on state bookshops disclosed a backlog of 2.7 million copies of unsold, let alone unread, books. After a new constitution in 1977 established the office of president as titular head of state, Brezhnev assumed that position as well. With good reason, A. N. Shelepin argues that 'Brezhnev was a great, very great mistake'.

Brezhnev consolidated not only his own power but also that of the partocracy: article 6 of the new constitution formally established the CPSU as the leading force in Soviet society. The party also expanded its presence through sheer growth: although the rate of growth after 1964 was slower, the party none the less increased its ranks from 12.5 million (1966) to 17.5 million (1981), an increase of 40 per cent.

But the most significant accommodation was Brezhnev's 'trust in cadres' and resolve to end 'the unjustified reshuffling and frequent replacement of cadres'. In contrast to Khrushchev, who sought to rejuvenate the party through democratization and turnover, Brezhnev left most members in their position until death or incapacitation. As a result, the average age of Politburo members rose from 55 to 68 between 1966 and 1981; by then half were over the age of 70 and would die within the next few years. The pattern was true of the Central Committee: because of the high rate of return (rising from 54 per cent in 1961 to 89 per cent in 1976–81), 44 per cent of the membership of the Central Committee was unchanged between 1966 and 1981, with an inevitable rise in the average term from 56 to 63. Low turnover rates also characterized lower echelons of the party; thus the proportion of *oblast* secretaries retaining their positions rose from 33 per cent under Khrushchev to 78 per cent in the period 1964–76.

This partocracy ossified into gerontocracy, devoid of dynamic leadership. It was not only inimical to change but physically incapable; Brezhnev himself, ravaged by ailments and strokes, gradually deteriorated into a breathing mummy. His colleagues were likewise so infirm that, shortly after his death, the Politburo solemnly addressed the issue of age and 'solved' the problem by setting limits on the hours and days that its members should work. This ossified leadership invited rampant corruption and crime, not only in the outlying republics of the Caucasus and Central Asia, but also in core Russian *oblasti* like Krasnodar, Rostov, and Moscow itself. Although the party periodically purged the corrupt (nearly 650,000 lost party membership on these grounds between 1971 and 1981), it did little to stop the rot, especially at upper levels. That decay even touched Brezhnev's own family, as police arrested close friends and associates of his daughter.

ECONOMY AND SOCIETY

Brezhnev's stewardship also brought sharp economic decline. Whereas national income rose 5.9 per cent per capita in 1966–70, thereafter it fell sharply, bottoming out at 2.1 per cent in 1981–5. GNP followed a similar trajectory: 6 per cent in the 1950s, 5 per cent in the 1960s, 4 per cent from 1970–8, and 2 per cent in subsequent years. This corresponded, predictably, to a decrease in the rate of growth in investment capital (from 7.6 per cent in 1966–70 to 3.4 per cent in 1976–80, including a mere 0.6 per cent in 1979). The regime deftly juggled statistics to mask the malaise: by emphasizing not physical output but 'rouble value' (showing a 75 per cent increase in 1976–83), it took advantage of the hidden price inflation and concealed the modest increase in gross production (a mere 9 per cent in the same period).

Agriculture was still the Achilles heel of the Soviet Prometheus. Agricultural output at first increased (by 21 per cent in 1966–70, compared to 12 per cent in 1961–5), but thereafter the rate of growth declined (to just 6 per cent in 1981–5). Apart from bumper harvests (for example, 235 million tons of grain in 1978), most crops were mediocre or outright failures. Thus the yield for 1975 was a mere 140 million tons—the worst since 1963 and 76 million short of the goal. And because of limited port capacities, the government could import only 40 million tons, the shortfall causing a higher rate of slaughter and long-term consequences for animal husbandry. A desperate regime made new concessions on private plots and even encouraged city-dwellers to have garden plots. By 1974 private agriculture consumed one-third of all man-hours in agriculture and one-tenth in the entire economy. The private plots were phenomenally productive: in 1978, for instance, they occupied just 3 per cent of arable land but produced 25 per cent of total agricultural output.

Agriculture became a drag on the whole economy, devouring an ever larger share of scarce investment capital. According to G. A. E. Smith, its share of investment rose from 23 per cent (1961–5) to 27 per cent in 1976–80; allocations to the entire agro-industrial complex (for example, fertilizer plants) increased from 28 to 35 per cent. The United States, by comparison, allocated a mere 4 per cent of investment capital to agriculture. Although total output did increase (the yield for 1976–80 being 50 per cent greater than that for 1961–5), it did not keep pace with demand or rising production costs (covered primarily by gargantuan government subsidies). Subsidized bread prices were so low that peasants even used government bread for fodder. Nevertheless, spot shortages and price adjustments remained a source of hardship that periodically triggered food riots, such as those in Sverdlovsk (1969), Dnepropetrovsk (1972), and Gorky (1980).

The regime could boast of better results in the industrial sector, yet still failed to match past performance or reach plan targets. It could claim salient achievements like the mammoth 'Baikal–Amur' project—a 3,000 kilometre railway north of the old Trans-Siberian and linking eastern Siberia with the Pacific. But the general record on output and productivity was dismal. Although the regime periodically spoke of revamping the system, it did little to raise critical indicators like product quality or labour productivity. Far more characteristic was the bureaucratic posturing, the attempt to solve economic problems with administrative decrees (which mushroomed to more than 200,000 in the late 1970s). Increasingly, the main goal was not reform but control, primarily through the formation of central industrial associations to ensure subordination and vertical integration in a specific sphere of industry.

This decline in industrial growth had many causes. Some were inherent in a 'command economy', with all its inefficiencies and bottle-necks, compounded by the incompetence of a superannuated leadership. Moreover, the hidden inflation of the Soviet price system (which allowed plants to reprice essentially

the same products) encouraged managers to ignore productivity and avoid retooling that involved short-term costs and unwanted—and unnecessary—risks. So long as the state provided a guaranteed market and set the prices, it was pointless to cut costs or even worry about cost-effectiveness.

Labour constituted another major problem. The difficulty was partly quantitative: whereas the labour force had increased by 23.2 million in 1960–70, that growth fell to just 17.8 million in 1970–80 and to 9.5 million in 1980–90. For a labour-intensive economy heavily dependent on manual labour, the sharp reduction in labour inputs was devastating. Labour was also maldistributed, being concentrated not in industrialized areas but in backward regions like Central Asia, where the willingness to relocate was minimal. Labour also showed a high turnover rate (25 to 30 per cent) that directly undermined continuity and training. Nor was labour so tractable; strikes, rare under Stalin, openly challenged the regime's authority. In 1968, for example, workers struck at twenty large industrial enterprises, chiefly because of grievances over wages and production norms, sometimes because of tactless management and unwarranted deductions.

Paradoxically, contemporaries saw the 1970s as a decade of unprecedented well-being. The Twenty-Fourth Party Congress (March 1971) renewed the perennial pledge to support heavy industry and defence, but also laid a new

Despite the rapid industrialization and urbanization, modernization bypassed the countryside, with productivity low and living conditions backward. As this photograph shows, this village still has no running water and must rely on water being delivered by horse.

emphasis on consumer goods. The Ninth Five-Year Plan (1971–5) even projected higher growth for consumer goods than for capital goods; although that goal was not met, it did signal a marked change. Given the precipitous decline in agricultural and industrial sectors, the 'mirage' of prosperity is puzzling.

Much of the explanation rests in fortuitous circumstances on foreign markets. The primary elixir was oil: after the 1973 oil crisis, the enormous profits from oil kept the leaky Soviet vessel afloat. A simultaneous commodity boom also increased revenues for an economy that exported primarily raw materials, making the terms of trade still more favourable. The surge in gold prices (for example, the 75 per cent increase in 1979) further added to state coffers. Although the USSR had already accumulated a substantial foreign debt (17 billion dollars), that sum paled in comparison with current revenues from hydrocarbon and raw material exports. As a result, the Soviet Union was able to use its hard-currency earnings to pay for the import of producer goods, consumer products, and endless shiploads of grain.

Alongside this inefficient state economy, a 'second' (or 'black') economy emerged to satisfy the demand for deficit goods and services. According to one estimate, some twenty million people worked on the black market to supply the demand for 83 per cent of the general population. Because of rampant corruption, repression of the black market became increasingly symbolic and inconsequential. The result was a subclass of 'underground' millionaires whose illicit earnings became a prime source of private investment after 1985.

'High Brezhnevism' also marked the apogee of the *nomenklatura*—a term denoting not merely the list of key positions, but the social and political élite who monopolized them. According to estimates for 1970, this élite included about 700,000 individuals: 250,000 people in state and party positions, 300,000 members in economic sectors, and another 150,000 in science and research. By 1982 this group had increased to some 800,000 people and, together with their families, comprised about 3 million people (1.2 per cent of the Soviet population).

Although a golden age for the *nomenklatura*, the Brezhnev era also attempted to improve the lot of the general population. Despite the rising cost of living (about 1 per cent per annum), real wages increased still more sharply (50 per cent between 1967 and 1977). The state also established a five-day working week, mandated a minimum vacation of 12–15 days, raised the minimum monthly wage (first to 60 roubles, later to 70 roubles), and expanded Khrushchev's social welfare (which increased fivefold between 1950 and 1980). The regime gave particular attention to the 'underclass', as in the decision of 1974 to provide an income subsidy to alleviate poverty. It also made a concerted effort to improve the lot of collective farmers, three-quarters of whom initially fell below the official 'poverty line' (with a quarter even below the official subsistence minimum). The goal was not just to ensure social justice but to cauterize social haemorrhaging—the flight of rural labour, especially youths and males, from the village. As a result, by the 1970s rural wages were only 10 per cent lower than those for urban workers and were supplemented by a significant income from the private plots.

Despite petro-dollars and state welfare, Soviet society revealed signs of acute stress. One was hyper-alcoholism: surplus income, amid widespread goods deficits, led to a massive increase in alcohol sales (77 per cent in the 1970s alone). Another disturbing indicator was infant mortality, which jumped from 22.9 (per 1,000 live births) in 1971 to 31.6 in 1976. Another cause of concern was the decrease in the average number of children per family (from 2.9 in 1970 to 2.4 in 1978). The demography carried ominous political and ethnic overtones: whereas the average family in the RSFSR in 1970 was 1.97, family size among the Muslim peoples of Central Asia was nearly three times higher—for example, 5.64 in Uzbekistan and 5.95 in Turkmenistan.

Détente

To counteract the international furore over the invasion of Czechoslovakia in 1968, the Brezhnev government embarked on a policy of calculated *détente*. Whatever the motive, it led to an impressive array of agreements on trade, arms, human rights, and even the German question. This environment also favoured a marked improvement in Soviet–American relations. The end to the Vietnam War, long a festering issue, doubtless helped. But both sides found an array of common interests, especially in trade and military security, which could foster collaboration in spite of significant spheres of difference. The first important sign was SALT-I, a 'strategic arms limitation treaty' in 1972 that set limits on offensive missiles and anti-ballistic missiles for five years. This agreement was followed by others—on nuclear accidents, joint space operations, and a further arms agreement finally signed in June 1979 as 'SALT-II'.

Nevertheless, the 1970s were years of instability and conflict. Apart from Western concern about domestic Soviet policy (especially with respect to human rights issues, including Jewish emigration and suppression of dissidents), Moscow continued efforts to increase its presence and influence around the globe, especially in underdeveloped countries. After failing to achieve a significant improvement in relations with China or to increase its authority in Asia, Moscow showed a growing interest in Africa and especially South Yemen (which became a Marxist republic in 1978). Moscow relied not only on subversion but subvention (to be sure, promises outpaced deliveries: of 13 billion dollars promised in 1954–77, only 7.2 billion actually materialized). And aid came increasingly in the form of military assistance and arms, as Soviet arms shipments increased exponentially.

The *coup de grâce* for *détente* was the decision to intervene in Afghanistan in December 1979. Ever since a Marxist faction seized power in April 1978, Moscow had given strong support to the regime in Kabul and its social and cultural transformation. Although willing to provide assistance (including Soviet

ВЬЕТНАМ ПОБЕДИТ!

АГРЕССОРА ВОН ИЗ ВЬЕТНАМА!

This May Day celebration, held before *détente* in the 1970s, reflects the acute tensions of the Cold War. Huge posters denounce American involvement in the Vietnam War, proclaiming that 'Vietnam Will Conquer!' and 'Throw the Aggressor out of Vietnam!'

'advisers' to guide the 'socialist transformation'), Moscow abjured a direct military role as likely to 'expose' the weakness of the Afghan government and to 'inflict serious harm on the international authority of the USSR and significantly reverse the process of détente'. In December 1979, however, a rump meeting of the Politburo elected to intervene militarily because of the region's strategic importance, popular opposition to the Afghan government, and rumours that Kabul was making overtures to the American government. Whatever the rationale, the result was catastrophic: the Soviet Union found itself snared in a military quagmire that consumed vast resources, cost enormous casualties, and had a devastating effect on the Soviet Union's international position.

Dissent

The 1970s also marked the emergence of two broad-based dissident movements—one in defence of human rights, the other representing national minorities, both sharing a common cause against an authoritarian regime. They steadily gained in strength, notwithstanding domestic repression and foreign ambivalence bred by *détente*. A KGB report of December 1976 (on thousands of cases) gives some idea of the main currents of dissent: 'revisionism and reformism' (35 per cent), 'nationalism' (33.7 per cent), 'Zionism' (17.5 per cent), 'religion' (8.2 per cent), 'fascism and neo-fascism' (5.6 per cent), and other miscellaneous matters. Although samizdat included many different works, the main voice for the movement was a samizdat journal *Chronicle of Current Events*, which appeared first in 1968 and managed to publish bi-monthly issues almost uninterruptedly (except for an eighteen-month gap in 1972–4).

Compared to the preceding decade, this dissident movement of the 1970s was different in several respects. First, although *belles-lettres* remained important, the movement itself became much more political. A KGB report in 1970 noted that the earlier samizdat had been primarily literary, but of late consisted chiefly of 'political programmatic' materials, influenced mainly by Yugoslav and Czechoslovak literature. Second, dissent was more widespread, spilling beyond secret circles and tiny demonstrations to envelop larger segments of society, with nearly 300,000 adherents (mostly supporters and sympathizers, including some 20,000 political prisoners and people under surveillance or investigation). That was a far cry from the '35 to 40' dissidents that the KGB reported a few years earlier. The growth of dissent was also apparent in the mushrooming of samizdat, which included some 4,000 volumes in 1979. The KGB warned that dissent was especially strong among the young—in its view, because they were denied access to professional organizations (for example, only 48 of the 75,490 members of the Union of Writers being under the age of 30). Third, dissent was better organized, especially after Andrei Sakharov (a full member of the prestigious Academy of Sciences and leading figure in Soviet nuclear development) and others founded the 'Human Rights Committee' in November 1970.

As the human rights movement gained momentum from the late 1960s, one major issue was the right of emigration, a demand most dramatically expressed in the case of Jews. A demonstration outside the Ministry of Internal Affairs in 1973 protests against the Soviet refusal to grant exit permits to numerous Jews. The various signs say: 'Let Us Go to Israel', 'Let me go to Israel', and 'Visas to Israel instead of Prison'.

Predictably, the dissident movement aroused growing concern, especially in the KGB. Dismayed by the Politburo's reluctance to deal with Sakharov, in September 1973 the KGB chief, Andropov, warned that the failure to act not only enraged honest Soviet citizens but also encouraged 'certain circles of the intelligentsia and youth' to flout authority. Their motto, he claimed, was 'Act boldly, publicly, involve Western correspondents, rely on the support of the bourgeois press, and no one will dare touch you'. Emphasizing the need to interdict the 'hostile activities of Solzhenitsyn and Sakharov', he proposed to put Solzhenitsyn on trial (afterwards offering him foreign exile) and to quarantine Sakharov in Novosibirsk. After Solzhenitsyn's forced extradition and deprivation of citizenship in 1974, the regime focused increasingly on Sakharov, whom the KGB accused in 1975 of 'evolution in the direction of open anti-Sovietism and direct support for the forces of international reaction'. Although the KGB urgently demanded vigorous action against Sakharov, the Politburo demurred—in large part for fear of the negative repercussions on *détente*. But patience wore thin, even for the timorous Brezhnev, who made this comment at a Politburo meeting of 8 June 1978: 'The reasons for our extraordinary tolerance of Sakharov are known to all. But there is a limit to everything. To leave his attacks without a response is impossible'. Western furore over Afghanistan removed the final inhibition; with nothing to lose, the regime approved a KGB proposal to exile Sakharov to the closed city of Gorky, thereby cutting off his access to Westerners.

While dissenters like Sakharov and writers like Solzhenitsyn captured world attention, no less significant was the political dissent sweeping minority nationalities. The most visible, for Western observers, was the Jewish movement, the product of official anti-religious repression (by the 1970s only thirty synagogues existed in European Russia) and an anti-Israeli foreign policy that fanned popular anti-Semitism. But powerful nationalist movements also appeared in all the republics, especially in Ukraine, the Baltic states, and the Caucasus. The intensity of nationalist sentiment was dramatically revealed in 1978, when mass demonstrations in Tbilisi forced the government to abandon plans to eliminate Georgian as the official state language inside the republic. Tensions also mounted in the Muslim republics of Central Asia, fuelled by a steady influx of Russian immigrants and the repression of Islam.

The government itself realized that it had failed to assimilate minorities. That failure was amply demonstrated in a secret report of 1978, which detailed the obstacles to Russification of schools, including a lack of qualified teachers: 'Many of the teachers in minority elementary schools have only a poor knowledge of Russian. There are cases where, for this reason, Russian is not taught at all'. The failure of linguistic Russification was clearly apparent in Central Asia: the proportion claiming total ignorance of Russian language ranged from 24 per cent among Uzbeks to 28 per cent among Tajiks and Turkmen. Even graduates of specialized technical schools had a poor command of Russian. In

As the movement of dissenters, minorities, and human rights activists gained momentum, the regime responded with vigorous persecution and harsh punishments. This photograph shows the outside wall of 'Camp No. 1', part of the notorious complex of labour camps in the Mordvinian Autonomous Republic.

response, the regime proposed to establish a special two- or three-month course in Russian for those due to perform military service. As Brezhnev admitted at the Twenty-Sixth Party Congress in February 1981, the government had made scant progress in its campaign to assimilate minorities and combat nationalism.

Towards the Abyss

When Leonid Brezhnev died on 10 November 1982, he bequeathed a country mired in profound systemic crisis. Its economic problems were daunting; amid falling prices on energy and commodities, the regime lacked the resources either to reindustrialize or to restructure agriculture. Although the KGB had seemingly decapitated the leadership of the democratic and nationalist movements, anti-regime sentiments were intense and widespread. Nor had the Brezhnev government achieved stability and security in foreign policy: the invasion of Afghanistan, débâcles elsewhere around the globe, even erosion of the Warsaw Bloc (especially in Poland) provided profound cause of concern and an endless drain on resources.

Neither of Brezhnev's immediate successors, the former KGB chief Andropov or the quintessential party functionary Konstantin Chernenko, survived long enough to address the ugly legacy of the 'years of stagnation'. Andropov placed the main emphasis on law and order, even for solving the economic crisis, with the explanation that 'good order does not require any capital investment whatever, but can produce great results'. He also waged a vigorous campaign against corruption and, lacking Brezhnev's veneration for 'stability of cadres', replaced

Symbolic of the regime's own debilitation was the rapid succession of deaths by the leaders—Brezhnev in 1982, Andropov in 1984, and Chernenko in 1985. This photograph shows the party leaders bearing Andropov's ashes for burial in the Kremlin Wall. In language typical of the time, Novosti offered this caption: 'The Soviet people, gripped by profound grief, bade their final farewell to Iurii Andropov.'

a quarter of the ministers and *oblast* secretaries in a desperate attempt to re-vitalize the system. But within fifteen months he too was dead, with power devolving on Chernenko—an elderly partocrat whose only distinction was to have been Brezhnev's chief adviser. In the end Chernenko became the old élite's last hurrah—an ageing and ailing leader, he 'reigned' but one year before dying from emphysema and respiratory-cardiovascular problems in March 1985.

As the Politburo assembled to confirm the accession of Mikhail Gorbachev to the post of General Secretary, the prospects for survival were bleak. Internationally, it had paid an enormous cost for the Afghanistan invasion and faced an awesome challenge from the aggressively anti-communist administration of Ronald Reagan in Washington. Domestically, its economy had ground to a halt, paralysed by profound structural problems in agriculture and industry and now deprived of lucrative revenues from the export of energy and raw materials. The new General Secretary, whatever his personal proclivities, had good cause to ponder the options for a fundamental 'perestroika'.

FROM PERESTROIKA TOWARDS A NEW ORDER
1985–1995

MARTIN McCAULEY

This era marks the inglorious end of one regime and inglorious beginning of another. Gorbachev's achievement was, however unwittingly, to dismantle the USSR, with a minimum of bloodletting—earning him admiration abroad and enmity at home. Yeltsin, a weak president in a strong presidency, presided over economic depression, loss of superpower status, and a state taken over by corrupt economic élites.

MIKHAIL GORBACHEV, a gifted politician, became the most revolutionary leader since Lenin. After his election as General Secretary of the Communist Party of the Soviet Union (CPSU) in March 1985, he set in train a process so radical in conception that the whole edifice of Soviet communism came tumbling down. He believed that the solution to the *malaise* that gripped the country was to return the USSR to its Leninist roots. *Perestroika* ('reconstruction and reform'), *glasnost'* ('publicity and openness'), and *demokratizatsiia* ('democratization') were to rejuvenate the socialist system and make it more efficient. Perestroika was to refashion all the institutions of state, society, and the economy. Glasnost was to expose abuses of the system, to generate new approaches, and to demolish obstacles to new ideas. Democratization, understood as guided participatory democracy, was to reanimate a stultified partocracy by tapping the dynamism and authentic involvement of the masses.

Basic democracy could be exercised from below, all culminating in the USSR Supreme Soviet at the top. However, Gorbachev found the Supreme Soviet cumbersome and deliberately slow, being replete with members of the Soviet élite (the *nomenklatura*), who were profoundly suspicious of his motives. His eyes then lit on the presidential systems that he had observed on his foreign travels; he eventually chose a combination of the American and French systems and had himself elected President. That, however, proved a fatal mistake: rather than seek a direct mandate from the people, Gorbachev chose the less risky option of being elected by the Supreme Soviet. He therefore lacked legitimacy, a weakness that was to haunt him when he later clashed with Boris Yeltsin and others who had been chosen through direct popular elections. As President of the USSR, Gorbachev possessed great nominal authority but in fact was powerless to implement his policies, in large part because he failed to create the requisite set of executive institutions. He also failed to clarify his vision of a new Soviet Union, thereby creating perpetual confusion and scepticism about his real objectives.

He had little interest in industry but a passion for agriculture. As a result, others dominated the economic agenda, notably Nikolai Ryzhkov, no advocate of market solutions; Gorbachev became a sideline participant in the critical debates over marketization and economic reform. He was easily persuaded of the need for radical market reforms, such as the 500-day programme, but did not foresee the structural complexities or internal opposition, mainly from state enterprise managers, that was bound to arise.

Glasnost and democratization opened the floodgates to reform and also reconfigured politics in the USSR. As the fear instilled by Stalin dissipated, people began to express their own views openly. Soviet institutions had scant claim to legitimacy (previous elections being correctly deemed a sham); hence the new politics posed a fundamental threat to the existing order. A resulting vacuum led to the creation of countless informal (so called because they were not officially registered) groups and movements claiming to represent various interest groups and constituencies. In non-Slav republics these quickly coalesced to form popular fronts, which articulated not only political but national aspirations. The new political movements began to challenge the CPSU and its monopoly of political power. The turning-point came in the elections to the USSR Supreme Soviet in 1989, when non-Communists were allowed to run for office; these elections were followed by others at the republican and local levels. Victory in these elections allowed popular fronts, especially in the Baltic republics, to claim legitimacy as the sole authentic voice of the people. Even more alarming for Gorbachev, the Baltic republics began to demand independence, thereby challenging the territorial integrity of the Soviet Union. In response the General Secretary proposed to fashion a new Soviet Union that was genuinely federal, but people in the Baltics would have nothing of it. Thus Gorbachev, who originally had been the radical, was soon overtaken by events and by 1990 found himself swimming against the tide.

But he enjoyed much greater success in the sphere of foreign and security policy. Convinced that defence was exacting a catastrophic toll on the economy, he embarked on breathtakingly original solutions. Together with Eduard Shevardnadze, he set out to charm the world and convince everyone that the Soviet Union was a normal state and no longer a menace to world peace. Gorbachev persuaded President Ronald Reagan to meet in Geneva; that first fireside chat set the tone for Soviet–American relations for the rest of his tenure in office. By making concessions, Gorbachev managed to slow, then stop the arms race, and ultimately even initiate disarmament.

By 1991 a coalition of interests stood opposed to Gorbachev. The foreign policy initiatives proved highly unpopular, especially with the Soviet military. Ethnicity was a further source of difficulty: the national republics were being seduced by the prospects of greater independence or even, as in the Baltics, came to demand complete independence. Such sentiments even began to pervade the Russian Federation, which found an inspiring leader in Boris Yeltsin. If Russia and Ukraine agreed that they did not need the Soviet Union, they could simply dismantle it. Moreover, leadership in the government and CPSU was riddled by tensions between moderate and radical reformers; it also included some categorical opponents of all reform, unless strongly led from the top, as inherently destabilizing and a threat to the hegemony of the CPSU. Some figures in the party, the KGB, and the military believed that the country could yet be saved from chaos (to them democracy was chaos) and that a strong centre could yet be re-established. This motley group, calling themselves the Emergency Committee, decided to strike on 18 August 1991. Practically everything they undertook was a miscalculation, but the bungled coup was fraught with important consequences. The coup demoralized the formerly dominant institutions, led to the banning of the party, and soon contributed to the demise of the Soviet Union, as Russia and Ukraine decided to become independent republics and to dissolve the USSR. Gorbachev, a well-meaning and decent man, an inspirational leader abroad but a failure at home, had set in train events over which he had no control.

Gorbachev as General Secretary

By most accounts, Iurii Andropov was the first to identify Mikhail Gorbachev as a future member of the Soviet élite. As head of the KGB Andropov had visited Stavropol Krai to enjoy its spas and relaxation; Gorbachev, as first secretary of the local party organization, officially welcomed him and other important guests, including Leonid Brezhnev. He had also earned a certain reputation for effectiveness in dealing with the intractable agricultural problem. In any event, in 1978 Gorbachev was summoned to Moscow to become Central Committee secretary for agriculture. Given the importance of the party apparatus under Brezhnev, this meant that he was in overall control of agriculture in the Soviet Union. The fact that he progressed from candidate and then to full member of the CPSU Politburo, despite the lack of agricultural success, revealed that he had powerful patrons. At the time of Brezhnev's death in November 1982, Gorbachev was the youngest member of the Politburo, as yet not in the direct line of succession.

A typical Gorbachev pose: listening, thinking, and observing.

Gorbachev was born into a peasant family in that same Stavropol Krai in southern Russia in March 1931. His grandfather was arrested as an 'enemy of the people' in 1937, an event that left a deep impression on the young Gorbachev. His formal schooling was interrupted during the war when his village was briefly occupied by the German *Wehrmacht*. After the war he continued his schooling and graduated from secondary school with a silver medal. In 1948 he was awarded the Order of the Red Banner of Labour for helping to produce a record harvest on his collective farm; not long afterwards he was admitted to candidate membership in the party. These factors, together with his lower-class background, helped him gain admission to the law faculty of Moscow State University in 1950. When he graduated in 1955 he was already married, to Raisa Maksimovna Titorenko—purportedly without the blessing of her family. On graduation Gorbachev was initially appointed to serve in the USSR Procurator's Office; apparently by a decision of superiors in the Soviet leadership, however, he was not permitted to assume the post. He was then posted back to Stavropol. He quickly tired of life as a lawyer and used his local connections to obtain a transfer to the Komsomol (the Young Communist League), where he blossomed and in due course moved into party work, eventually becoming first secretary of the local organization. He devoted enormous efforts to promoting agriculture in the krai, but at the price of neglecting to develop expertise in industrial affairs.

Although Gorbachev was Andropov's favoured successor, the old men in the Politburo elected Konstantin Chernenko instead, making Gorbachev the second secretary. This meant that he deputized for Chernenko whenever the latter was indisposed—which in fact began to occur more frequently. When Chernenko died in March 1985, Gorbachev was the clear front runner, but had to beat back challenges from two other candidates: Viktor Grishin, the Moscow party leader, and Grigorii Romanov, Central Committee secretary for the military economy and former Leningrad party boss. Gorbachev soon prevailed. Andrei Gromyko, the veteran Foreign Minister, fulsome in his praise (and emphasizing that Brezhnev himself had advanced Gorbachev's career), nominated Gorbachev for the post of General Secretary. The youngest man on the Politburo was elected unanimously.

As General Secretary his first task was to bolster his personal authority in the party by placing his own people in key positions. That meant replacing the Brezhnev generation with cadres who would implement the policies of the new leadership. Gorbachev was at a disadvantage from the beginning, however. Although normally the General Secretary headed the Secretariat, which controlled cadres assignments, Egor Ligachev was instead entrusted with this task. As a result, Gorbachev and Ligachev had to engage in intense bargaining and horse-trading on promotions and demotions. Gorbachev soon proved himself a skilful horse-trader: in April 1985 Ligachev and Nikolai Ryzhkov became full Politburo members, while Alexander Iakovlev, later to spearhead glasnost,

The Soviet leadership always maintained a sombre appearance, even on anniversaries. The 69th anniversary of the October Revolution—7 November 1986—was marked by the usual parade of senior civilian and military leaders on the top of the Lenin Mausoleum, Red Square, Moscow. From the left: President Andrei Gromyko, living up to his nickname of Grim Grom, Mikhail Gorbachev, for once unsmiling, General Petr Lushev, first deputy USSR Minister of Defence, and Nikolai Ryzhkov, USSR Prime Minister.

joined the Secretariat. On 1 July 1985 Romanov was dropped from the Politburo (ostensibly for 'health' reasons). Eduard Shevardnadze, party leader in Georgia, became a full Politburo member, and Boris Yeltsin was appointed Central Committee secretary responsible for the construction industry. The full significance of Shevardnadze's promotion became evident on 2 July when he was appointed USSR Foreign Minister, and Andrei Gromyko, Foreign Minister since 1957, became Soviet President.

The replacement of Gromyko reveals much about Gorbachev's tactical skills: he was able to remove the man who, just three months earlier, had nominated him as General Secretary of the party. Gromyko, who was clearly out of step with the 'new political thinking', thereby lost control over Soviet foreign policy and was shunted upstairs to the largely ceremonial post of President. Shevardnadze was an inspired choice: a Georgian, lacking a native command of Russian, devoid of experience in foreign policy and knowledge of Western languages, a loyal and valuable supporter of Gorbachev and his policies. The appointment also suggested that Gorbachev himself intended to play a key role in foreign policy.

In November 1985 Nikolai Ryzhkov replaced Nikolai Tikhonov as Prime Minister of the USSR. Ryzhkov came with impressive credentials: a successful manager of Uralmash (a huge defence industry plant in the Urals), then a deputy minister, later an official in Gosplan (the state planning agency), and finally a high-ranking member of the Secretariat. No one understood better than Ryzhkov the inefficiencies—and complexities—of the state economy, a fact that made him hesitate about reform. Later Gorbachev became frustrated with his caution.

In December 1985 Boris Yeltsin replaced Viktor Grishin (known as the 'Godfather' because of his corrupt stewardship) as first party secretary of Moscow. His charge included a mandate to clean up the capital. A few months later Yeltsin became a candidate Politburo member.

The Twenty-Seventh Congress of the CPSU (February–March 1986) afforded Gorbachev an opportunity to take full control of the Secretariat and put a new team in place. Almost two-thirds of department heads in the Secretariat, 52 per cent of the Central Committee members, and 40 per cent of the USSR ministers were replaced. Gorbachev could reflect with satisfaction on the fact that such a massive turnover of top- and middle-level officials—at least since the purges of the 1930s—had been unprecedented; none of his predecessors had been able to effect such changes in his first year of office. In the country at large about a third of party cadres were replaced and thousands of government officials moved. On the surface the new team was in place, but in fact many of them came from the same mould as their predecessors.

Policy Goals

Gorbachev admitted to a Warsaw audience in July 1988 that when he had come to power he had concentrated on economic reform and had not perceived the need for political reform. On 10 December 1984 he presented some policy preferences. He spoke of the need to effect 'deep transformations in the economy and the whole system of social relations', and to implement the policies of perestroika of economic management, the 'democratization of social and economic life' and glasnost. He underlined the need for greater social justice, a more important role for local soviets, and active participation of workers at the workplace. He sided with those who blamed the decline in the Soviet economy on the 'command-administrative' structure—i.e. the central ministerial bureaucracy and the enterprise directors, both of whom preferred the status quo and operated under the supervision of the party bureaucracy. Tatiana Zaslavskaia, main author of the famous Novosibirsk report (leaked in 1983), had warned that this structure, if not removed, could drag the whole state down.

The decline in economic performance was accompanied by a marked deterioration in discipline, order, and morality. By all accounts, the era of 'stagnation' had produced enormous corruption, privileges, 'breaches of the law, bureaucratism, parasitism, drunkenness, prodigality, waste and other negative phenomena'. Gorbachev believed that these abuses themselves were partly to blame for the economic decline and that, if they could be removed, growth rates would again rise. And this revitalization of the economy remained the primary goal, with a target of 4 per cent growth in national income. But Gorbachev also recognized the need for qualitative improvement, noting that the 'acceleration of scientific-technical progress' was also necessary. He therefore proposed to retool

Soviet industry through substantial injections of investment capital in machine-building and electronics. At the same time, however, he also promised to increase housing, consumer goods, and food supply. In effect, Gorbachev was simply following Andropov's strategy; his very terminology—'perfecting' of the system—was characteristic. And like Andropov, he sought to restore 'order and discipline', most notably in a vigorous anti-alcohol campaign that only earned him the sobriquet 'mineral water secretary' for his pains.

During his speech at the Twenty-Seventh Congress Gorbachev warned that the party could lose power if it became too self-assured and feared to air its own weaknesses. He stressed that there could be no political stability without 'social justice'—an expression that recurred nine times during his speech and underlined the need to afford every citizen equal opportunities. Gorbachev implicitly conceded that two nations existed in the Soviet Union: the privileged élite, who had special access to the good things of life, and the rest.

There were also two economies: the state economy and the 'second' economy of the black market that fed on the inability of the state economy to supply the necessary goods and services. Indeed, that second economy was expanding at a faster rate than the state economy, chiefly because of the latter's inefficiency. The black economy began to emerge under Khrushchev, obtained a firm grip under Brezhnev, and then received an enormous boost from Andropov's anti-alcohol campaign. It grew rapidly under Gorbachev, and once co-operatives were legalized in 1988, it became irresistible.

Glasnost

When Gorbachev's initial efforts failed to produce a resurgence of growth in the Soviet economy, he came increasingly to link economic and political reform. He was aware that constructive debate is essential in a modern economy and society, that problems can have a variety of solutions, that such openness could be a counterweight to the inertia and resistance in the partocracy. To gain legitimacy for this change, Gorbachev resolved to solicit the support of the intelligentsia, especially journalists and writers. The most dramatic sign of the change was the decision to free Andrei Sakharov—the moral voice of the nation—from exile in Gorky (since renamed Nizhnii Novgorod). Censorship controls were also relaxed; Iakovlev even promoted radical journalism, much to the ire of Ligachev. Very soon, the party leadership began to split into two distinct factions: moderate reformers, led by Ligachev and Ryzhkov, and radical reformers, lined up behind Gorbachev, Yeltsin, and Iakovlev. One major point of contention was party privilege. Whereas the moderates saw attacks on party privilege as veiled attacks on the party's leading role, the radicals viewed such criticism as a much-needed step towards restructuring and revitalizing the party.

On 26 April 1986 part of the Chernobyl, Ukraine, nuclear power station exploded killing some people and spreading radioactive waste over a large area. The Soviet leadership was slow to react and reveal the full implications of the disaster. However Gorbachev did address the nation and this was an important breakthrough for glasnost.

A plurality of views began to emerge not only in the party but in the country at large. The General Secretary's intention was to provoke debate and participation so as to make the Soviet Union stronger. However, the lack of clarity about his objectives (for instance, perestroika) generated a multiplicity of interpretations and opinions—and, in short order, informal groups and movements. Many of these had previously existed as small debating 'circles' of like-minded individuals, coming almost exclusively from the intelligentsia. In the non-Slav republics these circles coalesced into 'popular fronts', uniting all those opposed to Moscow's rule; the most aggressive movements appeared in the Baltic republics, which indeed had firmly resisted several decades of attempts to integrate them into the USSR. Interestingly, no popular front emerged in Russia itself, reflecting not only the ethnic diversity but also the lack of national consciousness in the largest republic. Most important, many of the new groups and movements were overtly political and soon raised an open challenge to the party's monopoly of political power. A Central Committee official wrote in *Pravda* that the party should not simply tolerate these groups but should consider 'co-operation, partnership, and even formal agreements' with them. Conservatives took a different view. Thus Viktor Chebrikov, Politburo member and former head of the KGB, denounced informal groups for pretending to support perestroika but in reality seeking to undermine both perestroika and the party.

Glasnost was put to the test on 26 April 1986 when a reactor at the nuclear power station at Chernobyl, in Ukraine, exploded. Gorbachev waited eighteen days before appearing on television to give an account of the worst nuclear power disaster in history. Until then the regime took refuge in silence and denial that bordered on the criminal: despite the obvious danger from radioactive fall-out, the party refused to cancel the May Day parade in Kiev a few days after the accident. The disaster had a profoundly negative effect on popular attitudes towards nuclear power and stimulated the emergence of a 'green' (environmentalist) movement. In the long term, however, the disaster had one positive consequence: it drove the regime to become much more open, not only about disasters, but about other problems, such as crime and drug abuse.

Reforming the Party

The perceived need for political reform, coupled with the unwillingness of many in the party apparatus to agree on an agenda, led Gorbachev to convene a party conference in June 1988. Its proceedings were conducted with a freedom of speech and criticism that had not been seen since the early days of the revolution. Gorbachev's overriding achievement was to emasculate the party Secretariat: it lost its power to vet all key nominations to government and soviet posts, to interfere in the economy and to dominate local party bodies. In effect, Gorbachev had stripped the party 'centre' of its power over the state, economy, and even lower-ranking bodies. All this accelerated the centrifugal flow of power to the periphery, a process that indeed had already gathered momentum in the late Brezhnev era. The conference further agreed to establish an executive-style presidency (Gorbachev being the President-in-waiting) and restricted party executives to five-year terms of office, renewable only once. They were also to be appointed after contested elections. Other resolutions welcomed the formation of new social groups in favour of perestroika but condemned 'any action aimed at destroying the socialist basis of society, inciting nationalism or racism, or advocating war, violence, or immorality'. Freedom of conscience and the right to take part in decision-making were listed as basic human rights. What was needed was an 'effective mechanism for free dialogue, criticism, self-criticism and self-control'. Gorbachev proposed to restore power to popularly elected soviets, but still within the framework of a one-party communist system. In order to win over party officials, he proposed that the local party secretaries chair the local soviets 'in order to confer legitimacy on them'. As some were quick to point out, however, this proposal was contradictory to Gorbachev's declared goal of transferring power to local soviets.

Power to the Soviets

According to the Brezhnev constitution of 1977, the USSR Supreme Soviet was the supreme legislative body, but in reality of course it ceded precedence to the Politburo and Central Committee. Its ceremonial function was evidenced by the fact that it normally adopted all resolutions unanimously. By October 1988, however, glasnost led to dissent appearing in the Supreme Soviet. At issue was the right of Ministry of Interior troops to enter private homes without a warrant, and the right to control demonstrations without reference to local authorities. On the first issue thirty-one deputies voted against, and on the second thirteen opposed the adoption of the decree.

On 29 November 1988 the Supreme Soviet adopted a law that was tantamount to its own dissolution when it established a new institution, the Congress of People's Deputies (CPD) with 2,250 members. Two-thirds were to be elected under the old system: 750 members were to represent nationalities, another 750 were to be chosen by electoral constituencies of the same approximate size. The remaining 750 were to be nominated directly by the CPSU, Komsomol, trade unions, the Academy of Sciences, and Churches. This CPD was then to elect a new USSR Supreme Soviet; comprised of two chambers (with 271 members in each), which were to function as a real parliament and to meet for three- to four-month periods in spring and autumn. Those nominated did not have to be party members, but electoral meetings normally favoured party candidates. To be elected, a candidate had to obtain over 50 per cent of the vote, even if he or she were the only candidate. If no one was elected in the first round, a second round had to take place not more than two months later. On this occasion the candidate with most votes was declared the winner. Candidates could put forward their own political programme and debate with one another.

When the CPD elections were held in March 1989, approximately a quarter of the 1,500 directly elected deputies faced no opposition in their constituencies. Over 80 per cent of the candidates were CPSU members; one-fifth were women. Some prominent party officials were defeated, including five members of the Central Committee. The most prominent casualty was Iurii Solovev, first party secretary of Leningrad *oblast*. Prominent radicals, such as Andrei Sakharov and

Roy Medvedev, were elected. Boris Yeltsin won a landslide victory in Moscow; voters took his side after the minutes of the Central Committee meeting of 21 October 1987, when he was humiliated and sacked as a member of the Politburo and the party secretary for Moscow, were published in an effort to undermine his popularity. Yeltsin, ever the populist, promised to 'free Moscow from the mafia of bureaucrats'. Gorbachev's failure to support Yeltsin in his conflict with Ligachev and the conservative Party élite led to the two falling out and the beginning of the titanic struggle that was to end in the Soviet leader's political destruction. Yeltsin was elected to the USSR Supreme Soviet after a Siberian deputy stood down and offered Yeltsin his mandate. This afforded Yeltsin a national platform for the first time, which he used to promote the interests of the Russian Federation and to attack party privilege, the failings of perestroika, the need for market-oriented reforms, and Gorbachev himself.

In republican and local elections in March 1990 radical electoral groups won in the major cities and many prominent party officials were defeated. In Moscow 'Democratic Russia' won 85 per cent of the capital's seats in the CPD of the Russian Federation and 56 per cent of the seats in the city soviet. In Leningrad, the group 'Democratic Elections 90' took 80 per cent of the mandates to the CPD and 54 per cent of the seats in the city soviet.

President Gorbachev

Gorbachev was duly elected head of state by the CPD. He chose Anatolii Lukianov as his Vice-President and Nikolai Ryzhkov as USSR Prime Minister; both were closely questioned by Congress. In fact, five of his nominees for senior posts in the Council of Ministers were rejected by Congress. The CPD also elected a committee, chaired by Gorbachev, to draft a new Soviet constitution to replace the increasingly obsolescent 1977 version. Groups formed in the Supreme Soviet, which increasingly began to operate like a normal parliament. But it also grew more conservative as the crisis deepened, tending to throw its support behind Gorbachev.

Yeltsin emerged increasingly as a counterweight, even competitor, to Gorbachev. A member of the constitutional committee, Yeltsin was determined to bolster Russia's sovereignty and already began to speak of forming a loose confederation of independent states. He was also mindful of the potential power of the presidency. In a speech in the Supreme Soviet on 31 May 1989, he warned of the dangers posed by the increased powers of the President and the continuing influence of the CPSU over parliament. He perceived a danger that the President, given the 'general economic crisis and sharpening ethnic tensions', might be tempted to 'solve our complex problems by force'. As a consequence, 'we may again find ourselves captive of a new dictatorship'. He therefore proposed that the President be subject to an annual vote of confidence. Yeltsin further argued in favour of shifting power from the party to soviets and urged the Supreme Soviet to provide a precise legal definition of the party's power.

Gorbachev himself became increasingly frustrated with the new USSR Supreme Soviet and looked for a new model to enhance his authority and capacity to act. He eventually chose an executive presidency based on a mixture of the US and French presidencies. Following American practice he needed a Vice-President and, after Nursultan Nazarbaev (the leader in Kazakhstan) and Eduard Shevardnadze had declined the post, chose Gennadii Ianaev. Radicals in parliament—who sought to strengthen parliamentary control over the government—were duly alarmed by the turn of events. Gorbachev had a fight on his hands; in the end, only 59 per cent of the CPD voted in favour of his election as executive President. That vote stood in sharp contrast to his experience ten months earlier, when 96 per cent had supported his election as head of state.

The new system substantially expanded the President's authority. He was empowered to nominate the chairman and members of the Council of Ministers, to chair the Defence Council, and to conduct international negotiations. He was also to sign decrees of the Supreme Soviet and to exercise overall responsibility for that body. The functions of the old Politburo devolved onto a new 'Presidential Council'.

Although a separate 'Presidential Council of the Federation' was created to represent the various nationalities, the centre and the non-Russian republics differed over the right of the central government to declare a state of emergency. Legislation under discussion would allow the centre to suspend the republican Supreme Soviets, countermand decisions of their governments, and appropriate their administrations during times of widespread violence. Eventually, the text was amended to require the President to warn republics of his intention to impose a state of emergency and to obtain their approval. If they refused, he needed to obtain a two-thirds majority in the USSR Supreme Soviet to proceed. The power of the President to impose a state of emergency and the role of the USSR Supreme Soviet and the republics were critically important for denying the attempted coup in August 1991 of its claim to legality and constitutionality.

An important new institution was the Constitutional Review Committee, which was to vet all new legislation. Gorbachev had wanted to appoint its members himself, but after protests this role was assigned to the chairman (speaker) of the USSR Supreme Soviet. It had fifteen members, mostly lawyers, and it demonstrated its independence in February 1991 when it ruled there were 'substantial flaws' in the President's decree setting up joint military-militia patrols in major cities.

The USSR Supreme Soviet gave Gorbachev special powers for a period of eighteen months to deal with problems in the economy, budget, property relations, and the 'strengthening of law and order'. The situation deteriorated to the extent that in November 1990 there were calls for emergency measures to cope with food and supply shortages. Yeltsin urged the formation of a coalition government.

Again Gorbachev was granted greater powers, with all organs of the central executive being directly subordinate to the President himself. The Presidential Council was replaced by a National Security Council that included representatives from the military, police, and KGB. Its members being nominated by the President, the Council was to 'implement USSR policy concerning defence' and 'to guarantee stability, law, and order'. The Council of the Federation was upgraded and was to be advised by a committee of experts nominated by the republics. In theory the President was bound by the Council's decisions. Although nominally the republics' voice in central decision-making, it also included the small autonomous republics and hence was too large to be effective. The Council of Ministers was replaced by a Cabinet of Ministers, subordinate to the President. The Cabinet was to include republican Prime Ministers but the latter would have preferred a horizontal structure, allowing them to take executive decisions, with Moscow playing a co-ordinating role.

It soon became clear that the key decision-making body was the National Security Council. Vadim Bakatin, a liberal Minister of the Interior, was replaced by Boris Pugo, the former head of the KGB in Latvia; General Boris Gromov became first deputy minister. Most of the President's radical advisers were sacked. In December 1990 Eduard Shevardnadze resigned and delivered an emotional speech in the Supreme Soviet warning of the threat of dictatorship. Tension rose as calls mounted for Gorbachev to take matters in hand—on one occasion, this took the form of a declaration by fifty-three prominent figures, ranging from General Moiseev (Chief of Staff) to Patriarch Alexi. As rumours of a state of emergency or even a coup proliferated, the President himself moved steadily rightward in the autumn of 1990 and the spring of 1991.

About 15 per cent of party deputies in the Russian CPD supported 'communists for democracy', a pro-Yeltsin reformist movement within the party. It was led by Colonel Alexander Rutskoi—subsequently Yeltsin's Vice-President, still later his arch-adversary. This opened up the possibility of radicals and reform-minded communists coming together to form a centre party alternative to the CPSU. 'Soiuz' ('Union'), a conservative faction in the CPD, talked of a third way between the conservative communists and the radicals, based on 'all-Russian patriotism'. In April 1991, however, Gorbachev and Yeltsin appeared to be groping towards a *rapprochement*, as they and eight other republican leaders signed a document acknowledging the gravity of the crisis and outlining ways of overcoming it—including the conferral of greater independence to individual republics.

The President's sorry political state in early 1991 was, to a large extent, the result of his own prevarications over reform. According to Alexander Iakovlev, an architect of perestroika and its chief theorist, the revolution from above reached a critical point at the Nineteenth Party Conference in June 1988. It gave Gorbachev a clear choice: either advance and transform perestroika into a 'genuinely popular democratic revolution, go all the way and afford society total freedom', or pull back, remain a communist reformer, and stay within the well-known milieu of the bureaucracy. The choice was between genuine or controlled democracy. That choice informed debates in a small group, formed in early 1988 and chaired by Anatolii Lukianov, to discuss elections to the Supreme Soviet. Lukianov himself proposed a two-stage election; although legal authority was to be vested in local soviets, the relationship between the party and local soviets remained vague. Fedor Burlatskii, who proposed direct elections to the Supreme Soviet, offered a clear democratic alternative, but only one member of the group—Iakovlev himself—supported him. Gorbachev could have effected a political revolution but, true to his low-risk strategy, sided with the Lukianov majority.

The Party Crumbles

The emergence of informal groups and movements brought into question Article 6 of the 1977 constitution, which explicitly guaranteed the party's leading role in society. But many reformers still believed that the party, the only organization with a nation-wide organization, was the most effective vehicle for change. Elections to the CPD in March 1989 stirred debate within the party, and Gorbachev appeared to have a solid constituency for change. Nevertheless, both radicals and conservatives were suspicious about his motives, the former because he moved too slowly, the latter because he was undermining the existing power structure. In April 1989 he persuaded about a quarter of the Central Committee members to retire; most, in fact, no longer occupied the positions that had ensured their election in the first place. Twenty-four new members were added. Gorbachev spoke enthusiastically about a 'new type of working person' who would 'feel like a human being' as a result of participating in the whole range of economic and social development.

In December 1989 Gorbachev underlined the party's role as a 'consolidating and uniting force' and defended article 6 that had legitimized this role. He was under pressure from Lithuania: the Communist Party of Lithuania had just removed a similar article from the Lithuanian constitution and, still more ominously, was preparing to break from the CPSU and form a separate national Communist Party. Gorbachev warned the Lithuanians 'not to cross the line' that threatened to destroy the CPSU 'as a single political organization and the vital consolidating force of the Soviet Union'.

As an inter-regional group (led by such radicals as Sakharov and Yeltsin) emerged in the Supreme Soviet, some party members began to break ranks and urge the formation of an opposition party. Gorbachev's decision to retain the leading role of the party may have been a tactical blunder; with hindsight it seems that he might have achieved more by splitting the party and assuming leadership of its radical wing.

The date for the Twenty-Eighth Party Congress was moved up to July 1990. Gorbachev's programme remained fundamentally contradictory: on the one hand, he called for the reform and renewal of the party, but on the other he revived Lenin's slogan of 'all power to the soviets'. He could not have it both ways, however: either the renewed party or the soviets were to exercise power, not both. The draft proposal, 'Towards Humane Democratic Socialism' (prepared for the Central Committee plenum in February 1990), was perhaps indicative of his thinking. The party would no longer exercise any state or government functions; hence it was to renounce its monopoly of power, enshrined in the Brezhnev constitution, and permit the emergence of multi-party politics. If the party wanted a leading role, it must first acquire it by popular mandate; it was to participate in the political process, but without special privileges or advantages. The document noted that the democratization was already under way and leading towards greater 'political pluralism'; the emerging political organizations and movements might coalesce to form regular political parties. The CPSU was prepared to 'co-operate' and enter into a 'dialogue' with all organizations committed to the Soviet constitution and the social system that it prescribed. It also proposed to water down the democratic centralism that had concentrated decision-making at the top and stifled debate and grass-roots initiative. Party branches, for example, were to play the 'decisive role' in electing delegates to the Congress.

Gorbachev's proposals ignited a fierce debate in the party and provoked growing criticism of his leadership. And as the Central Committee met in plenary session, a huge pro-reform demonstration gathered outside the walls of the Kremlin. In any event it agreed to deprive the Politburo of its dominant role in the state; henceforth it was to deal solely with internal party matters. Article 6 of the constitution was thus modified; the new text declared that the party merely 'participates' in running the country and vowed that it 'does not lay claim to full governmental authority. It seeks to be the political leader but without any claim to any special position laid down in the constitution'.

The programme elicited strong opposition from both conservatives and radicals. The fiercest radical critics of the plenum were Boris Yeltsin and the younger generation, who regarded the resolutions as a vain attempt to conciliate right and left. Egor Ligachev, expressing the fears of the conservative bureaucracy, called for party and national unity. In his view, the greatest danger to perestroika emanated from the 'powerful forces of a nationalist, separatist and anti-socialist tendency'.

Pravda, the party's own voice, had been lukewarm towards reform, but Gorbachev managed to install Ivan Frolov as editor. He duly praised Gorbachev as the 'leader of the progressive forces in the party'. That very statement, in effect, conceded that the 'monolithic Party' was a thing of the past, that it was riven with dissent. In March 1990 *Pravda* published the programme of the 'Democratic Platform', a radical faction in the party, which demanded the outright abandonment of a single ideology and the rejection of communism as the party's goal. The programme further urged the party to renounce democratic centralism and cells based on production units, and instead to build a democratic society and become one of several political parties based on freedom, justice, and solidarity. The programme, understandably, sent shock waves through the party.

The Politburo and Central Committee reacted in high dudgeon in an open letter to all members. They called for an end to factionalism, enjoined those involved to resign, expressly denounced the Democratic Platform, and expelled its leaders from the party. This caused Yeltsin and others to sign an open letter, which accused conservatives of 'making furious efforts on the eve of the Congress to effect a coup against perestroika in the party'. They did not recognize the 'right of party officials to impose their will on the rank and file'. Advocates of the Democratic Platform debated whether they should leave the party before the Congress or wait to see if it could regenerate itself. Although some supporters had already left the party, most opted to wait and see.

The Communist Party of the Russian Federation (CPRF)

Lenin had been adamantly opposed to the formation of a separate 'Russian Communist Party'—on the grounds that this would only open the door to Great Russian chauvinism and nationalism. A Russian bureau had briefly existed under Khrushchev, but was dissolved when Brezhnev became party leader. However, there was a growing feeling among Russian communists, who made up 60 per cent of party members and dominated the CPSU leadership, that the Russian Federation should have its own party. This was reinforced by the conviction that Russia was subsidizing the other republics. Gorbachev, not unnaturally, opposed the formation of such a party: it would unite the majority of CPSU members and, if it fell under the control of conservatives, would erode his own power. His fears were realized, however, when the constituent conference of the 'Communist Party of the Russian Federation' (CPRF) convened in June 1990. It was dominated by party officials who felt most threatened by reform. Gorbachev addressed the conference and boldly proposed the 'fastest possible move to the market economy'. Those who wanted to return the party to the old ways had 'lost touch with reality'. In reply Egor Ligachev bluntly called upon Gorbachev to resign as General Secretary. Colonel General Albert Makashov, one of the military firebrands, argued that the unification of Germany and the Soviet withdrawal from Eastern Europe had undermined national security. Although the conference approved the formation of a multi-party system and the transition to a market economy, Gorbachev failed to have his own candidate elected as party leader. Instead, Ivan Polozkov, a colourless conservative critic of the General Secretary, became leader. Polozkov promised to work closely with Boris Yeltsin—which appeared highly improbable—and distanced himself from Makashov's strictures on defence policy. Since the conservative leadership did not reflect rank-and-file opinion, many resigned from the party.

The Twenty-Eighth Party Congress

Although conservative party officials dominated the vigorous and outspoken debates at the Congress, its programme was quite radical—it even used the expression 'private property' and declared that the process of marketization was irreversible. Gorbachev was in his element and skilfully manipulated the various splits among delegates. He was strengthened by the fact that the right had no alternative leader or programme except to go backwards. Gorbachev's speech was long and rambling, as usual, but he concentrated his ire on the conservatives for trying to derail perestroika.

The Congress re-elected Gorbachev as General Secretary and declared that henceforth the right to appoint the party leader belonged to a party congress, not the Central Committee. It also created the new position of deputy general secretary; as Ligachev made a strong bid for the post and Gorbachev lobbied against him behind the scenes, the Congress eventually settled on an acceptable candidate—Vladimir Ivashko, the Party leader in Ukraine. The latter's decision to leave Kiev at such a critical moment in that nation's history in preference for a job that would soon disappear revealed his lack of sound political judgement. Gorbachev appealed for unity among the 'democratic, progressive forces dedicated to carrying through the democratization of society'. However, this was in vain as the Democratic Platform announced that it was leaving to form an 'independent, democratic, parliamentary party'. Yeltsin, always the master of the dramatic, asked for the floor and requested the party to retract the criticisms directed at him in 1987. When it declined to do so, Yeltsin thereupon resigned from the party and made his exit followed by the television cameras. Other prominent defections included Anatolii Sobchak (chairman of the Leningrad soviet) and Gavriil Popov (chairman of the Moscow soviet). The Politburo was expanded to include republican party leaders but holders of state and government offices were excluded.

In July 1991 Gorbachev submitted a new draft party programme to the Central Committee, which was to be debated at the Twenty-Ninth Party Congress in the autumn. This astonishing document proposed to jettison Marxism-Leninism as the party's ideology and its claim to represent the working class. The new programme, in effect, proposed to restructure the CPSU as a social democratic party. It also endorsed the market economy, privatization, and multi-party politics. Had the Congress in fact convened and adopted the programme, a moderate social democratic party might have emerged from the wreckage of the CPSU.

Economic Catastrophe

During the first four years of perestroika, the Soviet gross domestic product (GDP) was virtually stagnant. Unemployment hovered at about 4 per cent, but was highly concentrated in the labour surplus areas of Central Asia and the Caucasus. Inflation also remained low until 1989, but there were already disturbing signs of a systemic breakdown. For example, shortages, while endemic to all planned economies, became increasingly acute; by mid-1990 over 1,000 basic consumer goods were rarely available in state shops. Queuing reached monumental proportions; according to one estimate in 1990, it amounted to 30 to 40 billion man- (or rather woman-) hours a year. Rationing became widespread, with many goods being distributed at the workplace. The only thing that was not in short supply was money, which was printed in huge quantities to cover a budget deficit that first became evident in 1987 and increased sharply thereafter. Next came the Law on State Enterprises, which took effect in

Cigarettes, like every other consumer good, were in short supply. The picture shows a long queue before a kiosk selling tobacco products.

January 1988 and gave managers control over their enterprises' wage fund and allowed them to increase incomes faster than productivity growth. The State Bank lost control over the money supply: whereas the 1990 plan envisaged an increase of 10 billion roubles in the money supply, it actually turned out to be about 28 billion roubles. Social benefits skyrocketed, increasing 21 per cent after the USSR CPD in 1990 voted in favour of a whole raft of benefits. Because of the spendthrift CPD, economic austerity was virtually impossible.

But responsibility for the budget deficit lay with the Gorbachev administration. Traditionally, the real budget deficit had run at about 2–3 per cent of GDP, but all that changed after 1985. Because of Gorbachev's determination to achieve faster growth rates, he sent back the Twelfth Five-Year Plan (1986–90) three times to planners, with the complaint that the targets were not sufficiently ambitious. As a result, the deficit steadily increased: from 6 per cent in 1986 to 10 per cent in 1988. At the same time that the administration increased investment and defence expenditure, state revenue fell sharply—chiefly because of lost income from the anti-alcohol campaign and lower export prices. By 1991 the situation had become so dire that the economy was on the verge of collapse. To compound the problem, the government was no longer able to intervene decisively, at least in part because the Law on State Enterprises had reduced the personnel in central ministries and transferred greater powers to enterprise management. As the central distributive network broke down, regions were increasingly left to their own devices.

The leadership did not lack economic advice on how to remedy the situation. It was, however, hampered by the fact that the state planning agency, Gosplan, had no operational model of how the planned economy had in fact functioned. In effect, solutions fell into two main categories: the regulated approach or the market approach. Ryzhkov, the Prime Minister, who presented his first reform plan in December 1989, attempted to steer a middle course between planned and market economies. By early 1990, however, it had become clear that Ryzhkov's plan had failed; in May 1990 he therefore submitted a new economic plan, which envisaged a sharp increase in prices—double those of January 1990. His plan also provided for a second stage (marked by the emergence of a 'regulated market economy') and a third stage (with a 'demonopolization' of the economy).

His new plan only provoked a new torrent of criticism, with abuse being showered on the Prime Minister from all sides. Ryzhkov set about designing a third economic plan, but by now he had competition: Gorbachev and Yeltsin agreed to form a commission, which would base its proposals on the '500-day programme' (drafted by Stanislav Shatalin and Grigorii Iavlinskii). This plan, already adopted by the Russian parliament, envisaged an accelerated programme of privatization, with only 30 per cent of the enterprises left in state hands by the end of the 500 days. Given the opposition of the military-industrial complex, however, prospects for this scenario seemed anything but bright.

A shortage of workers at a time of bumper harvests meant that troops, factory workers, and students were sent by the government to help in the fields. Here soldiers help pick potatoes (1991).

While reaffirming the importance of a market economy in the future, Gorbachev conceded that the economy was in deep crisis and backed away from the plan in October. Although he still claimed to support economic reform (in four phases, without regard to any fixed schedule), the centre possessed neither the will-power nor the ability to enforce this programme, for individual republics simply refused to pay contributions. The Baltic republics and Russia even refused to participate in discussions about the 1991 budget. Ryzhkov suffered a heart attack and was succeeded by Valentin Pavlov (whose standing can be gauged from his nickname: pig-hedgehog, because he was corpulent and sported a crew cut). The new Prime Minister infuriated almost everyone by withdrawing all 50- and 100-rouble notes and giving citizens only a few days to exchange them. The maximum that could be exchanged was half of one's monthly salary or 1,000 roubles. Although he justified this measure on the grounds that the West was planning to undermine the rouble, the step was actually aimed at black marketeers and enterprises. In this it failed, however: black marketeers learned of the move beforehand and were able to get rid of their 50- and 100-rouble notes.

Foreign and Security Policy

Like Khrushchev, Gorbachev was more popular abroad than at home. He proved a brilliant diplomat and produced the smile that conquered the West. As Gromyko warned, however, Gorbachev might have a nice smile, but he had teeth of steel. That may be true, but by 1991 they had all been extracted.

None the less he dominated foreign policy decision-making, with Eduard Shevardnadze proving an able accomplice. He had far greater problems with security policy, where the Soviet General Staff had always enjoyed a monopoly and was more wary of taking risks than the President.

Gorbachev was well aware that defence costs were crippling the national economy and that the Soviet Union could not win an arms race with the United States. His 'new political thinking' amounted to renouncing the notion that security should be based on 'bayonets, tanks, and blood'. Instead, he argued, the security of all states was interdependent and could be promoted by recognizing national sovereignty and non-intervention as fundamental principles in the communist world as well. The new approach thus aimed to remove ideology from decision-making, to abandon the concept of an inevitable struggle between opposing camps (still inherent in the Khrushchev strategy of 'peaceful coexistence'), and to give untrammelled precedence to national interest. Gorbachev's strategy provoked opposition not only from the military, but also from conservative party leaders like Ligachev, who continued to uphold the traditional idea that international relations were particularly class in nature.

Critical to the new policy was a new relationship with the United States. The first Gorbachev–Reagan summit, held in Geneva in November 1985, produced a noticeable thaw in relations. The fireside chat (reminiscent of President Roosevelt) charmed the world, as did Raisa Gorbacheva—the first wife of a Soviet leader to exude grace and poise. The outcome of the summit was a joint declaration that proposed to make a 50 per cent reduction in the superpowers' nuclear arsenals. The next summit convened in Reykjavik in October 1986. This time, however, discussions broke down over the issue of the Strategic Defence Initiative (SDI—the famous Star Wars scheme to intercept incoming ballistic missiles), which the Americans were unwilling to abandon. The third summit in Washington in December 1987 was historic: the two sides agreed to eliminate a whole category of nuclear weapons—land-based intermediate and short-range missiles. The final result was the Intermediate Range Nuclear Treaty that Gorbachev and Reagan signed at their final summit in Moscow in May–June 1988. Serious differences still existed, however, especially with respect to verification. Significantly, Gorbachev and Reagan did not raise the SDI issue at the Washington and Moscow summits: the Soviets had made their stand at Reykjavik and lost—a clear sign of the Soviet Union's declining status as a superpower.

A collateral agreement at Geneva also dealt with the Afghanistan issue: the Soviets agreed to withdraw their troops, the last soldier finally leaving that country in February 1989. The withdrawal, which came nearly a decade after Brezhnev had blundered into Afghanistan, had exacted a heavy price in men (almost 14,000 casualties), military equipment, and goodwill around the world.

Relations were also good with the administration of George Bush. Several new summits produced two historic agreements: the CFE Treaty (November

1990) and the START Treaty (July 1991). So good were relations with Washington that Moscow joined the United Nations coalition, spearheaded by America, during the Gulf War in January 1991. That decision was doubtless fraught with much pain, for Iraq had been a long-standing ally of the Soviet Union.

The Gorbachev government also recommended perestroika to the East European regimes in the hope that more reform-minded leaderships would emerge. In a visit to east Berlin in October 1989, Gorbachev deliberately under-mined the position of the GDR leader, Erich Honecker. As a result, his actions not only failed to strengthen socialism in Eastern Europe, but actually dealt the *coup de grâce*. The opening of the Berlin Wall on 9 November 1989 signalled the end of the post-war order in Eastern Europe, a transformation that became possible when Gorbachev renounced the use of Soviet or local military force in the defence of communist regimes. The result was German unification, some-thing that Gorbachev himself had originally opposed.

At Strasbourg in July 1989 Gorbachev spoke of a 'vast economic space from the Atlantic to the Urals'. He coined the expression 'common European home' to make his vision of a general European security agreement more attractive. The Soviet leader promoted the vision of a nuclear-free world by the end of the century.

The Geneva 'fireside' summit of 19–21 November 1985 when Ronald Reagan and Mikhail Gorbachev met for the first time for an exploratory meeting about reducing nuclear arsenals. It was the first meeting of superpower leaders for six years. They hit it off and it led to subsequent meetings and agreements.

On 9 November 1989 the GDR authorities were forced to ease travel restrictions to the West. That night crowds began to dismantle the Wall. Erected on 13 August 1961 to prevent East Germans emigrating to the West, the Wall had made the GDR state viable. Its opening heralded the end of GDR.

Gorbachev, who struck up a warm relationship with Prime Minister Margaret Thatcher, similarly transformed Soviet–British relations. At their first meeting in December 1984, Mrs Thatcher was so taken by the man from Stavropol that she declared him to be a man with whom 'we can do business'. The Thatcher connection was crucial because of her close relationship with Presidents Reagan and Bush.

Gorbachev travelled the world in a vain attempt to attract large foreign investment. He placed high hopes in the International Monetary Fund (IMF) and the Group of Seven (G7) states, but here he had far less success. Japan, in particular, refused to help until the Kurile Islands issue was resolved, and most American businessmen generally regarded Gorbachev as a bad bet.

Relations with the Republics

RUSSIA

When the Russian CPD convened in May 1990, it proceeded to elect Yeltsin as chairman and to declare Russia a sovereign republic. Asserting that the laws of the Russian Federation take precedence over Soviet laws, the congress declared that any Soviet legislation contradictory to Russian law was null and void within the territory of the Russian Federation. Yeltsin announced that Russia would have a multi-party government, with its own defence, foreign, and foreign-trade ministries and central bank. His government also opened negotiations with the Baltic republics, Moldova, Ukraine, and Kazakhstan to establish direct bilateral economic and cultural links. A draft Russian constitution was prepared that made no mention of either the Soviet Union or socialism.

By January 1991 proposals for a popularly elected President of the Russian Federation generated widespread discussion. Yeltsin himself supported the idea, all the more because he found that he could not rely on a majority in the Russian CPD, where conservatives were even pressing for a vote of no confidence. To his aid came democratic forces in Moscow (especially Democratic Russia), which organized great demonstrations in his support. Ironically, the question of direct presidential elections was resolved by Gorbachev, who called for a nation-wide referendum on 17 March 1991 to consider his proposal of a new federal Union. In the Russian Federation the ballot added the question of whether the voter favoured a directly elected Russian President. After the majority voted yes, elections were held in June 1991, with Yeltsin winning 57 per cent of the votes. The list of defeated candidates included the infamous Vladimir Zhirinovskii, leader of the Liberal Democratic party. Yeltsin obtained strong support in the major cities, but fared much worse in the countryside, where the communists still held sway. Obstruction in the CPD led Yeltsin to set up four councils directly subordinate to him: the State Council, the Security Council, the Council of the Federation, and a Council of Ministers (concerned mainly with economic affairs). Governors, reminiscent of Muscovy, were to be sent to the regions to supervise the implementation of central policy.

UKRAINE

Formation of a multi-party system proceeded apace in Ukraine. The party leaders, who had been sceptical of perestroika, suffered a defeat in several cities during the March 1989 elections to the USSR CPD. Even earlier, the Chernobyl disaster had already stimulated the development of the Greens. A popular front movement, called 'Rukh' and led by Ivan Drach, published its programme in February 1989 calling for more decentralization and drew its main support from the intelligentsia. Rukh became increasingly nationalist, with its main stronghold in western Ukraine; communists, by contrast, continued to dominate in eastern Ukraine. In March 1990 Rukh announced its intention to become an

A man holds a banner showing the Baltic republics being cut free from the Soviet Union at an independence rally in Lithuania. In March 1991 Lithuania voted overwhelmingly for independence from the Soviet Union, which had forcibly annexed it after the Second World War.

opposition party and to campaign for independence from the Soviet Union. In July Ukraine followed the example of other republics by declaring sovereignty and claiming the precedence of Ukrainian over Soviet law. In the event a remarkable alliance of communists and nationalists emerged, as communists concluded that nationalism would triumph and therefore determined to lead the nationalist movement and maintain its hold on the reins of power.

In the all-Union referendum on 17 March 1991, some 80 per cent of the Ukrainian voters supported a proposal for a 'union of soviet sovereign states based on the declaration of sovereignty'. The Ukrainian Parliament adopted a market reform that envisaged the 'complete economic and political independence' of Ukraine.

THE BALTIC REPUBLICS

Unlike the Caucasus and Central Asia, which were rent by ethnic unrest and violence, the Baltic republics implemented reform gradually, with the violence coming from the Soviet authorities. Tension between the indigenous and Russian populations was greatest in Estonia. Glasnost provoked a deep crisis in the communist parties of the Baltics; ultimately they were all to split. By 1988 popular fronts were active throughout the Baltics; about one-third of their members were communists, with the radical wings pushing for independence, a Western-style market economy, and a multi-party political system. There were also pro-independence parties and movements representing immigrants, chiefly Russians.

On 1 January 1990 the Baltic republics embraced 'economic self-accounting', which was really a declaration of political, not just economic, autonomy. The formalities were not long in coming, as all three republics (with Lithuania in the forefront) declared formal independence in the course of the same year. Gorbachev responded by declaring the declarations illegal, and tension steadily mounted between the local populations and the Soviet military stationed there. When Soviet forces attacked the TV building in Vilnius in January 1991 (resulting in fourteen deaths), followed by violence in Latvia as well, Gorbachev appeared to be losing control of the forces of coercion. Yeltsin seized the opportunity to demonstrate solidarity with the Baltic republics by flying to Estonia and appealing to the UN Secretary-General to convene an emergency conference on the crisis. It appeared that the 'committees for national salvation' that formed in Lithuania and Latvia had attempted to seize power. The three republics refused to participate in the referendum in March 1991, holding instead their own vote on independence, which won with huge majorities and attracted the support of many non-indigenous voters.

THE CAUCASUS

Glasnost opened a Pandora's box of suppressed ethnic tensions in the Caucasus. In 1988 Armenians, who made up about 75 per cent of the population in the Azerbaijan district of Nagorno-Karabakh, demonstrated in favour of union with Armenia. The conflict caused Armenians in Azerbaijan to flee to Armenia and Azeris in Nagorno-Karabakh to take refuge in Azerbaijan. In response Moscow introduced a 'special form of administration' in January 1989, but made clear its opposition to any territorial transfer. After Moscow returned Nagorno-Karabakh to Azeri control in January 1990, a three-day pogrom of Armenians erupted in Baku and other towns; the bloodletting escalated, with the Armenians seeing themselves as a Christian island in an Islamic sea. Soviet troops finally interceded and opened fire in Baku, killing and wounding several hundred. The Azeri Supreme Soviet reacted by threatening to hold a referendum on secession. The conflict escalated when Nagorno-Karabakh and the neighbouring Shaumian *oblast* declared themselves independent of Azerbaijan. In the latter a popular front, which obtained official recognition in October 1989 and emerged as the dominant political force, aimed at full autonomy

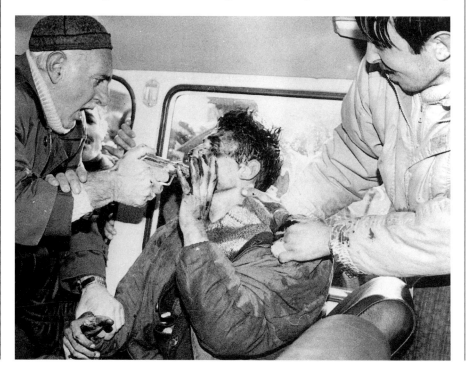

President Zviad Gamsakhurdia's supporters interrogate an opposition fighter suspected of firing at a rally of pro-Presidential supporters in Tbilisi, 3 January 1992.

within the Soviet Union, free association with Iranian Azeris and an end to the 'strongly pro-Armenian policy of Moscow'. When communists won the October 1990 elections, the popular front claimed electoral fraud.

In August 1990 Levon Ter-Petrosian was elected President of Armenia by popular vote. As the nationalist government considered full independence from the Soviet Union, armed militias began to form, attacking Soviet troops and seizing their weapons. The largest formation, the Armenian National Army, attacked the Azeri border but, in the spring of 1991, grudgingly acknowledged the authority of the Armenian government. Nevertheless, fighting between other militias and Soviet troops continued. As Armenia too began to accuse Moscow of siding with its adversary, both sides were now claiming that Moscow supported the other.

Georgia too was torn by increasing turbulence. Opposition to a huge hydro-electric scheme in September 1988 led to the formation of the nationalist movement, and by February 1989 demonstrators were openly demanding independence from Moscow. But the watershed came on 9 April 1989, when Soviet troops killed nineteen unarmed demonstrators in Tbilisi: many believed that Moscow had conducted a punitive operation, and a Georgian commission officially concluded that the soldiers had carried out a 'planned mass massacre'. Ligachev later claimed that the operation had been endorsed by the whole Politburo. The first anniversary of the massacre came shortly before elections to the Supreme Soviet on 25 March 1990, but unrest led to their postponement until 28 October. The Round Table–Free Georgia Alliance, led by Zviad Gamsakhurdia, won 155 of the 250 seats with the communists mustering 64 seats. As a result, the Communist Party lost power after having held it without interruption since 1921.

At the same time, Georgia suffered challenges from its own minorities. Thus the autonomous republic of Abkhazia raised demands that it be permitted to secede from Georgia and become a republic within the Russian Federation. Only about one-sixth of the population was Abkhazian, and their claims were fiercely resisted by Tbilisi. In September 1990 South Ossetia proclaimed itself a separate republic and sought reunion with North Ossetia in Russia. As armed conflict between Ossetians and Georgians mounted, Moscow threatened to intervene to restore order. In March 1991 Presidents Yeltsin and Gamsakhurdia agreed to set up a joint militia force to attempt to calm the situation. In a Georgian referendum on 31 March 1991, fully 99 per cent of the voters opted for independence. Although Gamsakhurdia was overwhelmingly elected as President by voters in May, his dictatorial tendencies and confrontational policies gravely aggravated internal tensions, especially in Abkhazia and South Ossetia.

410

The Attempted Coup

The odds were certainly in favour of a successful coup by the eight-man 'Emergency Committee' comprised of the heads of the military, police, KGB, and government. Although the nominal head was Gennadii Ianaev (Gorbachev's Vice-President, who was to assume the top position), the real mastermind was Vladimir Kriuchkov, the KGB chief. The announcement that the treaty to establish a union of sovereign states was to be signed on 20 August 1991 triggered the move. The plotters also believed that Gorbachev would accede to their demand that he resign in favour of Ianaev; they laid no contingency plan when, in a meeting at his dacha at Foros, Crimea, on the evening of 18 August, he flatly refused. At 6 a.m. the following day Moscow radio broadcast an 'appeal to the Soviet people', claiming that Gorbachev's policies had failed and left the country ungovernable and on the verge of collapse. The plotters sent tanks into Moscow but failed to arrest Yeltsin, who boldly made his way to the Russian White House, passing through the lines of tanks and daring anyone to arrest him. His refusal to acquiesce proved the turning-point: standing on a tank (reminiscent of Lenin's arrival at Finland Station in April 1917), Yeltsin demanded the restoration of Gorbachev as President, called for a general strike, declared the Russian Federation sovereign, and ordered all authorities to obey him. He called the *putsch* an attempt to crush Russia. Eventually, the military itself split, with some tanks and units changing sides and coming to defend the White House. The plotters had to abandon their plan to storm the White House and by 21 August had obviously suffered a complete rout, the entire *putsch* exacting just three fatalities. Gorbachev now returned to Moscow, but the capital in fact already belonged to Yeltsin.

The organization of the *putsch* itself had been astonishingly inept, but its most critical error had been the failure to identify and deploy loyal troops. The plotters had simply assumed that the military would obey. They had failed to grasp the political and social transformation that perestroika had wrought, that it was no longer possible to seize power by simply declaring that the President had retired on 'grounds of health'.

The attempted coup none the less had important consequences: above all, it destroyed prospects for a new union. As republics rushed to declare independence before another coup could succeed, Gorbachev tried desperately to salvage something from the wreckage. But when Ukraine voted for independence on

Cartoon satirizing Gorbachev as organ-grinder, who invokes the old Leninist promises of 'happiness' along with refrains of 'liberty, equality, fraternity'. As the clock suggests, time for Gorbachev has about run out.

Boris Yeltsin waves the Russian flag after the collapse of the August coup against Mikhail Gorbachev. It was generally held that Yeltsin's actions both helped defeat the coup and enhanced his own power over his rival.

1 December 1991, it dealt the Soviet Union a final mortal blow. One week later the three Slav republics—Russia, Ukraine, and Belorussia (renamed Belarus)—issued the 'Minsk Declaration' stating that the Soviet Union had been superseded by the Commonwealth of Independent States (CIS). On 21 December, in Alma-Ata (Kazakhstan), eleven states signed a protocol formally establishing the CIS. The other four republics of the former Soviet Union (Estonia, Latvia, Lithuania, and Georgia) refused to sign. Gorbachev waited until Christmas Day to resign and laid the Soviet Union to rest on 31 December, 1991.

The principal legal successor state to the Soviet Union was the Russian Federation. Thus it formally assumed the Soviet seat on the UN Security Council, took control of all the Soviet embassies and property around the world, and accepted responsibility for outstanding Soviet debts (approximately 60 billion dollars). Russia was by far the predominant power, accounting for 60 per cent of the GDP and occupying 76 per cent of the territory of the former USSR. Although its population (148 million) was now far smaller, Russia was the largest country in the CIS, with 51 per cent of the former Soviet population. It still occupied more than one-eighth of the globe's territory, wielded a vast arsenal of nuclear weapons, and could draw upon a rich wealth of natural and human resources.

Post-Soviet Economy: Privatization and Privation

The Soviet experiment ended, the peoples of the former Soviet Union appeared ready to embark on the building of an entirely new order. Each of the fifteen republics, and indeed regions within them, now claimed independence and the right to determine their own path of development. Each now had an opportunity to complete the transformation initiated by Gorbachev, above all, by replacing the authoritarian, single-party order with a democratic state, where real power devolved upon the people themselves. Even more tantalizing were the prospects for economic reform; blessed with immense natural resources and a highly educated labour force, Russia and the other states seemed poised to construct—with Western financial assistance—a market economy that would be far more productive than the stagnant order of the late Soviet era. Culturally, too, the shackles of communist control were sundered; the collapse of party cultural controls, paralleled by the emergence of a free, private press, promised to inaugurate a whole new golden age of cultural productivity. And after decades of 'deficitism', the shelves in shops were now lined with a superabundance of wares, including top-quality imports. These promises of change at home accompanied a significant easing in international relations, as the post-Soviet states (including Russia) attempted to improve relations with Western powers and to address such outstanding issues as disarmament, nuclear proliferation, and territorial disputes.

The first years of post-Soviet 'transition', however, were anything but pain-
less. Anxious to reconstruct the economy in the shortest possible time, the
Yeltsin regime—led by his Prime Minister, a young economist named Egor
Gaidar—attempted to apply 'shock therapy', that is, a radical programme to
accelerate price deregulation ('liberalization'), marketization, and privatization.
The immediate impact of such policies, especially in an economy dominated by
state oligopolies, was runaway inflation, as prices leaped 300 per cent the first
month and increased 2,591 per cent for 1992. That hyper-inflation wiped out
savings, devalued salaries and pensions, and left the entire economy in turmoil.
As ordinary citizens saw it, the Gaidar programme brought much 'shock' but little 'therapy'. Although in late 1992 Yeltsin replaced Gaidar with a more conservative figure, Viktor Chernomyrdin, the new Prime Minister reaffirmed his
commitment to its original programme, even if one moving at a somewhat
slower pace.

In the ensuing years, the Yeltsin regime indeed did much to restructure the
old Soviet economy. Most dramatic has been the formation of a large private
sector in the industrial and service sectors; by 1997, Russia had privatized
120,000 enterprises, which accounted for more than 70 per cent of the country's
GDP. The government had also deregulated most prices and eliminated many
forms of special subsidies and controls. Another goal was to create a new market infrastructure by encouraging the formation of a whole array of institutions, such as commercial banks, stock exchanges, and financial investment
companies. Russia also actively sought to obtain foreign capital, both through
loans from international financial agencies (such as the International Monetary
Fund) and through direct foreign investment. Observers were quick to discern
the appearance of the 'new Russians', a small but powerful stratum of wealthy
entrepreneurs and investors who reaped fabulous profits from the new opportunities of a free market economy.

These changes, however, were accompanied by acute economic crisis. Thus,
during the first five years (1991–6), the country's GDP fell every year, reaching
even double-digit proportions in some years. Unlike many other post-commun-
ist states, Russia and most other members of the CIS have not been able to
attract much foreign capital—not for lack of opportunity or desire, but because
investors were deterred by the rampant corruption, interminable red tape, legal
chaos, and political instability. Ominously, investment in fixed assets—the
dynamo of future growth and potential—has continually declined, falling
another 18 per cent in 1996 alone. Inflation has gradually declined (840 per cent
in 1993; 215 per cent in 1994; 131 per cent in 1995; 22 per cent in 1996), but it
remains high for a developed country. Although the *rate* of decline in GDP
slowed (4 per cent in 1995 and, disturbingly, 6 per cent in 1996), these data none
the less attested to a continuing decrease in the country's economic potential.
Even though economic reform (above all, the privatization of land) barely
touched the agricultural sector (where 90 per cent of the grain still comes from

the state and collective farms), the systemic economic crisis caused severe dislocation and decline in production. As a result, Russia now imports 35 per cent of its food products (including 50 per cent of its meat).

The cumulative effects have been enormous, as, year in and year out, output declined in industry, agriculture, and other branches. Altogether, during the first five years of independence, Russia's GDP fell by more than 40 per cent—a decline far greater than that experienced by the Western countries during the Great Depression of the 1930s. As a result, per capita GDP in Russia has fallen dramatically; Russia has declined from an economic superpower, as the gap behind the developed countries—where GDP continues to increase—only widened. A CIA Factbook, for example, reports that per capita income in Russia, which in 1989 had stood at 43 per cent of the level in the United States, shrunk to a mere 10 per cent by 1995. Economists and planners in Russia (and the other CIS states) estimate that, even if the economy stabilizes and modest growth resumes, it will require years or even decades to recover the levels in the late 1980s.

Behind these gross macroeconomic indicators, moreover, was massive evidence that the new economic order suffered from fundamental deficiencies. Above all, privatization itself has been riddled with miscalculation and corruption, as property was sold at below-market prices to special insiders; by 1996, even the pace of privatization had slowed considerably, being driven more by the government's frenetic attempts to raise funds rather than to revive the economy. Nor did the market economy prove capable of mobilizing domestic capital, partly because of hyper-inflation (which naturally discouraged long-term investment), partly because of the scandalous reputation of the banking sector (where only some 20 of the 2,300 commercial banks elicit public confidence, with an estimated 80 billion dollars being held in bank accounts abroad). Nor did 'transition' magically transform the inefficient state enterprises into sleek Western corporations; by 1997, nearly half of the firms were still listed as 'unprofitable', meaning that attempts to privatize, restructure, and retool had had scant effect. As a result, these and other marginal enterprises ammassed enormous debts, not only towards each other, but also towards their own employees. Thus, by 1997 less than one-third of the Russian labour force was receiving their wages on time, the rest still awaiting their wages from several months earlier.

This economic collapse, inevitably, entailed ominous consequences for society as a whole. Perhaps the most telling indicators for social conditions come from sheer demographic data: between 1990 and 1995, life expectancy fell sharply for both men (from 64 to 58) and women (from 74 to 70). As the country's mortality rate climbed and birth-rate fell, the population actually decreased by several hundred thousand in 1996. Behind such grim statistics lay the everyday realities of the post-Soviet economy—with 13 to 15 per cent unemployment (including the massive hidden underemployment), the precipitous drop in caloric intake (per capita meat consumption, for example, decreased from 69 to 52 kg. —compared to 115 kg. in the United States), and the appearance of a large underclass somehow surviving under the poverty line (20 per cent). Although the 'poverty line' is manipulable, it bears noting that by early 1997 some 11 per cent of the population lacked sufficient income to meet the bare subsistence minimum. Amidst the breakdown of basic public services (health, education, and public assistance), the country has also experienced an extraordinary explosion of crime, including much in the form of organized Mafias competing for power and wealth. Indicative was the surge in contract murders and a skyrocketing homicide rate (20 per 100,000 citizens—compared to 1 in Great Britain, 3 in Germany, and 9 in the United States).

Moreover, the new order has raised serious questions of social justice. Above all, that applies to income distribution, where the gap between rich and poor sharply widened. According to data on the 'decile coefficient' for 1994, the top 10 per cent of the population obtained 15.1 times more than the poorest 10 per cent; that was a far cry from the three reported in the 1960s. Although the gap has since narrowed slightly (dropping to 13.1 times by 1996), it none the less remains immense. Moreover, such stratification is hardly equivalent to social progress, and, especially, to the formation of a new 'middle class' or 'entrepreneurial élite'. As recent research has demonstrated, the majority of the new élites—75 per cent of those in politics, 61 per cent of the economic moguls— came from the old *nomenklatura*, who simply used their old status to achieve special privilege and property under the new order. As a result, the new order appears as corrupt and criminal as it is unjust, at least from the perspective of the vast majority of citizens.

Post-Soviet Politics: Domestic Instability and International Tension

The economic crisis, with all its alarming social consequences, significantly exacerbated the problems of building a new political order. Once the euphoria of defeating the *putsch* had subsided, the Yeltsin government soon found itself locked in a fierce struggle with the remnant of the old order, the CPD and its smaller body, the Supreme Soviet. Although Yeltsin replaced the unpopular Gaidar with the more cautious Chernomyrdin, and although the government slowed the pace of economic reform, its onerous programme remained extremely unpopular for the general population and inspired fierce opposition in the parliament. Indeed, post-*putsch* politics has been one long story of incessant conflict between President and parliament. Hence Yeltsin's primary goal was to neutralize his parliamentary critics and to replace the old 'Brezhnev Constitution' of 1977 with one that lent far more power to the President.

He took a critical step in that direction in April 1993 by holding a national referendum on his proposal to draft a new constitution. After winning by a slim majority and, in the face of rising parliamentary opposition, Yeltsin convened a constitutional commision to draft a new set of fundamental laws. As opposition of the parliament mounted (including attempts to impeach him), on 21 September 1993 Yeltsin summarily—and illegally—dissolved the existing parliament and announced plans to hold new elections and a referendum on his draft constitution. Hardline opponents in the parliament, supported by Yeltsin's own Vice-President (Alexander Rutskoi), occupied the 'White House' (the seat of parliament) and attempted to resist Yeltsin's unconstitutional actions. The dispute ended in a bloody battle, as government troops stormed the building to suppress the parliamentary rebels, leaving a large number of dead and wounded.

In the aftermath, Yeltsin attempted to construct a new regime. His parliamentary opposition now crushed, Yeltsin now hastened to solicit popular endorsement for his new constitution. It was a strongly 'presidential' order, one that assigned extraordinary powers to Yeltsin himself (to issue 'ukases' and determine ministerial appointments) and severely limited the authority and role of the parliament. The latter took the form of a bicameral system: a parliament called the State Duma (with 450 members) and a Federation Council (with two members from each of the eighty-nine regions). At the same time, Yeltsin attempted to strengthen his control over local government, chiefly by personally appointing local 'governors' until formal elections could be held. The new constitution won a slight majority in a national vote in December 1993 and immediately went into effect.

Although the new constitution greatly enhanced Yeltsin's presidential powers, it did not enable him to construct a supportive, or even stable new order. That was immediately apparent in the parliamentary elections of December 1993, where pro-reform factions (such as Egor Gaidar's 'Russia's Choice') elicited little support. Far more successful were the nationalist parties, above all, Vladimir Zhirinovskii's Liberal Democratic Party, which received the largest share of the vote (23 per cent). Not surprisingly, the new parliament proved nearly as recalcitrant as the last, and among its first acts was to declare an amnesty for Yeltsin's adversaries in the conflicts of August 1991 and October 1993. In the next parliamentary elections (December 1995), the results were still more dismaying, for the largest share of votes (22 per cent) now went to the Communist Party of the Russian Federation under Gennadii Ziuganov and other oppositionist parties. As a result, communists were elected to chair both the State Duma and the Federation Council, much to Yeltsin's dismay and chagrin. By late 1995, as Yeltsin's personal approval rating had descended to a single-digit level, his prospecs for the impending persidential elections in 1996 seemed extraordinary dim.

That election campaign, which dominated the political life of the country in the first half of 1996, reflected a miraculous turn-around for Yeltsin. Like incumbents everywhere, he dispensed largesse in a wild spending spree (giving lavish presents, such as automobiles, to some voters) that threatened to demolish his government's own programme of budgetary austerity. The President unabashedly exploited his near-monopoly over media coverage, especially television, where his opponents were portrayed very negatively if at all. And, despite a legal spending limit of 3 million dollars, Yeltsin's camp spent an estimated 140 million dollars (much of it coming from shadowy entrepreneurial circles, fearful that a communist victory would bring a new 1917). Outsiders, especially the International Monetary Fund and some foreign governments, exhibited overt sympathy towards Yeltsin and even provided some timely financial support.

Although the elections themselves had relatively few irregularities, these pre-election conditions proved decisive. Expoiting residual fear that the communists would return to power and their old ways, the unpopular Yeltsin managed to win an astounding 35 per cent of the vote in the first round of open elections; he was followed by Gennadii Ziuganov with 32 per cent and a retired general, Alexander Lebed, with 15 per cent. Since no candidate obtained a simple majority, the Russian constitution mandated a second run-off election. In a deft manoeuvre to obtain the support of Lebed's voters, Yeltsin co-opted the ambitious general into his own administration by appointing him as executive secretary of the Security Council. As a result, in the run-off election on 3 July between Yeltsin and Ziuganov, Yeltsin won 54 per cent of the vote—compared to 40 per cent for Ziuganov, with the balance voting against both men.

Despite that resounding victory, Kremlin politics remained as turbulent as ever. The presidential elections, deliberately scheduled so as not to coincide with the parliamentary vote, did nothing to resolve the conflict between an oppositionist parliament and the newly re-elected President. Moreover, Yeltsin's new government was ridden by internal squabbling and conflict; the dismissal of Lebed after just four months (October 1996) did nothing to eliminate the bitter feuding within the Kremlin itself. In no small measure, the problem lay with Yeltsin himself, who suffered serious health problems and underwent a quintuple bypass heart operation; beginning in mid-1996, Yeltsin was effectively removed from ongoing control over his own 'presidential' regime. Given the 'presidential system' (whereby the Yeltsin constitution of 1993 made so much dependent on the President himself), Yeltsin's health problems opened the door to backroom intrigues and growing doubts about his capacity to manage the Kremlin, let alone govern the country.

Nor was the Yeltsin regime able to build a system of effective administration, either at the centre or at lower levels. Characteristically, in recent years the government had difficulty performing even the most elementary functions, such as tax collection; in 1996, for example, revenues fell 15 per cent below the expected levels, thereby exacerbating the problems of a budget deficit and causing sharp cut-backs in support for essential social services like health care and education. Characteristically, the regime could find no better way to deal with the crisis that to re-establish a 'Cheka' for tax collection and to set ever higher duties on alcohol consumption. According to official sources, only 17 per cent of all Russian firms pay taxes on a regular basis; most are late, while one-third pay none at all. The confusion of laws (contradictory, arbitrarily applied), corruption, red tape—all attested to a steady degradation of central governance. To counteract or camouflage this weakness at the top, Russia (and, indeed, several other post-Soviet states—including Belarus, Uzbekistan, and Azerbaijan) have tended towards authoritarianism under the guise of 'presidential power', only exacerbating the political turmoil while failing to rebuild effective state power.

Perhaps more ominous still, Moscow gradually lost its control over local government, as the eighty-nine regions increasingly came to assert their own authority and prerogatives. Given the erosion of power at the centre, regional authorities were forced to address problems on their own—to find funds for public assistance, obtain energy and other resources, and rebuild local economies on their own. That 'regionalization' of power was first apparent in the autonomous ethnic areas, such as Tatarstan, which refused to recognize Moscow's hegemony and in February 1994 signed an agreement with the Yeltsin government acknowledging its right to conduct an independent foreign policy and control its own economic resources. In 1996, as the country held its first wave of regional elections (to replace those appointed by Yeltsin), the elections brought outright opponents to power and, more important, greatly increased the independence of local authorities.

In no place was the centrifugal forces more apparent than in Chechnia—a small Caucasus region with a long and bitter history of Russian rule (including Stalin's mass deportation for treason during the Second World War). In 1991, as the Soviet Union finally disintegrated, nationalists in Chechnia (led by a former Soviet general, Dzhokhar Dudaev) declared independence and effectively ceased to heed directive from Moscow. While Yeltsin initially tolerated such declarations (they came from many other areas as well, such as the 'Republic of Sakha' in Eastern Siberia), he gradually became persuaded that the secessionists in Chechnia posed a serious threat to Russian authority and, especially, the vital oil pipelines that traverse the area. In December 1994, without parliamentary approval, Yeltsin ordered a military invasion to re-establish 'law and order', thereby initiating a bloody war that would last some nineteen months and cost tens of thousands of lives. The conflict not only failed to restore Moscow's authority but also exposed the degradation of the Russian military machine and the acrimonious conflict among the various 'force ministries' (army, special forces, ministry of interior, and intelligence services). It all came to an ignominious end in August 1996, when Alexander Lebed negotiated the Khasaviurt Accords, which provided for a Russian withdrawal, new elections in Chechnia, and disposition of the 'sovereignty' question for Chechnia at some later point.

Nor did the Yeltsin regime have much success in dealing with other former Soviet republics. Despite the creation of a loose association as a 'commonwealth of independent states', and despite the continuing importance of economic ties, Russia's relations with most of the former Soviet republics have been marked by tension and conflict. That is particularly evident in the Baltics (Estonia, Latvia, and Lithuania), where anti-Russian sentiments not only impelled them to eschew membership in the 'Commonealth', but also to adopt discriminatory measures against their substantial Russian minorities (roughly a third of the populace in all three countries). Although Moscow continues to regard the post-Soviet space as its own special sphere of interest (referring to these independent states as the 'near abroad'), and although its influence is indeed substantial, it has thus far achieved little in schemes aimed at 'regional integration' through political, military, or economic unions. On the contrary, it faces many residual issues, as in Ukraine, where the two countries continue to wrangle over rights to the Black Sea fleet, a Russian naval base in Sebastopol, and the final disposition of the Crimea (formally transferred to Ukraine in 1954, but with an ethnic Russian majority).

Compounding problems in the 'near abroad' have been growing complications in Russia's relations with the 'far abroad'—especially the Western powers. Although Yeltsin's first Foreign Minister, Andrei Kozyrev, banked heavily on good relations with NATO and especially the United States, the cheerful assumptions about the possibilities for co-operation have gradually dissipated. In part, contrary to Russian expectations and promises by Western leaders, Russia received only a modest level of financial assistance and investment; organizations like the International Monetary Fund and the European Bank of Reconstruction and Development were far more generous with their advice and requirements than they were with aid and loans. Moreover, Western powers grew increasingly concerned about Moscow's inclination to sell military goods and nuclear technology to any bidder, especially international pariahs like Iran, regardless of the attendant risks of nuclear proliferation. And, most important of all, the Western powers became increasingly committed to the expansion of NATO eastward, thereby marginalizing and isolating Russia as its neighbours gradually gravitated towards partial ('Partners for Peace') and full membership.

Catastrophic economic decline, internal political instability, and loss of super-power status—all have fuelled domestic disenchantment and disillusion with the post-Soviet order. Public opinion surveys in late 1996, for example, revealed that only 11 per cent now approve the breakup of the Soviet Union, while the vast majority—rightly—believe that the 'transition' has drastically lowered their standard of living. Nor is there much faith that the government, itself in disarray and devoid of resources, will be able to address the problems of economic decline and attendant social problems. The former Soviet Union will leave the twentieth century much as it began it, with a wrenching crisis in ethnic relations, political institutions, and the economy. The demise of the Soviet authoritarian state heralded new possibilities for democratization, but left the country with a greatly diminished capacity to resolve the long-term problems of economic development, political integration, and social stability. Although Russia and the other post-Soviet republics frantically draft plans for long-term development and even predict imminent 'stabilization' and 'resumption of economic growth', in fact such predictions are neither new nor persuasive. And, even if true, it will take years, even decades, to return to the level of output, standard of living, and panoply of social services that the country had taken for granted in the final years of the *ancien* Soviet *régime*.

While such pessimistic assessments are widespread among specialists (and for good reason), one must not hasten to banish Russia to the ranks of a third-world country. Above all, it continues to possess immense natural and human resources; these include vast reserves of oil, gas, and other raw materials as well as a labour force that is highly educated and trained. Moreover, the data on economic 'decline' can be highly deceptive, partly because so much economic activity is hidden in the 'shadow economy' (to evade taxation), partly because the productive capacity, fixed capital, and infrastructure are merely under-utilized (not non-existent). If freed of neo-liberal economic dogma, 'transitionology' might well programme a far more efficient path to marketization and economic growth (as in China), largely by relying more, not less, on state intervention in the economy. And that, in turn, depends on the ability to rebuild the state itself, with a modern system of laws and institutions, democratic political culture, and effective system of governance.

MAPS

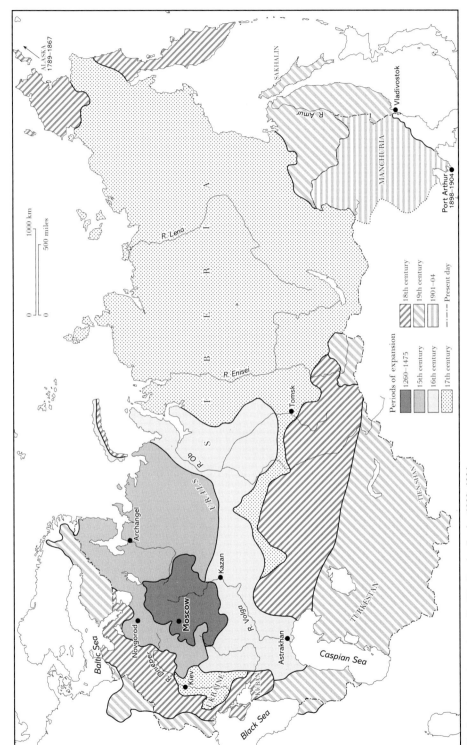

Territorial expansion and growth of the Russian Empire, 1260–1904

Periods of expansion

1260–1475	18th century
15th century	19th century
16th century	1901–04
17th century	Present day

423

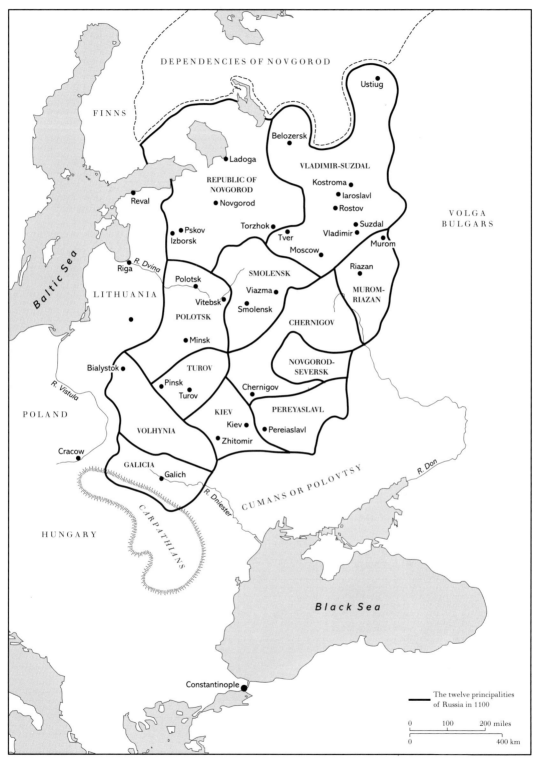

Kievan Russia, 1054–1238

Russia c.1396 and the rise of Moscow, 1300–1584

Moscow

▨	1300 (to Daniil)
▦	To 1389 (Ivan I-Dimitri)
☐	To 1462 (Vasily I, Vasily II)
▨	To 1533 (Ivan III, Vasily III)
⸭	To 1584 (Ivan IV)

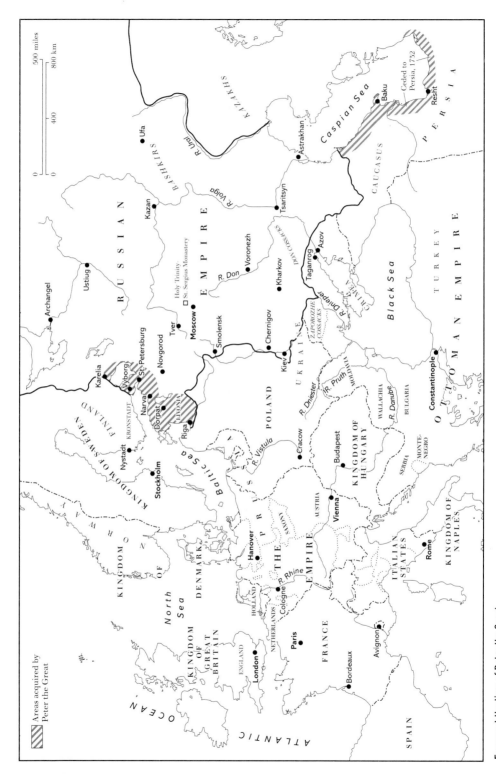

Europe at the time of Peter the Great

Areas acquired by
Peter the Great

500 miles

800 km

400

0

0

Ufa

R. Ural

KAZAKHS

BASHKIRS

Kazan

RUSSIAN

Astrakhan

Caspian Sea

Baku

Ceded to
Persia, 1732

Resht

PERSIA

CAUCASUS

R. Volga

Tsaritsyn

EMPIRE

Archangel

Ustiug

Holy Trinity
□ St. Sergius Monastery

R. Voronezh

DON COSSACKS

Black Sea

TURKEY

Voronezh

R. Don

Kharkov

Taganrog

Azov

CRIMEA

OTTOMAN EMPIRE

Tver

Moscow

Smolensk

Chernigov

Kiev

ZAPOROZHIE
COSSACKS

R. Dnieper

St. Petersburg

Novgorod

UKRAINE

R. Dniester

MOLDAVIA

R. Pruth

WALLACHIA

Constantinople

Karelia

Vyborg

Narva

Dorpat

LIVONIA

Riga

KRONSTADT

FINLAND

Nystadt

Stockholm

Baltic Sea

POLAND

Cracow

R. Vistula

Budapest

BULGARIA

R. Danube

KINGDOM OF SWEDEN

NORWAY

North
Sea

DENMARK

KINGDOM
OF

PRUSSIA

SAXONY

KINGDOM OF HUNGARY

Vienna

AUSTRIA

SERBIA

MONTE-
NEGRO

Hanover

THE

EMPIRE

R. Rhine

Cologne

ITALIAN
STATES

Rome

KINGDOM OF NAPLES

HOLLAND

NETHERLANDS

KINGDOM
OF
GREAT
BRITAIN

London

ENGLAND

Paris

FRANCE

Avignon

Bordeaux

ATLANTIC OCEAN

SPAIN

The provinces of European Russia

428

Russia, its Empire, and its neighbours in the 20th century

ARCTIC OCEAN

Murmansk
Barents Sea
Kara Sea
FINLAND
Leningrad (St Petersburg)
Moscow
Vorkuta
Norilsk
Iakutsk
Magadan
KAMCHATKA PENINSULA
Okhotsk Sea
SAKHALIN
R. Kolyma
R. Ob
R. Enisei
R. Lena
R. Amur
SIBERIA
Surgut
TRANS-SIBERIAN RAILWAY
KUZBASS
Bratsk
ALTAI
Irkutsk
Harbin
Vladivostok
JAPAN
KOREA
Port Arthur
Beijing
MANCHURIA
MONGOLIA
Caspian Sea
Aral Sea
KAZAKHSTAN
UZBEKISTAN
TURKMENISTAN
KIRGHIZSTAN
Alma-Ata
TADZHIKISTAN
IRAN
AFGHANISTAN
PAKISTAN
INDIA
TIBET
CHINA
PACIFIC OCEAN

uralsk
Sverdlovsk (Ekaterinburg)
Cheliabinsk
Omsk
R. Ob

| 0 | 200 | 400 | 600 | 800 km |
| 0 | 200 | 400 | 600 miles |

Boundary of former USSR

Magnitogorsk
Karaganda

L. Balkhash

KAZAKHSTAN

Aral Sea

UZBEKISTAN

Frunze
KIRGHIZSTAN

Tashkent

TADZHIKISTAN

Samarkand
Dushanbe

Bokhara

TURKMENISTAN

AFGHANISTAN

429

URAL MTS

FINLAND

Vyborg
●Vologda
Leningrad

Reval
Baltic
Sea
●Pskov
●Gorky

Riga
LATVIA
●Moscow

Memel
LITHUANIA
Tula
Kovno ●Vilna
Königsberg
●Minsk
Voronezh

Warsaw
●Pinsk
●Stalingrad

POLAND
●Lvov
GALICIA
Rostov

CZECH
Chernovtsy
Caspian
Sea

Budapest
Kishinev
BESSARABIA

HUNGARY
ROMANIA
Sevastopol

Belgrade ●
●Bucharest
Black Sea
CAUCASUS MTS

YUGOSLAVIA
BULGARIA

Sofia

Tirana●
ALBANIA
GREECE

TURKEY

Aegean Sea

| | Front line of German invasion forces, December 1941 |

0   200   400 miles
0   200   400   600 km

Territory annexed by Soviet Union 1939–40, reincorporated into Soviet Union in 1945

Former German and Czechoslovak territory annexed in 1945

The Great Patriotic War

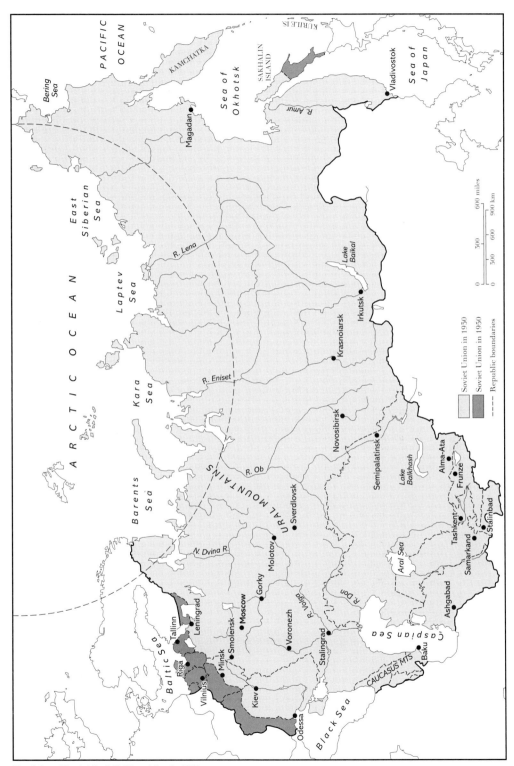

The Union of Soviet Socialist Republics in 1950

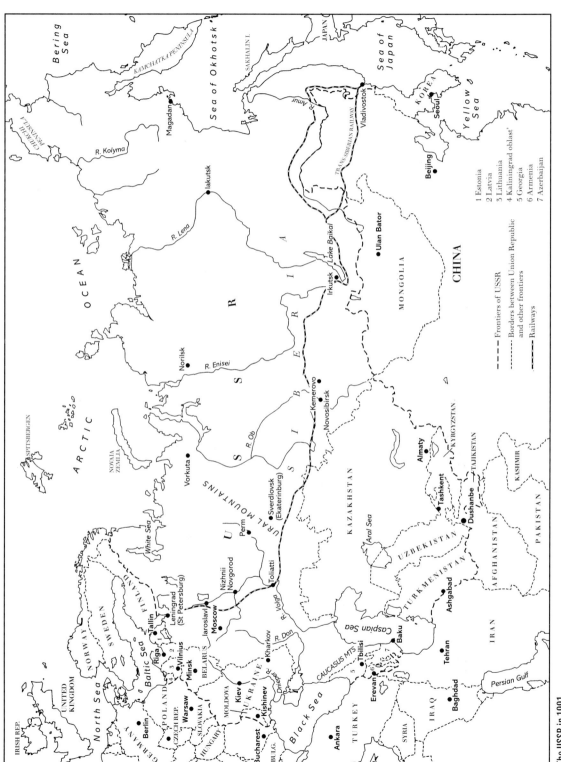

The USSR in 1991

Chronology

For a detailed chronology of Russian history, see Francis Conte (ed.), *Great Dates in Russian and Soviet History* (New York, 1994).

860–1240	**Era of Kievan Rus**
862	Traditional date for arrival of 'Riurik' of Varangians (Norsemen), founder of Riurikid dynasty (862–1598)
980–1015	Vladimir reigns as grand prince of Kiev
988	Conversion of Kievan Rus to Eastern Orthodox Christianity
1019–54	Iaroslav reigns as grand prince of Kiev
1037–46	Construction and decoration of Church of St Sofia in Kiev
1051	Hilarion consecrated as metropolitan of Kiev and all Rus
1055	Polovtsy appear on steppe
1061	Polovtsy attack territories of Rus
1072	Canonization of Princes Boris and Gleb
1096	Polovtsy attack Kiev and burn Pecherskii Monastery
1097	Princely conference at Liubech
1113–25	Vladimir Monomakh reigns as grand prince of Kiev
1132–6	Emergence of semi-autonomous Novgorod
1147	First chronicle mention of Moscow
1156	Construction of first kremlin walls in Moscow
1169	Armies of Prince Andrei Bogoliubskii of Vladimir sack Kiev
1191–2	Novgorod signs commercial treaty with Scandinavians and Germans
1223	Battle of Kalka: first encounter of Mongols with Kievan Rus
1237–40	Mongol conquest of Kievan Rus, culminating in the sack of Kiev
1240	Prince Alexander Nevsky defeats Swedes on the Neva
1240–1340	**Early Mongol Suzerainty**
1242	Prince Alexander Nevsky defeats Teutonic Knights at Lake Peipus
1300	Moscow conquest of Kolomna: beginning of 'in-gathering' of Russian land
1317–28	Metropolitan moves to Moscow
1327–41	Ivan I (Kalita), designated grand prince of Vladimir, by the Mongol khan
1340–1584	**Rise of Muscovy**
1337	Founding of Holy Trinity Sergius Monastery
1359–89	Dmitrii Donskoi reigns as grand prince of Moscow
1367	Construction of stone kremlin in Moscow
1380	Battle of Kulikovo
1389–1425	Vasilii I reigns as grand prince of Moscow
1425–62	Vasilii II reigns as grand prince of Moscow
1433–53	Civil war between Vasilii II and his kinsmen

1448	Bishop Iona of Riazan selected metropolitan, without the approval of Constantinople
1453	Fall of Constantinople
1462–1505	Ivan III (the Great) reigns as grand prince of Moscow
1463	Moscow acquires the principalities of Iaroslavl and part of Rostov
1478	Moscow annexes Novgorod
1480	Battle of Ugra, nominal end of Moscow subordination to Mongols
1485	Moscow conquers Tver
1497	Ivan III issues a brief law code (*Sudebnik*), with the first broad limitation on peasant movement
1499	Moscow acquires the principalities of Viatka
1505–33	Vasilii III reigns as grand prince of Moscow
1510	Moscow absorbs the city-state of Pskov
1514	Smolensk conquered
1521	Annexation of Riazan, last independent principality in central Russia
1533–84	Ivan IV reigns in minority as grand prince (1533–47), then tsar of Moscow (1547–84)
1537	Local judicial and administrative reforms, with the election of 'brigandage elders' (*gubnye starosty*)
1547	Ivan IV crowned tsar
1550	Law code (*sudebnik*) promulgated
1551	Church council ('Hundred Chapters' or *Stoglav*) proposes church reforms
1552	Conquest of Kazan
1555	Reform of local fiscal system (*zemskie starosty*)
1556	Astrakhan conquered
1558–83	Livonian War, ending with threats that cede lands to Poland-Lithuania and Sweden
1564	Publication of first book
1564–72	*Oprichnina*, Ivan's personal domain
1570	*Oprichnina* forces sack Novgorod
1571	Crimean Tatars storm and burn Moscow
1575	Ivan IV abdicates temporarily in favour of Semen Bekbulatovich
1580	First law forbidding peasants to change landlords
1582	Ermak's initial conquest of khanate of western Siberia
1584–1613	**Time of Troubles**
1584	Fedor Ivanovich reigns as tsar, with Boris Godunov ruling behind the scenes
1589	Law code (*sudebnik*); establishment of Patriarchate
1591	Death of Tsarevich Dmitrii
1598	Fedor dies, marking the extinction of the Riurikid dynasty
1598–1605	Boris Godunov reigns as tsar
1605–6	First False Dmitrii reigns as tsar
1606–7	Bolotnikov rebellion
1606–10	Reign of 'boyar' tsar, Vasilii Shuiskii
1610–13	Interregnum: boyar intervention, Polish rule

1612	Liberation of Moscow by Minin and Pozharskii (October)
1613–1689	**Muscovy: Restored and Reconstructed**
1613	Election of Michael Romanov, onset of new dynasty (1613–1917)
1613–45	Mikhail reigns as tsar
1617	Treaty of Stolbovo with Sweden
1618	Armistice of Deulino with Poland
1619	Filaret (Romanov) consecrated as patriarch
1632–4	Polish war
1645–76	Alexis reigns as tsar
1648	Moscow uprising
1649	Law code (*Sobornoe ulozhenie*)
1650	Novgorod and Pskov rebellions
1652	Establishment of separate foreigners' settlement (*nemetskaia sloboda*) in Moscow; consecration of Nikon as Patriarch
1653	First church reforms, which eventually led to schism (*raskol*)
1654	Cossacks under Bohdan Khmelnitskii recognize Moscow's suzerainty
1666–7	Church council: condemnation of Nikon, formal beginning of schism
1667	Armistice of Andrusovo with Poland
1667–71	Stenka Razin rebellion
1672	First theatrical performance
1676–81	First Russo-Turkish war
1676–82	Fedor reigns as tsar
1682–9	Regency of Sofia; nominal rule of Peter I and Ivan V
1682	Peter I proclaimed tsar, then co-tsar with older half-brother Ivan V; aboltion of precedence; Streltsy revolt
1686	'Eternal Peace' with Poland-Lithuania and joining Holy League against the Ottoman Turks
1687–9	Vasilii Golitsyn's failed campaigns against the Crimean khanate
1689	Russian–Chinese Treaty of Nerchinsk
1689–1740	**Petrine Russia and Aftermath**
1689	Peter I (the Great) assumes power, ruling until his death in 1725
1690	Birth of Tsarevich Alexis
1693–4	Peter travels to Archangel to sample sea voyages
1695–6	Azov campaigns: initial failure, eventual success
1697–8	Peter's 'Grand Embassy' to Western Europe
1698	Revolt of the Streltsy suppressed
1700–21	Northern War between Russia and Sweden
1700	Russian defeat at Narva; death of Patriarch Adrian; adoption of European (Julian) calendar
1701	Opening of the Moscow school of mathematics and navigation
1702	Manifesto welcoming foreigners to Russia; opening of first public theatre in Moscow
1703	Foundation of St Petersburg; publication of first newspaper (*Vedomosti*)
1705–6	Streltsy revolt at Astrakhan

1707–8	Cossack revolt on lower Don led by Bulavin
1708	Adoption of civil alphabet
1709	Russian victory at Poltava
1710	Russian conquest of Baltics
1711	Foundation of the Senate; marriage of Peter to Catherine; defeat at Pruth
1713	Court and many administrative agencies transferred to St Petersburg; earnest preparations for administrative reform commence
1714	Russian naval victory at Hangö; Naval Academy established in St Petersburg
1715–17	First Russian expedition to Central Asia
1716–17	Peter's second extended trip to Europe
1717–18	Administrative colleges (*kollegii*) established
1718	Investigation, trial, and execution of Tsarevich Alexis and other alleged conspirators
1721	Adoption of imperial title; publication of the *Ecclesiastical Regulation* and foundation of the Holy Synod
1722	New succession law; Table of Ranks promulgated
1722–3	Persian Campaign along the Caspian Sea
1722–4	Completion of first universal (male) census; first collection of 'soul tax'
1724	Foundation of the Imperial Russian Academy of Sciences at St Petersburg
1725	Death of Peter I; accession of Catherine I
1725–7	Reign of Catherine I; hegemony of Alexander Menshikov
1726–30	Predominance of Supreme Privy Council
1727–30	Reign of Peter II; downfall and exile of Menshikov
1730	'Constitutional Crisis' after the death of Peter II, accession of Anna Ivanovna as empress (1730–40); abolition of Supreme Privy Council; emergence of Biron as favourite
1733–5	War of the Polish Succession, Russia in alliance with Austria
1735	Orenburg founded on south-eastern border and southern Urals; Turkic Bashkirs resist Russian encroachment in a full-blown colonial war till 1740
1736–9	Russo-Turkish War
1740	Death of Anna Ivanovna
1740–1	Ivan VI, with Anna Leopoldovna as regent
1741–1801	**Age of Enlightenment**
1741–61	Reign of Elizabeth
1741–3	Russo-Swedish War
1754	Abolition of internal tariffs; establishment of Noble Bank
1755	Moscow University established
1756–62	Russian participation in Seven Years War
1760	Nobles given right to exile serfs to Siberia
1761–2	Reign of Peter III
1762	Manifesto freeing the nobility from obligatory service (18 February)
1762–96	Reign of Catherine II
1764	Secularization of Church lands and peasants

1766	Publication of 'The Great Instruction' by Catherine the Great
1767–8	Legislative Assembly (*Ulozhennaia komissiia*) convened
1768–74	Russo-Turkish War
1771	Bubonic plague; Moscow riots
1772	First Partition of Poland (July)
1774	Treaty of Kuchuk-Kainardji with Turkey, recognizing Russian protectorate over Christians in the Ottoman Empire
1773–5	Pugachev rebellion
1775	Statute on Provincial Administration
1781–6	Administrative absorption of Ukraine
1782	Law on Provincial Police
1785	Charter to the Nobility; Charter to the Towns
1787–92	Russo-Turkish War
1790	A. N. Radishchev's *Journey from St Petersburg to Moscow* published
1793	Second Partition of Poland
1794	Odessa founded
1795	Third and final partition of Poland
1796–1801	Reign of Paul
1797	Edict limiting corvée labour (*barshchina*) to three days per week; Law of Succession

1800–1855	**Pre-Reform Russia**
1801–25	Reign of Alexander I
1801	Annexation of Georgia
1802	Establishment of ministries
1804	Educational Reform; establishment of three additional universities; Pale of Settlement, restricting Jewish residency to the Western provinces
1804–7	Russian participation in alliance against Napoleon
1807	Peace of Tilsit
1807–11	Speransky Reforms
1809	Acquisition of Finland
1810	State Council established
1812	Napoleon invades Russia (June); Battle of Borodino; Moscow burnt (September); French retreat
1815	Holy Alliance; establishment of Congress Poland
1816–19	Landless emancipation of Baltic serfs
1819	Establishment of St Petersburg University
1825	Decembrist revolt
1825–55	Reign of Nicholas I
1830	Publication of *The Complete Collection of Laws of the Russian Empire*
1830–1	Polish rebellion
1833	First modern law code (*Svod zakonov*) published, taking effect in 1835
1836	Publication of P. Ia. Chaadaev's 'Philosophical Letter'
1837–42	State peasant reforms under P. D. Kiselev
1842–51	Construction of first Russian railway line (St Petersburg–Moscow)
1847	Exchange between N. Gogol and V. Belinskii

| 1849 | Petrashevskii circle |
| 1853–6 | Crimean War |

1855–1890   **Great Reforms and Counter-Reform**

1855–81	Reign of Alexander II
1856	Peace of Paris, ending the Crimean War; Alexander's speech to the nobility of Moscow, intimating the need to reform serfdom 'from above'
1857	Secret commission for serf reform established (1 January); Nazimov Rescript (20 November) inviting nobility to collaborate in reform; 'Chief Committee on Peasant Affairs' under Rostovtsev established to oversee emancipation
1859–60	Noble deputations come to St Petersburg (August 1859; January 1860)
1861	Emancipation Manifesto (19 February)
1862	Publication of I. S. Turgenev's *Fathers and Sons*
1863	Polish Rebellion; publication of N. G. Chernyshevskii's *What Is to Be Done?*; University Statute issued
1864	Zemstvo (local self-government) established; judicial reform; elementary school reform
1865	Censorship reform ('Temporary Regulations')
1865–85	Conquest, absorption of Central Asia
1866	Assassination attempt on Alexander II
1867–9	Church reforms (abolition of caste in 1867; restructuring of seminary; reorganization of parishes in 1869)
1869	Publication of P. Lavrov's *Historical Letters* and L. Tolstoy's *War and Peace*
1870	City government reform
1872	Russian publication of Karl Marx's *Das Kapital*
1874	Universal Military Training Act, culminating military reforms
1874	Populist 'going to the people'
1876–9	Revolutionary populist organization, Land and Freedom
1877–8	Russo-Turkish War
1878	Peace of Berlin
1879	Terrorist organization, People's Will, established to combat autocracy
1879–80	Publication of F. Dostoevsky's *Brothers Karamazov*
1879–81	'Crisis of Autocracy'—terrorism, 'dictatorship of the heart'
1881–94	Reign of Alexander III
1881	Temporary Regulations of 14 August 1881 (establishing 'extraordinary' police powers to combat revolutionary movement)
1881–2	Pogroms
1882	May laws (discriminating against Jews)
1882–4	Counter-reform in censorship (1882), education (1884), Church (1884)
1882–6	Reform acts to protect industrial labour
1884	First Marxist organization, under G. Plekhanov, established abroad
1885	Noble Land Bank established; abolition of poll-tax
1885–1900	Russification in borderlands
1889	New local state official, the 'Land Captain', established

1890–1914   Revolutionary Russia

1890	Zemstvo counter-reform (restricting autonomy and franchise)
1891–2	Famine
1891–1904	Construction of Trans-Siberian Railway
1892	City government counter-reform (restricting autonomy and franchise)
1892–1903	S. Iu. Witte as Minister of Finance
1894–1917	Reign of Nicholas II
1895	'Senseless dreams' speech by Nicholas II
1896–7	St Petersburg textile strikes; St Petersburg Union for the Liberation of Labour established
1897	Gold standard; first modern census
1898	Russian Social Democratic Workers' Party founded
1899	V. I. Lenin's *The Development of Capitalism in Russia* published
1901–2	Party of Social Revolutionaries (PSR) established
1902	Peasant disorders in Poltava and Kharkov (March–April); Lenin's *What Is To Be Done?* published
1903	Union of Liberation (left-liberal organization) established; RSDWP splits into Bolshevik (under V. I. Lenin) and Menshevik (under Iu. Martov) factions; south Russian labour strikes (Rostov-on-the-Don and Odessa); Kishinev anti-Semitic pogroms
1904	Corporal punishment abolished
1904–5	Russo-Japanese War
1905–7	Revolution of 1905
1905	Bloody Sunday (9 January); October Manifesto (17 October) promising political reform and civil rights
1906	First State Duma; Stolypin land reforms
1907	Second State Duma; *coup d'état* of 3 June
1907–12	Third State Duma
1909	Publication of *Vekhi* ('Signposts')
1911	Assassination of P. A. Stolypin (September)
1912	Lena Goldfields massacre and ensuing strike wave (March–May)
1912–17	Fourth State Duma

1914–1921   War, Revolution, Civil War

1914	Outbreak of First World War
1915	Progressive Bloc and political crisis (August)
1916	Central Asia rebellion; murder of Rasputin
1917	February Revolution (23 February–1 March); establishment of Provisional Government and Petrograd Soviet of Workers and Soldiers' Deputies (1 March); abdication of Nicholas II (2 March); 'Programme' of the Provisional Government (8 March); 'Appeal to All the Peoples of the World' by Petrograd Soviet (14 March); Lenin's return to Russia (3 April) and the 'April crisis' in the party; Petrograd crisis (23–4 April); coalition governments (May–October); first 'All-Russian Congress of Soviets' (June); 'July Days'; Kornilov mutiny (25–8 August); publication of Lenin's *State and Revolution*; Bolshevik seizure of power (25 October); elections for

	Constituent Assembly (25 November); establishment of the Cheka (7 December)
1918	Constituent Assembly meets (5–6 January); separation of Church and State; civil war commences; first Soviet constitution (July)
1919	Height of White challenge (autumn 1919); establishment of the Comintern
1920	Soviet–Polish War

1921–1929 Era of the New Economic Policy (NEP)

1921	Kronstadt revolt (2–17 March); Tenth Party Congress (8–16 March), which promulgated 'New Economic Policy'
1921–2	Famine
1922	Eleventh Party Congress (27 March–2 April); Stalin elected General Secretary (3 April); Genoa Conference, with Soviet participation (April); German–Russian treaty at Rapallo; Lenin's first stroke (26 May); Lenin's second stroke (16 December); Lenin dictates 'testament' (25 December)
1923	Lenin adds postscript to 'testament' calling for Stalin's dismissal as General Secretary (4 January); Lenin's third stroke (9 March)
1924	Death of Lenin (21 January); party launches 'Lenin Enrolment' campaign (February); Stalin publicizes 'Socialism in One Country' (December)
1925	Apogee of NEP (April)
1926	'United Opposition' of Trotsky, Zinoviev, and Kamenev emerges in the Central Committee (6–9 April); Zinoviev removed from the Politburo (14–23 July); Trotsky and Kamenev removed from Politburo (23–6 October); Bukharin replaces Zinoviev as chairman of Comintern; Family Code to reform marriage and divorce
1927	'War Scare' with Great Britain (May–August); Trotsky and Zinoviev expelled from Central Committee (21–3 October); Trotsky and Zinoviev expelled from party (15 November); Fifteenth Party Congress, which approves Kamenev's expulsion from the party (2–19 December); first Five-Year Plan
1928	Trotsky exiled to Alma-Ata (16 January); Shakhty Trial (18 May–5 July) and beginning of the 'cultural revolution'; first Five-Year Plan officially commenced (1 October)

1929–1940 Stalin Revolution

1929	Defeat of the 'Right Opposition' (Bukharin, Rykov, and Tomskii); ban on 'religious associations' and proselytizing (April); Stalin condemns 'right deviation' (21 August); Bukharin dropped from Politburo (10–17 November); celebration of Stalin's fiftieth birthday and beginning of the 'cult of the individual' (21 December); Stalin calls for mass collectivization and liquidation of kulaks (27 December)
1930	Mass collectivization launched (5 January); Stalin's 'Dizziness from Success' published in *Pravda* (2 March)
1932	Issue of internal passports (December)
1932–3	Famine in Ukraine and elsewhere

1933	Second Five-Year Plan (1 January 1933–December 1937)
1934	Seventeenth Party Congress (January); first congress of Union of Soviet Writers (August); assassination of Sergei Kirov (December)
1935	Model collective farm statute (February); Stakhanovite movement begun (September)
1936	New family law restricting abortion and divorce (June); show trial of Zinoviev, Kamenev, and others (August); Ezhov appointed head of NKVD (September); promulgation of Stalin Constitution (December)
1937	Show trial of Radek, Piatakov, and others (January); execution of Marshal Tukhachevskii and Red Army officers (June); height of 'Great Terror' (to late 1938)
1938	Third Five-Year Plan (1 January 1938–June 1941); trial of N. Bukharin, Rykov, and others (March); introduction of 'labour book' for workers (December); Beria succeeds Ezhov as head of NKVD (December)
1939	Nazi–Soviet pact (August); Soviet invasion of eastern Poland (September); Soviet–Finnish 'winter war' (November 1939–March 1940)
1940	Soviet annexation of Baltic states (June)

1941–1953 Great Fatherland War and Post-War Stalinism

1941	Nazi Germany invades USSR (22 June); formation of State Defence Committee (30 June); emergency legislation to mobilize labour, institute rationing, lengthen working day, and criminalize absenteeism (June–December); Stalin's speech to the nation (3 July); Germans reach Smolensk (16 July); beginning of siege of Leningrad (July); fall of Kiev (19 September); battle for Moscow (November–December); USA approves Lend-Lease aid for the USSR (7 November); Soviet counter-offensive (December 1941–February 1942)
1942	Anglo-Soviet alliance (May); fall of Sevastopol (July); Battle of Stalingrad (August 1942–February 1943)
1943	Surrender of von Paulus at Stalingrad (31 January); battle of Kursk (July); Stalin eases restrictions on Russian Orthodox Church (September); Teheran Conference (November); beginning of deportations of nationalities from northern Caucasus
1944	Siege of Leningrad broken (January); Belorussian operation and destruction of German army group 'Centre' (June–July); Soviet armies penetrate Poland, Romania, Yugoslavia, and Hungary (July–December)
1945	Soviet invasion of Germany (January); Yalta Conference (February); US and Soviet forces meet at the Elbe (25 April); German unconditional surrender (9 May); Potsdam Conference (July–August); Soviet invasion of Manchuria (9 August); formal Japanese surrender (2 September)
1946	Stalin's 'electoral speech' (February); attacks on leading intellectuals, onset of 'Zhdanovshchina'; decree on collective farms (September).
1947	Famine in Ukraine (1947–8); formation of Communist Information Bureau, or Cominform (September)
1948	Communist coup in Czechoslovakia (February); start of Berlin blockade (May)

1949	Leningrad affair; formation of NATO (April); end of Berlin blockade (May); Soviet atomic bomb test (August)
1950	Outbreak of Korean War (25 June)
1952	Nineteenth Party Congress
1953	Doctors' plot (January); death of Stalin (5 March)

1953–1985   From Stalinism to Stagnation

1953	G. Malenkov becomes head of state, Beria head of the NKVD and police, N. S. Khrushchev first secretary of the party; denunciation of doctors' plot; arrest of L. Beria (26 June; executed in December); first hints of de-Stalinization and cultural 'thaw'
1954	Publication of I. Ehrenburg's *The Thaw*; rehabilitation commission established (May); Khrushchev's 'Virgin Lands programme' adopted
1955	Malenkov replaced by Bulganin as head of state
1956	Twentieth Party Congress (Khrushchev's 'secret speech' denouncing Stalin); CC resolution 'On Overcoming the Cult of the Individual and Its Consequences' (30 June); Hungarian insurrection (November)
1957	Decentralization proposal (*sovnarkhozy*) adopted in May; anti-party group defeated (June); demotion of Marshal Zhukov (October); 'Sputnik' launched (October)
1958	Boris Pasternak awarded Nobel Prize for *Doctor Zhivago*; new penal code, eliminating category of 'enemies of the people' (December)
1959	Sino-Soviet split becomes public; Twenty-First Party Congress; Khrushchev launches maize campaign
1960	American reconnaissance plane, U-2, shot down inside Russia
1961	Capital punishment extended to economic crimes (May); Twenty-Second Party Congress (October); Stalin's body removed from Kremlin (31 October); first manned space flight
1962	Publication of A. Solzhenitsyn's *One Day in the Life of Ivan Denisovich*; Novocherkassk disorders (June); Cuban missile crisis (October)
1963	Exceptionally poor harvest
1964	Removal of N. S. Khrushchev (14 October)
1965	CC approves plan for economic reform (September); publication of A. Nekrich's *22 June 1941*
1966	Trial of dissident writers Iu. Daniel and Andrei Siniavskii (February); Twenty-Third Party Congress (March)
1968	Demonstration by Crimean Tatars (April); invasion of Czechoslovakia (August); first issue of *Chronicle of Current Events*
1970	Establishment of Human Rights Committee (November)
1971	Jewish demonstration in Moscow, beginning of large-scale Jewish emigration
1972	SALT-I (arms limitations); Shevardnadze becomes party boss in Georgia
1974	Deportation of Solzhenitsyn from USSR
1975	Helsinki agreement on European Security and Co-operation; Sakharov awarded Nobel Prize for peace
1976	Twenty-fifth Party Congress

1977	New Soviet constitution; Brezhnev becomes President of the USSR
1978	Trial of Anatolii Shcharanskii
1979	SALT-II (arms limitation agreement); Soviet intervention in Afghanistan
1980	Exile of Sakharov to Gorky (January)
1981	Twenty-Sixth Party Congress
1982	Death of L. I. Brezhnev (10 November), replaced by Andropov
1984	Andropov dies, replaced by Chernenko (February)
1985	Chernenko's death, replacement by Mikhail Gorbachev (11 March)

1985–1996 **From Perestroika to Dissolution of the USSR**

1985   Mikhail Gorbachev elected General Secretary (11 March); Eduard Shevardnadze appointed Foreign Minister (2 July); first superpower summit between Gorbachev and Ronald Reagan in Geneva (November)

1986   Tbilisi disorders, with twenty demonstrators slain by Soviet troops (9 April); Chernobyl disaster (26 April); riots in Alma-Ata (December)

1987   Twenty-Seventh Party Congress (February–March); new law on 'socialist enterprise'; Yeltsin dismissed as Moscow party chief (November)

1988   Nineteenth Party Conference transforms role of Communist Party (June)

1989   Ethnic conflict erupts in Nagorno-Karabakh (February); USSR Congress of People's Deputies elected in partly democratic elections (March); anti-perestroika letter by Nina Andreeva; Gorbachev announces plan to withdraw from Afghanistan (April); miners' strike (July 1989); first national movement, Sajudis, forms in Lithuania (November)

1990   Election of People's Deputies of Russian Federation (March); formation of Communist Party of the Russian Federation, with Ivan Polozkov as leader (June); Twenty-eighth Party Congress, with defection of Boris Yeltsin and leaders of Democratic Platform to establish their own party; Gorbachev elected President of the USSR (September).

1991   Soviet troops attack TV centre in Vilnius, killing 14 (January); Boris Yeltsin elected President of the Russian Federation (June); ultimatum to Gorbachev to resign in favour of Gennadii Ianaev signals beginning of attempted coup (18 August); Yeltsin makes his way to White House to lead opposition to *putsch* (19 August); attempted coup collapses (21 August); Yeltsin announces plans for economic reform (October); Estonia, Latvia, Ukraine, Belarus, Moldova, and Azerbaijan declare independence (August–September); Chechnia declares independence (November); Russia, Ukraine, and Belarus agree on formation of Commonwealth of Independent States (CIS) (8 December); CIS formally constituted in Alma-Ata, Kazakhstan (21 December); resignation of Gorbachev (25 December); formal dissolution of the USSR (31 December)

1992   Gaidar introduces radical 'shock therapy' economic reforms (January); constitutional referendum (April); Tashkent summit (March); Black Sea accord between Ukraine and Russia (August); privatization vouchers issued (1 October); Yeltsin appoints V. Chernomyrdin as Prime Minister (14 December).

1993	START-II signed by United States and Russia (3 January); leaders of Central Asia agree in principle on loose union (January); mounting conflict between Yeltsin and Parliament, which votes to strip the President of his economic powers (March); national referendum of 25 April shows support for Yeltsin (58 per cent of votes) and constitution; Yeltsin dismisses parliament and announces new elections (21 September); after parliament impeaches Yeltsin and poses armed resistance, Yeltsin storms the Parliament building, with upward of 200 killed (3–4 October); many CIS states (Kazakhstan and Uzbekistan, followed by others) establish their own national currencies (November); national vote to approve constitution (57 per cent) and to elect new Duma, with nearly a quarter of the votes for V. Zhirinovskii's nationalist party (12 December).
1994	Russian–Belarus economic union (5 January); Yeltsin's initial core group of reformers, including E. Gaidar, resigns (16–20 January); plotters of August 1991 *putsch* are amnestied by Duma (23 February); MMM stock fund fails (29 July); clashes between D. Dudaev and pro-Russian forces in Chechnia (September); crash of rouble (11 October); Russian invasion of Chechnia (11 December)
1995	Rehabilitation of 1.5 million victims from Second World War in Gulag (25 January); election of Duma, with the Communist Party emerging as the largest party (17 December)
1996	Presidential election, with Yeltsin defeating Communist candidate Gennadii Ziuganov (3 July); Khasaviurt accords, negotiated by Alexander Lebed, for peaceful resolution of Chechen conflict (August); quintuple bypass operation for Yeltsin (November)

FURTHER READING

BIBLIOGRAPHICAL GUIDES

American Historical Association, *Guide to Historical Literature* (2nd edn., New York, 1961 and 3rd edn., New York, 1995), comprehensive guides to bibliography and specialized literature, the 2nd edn. containing the classical titles, the latter emphasizing the literature of the last three decades.

GENERAL HISTORIES

R. Auty and D. Obolensky (eds.), *An Introduction to Russian History* (Cambridge, 1976), valuable collection of essays, broad in scope and rich in bibliography.

M. T. Florinsky, *Russia: A History and Interpretation* (2 vols., New York, 1953), detailed account to 1917, drawing heavily on pre-revolutionary scholarship.

V. O. Kliuchevskii, *History of Russia* (5 vols., New York, 1911–31), classic pre-revolutionary history to 1825.

P. I. Liashchenko, *History of the National Economy of Russia to the 1917 Revolution* (New York, 1949), informative, rich history from Soviet perspective.

N. V. Riasanovsky, *A History of Russia* (5th edn., New York), standard textbook survey.

I. From Kiev to Muscovy: The Beginnings to 1700

GENERAL HISTORIES AND MONOGRAPHS

J. Blum, *Lord and Peasant in Russia* (New York, 1969), economic and social history from the era of Kiev Rus to the abolition of serfdom in 1861.

R. O. Crummey, *The Formation of Muscovy, 1304–1613* (London, 1987), informed and highly readable interpretive survey.

R. S. Hellie, *Slavery in Russia, 1450–1725* (Chicago, 1982), thorough study of law and practice of slavery.

D. H. Kaiser, *The Growth of the Law in Medieval Russia* (Princeton, 1980), on the evolution of triadic state-initiated legal institutions and concepts by Ivan III's time.

J. L. H. Keep, *Soldiers of the Tsar* (Oxford, 1985), detailed history of army until 1874 conscription reform.

E. Levin, *Sex and Society in the World of the Orthodox Slavs, 900–1700* (Ithaca, NY, 1989), study of ecclesiastical sources on such matters as marriage, sexual crimes, sexual deviance.

J. Martin, *Medieval Russia, 980–1584* (Cambridge, 1995), comprehensive survey, drawing upon most recent scholarship with new interpretations and analysis.

A. E. Presniakov, *The Tsardom of Muscovy* (Gulf Breeze, Fla., 1978), classic pre-revolutionary account.

G. Vernadsky, *A History of Russia* (5 vols., New Haven, 1943–69), survey from pre-history to 1682 from the perspective of the Eurasian school.

1. FROM THE BEGINNINGS TO 1450

S. Cross and O. P. Sherbowitz-Werzor (eds. and trans.), *The Primary Russian Chronicle: Laurentian text* (3rd edn., Cambridge, 1973), basic source for early history.

F. L. I. Fennell, *The Emergence of Moscow, 1304–1359* (Berkeley and Los Angeles, 1968), detailed examination of Moscow's growing political importance, emphasizing inter-princely conflicts, Mongol influence, and relations with neighbouring principalities.

—— *The Crisis of Medieval Russia, 1200–1304* (London, 1983), detailed political narrative.

C. J. Halperin, *Russia and the Golden Horde* (London, 1987), reinterpretation of Mongol impact, counterbalancing destructive aspects with evidence of close, pragmatic Mongol–Rus relationships.

J. Martin, *Treasury of the Land of Darkness* (Cambridge, 1986), on international fur trade from the ninth to fifteenth centuries.

B. A. Rybakov, *Kievan Rus* (Moscow, 1989), Marxist interpretation by leading Soviet historian.

Ya. N. Shchapov, *State and Church in Early Russia* (New Rochelle, NY, 1993), collection of essays on the institutional structure of the Church and its relations with the princes of Kievan Rus.

2. MUSCOVITE RUSSIA, 1450–1598

G. Alef, *Rulers and Nobles in Fifteenth-Century Muscovy* (London, 1983), essays on institutions, symbols of autocracy.

Bushkovitch, P. *Religion and Society in Russia* (Oxford, 1992), on the change in élite religious life.

R. O. Crummey, *Aristocrats and Servitors: The Boyar Élite in Russia, 1613–1689* (Princeton, 1983).

H. W. Dewey (comp., trans., ed.), *Muscovite Judicial Texts, 1488–1556* (Ann Arbor, 1966), texts of the law codes of 1497 and 1550 and other key documents.

J. L. I. Fennell, *Ivan the Great of Moscow* (London, 1963), political biography.

R. S. Hellie, 'Zemskii sobor (Assembly of the Land),' in *Modern Encyclopedia of Russian and Soviet History* 45 (1987), 226–34.

E. L. Keenan, Jr., *The Kurbskii-Groznyi Apocrypha: The Seventeenth-Century Genesis of the 'Correspondence' Attributed to Prince A. M. Kurbskii and Tsar Ivan IV* (Cambridge, Mass., 1971).

V. O. Kliuchevskii, *A History of Russia*, 5 vols. (London, 1911–13).

N. S. Kollmann, *Kinship and Politics* (Stanford, Calif., 1987), shows family and clan at the heart of Muscovite power hierarchy and political conflict.

Levin, E., 'Supplicatory Prayers as a Source of Popular Religious Culture', in S. H. Baron and N. S. Kollmann (eds.), *Religion and Culture in Early Modern Russia and Ukraine* (DeKalb, Illinois, 1997), 96–114.

S. F. Platonov, *Ivan the Terrible* (Gulf Breeze, Fla., 1974), still the best biography.

A. E. Presnaikov, *The Tsardom of Muscovy* (Gulf Breeze, Fla., 1978), excellent introduction to the early history of autocracy and its institutions.

R. G. Skrynnikov, *Ivan the Terrible* (Gulf Breeze, Fla., 1981), political narrative.

S. B. Veselovskii, *Issledovaniia po istorii oprichniny* (Moscow, 1963).

A. A. Zimin, *Reformy Ivana Groznogo* (Moscow, 1960).

3. FROM MUSCOVY TOWARDS ST PETERSBURG, 1598–1689

C. Bussow, *The Disturbed State of the Russian Realm* (Montreal, 1994), translation of important contemporary account.

R. O. Crummey, *Aristocrats and Servitors* (Princeton, 1983), social and political history of aristocracy in seventeenth-century Russia.

R. S. Hellie (ed. and trans.), *Muscovite Law Code (Ulozhenie) of 1649* (vol. i, Irvine, 1988), parallel Russian and English texts of critical, formative law code.

—— *Enserfment and Military Change in Muscovy* (Chicago, 1971), parallel studies of enserfment and landed military élite.

L. Hughes, *Sophia: Regent of Russia, 1657–1704* (New Haven, 1990), on the origins of the Petrine reform era.

P. Longworth, *Alexis, Tsar of all the Russias* (London, 1984), broad survey of mid-seventeenth-century Muscovy.

S. F. Platonov, *The Time of Troubles* (Gulf Breeze, Fla., 1970), sweeping pre-revolutionary analysis, emphasizing interaction of dynastic, social, and national crises.

—— *Boris Godunov* (Gulf Breeze, Fla., 1973), classic liberal account.

R. G. Skrynnikov, *The Time of Troubles* (Gulf Breeze, Fla., 1988), detailed, nationalistic account.

C. Stevens, *Soldiers in the Steppe* (De Kalb, Ill., 1995), on military reform and social development in Muscovy.

II. Imperial Russia, 1689–1917

GENERAL HISTORIES AND MONOGRAPHS

P. Avrich, *Russian Rebels, 1600–1800* (New York, 1976), on four great popular insurrections.

R. O. Crummey, *The Old Believers and the World of Antichrist* (Madison, 1970), pioneering case study of dissenting Old Believers.

W. Fuller, Jr., *Strategy and Power in Russia, 1600–1914* (New York, 1992), informed and sweeping analysis of military strategy and policy.

P. Gatrell, *The Tsarist Economy, 1850–1917* (New York, 1986), general survey.

D. Geyer, *Russian Imperialism* (New Haven, 1987), on interaction of foreign and domestic policy to 1914.

B. Jelavich, *A Century of Russian Foreign Policy, 1814–1914* (Philadelphia, 1964), excellent survey.

H. D. Löwe, *Tsar and Jews* (Chur, Switzerland, 1993), up-to-date analysis of the Jewish question in the Russian Empire.

T. C. Owen, *The Corporation under Russian Law, 1800–1917* (Cambridge, 1991), study of support and impediments to the development of corporations.

W. M. Pintner and D. K. Rowney (eds.), *The Bureaucratization of Russian Society from the Seventeenth to the Twentieth Century* (Chapel Hill, NC, 1980), important essays on bureaucracy and civil service.

M. Raeff, *Understanding Imperial Russia: State and Society in the Old Regime* (New York, 1983), broad synthetic study of Russia from the eighteenth to early twentieth centuries.

D. Ransel, *Mothers of Misery* (Princeton, 1988), pioneering study of child abandonment and foundling care in the eighteenth and nineteenth centuries.

H. Seton-Watson, *The Russian Empire, 1801–1917* (Oxford, 1967), detailed account, with particular attention to institutional, diplomatic, and minority history.

R. S. Wortman, *Scenarios of Power* (vol. i, Princeton, 1995), on symbols and culture of rulership.

4. THE PETRINE ERA AND AFTER, 1689–1740

M. S. Anderson, *Peter the Great* (London, 1978), traditional biography, with emphasis on foreign policy.

E. V. Anisimov, *The Reforms of Peter the Great* (Armonk, NY, 1993), revisionist interpretation.

G. Barany, *The Anglo-Russian Entente Cordiale of 1697–1698* (Boulder, Colo., 1986), on the 'Grand Embassy'.

J. Cracraft, *The Petrine Revolution in Russian Architecture* (Chicago, 1988), beautifully illustrated and broadly conceived.

—— (ed.), *Peter the Great Transforms Russia* (3rd edn., Lexington, Ky., 1991), anthology of major interpretative essays.

M. Curtiss, *A Forgotten Empress* (New York, 1974), the only book-length treatment on Anna in English.

A. Lentin (ed. and trans.), *Peter the Great: His Law on the Imperial Succession in Russia* (Oxford, 1995), translation of important defining political statement, 'The Truth of the Monarch's Will'.

E. J. Phillips, *The Founding of Russia's Navy* (Westport, Conn., 1995), new interpretation on the origins of the Russian navy.

I. Pososhkov, *The Book of Poverty and Wealth* (Stanford, Calif., 1987), important contemporary writing by merchant.

N. V. Riasanovsky, *The Image of Peter the Great in Russian History and Thought* (New York, 1985), analysis of rhetorical and historical representations of Peter.

5. THE AGE OF ENLIGHTENMENT, 1740–1801

J. T. Alexander, *Catherine the Great* (New York, 1989), modern scholarly biography.

E. V. Anisimov, *Empress Elizabeth* (Gulf Breeze, Fla., 1995), important study of critical period of state building.

G. L. Freeze, *The Russian Levites: Parish Clergy in the Eighteenth Century* (Cambridge, 1977), on transformation of the married parish clergy into a social and cultural caste.

R. E. Jones, *The Emancipation of the Russian Nobility, 1762–1785* (Princeton, 1973), careful study of the politics of terminating obligatory state service for the nobility.

—— *Provincial Development in Russia* (New Brunswick, NJ, 1984), valuable case study of provincial life and administration.

W. G. Jones, *Nikolay Novikov* (Cambridge, 1984), standard work on leading publisher and intellectual figure in Catherinean Russia.

J. D. Klier, *Russia Gathers Her Jews* (DeKalb, Ill., 1986), on formation of the Pale of Settlement.

J. P. LeDonne, *Ruling Russia* (Princeton, 1984), controversial attempt to provide 'class' interpretation of state and policies.

I. De Madariaga, *Russia in the Age of Catherine the Great* (New Haven, 1981), sweeping account of Russian state and society in the second half of the eighteenth century.

G. Marker, *Publishing, Printing, and the Origins of Intellectual Life in Russia, 1700–1800* (Princeton, 1985), on role of state and public in development of print culture.

M. Raeff, *Origins of the Russian Intelligentsia* (New York, 1966), imaginative attempt to explain how Petrine servitors became the disaffected intelligentsia.

—— *The Well-Ordered Police State* (New Haven, 1983), comparative study of cameralism as transplanted to imperial Russia.

D. L. Ransel, *The Politics of Catherinean Russia* (New Haven, 1975), original analysis of clan and politics.

6. Pre-Reform Russia, 1801–1855

W. L. Blackwell, *The Beginnings of Russian Industrialization, 1800–1860* (Princeton, 1968), on obstacles and achievements of economic growth in pre-reform era.

A. von Haxthausen, *Studies on the Interior of Russia* (Chicago, 1972), informed and influential German analysis of Russia in the 1840s.

S. L. Hoch, *Serfdom and Social Control in Russia* (Chicago, 1986), case study of serf village in Tambov province.

W. B. Lincoln, *In the Vanguard of Reform* (De Kalb, Ill., 1982), on the Nicholaevan pre-reforms and figures who prepared for Great Reforms.

—— *Nicholas I, Emperor and Autocrat of all the Russias* (De Kalb, Ill., 1989), positive reassessment of emperor, with good overview of state policy.

M. Malia, *Alexander Herzen and the Birth of Russian Socialism, 1812–1855* (New York, 1971), broad intellectual history, not mere biography of seminal figure in the development of Russian agrarian socialist thought.

D. Moon, *Russian Peasants and Tsarist Legislation on the Eve of Reform* (Houndmills, Basingstoke 1992), on serf question and stability in Nicholaevan era.

M. Raeff, *Michael Speransky* (The Hague, 1957), political biography and guide to institutional development in the early nineteenth century.

M. Stanislawski, *Tsar Nicholas I and the Jews* (Philadelphia, 1983), revisionist study of Jewish policy.

E. K. Wirtschafter, *From Serf to Russian Soldier* (Princeton, 1990), on social conditions of lower ranks in pre-reform era.

7. REFORM AND COUNTER-REFORM, 1855–1890

D. R. Brower, *The Russian City between Tradition and Modernity, 1850–1900* (Berkeley, 1990), best recent synthesis of urban history in post-reform era.

B. Eklof, *Russian Peasant Schools* (Berkeley, 1986), on peasant role in shaping content of elementary education.

—— and J. Bushnell (eds.), *Russia's Great Reforms, 1855–1881* (Bloomington, Ind., 1994), important collection of essays on individual great reforms.

T. E. Emmons and W. Vucinich (eds.), *Russia: An Experiment in Local Self-Government* (Cambridge, 1982), on the composition and role of the Zemstvo in post-reform era.

D. Field, *The End of Serfdom* (Cambridge, Mass., 1976), close analysis of noble and state interaction in preparing the terms of emancipation.

—— *Rebels in the Name of the Tsar* (Boston, 1989), penetrating analysis of two major peasant disorders in 1860s and 1870s.

G. L. Freeze, *The Parish Clergy in Nineteenth-Century Russia* (Princeton, 1983), on reform—goals, politics, problems—in the Church, with ramifications for larger problems of change.

C. Johanson, *Women's Struggle for Higher Education in Russia, 1855–1900* (Kingston, 1987), on barriers and response to university and women.

W. B. Lincoln, *The Great Reforms* (DeKalb, Ill., 1990), best general overview of great reforms.

S. F. Starr, *Decentralization and Self-Government in Russia, 1830–1870* (Princeton, 1972), on under-institutionalization and zemstvo reform of 1860s.

R. Stites, *The Women's Liberation Movement in Russia* (2nd edn., Princeton, 1991), general survey of different streams of women's movement.

F. Venturi, *Roots of Revolution* (Chicago, 1983), massively detailed narrative account.

P. A. Zaionchkovskii, *The Russian Autocracy under Alexander III* (Gulf Breeze, Fla., 1976), on counter-reforms of 1880s.

—— *The Russian Autocracy in Crisis, 1878–1882* (Gulf Breeze, Fla., 1979), on dramatic confrontation of autocracy and revolutionary terrorism.

R. E. Zelnik, *Labor and Society in Tsarist Russia* (Stanford, Calif., 1971), on early history of labour movement and state response.

8. REVOLUTIONARY RUSSIA, 1890–1914

A. Ascher, *The Russian Revolution of 1905* (2 vols., Stanford, Calif., 1988–92), best synthesis of recent scholarship.

V. E. Bonnell, *Roots of Rebellion* (Berkeley, 1983), detailed account of worker politics and mobilization, 1905–14.

J. Bradley, *Muzhik and Muscovite* (Berkeley, 1985), urban history of Moscow in late nineteenth and early twentieth century.

J. Brooks, *When Russia Learned to Read* (Princeton, 1985), study of popular reading culture, consumption, and major themes.

J. Bushnell, *Mutiny and Repression* (Bloomington, Ind., 1985), close analysis of uneven pattern of soldiers' involvement in revolution.

B. E. Clements *et al.* (ed.), *Russia's Women* (Berkeley, 1991), on women's experiences and problems in modern Russia.

E. W. Clowes *et al.* (eds.), *Between Tsar and People* (Princeton, 1991), on the emergence of civil society.

O. Crisp and L. H. Edmondson (eds.), *Civil Rights in Imperial Russia* (Oxford, 1989), on reform and civil rights in early twentieth century.

T. Emmons, *Formation of Political Parties and the First National Elections in Russia* (Cambridge, 1983), on liberal and moderate parties as they prepare for the first duma.

L. Engelstein, *The Keys to Happiness* (Ithaca, NY, 1992), a study of Russian society and culture seen through the prism of sex and gender.

W. C. Fuller, Jr., *Civil–Military Conflict in Imperial Russia, 1881–1914* (Princeton, 1985), study of tension between military professionalism and civil service.

M. F. Hamm (ed.), *The City in Late Imperial Russia* (Bloomington, Ind., 1986), case studies of several leading cities.

J. F. Hutchinson, *Politics and Public Health in Revolutionary Russia, 1890–1913* (Baltimore, 1990), study of medical profession and its response to issues of public health and politics.

D. C. B. Lieven, *Russia and the Origins of the First World War* (New York, 1983), on domestic causes of Russian entry into war.

—— *Russia's Rulers under the Old Regime* (New Haven, 1989), prosopographical and biographical study of State Council.

R. T. Manning, *The Crisis of the Old Order in Russia* (Princeton, 1982), on shift of gentry from opposition to conservative defence of old order.

L. McReynolds, *The News under Russia's Old Régime* (Princeton, 1991), on the development of a mass circulation press.

J. Neuberger, *Hooliganism* (Berkeley, 1993), on youth and crime in St Petersburg.

A. J. Rieber, *Merchants and Entrepreneurs in Imperial Russia* (Chapel Hill, NC, 1982), sophisticated account of merchant-industrial élites in post-reform era.

R. G. Robbins, *The Tsar's Viceroys* (Ithaca, NY, 1987), on profile and role of governors at end of old regime.

H. Rogger, *Jewish Policies and Right-Wing Politics in Imperial Russia* (Berkeley, Calif., 1986), an important series of essays on the complexities of state policy and politics.

E. C. Thaden (ed.), *Russification in the Baltic Provinces and Finland, 1855–1914* (Princeton, 1981), valuable collection of essays on post-reform minority policy.

A. M. Verner, *The Crisis of Autocracy* (Princeton, 1990), close analysis of emperor and bureaucratic élite responses to revolution.

T. H. Von Laue, *Sergei Witte and the Industrialization of Russia* (New York, 1963), the standard account of Witte and his industrialization policies.

N. B. Weissman, *Reform in Tsarist Russia* (New Brunswick, NJ, 1981), on the problem of rebuilding a more effective system of local government.

A. L. Wildman, *The Making of a Workers' Revolution: Russian Social Democracy, 1891–1903* (Chicago, 1967), on the relations between Marxist intellectuals and politicized workers.

III. Soviet History and Beyond

GENERAL HISTORIES AND MONOGRAPHS

K. E. Bailes, *Technology and Society Under Lenin and Stalin* (Princeton, 1978), path-breaking study of the Soviet technical intelligentsia.

J. S. Curtiss, *The Russian Church and the Soviet State, 1917–50* (New York, 1953), balanced treatment of Soviet religious policies.

R. W. Davies *et al.* (eds.), *The Economic Transformation of the Soviet Union, 1913–1945* (Cambridge, 1994).

J. Degras (ed.), *Soviet Documents on Foreign Policy, 1917–41* (3 vols., New York, 1978), important collection of documents.

M. Fainsod, *How Russia Is Ruled* (2nd edn., Cambridge, 1965), classic institutional and political history from pre-revolutionary to Khrushchev eras.

J. L. Gaddis, *Russia, the Soviet Union, and the United States* (2nd edn., New York, 1990), good overview of Soviet–American relations.

W. Z. Goldman, *Women, the State, and Revolution* (Cambridge, 1993), on Soviet family policy from the revolution to the mid-1930s.

L. R. Graham, *Science, Philosophy, and Human Behavior in the Soviet Union* (New York, 1987), treats the impact of ideology on science.

M. Heller and A. Nekrich, *Utopia in Power: The History of the Soviet Union from 1917 to the Present* (2 vols., New York, 1992), vigorously anti-Soviet *émigré* history, with fresh detail on many subjects.

G. A. Hosking, *The First Socialist Society: A History of the Soviet Union from Within* (2nd edn., Cambridge, 1990), excellent, well-informed account.

P. Kenez, *The Birth of the Propaganda State* (Cambridge, 1985), insightful treatment of propaganda as critical instrument in early phase of Soviet state-building.

—— *Cinema and Soviet Society, 1917–1953* (Cambridge, 1992), original reinterpretation of film and its impact.

M. Lewin, *The Making of the Soviet System* (New York, 1985), analysis of the early USSR by the doyen of social historians of the Soviet period.

M. McAuley, *Soviet Politics, 1917–1991* (rev. edn., Oxford, 1992), standard survey of political history.

R. McNeal *et al.* (eds.), *Resolutions and Decisions of the Communist Party of the Soviet Union* (5 vols., Toronto, 1974–82), basic set of translated official party resolutions.

M. E. Malia, *The Soviet Tragedy: A History of Socialism in Russia, 1917–1991* (New York, 1994), lively, critical account of Soviet ideology and rule.

J. L. Nogee and R. H. Donaldson, *Soviet Foreign Policy since World War II* (4th edn., New York, 1992), authoritative, wide-ranging account of foreign policy.

A. Nove, *An Economic History of the USSR, 1917–91* (3rd edn., Harmondsworth, 1992), best single-volume history of Soviet economy.

W. G. Rosenberg (ed.), *Bolshevik Visions* (2 vols., Ann Arbor, 1990), valuable collection of documents on the cultural revolution.

L. Schapiro, *The Communist Party of the Soviet Union* (2nd edn., New York, 1971), full political history of the Soviet Communist Party.

G. Simon, *Nationalism and Policy towards the Nationalities in the Soviet Union* (Boulder, Colo., 1991), systematic overview of Soviet nationality policies.

R. Stites, *Revolutionary Dreams* (New York, 1991), sweeping account of utopian vision in early Soviet culture.

9. RUSSIA IN WAR AND REVOLUTION, 1914–1921

E. Acton, *Rethinking the Russian Revolution* (London, 1990), critical analysis of historiography on 1917.

P. Avrich, *Kronstadt, 1921* (Princeton, 1991), standard account of this critical rebellion.

F. Benvenuti, *The Bolsheviks and the Red Army, 1918–22* (Cambridge, 1988), on party–military relations.

R. P. Browder and A. Kerensky (eds.), *The Russian Provisional Government, 1917: Documents* (3 vols., Stanford, Calif., 1961), valuable collection of documents in translation, but not always reliable.

E. N. Burdzhalov, *Russia's Second Revolution: the February 1917 Uprising in Petrograd* (Bloomington, Ind., 1987), masterful, richly detailed account of the Petrograd revolution.

E. H. Carr, *The Bolshevik Revolution, 1917–1923* (3 vols., London, 1985), classic study of the revolution and civil war.

W. H. Chamberlin, *The Russian Revolution, 1917–1921* (2 vols., Princeton, 1987), reprint of well-informed, highly readable account.

H. Carrère d'Encausse, *The Great Challenge* (New York, 1992), on Bolshevik policy towards minorities from the Revolution to the great turn.

B. Farnsworth, *Alexandra Kollontai: Socialism, Feminism, and the Bolshevik Revolution* (Stanford, Calif., 1980), excellent biography of leading feminist, providing good introductions to 'women's question' in early Soviet era.

M. Ferro, *October 1917: A Social History of the Russian Revolution* (London, 1980), rich in material on attitude of different social groups.

O. Figes, *Peasant Russia, Civil War: The Volga Countryside* (Oxford, 1989), well-researched regional study of peasant role in the civil war.

S. Fitzpatrick, *The Commissariat of the Enlightenment: Soviet Organization of Education and the Arts under Lunacharsky, October 1917–1921* (Cambridge, 1970), standard account of cultural politics during the civil war.

A. Gleason, P. Kenez, and R. Stites (eds.), *Bolshevik Culture: Experiment and Order in the Russian Revolution* (Bloomington, Ind., 1985), important collection of essays.

W. Husband, *Revolution in the Factory: The Birth of the Soviet Textile Industry, 1917–1920* (New York, 1990), on workers, trade unions, and revolution.

J. L. H. Keep, *The Russian Revolution: A Study in Mass Mobilization* (New York, 1976), broad, detailed synthesis.

D. P. Koenker and W. G. Rosenberg, *Strikes and Revolution in Russia, 1917* (Princeton, 1989), careful analysis of strikes and labour protest.

—— and R. G. Suny (eds.), *Party, State, and Society in the Russian Civil War: Explorations in Social History* (Bloomington, Ind., 1989), valuable collection of essays.

M. McAuley, *Bread and Justice* (Oxford, 1991), broad-ranging study of Bolshevik policies and institution-building in Petrograd.

M. McCauley (ed.), *The Russian Revolution and the Soviet State, 1917–1921* (London, 1988), valuable collection of primary sources.

R. Pipes, *The Russian Revolution* (New York, 1991), anti-revisionist, political account.

—— *Russia under the Bolshevik Regime* (New York, 1994), popular survey, casting blame on intelligentsia and traditional Russian political culture for rise of authoritarian regime.

A. Rabinowitch, *Prelude to Revolution* (Bloomington, Ind., 1968), close study of the July uprising in 1917.

D. J. Raleigh, *Revolution on the Volga* (Ithaca, NY, 1986), case study of revolution in Saratov.

T. F. Remington, *Building Socialism in Soviet Russia* (Pittsburgh, 1984), on self-defeating attempts at mass mobilization.

R. Sakwa, *Soviet Communists in Power* (New York, 1988), on politics and government in Moscow during the civil war.

S. A. Smith, *Red Petrograd: Revolution in the Factories, 1917–18* (Cambridge, 1983), sensitive analysis of Petrograd workers during the revolution.

J. D. White, *The Russian Revolution, 1917–1921* (London, 1994), recent general account.

A. K. Wildman, *The End of the Russian Imperial Army* (2 vols., Princeton, 1980–7), massively researched, standard account of the devolution of the army in 1917.

10. The New Economic Policy and Revolutionary Experiment, 1921–1929

A. M. Ball, *Russia's Last Capitalists* (Berkeley, 1987), solid analysis of NEP and 'nepmany'.

—— *And Now My Soul Has Hardened* (Berkeley, 1994), study of the homeless orphans (*bezprizorniki*) during NEP.

E. H. Carr, *The Interregnum, 1923–1924* (Harmondsworth, 1969), *Socialism in One Country, 1924–1926* (3 vols., Harmondsworth, 1970), and (with R. W. Davies), *Foundations of a Planned Economy, 1926–1929* (2 vols., Harmondsworth, 1971–4), magisterial study of the first decade of Soviet rule.

W. J. Chase, *Workers, Society, and the Soviet State* (Urbana, Ill., 1987), on Moscow workers during the 1920s.

S. F. Cohen, *Bukharin and the Bolshevik Revolution* (Oxford, 1980), political and intellectual biography of leading Bolshevik.

V. P. Danilov, *Rural Russia under the New Regime* (Bloomington, Ind., 1988), analysis of peasants in the 1920s by the doyen of Russian agrarian historians.

S. Fitzpatrick, *Education and Social Mobility in the Soviet Union, 1921–1934* (Cambridge, 1979), provocative study of social changes and formation of a new élite.

—— A. Rabinowitch, and R. Stites (eds.), *Russia in the Era of NEP* (Bloomington, Ind., 1991), collection of essays by leading scholars.

C. Gray, *The Russian Experiment in Art, 1863–1922* (New York, 1986), valuable study of the artistic turmoil and experimentation in the 1920s.

L. E. Holmes, *The Kremlin and the Schoolhouse* (Bloomington, Ind., 1991), interesting assessment of the attempt to use education to engineer social change.

J. Hughes, *Stalin, Siberia, and the Crisis of the New Economic Policy* (Cambridge, 1991), shows how Stalin's experience in Siberia provided the impetus to collectivization.

R. Pethybridge, *The Social Prelude to Stalinism* (New York, 1974), examines the clash between Bolshevik ambitions and Soviet realities, with much data about party, society, and culture.

L. H. Siegelbaum, *Soviet State and Society Between Revolutions, 1918–1929* (Cambridge, 1992), comprehensive review of scholarship and major issues.

R. C. Tucker, *Stalin as Revolutionary, 1879–1929* (New York, 1973), biography of Stalin's origins and rise to prominence.

C. Ward, *Russia's Cotton Workers and the New Economic Policy* (Cambridge, 1990), original and penetrating look at factory life during NEP.

M. von Hagen, *Soldiers in the Proletarian Dictatorship* (Ithaca, NY, 1990), study of military and politics in early Bolshevik state.

S. White, *The Bolshevik Poster* (New Haven, 1988), excellent analysis with rich collection of illustrations.

D. J. Youngblood, *Movies for the Masses* (Cambridge, 1992), on debates, films, and reaction of critics and viewers.

11. BUILDING STALINISM, 1929–1941

V. Anderle, *Workers in Stalin's Russia* (New York, 1988), sociological analysis of workplace interaction.

R. Conquest, *The Great Terror: A Reassessment* (New York, 1990), updated version of classic account from the perspective of the 'totalitarian' school.

R. W. Davies, *The Industrialization of Soviet Russia* (3 vols., Cambridge, 1980–91), continuation of the E. H. Carr multi-volume history.

M. Fainsod, *Smolensk under Soviet Rule* (Cambridge, 1958), path-breaking analysis based on the Smolensk party archive.

S. Fitzpatrick (ed.), *Cultural Revolution in Russia, 1928–1931* (Bloomington, Ind., 1979), treats upheavals in professions from perspective of social history.

—— *The Cultural Front* (Ithaca, NY, 1992), ten essays on the complex relationship between the intelligentsia and political authority.

—— *Stalin's Peasants* (Oxford, 1994), on peasant response and adaptation to collectivization.

D. Filtzer, *Soviet Workers and Stalinist Industrialization* (Armonk, NY, 1986), on regime's attempt to subdue worker resistance.

V. Garros, N. Korenevskaya, and T. Lahusen (eds.), *Intimacy and Terror* (New York, 1995), fascinating collection of diaries from the 1930s.

J. A. Getty, *Origins of the Great Purges* (Cambridge, 1985), 'revisionist' account of inner-party politics, drawing mainly on the Smolensk party archive.

—— and R. T. Manning (eds.), *Stalinist Terror: New Perspectives* (Cambridge, 1993), fourteen essays that draw upon recently opened Soviet archival materials.

G. Gill, *The Origins of the Stalinist Political System* (Cambridge, 1990), on formation of Stalinist dictatorship as break with Leninist system.

Boris Groys, *The Total Art of Stalinism* (Princeton, 1992), on Stalinism as cultural system.

M. Hindus, *Red Bread* (Bloomington, Ind., 1988), perceptive account by empathetic eye-witness.

J. Hughes, *Stalinism in a Russian Province* (New York, 1996), on collectivization in Siberia.

H. Hunter, 'The Overambitious First Five-Year-Plan', *Slavic Review*, 32 (1973), 237–57, famous essay on dysfunctions of inflated plan objectives.

H. Kostiuk, *Stalinist Rule in the Ukraine* (Munich, 1960), detailed account of terror in the Ukraine.

S. Kotkin, *Magnetic Mountain* (Berkeley, 1995), analysis of Stalinism as functioning social system.

M. Lewin, *Russian Peasants and Soviet Power* (New York, 1975), systematic analysis of collectivization.

N. Mandelshtam, *Hope against Hope* (New York, 1970), valuable memoir on the intelligentsia experience of the 1930s.

R. A. Medvedev, *Let History Judge* (2nd edn., New York, 1989), gold mine of information by dissident Soviet historian.

Iu. A. Poliakov, *A Half Century of Silence: the 1937 Census* (New York, 1992), interesting data on the suppressed census of 1937.

G. T. Rittersporn, *Stalinist Implications and Soviet Complications* (Chur, Switzerland, 1991), revisionist critique of totalitarian historiography.

W. G. Rosenberg and L. H. Siegelbaum (eds.), *Social Dimensions of Soviet Industrialization* (Bloomington, Ind., 1993), thirteen essays on social mobility, workplace politics, and labour culture.

J. Scott, *Behind the Urals* (Bloomington, Ind., 1966), graphic account of the building of Magnitogorsk.

L. H. Siegelbaum, *Stakhanovism and the Politics of Productivity in the USSR, 1935–41* (Cambridge, 1986), on the Stakhanovite movement as a window on to industrial relations.

P. Solomon, *Soviet Criminal Justice under Stalin* (Cambridge, 1996), close study of key institution.

D. Thorniley, *The Rise and Fall of the Soviet Rural Communist Party, 1927–39* (New York, 1988), shows party weakness and failure to establish control over the village.

R. C. Tucker (ed.), *Stalinism* (New York, 1977), important collection of essays.

—— *Stalin in Power* (New York, 1990), treats Stalin Revolution as a reversion to the developmental mode in prerevolutionary Russia.

L. Viola, *Peasant Rebels under Stalin* (New York, 1996), innovative examination of the culture of peasant resistance and collectivization.

D. Volkogonov, *Stalin* (New York, 1991), draws heavily upon new archival materials.

12. The Great Fatherland War and Late Stalinism, 1941–1953

C. Andreyev, *Vlasov and the Russian Liberation Movement* (Cambridge, 1987), excellent account of anti-Soviet units formed from Soviet prisoners of war.

J. A. Armstrong, *Ukrainian Nationalism* (3rd edn., Englewood Cliffs, NJ, 1990), study of nationalist movements in the Ukraine during the Second World War.

J. Barber and M. Harrison, *The Soviet Home Front, 1941–45* (London, 1991), pioneering study examines how Soviet system withstood Nazi invasion.

O. Bartov, *The Eastern Front, 1941–45* (New York, 1986), discusses the German prosecution of the eastern campaign as a 'race war'.

F. Belov, *The History of A Collective Farm* (New York, 1955), inside account of life on a collective farm.

Y. Boshyk (ed.), *Ukraine during World War II* (Edmonton, 1986), articles on German occupation and Ukrainian resistance.

R. Brody, *Ideology and Political Mobilization* (Pittsburgh, 1994), on benefits and limits of Soviet ideology in validating the regime's authority and controlling its citizens during the war.

R. W. Davies, *Soviet History in the Gorbachev Revolution* (Bloomington, Ind., 1989), on the historiography of the war.

M. Djilas, *Conversations with Stalin* (New York, 1962), classic account of three encounters between Stalin and Yugoslav communists in the 1940s.

T. Dunmore, *Soviet Politics, 1945–53* (New York, 1984), general survey, contesting totalitarian thesis and showing bureaucratic conflict as key to decision-making.

J. Erickson, *The Road to Stalingrad* (New York, 1975), superior analysis of war up to Stalingrad.

—— *The Road to Berlin* (Boulder, Colo., 1983), still the best history of the war from 1942 to its conclusion.

H. Fireside, *Icon and Swastika* (Cambridge, 1971), on revival of Orthodox Church under German occupation and *rapprochement* between State and Church in 1943.

J. Garrard and C. Garrard (eds.), *World War II and the Soviet People* (London, 1993), articles on the home front during the war.

D. Glantz and J. House, *When Titans Clashed* (Lawrence, Kan., 1995), operational military history.

S. N. Goncharov, J. W. Lewis, and X. Litai, *Uncertain Partners* (Stanford, Calif., 1993), collective work of international team drawing on new archival documentation.

M. Harrison, *Soviet Planning in Peace and War, 1938–45* (Cambridge, 1985), good study of wartime economy and subsequent implications.

D. Holloway, *Stalin and the Bomb* (New Haven, 1994), superb study of Soviet atomic bomb programme.

W. Moskoff, *The Bread of Affliction* (Cambridge, 1990), first-rate study of agriculture and food supply during the war.

A. M. Nekrich, *The Punished Peoples* (New York, 1978), on deportation of nationalities during the Second World War.

C. Porter and M. Jones, *Moscow in World War II* (London, 1987), social history from perspective of sympathy for the Soviet government.

A. Resis (ed.), *Molotov Remembers* (Chicago, 1994), provides insights into Soviet policy in the 1940s and 1950s.

D. Reynolds (ed.), *The Origins of the Cold War in Europe* (New Haven, 1994), collection of articles highlighting post-Cold War scholarship.

H. Shukman (ed.), *Stalin's Generals* (New York, 1993), short biographies of top Soviet commanders during the war.

G. L. Weinberg, *A World at Arms* (Cambridge, 1994), prize-winning general history of the second world war.

13. FROM STALINISM TO STAGNATION, 1953–1985

S. Bialer, *Stalin's Successors* (Cambridge, 1980), on party leadership in post-Stalinist era.

G. W. Breslauer, *Khrushchev and Brezhnev as Leaders* (London, 1982), penetrating assessment of leadership styles and achievements.

R. A. Divine (ed.), *The Cuban Missile Crisis* (2nd edn., New York, 1988), contains new information and recollection of key participants.

J. Ellis, *The Russian Orthodox Church* (Beckenham, 1986), informed contemporary history.

G. A. Hosking, *Beyond Socialist Realism* (New York, 1980), scintillating analysis of 'village writers'.

J. L. H. Keep, *Last of the Empires* (Oxford, 1995), sweeping recent history of post-war USSR.

N. S. Khrushchev, *Khrushchev Remembers* (3 vols., Boston, 1970–90), edited versions of memoirs.

S. N. Khrushchev, *Khrushchev on Khrushchevism* (Boston, 1990), memoir of Khrushchev's son.

N. Lubin, *Labour and Nationality in Soviet Central Asia* (Princeton, 1984), on complex problems of labour and economic development.

A. McAuley, *Economic Welfare in the Soviet Union* (Madison, 1979), on poverty and income distribution.

M. McCauley (ed.), *Khrushchev and Khrushchevism* (Bloomington, Ind., 1987), useful collection of essays.

—— *Nikita Khrushchev* (London, 1991), reliable, up-to-date biography.

R. Medvedev, *Khrushchev* (Garden City, NY, 1984), informed biography with fresh detail.

J. Millar (ed.), *Politics, Work, and Daily Life in the U.S.S.R.* (New York, 1987), results of survey of former Soviet citizens.

M. Shatz, *Soviet Dissent in Historical Perspective* (New York, 1980).

M. J. Sodaro, *Moscow, Germany, and the West from Khrushchev to Gorbachev* (Ithaca, NY, 1990), expert account.

A. P. Van Goudoever, *The Limits of Destalinization in the Soviet Union* (London, 1986).

14. FROM PERESTROIKA TOWARDS A NEW ORDER, 1985–1995

A. Aslund, *Gorbachev's Struggle for Economic Reform* (2nd edn., Ithaca, NY, 1991), penetrating analysis by perceptive critic of Gorbachev's reforms, arguing in favour of a rapid transition to the market economy.

A. Brown, *The Gorbachev Factor in Soviet Politics* (2nd edn., New York, 1992), incisive analysis of Gorbachev's role and significance.

M. Buckley (ed.), *Perestroika and Soviet Women* (Cambridge, 1992), on the women's question in the Gorbachev era.

G. J. Gill, *Collapse of a Single-Party System* (Cambridge, 1994), penetrating account of the demise of the Soviet system.

M. S. Gorbachev, *Perestroika* (rev. edn., 1988), discussion of the 'new thinking' that shows the lack of clear vision, especially on realizing perestroika.

G. A. Hosking, *The Awakening of the Soviet Union* (rev. edn., Cambridge, Mass., 1991), balanced survey of Gorbachev era.

—— et al., *Independent Political Movements in the Soviet Union 1985–91* (London, 1992), detailed, well-researched treatment.

International Monetary Fund, *A Study of the Soviet Economy* (3 vols., Washington, 1991), wide-ranging survey of the Soviet economy just before its dissolution.

R. Sakwa, *Gorbachev and His Reforms, 1985–1990* (New York, 1991), positive assessment of Gorbachev as reformer.

G. Smith (ed.), *The Nationalities Question in the Soviet Union* (London, 1990), wide-ranging coverage.

R. G. Suny, *The Revenge of the Past* (Stanford, Calif., 1994), on nationalism and the demise of the Soviet system.

S. White, *Gorbachev and After* (3rd edn., Cambridge, 1992), best short narrative of perestroika.

B. Yeltsin, *Against the Grain* (London, 1990), autobiography, with revealing insights into Yeltsin's rise to power.

PICTURE ACKNOWLEDGEMENTS

109, 114 Novosti (London)
115 Robert Harding Picture
     Library
117 Novosti (London)
118 © British Museum
123 Russian State Library Moscow
128 Victor Kennett/V & A Picture
     Library
129 Private Collection
131 P S Pallas: Travels through the
     Southern Provinces of the
     Russian Empire in the years
     1793 and 1794/British
     Library 567h4
135 Mary Evans Picture Library
139 © British Museum
143 Getty Images
146 Chateau de Malmaison/
     Giraudon
148 © British Museum
152 Versailles/Giraudon
153 Bibl. Marmottan/Giraudon
156, 161 Novosti (London)
163 Getty Images
165 E T Archive
166 Courtesy of the Director,
     National Army Museum,
     London/ Andromeda
168 Russian State Library Moscow
170 Russian State Archive of Film
     and Photographic Documents
     Krasnogorsk
176 Novosti (London)
181 David King Collection
182 Russian State Archive of Film
     and Photographic Documents
     Krasnogorsk
183, 184 David King Collection
189 Private Collection
190 Russian State Archive of Film
     and Photographic Documents
     Krasnogorsk
195 David King Collection
197 Russian State Library Moscow
198 Russian State Archive of Film
     and Photographic Documents'
     Krasnogorsk
199 Bibliotheque Nationale de
     France
200 Novosti (London)
203 Photo courtesy of Wendy
     Salmond
204 Mary Evans Picture Library/
     Alexander Meledin Collection
207 Foss Collection Hoover
     Institution Archives

213 David King Collection
216 Novosti (London)
219 From the Archives of the
     YIVO Institute for Jewish
     Research
220 Getty Images
223 Netta Peacock/V & A Picture
     Library
227 Russian State Library Moscow
228 Popperfoto
229 David King Collection
231 Rex Features
233 Central State Archive of Cine-
     Phono- and Photographic
     Documents St Petersburg
236, 238 Russian State Archive of
     Film and Photographic
     Documents Krasnogorsk
242 University of Helsinki Slavic
     Library
245 Russian State Archive of Film
     and Photographic Documents
     Krasnogorsk
247, 248 David King Collection
249 Rex Features
256, 259, 261, 263, 264 David King
     Collection
267 Central State Archive of Cine-
     Phono- and Photographic
     Documents St Petersburg
269 David King Collection
275, 276 Russian State Archive of
     Film and Photographic
     Documents,Krasnogorsk
279 David King Collection
281 Novosti (London)
285, 286 David King Collection
288 Museum Of Architecture
     Moscow
289, 291 Russian State Library
     Moscow
293 Arcady Shaikhet/ Mary Evans
     Picture Library/ Alexander
     Meledin Collection
295 David King Collection
298 Russian State Library Moscow
299 Dmitry Dyebabov/ Novosti
     (London)
303 David King Collection
306, 309 Society for Co-operation
     in Russian and Soviet Studies
310 Novosti (London)
314, 315, 317, 319 David King
     Collection
320 Robert Hunt Library
324, 325, 327, 329, 331 Mary

Evans Picture Library/
     Alexander Meledin Collection
335 Novosti (London)
336 Aid to Russian Christians
337 David King Collection
339 Getty Images
340 David King Collection
344 Rex Features
347 Camera Press
351 Novosti (London)
352 Russian State Archive of Film
     and Photographic Documents
     Krasnogorsk
362 Krokodil 30 September 1953
367 Don Hunstein/FPG/Robert
     Harding Picture Library
370 Camera Press
372 Novosti (London)
375 Camera Press
378 Camera Press (TS/RBOR)
379 Corbis-Bettmann/UPI
381 Aid to Russian Christians
382 V Koshevoi/Novosti (London)
385, 386 Sepp Spiegl/Camera
     Press
388, 391 Novosti (London)
401 Graham Turner/Camera
     Press
403 Laski/ Rex Features
405 Terry Arthur/Camera Press
408 Chip Hues-Gamma/Liaison/
     Frank Spooner
409 Tass/Camera Press
411 Robert Wallis/Rex Features
412 Roberto Koch/Contrast/Katz

In a few instances we have been
unable to trace the copyright holder
prior to publication. If notified, the
publishers will be pleased to amend
the acknowledgementas in any
future edition.

Picture research by Anne Lyons

Additional research in Moscow by
Valery Medvedev

Photography at the Russian State
Library by Anatoly Petrovich
Popov and Aleksander
Mikhailovich Perfiliev

INDEX

461